More praise for *Life and Death on the New Yo

"Tim Lawrence brings the author
history *Love Saves the Day* to club
ment, when hip hop, punk, and disco transformed one another,
with input from salsa, jazz, and Roland 808s. If you never danced
yourself dizzy at the Roxy, the Paradise Garage, or the Mudd
Club, here's a chance to feel the bass and taste the sweat."
—**WILL HERMES**, author of *Love Goes to Buildings on Fire: Five
Years in New York That Changed Music Forever*

Praise for *Love Saves the Day*

"Tim Lawrence's disco culture tome is one of the sharpest books
on dance music to date, striking a balance between you-are-there
club descriptions, socioeconomic analysis, and musical critique."
—**TRICIA ROMANO**, *Village Voice*

"[E]verything a good history should be—accurate, informative,
well-organized, and thoughtful. It is also everything a quality read
should be—fresh, thoughtful, and provocative. . . . *Love Saves the
Day* is, as so many critics have noted, the definitive book on dance
music in the 1970s."
—**LISA NEFF**, *Chicago Free Press*

"*Love Saves the Day* is what we need for generations to come: it's
the real history of dance music and DJ/club culture."
—**LOUIE VEGA**, DJ/producer, Masters At Work & Nuyorican
Soul

"*Love Saves the Day* not only gets dance music history right—it
refocuses that history to include those unjustly excluded from it."
—**ETHAN BROWN**, *New York Magazine*

"[T]his is as close to a definitive account of disco as we're likely to
get, and as entertaining as a great night out."
—**RICHARD SMITH**, *Gay Times*

"Lawrence's astounding research and wide focus make this the
music's definitive chronicle so far."
—**MICHAELANGELO MATOS**, *Seattle Weekly*

"An extraordinarily rich work that ought to transform the ways we write the history of popular music."
—MITCHELL MORRIS, *Journal of Popular Music Studies*

Praise for *Hold On to Your Dreams*

"[T]he most fascinating recount of the unfairly condemned-to-obscurity experimental musician. . . . Russell's unprecedented genre-merging deserves this kind of exploration, and Lawrence approaches with a delicacy and direct intimacy reminiscent of the music itself."
— *Oxford American*

"With rich and animated detail, Tim Lawrence tracks Arthur Russell's insatiable drive to integrate so-called serious music and pop. This definitive biography is both an engrossing record of Russell's musical ambitions and a compelling account of the fertile downtown scene that supported his admirable dreams."
—MATT WOLF, director of *Wild Combination: A Portrait of Arthur Russell*

"A monumental work."—KRIS NEEDS, *Record Collector*

"Lawrence's writing is up to the task of telling this narrative in a way that makes the pathos of Russell's life a deeply compelling window onto the 'Downtown' music scene of the 1980s and '90s."
—GUSTAVOS STADLER, *Social Text*

"*Hold on to Your Dreams* sets a new standard for musical biography by virtue of its research methodology and focus on seemingly minor figures. Lawrence makes a strong case for the importance of Russell's music to our understanding of late-twentieth-century cultural life and, perhaps most importantly, shows the value of historical biography written with an emphasis on musical mediation and social networks."
—RYAN DOHONEY, *Journal of the Society for American Music*

**LIFE AND
DEATH
ON THE
NEW YORK
DANCE
FLOOR**
1980–1983

Dear Matt

Welcome to the Lucky
Cloud Sound System
dance community –
and thanks for your
record-breaking support!
LSD,
Tim x

Tim Lawrence

LIFE AND DEATH ON THE NEW YORK DANCE FLOOR 1980–1983

Duke University Press
Durham and London 2016

Cover designed by Natalie F. Smith
Interior designed by Mindy Basinger Hill
Typeset in Minion Pro by Westchester Publishing Services

Library of Congress Cataloging-in-Publication Data
Names: Lawrence, Tim, [date]
Title: Life and death on the New York dance floor, 1980–1983 /
Tim Lawrence.
Description: Durham : Duke University Press, 2016. | Includes
bibliographical references and index.
Identifiers: LCCN 2016007103 (print)
LCCN 2016008598 (ebook)
ISBN 9780822361862 (hardcover : alk. paper)
ISBN 9780822362029 (pbk. : alk. paper)
ISBN 9780822373926 (ebook)
Subjects: LCSH: Dance music—New York (State)—New York—20th
century—History and criticism. | Popular music—New York (State)—
New York—1981–1990—History and criticism. | Popular culture—New York
(State)—New York—20th century—History and criticism.
Classification: LCC ML3411.5 .L379 2016 (print) |
LCC ML3411.5 (ebook) | DDC 781.64—dc23
LC record available at http://lccn.loc.gov/2016007103

Cover art, clockwise from upper left: Ruza Blue at Danceteria, 1984;
photograph © Rhonda Paster. Danceteria dance floor, 1980; photograph
© Allan Tannenbaum / SoHo Blues. From left to right: Keith Haring,
unknown, Grace Jones, and Fab 5 Freddy at the Fun Gallery, ca. 1983;
photograph © Ande Whyland. Dancers at the Roxy, 1983; photograph
© Bob Gruen.

CONTENTS

PREFACE

Sanity dictated that this book should have told the history of 1980s dance culture in the United States in the way that my first book, *Love Saves the Day*, excavated the 1970s, charting the chaotic renewal of the post-disco party scene in early 1980s New York, the mid-decade rise of Chicago house and Detroit techno, and the culture's end-of-decade decline as its center of gravity shifted to Europe. But sanity failed to anticipate the way the early 1980s would reveal themselves to be one of the most creatively vibrant and socially dynamic periods in the history of New York. Nor did it foresee how those superficially amorphous years contained some kind of coded lesson about creativity, community, and democracy in the global city. So instead of depicting the 1980–1983 period as a mere bridge that connected the big genre stories of 1970s disco and 1980s house and techno, I submitted to its kaleidoscope logic, took my foot off the historical metronome, and decided to *take it*—the book—*to the bridge.*

The truncated time frame didn't exactly make it easier to write this book, in part because the period didn't present an obvious start or endpoint and in part because its modus operandi was one of interaction, openness, and freedom in which everything seemed to be tied to everything and nothing really had a name. Negotiating disco's recent collapse, rap's battle to become more than a passing fad, and punk's aesthetic exhaustion, New Yorkers were so unbothered about defining the culture they were bringing into existence it was left to the British to coin the names of mutant disco and electro, with postpunk popularized later. That left the period appearing to lack an identity as well as the kind of clean-cut generic innovation that can provide an easy anchor for chroniclers and readers alike, while its sandwiching between disco plus house and techno added to its antinarrative personality. When Chicago DJ Frankie Knuckles argued that house music amounted to "disco's revenge," he inadvertently contributed to the idea that the music and culture of the early 1980s were only of passing consequence. This book aims to show how, at least in New York, revenge wasn't even a conversation topic as the city's party culture entered into what would turn out to be—at least at the time of writing—its most prolific phase.

The 1980–1983 period hasn't remained completely off the radar. Steven Hager's *Art after Midnight*, which charts the artist incursion into the city's club scene, remains the most significant contribution to the historicization of the period. Jeff Chang (*Can't Stop Won't Stop*), Bernard Gendron (*Between Montmartre and the Mudd Club*), Simon Reynolds (*Rip It Up and Start Again*), and Peter Shapiro (*Turn the Beat Around*) have added chapters that explore the way hip hop, postpunk, and mutant disco proliferated in early 1980s New York. Yet while these authors capture a slice of the city's cultural history, their angled approach inevitably slices up an era that was arguably defined by its synergy and its interconnectedness. Although affiliations to certain sounds, venues, and scenes were often real and impassioned, they routinely came second to the broadly accepted idea that the city's party spaces doubled as environments of possibility and community. The challenge has been to write a book that captures the breadth of what happened and the spirit in which it unfolded.

The complexity and interactivity of the New York party scene required this book to adopt a crablike syncretic approach, spending more time moving sideways than forward. The events of each year are presented in four parts, each subdivided into chapters that take on the city's art-punk, post-disco dance, and hip hop party scenes; the music linked to these scenes; the relationship between the culture and the broader music industry; and sociopolitical matters (ranging from city and national government matters to the spread of AIDS). If it wasn't for the two-year gap, this book could almost be the successor to *Love Goes to Buildings on Fire*, Will Hermes's account of the city's music culture of 1973–1977. Yet whereas the disco, punk, and prerecorded rap scenes charted by Hermes remained largely unto themselves, *Life and Death* explores their meeting and synthesis during the opening years of the 1980s, with each chapter being semipermeable. In short, the party culture of the early 1980s is of interest not in spite of its lack of generic clarity but because its itinerant leanings opened up so many social and sonic possibilities. This book places the era's indiscipline at the center rather than the margins.

In keeping with the nebulous quality of its scenes and sounds, the 1980–1983 period doesn't have a clear start and endpoint. The turn toward mutation can, for instance, be traced to Dinosaur's "Kiss Me Again," Cristina's "Disco Clone," and the opening of the Mudd Club, all of which unfolded during the autumn of 1978. At the other end of the time frame, venues such as Danceteria and the Paradise Garage entered 1984 in something akin to full flow while Strafe's "Set It Off" traveled between the city's venues in a manner that suggested that interscene records could make their mark just so long as the beat combination was right. Yet it remains the case that disco continued to hog the story of party culture during 1979, even if many of the headlines were turning negative, and it was only during 1980, after the majors shifted into post-backlash retrenchment mode and the national media lost interest in disco, that the shift into a mongrel era became explicit. Similarly, 1983 amounted to a tipping point in the city's history as AIDS reached epidemic proportions while the influences of real estate inflation and Wall Street began to climb exponentially. The continuation of those trends, the onset of the crack epidemic, and the reelection of Ronald Reagan during 1984 marked the beginning of a much more conflictual and divisive era that turned records like "Set It Off" into a rarity.

Somewhat regrettably, this book restricts its coverage to New York, but if anything the city was even more dominant during the early 1980s than it had been during the 1970s, when Boston, Los Angeles, Philadelphia, and San Francisco fed much more heavily into party culture—including New York party culture. Of the urban centers omitted, San Francisco supported a vibrant yet somewhat isolated white gay scene and not a great deal more, so it is referenced primarily in relation to the way some of its independent label recordings traveled eastward. Although Chicago remains significant thanks to the run of Frankie Knuckles at the Warehouse between 1977 and 1983, its party scene exerted no significant influence on other cities during this period (with house emerging in 1984 and breaking out a year later). Elsewhere, Detroit supported a significantly less developed local scene than Chicago and an equally limited national profile, while Philadelphia existed as a shadow of its former self, its towering musical output of the 1960s and 1970s dramatically diminished. Newark's impact was more marked, largely because of Zanzibar, and is discussed in the pages that follow, as are some of the important transatlantic links established with the United Kingdom, particularly Manchester. Yet it remains the case that during the opening years of the 1980s, New Yorkers had fewer reasons to track external developments than at any time in recent memory. Their own productivity provided added reason to stay put.

Life and Death aims to contribute to the "archive of the ephemeral" evoked by the late José Muñoz, for while some art and most recordings survive in material form, many efforts—DJ sets, band performances, theatrical explorations, immersive happenings, fashion shows, dance styles, and graffiti/xerox/

found-object art efforts—assumed a transient form.[1] As well as describing and acknowledging this other strand of creativity, the pages that follow seek to shape a form of collective memory that foregrounds what Judith Halberstam describes as "the self-understandings of cultural producers."[2] They do so by drawing heavily on interviews and email conversations with some 130 participants (interviews are conducted by myself unless otherwise referenced) as well as the vibrant, sometimes urgent accounts of contemporaneous writers, including Vince Aletti, Brian Chin, Nelson George, Richard Grabel, Steven Hager, Steven Harvey, Robert Palmer, John Rockwell, and Stephen Saban, plus neglected yet invaluable sources such as *Dance Music Report*, the *East Village Eye*, and the *New York Rocker*, respectively edited by Tom Silverman, Leonard Abrams, and Andy Schwartz.

If a guiding concept runs through this book it lies in Henri Lefebvre's description of the ideal city as "the perpetual *oeuvre* of the inhabitants, themselves mobile and mobilized for and by this *oeuvre*," where a "superior form of rights" emerges: the "right to freedom, to individualization in socialization, to habitat and to inhabit."[3] Did New York's inhabitants realize themselves in such a way during the early 1980s? The portents weren't promising, given that their city is widely assumed to have collapsed during the 1970s, with the fiscal crisis, deteriorating public services, and rising crime rates pummeling its inhabitants. But although the ride was often bumpy, and although certain problems appeared endemic, New York entered the new decade with its public services operational and its debt manageable. Rarely referenced, President Ford delivered a $2.3 billion loan soon after the *New York Post* reported him telling the city to drop dead, real estate values dipped yet never collapsed, heroin use was far less ubiquitous than is routinely implied, the murder rate barely rose between 1971 and 1979, and muggers were frequently greeted with the comment "Sorry, I haven't got any money," recalls downtown actor Patti Astor. With the cultural renaissance already gathering momentum, the city was set for an explosion of creative activity that came to be distinguished by its participatory nature as well as the ability of those involved to reinvent themselves and their surroundings.

Although the primary task of this book is to chronicle the relentless activity of the era, it is also concerned with the policies that were introduced to combat the perceived failure of the 1970s. These included reductions in government spending and welfare, the deregulation of the banking sector, tax cuts for the wealthy, and the introduction of additional tax breaks to stimulate corporate investment in the city. Conservatives argued that such measures were necessary to revive the city, pointing to garbage piled high on the sidewalks, citizens supposedly afraid to step out of their front doors, and graffiti that overran the

subway system. But while life in New York undoubtedly produced its discom-
forts and its hairy moments, the New Yorkers I spoke to recounted to a person that even if city life caused occasional trepidation, they felt more anxious
about what they would miss if they had to leave the city for a few days, with
Ronald Reagan's trigger-happy references to nuclear war their greatest political concern. It was only during 1983 that another set of more anxiety-inducing
fears started to take shape as real estate inflation began to rocket, rents started
their mountainous climb, and Wall Street headed skyward, which conspired
to transform the city into a less democratic space. That year AIDS also reached
epidemic proportions, with crack consumption spiraling out of control the
following year, scaring the shit out of participants and decimating communities. Lefebvre's moment began to recede, even if memories of what had just
passed would sustain his ideals.

This book makes three core arguments. First, New York experienced a
community-driven cultural renaissance during the early 1980s that stands as
one of the most influential in its, and perhaps in any city's, history. Second,
the renaissance was rooted in opportunities that came to the fore during New
York's shift from industrialism to postindustrialism, and it began to unravel
when New York assumed the character of a neoliberal city organized around
finance capital, gentrification, real estate inflation, and social regulation. Third,
although party culture is routinely denigrated as a source of mindless hedonism and antisocial activity, it revealed its social, cultural, and even economic
potential during the period examined here. None of this means that early 1980s
New York achieved some kind of utopia. After all, day-to-day life came with
its struggles, integration might have moved faster and gone further, and participants became embroiled in their fair share of falling outs, betrayals, and
rivalries. With the benefit of hindsight, it can also be argued that a certain
naïveté—a collective belief that conditions would always remain favorable—
underpinned much if by no means all of the activity. Then again, a careful
examination of the early 1980s also confirms that valuable freedoms have diminished since the city entered the neoliberal era. Given that corporations
received heavy subsidies to set up shop in the first place, and given that so
many of them have subsequently pioneered ways of minimizing their tax bill,
this history also begs the question: what might have happened if a different
path had been chosen?

Caveats apply, beginning with the standard acknowledgment that much
of this history relies on recollections that can only be filtered through the
present and are to varying degrees partial. If "some memories are hazy," as

David DePino, a close friend of Larry Levan, the DJ at the Paradise Garage, puts it, conscious of the wear-and-tear that late-night living can cause, it remains the case that hindsight brings its own rewards, while the value of capturing the memories of those who are still around is surely highlighted by the passing of so many protagonists (among them Levan). Because the story of a person can never be fully re-created, it follows that the portraits developed here will inevitably appear slim, yet the broad intention is to show how the multitude of participants, the overwhelming majority unnamed, helped create and in return received sustenance from a towering scene. Introducing another qualification, although a significant proportion of the material introduced is original, some aspects will inevitably be familiar to readers. Rather than leave out the era's better-known DJs or parties or recordings, the plan is to convey them with fresh detail and insight.

As for this book's title, the reference to life is intended to evoke the way that New York party culture didn't merely survive the hyped death of disco but positively flourished in its wake. If the backlash held sway in the suburbs of the United States as well as the music corporations that gauged success according to national sales, the sense of possibility, opportunity, and exploration remained palpable for those who experienced the culture via the city's private parties and public discotheques. As for the evocation of death, the primary reference is to AIDS, which devastated the queer population that contributed so powerfully to the city's party scene, with heroin users and others also embroiled. Death also refers to the reorganization of the city around a neoliberal ethos that has ultimately resulted in the radical curtailment (if not total eradication) of its party culture.

In some respects this book is written as an outtake of Jane Jacobs's monumental work *The Death and Life of Great American Cities*, which describes the organic interactions that were the stuff of city life and the way in which grandiose planners could suffocate such activity. At the same time it acknowledges Sharon Zukin's observation that the greatest threat to mixed-income communities lies not in the activities of planners but in the relentless march of gentrification, the breakneck rise of housing as an investment opportunity, and the shift toward a deregulated and globalized economy that has accelerated these developments.[4] The clampdown on party culture has taken place in the interests of the few rather than the many, who no longer have the opportunity to engage in the kind of democratic art and music culture that was once integral to Manhattan. "I believe that nightclubs are these terribly important places where all kinds of things happen," argues dominatrix doorwoman, barwoman, promoter, performer, and self-described "nightclub utopian" Chi Chi Valenti. "They're kind of underrated, but if you look at the things that have been formed and born in clubs, especially but not only in New York, the results are extraordinary."

One small hope carried through this book is that its detailing of the city's recent past can suggest what it might become again.

ACKNOWLEDGMENTS

This is the third time I have found myself immersed in the act of "community history writing," as a friend and colleague recently described my books. The work is both collective and interactive, with a chorus of a hundred-plus voices that made a scene enabling this particular narration. All manner of thanks are due.

Once again I would like to begin by acknowledging the generosity and perseverance of those who have granted interviews, many of which ran to several hours, some even longer, with a high proportion willing to contribute to a sometimes ridiculous number of email follow-ups. Thanks for this and more to Sal Abbatiello, Leonard Abrams, Vince Aletti, John Argento, Patti Astor, David Azarch, Arthur Baker, Ivan Baker, Afrika Bambaataa, John "Jellybean" Benitez, Chris Blackwell, Bob Blank, Ruza Blue, Fred "Fab 5 Freddy" Brathwaite, Gail Bruesewitz, Vito Bruno, Archie Burnett, Brian Butterick/Hattie Hathaway, Kenny Carpenter, Ray Caviano, Ken Cayre, James Chance, Mel Cheren, Brian Chin, Carol Cooper, Diego Cortez, Frankie Crocker, Chuck D, Michael de Benedictus, Jeffrey Deitch, David DePino, Alan Dodd, Leslie Doyle, Keith Dumpson, Johnny Dynell, Brent Nicholson Earle, Willie "Marine Boy" Estrada, Jim Feldman, Michael Fesco, Bruce Forest, Jim Fouratt, Michael Gomes, Charlie Grappone, John Hall, Alan Harris, Steven Harvey, Michael Holman, Tony Humphries, Afrika Islam, Boyd Jarvis, Dany Johnson, Bill T. Jones, Mark Kamins, Louis "Loose" Kee Jr., François Kevorkian, Steve Knutson, Danny Krivit, Jorge La Torre, Stuart Lee, Manny Lehman, Robbie Leslie, Joey Llanos, Monica Lynch, Ann Magnuson, David Mancuso, Steve Mass, Howard Merritt, David Morales, Man Parrish, Shep Pettibone, Rudolf Piper, Kenny Powers, Sal Principato, Kenneth Reynolds, Mark Riley, John Robie, Judy Russell, Anita Sarko, Marvin Schlachter, Renee Scroggins, Jonny Sender, Terry Sherman, Hank Shocklee, Tom Silverman, Tony Smith, Will Socolov, Steve "Steinski" Stein, Marsha Stern, Mike Stone, Justin

Strauss, Curtis Urbina, Chi Chi Valenti, Barry Walters, Judy Weinstein, Sharon White, and Michael Zilkha.

Various participants provided important information via email, including Charlie Ahearn, Mustafa Ahmed, Animal X, Stuart Argabright, Emily Armstrong, Ken Aronds, Peter Artin, Max Blagg, Ross Bleckner, Richard Boch, Jeff Brosnan, Tim Broun, Sean Cassette, John Ceglia, Rhys Chatham, Denise Chatman, Leslie Cohen, Jane Dickson, Alan Fierstein, Michelle Florea, Joshua Fried, John Giove, Frank Holliday, John Holmstrom, David King, Barbara Kirshenblatt-Gimblett, Kirk Leacock, Garrett List, Tom Moulton, Paul Outlaw, Rhonda Paster, Patricia Ragan, Gonnie Rietveld, Joni Rim, Iris Rose, Barbara Russo, Kenny Scharf, and Fred Schneider. Interviews with Joaquin "Joe" Claussell, Jim Feldman, Kit Fitzgerald, Ozkar Fuller, Peter Gordon, Victor Rosado, Diane Strafaci, Ned Sublette, Danny Tenaglia, Hippie Torales, and Bobby Viteritti have also informed aspects of this book, even though they are not quoted directly. Those who contributed to the book's artwork—much of it rare due to the relatively high cost of photography as well as restrictions placed on photographic activity in the city's private venues—are acknowledged in the pages that follow. I also remain grateful to Laurie Simmons and Mary Simpson at the Jimmy DeSana estate for the permission to reproduce Jimmy DeSana's work, and to Michael Holman for the introduction to Nicholas Taylor.

All manner of generous support has come my way while researching and writing this book. Leonard Abrams provided access to the full collection of the *East Village Eye*; John Argento allowed me to go through his collection of Danceteria flyers and newsletters; Robbie Leslie sent me articles, flyers, and photos; Stephen Pevner made available the Saint-at-Large's archive of Saint memorabilia; and Tom Silverman provided access to his *Dance Music Report* collection. On the music tip, Lee White turned me on to numerous recordings from the era; Greg Wilson offered thoughts on parallel electro-funk developments in the United Kingdom and sent over music files; and additional discographical assistance came from Marsha Stern (for Roy Thode's discography), David DePino (for Larry Levan), and Afrika Islam and Ruza Blue (for Afrika Bambaataa at Negril and the Roxy). Additional archive information and pointers came from Tim Broun, Laura Forde, Simon Halpin, Helena Kontova, Michael Koshgarian, Conor Lynch, Steve Mass, James McNally, Iris Rose, Victor Simonelli, David Steel, and James W. Weissinger.

It's been a pleasure as well as an education to present the working ideas of this book to audiences in the United States, the United Kingdom, and Europe, so I'd like to extend further thanks to those who made this possible, namely Mirko Bartels, Chris Bell, Marcel Bisevic, Rajendra Chitnis, David Clarke, Tom Cole, Martin Colthorpe, Roberta Cutolo, Robert Dansby, Ashley Dawson, Conor Donlon, Yusuf Etiman, Hendrik Folkerts, Jeremy Gilbert, Stephen Graham, Henrik Hallberg, Lindsey Hanlon, Julian Hellaby, Hua Hsu, Martha Kirszenbaum, Iván López Munuera, Matthew Lovett, Paul Luckraft, Dino Lupelli, Conor Lynch, Kingsley Marshall, Angela McRobbie, Ricardo Montez, Anne Hilde Neset, Francesco WARBEAR Macarone Palmieri, Ryan Powell, Wiebke Pranz, Alberto Randi, Christian Rogge, Walter Rovere, Sukhdev Sandhu, David Sanjek (rest in peace), Gustavos Stadler, Andreas Stolzenberg, Hans Stützer, Maciej Szalonek, Stefan Thungren, Rui Torrinha, Sven von Thuelen, and Eric Weisbard. Commissions from editors and publishers Bernardo Attias, Stuart Baker, Lisa Blanning, Todd Burns, Anna Gavanas, Tony Herrington, Richard King, Julie Malnig, Mike McGonigal, Angela McRobbie, Anne Hilde Neset, Piotr Orlov, Benjamin Piekut, Hillegonda Rietveld, Quinton Scott, Gustavos Stadler, Graham St. John, Karen Tongson, Sven von Thuelen, and Derek Walmsley have also helped me process ideas. Maggie Humm and Hua Hsu provided useful editing suggestions.

Informal conversations about culture and politics with friends and colleagues have been just as valuable, including (at the risk of repeating some names) Andrew Blake, Lisa Blanning, Dhanveer Brar, Ilaria Bucchieri, Garnette Cadogan, Rob Calcutt, David Campbell, Lili Capelle, Guillaume Chottin, Cyril Cornet, Roberta Cutolo, Robert Dansby, Ashley Dawson, Alan Dixon, Clod Dousset, Estelle du Boulay, Angus Finlayson, Mark Fisher, Mary Fogarty, Jeremy Gilbert, Steve Goodman, Peter Gordon, Jack Halberstam, Simon Halpin, Darren Henson, Tony Herrington, Louise Hisayasu, Hua Hsu, Maggie Humm, Jo Kemp, Roshini Kempadoo, Jason King, Charlie Kronengold, A. J. Kwame, Cedric Lassonde, Fabien Lassonde, Jo Littler, Iain Mackie, David Mancuso, James McNally, Pauline Moisy, Ricardo Montez, Darren Morgan, Pete Morris, José Muñoz (rest in peace), Colleen Murphy, Mica Nava, Anne Hilde Neset, Andrew Pirie, Alejandro Quesada, Amit Patel, Aneesh Patel, Susannah Radstone, Helen Reddington, Sharon Reid, Simon Reynolds, Sukhdev Sandhu, David Sanjek, Maureen Schipper, Quinton Scott, Gustavos Stadler, Christabel Stirling, Ned Sublette, Dave Tompkins, Jason Toynbee, Alexandra Vázquez, Derek Walmsley, Danny Wang, Tim Watson, Shannon Woo, and Peter Zummo. A big shout also goes out to (repeating some more names) Guillaume Chottin, Jeremy Gilbert, Simon Halpin, Colleen Murphy, and the rest of the Lucky Cloud Sound System crew; the dear dancers who come to our parties at the Rose Lipman Building; Jeremy Gilbert, Stephen Maddison, Ash Sharma, and Debra Shaw of the Centre for Cultural Studies Research; and other valued colleagues too numerous to name in the School of Arts and Digital Industries and beyond at the University of East London.

I'm grateful for support from the Arts and Humanities Research Council (research leave), the Research and Development Support team at the University of East London (Angus Finlayson internship), the School of Arts and Digital Industries in the University of East London (artwork funding, conference travel, sabbatical leave), Red Bull Music Academy (artwork funding; additional thanks to Todd Burns and Torsten Schmidt for facilitating), and the librarians at the British Library, the New York Public Library, and the University of East London. As was the case with *Love Saves the Day* and *Hold On to Your Dreams*, it's been a privilege to publish with the Duke University Press team, including Elizabeth Ault, Amy Ruth Buchanan, Danielle Houtz, Michael McCullough, Laura Sell, and my editor, Ken Wissoker. A special word of thanks goes to Ken, whose boundless engagement with the world continues to amaze and inspire. In addition to being a great friend and editor, Ken has stuck with me while I've headed off on a 1,500-page prequel to the book he commissioned me to write back in 1997—a history of house music. This effort takes me to the cusp of honoring that original agreement (if he's still interested).

So many figures who contributed to the New York party scene of the early 1980s have passed away, among them Jean-Michel Basquiat, Michael Brody, Jim Burgess, Arch Connelly, Patrick Cowley, Ann Craig, Jimmy DeSana, Juan DuBose, Ethyl Eichelberger, Kenneth Eubanks, Walter Gibbons, Gwen Guthrie, Keith Haring, Tseng Kwong Chi, Barry Lederer, Larry Levan, Tina L'Hotsky, Bruce Mailman, Robert Mapplethorpe, Malcolm McLaren, Haoui Montaug, Sergio Munzibai, Klaus Nomi, Larry Patterson, Anya Phillips, Ruth Polsky, Sharon Redd, Arthur Russell, Tee Scott, John Sex, Sylvester, Roy Thode, Arturo Vega, Andy Warhol, Arthur Weinstein, Michael Wilkinson, David Wojnarowicz, and dancers too many to mention. Mel Cheren, Frankie Crocker, Loleatta Holloway, Mark Kamins, Anita Sarko, and Mike Stone also passed during the gap between our interviews and the completion of this book. (Mark was engaging, perceptive, and sweet, and I was looking forward to him reading a book about party culture that fully credited his contribution. Fired up and compelling, Anita told stories about her time at the Mudd Club, the Rock Lounge, and Danceteria, never hinting she would take her own life.) Thoughts always go out to my mum and dad, Muriel and Leo Lawrence, whose parental devotion and intellectual adventure continue to move and guide me, years after their passing. Family love also goes out to my uncle and aunt, Helen and David, who have always been there for me, as well as to Tess, Greg, Angie, Kevin and Camilla, Rita, Giorgio, Elsa, cousins too numerous to name, Sheila and Lionel, and the Franks clan. More love goes to the wider community of friends I meet in front of the school gate, in yoga class, and over the dinner table. Special delivery love goes to Enrica Balestra and our girls, Carlotta and Ilaria, both of whom are amazing dancers, even if they don't yet fully appreciate their parents' moves.

INTRODUCTION

New Year's Eve 1979 carried the promise of a break with a decade marked by defeat in Vietnam, the Watergate scandal, the first recession of the postwar era, an ongoing hostage crisis in Iran, and the culture most heavily associated with the 1970s — disco. Polls conducted during the year indicated that only 19 percent of U.S. citizens were satisfied with the country's direction while trust in government hit a record low of 29 percent, crashing from a 1967 peak of 76 percent.[1] Public confidence suffered some more in October when the Federal Reserve tightened monetary supply in order to curb the spiraling inflation that accompanied weakening economic growth, which fell from more than 6 percent to under 2 percent during the year. Then, on 31 December, the *New York Times* reported that "the much heralded recession is starting fitfully."[2] Sages read the national mood and announced that it called for belt-tightening, hard work, and a reassertion of traditional values. It had become, in short, a bad time to discuss the pleasures of the dance floor with one's bank manager.

New York Magazine captured the zeitgeist in its 31 December issue. "The media have already been at work defining it all," ran the introductory piece. "The key words seem to be 'Me,' 'Self,' 'Disco,' 'Woody Allen,' 'Third World,' 'Liberation (usually women's possibly anybody's),' 'Cocaine,' 'Style,' and, above all, 'Energy.'"[3] The publication noted that the words could be joined together, so a "shortage of energy" could be "relieved by cocaine," which could provide "the strength to dance the night away," with disco movie star John Travolta "dancing with a degree of self-absorption that would glaze over the eyes of Narcissus" in *Saturday Night Fever*.[4] The magazine positioned the 1970s as "the decade of the last free ride" and forecast that the 1980s would "find us paying our dues for the debts and obligations we took on during the 1970s."[5] It also suggested that the anonymous Studio 54 dancer who said "this is as near to heaven as I'll ever get" might have been right, because the 1980s didn't look as though they were "going to be that much fun."[6] It didn't seem to matter that *New York Magazine* had published the semifictional article that inspired the making of *Saturday Night Fever* in the first place. The time had come to rein in consumption, cut down on the partying, and lie on a bed of nails.

None of the talk would have discouraged hardened revelers from heading out to a subterranean party scene that bore only a passing resemblance to the flashier side of disco. At the Loft, musical host David Mancuso selected a panoramic range of danceable sounds for a crowd that had frequented his spot since the beginning of 1970. At Better Days, DJ Toraino "Tee" Scott delivered a blend of soul, funk, R&B, and disco that lured his black gay followers into the timeless flow of the rhythm section. At Flamingo and 12 West, DJs Howard Merritt, Richie Rivera, and Robbie Leslie played to a white gay crowd that had helped set disco in motion before side-stepping its commercial conclusion. At the Paradise Garage, DJ Larry Levan created a tapestry that lay somewhere between the range of Mancuso and the steady drive of Scott. At Club 57 and the Mudd Club, Dany Johnson, David Azarch, Johnny Dynell, and Anita Sarko selected funk, new wave, no wave, punk, R&B, and sometimes even disco in between offerings that included live bands, art, immersive happenings, participatory theater, and experimental film. Meanwhile Disco Fever, located up in the Bronx, presented DJ and MC combinations that worked the floor by mixing disco, funk, and the nascent sound of rap. Giving up the ritual wasn't even a consideration.

The culture continued to thrive because the conditions that had led DJ-ing to take root in New York in the first place remained largely unchanged. The city housed the highest concentration of gay men, people of color, and women in the United States, if not the world, and just as these groups had joined forces with miscellaneous others to conquer, recalibrate, and properly ignite the withering discotheque scene during the early 1970s, so they continued at the beginning of the new decade, because going out to party had become a way of life. The music industry's historic presence in the city had also helped it become the national capital for disco and new wave, with musicians encouraged to migrate to the city in the knowledge that they would enjoy a better-than-average chance of making a go of it if they played and recorded there. Usually broke, musicians were able to pursue this kind of dream because real estate remained cheap, thanks to the impact of deindustrialization, the flight of the white middle class to the suburbs, and the city's mid-decade nosedive into bankruptcy.

New York remained raw and ardent. Rolled out during the second half of the 1970s, budget cuts placed the city's services under such severe strain they were still deteriorating as the new decade got under way. More murders, robberies, and burglaries were recorded in 1980 than in any year since records began forty-nine years earlier; subway breakdowns rose from 30,000 in 1977 to 71,700; and the city's public schools lagged far behind their private counterparts.[7] Meanwhile a significant element of the housing stock went up in smoke as landlords ran down decrepit buildings before resorting to arson, aware they could often make more money from insurance than by renting to low-earning tenants. During 1979 alone, close to ten thousand premeditated blazes raged through the city, with almost half of them occurring in occupied buildings. "Arson is the cremation ritual of a diseased housing system," lamented the *Village Voice* in June 1980. "In housing, the final stage of capitalism is arson."[8] With heroin dealing taking root in the Lower East Side, it was no wonder that some believed the city amounted to a study in nihilism, as was the case with punk vocalist Lydia Lunch, who described it as a "filthy specter" constructed out of "blood-soaked bones."[9]

There were times, however, when the doomsday headlines failed to capture the city's openness, communality, and durability. Even though friends had warned her that the Lower East Side was so dangerous nobody would visit, for instance, the Cincinnati-raised downtown movie actor Patti Astor discovered the area to be "actually quite pastoral, with firmly established Russian, Italian and Hispanic communities" when she moved into a dirt-cheap three bedroom walk-up on East 10th Street and Second Avenue.[10] The ceiling fell in at her next apartment, on 3rd Street between Second Avenue and the Bowery, but that, she says, was nothing and it also gave her a reason to not pay the rent. "We just ran wild in the streets, wearing our little outfits," reminisces Astor. "We all lived in these *horrible* little apartments so we really didn't want to stay inside, and we kind of made that whole neighborhood one big playground. The parents were gone." Even the threat of violence usually ended in a slapstick standoff. "Being stuck up by somebody with a knife wasn't that big of a deal," she adds. "They'd go, 'Give me your money!' And we'd reply, 'We don't *have* any money! Why do you think we're out on the *same street*?!' Then the guy would go, 'Oh, okay. Here, have a cigarette.' For real." Only the Alphabets, as the alphabetized avenues at the eastern end of the Lower East Side were known, were deemed to be out of bounds (thanks to the local heroin trade).

Creativity flourished under these conditions. "It was a time when people could literally pay $100 a month in rent and there was a tremendous freedom to that," argues Chi Chi Valenti, a native New Yorker and party animal who shared a $400-per-month loft on 14th Street with three roommates. "They didn't have to have a career. There was a great fluidity." Getting by with very little money, Valenti and her peers flocked to the Odessa, a cheap diner located on Avenue A and St. Mark's Place, as well as the ubiquitous ethnic cafés and restaurants of the East Village, where the enormous plates of food could suffice for a day. Those who got to know the door staff of downtown's clubs gained free entry and often free drinks. Transport couldn't have been cheaper because everyone walked everywhere. "It's amazing how little we needed," adds Valenti, whose uniformed outfits, severe aura, and dominant personality made her a recognizable presence. "That was terribly important."

Taking shape after creative workers flooded into Lower Manhattan during the 1960s and 1970s, the downtown art scene coexisted with the clandestine end of the city's party network. The experimental Kitchen Center for Video and Music operated out of the Mercer Street Arts Center, which was situated around the corner from Mancuso's first Loft on Broadway and Bleecker Street. Paula Cooper's gallery on 96 Prince Street, the first of its kind when it opened in SoHo in 1968, became neighbors with the second incarnation of the Loft when Mancuso moved to number 99. Leo Castelli, the most influential dealer in American contemporary art, opened a gallery at 420 West Broadway in SoHo in 1971, little more than a hop, skip, and jump away from Nicky Siano's second Gallery, a Loft-style venue located on Mercer Street and Houston. La MaMa Experimental Theatre Club had already been running on East 4th Street for twelve years when future punk hangout CBGB set up shop at nearby 315 Bowery. Students from the School of Visual Arts on East 23rd Street were happy to make the short hike to Club 57 on St. Mark's Place. And the Performing Garage, home of the experimental theater group the Wooster Group, turned out to be a twelve-minute saunter from the Paradise Garage, located at 84 King Street. With so much at their doorsteps, downtowners rarely felt the need to leave.

Negotiating streets that were still unlit at night, artists, actors, choreographers, composers, dancers, DJs, musicians, performance artists, theater directors, video filmmakers, and writers tended to collaborate and socialize within discrete groups at first, drawn to those who shared their vocabulary. Yet whether they ended up living in an expansive loft in SoHo or a run-down tenement in the East Village, the density of their living arrangements, the sheer level of their activity, and the shared desire to make a stand led the divergent strands of this definitively postindustrial generation to come into increasing contact, and from the mid-1970s onward a constellation's worth of meetings and collaborations began to unfold. "Artists worked in multiple media, and collaborated, criticized, supported, and valued each other's works in a way that was unprecedented," argues archivist and critic Marvin J. Taylor in *The Downtown Book*. "Rarely has there been such a condensed and diverse group of artists in one place at one time, all sharing many of the same assumptions about how to make new art."[11]

Locales such as the Broome Street Bar (on Broome Street), Fanelli's Bar (on 94 Prince Street), the One Fifth (at 1 Fifth Avenue), Phoebes (on the corner of 4th Street and the Bowery), Raoul's (on 180 Prince Street), and the Spring Street bar (on Spring Street) encouraged the interaction. "Personally, I loved Phoebes," recalls composer and musician Garrett List, who worked as music director of the Kitchen between 1975 and 1977, where he made it his business to introduce downtown loft jazz musicians into the schedule. "It was a kind of inter-disciplinary bar (avant la lettre) with a weird kind of mix: the black new jazz thing, actors and theater people, poets and white avant-garde musicians." Meanwhile, Max's Kansas City (on Park Avenue South and 17th Street) followed by CBGB (on the Bowery) introduced experimental rock into the mix, with the latter becoming a key hangout after the closure of the Mercer Street Arts Center pushed a bunch of proto-punk bands into its midst. Then, as the decade reached its denouement, the scene began to motor as Hurrah opened as the first rock discotheque, the Mudd Club followed by Club 57 mixed DJ-ing with various forms of performance, and the Paradise Garage opened as an expanded version of the Loft and the Gallery. By the time the clocks struck midnight on 31 December 1979, then, revelers could survey the downtown scene and conclude that the cross-fertilizing energy was, if anything, about to intensify. "Downtown was like this kaleidoscopic, smörgåsbord of activity," recalls party organizer and performance artist Ann Magnuson. "All of these ideas were out there. It was like Halloween every night."

The beginning of the new decade bore uncanny similarities to the beginning of the last. As before, New York faced deep-seated economic challenges, with austerity matching the earlier challenge of white flight and spiraling debt. Both junctures were also marked by foreign-policy emergencies that undermined the country's global authority as the ongoing Iran hostage crisis dominated the headlines in a manner reminiscent of Vietnam. In another parallel, conservatives lambasted the perceived moral excesses of both outgoing decades, with the counterculture followed by disco blamed for cultivating hedonistic practices that undermined productivity as well as the social order. The game of parallels even extended to discotheque culture, which experienced its first crash when the twist along with rock and roll crashed out of fashion toward the end of the 1960s, only to experience an even more dramatic collapse when the backlash against disco peaked in 1979. Just as commercial tendencies had corroded the core values of the counterculture a decade earlier, so a form of insidious commercialism undermined disco from within after it outsold rock during 1978.

Revelers old enough to remember the ebbs and flows of the previous decade still had good reason to be cheerful. Just as the disintegration of the first wave of flashbulb discotheque culture paved the way for an organic alternative to take root at the Loft and the Sanctuary, where David Mancuso and Francis Grasso, respectively, selected records as if they were engaging in a democratic conversation rather than delivering a disjointed rant, so the domino collapse of the join-the-dots discotheques that had opened in the slipstream of *Saturday Night Fever* signaled the beginning of a period that would see venues such as Danceteria, the Funhouse, Pyramid, the Roxy, the Saint, and even Studio 54 reenergize the night. If the spluttering economy at both ends of the 1970s meant that money was often scarce, party promoters could also find affordable spaces with relative ease while locals viewed dancing as a cheap and cathartic form of entertainment. Finally, just as the opening of the 1970s heralded a period of social and sonic openness, when people and sounds came together in ways previously unimagined, so the same would come to pass during the early 1980s.

Four key differences would also take effect, beginning with the city's party infrastructure, which amounted to a spent force on New Year's Eve 1969 as discotheque audiences dwindled following the exhaustion of the twist craze and the rise of countercultural alternatives, after which Mancuso turned his home into a private party that came to be known as the Loft and two West Village gay bar owners who went by the names of Seymour and Shelley revived a stuttering public discotheque known as the Sanctuary. That, more or less, was that, with alternative destinations few and far between during the opening months of 1970. Yet New Yorkers who headed out on New Year's Eve 1979 were spoiled for choice, at least in Manhattan, where dance venues continued to thrive in spite of the wider backlash against disco. Moreover, in stark contrast to the decade's beginning, when companies were oblivious to the dance storm that was about to unfold, the cluster of independent labels that had emerged to serve the party scene remained operational, albeit chastened and somewhat slimmer. Whereas 1970 marked the beginning of a story, 1980 represented its complex, multidirectional continuation.

Second, the geographic origins of the music played in the city's party spaces shifted markedly between 1970 and 1980. Back in the very early 1970s, for instance, first-generation DJs scoured record bins in search of viable music that, when they checked the publishing details, usually came from Detroit or

Philadelphia. As the decade gathered pace, however, a series of New York–based independents began to service the city's selectors with R&B-oriented disco grooves; CBGB became the incubator for a breakthrough generation of punk and new wave bands; venues such as Artists Space, the Kitchen, and Tier 3 provided a platform for the no wave lineups that succeeded them; and Bronx-based DJs and MCs inspired the first cluster of rap releases. Thanks to these developments, New York DJs found themselves drawing on a rising proportion of locally produced records as they became the midwives of the disco boom, and both they and the companies that had invested in the city's buoyant musical networks were keen to maintain the flow after disco veered into an aesthetic cul-de-sac at the decade's tumultuous close. Far more evolved than anything that had existed ten years earlier, the city's independent labels were all set to explore new combinations in dance.

Third, the soundscape went through a triple somersault that played havoc with notions of marketing as well as form. With party DJs taking three or four years to establish their promotional worth, disco's rise out of funk, soul, and R&B was such a subtle affair that label heads and journalists didn't agree that a new genre had come into being until 1974. However, once disco had been established, and once punk started to make itself heard a couple of years later, record labels switched up the gears as they threw their know-how into selling the sounds as competing, discrete, and in many respects inverse phenomena. The strategy lasted until disco nosedived in tandem with the U.S. economy during 1979, and with punk and new wave having failed to convert their early promise into major sales, and with the late-arriving sound of rap widely judged to be a passing fad, all calculations pointed to the same conclusion: the beat was set to change as its creators sought out subtler, more imaginative ways to engage audiences that paid much less attention to genre and etiquette. "If the music was good and people connected to the conversation you were musically having with them, they didn't give a toss if you took a sharp left or paused or stopped or generally messed with their heads," Mudd Club DJ Anita Sarko notes of the parallel shift in listening habits. "They welcomed it!" Mutation, convergence, and freedom were about to define the night.

Fourth, the national political climate appeared to be more conducive at the beginning of 1980 than it had been ten years earlier. Inaugurated in January 1969, President Nixon presided over the bombing of Cambodia, the failed assault on Vietnam, and the beginning of a recession as songs such as "War" by Edwin Starr, "Black Skin Blue Eyed Boys" by the Equals, "What's Going On" by Marvin Gaye, and "Back Stabbers" by the O'Jays fed into a culture of protest. Ten years later, Carter presided over a slowing economy yet engineered several international peace initiatives, including the Camp David Israeli-Egyptian peace agreement and the Strategic Arms Limitation Talks II accord. Rather than attack perceived international threats, Carter headed so far in the other direction he appeared ineffectual as he struggled to find a solution to the Iran hostage crisis, which broke in November 1979. Leftists criticized Carter for initiating a program of deregulation and for achieving little in terms of wealth redistribution, but at least he wasn't a warmonger, and at the beginning of 1980 he also stood at 62 percent in the polls, comfortably ahead of Republican candidate Ronald Reagan, who lagged at 33 percent.[12] Reagan would sweep the November election and haul the country into a decade marked by inequality and polarization. But before that the national outlook looked benign and set to continue.

Come January, then, as journalists pondered the need for atonement and the economy veered toward recession, partygoers continued an odyssey already begun, greeting the night as a hallowed time when they could immerse themselves in an alternative milieu. Drawn to DJs who selected a wide spectrum of sounds, and often heading to venues where creativity and community flourished hand-in-hand, they headed out because the city's party spaces seemed to operate as sites of progress and pleasure. Also wary of the commercialism that had blunted disco's edge, participants weren't in a hurry to name their activity. A new kind of freedom was set to rule the night.

PART I

1980

THE RECALIBRATION OF DISCO

STYLISTIC COHERENCE DIDN'T MATTER AT ALL

Born in 1942, Steve Mass grew up in Macon, Georgia, the oldest son of Chicagoan-Jewish parents, his physician father head of the only radiology department in town. His childhood was a privileged one, yet the presence of a church on every block reminded him that he was an outsider, his interest in the arts provoked jeers at school, and visits to the country club, where his parents were required to socialize with other local notables, many of them with southern aristocratic roots and golf panache to spare, left him convinced of his inferiority. For a while he didn't even know that half the local population was African Americans, so severe was the separation between whites and blacks, but he got to spend time in the same room as African Americans — albeit a segregated one — when he began to head to concerts held in downtown Macon with his closest school friend, Phil Walden, who went on to found Capricorn Records and spearhead the development of southern rock. The experience of seeing the likes of Chuck Berry, Bo Diddley, James Brown, and Little Richard virtually levitate before his eyes was formative. Thanks to his father's line of work, Mass already knew about the steady stream of unsolved murders that were clearly related to Ku Klux Klan activities, and he came to regard these performers as heroes, conscious that when he and other teenagers screamed during their shows, the Klan judged that to be "dangerous."

Mass studied anthropology at Northwestern and creative writing at the Iowa Writers' Workshop, after which he moved to New York to forge ahead with a publishing venture initiated with a Ceylonese aristocrat, determined to take the artistic-curatorial-business pathway because "there was no hope in those days" of earning a living from art. The city was so cheap he launched a printing press in SoHo for "virtually nothing," only to see the venture founder, following his decision to organize it around a wondrous yet inefficient 1938 printing press. He bounced back with a business that provided an out-of-hours ambulance service to the membership of a large medical insurance company, which enabled him "to see how the city really worked" when he stepped into one of his adapted vans to cover for a sick driver. With no daytime responsibilities and a significant level of freedom at night, given that he could coordinate his business via two-way radio, he also started to pursue his poetic passions, assisting underground cinema pioneer Jack Smith on "a few small films," hanging out with punk director Amos Poe when the opportunity arose, and purchasing a 16mm Frezzolini camera so he could film bands at CBGB, the down-and-out (yet very in) Bowery venue where punk and new wave acts such as Blondie, the Ramones, Talking Heads, and Television had built a following. When New York descended into semi-anarchy during the summertime electricity blackout of 1977, he headed out with his camera to capture "the explosive social ramifications of the machine stopping."

Mass edged deeper into the city's subterranean theater when Poe introduced him to Anya Phillips, a Taiwanese-born designer, dominatrix, ex–Times Square stripper, and art-punk scenester. "Anya had a little circle of friends," he recalls. "They were all designers, they were working with spandex, they were wearing stiletto heels. All of this fascinated me. I was interested in Anya more than the bands." It was through Phillips that Mass also became friends with Diego Cortez, an Illinois-raised artist, performer, and fledgling filmmaker who immersed himself in the SoHo art scene until lead singer David Byrne invited him to see Talking Heads play live at CBGB. "I was brought into another scene that I thought was more vital than my own," reasons Cortez, known as Jim Curtis before he moved to New York. "The conceptual art scene of the 1970s was radical but it was a little bit too much removed from reality for my taste." On-off roommates, Cortez and Phillips were happy to spend time with Mass. "Steve would take Anya and I to dinner and we would hang out a bit," remembers Cortez. "He was one of the few people who had any money in the scene we were part of."

When Cortez directed a "schizo documentary" about Elvis that interspersed the story of the artist's time serving in the U.S. military in Germany with the trials of the country's militant Red Army Faction, he cast himself in the part of Elvis, handed Phillips the role of Priscilla, and brought in Mass to take on the role of cinematographer. The project took them to Memphis, where they drove in one of Mass's vans in order to film outside Graceland, Presley's mansion home, where fans were gathering in the wake of the artist's death on 16 August. After that they took a long route back via Chicago, because Cortez and Phillips had started to toy with the idea of setting up an alternative to CBGB and Max's that would mix live music with DJ-ing, performance art, and exhibitions, and having proposed the idea to Mass on the road to Memphis,

Anya Phillips and Diego Cortez, ca. 1978–1979. Photograph
by Jimmy DeSana; courtesy of the Jimmy DeSana Trust.

they wanted to show him a trailblazing punk discotheque called La Mere
Vipere located on North Halstead Street that could provide them with a reference point. The experience of seeing some fifty punks thrashing about in
black made an impression on Mass, as did the shattered skylight that was positioned above the DJ booth. "I saw the urban terrain as consisting of all these
eruptions and moral panics and riots," he recalls. "I thought, 'If neighbors
were throwing bricks through the window, then these people must be doing
something right.'" Mass confirmed later that the visit "inspired" him and had
a "strong influence" on his decision to open a club.[1]

Three factors tempered the southerner's enthusiasm. First, he didn't have
any spare money. Second, he still hoped to make it as a filmmaker. Third,
the tumultuous events of the summer, which also saw David "Son of Sam"

Berkowitz terrorize New Yorkers, left him feeling cautious because "everything was going wrong." Yet the commotion also coincided with his growing interest in Situationist philosophy and in particular Guy Debord's call in *Society of the Spectacle* for citizens to overturn the commodification of social life by constructing "situations" that re-ordered life, politics, and art.[2] At the same time he calculated that Jack Smith's skill at transforming a ramshackle cast into an expressive community could be partially replicated in a club situation. A self-described loner in search of a community, Mass concluded that the idea of opening a venue for "the moral panic crowd" rippled with potential.

The plan to open an art-punk discotheque remained speculative until Mass and Phillips hit on a dilapidated textile warehouse owned by artist Ross Bleckner, located at 77 White Street, a dead-end part of town that nevertheless lay at the hub of a series of discrete yet vital neighborhoods. To the north, SoHo had come to host the greatest artistic migration the country had ever seen. To the northeast, CBGB remained the choice destination for punks and new wavers. To the east and southeast, industrial Chinatown loomed large. To the south, the New York Metropolitan Correctional Center and New York City Hall hovered with authoritative intent. And to the west, TriBeCa, so called because it formed a triangle below Canal Street, hosted loft happenings that dated back to the early 1960s. "The whole 'science of location' idea — I threw that out of the window," recalls Mass. "I wanted a place that dragged along the bottom of the urban ocean. Whatever it picked up in its net I would deposit in this space." The prospective owner didn't mind that the building had no distinguishing features, drawn as he was to its industrial character as well as its status as an "appendage coming off the city hall and port system." When Bleckner expressed concerns about Mass's proposal, Cortez, who happened to be an ex-tenant of Bleckner's, reassured him that the venue would feature low-key experimental performances and most definitely not "constantly loud music." Mollified, Bleckner offered Mass a lease.

That spring Mass sold a house he owned in Massachusetts in order to raise a shoestring refurbishment budget of $15,000; Phillips became involved with James Chance, founder of the Contortions, which together with DNA, Mars, and Teenage Jesus and the Jerks had started to break with punk and new wave to forge a disruptive and deconstructive sound; and Cortez worked on his Elvis documentary, edited a *Private Elvis* book, and semimanaged some of the bands that had also impressed Phillips, drawn to the way they were "doing something more extreme" than the CBGB breakthrough lineups that had landed contracts with Sire.[3] "Those bands all had a strong concept," recalls Chance. "They had a look, an image of what they wanted to be, and that im-

Steve Mass and Diego Cortez, Lower East Side, 1978. Cortez first headed to CBGB following an invite from Talking Heads guitarist and lead singer David Byrne. Photograph by and courtesy of Bobby Grossman ©.

pressed me, but they were all using the same old rock and roll chord changes. None of them were taking it any further than the Velvet Underground or the Stooges — in fact they were more conservative — and none of them had an overt black influence."

Raised in Milwaukee, where he studied piano at a conservatory before switching to sax, Chance moved to New York because "that was just the place to go to make it in jazz," but he quickly gave up on the loft jazz scene because its white hipster and hippie contingents annoyed him too much. Instead he gravitated to CBGB and Max's, where he met Cortez, who encouraged him to explore punk, which led him to join Lydia Lunch's Teenage Jesus and the Jerks until Lunch kicked him out because his sax was wrecking her minimalist aesthetic. Chance responded by founding the Contortions, a James Brown–inspired outfit with added atonality and sax solos that debuted in December

1977 and played at an *X Magazine* benefit held in an East 4th Street hall the following March. "All these people started sitting and crouching on the floor, and it made me go crazy because that's what all those people did in the jazz lofts," he recalls. "That was the first time I attacked people in the audience." Phillips had looked right through Chance the first time he tried to talk to her but now approached him. "We ended up hanging out for two days straight," he reminisces. "Soon after she started talking about this club idea. Steve was the money man and Anya was going to be the manager."

A short while later, a mutual friend told Cortez that Brian Eno — cofounder of Roxy Music, producer for David Bowie, and composer of the landmark ambient album *Discreet Music* — was traveling to New York on 23 April to master the Talking Heads album *More Songs about Buildings and Food*. Cortez invited the Englishman to Mass's duplex apartment on 8th Street to persuade him to record a soundtrack for his Elvis film. Just under two weeks later, Eno attended a five-night music series at the TriBeCa gallery and performance venue Artists Space that featured ten bands, among them the Contortions, Teenage Jesus and the Jerks, Mars, and DNA. With Cortez, Phillips, and Arto Lindsay of DNA facilitating a process that began with further meetings on 8th Street, Eno recorded a showcase *No New York* compilation album that captured their post–new wave sound, soon to be known as no wave.[4] Lodging on the spare floor in Mass's duplex, Eno ended up extending his visit from three weeks to seven months. "It turned out that I happened to be in New York during one of the most exciting months of the decade, I should think, in terms of music," Eno recalled in 1980. "It seemed like there were 500 new bands who all started that month."[5]

Back on White Street, Cortez and Phillips persuaded Mass to name his venue the Molotov Cocktail Lounge after the MCL letters inscribed on the building's frontage, only for the entrepreneur to backtrack on the basis that the name was too inflammatory. After all, whereas Cortez and Phillips were free to take chances, he had a medical business service to protect, plus he wanted the liquor license application process to be smooth. As an alternative he proposed the Mudd Club Lounge, which both referenced Samuel Alexander Mudd (the southerner physician who treated John Wilkes Booth for the injury he suffered after he assassinated President Lincoln) and somewhat obliquely evoked his anthropological interest in indigenous peoples. The suggestion riled Cortez and Phillips, however, and a subsequent meeting between Mass and Phillips culminated in a blow-out argument. Unable to remember the details of the altercation, Mass wonders if Phillips took umbrage to the news that he was applying for a liquor license in his own name, yet

Cortez maintains that Mass's sole ownership was never in doubt. "We were never financial partners with Steve and we didn't want to be part of any administrative machine," he points out. "It was just our idea." Chance confirms that Phillips couldn't have cared less about the liquor application. "In Anya's mind she was going to be the manager of the club and the guiding spirit behind the whole thing, and Steve would stay in the background," he recalls. "But she absolutely hated the Mudd Club name and all of a sudden she was completely out."

Mass proceeded with the renovation of the White Street space as if nothing had happened. He organized the main room around a long bar embedded with his personal collection of aviation maps and equipped with two turntables. At the far end of the room he installed a small, collapsible modular stage that could be easily erected and dismantled so the room could support live music followed by dancing. For the sound system he teamed up with Eno to re-create the studio conditions he had experienced during the recording sessions of *No New York* so his future crowd could listen to punk's Rimbaud-style symbolist lyrics with absolute clarity. Outside he left the building's nondescript frontage untouched in order to contribute to the impression the club existed several urban layers deep. He also employed a local blacksmith to create an industrial chain and stanchion that would offer a symbolic challenge to the velvet rope deployed by Manhattan's elitist midtown discotheques. "The velvet rope was designed to keep the people lacking taste, the underclass, away," notes Mass. "But I took the velvet rope and devalued it."

With typesetter Alex Blair facilitating — she knew Eno and through Eno knew Mass — *Punk* magazine staged the first event at the Mudd Club, an awards ceremony afterparty that happened to fall the day after Sid Vicious was arrested for killing his girlfriend, Nancy Spungen (on Friday, 13 October). "There were all these people there, all these movers and shakers — Amos Poe, Anya Phillips, rock and roll people like David Johansen [of the New York Dolls]," recalls novice DJ David Azarch, a sales assistant in a record store called Jimmy's Music World. "I was, 'Wow, wow, wow, wow!'" Having maintained standoffish contact with Mass because she had started to manage the Contortions as well as date Chance, and hoping to be able to arrange for the Contortions to perform at the new venue, Phillips staged a party that featured Chance lip-synching to James Brown records a week or so later. Mass then held an unofficial launch on Halloween, during which local punk band Xerox took to the stage wearing blacklight outfits and the Georgian new wavers the B-52's performed in girdles. "It was just an amazing night," recalls Azarch, who showed up to DJ without even knowing the B-52's were going to play. "The downtown arts scene mixed with the rock and roll scene from a little bit north. It was just a magical mix. The place was electric."

Hosted by Tina L'Hotsky, a Cleveland Institute of Art graduate, underground film director/actor, and organizer of several impromptu parties in rubble-strewn lots on Avenue C, the "Cha-Cha Party" of 5 December hinted at the creative bedlam that was about to unfold in the Mudd Club. Breaking with the East Village punk scene's benign disinterest in the local migrant community, the night celebrated Caribbean, Latin, and East Village storefront culture as revelers dressed "Rican," the room was hung with bananas and southern religious icons, waiters served Spanish sherry and pork rinds, a local Hispanic television celebrity sang ethnic songs, and L'Hotsky celebrated the publication of her photo-fiction book, *Muchachas Espanola Loca* (*Crazy Spanish Girls*).[6] The night amounted to a rare flash of exuberance as Steve Mass waited for his temporary license to be made permanent. Then, once the owner was satisfied the certification was in order, he took the Mudd Club on a run of activity that knew no obvious nightlife precedent in terms of curatorial range and visceral fire.

Held approximately once a month, immersive parties drew inspiration from the Fluxus happenings of the 1960s that saw avant-garde artists and musicians integrate a range of media and disciplines to challenge received assumptions about art and commerce. Staged at the beginning of 1979, the "Hawaiian Beach Party" featured hula dancers, Polynesian music and decor, tropical drinks, and another set from the B-52's. Taking its name from the abuse-and-survival memoir published by one of Joan Crawford's adoptees, the "Joan Crawford 'Mommie's Dearest' Mother's Day Celebration" featured a complete 1950s kitchen installation plus a large party cake furnished with a gagged and bound baby doll tied to a Styrofoam bed post, around which Joan Crawford lookalikes mixed and mingled with partygoers who dressed up as battered and abused children.[7] Commemorating D-Day, the "War Games: Combat Love Party" included a live set from Shrapnel, refreshments in the form of World War II–style K-rations, and a Jane Fonda protest doll for target practice, with participants dressing as members of the Women's Army Corps, Stormtroopers, generals, protestors, geishas, Nazi dykes, USO (United States Organization) chorus girls, and related figures (as the flyer instructed).[8] Then there was the "Rock 'n' Roll Funeral Ball Extravaganza," which staged a mock funeral procession of dead rock stars Mama Cass, Janis Joplin, Jim Morrison, Elvis Presley, and Sid Vicious, who were laid to rest in coffins in tableau-style

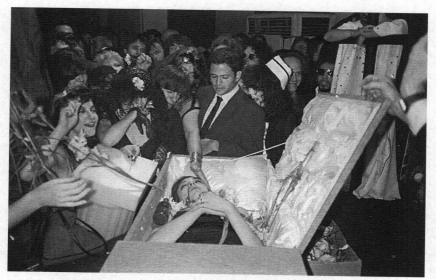

"Rock 'n' Roll Funeral Ball Extravaganza" at the Mudd Club. Photograph by and courtesy of Allan Tannenbaum/SoHo Blues ©.

recreations of their death scenes, from the syringe that pierced Joplin's arm to the plate of ham sandwiches on which Cass reputedly choked to death. "The parties took American institutions and parodied and destroyed them in one way or another," comments Mass. "All kinds of unexpected things would happen."

Mass simultaneously curated a live music program that saw the B-52's, Marianne Faithfull, and Talking Heads take to the same, modular stage as new wave and no wave outfits Boris Policeband, DNA, the Feelies, the Fleshtones, Material, the Necessaries, Suicide, and Tuxedomoon. The owner also booked the composer-performer-guitarists Rhys Chatham and Glenn Branca, who created minimalist drone sounds played at ear-splitting volume. Yet while many of these lineups bolstered a dissonant aesthetic reminiscent of the one already shaped at CBGB and Max's, Mass made a point of embracing a radical eclecticism that saw him schedule the experimental composer-musicians Laurie Anderson, Harold Budd, Peter Gordon, and David van Tieghem; heavy metal terrorizers Judas Priest; ska and reggae lineups such as the U.K. breakthrough band Madness; macabre R&B performer Screamin' Jay Hawkins; New Orleans vocalist and pianist Professor Longhair; pioneering girl groups the Crystals and the Shirelles; and the "Queen of Motown," Mary Wells. "I thought that there were similarities between all these different types of music," explains the owner. "I didn't care what the audience thought. I wasn't trying to supply the audience with a punk repertoire. To me stylistic coherence didn't matter at all." He also saw black music as part of an "extraordinary revolutionary phenomenon" that was as politically and conceptually radical as the white rock and punk music that was more readily lauded in downtown circles. "The punks," he thought, "were privileged to even rub elbows" with black musicians.

With screenings scheduled between 7:00 and 9:00 PM, the innovative visual culture was more aesthetically and socially coherent. Downtown video artist teams Emily Armstrong/Pat Ivers and Kit Fitzgerald/John Sanborn were among the first to show their work using the venue's huge, bullet-shaped, black-and-white projector. *Interview Magazine* editor Glenn O'Brien and Blondie guitarist Chris Stein filmed several episodes of their punk-oriented cable access program TV *Party* in the venue. No wave directors Kathryn Bigelow, Jim Jarmusch, Eric Mitchell, James Nares, and Amos Poe contributed to screenings that took place once every two weeks or so. "Clubs didn't have film before the Mudd Club," points out Mass, who played the part of the entrepreneur abducted and abused by blunted bohemians in Mitchell's 1978 film *Kidnapped*. "But all of these people were my friends. That was my initial entry into the club scene — through film."

Alternative fashion also figured prominently as Mass commissioned a "whole army" of young punk-inspired designers to put on shows. "I was always trying to involve them in the life of the Mudd Club," comments the owner. "That was part of the sociology of the scene that really interested me because they were deconstructing the commodity. They were living examples of the Situationist strategy." Betsey Johnson, Maripol, Stephen Sprouse, Anna Sui, and Tish and Snooky helped shape a style that combined the dressy and the homemade. "There was this really big and strong DIY ethos everywhere, and that also became what was in fashion," explains Chi Chi Valenti, a window display designer, who for "Combat Love" dressed in the Nazi regalia worn by the former concentration camp prisoner when she begins a relationship with her ex-guard in the film *The Night Porter*. "We didn't want our outfits to look too studied. The look was not just punk but low rent, xeroxy. It was really about creating something from nothing."

Meanwhile the spiky-haired, Beatle-booted Azarch continued to select records for $5/hour, with Sean Cassette, Mark Fodiatis, and Danny Heaps working as alternates. "My attitude from the very first time I did it was to play music that I liked," notes Azarch, who was eighteen years old at the time. "People were just into the music. They didn't say, 'Let's go dance.' It was, 'Check this song out' and the next thing you know people were on the dance floor. It just escalated from there. There weren't very specific markings as to how it happened." Warming up with tracks by the likes of Eno and Kraftwerk before he turned to Blondie, David Bowie, the Clash, Cold Hero (later the Cure), Elvis Costello, ELO, the Only Ones, Tom Petty, Iggy Pop, Lou Reed, the Sex Pistols, and Talking Heads, Azarch felt his way into the novice role of the punk rock DJ. "David Bowie came to the club one night and Steve Mass came to me and said, 'David Bowie's here,'" he recalls. "I said to myself, 'The last thing David Bowie wants to hear is David Bowie,' so I played everything he'd played sax on or produced. I was like, I have *Transformer* [by Lou Reed], I have Iggy Pop — things he was involved with over time. It was just my response."

Mass nevertheless believed that the DJ-ing profession had yet to throw up the kind of artist figure he would have liked to employ, so he "tried to make up for it" by instructing Azarch to make a specific selection whenever it took his fancy. "I would actually impose my eclectic taste, throwing in all kinds of strange stuff," comments the owner. "As the dance floor was erupting in a magical, orgiastic moment, I might switch into a soundtrack of roaring tornadoes hitting a small town in Texas. I actually had one woman come up to me, crying, and say, 'How could you do something so awful?' Like I was a war criminal." Azarch recalls Mass would approach him during the middle of the night with a 45 of "Betty Lou Got a New Pair of Shoes," an obscure song from the 1950s, and order him to play it five or six times in a row. "He'd stand in the booth sipping his drink, loving that I was playing this record," remembers the DJ. "People would be standing, looking at me, saying, 'What are you doing?'"

The Mudd Club became the preferred hangout for a group of miscellaneous bohemians, many of them one-time Max's and CBGB regulars who found themselves drawn to the White Street spot's wider range of creative engagements. In addition to the musicians, film directors, and fashion designers who socialized as well as worked at the spot, regulars included Andy Warhol and Warhol Superstars Jackie Curtis and Nico, beat writers William Burroughs and Allen Ginsberg, poet John Giorno, post-Marxist intellectual Sylvère Lotringer, *East Village Eye* editor Leonard Abrams, graffiti artist Jean-Michel Basquiat, art critic Edit deAk, and the poet-actor-painter Rene Ricard. Numerous others hung out at the spot, even if they didn't perform there during its opening months, among them Debbie Harry and Chris Stein of Blondie, Arto Lindsay, John Lurie of the Lounge Lizards, German countertenor Klaus Nomi, the band members of the Ramones, and Johnny Thunders of the New York Dolls. Experimental writer Kathy Acker and underground cinema star Patti Astor joined L'Hotsky, Lunch, and Valenti to form an active contingent of third-wave feminists. Critic Bernard Gendron argues the

Klaus Nomi at the Mudd Club. Photograph by and courtesy of Nicholas Taylor ©.

venue resembled a modern-day reincarnation of either Le Chat Noir, the late nineteenth-century cabaret that served the bohemian Montmartre district of Paris, or Cabaret Voltaire in Zurich, Hugo Ball's mutinous cabaret that inspired the Dada movement.[9] "The Mudd Club wasn't a destination; it was a place for locals to hang out," observes Azarch. "The people who were coming to hang out were people of some notoriety or people who later on became people of notoriety. I would turn around and there'd be Jean-Michel Basquiat or Allen Ginsberg. Here I was, not only in their presence but entertaining them."

A new type of hangout had come into being—one that made CBGB's exclusive focus on live music appear anachronistic. "The Mudd Club wasn't just a new club," comments Johnny Dynell, who traveled to New York to go to art college, joined a no wave band, and lived in Bleckner's painting studio. "It was a new concept." Having kickstarted her film career at CBGB after meeting Poe there, Astor began to head to White Street on a nightly basis as soon as it opened. "That's where you met everybody," she comments. "It became the only place to go." Because of the scarcity of phones never mind answering machines, many gravitated to Mass's spot not only to socialize but also to find out what was going down: who was making what film or planning what special party or putting together what fashion show or staging what theater production. In short, it operated as both a scene unto itself and also a scene generator, or a place where it was possible to make connections and begin collaborations. "There were so many people who got their start at the Mudd Club," adds Dynell. "When the Mudd Club opened, it wasn't just a new club. It was a new generation."

Troubled when he learned that a key figure from the art scene had been refused entry one night, Mass employed local artist and Max's/CBGB habitué Richard Boch to run the door four months after opening. Sometimes following and sometimes ignoring the owner's "off-the-wall" guidelines, Boch drew on gut instinct as well as scenester knowledge as he welcomed artists, the rock and roll crowd, the fashion set, and celebrities such as David Bowie, Mick Jagger, Iggy Pop, and Lou Reed while refusing entry to tourists as well as anyone who "seemed like a jerk" or "came on strong" (unless they enjoyed a connection to Mass or the venue). "The Mudd Club was often on the edge of being out of control," observes Boch. "It was its ability to not tip over the edge that made it what it was. When the door was handled well it rarely toppled over." Mass came to view Boch as a linchpin who knew to admit Robert Rauschenberg if he showed up "in a drunken state, disheveled, holding onto some sixteen-year-old boy," yet would also make record company executives, tastemakers, and anyone who rolled up in a limousine wait "while some sixteen-year-old punkette got in ahead of them." *SoHo News* ad salesperson and *Living Eye* fanzine editor Ken Aronds benefited the night he showed up with Susan, a two-and-a-half-foot, hunchbacked punk who walked with a cane. "The doorkeepers gawked at us and let us in," he recalls. "We were a freak show, something different, and that's why we were admitted."

As the pressure on the door mounted, especially over weekends, Mass extended the club into the second floor, shaping it as a breakout lounge space, which he could open when the first floor became packed, as well as a room where he could position the installations he commissioned for the happenings. Equipped with ugly banquettes purchased in an auction plus a Zodiac Wurlitzer jukebox that he stocked with records that ranged from the Sex Pistols to Pat Boone, the lounge soon doubled as a retreat for regulars who wanted to congregate away from the hurly-burly of the first floor, and it acquired VIP status when Valenti became its doorkeeper during weekends. A foreboding presence who boasted an exquisite line in dominance outfits, Valenti received $75 for her 2:30 AM to 6:30 AM shifts, and although Mass maintains that he never intended the second floor to become an exclusive domain, with the basement his preferred hideaway for celebrities such as Bowie, that's how his crowd imagined it. "Steve started to go up the floors," recalls Astor. "He kept that VIP room pretty tight. The original people were always taken care of. I didn't pay for a drink for four years."

It was the second-floor lounge space and in particular the Wurlitzer's juxtaposition of punk and easy listening pop that caught the attention of Anita Sarko when she visited the Mudd Club for the first time soon after the second-floor lounge opened in the spring. A radio DJ based in Atlanta, she heard about the spot from local band the B-52's and arrived with high expectations, only to experience a twang of disappointment at what she judged to be the conservative rock selections of whoever was DJ-ing that night. Raised on an eclectic diet of musical theater, gospel, Elvis, Motown, English rock, and Michigan punk, Sarko concluded that she "could do better," returned home to gather her possessions, headed back to New York, and met Mass when she gatecrashed an uptown party for the Who. The owner offered her Mondays and Tuesdays, having started to DJ himself in order to fill a vacancy that appears to have emerged when Cassette left to play at a struggling midtown rock discotheque called Hurrah. Azarch held onto the busiest nights of the week while Sarko took to selecting music for the start-of-the-week diehards.

Dressing in outfits that combined glam, vintage, and punk, Sarko confronted expectations by integrating funk, jazz, R&B, soul, folk, reggae, and "lots of foreign" alongside more obvious punk, new wave, and no wave cuts. "My style was to mix all sorts of music together so nobody ever knew what was going to happen next," she explains. "I always had hundreds of records surrounding me because I could only think in a free-form, improvisational way. I never knew what the energy would be that night or what I would be in the mood for or how the guests would feel." Unable to grasp the concept of thinking outside the box because she had never been able to locate the "fucking box" in the first place, the DJ also introduced noise, classical, and spoken-word cuts, toying with variables to discover "what reactions could occur through the abstraction of sound." For the "Rock 'n' Roll Funeral Ball Extravaganza," when revelers were required to dress as someone who was dead or should be dead, she played records within the same parameters. "Obviously Paul McCartney was included because of the rumor that he had died and been replaced by a lookalike," she remembers. "That had always been the explanation for Wings [McCartney's post-Beatles lineup]."

If Mass wondered at how he had come to run the hottest off-the-radar spot in the city as a result of discussions with Cortez and Phillips plus a $15,000 budget, the radar began to track his venue when *People Magazine* became the first national outlet to cover the spot in July 1979. "Ever on the prowl for outrageous novelty, New York's fly-by-night crowd of punks, posers and the ultra hip has discovered new turf on which to flaunt its manic chic," reported the publication. "For sheer kinkiness, there has been nothing like it since the cabaret scene in 1920s Berlin." The tabloid gorged on the unfolding scene, noting that it amounted to a "depraved version" of *Let's Make a Deal* and feigning shock that "one man gained entrance simply by flashing the stump of his amputated arm." The Mudd Club, it added, had made the midtown discotheque and celebrity magnet Studio 54 seem almost passé in six months flat as it assembled its crowd "like some sort of perverse trash compactor."[10] If anything, Mass set out with the thought that the Mudd Club would operate as the polar opposite of Studio, with its industrial chain and unlit entrance symbolic of its opposition to midtown disco's rootedness in hierarchy, flashiness, and materialism. But as the *People* article fomented demand, the owner began to feel that "something got out of control" and even began to fear that the "whole thing couldn't go on." Then again, disco was about to implode, and not even the punk crowd had got around to calculating the consequences of that.

A strong anti-disco feeling ran through the Mudd Club. "The music became monotonous and there was this celebration of people not getting in, of social exclusivity, so I knew I wanted the Mudd Club to be the opposite of the glitz of the disco ball," Steve Mass explains. "I think it was a mistake, but we had no appreciation of disco whatsoever. This went across the board, from Diego to the lowest thug working for Warner Bros." Mass judged Studio 54 to be symptomatic of the society of the spectacle while Cortez confirms that he and Phillips imagined the Mudd Club as being "anti-disco from the beginning" because "we wanted a place to dance but not to the innocuous auto-beats of the large NYC disco." Azarch notes that he "was not a big fan" of disco, especially the "standardized" tracks that were being "pumped out." Arguing that disco sounded like "musical wallpaper" and that disco-style beat mixing "didn't allow one to change direction or enmesh different sounds and moods," Sarko maintains that her approach to DJ-ing amounted to "the antithesis of disco."

Punk opposition to disco came to the fore during 1976 when *Punk* magazine editor John Holmstrom rallied against its rootedness in the studio and repetition.[11] Feelings of hostility peppered with disgust intensified when Studio 54 opened the following spring and the Brooklyn disco movie *Saturday Night Fever* began its record-breaking run in November, leading disco to become associated with velvet-rope elitism on the one hand and working-class suburbia on the other. The Mudd Club opened toward the end of 1978, just before Warner Bros. became the first major label to open a disco department and just before analysts confirmed that the year saw the dance genre surpass rock in terms of sales. When author Vita Miezitis toured New York's night clubs during the summer of 1979 to research a book published in 1980, she was struck by the Mudd Club's "anti-disco dress code" as well as the way the DJ that night would select "every kind of music but disco."[12]

Yet although the White Street venue appeared to exist as the perfect counterpoint to disco, its crowd soon came to contain too many disco habitués for it to mount a credible stand against the culture. With Warhol leading the way and the high-profile federal raid on Studio 54 in December 1978 encouraging others to follow, midtown regulars started to gravitate to White Street soon after it opened, reassured that the door queues and atmosphere of exclusivity offered important continuities. When Victor Hugo performed at the spot in July 1979, a photographer caught Studio 54 co-owner Steve Rubell slouching on a sofa beside his lawyer Roy Cohn. "My evenings were pretty much equally divided between the Mudd Club and Studio 54," adds Monica Lynch, a onetime regular at La Mere Vipere who worked on 54th Street. "Steve Rubell always hired fun young kids to decorate the room at Studio 54 and the younger kids like myself would also venture downtown. Stirling St. Jacques might not have been going to the Mudd Club but there was more overlap than people thought. They were both discos, frankly." Peaking when Chicago talk DJ Steve Dahl blew up forty thousand disco records during an anti-disco rally, also in July 1979, the frequently homophobic, racist, and sexist backlash against disco rendered punk's opposition anachronistic. "We all had to face the reality that we were, with our disco hatred, aligning ourselves with the forces of reaction," remembers Aronds. "At that point I began to examine my prejudices and I didn't like what I found."

It was in this setting that Johnny Dynell executed what he perceived to be the ultimate punk move by selecting disco, having started to DJ around the time of the "Rock 'n' Roll Funeral Ball Extravaganza." "I was hanging out," he recounted later. "I needed money. I needed a job and Steve just said, out of the corner of his mouth, 'Well, uh, what do you want to do? Do you want to be a bartender? What exactly do you want to do?' So, out of the blue, I just said, 'I want to be a deejay.'"[13] Cast in the role of Elvis for the funeral ball, Dynell started to appear between Azarch's and Sarko's sets. "I was doing disco as a kind of art," he explains. "I was dressing in tight Jordache jeans — they were the look of uptown disco, of Studio 54 — and I had my hair cut like John Travolta." He even penned a spoof *National Enquirer*–style article titled "How I Beat Cancer by Listening to Disco Music" in the *SoHo News* under the name of Pablo "Cuchi-Frito" Cordova that featured a mock interview with Johnny Savas (his original family name). "I can assure you I haven't the slightest desire to return to my old body-destroying slow-death listening diet," declared Savas. "It's marvelous how your sensibilities become more sensitive to the many varieties of artists playing disco music today."[14]

Dynell didn't share any contempt his Mudd Club peers might have felt toward disco, including those who approached him during the night to ask "What is this nigger-shit?" or to declare "Go back to Studio 54 where you belong."[15] It wasn't just that his ears heard the "Uh-huh, uh-huh" chorus of KC & the Sunshine Band's "That's the Way (I Like It)" to be a kind of punk chant. He also might have been the only White Street regular to frequent the downtown dance scene, which took root prior to the rise of disco as well as punk when David Mancuso started to hold private parties in February 1970 and the Sanctuary re-opened as the first public discotheque to welcome gay men around the same time. "I went to the Loft, I went to the Paradise Garage, I went to hear Danny Krivit at One's, I went to the first Limelight, I went to Buttermilk Bottom, so I was much more comfortable with disco than the other Mudd Club DJS," he notes. "Disco became this thing and a lot of people wanted to distance themselves from it, but I never thought of the Loft and the Paradise Garage and One's as discos in the first place." Yet with Dahl and the federal raid of Studio instilling the backlash with a reactionary complexion, the Mudd Club crowd's response to Dynell turned out to be remarkably enthusiastic. "I was like, 'If people wanted to dance to disco music, why didn't they go uptown for that?'" remembers Azarch. "But so many people wanted to hear it I was like, 'Wow, this is interesting.'" Recognizing that some of Dynell's selections were "really good," he tweaked his style accordingly. "I'd play 'Mr. Big Stuff' [by Jean Knight] first and then 'Hot Stuff' by the Stones and then 'Hot Stuff' by Donna Summer, so I'd create these themes."

The Mudd Club had come a long way from Max's (where Dynell had been thrown out for dancing) and CBGB (where James Chance "really hated" the lack of a dance floor).[16] It was true that nobody was "commanded" to dance in the White Street spot, as Valenti puts it, but while Sarko could get away with her idiosyncratic selections on the comparatively quiet nights of Mondays and Tuesdays, the rest of the week became notable for its kinetic crescendos. As much as Cortez enjoyed talking, he "danced all the time as well," he recalls, while Lynch remembers "ferocious dancing" at the spot. "We were making fun of Studio 54 and Les Mouches, but people started dancing and the Mudd Club changed into this major dance club," argues Dynell. "It was a joke and nobody expected the whole thing to blow up." The venue was helping establish the foundations for a renaissance marked by convergence and exploration. "Very quickly the Mudd Club had a sound that was edgy and

The Mudd Club dance floor, 1979. Photograph by and courtesy of Allan Tannenbaum/ SoHo Blues ©.

alternative — Ian Dury, 'Reasons to Be Cheerful'; Flying Lizards, 'Money'; the Slits, 'Heard It through the Grapevine'; Marianne Faithfull, 'Why D'Ya Do It?,'" adds Dynell. "But these records had a beat and the basic beat was disco."

The Hegelian struggles of the 1970s were approaching the point of implosion. Punk and disco had respectively challenged the stagnant status quo, only to swerve into a dialectical battle of their own. But instead of concluding with a winner, the bout ended in a draw as the contestants clasped one another, exhausted, and in that moment grasped that victory could lie in amalgamation rather than annihilation. "If the thing you're fighting is no longer there then you're fighting windmills," points out Sarko. "But in this case Mudd Club did have an identity of its own. It was art-based, postmodern and postpunk, and it was also about expression and humor and creativity, not fame or wealth or the desire to be recognized by those who were part of the agreed-upon establishment. It was about pushing boundaries and continually being open to new ideas and forms, which was why we all dabbled in each other's art, whether that be acting, painting, DJ-ing or putting on shows." The more philosophical, adds Sarko, were more interested in "the process than the outcome."

An unpredictable, mutant, and at times indelibly strange period in the history of New York party culture was about to unfold, and at its vanguard stood a fledgling nightlife operator who placed experimentation and contradiction at the heart of his operation. "I wasn't for or against either side," reasons Mass. "I felt the only way to run a club was to be constantly turning things upside down. As far as I was concerned, this is the kind of atmosphere creativity thrives in. This was my aesthetic theory." The downtown party scene was heading in a direction that was unpredictable, darkly humorous, inventive, and participatory.

THE BASEMENT DEN
AT CLUB 57

A self-described suburban refugee of West Virginia, Ann Magnuson studied theater and cinema in Ohio before moving to New York in January 1978 to complete her studies by working as an intern director. She arrived somewhat disappointed that the Great Lakes College Association had assigned her to work at the Ensemble Studio Theater, an Off-Broadway theater company based on 52nd Street, rather than an avant-garde, downtown setup. But within days she threw herself into the sunless substrata of CBGB and Max's Kansas City, where she headed "every night" except the one when she checked out Studio 54, which held her attention for all of fifteen minutes. "The punk bands at CBGB opened everybody's eyes and made us think, 'Yeah, pick up an instrument, pick up a paintbrush, there's nothing to stop you!' " she reminisces. " 'There are no limits, there are no rules! Let your freak flag wave high!' " Fair-skinned, doe-eyed, and inspired, Magnuson resolved to combine her two worlds of theater and nightclubs. By June she was so immersed she refused to attend her graduation ceremony.

That autumn Magnuson teamed up with CBGB friends Susan Hannaford and Tom Scully to stage a four-night "New Wave Vaudeville" variety show at Irving Plaza, a Polish veterans' club located at 15th Street and Irving Place. With punk-art energy charging the rehearsals, which included debutant Klaus Nomi singing an aria from the opera *Samson et Dalila* dressed in alien drag, building manager Stanley Strychacki invited the audacious organizers to view another spot he ran, Club 57, previously the East Village Student Club, which was located in the basement of the Holy Cross Polish National Church at 57 St. Mark's Place. Strychacki had already started to schedule punk concerts and film screenings in the spot, including the April 1978 Reelin', Rockin' Film Festival.[1] But there were limits to what he could manage, plus neighbors complained about the live music, so he decided to head in the direction of the

"New Wave Vaudeville" cabaret. The Mudd Club had only just got going and was barely open to the public. There was plenty of slack to take up.

Hannaford, Magnuson, and Scully checked out the St. Mark's Place spot and then returned with friends to test opinion. "We entered into this small dark room with low ceilings and random institutional pieces of furniture scattered around," recalls School of Visual Arts (SVA) student Frank Holliday. "There was an old wooden bar on the left side, much like other Polish bars in the neighborhood, but smaller, and there was some old lamp. It smelled like a church — it was musty, old, dark." Holliday remembers that "it really didn't look like much," but Scully could barely contain his excitement as he explained how the spot could be used to stage parties and screenings, and Strychacki couldn't have been happier when the three friends agreed to accept his offer. "I fell in love with them and I got them!" recalls the Polish manager.[2]

Strychacki continued to schedule events during the long, hard winter of 1978–1979, among them Double Exposure, a four-night film and performance festival that featured subterranean stars such as Kathy Acker, John Lurie, and James Nares. Then, beginning in April, Hannaford, Magnuson, and Scully cleaned and painted the basement spot while Strychacki persuaded Magnuson to take on a managerial role. A month later, Hannaford and Scully launched the weekly Monster Movie Club with a screening of the sci-fi comedy *Invasion of the Saucer Men*, and the night soon started to attract SVA students, who took to punctuating films with riotous comments as joints and mushrooms accentuated the fun. The venue quickly settled into a quiet routine that featured movie nights, theatrical performances, St. Mark's Poetry Project events, and, beginning in August, meetings of the Ladies Auxiliary of the Lower East Side, a Magnuson-led feminist group that resembled a punk version of the Junior League. "There was this guy at one of the St. Mark's Poetry Project nights doing this off-the-wall stuff and they all hated him," recalls Magnuson, who was managing the venue that night. "When he came up to the bar I said, 'You're my favorite poet!' That was the first time I met Keith and we became friends."

Raised in Kutztown, Pennsylvania, Keith Haring was already combining calligraphy, energetic shapes, semiotics, and the cutup language of William Burroughs and Fluxus with a passion for performance, music, and partying when SVA and pot-smoking buddy Holliday introduced him to Club 57. Soon after, Haring started to usher other college friends into the denlike spot. One of them, Kenny Scharf, a University of California graduate, melded pop art, surrealism, suburban culture, and space-age imagery. Another, John McLaughlin, shifted

Club 57 entrance. Photograph by and courtesy of Harvey Wang ©.

his focus from painting to performance art as he restyled his hair into a blond pompadour, took on the persona of a Las Vegas lounge singer/alternative burlesque performer, and started to go under the name of John Sex. A third, Drew Straub, who also hailed from Kutztown, started to make art out of pennies. A fourth, Wendy Wild, who was dating Sex, flung herself into performance opportunities and took on the celebrated role of preparing the mushroom punch. "Club 57 attracted a particular kind of art student, as well as people who never went to art school but were attracted to that kind of aesthetic," remembers Magnuson, who signed all comers up to a $2-a-head membership system, introduced in case the cops asked why alcohol was being served in the unlicensed club. "Everybody started to meet each other and it just built."

Following a stifling August, Magnuson began to curate and organize nights at a bewildering pace, with Hannaford and Scully, the SVA posse, and regulars such as Dany Johnson, William Fleet Lively, Andy Rees, Naomi Regelson, and the Ladies Auxiliary troops contributing to a program that started to run six nights a week during the autumn. Screenings remained at the core of the program. Jerry Beck's "Cartoons You Won't See on TV" presented animation that featured violence, sex, and racism. "Home Movie Torture" showcased embarrassing moments captured on video. Beck and Magnuson's retro TV night "Television Nostomania" replayed episodes of TV shows from the 1950s and 1960s. Bill Landis, the creator of grindhouse-movie scene journal *Sleazoid Express*, presented films that captured the sex and drugs culture of Times Square. Film also merged with performance and partying, as was the case the night Fellini's *La Dolce Vita* played during the "Decadent High Fashion Bacchanal Party." Meanwhile Hannaford and Scully augmented their Monster Movie Club by initiating a second weekly slot that screened films ranging from *Belle de Jour*, Luis Buñuel's tale of a housewife's sadomasochistic fantasy, to Russ Meyer's exploitation film *Faster, Pussycat! Kill! Kill!* The curatorial efforts of her partners shaped the emergence of a "Hammer-vampire-Texas-Chainsaw-astrozombie knowledge," Magnuson argued in 1982.[3]

Club 57 also introduced a vibrant combination of artistic and performance-based events that knew no obvious precedent in the city, in part because noise problems prevented Magnuson and company from developing the kind of live music schedule that Steve Mass had championed at the Mudd Club. Scharf staged the venue's first exhibition, *Celebration of the Space Age*. Haring curated a multi-artist *Xerox Art* show and an open *Club 57 Invitational*. Sex's participatory "Acts of Live Art" nights integrated all manner of weird and wild performances, including wheelchair-bound convulsions, the Bertha Butt Boogie caveman dance, naked rapping, majorette tap dancing to disco, and a matador striptease. Participatory events such as the punk rock game show "Name That Noise," the photo dance party "Pictures You Can Dance To," and the performance night "Rapper Party, Psycho Disco with Special Guests" kept the fun and inventiveness flowing. If there was live music, it usually came courtesy of in-house bands, the Man Rays, who performed with tin foil wrapped around their heads so that they resembled human baked potatoes (as Kai Eric, a front man, conceptual artist, and boyfriend of Magnuson, liked to put it), or from featured bands, that didn't push the decibels too hard, as was the case with ART, the Only Band in the World.

Special parties completed the schedule. The Ladies Auxiliary started things off with a packed "Stay Free Mini Prom." Magnuson channeled her obsession with the communist bloc at "Radio Free Europe," where she launched her Russian pop-star character Anoushka. Revelers messed about with model kits, glue, and (for those who wanted to sniff the glue) paper bags at "Dada Disco GoGo Cavalcade/Model World of Glue," after which the Man Rays performed "Dada Disco." The "Putt-Putt Reggae Party" featured a miniature eighteen-hole-golf-course-cum-Jamaican-shantytown made out of refrigerator boxes. "Iran, Iraq and Iroll" satirized the stalled Iran hostage crisis as Scully

DJ-ed in a headdress made out of a U.S. flag. "Ladies Wrestling Night" featured raucous battles, faux coaches, and camp refereeing. The "Bongo Voodoo" event combined chicken cursing, secret rituals, and frenzied ceremonial dancing. And the "Debutante Ball" foregrounded elegant outfits, couples dancing, and MC Kristian Hoffman of punk outfit the Mumps crooning ballads. And so the theme parties rolled until the calendar crescendoed with the "Elvis Memorial Party," held in mid-August 1980, which brought together Elvis lookalikes, impressionists, memorabilia, and a screening of *King Creole*, only for a faulty air conditioner to burst into flames and break up the festivities. Revelers proceeded to clamber onto the fire truck until angry Polish residents doused them with bathwater.[4]

Dancing became central to the fun as Club 57-ites honed retro styles such as the twist, the shimmy, the frug, and the jerk, usually in bursts of an hour or two before and after the billed attraction. Initially Scully supplied the music via a jukebox, but then the cofounder started to DJ, sometimes putting on themed nights such as "British Invasion" and "The Wild, Wild World of Speed," with Naomi Regelson and Dany Johnson also taking turns. Notable for her mix of boogaloo, go-go, funk, and new wave, and favoring what she calls "campy records" sourced in neighborhood junk shops, Johnson became the main DJ over time. "Dany always knew how to make us shake hard and fast," recalls Scharf. "The spoof atmosphere was part of the fun." Packed with just fifty people and rammed when one hundred showed up, the floor heated up quickly. "There'd be so much dancing the DJ equipment would start to vibrate and the music would skip," remembers Magnuson, who also played records from time to time. "That was a huge problem. It'd put a dampener on proceedings and sometimes we'd just resort to the jukebox." Eric, another occasional DJ, described Club 57 as an envirothèque — or an environmental discotheque.

SELECTED DISCOGRAPHY

DANY JOHNSON, CLUB 57 (1980)

Ray Barretto, "Midnight Boogaloo"
The B-52's, "Dance This Mess Around"
The B-52's, "Planet Claire"
Blondie, "I Know but I Don't Know"
Bootsy's Rubber Band, "Bootzilla"
James Brown, "The Payback"

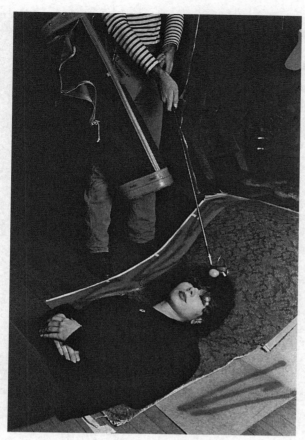

Susan Hannaford at the "Putt-Putt Reggae Party."
Photograph by and courtesy of Harvey Wang ©.

The Bush Tetras, "Too Many Creeps"

Bobby Byrd, "Hot Pants — I'm Coming, I'm Coming, I'm Coming"

Edd Byrnes, "Kookie's Mad Pad"

Cannibal & the Headhunters, "Land of 1,000 Dances"

Jimmy Castor, "The Bertha Butt Boogie"

Chakachas, "Jungle Fever"

Petula Clark, "I Know a Place"

Lynn Collins, "Rock Me Again & Again & Again & Again & Again &
   Again (6 Times)"

Count 5, "Psychotic Reaction"

The Cramps, "I'm Cramped"

Ann Magnuson on the floor during the "Ladies Wrestling Night." Photograph by and courtesy of Harvey Wang ©.

Delta 5, "Mind Your Own Business"
Manu Dibango, "Soul Makossa"
Duane Eddy, "Peter Gunn"
Shirley Ellis, "The Clapping Song (Clap Pat Clap Slap)"
Fatback Band, "King Tim III (Personality Jock)"
Fela and Afrika 70, "Zombie!"
Aretha Franklin, "Rock Steady"
Incredible Bongo Band, "Bongo Rock"
The Joe Cuba Sextet, "Bang! Bang!"
King Swallow, "Please Don't Stop the Party Party Party"
Little Richard, "The Girl Can't Help It"
Lene Lovich, "Lucky Number"
Lulu, "The Boat That I Row"
Marie et les Garçons, "Re-Bop"

Mitch Ryder and the Detroit Wheels, "Devil with a Blue Dress On"

Mo-Dettes, "White Mice"

Sandy Nelson, "Let There Be Drums"

Parliament, "Tear the Roof Off the Sucker (Give Up the Funk)"

People's Choice, "Do It Any Way You Wanna"

Pete Rodriguez y Su Contunjo, "I Like It (I Like It Like That)"

Pylon, "Gravity"

Ricardo Ray, "The Nitty Gritty"

Nancy Sinatra, "Lightning's Girl"

Millie Small, "My Boy Lollipop"

Frankie Smith, "Double Dutch Bus"

Spoonie Gee Meets the Sequence, "Monster Jam"

Yma Sumac, "Taki Rari"

The Supremes, "Love Is Like an Itching in My Heart"

Sylvia, "Pussy Cat"

Talking Heads, "Warning Sign"

Toys, "Attack"

The Ventures, "Out of Limits"

Betty Wright, "Clean Up Woman"

Club 57 was a creature of the East Village, where cheap tenement accommodation drew in East European Jews during the nineteenth and first half of the twentieth centuries followed by Puerto Ricans and Dominicans in the postwar era. The area also emerged as a hotbed of countercultural activity during the late 1960s and early 1970s when the Fillmore East on Second Avenue and the Electric Circus on St. Mark's Place combined psychedelic rock performance and immersive multimedia effects supplied by groups such as the Joshua Light Show. Punk aesthetics surged to the fore when it became acceptable to sleep with a hippie but not be one during the 1970s. When Allen Ginsberg moved to 437 East 12th Street in 1975, having relocated to the East Village in 1952, he was joined by so many like-minded artists the tenement came to be known as the Poets Building. Because space was so tight, residents got out as much as they could, and the willingness of the SVA student crowd and others to turn Club 57 into an expanded living room became a major factor in the venue's development.

Even if Strychacki was the first to shape Club 57 as an East Village hangout, and although he continued to tend the building while smoothing neighborly relations, his main contribution turned out to be his empowerment of "chief scientist" Magnuson, who "had the enthusiasm, the energy and the stamina to take the crazy brilliance of the club and the ideas of its members and turn them into things that really happened."[5] Harnessing the energy of punk, the thrill of suburban escape, the freedom of cheap living, the comic potential of kitsch pop culture, and the twist of hallucinogenics, the venue came to resemble a giant television set that could be tuned to a different channel at the click of a suggestion, just as Magnuson dreamed it. "I lived for creating a new theater experience every night," she recalls. "The vibe was just total freedom." When *New York Magazine* referenced the venue in March 1980, it described it as "one of the wittiest of the new clubs."[6] Anarchy, parody, libidinousness, and performance were making a stand.

The Mudd Club had been open for a year before a vague rivalry began to take shape. Dressed as a character in Jean-Luc Godard's *Alphaville*, Magnuson approached Amos Poe at the White Street launch, hoping to land a role in a future movie, and she returned on a regular basis right through the spring of 1979. "My first impressions of the Mudd Club were, 'Great, a new place to go on our nightly club-hopping escapades!'" she remembers. Admittedly she didn't identify with the Mudd Club's atmosphere of exclusivity and also recalls being "a little suspicious" of Steve Mass, "who seemed to be this weird, moneyed nerd who wanted to exploit a downtown aesthetic" that she "felt was already well in place." Yet it was only when Club 57 started to motor in the autumn of 1979 that a low-key, largely jocular competitiveness emerged. Soon after Mass began to hire Magnuson and her friends to work at his spot.

At times Club 57 and the Mudd Club 57 resembled chalk-and-cheese siblings. Whereas the St. Mark's locale attracted a barely-out-of-college crowd that turned out to be ever-willing to engage in frivolous activity, the White Street spot drew in a more mature and self-consciously serious demographic that included some who looked down on their precocious counterparts. "They were more of an annoyance than anything else," notes Ken Aronds of the Club 57 posse and their whacky activities. Distinguishing the spots in polar terms, Straub concludes that whereas Club 57 was grounded in "creation," the Mudd Club reveled in "destruction," and his view was echoed by Scharf, who characterizes the St. Mark's spot as "groovy" and the White Street venue as "cool."[7] Dressing for special parties, Club 57-ites tended to piece together vintage outfits, whereas Mudd Clubbers regulars preferred s/m gear, severe uniforms, and minimalist chic. "They dressed like characters in a new wave film, whereas we were much more into laughing and bright psychedelic colors," observes Magnuson. "We tended to take nothing seriously and that can be an affront to people who are taking things way too seriously."

(Left to right) Ann Magnuson, Dany Johnson, and Min Thometz (now Sanchez) of the Ladies Auxiliary of the Lower East Side. Photograph by and courtesy of Harvey Wang ©.

Environmental factors played their part. With East Village neighbors to pacify, Magnuson and friends placed cabaret and screenings at the center of Club 57's activity, whereas the relative desolation of White Street made it possible for Mass to place live music and DJ-ing at the heart of his program. More important, whereas the Mudd Club operated as a fully licensed venue that generated revenue that Mass could reinvest in elaborate happenings, Club 57 resembled a ramshackle youth club that ran a limited, semilegal bar and could barely fund its basic upkeep. Although the St. Mark's venue could attract crowds of up to a hundred, sometimes more, gatherings tended to be intimate, with some fifteen people turning up to the "Putt-Putt Reggae Party," and the venue rarely experiencing the kinds of queues that became standard at the Mudd Club. "Club 57 was not like a real bar or a business in any way," points out Johnson, who contributed to the makeshift operation by variously tending the bar, running the door, helping out at the coat check, operating the projector, and sweeping up at the end of the night in addition to her DJ-ing duties, depending on circumstances. Offering further contrast, Magnuson was younger, poorer, more sociable, and more artistic than Mass, whose entrepreneurial and managerial reputation offset his formidable creative and intellectual qualities.

Yet talk of difference concealed important ties. Participant and critic Steven Hager would go on to argue that the Club 57 crowd was "more interested in the sort of sensibility embodied by the B-52's" than its Mudd Club counter-part, preferring grooviness, camp, and color to dissonance, seriousness, and black, yet the B-52s performed at the Mudd Club several times, Fred Schneider worked at the White Street spot, and his cohosting of the "Hawaiian Beach Party" set the tone for future forays into kitsch and irony.[8] Twisting in the other direction, Mudd Club diehards Amos Poe and James Nares screened films at Club 57, the Contortions performed at the St. Mark's spot long before they debuted on White Street, and Anita Sarko started to head to Club 57 when she wasn't working, "honored" to have witnessed what she took to be a parody of herself DJ-ing the first time she headed to the venue. "Most of the things were extreme and very sexual, gender-bending or campy — a cross between drag shows and social critique," recalls Diego Cortez, another participant whose social allegiance was never singular. "It was high-level camp and interesting from a theatrical point of view. I went there all the time." Nor did clichés about drug consumption straightforwardly apply, for while mushrooms were popular on St. Mark's Place, heroin hardly went down at all on White Street, in part because coke was the drug of choice, in part because of the sheer impracticality of shooting up in a bar. "Early on there was a bit of a rivalry," observes Magnuson. "But I hesitate to even call it that now, even though I've been quoted saying as much."

For a while Mass carried on as if Club 57 didn't even exist as a pimple on the face of the downtown scene, with live music still central to his seven-nights-a-week offering during 1980. The punk, rock, new wave, and no wave schedule included shows by the likes of Bad Brains, Bauhaus, Jayne County, the Del-Byzantines, DNA, the Go-Go's, Gray, Nina Hagen, Jonathan Richman, Polyrock, Pylon, Psychedelic Furs, the Raincoats, Tom Robinson, Johnny Thunders, and, with the Mudd Club still punching above its size, Captain Beefheart, the Damned, Frank Zappa, and U2. Mass also booked bands that didn't quite fit the mold, ranging from the punk-meets-funk sound of the Bush Tetras and Snuky Tate to the downtown disco of Kid Creole and the Coconuts and the Love of Life Orchestra to the R&B of Percy Sledge and Junior Walker to the straight-up funk of George Clinton and the Brides of Funkenstein to the roots reggae of Burning Spear. Meanwhile Rhys Chatham scheduled experimental composers and musicians, including Boris Policeband, to perform early evenings. "[Policeband] was known for playing electric violin and being radically into noise," recalls Chatham. "However, for this concert he played an evening of Bach violin sonatas, totally surprising everyone."

Among the venue's now predictably unpredictable array of nonmusical events, London-based New Romantic pioneers Steve Strange and Rusty

Egan presented a fashion show that featured ballgowns as a form of Dada-esque creativity, underground filmmaker Nick Zedd screened his twisted death rockers vs. disco mutants film *They Eat Scum*, and Gary Indiana appeared in a benefit staged for himself that also included three films selected by Tina L'Hotsky plus a drag performance by Ethyl Eichelberger.[9] Mass also continued to roll out happenings at regular intervals, with the "Soul Party" featuring a pimp's bedroom and beauty parlor installations, soul food, and Clarence Carter; the "Catholic Schoolgirls Party" celebrating Mary Magdalen de Pazzi, whose proto–East Village life was marked by ecstatic and mystical experiences as well as an ability to read minds and predict the future; the "National Geographic Night" showcasing voodoo, human sacrifice, women wearing leopard skins, and a freshly roasted pig; and the "Mudd Club Playboy Party," which beckoned appropriately dressed participants to mix cocktails, play Scrabble, nibble on an hors d'oeurve or two, enjoy some mood music, and "have a quiet discussion on Picasso, civil rights, jazz, or sex."[10]

Mass couldn't straightforwardly ignore developments at Club 57, however, and beginning in the summer of 1980 he started to offer work to several core members, hiring Magnuson and Johnson to help refurbish the second-floor lounge, Susan Hannaford and Samantha McEwen to work the coat check, Stacey Elkin to organize a cocktail-dress fashion show, and Scharf to take part in performances and help out on the door — until he refused entry to a Bowie lookalike who turned out to be Bowie.[11] "He also borrowed an idea or two, so after Magnuson staged a "Playboy Party" at Club 57 in July Mass arranged for her to stage an equivalent event on White Street in October. (Assuming the role of "hutch mother," Magnuson performed alongside Wendy Wild in Barbie and the Heftones, the imagined band of *Playboy* magnate Hugh Hefner, played by Mass.) The Mudd Club owner denies making a particular beeline for the Club 57 crowd, noting that he was constantly recruiting new talent anyhow, yet he would have happily employed Magnuson as a right-hand woman alongside Tina L'Hotsky if she'd been available. Club 57-ites were happy to collaborate. "We would have preferred to have made money at Club 57 and not gone anywhere else, but we weren't set up like that," explains Magnuson. "So although there was a reluctance to do these things at the Mudd Club we did them and we had fun and we were going there a lot anyhow."

Meanwhile the slow-burn closure of Studio 54 — which saw a judge find Steve Rubell and co-owner Ian Schrager guilty of tax evasion in January, scratch their liquor license in February, and send them to prison in March — modified the makeup of the White Street crowd. "There was this really bad change, even on the upstairs door," remembers Chi Chi Valenti. "There was this big influx of Diana Ross celebrity types, who were fine, and all of the people who wanted to see them, who weren't." The pressure eased the night in late January when Valenti, wearing a white satin gown and a fox coat, and Johnny Dynell split a quaalude as they retired to Ross Bleckner's painting studio. But some three weeks later, Dynell and Valenti quit the Mudd Club after rowing with Mass, and that left the second-floor lounge in a state of flux at the very moment when a fresh wave of media coverage added to the pressure on both doors. "Competition to gain entrance is intense and slightly desperate," *New York Magazine* noted of the VIP doorway in March, "although, to the casual observer, it would seem that nothing much is really *going on* up there."[12] Richard Boch observes that numerous Studio regulars had already made the move to White Street, and "with one less club in the mix our door became even tighter."

The year also witnessed Anita Sarko consolidate her position as the Mudd Club's most contentious DJ. "Everyone thought the Mudd Club was a punk club but I would put on Pat Boone singing 'April Love,'" she notes. "People would get enraged because they didn't understand that the true punk attitude was to be reactionary — to react against. I reacted against what everyone thought was going to happen." The DJ discovered individual tipping points when customers hurled objects (including glasses) at her while she worked. "It was dangerous but Mudd Club was dangerous relative to any other club," she reasons. "I learned to duck." Yet her most equivocal listener turned out to be Mass, who wanted his DJs to inspire dance-floor action, because his business depended on the bar remaining busy, and concluded that Sarko wasn't the best fit. "I regarded her style as interesting and eclectic but it wasn't along the lines that I wanted," he explains. "I believed this kind of eclectic mix could work and be danceable. Anita never grasped that." Begging to differ, Sarko simply "didn't give a shit" if people danced or not. "If I could think of the furthest thing from my mind it was that," she remarks.

The tension between Sarko and Mass ran back to the start of her run at the Mudd Club, when the owner's repeated criticisms soon escalated into a form of bullying, claims the DJ. One of several who maintain the owner's substance use wasn't always in hand, the DJ maintains that his tirades appeared to coincide with his getting high. "His whole theory of being a bastard was that I had to learn to be tough," she adds. "He used to say, 'You are not in the Midwest or the South anymore. You are in New York. You need to toughen up. I'm doing you a favor by being so hard on you!'" Mass maintains he would only fault her selections "if, in the heat of the battle at one o'clock in the morning, the crowd started to exit the door because her selections were undanceable," at which point he would use his "directorial prerogative" to "strenuously criticize" her approach. Observers witnessed two strong-minded, highly unorthodox characters who might have needed one another more than they liked to admit. "Steve was creative and *very* odd," notes Boch. "He was never abusive to me in any way although he could be reticent and obtuse in his communication. However, he and Anita had a prickly relationship from the start." Dynell posits that Mass "could be sadistic" but adds that "as in any rocky relationship, it takes two rocks. I think on some level they both enjoyed the drama."

The difficult relationship careered into its first major breakdown when Mass turned on Sarko sometime during the summer and the DJ quit on the spot, only for *Interview* to coincidentally publish an article by Glenn O'Brien the following day that pronounced Sarko to be the best DJ in New York. "That's what made me because in New York nobody gives you any credit unless they've read about it," she remarks. "Some people can't even digest the food they ate at dinner until they read about it the next day." A couple of weeks later Mass tracked down Sarko and persuaded her to see the booth in his renovated lounge, which he had devised as a floor-to-ceiling Plexiglas art installation that cast DJs as if they were fruit flies trapped in a jar, except in Sarko's case it would offer her protection from flying objects. Sarko agreed to return when Mass increased her pay from $40 for eight hours' work, ostensibly because she had become the club's most requested DJ, as the owner's assistant confided to her one day. Mass still questions Sarko's popularity, maintaining that if she had been such an attraction he would have reinstated her on the first floor instead of switching her to the lounge, but he did lure her back.

The casualties were nevertheless beginning to pile up. After agreeing for her to stage the James Brown lip-synching party, Mass fell out with the combustible Anya Phillips once and for all after stringing her and James Chance along as she tried to book the Contortions at the venue. (Already disdainful of Mass's grungy interior design, the couple didn't return to the Mudd Club once, recalls Chance.) The owner also started to behave in a "very weird" way around Dynell and Valenti before an explosive confrontation forced the couple to seek alternative spaces. ("He didn't seem to like that we were together," recalls the DJ. "He threw a bottle at me as we were leaving and it smashed over my head. It was very dramatic.") Mass's furious response when Scharf painted a mural on the Plexiglas booth also appeared disproportionate. By then Cortez had also more or less stopped going to the White Street spot altogether. "Steve was starting to be a total lunatic," he reasons. "He was very bossy and manipulative."

Anita Sarko DJ-ing at the Mudd Club, ca. 1980. Photograph by and courtesy of Scott Morgan ©.

Mass was fine so long as those playing for him were sufficiently subservient, as was the case with Justin Strauss, a onetime rock musician who started to DJ at the Mudd Club in early 1980 after an ex-girlfriend who knew David Azarch made an introduction. Selecting "everything from James Brown to Ian Dury and the Blockheads to Lena Lovich to ska and Two Tone" during his Thursday-night appearances, Strauss felt comfortable with the irregular setup. "Steve Mass was a crazy dude," he reminisces. "While I was DJ-ing he would decide he wanted to play some records, so he'd just put on some rockabilly or reggae or whatever he felt like hearing at the time, whether it made any sense or not. It was weird but in a great way. He just had an instinct, an intuition, about all of this culture." But then onetime owner of the Electric Circus Jerry Brandt opened the Ritz as a venue for live music in an art deco nightclub on 11th Street in May 1980, and Strauss accepted his offer to work for him because he believed the unpredictable Mass could sack him "tomorrow" and because the Ritz was a larger venue that would bill him as its primary DJ.

Mass was happy to be regarded as downright peculiar. As an outsider-loner figure who was once removed from the Mudd Club crowd by age as well as status, he assumed the character of Dr. Mudd, a harebrained, slightly sinister scientist who maintained a low public profile as he sent out warped pronouncements about the importance of morality, order, dedication, intensity, progress, and initiative through newsletters and ads that promoted his "world famous laboratory for youth."[13] Cortez rated the idea before he became disillusioned with Mass, in part because "downtown was a big science lab anyway." Meanwhile Leonard Abrams came to view Mass as an "intelligent, creative and somewhat demented individual who had people doing all kinds of events," which was enough to make the Mudd Club his favorite club. "I was a generation older than these people and my goal was to provide a foil for them," explains Mass. "I self-styled myself as an authority figure who was warning them against dangerous sex and risky behavior. In practice I was an extremely permissive authoritarian. But I did also have this idea that I was controlling everything as if I was directing a film. I thought I was Cecil B. DeMille."

The director of Hollywood epics including *Cleopatra* and *The Ten Commandments*, DeMille was prone to displaying a form of tyrannical behavior that Mass understood. "Once you're in a film you're obliged to do everything the director tells you," he notes. "If you try and alter one comma in the script he's going to come down on your case. That's his prerogative." Mass also viewed the Mudd Club as his "private laboratory" and was prepared to enforce his ideas if subtler means of persuasion didn't work in the knowledge that, in comparison to other club owners, he had taken measures to make sure he wasn't "beholden" to a partner or a booking manager or an investor. Mass went on to consolidate his directorial position when he bought the White Street building from Bleckner in late 1979 and sold his medical services business in 1980. Also imagining himself as a head of a political party or the leader of a revolution, the owner recalls that manic states would possess him as fantasy assumed a form of reality. "If you pretend to be a famous film director and start making films with a Super 8 you're not just faking it but making it," he reasons.

Mass was at his most imperial when, drawing on his long-standing fascination with anthropology, history, and political theory, he hatched the ideas for the major happenings before forming a committee to develop and execute the event. The Military Party Committee formed for the "War Games: Combat Love Party," for instance, featured Tina L'Hotsky, Legs McNeil (cofounder of *Punk* magazine), Arturo Vega (creative designer for the Ramones), and his good self, with the likes of Animal X, Gary Indiana, Ann Magnuson, Fred Schneider, and sisters Tish and Snooky Bellomo among those who contributed significantly to other large-scale events.[14] Mass would go on to tell the *East Village Eye* that he could cite "a hundred" people who were involved in the happenings, yet in his mind the small army of creative innovators needed a leader. "I feel inhibited about naming names because there are so many people involved that it's not fair to give anyone extra credit," he added. "We all fused together these ideas under my general direction, because someone has to sit there and direct."[15]

There were times, however, when Mass's role was closer to that of a producer who enabled others to unleash their wildly creative imaginations. L'Hotsky was the most influential, thanks to her pivotal contribution to numerous happenings, several of which she directed, including the "Birthday Ball," "Blonde Night," the "Pyjama Party," and the "Monster Party" plus the "Cha-Cha Party."[16] "Tina was like an assistant director and sometimes a director," acknowledges Mass. "She had a surrealistic mind that combined Marxism with extraterrestrial phenomena with [American etiquette authority] Amy Vanderbelt. We also shared this interest in Puerto Rican kitsch culture. So we were on the same wavelength." Magnuson also emerged as a key figure and remembers welcoming Mass's suggestions so long as she "got to do 90 percent" of what she wanted. "I usually went into those first meetings with ideas in longhand or already typed up," she recalls. "But Steve also made stuff happen and took things up many notches. The Mudd Club became vibrant and then dominant because he was so willing to throw money around in ways other club owners wouldn't or couldn't."

An authoritarian and volatile figure operating in a highly charged environment where a small amount of financial capital unleashed a disproportionate amount of cultural capital, Mass could become frustrated when others were deemed to be the true inspiration behind his spot, including the time when he heard that some were referring to L'Hotsky as the "Queen of the Mudd Club." Sarko recalls that the owner introduced a rule that no employee could speak about the Mudd Club in an interview so that he would "take credit for everything." Yet if Mass could feel underappreciated, he also remained a significant employer and enabler of downtown talent as well as the "crystallizing force" behind the Mudd Club, in the words of Dynell. "Steve Mass would bring really crazy, genius people together and give them an opportunity to do something, and that's what the Mudd Club was," argues the DJ. "I wouldn't say the Mudd Club was Steve Mass. But he was the owner, he was the one with the money, and he was also a brilliant artist, the diabolical Dr. Mudd, who was as creative and out there as any of the 'ideas people' on the scene." Dynell adds that if Mass ran his empire like Caligula, playing the role of an insane tyrant, "how much of that was truly him is open to interpretation."

Scenesters learned to live with such tensions as Mass summoned all his energy to keep the Mudd Club "on the cutting edge" throughout 1980. But the very success of his venture encouraged others to attempt to imitate its basic idea, and that, in turn, gave the likes of Azarch, Sarko, and scores of others a better sense of their artistic and financial value, especially as they observed Strauss improve his income and profile at the Ritz. "The Mudd Club was a sensation," remembers Mass. "In every story in every paper, the first sentence always referred to the fact I had opened on a budget of $15,000. I was this guy who had turned dirt into gold. Nobody believed it. And this $15,000 launched a thousand other ships — people who wanted to do the same thing."

A new epoch in downtown partying beckoned.

DANCETERIA MIDTOWN FEELS
THE DOWNTOWN STORM

Danceteria sent shockwaves through the city's party scene when it opened in May 1980, all the way down to the Mudd Club, where its owners had spent a fair amount of time hanging out. Dedicating the basement to DJ-ing, the first floor to live bands, and the second floor to video, the venue presented revelers with a novel element of choice, not because of the range of entertainment but because all of the options were available at once. The shift to sensory overload was unmistakable as two bands appeared live every night, two DJs shared the turntables, and experimental filmmakers curated showings within a groundbreaking video lounge. In isolation, each floor oozed with the alternative inventiveness of downtown. Taken together, they offered a level of explorative creativity that threatened to dwarf the offerings of Club 57 and the Mudd Club. Yet in contrast to both of those spots, Danceteria was located not in downtown but midtown, toward the Eighth Avenue end of 37th Street, where commerce ruled the streets. With Jim Fouratt and Rudolf Piper at the helm, the mongrel explorations of the Lower Manhattan party scene were set to storm the city center.

Raised in a working-class Irish Catholic family, Fouratt moved from Rhode Island to New York in 1961 to study with Method acting pioneer Lee Strasberg, whose insistence that he be true to himself persuaded Fouratt to accept his homosexuality. Radicalized several years later when a judge ruled against him for his behavior at an antiwar demonstration, Fouratt cofounded the Youth International Party (or the Yippies) and a little later the Gay Liberation Front, having witnessed the early flash points of the Stonewall rebellion. To relax, he headed to Max's, CBGB, and Studio 54, although he rarely told his comrades about his trips to the midtown venue. Then, in the summer of 1978, a friend took him to Hurrah, a onetime fashion-conscious club located at 62nd Street that re-branded itself as the city's first rock discotheque after Studio 54 stole its crowd. Introduced to the owners, Fouratt told them how he thought the spot could be improved. In early 1979, or thereabouts, he landed the task of reviving it.

An occasional visitor to the Mudd Club, which he thought of as being rooted in the social interaction of its customers rather than its entertainment offering, Fouratt hired the White Street alternate Sean Cassette to work as his DJ, oversaw the installation of video screens above the dance floor, and booked punk and new wave bands such as Gang of Four, Pylon, the Rotating Power Tools, and Ultravox. "Disco was something we were moving away from," he observes. "I wanted to fuse Hurrah with a downtown sensibility that was very art-driven. I wanted to book the same kind of art-damaged acts that would play CBGB." Yet the promoter also distanced his venue from the leather-jacket roughness of the Bowery spot by introducing the fashion-conscious "See and Be Scene" slogan as well as a door policy that required groups of young men to wait while gay men were let in, only for his run to end the night the owners demanded he pay Klaus Nomi less money, even though seven hundred people had packed the club.[1] Fouratt stormed out, but he regretted his decision the following morning, by which time the owners had placed a padlock on his office.

As for Fouratt's soon-to-be business partner, the West German–raised Piper made his fortune working as a stockbroker and then running a restaurant business in Brazil before he decided to open a club in New York. (He was smoking a joint and enjoying the company of women on an Ipaneman beach at the time of the decision.) "There was Studio 54, which was the greatest in the world, and Xenon and Hurrah, but as a place midtown was lame," he concluded soon after arriving in the city. "Downtown there was just the Mudd Club, which was far too spartan in its amenities and didn't have a good layout, and CBGB, which was this piece of aesthetic shit. I thought, 'Man, somebody's going to have to do more than this.'"

Piper headed to the Mudd Club on a near nightly basis all the same, in part because it was "intellectually rewarding without being boring," in part because it was the "perfect place" to get to know the "downtown celebrities of the day," in part because it was the "best place to pick up chicks" (whom he took back to his room in the Chelsea Hotel with such regularity that nightlife commentator Stephen Saban published a piece in the SoHo News about his activities titled "German Sexual Response"). As the queues on White Street lengthened, Piper concluded that it would be perfectly viable to open an alternative spot, especially if it offered the artist community a place where they could show their art. "I loved the Mudd and it motivated and inspired me," he confirms. "Ultimately, and now it can be told, I wanted to do a club

Sean Cassette at the Mudd Club, ca. 1978–1979.
Photograph by Tony Baker ©; courtesy of Sean Cassette.

that would be better than the Mudd!" Steve Mass recalls that Piper virtually lived in the Mudd Club. "He was very friendly, charming, and suave," notes the owner. "He had this kind of European playboy presence. I didn't know he was going to start a place of his own."

Careful not to blab that he was, as far as he was aware, the wealthiest person living downtown, Piper had the power to "make things happen" and purchased a three-story building on Crosby Street in SoHo. He planned for "basement activity" in the basement, dancing on the first floor, and a gallery for local artists on the second, because the SoHo galleries "were never interested in the downtown scene," only to face concerted opposition from artists and the community board to his plans. At that point Cassette introduced the hyper-articulate Fouratt to Piper on the basis that the ex-Hurrah promoter could talk the project out of trouble, and the three of them held brainstorming sessions in Fouratt's office on Waverly Place, "where the whole concept came together," recalls Piper. Fouratt made good progress until Piper's building contractor threatened one of the protestors, after which negotiations broke down.

Naming his venue Pravda after he stumbled across the reference in *File* and *Wet* magazines, Piper opened all the same. "It was one of the most fabulous nights in the city," the owner claims of the launch, which took place on

David King draft graphic for Pravda. "Jim asked me to
start thinking about graphics, so I produced this rough,
which I was pleased with," comments King, designer of
the iconic logo for punk band Crass. "Disappointingly, the
whole venture fell through and this graphic sketch is all
that remains. It's been in a file drawer since it was made."
Designed by and courtesy of David King ©.

Thursday, 8 November 1979, and featured a fashion show by Betsey Johnson.
"Absolutely everybody in town was there. It was the beginning of this bizarre
new style." The party brought together Bauhaus, the iconography of David
Bowie's *Heroes*, Soviet aesthetics, and postmodern irony. "There were a lot
more fashion people, a lot more trendy people, a lot more uptown people than
there were at the Mudd Club, and they were dressed in a new way," recalls
Leonard Abrams. "There were all these people who were meeting each other
for the first time who were doing all these creative things. They were influenced by punk and were reinventing themselves, investing themselves for the
first time in throwing out all these ideas. It created a big impression." Chi Chi

Valenti remembers the night captured the zeitgeist by being "almost Russian constructivist yet fetishy at the same time."

Only the neighbors were underwhelmed and, having registered their unhappiness, city inspectors closed the spot the following day.[2] Piper argued during subsequent negotiations that he wanted Pravda to operate as a venue for the local community, maintaining that SoHo could come to resemble bohemian Paris of the 1920s if it opened itself to pleasure. Distrustful, residents replied that he had lost control of the opening-night party and couldn't be trusted to run a peaceable venue.[3] "The neighbors wanted to keep SoHo as an exclusive artistic enclave," reasons the German. "They were too fucking serious and did not understand the concept of uniting art and nightlife. But Pravda made my entire career in New York. The fact that it closed after one night added to the myth."

Fouratt hit on the venue that would become Danceteria when he agreed to represent a group that was booked to play at Armageddon, a nightclub located on 37th Street between Seventh and Eighth Avenues. When the venue's Mafia manager told him at the end of the night that he couldn't afford to pay the performers, pulling out a gun to demonstrate his sincerity, Fouratt offered to tell the manager how he could turn his club around if he settled. The manager paid up and asked Fouratt to take over the venue. "The first thing that Jim said is, 'We can cut a deal as long as you guys stay away,'" recalls Piper of subsequent negotiations. "They honored their commitment and that was important because downtown people don't like the mob, because the mob were Guidos and dressed ridiculously." Initially skeptical, Piper came round to the idea of opening in midtown after Fouratt took him on a tour of the streets that surrounded the venue, where garment manufacturers and trade retailers imbued the area with a gritty character.

The duo threw themselves into a collaboration that would leave an indelible mark on the era's party scene. A trained architect, Piper introduced 1950s-style wallpaper, furniture, and motifs as an "absurd joke" that mocked that decade's "dream of finding happiness through domesticity and mindless consumerism," and he also hired young artists, including Keith Haring, to cover the venue's walls with xerox art. Fouratt oversaw the upgrade of the venue's sound system as well as the construction of the second-floor video lounge, which he developed in conjunction with video artists Emily Armstrong and Pat Ivers, who had contributed a video installation called the "Rock and Roll Classroom" to the opening of Long Island City gallery PS1. Having vehemently objected to Piper's suggestions of the Bunker and the Eagle's Nest, both of which carried Nazi associations, Fouratt also came up with a name

Opening night at Pravda, 8 November 1979. Photograph by and courtesy
of Allan Tannenbaum/SoHo Blues ©.

for the venue while walking in front of either a carpet store called Carpeteria
(as Fouratt remembers it) or a cafeteria, probably Dubrow's, a postwar eatery
that sported a classic 1950s neon sign (as David King, a British graphic designer, musician and friend of Fouratt, recalls). "That's it," Fouratt exclaimed
the moment it struck him that the club would present customers with a menu
of options, like a cafeteria or the carpet store that played on the café concept.
"Danceteria!"

Running from 8:00 PM to 8:00 AM, the opening-night party of 9 May 1980
attracted a similar crowd to the one that gathered at Pravda. "We were appre-
hensive that the venue was outside of downtown's holy land so we plastered
posters all over town," remembers Piper. "In the end we were jammed beyond
belief. There was almost a mass hysteria." With the sensational ephemerality
of Pravda feeding the excitement, Fouratt introduced bands on the first floor,
Armstrong and Ivers screened video footage recorded at CBGB plus other independent offerings on the second, and Mark Kamins joined Sean Cassette
behind the turntables in the sweaty basement.[4] "From the first night the mix
of art, live music, video, fashion, staff and DJ-ing was the formula," notes Fouratt, who booked the bands and hired the DJs. "Hurrah was the incubator but
because it had one floor it was limited to the linear moment. Having three
floors on 37th Street changed everything. The DJs weren't in competition with

Original Danceteria graphic (left) and opening-night flyer (right), both featuring the Danceteria Lady. "When it was time to do the graphics, I immediately thought of depicting a uniformed waitress from a similar period as the large period sign that said 'Cafeteria' where Jim came up with the Danceteria name," recalls designer David King. "If we were walking north on Seventh Avenue then it was probably Dubrow's café." Graphic and flyer designed by and courtesy of David King ©.

the bands and the video lounge. The floors offered a nonstop choice." Even midtown had taken a leap into the hybrid unknown.

Regarding the dance floor, Fouratt had wanted to find someone to double up alongside Cassette on the basis that it would be tough for one DJ to play back-to-back twelve-hour sets and more interesting to have two DJs share the turntables if the chemistry was good. Raised in midtown Manhattan on 49th Street and First Avenue, Kamins offered contrast, having met "all the gay DJs" while working in a record store before he landed a job working the lights and then the turntables at Trax, a 72nd Street discotheque that showcased live bands. "At the time you could go to a disco and hear four-on-the-floor all night," notes Fouratt, who went to hear Kamins play at the spot following a tip-off from Nancy Jeffries, an A&R talent scout who had helped sign disco diva Evelyn "Champagne" King and new wave outfit Polyrock to RCA —

precisely the kind of combination that he was after. The promoter concluded that Kamins was "much more sophisticated and eclectic" than most disco DJs and would strike "a good balance" with Cassette's punk-oriented mindset. "I decided he was in touch with what I was trying to do aesthetically," he says.

The DJs struck up a quick camaraderie, playing mini-sets of two or three records each. "We had no idea how it would work when it was suggested but we agreed to try," recalls Cassette. "After the fourth spin, having played two records each, the bout started and we seemed to have something. We bounced off each other — it was a dialogue. The secret was we never tired of trying to outdo each other, so the energy came through." The fact that they were hired to play for twelve hours encouraged the DJs to explore contrasts and correspondences as they juxtaposed Public Image Ltd (PiL) and Bohannon, Killing Joke, and Donna Summer, while the fresh wave of recordings that started to layer punk sounds on top of a disco beat provided them with common ground. "We could change the tempo but the vibe — the heart — would stay the same," remarks Kamins. "The people that liked punk got into Bohannon and the people that were into my underground black music got into English punk and new wave because the vibe was the same."

SELECTED DISCOGRAPHY

SEAN CASSETTE AND MARK KAMINS, DANCETERIA (1980)

Big Youth, "Hit the Road, Jack"
Black Uhuru, "Guess Who's Coming to Dinner"
Bohannon, "Let's Start the Dance"
James Brown, "Get Up Offa That Thing"
The Bush Tetras, "Too Many Creeps"
The Clash, "London Calling"
The Clash, "Police and Thieves"
The Cure, "A Forest"
The Cure, "Killing an Arab"
Dead Kennedys, "Holiday in Cambodia"
Delta 5, "Mind Your Own Business"
Derrick Laro & Trinity, "Don't Stop Till You Get Enough"
Ian Dury, "Reasons to Be Cheerful (Part Three)"
Flying Lizards, "Money"
Gang of Four, "Damaged Goods"

Eddy Grant, "Living on the Frontline"

Instant Funk, "I Got My Mind Made Up"

Joy Division, "Disorder"

Joy Division, "She's Lost Control"

Killing Joke, "Wardance"

Lene Lovich, "Lucky Number"

Martha and the Muffins, "Echo Beach"

The Normal, "Warm Leatherette"

Gary Numan, "Cars"

PiL, "Death Disco"

PiL, "Swanlake"

Psychedelic Furs, "India"

The Ramones, "Blitzkrieg Bop"

The Slits, "Heard It through the Grapevine"

Lonnie Liston Smith, "Expansions"

The Specials, "Ghost Town (Extended Version)"

Spizzenergi, "Soldier Soldier"

Steel Pulse, "Ku Klux Klan"

Trance, "Time Devours"

On the floor above, live bands combined the sophisticated with the popular. "I wanted to try and treat seriously the art that was being developed but to do it in a nonserious environment that was closer to the mode of pop culture," Fouratt notes of his curatorial approach. "I always used to introduce the acts and explain why I had booked them. I'm sure I was insufferable but I wanted to provide a window of understanding to the audience." Devo, the Feelies, Gang of Four, the Go-Go's, Ministry, the Plastics, Polyrock, Tito Puente, Pylon, Sun Ra, the Raybeats, Pere Ubu, and X played live. On one occasion Generation X lead vocalist Billy Idol jumped on stage during a solo performance by Alan Vega, a member of the punk-electronic duo Suicide, and they started to sing country and western songs. "People liked to pit the Mudd Club against Danceteria," notes Fouratt. "The Mudd Club was hipper, the Mudd Club was downtown, whereas we were more populist and placed live performance at the core of the club. But I always thought of ourselves as doing the same thing. We spoke the same language aesthetically."

Unconcerned by sub-rudimentary bathrooms, two thousand punks, rockers, New Romantics, junkies, whores, sadomasochists, artists, Studio 54 exiles, and ne'er-do-wells flocked to the venue every Friday and Saturday,

Danceteria dance floor, 1980. Photograph by and courtesy of
Allan Tannenbaum/SoHo Blues ©.

prompting the *East Village Eye* to remark that the crowd "exhibits that lower
east side aesthetic (stiletto heels, purple hair and pointy sunglasses)."[5] It certainly began to seem as though downtown was more a "state of mind" or "an
identification" than a geographical location, as Fouratt puts it, with the concentration of artists, musicians, performers, photographers, and writers who
worked at the 37th Street spot illustrative of the way a community and its way
of life could shift almost seamlessly between different parts of the city as circumstances required. "I think it spread word-of-mouth because most of the
people who worked there were friends anyway," comments writer, performer,
and poet Max Blagg, who joined a team that included Karen Finley, Keith
Haring, Alexa Hunter, Zoe Leonard, David McDermott, Peter McGough,
Haoui Montaug, Chuck Nanney, Michael Parker, and David Wojnarowicz. "So
many wildly talented people worked there." Asked to remove his moustache if
he wanted to remain employed, Fouratt having decreed that anyone with facial hair should be automatically turned away at the door, Kamins maintains
that it was at Danceteria that he learned that a successful club had to have the
"perfect mix" of staff. "The doorman mixes the people, the bartender mixes

the drinks, the DJ mixes the music, and all three mix the whole fucking cake," comments the DJ.

Ignoring the blistering heat and lack of air conditioning, dancers partied as though their lives depended on it that summer. Fouratt and Piper held a special event for the Rolling Stones one night and premiered David Bowie's "Ashes to Ashes" video on another. "Danceteria was very modern and current," observes Brian Butterick, a Bronx-born drag queen who ended up joining the staff. Piper marveled at the unfolding scene. "Objectively one cannot describe this but Danceteria was one of the greatest places ever in terms of its energy," he reminisces. "There was just something in the air." Yet his and Fouratt's exhibitionist streak, readiness to take out ads in the *New York Times*, and irreverent approach to selling unlicensed alcohol positioned Danceteria as a car crash waiting to happen, and both were absent when authorities raided the venue on 4 October, arresting and charging Armstrong, Blagg, Butterick, Haring, Ivers, Montaug, Wojnarowicz, and fourteen others as they went about their business.[6] "The dance floor was an inch deep in pills and glassine envelopes," remembers Blagg. "I was stupid enough not to get out from behind the bar in time and the cop who arrested me stole my tips, the *lowdown scum*." Fouratt instructed his attorney to arrange for the employees to be released and headed to the local precinct to ameliorate the situation. "I felt really awful," he recalls. Blagg notes that "the owners were no heroes," however, while Armstrong recalls that Ivers was named as the venue's manager at the eventual hearing. "Danceteria had absolutely no permits whatsoever — it was insane," reasons Piper. "Then we got busted and we said, 'OK, next!'"

The partners hit on a new spot after Fouratt went on a reconnaissance trip to G. G. Barnum's Room, a transsexual-trapeze-disco-hustler bar located on West 45th Street that had recently lost its liquor license after a murder took place on its premises. Checking the basement, Fouratt discovered old signage for the Peppermint Lounge, the original home of the twist, and hurried to tell Piper they had to reopen the legendary spot. They struck a deal, rehired the 37th Street team, and launched in November.[7] Fouratt maintained his edge, booking acts such as Black Flag, the Cramps, Gang of Four, Philip Glass, and X, and he also persuaded David Azarch to move over to the reopened spot. Agitated that Steve Mass was handing Johnny Dynell and Anita Sarko more time behind the turntables, Azarch knew that the new setting could never match the "clientele chemistry" of the Mudd Club and it didn't. But the DJ also appreciated the eclecticism of the shows, the freedom he enjoyed in the booth, the records Fouratt passed his way, and the tripling of his pay. "DJs such as David Azarch left me when they got offered much better deals or work by promoters who respected them and gave them a long leash to do what they wanted to do," observes Mass.

Fouratt's and Piper's run at the Peppermint Lounge turned out to be a short one. Within weeks the management began to grumble about Fouratt's outgoings, including the $100 fee the promoter offered to a performance artist who dressed in a diaper to lip-synch Bowie songs. As tensions mounted, the venue's spotter — the employee tasked by the management to check that the bar staff weren't skimming cash — offered to give Fouratt a lift downtown after the venue closed one night. "You know, I remember you from the Stonewall and you're a good kid," the spotter revealed in the car. "I'm going to have to kill you but I just want you to know it's nothing personal." Fouratt opened the door and rolled out of the moving vehicle as it revved down the West Side Highway. Initially skeptical about Fouratt's account, Piper grasped the severity of the situation when a manager sent him tumbling down a set of stairs the next time he visited the spot.

The promoters responded by putting an ad in the *Village Voice*. "Jim and Rudolf have left the Peppermint Lounge," it ran. "We will tell you where the new place is. The beat goes on." OK, next.

4

SUBTERRANEAN DANCE

David Mancuso read about Steve Dahl's anti-disco rally — which saw the Chicago rock DJ detonate a small mountain of forty thousand disco records during a baseball double-header — in the paper and that was it. "The disco sucks movement was more of an out-of-New-York phenomenon," notes the Loft party host. "New York was and remains different to the rest of the States, including Chicago. Out there they had this very negative perception of disco, but in New York it was part of this mix of cultures and different types of music." Mancuso had become a key figure in the popularization of disco when he cofounded the New York Record Pool, the first organization to arrange for record companies to provide DJs with promotional copies, yet he became wary when Studio 54 instituted a hierarchical door policy while promoting a wall-to-wall disco soundtrack that didn't embrace "the range of music that was coming out." That had never been an issue at the Loft, where maybe a third of Mancuso's selections could be categorized as disco, but as the juggernaut gained momentum the music's exhilarating potential became harder to hear. "If people had been able to listen to disco alongside other sounds they might not have thought it was so bad, but they were being hammered with it," adds Mancuso. "Once it became a formula you knew there was going to be a change. People didn't want a set of rules. They wanted to dance."

The Loft dated back to Saturday, 14 February 1970, when Mancuso staged a "Love Saves the Day" Valentine's bash that synthesized a startling range of influences. The flight of manufacturers from downtown enabled Mancuso to move into a warehouse space at 647 Broadway and shape an expansive form of partying. The advances of the golden age of stereo enabled him to maximize the musicality and, it followed, the social potential of the party experience. The Harlem rent-party tradition that dated back to the 1920s suggested a community-based model of unlicensed, private partying that could be sustained by donations. The civil rights, gay liberation, feminist, and antiwar movements fed into the rainbow coalition identifications of his come-as-you-are crowd. And Sister Alicia, who put on regular parties for the kids she cared for in the children's home where Mancuso grew up, inspired his unswerving desire to nurture an extended family of dispossessed dancers as well as his comforting use of children's birthday-party décor. The Loft host's balloon supplier must have counted him as its most lucrative customer.

Thinking of himself not as a DJ but as a party host who happened to select music, Mancuso pioneered the practice of weaving together records according to their lyrical messages as well as their instrumental grooves, forging a narrative arc of acid intensity as the songs harmonized across the course of a night. He also expanded the sonic range of the New York dance floor by selecting records such as "City, Country, City" by WAR, "I'm a Man" by Chicago, "Girl You Need a Change of Mind" by Eddie Kendricks, and "Soul Makossa" by Manu Dibango, which introduced Latin, African, rock, gospel, breakbeat, and even country elements while bedding an aesthetic that favored explorative records that reached dramatic crescendos. Admirers went on to model the Tenth Floor, the Gallery, Flamingo, 12 West, the Soho Place, Reade Street, and the Paradise Garage after Mancuso's party, making it the most influential of the 1970s. But following a troubling period that saw authorities close down the Broadway Loft and trigger a move to Prince Street that became embroiled in a legal struggle, the party regained its equilibrium. "A lot of LSD was being dropped in those days and a trip lasted twelve hours, so even if you weren't taking acid that was the vibe," notes the host. "By 3:30 the place would be packed and the parties would carry on until one in the afternoon, sometimes later. It was the whole cycle."

Invited to check out the Loft while dancing at a Long Island party in early 1980, Louis "Loose" Kee Jr. had already partied in Manhattan when his best friend (whose sister was dating Eddie Murphy) got him into Studio 54. He lapped up the theater of the entrance, the pyrotechnics of the interior, and the glamour of the crowd, yet none of that prepared him for the moment when he entered the Loft via the party's basement entrance on Mercer Street and immediately witnessed three guys, one with his legs spread, the other two positioned at the other end of the room, each waiting their turn to take a run at the first guy, fall onto their knees, and slide through his legs while doing a backbend. "I was like, 'Wow, where am I?'" he reminisces. "I knew I was home. I had been doing freestyle and doing the hustle in Long Island clubs for at least four years, and this was the first time I met people who were in a higher caliber than I was—and I was *very good* in Long Island."

Going to the Loft provided Loose with his first experience of dancing "with blacks, whites, old, young, straight, and gay in the same room," and he soon joined a "secret society" of Long Islanders who headed to the city every weekend as he wrapped up his shift at Blimpies at midnight, grabbed his bag, and headed straight to Prince Street. Mancuso's party was the "complete opposite" of Studio 54, where dancers would buy expensive outfits in order to be somebody and narcissism reigned. "The Loft wasn't about your dress and attire," he explains. "It was about being communal." Dancers wore functional T-shirts, military-style gas pants, and either Capezio jazz-dance shoes or five-dollar Chinese slippers. Many shredded the sleeves of their tees, threading beads onto the shred so they hung like braids. Some also attached an alligator clip adorned with a long feather to part of their clothing as an ornamental smoking accessory for when their joints burned down to the roach. "People dressed creatively and practically," notes the dancer.

The comparatively uncrowded basement became a favorite destination for those who needed a little more space. One popular maneuver involved dancers taking a so-called swan dive, or leaping in the air, landing on their hands, and taking their head through their arms. Zuleka, one of the regulars, liked to stand on her hands and bring her legs around until her toes were touching the front of her head. "You could find people doing tap dancing, you saw people doing ballet, you would see gymnastics, you would see early aerobics, you would see people who were inspired by martial arts movies," reminisces Loose. "There was one guy who had a bandana around his head and he would jump rope to the music or do push-ups to the music. One guy named Magic, he did magic. He would do card tricks or take a coin out of his ear. Then there was one girl who used to use her dress as a flag; that was the way she danced." Complementary styles proliferated. "You could do anything physical so long as it was fun. Anyone who was free-spirited was accepted."

Archie Burnett started to head to the Loft around the same time. Raised as a Seventh-day Adventist, he wasn't permitted to wear tattoos and was only supposed to dance in honor of God. "Friday night sunset to Saturday night sunset, you didn't do anything," he notes. "I was living at home so I had to do this on the sneak." A graphic design student who worked as a part-time usher at the Gramercy Theater, Burnett tested out moves he had seen on TV at Studio 54 rival New York, New York, until a friend from the playhouse took him to Prince Street. "At first I was freaked out by the noise," he remembers. "When David played certain tracks the screaming was so deafening I didn't know what was going on." Burnett appreciated the contrast with midtown—the lack of gawking, the way dancers showed respect for each other's space,

David Mancuso. A highly
sensitized host who maintained
a fierce, trancelike concentration
during parties. Date unknown,
photographer unknown; courtesy
of Sharon White.

and the informal dress code. "I came in with my L.A. style, knowing nothing at all," he adds. "I was very upright, had my arms swinging, and didn't shift my body weight." Learning from others, Burnett started to become part of the music. "If a track had syncopation I would dance to the drums," he explains. "On other tracks I would pick out the bass or whatever my instincts would tell me to ride on. I would also act out the vocals."

With Alvin Ailey of the multiracial Alvin Ailey American Dance Theater a presence alongside coteachers and students, the Loft doubled as a place of mutual learning, especially downstairs, where dancers continually exchanged moves. At the same time the nurturing environment encouraged partici-pants to experience a sense of childlike freedom, allowing them to "regress to when" they "were nine years old," notes Burnett. (As domestic tensions deep-ened, the partygoer's mother told him, "You're doing the Devil's work! Come back to God!" But Burnett didn't agree and never missed a party.) Above all, the floor drew dancers into a web of interlocking, dynamic relationships in which sociality assumed forms that weren't immediately recognizable. "I could dance with two or three people at the same time," explains Loose. "Everyone gives you different rhythms, moves, and emotions, so on every turn I could pick up a little bit of what they were doing and add it to the repertoire of the dance." During peak hours dancers had to rein in their moves if they were

Louis "Loose" Kee Jr. and Roxana Tash preparing to go
to a party at the Prince Street Loft in 1982. Photographer
unknown; courtesy of Louis "Loose" Kee Jr.

on the main floor, yet by 8:00 AM they could start to stretch out as Mancuso
introduced records such as "America" from *West Side Story*. Come the afternoon, as the marathon drew to a close, the party host might put on *The Nut-
cracker* as his cat Sir Wolfie scampered around the room. "A lot of the guys
who came to the parties had rough lives on the outside," offers Burnett. "The
Loft was a sanctuary."

At the far western end of SoHo, meanwhile, the Paradise Garage offered
a spectrum of danceable music to a mixed crowd on Fridays and to a multiracial gay male gathering on Saturdays. With Reade Street forced to close,
owner Michael Brody had started to hold construction parties in the side
room of his new venue, a gargantuan ex–parking lot situated on King Street,

safe in the knowledge that Mancuso's move to Prince Street set a legal precedent for his ambitious project, which officially opened in September 1978. Fridays were a success from the get-go and attracted a diverse crowd that was similar to the one at the Loft. Yet to Brody's frustration the Garage didn't appeal to the white gay dancers who headed to Flamingo and 12 West, and his disappointment was shared by Mel Cheren, an ex-lover and the co-owner of West End Records, who lent him money to purchase equipment for his new venture. "There was a mix on the Friday-night parties but there weren't that many white people," confirms Mark Riley, a Loft and Paradise Garage regular who was friendly with Brody. "Michael found out pretty early on that the Flamingo crowd was not going to come to the Garage if there was this critical mass of black gay people as well."

Conscious that they were struggling, Cheren proposed that Brody turn Saturdays into a white gay night in the hope that any new arrivals would subsequently integrate with the Friday crowd.[1] Given that Flamingo and 12 West were flying, and that the Flamingo crowd was particularly eager to dance in a homogeneous setting, the proposal was naive, yet the Garage implemented it in the autumn of 1979, inviting white gay dancers to purchase black membership cards that provided Friday and Saturday access while offering others red cards that provided Friday-only access. "A new manager was brought in from 12 West and he started making all these changes," remembers David DePino, Garage DJ Larry Levan's best friend, who policed the entrance to the booth. "Then we were hit with the news that it was going white. That was blindside." Many remained sanguine. "Nobody cared because who wanted to be there on Saturdays anyway?" remarks Boyd Jarvis, a window dresser who first heard about the spot from Brooklyn neighbor and Brody employee "aunty" Kenny Eubanks. "I wanted to be there when the shit was hot and that was Fridays." Others, however, channeled their fury into a campaign that saw them write letters of complaint, hurl eggs, and take the story to radio. Deeply influenced by the integrationist ethos of the Loft, where he had started to dance around the time of his sixteenth birthday, Levan objected to the split on ethical grounds, and his opposition intensified when the Saturday manger told him a few weeks into the trial that he was going to be replaced by a white gay DJ — because Saturdays were still foundering. Levan showed his face merely to keep up appearances, including the night when Fire Island and Studio 54 DJ Roy Thode played on 20 October.[2]

Brody abandoned his Saturday-night experiment a month or two later, by which time it had become humiliatingly clear that the white gay crowd wasn't about to favor his spot. Picking up the pieces, he reinstated a told-you-so Levan to Saturdays and tweaked his membership system, providing gay men of any color with full access and restricting straights to Fridays only. For his part, Cheren told friends he wouldn't have proposed the change if he'd "known where it was going to lead."[3] Yet black and Latin dancers contained their excitement and largely steered clear of Saturdays until Levan invited mentor figure Toraino "Tee" Scott to play a weekend toward the end of the year. One of the first African Americans to hold down a residency in a profession initially dominated by Italian Americans, Scott was renowned for the fierce brand of disco, funk, and R&B he selected at Better Days, an intimate spot located on 49th Street and 8th Avenue that attracted a streetwise black gay crowd. Working with a smile on his face and a towel slung over a shoulder, ready to mop his brow as the Better Days floor reached cauldron intensity, the DJ also took to sharing his turntables with Levan when he rolled in for a boogie, nicknaming him Robin after Levan started to call him Batman. Then the Garage DJ, preparing for a weekend out of the city, asked Scott to cover for him, conscious the veteran could handle the pressure and wouldn't try to grab the precarious night for himself.

When Scott's Friday-night set went down a storm, the first huge Saturday-night crowd of Brody's run on King Street showed up for more of the same. "Tee really turned out the Garage," remembers Riley. "As a matter of fact, he bottomed the system out and blew a bunch of speakers right at the climax of Dan Hartman's 'Relight My Fire.'" Scott insists he only "blew one or two speakers that night," yet the incident became a topic of hot gossip, and the following week another big crowd showed up for both the Friday and Saturday parties to see if Levan could match Scott's performance — which he did.[4] From that point on, Saturdays picked up momentum while Levan entrenched his position. "It took a good six months to get most of the core members back," recalls Danny Krivit, a Garage regular who DJ-ed at the Ninth Circle and One's before taking up a job at Trude Heller's. "Larry was reminded of his importance and made Michael pay for anything and everything he asked for, including a duplex apartment on Gold Street. Larry had always been a bit of a diva, but now he was tried and true." Levan blamed Cheren more than Brody for the Saturday-night switchover. "It seemed like Larry and Mel really weren't talking for at least a few years," adds Krivit.

Brody gave Saturdays an extra boost when he started to schedule regular live shows, having clocked the huge crowds that rolled in when Dee Dee Bridgewater, First Choice, McFadden & Whitehead, and Karen Young appeared at special parties. "Michael knew the place would be packed on show nights so he started doing them once a fortnight," recalls DePino. "The shows

made them come to the party and then coming to the Garage became a habit,
so they would come even if there wasn't a party. Saturdays caught on in 1980."
Judy Weinstein became key to the strategy, thanks to her directorial position
at For the Record, the city's most powerful record pool, which counted Levan
among its 125 members, having come to the fore after Mancuso allowed his
own pool to run down. "Because of the record pool, most labels came to me
to organize promotional tours in New York City," she remarks. "Whenever
the record companies had an artist coming through town — whether it was
Jerry Butler or Candi Staton or Jackie Moore or Al Hudson — they would
call me and I would book these acts." Brody maintained at least some involvement throughout; Kenneth Reynolds, a promoter at CBS and then Polydor, remembers dealing only with the Garage owner when he took Cheryl
Lynn, Stephanie Mills, Junior, and Central Line to King Street. Then, when
Weinstein booked some "duds" because "record companies were asking her
for favors," the record pool head "took herself out of that position and only
got acts when Michael asked for them," adds DePino.

In the spring of 1980 Brody circulated a letter reporting that the Saturday-
night membership list was full. In contrast to Fridays, when members could
bring along as many women as they liked, members could only introduce
one woman on Saturdays, he added.[5] A child of the counterculture, Mancuso
wondered if the division was necessary, but gay men who wanted a night they
could call their own welcomed the system while a small number of women —
most of whom worked in music or fashion — were also granted Saturday
memberships. One of them, record store assistant Judy Russell, estimates that
out of a crowd of two thousand, one hundred were women who "wanted to
dance and were into the music." Krivit notes that female dancers "were in the
booth and in the middle of the dance floor so even a small contingent seemed
to diversify the crowd." Ultimately the venue catered to music lovers who got
down to what Levan was playing. "There was an open atmosphere," adds the
Trude Heller's DJ.

Although the Saturday-night drama hurt Levan, Brody's failure to lure the
white gay crowd left him in an unrivaled position to shape the taste of a city.
With Mancuso and Nicky Siano of the Gallery his primary teachers, the DJ
embraced a philosophy that held that dance music could be many things instead of one thing, and also that the dance floor should provide partygoers
from different backgrounds with an opportunity to explore alternative ways
of being. Levan's willingness to intersperse disco and R&B with new wave, rock,
dub, and gospel came as no surprise to those who got to know him. On one

The Paradise Garage dance floor, 1979. Photograph by Bill Bernstein ©;
courtesy of David Hill.

telling occasion, Mark Riley watched the DJ work his way through a huge
folder of menus and order fried chicken from every delivery restaurant in
the Village, inquisitive and voracious to the last. "In the end he didn't eat
anything," recalls Riley. "But it was like he was going to figure out which fried
chicken was the best out of all these different fried chicken places." Levan also
revealed "a specific ear for the unknown, for the untried," when he went on
shopping trips with Scott, who would often wrinkle his nose in disapproval
at his friend's selections only to then shout "Holy cow!" when he heard him
play them at the Garage.[6]

For a while Levan demonstrated he could "flawlessly mix the entire night,"
remembers Krivit, but as his confidence grew he became less and less interested in this technical aspect of DJ-ing. In part he simply wearied of battling
with the sluggish vari-speed controls of his Thorens turntables, which made
it difficult to sync two records together. In part he grasped that mixing two

records together according to their similar beat-per-minute tempo risked forsaking alternative, more adventurous transitional modes. Like Mancuso and Siano, he preferred to imagine how two records might join together to form a new lyrical narrative, or how two tracks might speak to one another in terms of their instrumentation, key, and energy. Creating mini-sets of thematically linked records, he also introduced pauses (sometimes by way of a sound effect) before moving to a new idea. Garage regular Manny Lehman recalls that "at other clubs there'd be seamless mixing and everyone would know the DJ" but that at the Paradise Garage "people understood the music, they felt it."

SELECTED DISCOGRAPHY

LARRY LEVAN, THE PARADISE GARAGE (1980)

Gayle Adams, "Stretch In Out"

Gayle Adams, "Your Love Is a Life Saver"

Aurra, "When I Come Home"

Edwin Birdsong, "Rapper, Dapper, Snapper"

Blondie, "Rapture"

Kurtis Blow, "The Breaks"

Brass Construction, "We Can Do It"

Dee Dee Bridgewater, "Bad for Me"

Ramona Brooks, "I Don't Want You Back"

Cameron, "Let's Get It Off"

Change, "Lover's Holiday"

Convertion, "Let's Do It"

Marianne Faithfull, "Why'd Ya Do It?"

Fantastic Aleems, "Hooked on Your Love"

Fantasy, "You're Too Late"

First Choice, "Double Cross"

Taana Gardner, "When You Touch Me"

Taana Gardner, "Work That Body"

Eddy Grant, "Living on the Frontline"

Johnny Harris, "Odyssey"

Loleatta Holloway, "Love Sensation"

Jimmy "Bo" Horne, "Is It In"

Geraldine Hunt, "Can't Fake the Feeling"

Instant Funk, "Everybody"

Grace Jones, "Warm Leatherette"

Kano, "I'm Ready"

Chaka Khan, "Clouds"

LAX, "All My Love"

Loose Joints, "Is It All over My Face? (Female Vocal)"

Janice McClain, "Smack Dab in the Middle"

Mtume, "So You Wanna Be a Star"

Billy Nichols, "Give Your Body Up to the Music"

Phreek, "Weekend"

The Police, "Voices inside My Head"

Queen, "Another One Bites the Dust"

Sharon Redd, "Can You Handle It?"

Rod, "Shake It Up (Do the Boogaloo)"

Rufus and Chaka, "Any Love"

Patrice Rushen, "Haven't You Heard"

Skyy, "Here's to You"

Skyy, "Skyyzoo"

Sun Palace, "Rude Movements"

Sylvester, "I Need You"

Talking Heads, "I Zimbra"

Trussel, "Love Injection"

Two Tons o' Fun, "I Got the Feeling"

Two Tons o' Fun, "Just Us"

Unlimited Touch, "I Hear Music in the Streets"

Theo Vaness, "I Can't Dance without You"

Young & Company, "I Like (What You're Doing to Me)"

Again following Mancuso and Siano, Levan wove records into an arc of intensity, yet he also demonstrated a newfound willingness to play games within this established meta-flow. He would often play a snatch of a record before introducing it later on in the evening, play the same record several times during the course of a night if he wanted it to have a particular impact, manipulate the equalizer in order to create spontaneous remixes of individual records, and even seize control of the lights from operator Robert DeSilva when he wanted to cultivate a specific atmosphere during a particularly important selection. When Peter Brown's "Do You Wanna Get Funky with Me" cut to the lyrics "It's so hot, I'm burning up" at the 1980 Halloween party, the DJ activated the dry ice machine while selecting red and orange lights, leaving

Loft and Paradise Garage dancers continue the party in Central Park, ca. 1980.
"This wasn't no scheduled party," says Boyd Jarvis, a participant. "This was us
saying, 'We're going to the park to turn it out. Everyone was clean and colorful."
Photograph by and courtesy of Kirk Leacock.

the crowd to dance in "slow motion" to "all these earth tones," recalls Victor
Rosado, a recent recruit to the spot.[7]

There were times when the Garage entered into an environmental plane of
affect and understanding. "What he was feeling, what he was thinking, what
he was going through at that particular point, the Garage took on that whole
ambience," Scott explained to Riley in a later interview. "It was like being on
a transcendental communication level with the people that he knew and that
he loved and partied with."[8] Experience taught the Better Days DJ to head to a
secluded spot whenever he went onto the floor because if Levan spotted him
from his booth he would pick out records to keep him dancing until he had
lost "10 or 15 pounds."[9] Usually relaxing the intensity of his selections around
the time his mother, Minnie, dropped by to pick up the money he gave her
each month in exchange for a home-cooked meal, Levan would put on the
kind of ethereal gospel she used to play when he was a child, including "Mary
Don't You Weep" by Aretha Franklin. "Around ten or eleven or twelve I'd get

in a fight with Larry," recounts Joey Llanos, who started to work on the security team during 1980 after Riley introduced him to the venue. "There'd be just ten people on the dance floor and Larry would be playing something very serene. He didn't want me to close the club until he was done."

Casting a spell that was unprecedented in terms of its emotional range and impact, Levan embodied the potential of the DJ to function as a highly evolved and responsive processor of sonic information. "Larry had no limits, no frontiers, just a wide open mind," argues François Kevorkian, a remixer, DJ, and regular presence in the Garage booth. "He was someone who truly did not discriminate and he was really ahead of his time. Yet he was also so mindful of the basics of what dancing and DJ-ing should be about — about the need to keep your flow with selections that are funky and tough." For Weinstein, a somewhat intimidating authority figure in the booth, Levan turned dancing into an adventure. "You never knew what he'd do next," she explains. "He played according to his mood. If he was in love, you'd hear love. If he felt dark, you'd hear dark. His mixing was so much more creative than anyone else who was playing."

The Paradise Garage realized its potential at the very moment when the backlash against disco raised questions about the future of dance music. "It was like we'd come through a war," remembers Krivit. "I thought, 'God, I hope I'm not going to have to become a new wave DJ or invent something.' The Garage gave me that reassurance. It made me think, 'Wait a minute, this music doesn't have a title, it's just good music that I dance to. It's still going on and there's still an audience that loves it.'" Levan reassured the largest dance crowd in the city that generic affiliations were of passing relevance. "They'd hear Larry play different types of music and they'd go, 'Wow, this stuff gets played with this stuff and it all make sense,'" adds Krivit. "'It's not just this or that. There are really no rules here.'"

With the Loft more than holding its own, the hardest partygoers could head to King Street and Prince Street over the course of a weekend or an elongated night, while those who felt a strong sense of loyalty to one particular spot could subdivide without troubling anyone. With their rivalry never less than friendly, dancers from both spots funneled to Washington Square Park or Central Park to mess around and share a joint on Sunday mid-morning and afternoon. "People would have their radios," recalls Jarvis. "We would line them up, tune them onto one station and continue the party right there until three in the afternoon." Tribal allegiances melted as the sun rose. "We were just dancers coming together," adds the Brooklynite. "There was no contest between the Garage and the Loft. None of that shit existed. It was just us getting down."

5

THE BRONX-BROOKLYN
APPROACH

As punk, new wave, no wave, Jamaican dub, pop art, performance art, live bands, experimental film, parodic kitsch, s/m, theme parties, homemade fashion, cutup, autobiography, psychedelia, the carnivalesque, gay liberation, disco, gospel, African American antiphony, audiophile sound-system culture, and the rest fed into Lower Manhattan's bewilderingly vibrant party scene, discrete practices that had taken root in the Bronx and Brooklyn started to permeate its outer margins. Quick-mix DJ-ing, MC rapping, the dance style known as breaking, and graffiti art were set to enter the syncretic storm.

Dating back to the late 1960s, when Greek writer Taki 183 and others started to cover the city's buildings and subway trains with their tags, graffiti was predestined to breach the downtown party scene first. After all, its nocturnal practitioners cultivated a guerrilla/art/poverty outlook that overlapped with the one that reigned at Club 57, Danceteria, and the Mudd Club, so someone just needed to introduce the groupings to one another. Cue Brooklyn graffiti artist Fred Brathwaite, who grew up in a household where chess, art, politics, and, above all, jazz were the stuff of life, as befitted someone who was also the godson of the jazz drummer Max Roach. A member of the Fabulous 5 collective, which gave him his Fab 5 Freddy tag, Brathwaite entered Lower Manhattan's punk/new wave/no wave milieu during 1979 while enrolled as an art student at the Medgar Evers College in Brooklyn. "I was involved in the arts and as a young kid I was aware of pop culture," notes Brathwaite. "I thought the graffiti art we were doing could be the descendant of pop art. Pop art converged with rock and roll in the 1960s, and when I saw the new wave and punk scene develop I was interested to see if I could find some like-minded people."

Michael Holman made the introduction after reading a short article about the Fabulous 5 in the *Village Voice* in early 1979. A mixed-race kid who had grown up in Europe and on the West Coast, Holman dropped out of the

University of San Francisco to perform in the theatrical camp rock band the Tubes, returned a year later to complete his economics degree, and then bolted to New York where he landed a job with Chemical Bank, partied on the weekends, and hooked up with London artist Stan Peskett, a friend of another Tubes band member. Peskett announced his intention to open a downtown spot around the time Brathwaite told the *Voice* that it was "time everyone realized graffiti is the purest form of New York art. What else has evolved from the streets?"[1] "I thought, who are these kids?" recalls Holman. "I'd seen these trains covered top to bottom in these graffiti burners and had wondered, 'What the hell is this about?' When I saw the blurb I called Freddy and said, 'Come over man, let's hang out!'"

Named after its 533 Canal Street location and held on 29 April 1979, Canal Zone's opening-night party featured thirty-by-forty-foot murals created by Brathwaite in tandem with Fabulous 5 collaborators Lee Quiñones (who had grown up on the Lower East Side, where his huge handball-court murals were legendary) and Slave (who hailed from Crown Heights, Brooklyn). Fancy dress, ketamine, and Peskett's home stereo fed the party, which vibed a little harder when downtown scenesters Glenn O'Brien, Debbie Harry, Rudolf Piper, Andy Warhol, and gallery owner Tony Shafrazi made their entries. As a hyped-up Holman pointed a video camera at guests and asked them juvenile questions, a young, black dreadlocked artist showed up unannounced, asked if he could paint, took hold of a spray can, and then wrote the question, "WHICH OF THE FOLLOWING IS OMNIPZNT? Harvey Oswald Coca Cola Logo General Melonry SAMO." The most celebrated graffiti artist on the downtown scene had just cast off his cloak of anonymity.

Raised in Brooklyn by his Haitian father and Puerto Rican mother, Jean-Michel Basquiat created the SAMO tag with schoolfriend Al Diaz while the two of them were smoking a joint, which inspired the phrase "same old shit" and out of that "SAMO." Developing their collaboration in school before hitting Lower Manhattan, they covered enough walls with their enigmatic slogans to prompt the *Village Voice* to cover their work in December 1978.[2] Basquiat had left home by then, having dropped out of school while still in the tenth grade, after which he took to selling hand-painted postcards and T-shirts to make some money. Drawn to the SVA café, he asked Keith Haring to escort him past security one day, and when Haring noticed on leaving later that day that the nearby walls had been freshly covered with the SAMO tag, he clocked that Basquiat was the mystery graffiti artist. Meanwhile Basquiat headed regularly to the Mudd Club, where Steve Mass gave him free rein and even let him sleep in the basement sometimes. Then, in early 1979, follow-

ing an argument with Diaz, Basquiat started to daub "SAMO is dead" slogans
around downtown. Haring performed a eulogy for the decommissioned tag
at a Club 57 poetry night soon after.

During the course of the Canal Zone party Basquiat bonded with Brathwaite, this despite the best efforts of a shit-stirring friend of Peskett's, who
ribbed the Fabulous 5 artist with the words, "Guess what, Fred? Guess who's
here? SAMO's here. How do you feel about that?"[3] The windup failed because
Basquiat and Brathwaite weren't about to let a little teaser stop them striking
up a conversation, cognizant that black guys were few and far between on
the downtown scene. "If you know about somebody's graffiti and recognize
their efforts, style and skill, you want to meet them because they're part of the
graffiti brotherhood," Brathwaite explained in a later interview. "Jean was
the same way."[4] Basquiat also bonded with Holman, asking him if he wanted
to join a band, to which the host replied, "Yes," Warhol, the Velvet Underground, and punk having established a trend in which it had become almost
irregular for an artist not to try her or his hand as a musician. "In one night
Jean and I meet for the first time, Freddy Brathwaite and Jean meet for the
first time, Jean meets Lee Quiñones for the first time, the downtown scene
and the graffiti scene meet for the first time, and Gray [as Basquiat and Holman would name their band] is started," adds Holman of the social frenzy. "In
one night. That was typical. Shit like that happened all the time."

Vibing off their shared Brooklyn background and interest in art, Basquiat
and Brathwaite split a studio space in Canal Zone and resolved "to be on the
scene and in the clubs," with the Mudd Club their most frequent destination.
Basquiat had recently entrenched his presence in the White Street spot after
Glenn O'Brien interviewed him for a graffiti piece he was writing for High
Times and warmed to him so much he invited him to appear on TV Party.
"He came on that week and never left," recalls O'Brien of the first episode to
feature the artist, which was broadcast four days before the Canal Zone party.
"Sometimes he got in front of the cameras, sometimes he ran a camera, but
he really loved running the character generator in the control room. On the
shows that have writing running across the screen, that's him improvising
poetry on top of the live action."[5] Basquiat also helped decorate Danceteria,
only for Rudolf Piper to fire him when he did a "fucking terrible job" painting
a wall. Basquiat hung out on 37th Street all the same and also contributed a
piece to Keith Haring's "Club 57 Invitational," yet harbored reservations about
the kitsch aesthetic that reigned at the St. Mark's Place venue.

Brathwaite, meanwhile, confirmed his theory that graffiti and punk spoke
a common pop-art language when he saw band names scrawled all over the

Jean-Michel Basquiat at the Mudd Club, 1979. "I met Jean-Michel on the MCL dance floor, where we danced often together," recalls Diego Cortez, who thinks he may be pictured wearing sunglasses, at left. Photograph by and courtesy of Nicholas Taylor ©.

walls of the urinals at CBGB. Yet it was at the Mudd Club rather than on the Bowery that he met Warhol and started to hang out with O'Brien, Debbie Harry, and Chris Stein, especially after calling O'Brien to say he was a fan of TV Party. O'Brien invited him into the studio and gave him impromptu camera work when a scheduled operator didn't show up (not knowing how to work the equipment being a qualification for the job). "The cool, hipster, new wave, artist creative types got in first and the people who came from Studio 54 were made to wait," Brathwaite notes of the Mudd Club, which is where he and his new TV Party family would head at the end of each show. "It was a declaration that we were here and were about to lay down what culture in New York City was going to be at the time — like a changing of the guard." Inside, a community took shape. "It was like, 'Hey, I'm going to do this!' and 'Hey, I'm making some paintings!' and 'Hey, I'm making a film!'" continues the graffiti artist. "Down-town was just an energy at that moment. There was this sense of commonality and reciprocity, this idea that different things could happen and were possible."

There were times, however, when Basquiat and Brathwaite struggled to get into a club, especially before they became more recognizable, with the city's art-punk club scene lagging behind the downtown dance and loft jazz scenes (and to a lesser extent the contemporary dance and experimental music scenes) when it came to integrating people of color. Perhaps it was inevitable progress would be slow. After all, Diego Cortez had abandoned the SoHo art scene because it consisted of white people drinking white wine in gallery rooms that were painted white.[6] "The absence of this mix was too much for me to take," he comments. Admittedly going to see the Ramones and the Dictators play at CBGB "was almost like a Nazi rally," yet the Bowery crowd's determination to challenge SoHo instilled it with an underlying promise.[7] "It was in the punk scene that I actually met people in European cinema, I met people in civil rights, I met black artists, South American artists, Asian artists, people from all over the world who were attracted to this dissonant music scene," argues Cortez. "In the end it led me to Jean-Michel Basquiat, Keith Haring, Fab 5 Freddy, and the emerging graffiti and rap scenes." The meeting with Basquiat took place at the Mudd Club, before Cortez knew about Basquiat's SAMO alter ego, but after seeing some thirty to forty graffiti pieces during a subsequent walk through SoHo, Cortez made a proposal. "I told him, 'You should start making drawings and paintings,'" he recounts. "'I can sell them. You're a really good artist.'"[8]

Meanwhile Basquiat and Holman rattled through several names for their band before settling on Gray, after *Gray's Anatomy*, Basquiat's favorite reference book. The choice stuck because even though they didn't know how to play their respective instruments — in Basquiat's case the clarinet and Wasp synthesizer; in Holman's, the drums — they liked the idea of dissecting sound. Joining the group in time for its debut at Hurrah, keyboard player Wayne Clifford and trumpeter Shannon Dawson also lacked conventional skills. "During those first three or four months we were playing our instruments in an attempt to emulate free jazz, when almost anything happened," notes Holman, who quit his job at Chemical Bank a couple of months after the Canal Zone party, having concluded he couldn't sustain the double life of working nine-to-five and partying all night. "But they were trained musicians and we were emulating it through a lack of skill."

The band shifted into its deconstructive phase after Holman and Basquiat concluded that Dawson had to go because his style was holding the group back. Fearing for his own position when Basquiat started to wince at his bombastic drumming style soon after, Holman became more experimental, placing a microphone on his drum and turning the reverb up high before he played it using metal sticks extracted from a toy piano, dropping ball bearings on it, and even attaching and then pulling off masking tape, which prompted everyone to turn to him and say, "*What the fuck was that*?!" From then on, Basquiat, Clifford, Holman, and new recruit Nick Taylor approached their instruments like aliens from another world, clueless as to how they should be played yet appreciative of beautiful music when they heard it. Basquiat loosened the strings of an electric guitar and dragged a metal file along them, Clifford ran his sweaty fingers across the face of an African xylophone box to create a plaintive horn sound, and Taylor scraped a pick up his guitar's striated neck. "We approached our instruments like a painter," remarks Holman, who cemented his rising status by joining the team that planned the Soul Party at the Mudd Club. "We were concerned with color, composition, sculpture. We were being tactile, we were being primitive, and when we did something purposefully wrong and it sounded right, that's what we would call 'ignorant.' We'd say, 'Oh, man, that is so *ignorant*!' That was like the greatest compliment you could ever get!"

Basquiat took on the role of unofficial leader because he had initiated the band and he also exuded a charismatic authority that set him apart from the others as well as Gray apart from other no wave lineups. If Basquiat didn't want someone in the band, there was no way that person could stay, end of story. If he wanted someone to join, they would join, because it was hard to resist his force of personality. If he grimaced during rehearsals, the culprit tried something different or risked being thrown out, as Holman learned from Dawson. "We talked about him being a realized human being," reminisces Holman. "He was not like the rest of us. He really transcended humanism as we understand it — his sensitivity, his genius, his vision, the way he looked, the way he spoke, his sexuality, his attractiveness, the way people wanted to hang out with him and talk with him and share ideas with him. Even before he became famous he was just this flame that we were all moths to. He was this special human being."

O'Brien interviewed Basquiat along with Brathwaite and Quiñones for his graffiti piece, an epic five-page account that appeared in *High Times* in June. The TV *Party* host tracked the history of the style from cave art to its breakthrough in New York to the rise of a new, complex form of three-dimensional, overlapping, semilegible lettering known as Wild Style. Many writers had come to think of themselves as artists, as Brathwaite and Quiñones demonstrated when they covered a subway car in Warhol-style Campbell's Soup cans, painted a whole ten-car train with such panache that passengers waiting on the plat-

Gray performing at Hurrah, 1979. Jim Fouratt booked the show. Basquiat (left), Holman (center, left), Wayne Clifford (center, right), and Shannon Dawson (right). Photograph by and courtesy of Nicholas Taylor ©.

Basquiat (left), Holman (center), and Shannon Dawson (right). Photograph by and courtesy of Nicholas Taylor ©.

form often applauded as it rolled into a station, and landed gallery shows in Italy. If the Metropolitan Transit Authority was prepared to spend several million dollars a year cleaning cars and committing offenders to community service, that service enabled writers to make new acquaintances and plot future forays. "Graffiti fights the fascism of design, the ultimate subliminal weapon for grinding down the human spirit," argued O'Brien. "Subway riders, afraid to look at one another, are expected to look at the ads, neatly boxed in lit panels over the windows. But they have to look at the graffiti — reminders that there are some things that can't be controlled, thousands of individual identities asserting themselves in wild color and bold hand across the tabula rasa of modern corporate planning."[9]

Coinciding with the publication of O'Brien's feature, the graffiti-downtown encounter blew up when the public art campaign group Collaborative Projects (Colab) opened the *Times Square Show* in a vacant ex–massage parlor located on 41st Street in Times Square at the beginning of June. Five months earlier Colab had broken into an abandoned building on Delancey Street to stage the *Real Estate Show* as a critique of the Lower East Side real estate market; officers made the exhibition's point perfectly by repossessing the property three days later. The ensuing publicity encouraged Colab sculptors John Ahearn and Tom Otterness to venture into Manhattan's seediest neighborhood in order to draw attention to the availability of empty buildings at a time when affordable housing was in short supply. "It had to be in this area," argued Ahearn, who contributed head casts of people who were local to the South Bronx Fashion Moda gallery where he worked. "Times Square is a crossroads. A lot of different kinds of people come through here. There is a broad spectrum and we are trying to communicate with society at large. There has always been a misdirected consciousness that art belongs to a certain class or intelligence. This show proves there are no classes in art, no differentiation."[10]

The show consisted of low-budget efforts constructed out of cheap materials that foregrounded a series of themes that were largely submerged within the established art world, including sex, domestic life, violence, business, commodification, and, in particular, race. In a wide-ranging review of the show published in *Art in America*, investment adviser Jeffrey Deitch judged Ahearn's brightly colored head casts of South Bronx residents to best represent the exhibition, describing the works as a "raw slice of South Bronx life." "It was so exciting sharing divided cultures that were hungry to experience what the other had to offer," recalls Anita Sarko, one of the DJs. "It was a very pure artistic experience completely devoid of ego or territorialism or macho

Fred "Fab 5 Freddy" Brathwaite at the *Times Square Show*, 1980. Photograph by and courtesy of Bobby Grossman ©.

posturing." The exhibition also presented pieces made by the up-and-coming artists who had hitherto channeled their efforts from the club and the street. Fred Brathwaite displayed graffiti pieces, Keith Haring showed a piece featuring pink penises, Kenny Scharf customized one of the building's air conditioners, and Basquiat's wall of graffiti amounted to "a knockout combination of de Kooning and subway paint scribbles," added Deitch.[11]

A new kind of presence on the downtown scene, Deitch had moved from Massachusetts to New York in 1974, the day after he graduated. For a couple of years he went with the flow as he worked in a gallery, headed to CBGB, staged an independent exhibition, wrote art reviews, and for a while claimed unemployment. But he also aspired to make some kind of living and, reluctant to take on a minimum wage job to augment his writing, he went to study for an MBA at Harvard in the autumn of 1976. Deitch returned to New York two years later and took up a position working in Citibank's art investment service, where he courted and guided some of the "biggest collectors in the world." None were interested in new art, yet Deitch still enjoyed showing colleagues around the *Times Square Show* during his lunch break. "It's where the graffiti artists met the art school artists," he recalls. "It wasn't just an exhibition you visited once; it was like a clubhouse. People would hang out there every day." A onetime member of Colab who heard the show's organizers had stolen the artist list he was compiling for an exhibition of his own, Diego Cortez balked, judging the show to be "half-assed."

Yet it was at the exhibition that Brathwaite introduced himself to Charlie Ahearn, the downtown filmmaking brother of the organizer John, a Mudd Club regular who had already started to eye up graffiti culture and in particular the work of "underground Picasso figure" Quiñones, which he noticed while filming *The Deadly Art of Survival*, a Lower East Side kung fu movie featuring black and Puerto Rican kids.[12] A fan of the film, Brathwaite pitched an idea to Ahearn at the show's opening party. "Fred told me that he wanted to make a movie with me," Ahearn told hip hop historian Jeff Chang. "He said, 'We should make a movie about this graffiti thing,' and he said he knew Lee Quiñones."[13] Taking one step at a time, Ahearn said if Brathwaite returned with Quiñones the next day he would pay them $50 to paint on a wall outside the show's building, which came to pass. Then, when the show wound down at the end of June, Ahearn, Brathwaite, and Quiñones started to run with the idea of making a movie and decided to call it *Wild Style* — after the newly popularized graffiti style.

Brathwaite initially argued that they should shoot downtown, but Ahearn felt the Bronx would be more interesting, having screened *The Deadly Art of Survival* at Fashion Moda the previous year, and he won the argument after Brathwaite checked out the borough. Their first trip took them to a park located on the north side, where a dub band vied for attention with a party crew. Certain that everyone assumed he was a cop, Ahearn made his way to the party crew stage while Brathwaite gawped at the sight of a thousand kids gathered to listen to "this thing, rapping."[14] When one of the crew, MC Busy Bee Starski, asked Ahearn what he was doing, he explained he was a movie producer and wanted to make a film about the rap scene, at which point Starski put his arm around Ahearn, led him onto the stage, and announced, "This here's Charlie Ahearn. He's my movie producer and we're making a movie about the rap scene." The director notes that Starski didn't lose a second. "That's how people were," he observes. "They were hungry."[15]

Of all the parties that made up the Bronx scene, the most prescient was the one organized by the Jamaican-born Kool Herc in the rec center where he lived on Sedgwick Avenue back in August 1973. The following summer he began to cut together funk and disco breaks in a "merry-go-round" technique that established him as the most progressive DJ in the borough, at least until Afrika Bambaataa started to hold Zulu Nation parties in the Bronx River Community Center in November 1976 and stretched out the sonic range. Dividing his appearances between one-off jams (as they were known) and regular club spots such as Italian American Sal Abbatiello's Disco Fever, Grandmaster Flash broke through around the same time, thanks to his ability to quick-cut and spin-back with virtuoso speed and accuracy (as well as carry out mixes with his feet). Herc and Bambaataa also picked up indoor residencies at spots such as the Hevalo and T-Connection, but when the weather was warm the DJs headed outdoors, where the open space made it easier for their previously warring gang-crews to channel their competitive energies into sound-system, DJ-ing and MC contests. Peace correlated with noise until Herc was stabbed while trying to break up a fight during 1977 in an incident that highlighted the fragility of the party-led détente. He never fully recovered his earlier prowess.

Ahearn and Brathwaite stumbled into a scene where no clear lines had been drawn between disco and funk. Just as downtown dance DJs had drawn heavily on records that were also played in the Bronx during the first half of the 1970s — including Babe Ruth, "The Mexican"; James Brown, "Give It Up"; Bobby Byrd, "Hot Pants"; Lynn Collins, "Think"; Cymande, "Bra"; Isley Brothers, "Get into Something"; Gil Scott-Heron, "The Bottle"; and Lonnie Liston Smith, "Expansions" — so Herc and Bambaataa blended disco with funk for audiences that would have expected nothing less, in part because disco was often funky. "People don't recognize this but we killed Disco!" points out Coke La Rock, Herc's DJ and MC partner.[16] Bambaataa adds that he "used to play a lot of disco for the people who were heavy into the hustle" because all sorts of dance styles were in play at the time. Afrika Islam, who carried Bambaataa's record crates and helped set up the Zulu Nation sound system, confirms that sound was a liquid force. "The Bronx was hip hop, but when I say hip hop I'm not talking about just James Brown and Sly Stone," he argues. "I'm talking about James Brown and Sly Stone and Inner Life and Sylvester and Roy Ayers. I'm talking about all of it. That was the sound of the Bronx."

If disco "grew and was built in the New York streets," as Brathwaite puts it, the centrality of African Americans to the culture faltered when it became clear that Steve Rubell "wasn't letting unattached black men into Studio 54 — not unless he knew them," notes Mark Riley. The privileging of Italian American suburban disco and the white-sounding fare of the Bee Gees in *Saturday*

Night Fever gave black partygoers further pause for thought. Yet concerns about appropriation didn't result in straightforward denunciation. "We were anti-disco because disco was John Travolta and *Saturday Night Fever* and Studio 54," declares Islam. "We were wearing Levi's jeans and Pumas so we didn't look like John Travolta, but it didn't mean we didn't listen to the music or dance to it." While Bambaataa started "pulling back to the funk" when radio stopped playing James Brown and Sly and the Family Stone, he still "used a lot of disco breaks" and even integrated the whiter end of the sound when he hammered Eurodisco records such as Cerrone's "Rocket in the Pocket." "A lot of disco records became hip hop classics," remarks the DJ. Then the backlash against disco played itself out, leaving local DJs who had grown to resent the sound with little to oppose, rather like their art-punk counterparts.

That autumn Ahearn and Brathwaite returned to party after party, introduced themselves to key figures, and persuaded their Mudd Club pals Debbie Harry and Chris Stein to sample the culture. "The scene was full-speed ahead up there and it was very much paralleling what was going on downtown," Stein recalls of a party held at the Police Athletic League. "It was so communal, almost like there was no boundary between the audience and the stage. The performers were just doing their thing in the crowd. I remember coming away super-buzzed."[17] Brathwaite, meanwhile, recalled reading that for a scene to be successful it needed a sound and a dance as well as a visual style, so he resolved to conjure a hypothesis that MC-ing, DJ-ing, and breaking formed part of the same energy as graffiti, not to mention punk. "At that time, this rapping, breaking, and graffiti scene was not really connected as one thing," he notes. "My idea was that this whole thing was one culture and that it should be shown as that. I felt that making a film about it would be a great way to show everybody that it was one thing."[18]

Although DJ-ing and MC-ing had indeed become tightly intertwined, graffiti and breaking only existed on the margins of the Bronx party scene. After all, writers carried out their work in train depots, in handball courts, and on vacant walls rather than party locations, while breakers were never more than a minority contingent at MC jams and carried out most of their moves in front of a boom box, not a DJ. Of the numerous parties he attended that autumn and winter, Ahearn recalls that the "MCs were onstage and people were looking at them," rap had become "the focal point," the DJs were "no longer at the center of the music," and "nobody was dancing."[19] Indeed the director only got to see breaking for the first time when Queens graffiti artist Lady Pink (selected to play the girlfriend of lead actor Quiñones in the movie) arranged for the Bronx- and Manhattan-based breaking outfit the Rock Steady Crew to dance at a twenty-first birthday party held for Quiñones. Hip hop — as the combination of Bronx DJ-ing, MC-ing, breaking, and graffiti writing would soon be named — was already "dead by 1980," at least in the Bronx, Ahearn would go on to tell Chang. In truth it had never existed as a cohesive culture in the first place.

Such niceties didn't stop Johnny Dynell from developing his own connection to Bronx party culture when he started to head to the borough around the same time as Harry and Stein, having heard Grandmaster Flash play in a church basement in Brooklyn. "Coming from an art school perspective, I was like, 'These people are taking these found objects and putting them to their own use,'" recalls Dynell, who was still DJ-ing at the Mudd Club. "I was getting all Marcel Duchamp on them and started screaming at people like Andy [Warhol], 'They're doing what you do but with records!' Andy was totally uninterested." Dynell's rap selections went down a storm, however, and Brathwaite remembers the DJ being "one of the few people who was aware of early rap music" and "representative" of those who "were open to new music." With time on his hands after he and Chi Chi Valenti fell out with Steve Mass, Dynell pulled together a horns-and-percussion backing outfit known as New York 88 and might have become the first white artist to rap in public when, mixing street talk with references to retro dance styles, he performed the rap-funk number "Jam Hot" at the *Times Square Show*.

Up to this point no Bronx graffiti artist had made a downtown stand in the manner of Basquiat, Brathwaite, or Quiñones, but the Bronx-based Funky 4+1 (four guys plus Sha Rock, the first woman rapper to break through on the scene) became the first MC lineup to crash the art-punk end of the party scene. They did so at the experimental venue the Kitchen, when Edit deAk, a Hungarian-born critic and ex-editor of the punk-influenced *Art-Rite* magazine, included them in a three-night "Dubbed in Glamour" spectacle, which showcased the "energies of the Para-Soho luminaries, that part of the art world which never had a loft, is younger than the art world and hangs out in the clubs," as the flyer for the event declared.[20] Held on the weekend of 21–23 November 1980, the event also included burlesque, fashion, gymnastics, readings, video, film, slides, live performance, and DJ-ing from the likes of Patti Astor, the Bush Tetras, Debbie Harry, Tina L'Hotsky, Glenn O'Brien, Anya Phillips, Amos Poe, Anita Sarko, and Chi Chi Valenti. If the Funky 4+1 appearance raised questions about the potential exoticization of rap, it remained the case that barely eighteen months had passed since the near-blanket exclusion of African

Americans from the venue's high-profile New Music, New York festival of June 1979 had come in for deserving criticism. The audience whooped it up and the rappers concluded their show by saying that it had been "a real pleasure" to perform.[21]

Basquiat, meanwhile, maintained his pre–*Times Square Show* momentum when Gray played a second time at the Mudd Club on 3 August 1980. Preparing for the concert, Holman re-jigged the twelve concentric blocks that made up the venue's modular stage by removing the center pieces and placing his drum kit in the cavity. He then headed to the Bronx to rent $100 worth of scaffolding and, with new recruit Vincent Gallo assisting, constructed a geodesic dome made up of metal pipes plus street lumber and garbage. The end result, which they completed by the time Basquiat showed up at 7:30 PM, resembled a three-dimensional spider's web. "I looked at Jean-Michel in a coy way and said, 'Well, I told you what time we were going to start building this,'" remembers Holman. "Inside I'm saying, '*I got you. I blew you away, Jean-Michel Basquiat.*'" Basquiat walked out and returned some five minutes later with a wooden shipping crate that measured approximately three feet by three feet, which he threw onto the stage, allowing the box to tumble around until it landed with the open side facing outward. Then the artist squeezed his body into the container, pulled his synthesizer toward him, and smiled. "He had gone out and within a few minutes had found something that not only fit but also made him the center of attention," remarks Holman. "It filled out the set so ingeniously. I was like, 'You motherfucker!'"

Getting ready for the show, Holman climbed into his hole so that the audience could only see his head, Gallo and Wayne Clifford strapped themselves from the geodesic dome so they and their keyboards hung out at forty-five degrees, Nick Taylor shifted on top of the structure with his guitar until only his lower legs were visible, and Basquiat wriggled into his box. The band started playing just before the venue's curtain — a metal store-front gate — cranked up and contributed to the cacophony of instrumentation through the noise of its grind. Twelve minutes and ten songs later the performance was over. "I remember looking out into the audience and everybody looked like the figure in Edvard Munch's painting 'The Scream,'" adds Holman. "They were holding their hands to their faces and their mouths were wide open. They were like, '*What the fuck am I looking at?*' They were all just looking up at this set like, '*What is going on?*'"

Gray cranked up the volume some more in September when they performed at SoHo gallery trailblazer Leo Castelli's birthday party. Curated by

O'Brien, who had become good friends with Basquiat, the event took place at the Rock Lounge, another addition to the rock discotheque movement opened by New York, New York owner Howard Stein on 285 West Broadway, right below Canal Street. Of the two songs Gray played that night, the second featured a shopping cart fitted with an industrial electric motor that drove a bent shaft, which caused the machine to make a huge clanging noise and thrash about in a reasonably dangerous manner as it beat against a truck spring welded to its bumper. "Jean-Michel plugged it into a socket and this thing rattled around like hell was coming through the door," reminisces Holman. "It was like *rrraaahhh, rrraaahhh, rrraaahhh, rrraaahhh*. The shopping cart leapt around and I remember seeing Leo Castelli holding his hand to his chest, his mouth wide open, his eyes right open. It was, 'Oh my god, this thing is going to jump off the stage and into the audience.'"

Already tipped off by Cortez that Basquiat was the most interesting new artist on the scene, Deitch learned that night that the dreadlocked guy playing the noise machine was the elliptical SAMO. Cortez proceeded to take the investment adviser — a friend since 1975 — to the Lower East Side apartment of Basquiat's girlfriend, Suzanne Mallouk, where Basquiat was living at the time, having given the artist some money to buy some paper and prestretched canvases to press ahead with his post-SAMO career. Deitch was stunned to enter a room strewn with art that featured recurring crowns, heads, letters, and numerals. "This is the most amazing work I've seen by anyone of this generation," he told Basquiat before picking out what he judged to be the four outstanding efforts. Basquiat requested $50 apiece and accompanied Deitch to a nearby cash machine. Deitch remembers clocking a look on Mallouk's face that suggested she knew her boyfriend would immediately head off to score rather than help pay the rent.

Although his contribution attracted less attention than Basquiat's, Keith Haring also experienced the *Times Square Show* as pivotal. "It was the first time that every kind of underground art could be seen in one place," he told biographer John Gruen, "and that included graffiti art."[22] Immediately attracted to the color, scale, pop imagery, guerrilla underpinnings, and audience appeal of graffiti when he first saw it on the subway, the Pennsylvanian artist met Brathwaite during the exhibition and the two of them, along with Basquiat, Scharf, and Futura 2000 (a graffiti artist who grew up on the Upper West Side), became "a sort of posse" when it wound down.[23] Brathwaite, Haring, and Scharf became particularly close as they hung out in the midtown apartment Haring and Scharf had started to share, consuming mushrooms in

Shopping cart used by Gray. "Jean liked my work a lot and came to the presentation where I showed the shopping cart and a film that I had made," recalls Cooper Union art student and experimental instrument builder Peter Artin. "Afterward he asked if he could use the machine with his band, which was cool with me. When I originally showed it, I would plug it in and it would go crazy until it pulled its plug out of the outlet. For Jean, I put a switch on the cord so he could turn it on and off and so 'play' it like an instrument." Photograph by Peter Artin ©; courtesy of Michael Holman.

an upstairs closet decorated in fluorescent colors by Scharf.[24] "Kenny would play psychedelic music and Keith would bring out paper and say, 'Let's draw,'" reminisces Brathwaite.

If the B-52's, Klaus Nomi, and the scene at CBGB encouraged Haring to pursue his vision, the skinny, bespectacled artist now judged Club 57 to be his standout influence, in part because the venue's spirit of childlike play, supernatural energy, and sexual vibrancy had started to imbue his life and work, and in part because its intimate environment, low-income accessibility, and spirit of openness helped him to develop his voice and make connections. "Club 57 not only meant dancing and drinking and sex and fun and craziness, but the beginning of a whole career as the organizer and curator of some really interesting art shows," Haring told Gruen. "This was the period in New York where people were trying to do things *outside* the gallery system — doing things more in the community."[25] As he oversaw the *Xerox Art* exhibition and the *Club 57 Invitational*, Haring created works that featured flying

Keith Haring (left) and Tseng Kwong Chi at Club 57, 1980. Photograph by and courtesy of Harvey Wang ©.

saucers, animal figures, humans having sex with humans, humans having sex with animals, energetic symbols, and crowds of people — symbols that would define his aesthetic. "Keith made every idea a reality," comments Ann Magnuson. "And he made artists out of us all when he curated the first Club 57 art shows and invited everyone to be part of it. His energy was boundless and inspiring." When the artist teamed up with Frank Holliday to stage a "Tribute to Gloria Vanderbilt" party — Vanderbilt being the actor, heiress, and designer of tight-fitting designer jeans — the flyer carried the summative slogan "any excuse for a party."

That spring Haring experienced an epiphany, having started to work as an assistant for Tony Shafrazi. An Iranian-raised, English-educated gallerist, Shafrazi had provoked headlines back in 1974 when he strolled into the Museum of Modern Art and spray-painted Picasso's *Guernica* with the words "KILL LIES ALL" in order to re-radicalize the painting in protest against the Vietnam War. Haring felt ambivalent about the act yet admired the doing and also appreciated the opportunity to gain hands-on experience at Shafrazi's gallery on Lexington Avenue. Invited to Haring's *Club 57 Invitational* in May, the gallerist judged it to be an "extraordinary assemblage of downtown art."[26] But at the end of the month Haring became deeply disillusioned at the opening of a show by Keith Sonnier, an established postminimalist artist and one of his tutors at SVA. Serving drinks, Haring tuned into the client conversations and concluded that they were "ridiculous and stupid," while Sonnier "didn't seem very happy," even if his show was judged a success.[27] Haring went outside, cried his heart out, and returned with his mind made up. "It wasn't that I wanted out of the art world," he explained to Gruen. "I just felt that the whole gallery situation was incredibly confining and it seemed very false. . . . There had to be a whole other reason for making art beside looking for success within the art world."[28]

Spurred on by the *Times Square Show*, Haring moved further away from gallery culture when he journeyed to the West Village on the eve of gay pride to plaster xeroxes taken from a book on sex and married life. Soon after he used stencils to spray "Clones Go Home" on the streets that divided the East Village and West Village, underscoring his efforts with the letters FAFH, which stood for Fags Against Facial Hair (because he and his friends "didn't want the preppy types of the West Village invading our territory — the East Village").[29] That autumn he curated *Anonymous Art* at Club 57, presenting art he had found on the street, and also presented drawings at an exhibition held at P.S. 122, an alternative art space located on 1st Avenue and 9th Street, which garnered him his first review courtesy of the *SoHo News*.[30] Then, toward the end of the year, he began to cover New York's subways with a distinctive style of graffiti.

Haring timed his entry to perfection. A few months earlier, back in August, Mayor Ed Koch proposed that dogs be placed around subway storage depots in order to prevent graffiti artists (or "vandals" in the terminology of the *New York Times*) from scrawling on the trains, regretting only that he couldn't use wolves instead.[31] In September, photographer Henry Chalfant, a Stanford University graduate who had started to document the art phenomenon, organized an exhibition at the OK Harris gallery in SoHo during which he "must have met every writer in the city," as "they came to the gallery as if on a pilgrimage," he told the *East Village Eye*.[32] In October, the *Times* compared riding on the subway to "standing in some awful forest," likening graffiti to a plague that was costing the city $10 million a year in maintenance and lost fares.[33] "Just within the last few months, the Transit Authority has reorganized its attack on graffiti and other forms of subway vandalism," noted the newspaper. "Arrests have doubled, and a program has been instituted requiring that subway vandals or their parents pay clean-up costs. A special plainclothes squad has been organized to combat graffiti." It added that Koch's canine unit was also being trained up.[34]

Hitting the subway, Haring started out by embellishing a whisky ad with babies and a flying saucer. After that he started to create chalk drawings on the black panels that covered unused advertising spaces, which was his way of participating in graffiti without copying the artists who had broken into yards to paint on trains.[35] Encouraged by Brathwaite and clear in his own mind that the graffiti community was evenly mixed between blacks, whites, Hispanics, and Chinese, Haring would complete "thirty or forty" drawings in one day as he rode from station to station, with Club 57 friend and photographer Tseng Kwong Chi tracking him along the way.[36] Animals that evolved into dogs, flying saucers that zapped proximate objects, and babies who emitted rays of energy enticed thousands of journeyers to view Haring's playful yet sophisticated code. "In the back of my mind was this idea of wanting the respect of the graffiti artists," Haring told Gruen. "It was much more important to me to have their respect for the work rather than that of the art world, because it was more of a challenge to obtain."[37] He added that, if anything, his decision to draw on the black panels rather than head into the yards made him "more vulnerable to being caught by the cops — so there was an element of danger."[38]

Sha Rock returned to Manhattan on New Year's Eve when Funky 4 + 1 promoter Ray Chandler booked the crew to appear at the Hotel Diplomat on 43rd Street. The MC outfit the Fantastic Freaks, rapper Kurtis Blow, and Grandmaster Flash shared the stage, Blow and Flash having already appeared at the venue in 1977 when the Queens-based Russell Simmons organized a Bronx-style event there. But instead of enjoying a happy reunion, Flash's MC crew the Furious Five — Cowboy, Melle Mel, Kid Creole, Rahiem, and Mr. Ness — eyed the size of the crowd and demanded a higher fee. Chandler stood his ground and so did the rappers as they walked away from the party. "How do I spin my way out of this?" Flash wondered.[39] He opted for the usual combination of mixing dexterity, instinct, speed, and bravado.

If Brooklyn had led graffiti's charge into Manhattan, at least one Bronx DJ and a dozen or so MCs from the same part of town were now contributing sounds to its party mix. Then there were the two filmmakers who were heading in the reverse direction in order to give some storytelling shape to the swishes, swirls, flows, and breaks. Come the year's end, borough-based forms were all set to take downtown by storm.

THE SOUND BECAME
MORE REAL

Michael Zilkha traveled to New York in June 1975, right after graduating from Oxford University. A cultural refugee of privileged upbringing — his Iraqi Jewish father was the founder of the U.K. chain store Mothercare, and his stepfather was the Labour MP Harold Lever, who was jokingly referred to as the Member of Parliament for the Côte d'Azur — he made his first trip to CBGB three days later. The venue appeared to be located a million metaphorical miles away from the university common room where a hereditary elite-within-an-elite left him feeling like an outsider. "I was a short child and puberty didn't come until nineteen, and what I knew more about than anyone else was music," he comments. "Music was absolutely everything to me and knowing more about it than other people gave me an identity." Zilkha interpreted the "disco sucks" graffiti on the bathroom walls as an expression of middle-class misfit ennui, not punk anger. "It was a deeply intellectual exercise," he argues of the wider venue. "The Ramones were high concept, Debbie Harry was high concept and the irony was built in. That didn't mean it wasn't great pop music, but anything scrawled on the walls of CBGB was tongue-in-cheek. The record burning that took place in Chicago was much more serious. You know, New York is a very fluid place."

Zilkha tried his hand in journalism before Velvet Underground musician John Cale proposed they start a punk label at the end of an interview. Forming Spy Records, they released a couple of tracks and laid down a spoof disco song titled "Disco Clone" before Zilkha concluded that he and Cale were never going to hit it off as partners. Around the same time, French producer Michel Esteban (who had introduced Marie et les Garçons to Spy) proposed they form their own company, and so ZE Records was born, named as a composite of the first letters of their surnames. "I saw how the *Saturday Night Fever* soundtrack was selling," remembers Zilkha. "Even though the Bee Gees had attained a level of perfection I could never aspire to, I wanted to make dance records that you could listen to repeatedly as records. I wanted to use the dance framework to paint a wild picture within."

For ZE's first release Zilkha re-recorded "Disco Clone" with his Franco-American girlfriend, Cristina Monet-Palaci, a Harvard dropout and *Village Voice* contributor. Engineered by Bob Blank, who had risen to industry renown with sharp, tight disco mixes such as Musique's "In the Bush," the result placed the four-on-the-floor bass drum, metronomic hi-hats, and Latinized piano lines of disco under the vocalist's shaky incantation of the line "I'm a disco clone." The ingeniousness of recording a disco track that poked fun at the genre's assembly line quality was only let down by its inauspicious execution. "Cristina was very, very clever, but she wasn't really a singer, and it also had twenty-four violinists doubled up and many, many horns," recalls Zilkha. "It was a ridiculously expensive production. But I was also learning about the recording studio." Blank preferred to accentuate the positive. "The record sounded terrible," he notes. "Michael was being ironic."

Zilkha went to watch the Contortions play live around the same time and, smitten by the coolness of James Chance and Anya Phillips, asked if they would record a track for his label. With "Disco Clone" still in the pipeline, Chance and Phillips declined to take the band to the fledgling label but agreed to record an album featuring another lineup, James White and His Blacks. Modifying the name to James White and the Blacks, which he felt more comfortable with, Zilkha proposed that if the Contortions weren't going to record with ZE then perhaps the bandleader could create something that would combine punk and disco. "The idea didn't bother them in the slightest," remarks the fledgling label boss, ever more convinced that if the relationship between a drummer and a bass player was right the introduction of added weirdness would provide contrast and adventure. "Their response was, 'You think we can make money in this way?' James was open to everything."

Pre-prepared for the outwardly surprising move, Chance had grown up in the Midwest, where "everybody danced," and during the early 1970s he started to head to a gay Milwaukee club called the River Queen that played the "hippest mix" of funk, R&B, and proto-disco. When Phillips landed the Contortions a residency at Max's in the summer of 1978, Chance was delighted to become a "headliner at a good club" yet resented the way that the venue lacked a dance floor, just like CBGB. Of Zilkha's album idea, he remembers thinking: "I'll come up with something that has a vague relationship to disco and then I'll do the rest the way I want."[1] In January he prepared followers for the move when he told the *SoHo Weekly News* that although he found disco "disgusting," he was interested in its monotony. "It's sort of jungle music, but

James Chance and Anya Phillips, ca. 1980. Phillips negotiated a two-album advance with ZE Records. Photograph by and courtesy of Bobby Grossman ©.

whitened and perverted," he argued. "On this album I'm trying to restore it to what it could be. Really primitive."[2] Four months later he even claimed that new wave and no wave had become outdated drivel. "So dislocate yourself. Get slick, move uptown and get trancin' with some superadioactive disco voodoo funk," he commanded.[3] Combining demented syncopation, freeform jazz, and fraught vocals, "Contort Yourself" turned out to be the standout track on the summer release of *Off White*. It also blazoned the arrival of a fresh punk-funk sound. Zilkha's mission to overhaul the city by combining rhythm and weirdness was up and running.

Appreciative of Esteban's artwork and liaison skills until he went on tour with Marie et les Garçons and forgot to pay any bills, Zilkha began to run ZE as a solo operation from the spring of 1979 onward. Winning over scenesters with his infectious enthusiasm, bold intelligence, and sharp taste, he produced Cortez's and Phillips's Elvis documentary; teamed up with Chance to coproduce the film's soundtrack; released records by no wavers Mars and Teenage Jesus and the Jerks; dug out the money to issue Suicide's electronic-protopunk "Dream Baby Dream," which he licensed to Island; and put out

Buy by the Contortions after Phillips and Chance "decided they had found a home," he reminisces. Maintaining the momentum during 1980, Zilkha cast punk poet Lydia Lunch as a torch singer on the solo album *Queen of Siam*. (Barry Lederer, author of the *Billboard* "Disco Mix" column, recommended the record to "the adventuresome deejay.")[4] Released around the same time, Cristina's eponymous debut album prompted *Dance Music* to declare that "the people at ZE are rapidly gaining a reputation as the 'wizards of weird.'"[5] Zilkha rode the wave. "Basically I signed all of downtown because no one else wanted it," he remarks. "I was building a repertory company."

August Darnell became a pivotal creative figure at the label after Bob Blank introduced him to Zilkha. The Bronx-raised son of a French-Canadian mother and Dominican father, Darnell made his name as the coleader of the disco-meets-swing-jazz outfit Dr. Buzzard's Original "Savannah" Band and the producer of Machine's late disco anthem "There but for the Grace of God Go I." When Zilkha invited him to remix "Contort Yourself," he jumped at the opportunity on the basis that it would expand his "horizons as an individual" to "get involved with something like that."[6] Zilkha hovered in the studio as Darnell obsessed over the record's kick drum, slowed its tempo, and softened its texture while retaining its swagger and menace. "Although James White and the Blacks were meant to be a disco band," observes the label boss, "it wasn't until that remix that the vision was truly realized." Darnell's production of Don Armando's Second Avenue Rhumba Band's "Deputy of Love" became the first ZE Record to rock the Paradise Garage while his debut album with Kid Creole and the Coconuts, *Off the Coast of Me*, anchored the label's polyglot credentials in name as well as sound. "It's rock. It's calypso. It's latin. It's swing. It's new wave. It's dance music," noted *Dance Music* in its March 1980 review. "No one in pop music today is as experimental as August Darnell."[7] The melting-pot producer also brought his sensibility to Cristina's debut album. "It had a cinematic quality," notes Zilkha. "It was like Kid Creole without someone who could sing very well." When the ZE owner hosted a showcase event at Hurrah a few weeks later, Darnell's band stole the show.[8]

Zilkha maintains that the entire ZE operation came together when he signed "Wheel Me Out" by Was (Not Was), a Detroit outfit that featured two white Jewish kids (David Weiss and Don Fagenson) plus a selection of George Clinton musicians. A jazz critic for the *Herald Examiner* in L.A., Weiss had tipped him to listen to "Wheel Me Out" without mentioning his vested interest, after which Fagenson traveled to New York to present the record to the ZE boss. Zilkha concluded that its combination of danceability and nihilism amounted

Michael Zilkha, New York, 1979. Photograph by and courtesy of Kate Simon ©.

to "everything [he] had been trying to do but done better." Shortchanged on the distribution deal for "Deputy of Love" and lumbered with the debts left by Esteban, he issued "Wheel Me Out" with Chris Blackwell's subsidiary label Antilles in the United States and Celluloid/ZE in Europe, settling for fifty cents on the dollar for the money he was owed on "Deputy" in order to begin recording an album with the outfit.

Born into a Jamaican plantation-owning family, Blackwell founded Island Records in 1959, opened a U.K. office in 1963, and scored his first international hit with Millie's "My Boy Lollipop" in 1964. Three years later he signed Steve Winwood's band Traffic as part of a fairy-dust shift into the white rock market that saw him also sign Emerson, Lake and Palmer, King Crimson, Robert Palmer, and Roxy Music. Bob Marley followed in 1972. "He was trying to get a hit on American black radio and I said I thought he should basically be a black rock act," recalls the label head. Blackwell went on to sign Grace Jones after British rock journalist Nik Cohn recommended he check out this "unbelievable looking Jamaican girl." Then, as the decade drew to a close, Blackwell hired Mark Kamins to work as his finger-on-the-pulse A&R rep, and he extended his interest in the city's party network through his friendship with the "amazingly knowledgeable" Zilkha, whom he met at a Marley concert in 1976. The Island head went on to mix "Disco Clone" after failing to persuade Tom Moulton to take on the job. (The pioneering disco remixer refused on the basis that it was "making fun of disco.") Blackwell gave Zilkha the money to sign James White and the Blacks in return for distribution rights. Repeated regularly, the arrangement provided Zilkha with the money he needed to keep going. Meanwhile Blackwell made a particularly easy connection with *Off the Coast of Me*. "It was tropical," he observes.

Blackwell also took on the role of producing Grace Jones during 1980, concerned that her third album, *Muse*, sounded no more than "standard." He resolved she should head to Compass Point, the studio he founded in Nassau, Bahamas, in 1977, because its isolation from the powerhouse capitals of London and New York would offer her a sense of freedom. On arrival he took out a five-foot-by-five-foot blow-up photo of Jones posing with her arms crossed, hair cut GI-short, and eyes fixed cold, and he told the lineup to create a sound that matched the image. With the disco era on its knees, the group recorded covers of "Warm Leatherette" by punk band the Normal plus songs by Tom Petty, Smokey Robinson, the Pretenders, and Roxy Music, all of them picked out by Blackwell. Released as *Warm Leatherette*, the result brought together the bass and drums of reggae, the midrange energy of rock, and the textural principles of disco — as if Blackwell hoped to synthesize his label's output on a single record. "I wanted to get something more exciting, more edgy, because I thought Grace was edgy," recalls the owner.

Back in New York, composer and guitarist Glenn Branca, a regular customer at 99 Records, a record store located at 99 MacDougal Street, handed owner Ed Bahlman a finished tape, having complained to him regularly about the lack of independent labels in the United States. His effort became "Lesson No. 1 for Electric Guitar"/"Dissonance," the debut release of 99 Records. Then came the Bush Tetras, a band initiated by Pat Place, the ex-guitarist for the Contortions, who wrote the lyrics to "Too Many Creeps" after people started to annoy while she was working one night in the Bleecker Street Cinema. Formed in January 1980, the Bush Tetras played their first gig at TR3 (previously Tier 3, a cutting-edge live venue opened by East Villager Hilary Jaeger in TriBeCa) in early February. A second gig at Irving Plaza in March had the audience dancing to a sound characterized as "mean & clean spunk-funk" by an *East Village Eye* reviewer.[9] During filming for the lo-fi video of "Too Many Creeps," lead vocalist Cynthia Sley had no choice but to dance.

Along with "Contort Yourself," the Bush Tetras debut confirmed that if no wave wasn't over it had passed its 1978 peak, with pioneers moving away from atonality, antistructure, noise, nihilism, and demolition-rhythm to a set of punk sounds that integrated a disco-funk groove. The irreverent Frank Zappa had helped signal the way with the inclusion of the parodic disco track "Dancin' Fool" on his 1979 album *Sheik Yerbouti*, which, whatever its ironic intent, got people dancing. When Zappa guest DJ-ed on WPIX-FM in November, one of his first picks was Snuky Tate's "He's the Groove," a grainy, in-your-face disco-punk track that hailed Pope John Paul II as a new kind of pop star with the lyric, "He's the groove, he's the man/He's the pope in the Vatican." The station boss proceeded to ask Zappa not to play the record again and Tate later told Leonard Abrams he received a call from the FBI for his misdemeanor. Reporting on a Tate performance at the East Village Artists Benefit in the summer of 1980, the *East Village Eye* commented that his songs "make you want to dance, urgently." In what was presumably a reference to passing fads of new wave and no wave, Tate commented that his music was "permanent wave."[10] As for the Bush Tetras, there was simply too much "yes" in "Too Many Creeps" for it to be characterized as no wave, even if its creators had graduated from that scene.

The members of Talking Heads fueled the shift when they traveled to Compass Point to finalize their break with the taught, frigid sound of their early recordings. Joined by session musicians, the quartet started out with improvised riffs instead of songs, limited themselves to one chord per track, and introduced a multitude of antiphonal voices. The experience of seeing James Brown play live convinced lead singer and guitarist David Byrne that a change of direction was overdue. "With the new wave bands I'd seen in the last year I thought, 'This doesn't move my body at all — is there something wrong with me? Have I lost something?'" Byrne revealed in November 1980, shortly following the release of *Remain in Light*, as the Compass Point effort was titled. "And then I saw him [Brown] and thought, 'No, it's definitely not me. It's that there's nothing happening in the music.'"[11] Byrne argued that most innovation in popular music during the last ten years had taken place in disco and funk, only for his interviewer to inform him that some were disappointed that Talking Heads no longer sounded like Talking Heads. Giving it a mark of nine-and-a-half out of ten, *Dance Music* countered by describing *Remain in Light* as "one of the year's most important albums."[12]

New wave also combined with Bronx aesthetics after Fred Brathwaite took Debbie Harry and Chris Stein to sample the borough's party scene. "I like to describe our relationship as a cultural exchange," recounts the graffiti artist, who appreciated Anita Sarko's taste in funk and R&B yet regretted the way that the Mudd Club and other downtown spots were "under the spell" of U.K. bands. "They were introducing me to their scene—I met Andy Warhol through Debbie and Chris—and then I took them up to the Bronx. They came uptown and were interested. There were a few people who were open." Blending new wave, disco, funk, and rap, the Blondie duo penned "Rapture," a twelve-inch single that melded their downtown, midtown, and uptown journeys. "Fab 5 Freddy told me everybody's fly/DJs spinning I said my, my/ Flash is fast, Flash is cool/François sais pas, Flashe no deux," rapped Harry on the track, which first appeared on *Autoamerican*, released in November. In the video, Brathwaite and Lee Quiñones applied the finishing touches to a graffiti mural while Basquiat played at being DJ behind the turntables, Brathwaite having failed to persuade Flash to show up (because Flash didn't believe him when he said he was with Blondie).

The figure of the MC rapper—whose genealogy included the Sunday morning sermons of church preachers, the fighting stanzas of Muhammad Ali, the radio patter of Frankie Crocker, the spoken words of the Last Poets, the incantations of Jamaican party hosts, and the microphone banter of DJs Hollywood, Eddie Cheba, and Kool Herc—set the Bronx party scene apart from Manhattan, as Mark Riley discovered when he DJ-ed at Harlem World in the summer of 1979. "This guy had heard me do the 'Disco Party' on BLS—I played music on BLS between 1977 and 1979—and he hired me to play at his club," recalls Riley. "I got there and started playing and the guy came out and he said, 'When are you going to start talking?' I said, 'I don't talk over music, the music is supposed to speak for itself,' which is a direct quote from David Mancuso. He said, 'No, no, you don't understand, we expect our DJs to talk over the music.'" It was then that Riley grasped he had walked into a "parallel universe."

Released during the second half of 1979, the first wave of rap tracks filled a vacuum, for as Cheba told *Billboard* in May of that year, "most of the records" the companies were sending him wouldn't go down in the Bronx.[13] Yet Bronx MCs also delivered many of their lines over funkified disco riffs, which effectively made rap a form of mutant disco, and the disco connection was reinforced when the cofounder of All Platinum Records, Sylvia Robinson, employed the disco-funk outfit Positive Force to recreate the rhythm section of Chic's "Good Times" on "Rapper's Delight," the debut release on Sugar Hill Records. Having operated Enjoy Records out of his Harlem record store since 1962, Bobby Robinson kept the groove going with the release of Funky 4 + 1 More's "Rappin and Rocking the House" and Grandmaster Flash & the

Furious Five's "Superappin.'" Amid a mini-flurry of other rap releases, the Furious Five appeared as the Younger Generation on "We Rap More Mellow," issued on Brass Records, and Paul Winley of the Harlem-based doo-wop label Paul Winley Records released his daughters Paulette and Tanya Winley with the Harlem Underground Band rapping on "Rhymin' and Rappin.'" Then, as the year's end approached, Mercury became the first major to enter the field with Kurtis Blow's "Christmas Rappin.'"

Billboard dampened expectations when it reported in February 1980 that many already viewed rap as a "passing novelty that will soon go the way of all fads."[14] But Blow's follow-up, "The Breaks," which featured a self-aggrandizing rap delivered over a breezy, uptempo disco-funk rhythm track, went gold, while Grandmaster Flash & the Furious Five switched from Enjoy to Sugar Hill to release "Freedom," which featured the label's house band approximate one of Flash's mixes (Flash having begun to provide studio demonstrations of how the players could generate more interesting sonic combinations). A little behind Flash in studio terms, Afrika Bambaataa struck a deal with Winley to release "Zulu Nation Throwdown," a raw, percussive track that featured the Cosmic Force and the Soul Sonic Force. Disco DJs might have long since stolen a substantial lead when it came to landing remix commissions, but their Bronx counterparts were bypassing that route in favor of instant artistry.

Meanwhile independent labels distanced themselves from disco's commercially driven lurch into join-the-dots monotony by ramping up the funk and R&B elements of their output. Established by Marvin Schlachter back in 1976, Prelude Records led the charge with "Stretch In Out" by Gayle Adams, "Can You Handle It?" by Sharon Redd, "I Hear Music in the Streets" by Unlimited Touch, and "I Can't Dance without You" by Theo Vaness, all of them released during 1980. "I Hear Music" put the city's epochal shift from slick production to an earthier aesthetic into words. "I hear music in the street," sang the band, founded in 1980 by members of Brooklyn disco-funk outfit Crown Heights Affair. "Yes I hear the funky beat/And I get down/Ooh I get down." The record reinforced the impression that borough innovation extended well beyond the Bronx.

François Kevorkian made a key contribution thanks to his mixes of the Adams, Unlimited Touch, and Vaness songs. The Frenchman had traveled to New York at twenty-one in order to get closer to the psychedelic rock, soul, and jazz of Miles Davis, Herbie Hancock, and Jimi Hendrix, only to veer down Disco Avenue when he landed work playing drums alongside the groundbreaking DJ Walter Gibbons at Galaxy 21. Kevorkian went on to become the resident DJ at New York, New York, and it was during that period

Grandmaster Flash & the Furious Five, 1981. Photograph by and courtesy of Laura Levine ©.

that Schlachter handed him an A&R role, having clocked that his feedback was consistently insightful. A week later Kevorkian established himself as a hot new studio hand when he mixed Musique's "In the Bush." When the backlash struck a year later it barely touched Prelude because the label was "tied to R&B and black music as well as disco," argues Kevorkian, who augmented his label work with bootleg mixes such as "X Medley," a 1980 issue that mashed up eleven tracks. "When Larry put 'X Medley' on at the Garage the whole place just jumped up to the ceiling," recalls the mixer, who hand-delivered all his efforts to the DJ. "It was like madness."

Salsoul Records also adapted to the changing times, having succumbed to the dark side when it tripled its album output during 1978. "A lot of it was just inferior garbage that we never should have put out," confesses label boss Ken Cayre. Having established Salsoul as easily the most popular independent among New York's DJ-ing community during the mid-1970s, Cayre refocused on the core business of recording fresh-sounding tracks that would inspire the city's polyglot dance contingent when he invited Larry Levan to put the finishing touches to Gibbons's mix of Instant Funk's "I Got My Mind Made Up" (the ex-Galaxy 21 DJ having quit toward the end of the job when he turned against the song's flagrantly sexual lyrics). "I worked for weeks on

the record," remembers Bob Blank. "Walter started on the mix but then refused to carry on because he became very religious. I remember him saying
very specifically, 'I really don't think I'm going to be working on this record
anymore.'"[15]

Cayre consolidated Salsoul's standing through the figure of Levan, who
worked almost exclusively for the label during 1980 as he delivered particularly fierce mixes of First Choice's "Double Cross," Loleatta Holloway's "The
Greatest Performance of My Life," the Salsoul Orchestra's "How High," and
Sparkle's "Handsome Man" for *Larry Levan's Greatest Mixes Vol. Two* (which
in the absence of *Vol. One* became the first album to feature a remixer's name
in its title). Tearing through nightspots that were still receptive to ecstatic
dance music, Tom Moulton's mix of "Love Sensation" by Loleatta Holloway
confirmed that life did indeed exist after death. "We never really believed the
word 'disco' meant anything anyway," remarks Cayre. "In the beginning we
were R&B and dance, so we just moved a little more towards R&B in '79 and
'80 because we weren't getting the hits from our producers on the disco side.
In 1980 we got back on track."

Levan might have been expected to devote at least equal energy to West
End Records, having turned out incendiary reworkings of Taana Gardner and
Billy Nichols for the label during 1979. But his argument with Mel Cheren
over the whitening of Saturday nights at the Paradise Garage must have taken
its toll because the DJ only remixed "Is It All over My Face?" for the label during 1980, and even that was carried out on the sneak as Levan grabbed the
multitrack tapes from West End's office one lunchtime before heading across
the corridor to Opal Studios to cobble together a lightning effort.[16] "It was
literally done in an hour or two," recalls David DePino. "When Larry heard
them coming back he took what he had done and left. Mel got mad because
Larry took the tape without asking permission, but that was Larry."[17] The DJ
completed the job while hanging out with Kevorkian in the Garage booth one
afternoon. "All I did was follow Larry's directions," notes the Prelude mixer,
who introduced echo, reverb, and panning, yet declined Levan's offer of a
cocredit due to his contractual obligations to Schlachter. "It was really Larry's
gig but it was fun. We did it in like three or four hours, and a good edit can
take days."

Doubling as a parable of disco's shift into mutation, the record dated back
to the moment when Cheren handed a $10,000 budget to pioneering Brook-
lyn DJ Steve D'Acquisto and Iowan-raised cellist/composer/songwriter Arthur Russell to produce a song that would capture the incandescent energy

of the dancers who played percussion instruments and sang out loud as the Loft party ran its weekly course. "It was like a circus," engineer Bob Blank remembers of the all-night recording session that featured Philadelphian rhythm section the Ingram Brothers play alongside amateur percussionists and vocalists. "It was really important to let these people, who were regulars at the party, perform with the music because it was all felt."[18] Released under the artist name of Loose Joints, which referenced the prerolled marijuana joints that could be purchased at Washington Square Park while evoking the limberness of the dancers who gathered at the Loft, the result exemplified the "anything goes" philosophy of the post–disco sucks era, noted *Dance Music Report*, but "bombed," recalls Cheren.[19] Apparently sourced from a different studio take of the same song, Levan's remix featured a previously unused spacey keyboard solo played by Russell, a freakily asymmetrical incantation of the main verse sung by Loft dancer Melvina Woods, and a much sleazier sounding rhythm section. Angry with Levan, Cheren nevertheless accepted Levan's offering because he urgently needed to generate some low-cost sales, West End's bank account having started to "shrivel" in the tightening economic climate.[20] "There's no doubt that Loose Joints saved our collective ass in 1980," concedes the record label owner.[21]

As the remix's druggy, draggy groove pulsed through New York radios, boom boxes, and sound systems, D'Acquisto and Russell's premise that dance music needed to abandon its slick, streamlined incarnation in order to reconnect with the floor coincided with the inverse move of those punk and new wave musicians who resolved to engage with disco and funk. No other record sounded like "Is It All over My Face?"; even the original and the remix barely seemed to be connected to one another, never mind any other dance track. Yet both versions explored a similar language to the one that could be heard in the output of Island, 99 Records, Prelude, Salsoul, Sugar Hill, and above all ZE. "The early 1980s turned out to be some of the best years because the sound was like everything before but it became more real," argues Michael Gomes, the onetime author of *Mixmaster* and now a promoter at Prelude. "It was no longer the industry creating this mushy elevator music, which was generic and fabricated. It was quirky. The little labels really took off."

Early on, disco's pioneering DJs, producers, and remixers had advanced a utopian ideology as they integrated a panoply of sounds into a modular four-on-the-floor structure, encouraging a rainbow coalition of dancers to forge a pluralistic unity within its groove. Then came repetition, the bottom line, and a partial breakdown in the relationship between dancers and producers as executives sought to maximize profits by marketing the sound through radio rather than party DJs. But with the majors now beating a retreat, New York's independents locked back into a coarser, less predictable sound as they released records that combined disco, funk, punk, and dub. The results were edgy, complex, and newly democratic. Sonic codes were breaking down. New combinations were coming into play.

MAJOR-LABEL CALCULATIONS

There was an argument to be had about the small print of disco's failure, for while the total number of disco LPs that went gold fell by close to 50 percent during 1979, the genre more than doubled its share of a declining market, at least according to figures crunched by *Dance Music Report*. Admittedly the figures concealed the month-by-month data that might have revealed disco performing well during the first half of 1979 and poorly during the second. Yet it also remained the case that Chic's "Good Times" topped the Hot 100 in August, after which disco chalked up five chart-topping records (including "Don't Stop 'Til You Get Enough" by Michael Jackson, "Pop Muzik" by M, "Dim All the Lights" by Donna Summer, and Summer again on "No More Tears (Enough Is Enough)," which she released with Barbra Streisand) in the autumn.[1] "Disco didn't crash the music business," argues CBS promoter Kenneth Reynolds, who enjoyed an expense account that pitched in at a few thousand dollars less than his salary until he was sacked toward the middle of the year. "Companies were enjoying great sales from disco. However, they weren't monitoring the market and were spending far more on promotion than they should have been."

The fact that all but one of the major record companies axed their disco departments completely rather than tapering their response indicates that disco had become a scapegoat for a deeper crisis, with executives loath to analyze what could be salvaged from a culture they had always viewed with skepticism. Author of the "Disco File" column at *Record World*, Brian Chin watched many of his professional acquaintances lose their jobs in promotion during the second half of 1979. "I felt harassed and threatened by the coming of new wave and the ceaseless proclamation that disco had died that year," he recalled later. "I don't think there was a person involved in the business that had grown up around clubs and club music who didn't wonder secretly, or even publicly, whether it was all over."[2] Barry Lederer noted in his *Billboard*

"Disco Mix" column in January 1980 that "a recent New York party held for the disco persons displaced by the record companies bought home . . . the gravity of the situation."[3]

Only Warner Bros. held its ground. "The majors are closing their disco departments — they believe what they read in magazines," head of disco Ray Caviano told the *New York Post* in January 1980. "I've got a 16-man department and a regional staff, and my only competition is from independents."[4] Caviano maintains that senior executives at the company only concluded they needed to rein in their disco department after reading about declining sales in the *Wall Street Journal*. After that, any sign of a backlash "legitimized" the idea they had committed too much money to promoting the sound in the first place. "I didn't try to convince them they were wrong," he recalls. "Instead I went on a 12-day tour around the country to counterattack the backlash against disco. I tried to make the case that people were never going to stop dancing. Disco was just a semantic pigeonhole that put us in a box, so I pivoted to change the name to dance." Relentlessly self-assured, Caviano argued that he could make money selling 75,000 to 100,000 records if he had "a tight deal," adding that such figures were achievable because New York's black, Latin, and gay communities had driven disco in the past and would do so again. "I'm looking for hit records that are danceable," he added to the *Post*. "It's a fusion now, but people are still going out, people are still dancing."[5]

The dregs of the disco industry convened at the Century Plaza, Los Angeles, to attend the seventh *Billboard* Disco Forum in February 1980. Dating back to January 1976, the forums had morphed into a disco-business hybrid where marketspeak suffused panels on pleasure and labels sponsored lavish parties that ran through the night, yet the mood at the L.A. meeting was "much more sedate," reported *Dance Music*, the successor publication to *Disco News*.[6] With attendance figures down, Caviano asserted that while some were "waiting to shovel disco into its coffin," the scene was forging "a new kind of musical fusion between black music, white music, traditional disco, and danceable rock."[7] A pioneering disco columnist for *Record World* before he joined Caviano's team at Warner Bros., Vince Aletti argued that disco's "hybrid" quality would "keep it going."[8] But would fusion and hybridity deliver the kind of commercial success they needed to placate their boardroom providers?

The challenge facing Caviano came into focus during the February Grammy Awards. Former Doobie Brothers performer Michael McDonald gathered four prizes while Donna Summer, who had been expected to dominate the night, picked up just one for best female rock vocal performance. That same month Summer filed a suit against her label, Casablanca Records, the most commercially successful imprint of the disco era, seeking termination of her contract and damages of $10 million. Days later PolyGram, which had acquired a 50 percent stake in Casablanca in 1977, forced label head Neil Bogart to stand down. Having come to embody disco's voracious hedonism, Bogart struck a contemplative tone during his keynote to the National Association of Recording Merchandisers in April. "People keep asking me: Where did we go wrong?" he asked. "Perhaps it was all of us. Perhaps we've all been conspirators in a suicide pact."[9] "Funkytown" by Lipps, Inc. reached the top of the charts a month later only for Casablanca to close its East Coast office that same week. "We had so much product and half the stuff I listened to was horrible," recalls DJ Howard Merritt. "But Casablanca wasn't the cause of the downfall by any means. It was just a small label that became big."

The conference also provided independent labels with an opportunity to describe their response to the turbulent market, which led them to scale down operations while maintaining core activity. "We can't afford to send out the same amount of promotional 12-inch singles we've been sending because both promotional and commercial sales have diminished," Mel Cheren reasoned, just as the scale of his losses on the original Loose Joints release crystallized. Contributing to the same panel, Prelude president Dan Hoffman announced he would rein in the label's twelve-inch output because it ate into the "more profitable" LP market. A couple of weeks later, *Dance Music* denounced the "conservative release of new product" while noting the shortsightedness of the attempt to save money by switching formats. "With no [twelve-inch] records coming out, the few that are around are literally selling out in many areas and single sales seem to be picking up," the publication noted.[10]

The arguments continued through to the eighth *Billboard* Disco Forum, held at the Sheraton Center in New York in July 1980. Conceding that disco had become a "dirty word" and wasn't selling like before, Caviano maintained that discotheques could still generate sales of fifty thousand in New York, establishing the basis for bigger sales in radio, only for PolyGram's Bob Haywood to argue back that a record could sell fifty thousand in New York yet struggle to sell as many again in the rest of the country — and ultimately the majors regarded sales of a hundred thousand as a springboard rather than a goal.[11] The confab also resolved to lay the disco moniker to rest. "What's in a name?" asked *Billboard* editor Bill Wardlow when a delegate accused him of selling out to rock and new wave. "Call it new wave, rock-fusion, or R&B/pop, it all boils down to dance music, and that is just another five-letter word for disco."[12] The point was valid given that disco started out as a name for the range of sounds that could be heard in a discotheque, yet having shaped it to become a marketing device for an international sound, Wardlow was poorly positioned to champion its hybrid survival. Chin recalls that the term had been "ridden too hard" and "needed a rest." The eighth Disco Forum turned out to be the last of its kind.

New wavers preyed on disco's demise. Back in February, Sire's Seymour Stein claimed that "rock and roll is staging a major comeback under the guise of 'new wave' and 'new rock'" and that "disco appears to be on a sharp decline giving way to 'Dance Oriented Rock [DOR].'"[13] The April release of Giorgio Moroder's production of Blondie's "Call Me," along with the appearance of the Clash on the front page of *Dance Music* under the headline "DOR is finally coming of age," supported his claim.[14] Three months later Danny Heaps and Mark Josephson of the rock-oriented record pool Rockpool fronted the first New Music Seminar, timing their event to coincide with the first day of the July Disco Forum. Yet the idea that the disco shakeout was about to spawn a paradigm shift struck some as premature. "I thought there was a little too much fervor and excitement that rock dance had to replace what had gone on before," recalls Danny Krivit. "The industry felt the need for us to latch onto something. It was like, 'What's going to replace disco?' Names were popping up left, right, and center, but they didn't come close to replacing disco, and what they came up with was often disco masquerading as something else."

Caviano turned out to be more resilient than the *Billboard* Disco Forum. He had already demonstrated his ability to preempt the changing times as well as adapt to them when he promoted "Rock Lobster" by the B-52's, one of the surprise dance hits of 1978, and following the July confab he started to plug "Whip It" by new wave outfit Devo, working spots like Hurrah and Danceteria as he helped the group to its first Hot 100 hit. Interviewed by the music business information service *New on the Charts* in September, he crowed that his subsidiary label RFC was close to achieving sales of five hundred thousand for the album *The Glow of Love* by Change, a studio lineup featuring Luther Vandross. "The odds for a new operation to achieve a gold record so quickly is very encouraging to us and has, quite frankly, given us immense credibility in our quest for further signings," he proclaimed.[15] The promoter wondered out loud how disco could be pronounced dead when a chart hit like "Another One Bites the Dust" by Queen recycled the signature bass line of Chic's "Good Times." Produced by Bernard Edwards and Nile Rodgers of Chic, "Upside Down" by Diana Ross reached number one on the pop charts that same month.

Yet Caviano's RFC roster only included Change plus his 1979 signings Gino Soccio and Janice McClain, and there was good reason to ask if that justified

The B-52's at Hurrah, 1979. Photograph by and courtesy of Harvey Wang ©.

the cost of employing sixteen (going down to nine) members of staff.[16] Almost invariably rejecting the tapes that Aletti preselected for him each week, Caviano noted the need for quality. But senior executives could also question that because Soccio's 1980 releases didn't match his 1979 breakthrough, "Dancer," while McClain failed to come out with anything during the year. "Change was a huge record for us," notes Aletti. "It was our most successful signing. But it wasn't an act that had a built-in continuity factor. The people who sang on the record were not signed to the group — it was a studio thing — and when we tried to put them on the road we had to find other people to recreate what they did. It didn't quite work."

Caviano and Warners parted company with one another at the end of the year. "I tried to make the argument and it didn't prevail," he remembers. "Mo Ostin [the executive to whom Caviano was answerable] was the consummate gentleman but he reported to a higher authority at Warner Communication. I went into his office and he gave me a sizeable settlement to leave. I was resigned to the reality and I knew I could take my artists with me." Caviano resolved to set up as an independent promoter while Aletti decided to follow his charged-up chief out of the office door. "It was partly due to Ray's out-spoken personality and partly due to his reluctance to continue under the same contract," recounts Aletti of the endgame. "Warners called his bluff, Ray left, and I foolishly chose to follow. I could have stayed, but Ray and I thought alike and heard records in the same way, and I didn't think I'd find this in another boss."

The first major label to back disco had withdrawn from the dance market, condemning it to return to the margins of U.S. culture. But it was there that DJs and dancers had shaped their synesthetic revolution in the first place, and with the city's independent labels leaner and sharper for having survived the crash, the white flag of Warners would hardly register. From the point of view of the floor, the party scene was set to burst through the roof.

THE SAINT PETER
OF DISCOS

Surveying the city in his 1980 travelogue *States of Desire*, Edmund White argued that New York's gay male residents were "justifiably proud of their status as taste-makers for the rest of the country" and added that "our clothes and haircuts and records and dance steps and decor — our restlessly evolving style — soon enough become theirs."[1] The author didn't question the genesis that traced the birth of disco back to the summer of 1970, when the Ice Palace and the Sandpiper opened on Fire Island, the favored holiday destination for many white gay men, rather than the beginning of that year, when multicultural crowds gathered at the Loft and the Sanctuary. Instead, he explained how members of Flamingo, the most exclusive white gay private party, were expected to be on an upward career trajectory as well as "produce good conversation, good food, good sex, attract the right friends, dance all night, jog three miles, press 200 pounds and have an opinion about Caballeé pianissimo."[2] At least they weren't supposed to do all of these things at the same time.

Flamingo dancers believed that while the spread of disco confirmed their position as leading tastemakers, the subsequent backlash revealed that the mainstream was incapable of properly embracing gay male innovation. How, for instance, could anyone ever imagine that the suits worn in *Saturday Night Fever* were appropriate for the dance floor? As for the popularity of the Village People, the group had long since ceased to be credible on the gay scene. "The backlash against disco went a little too far with the record burning in Chicago," argues Howard Merritt. "But it just pushed the culture back underground, where the gay boys had it to begin with, and all of a sudden we didn't have to deal with a ton of disco garbage." Nicknamed "Bongo Richie" because of his penchant for percussive records, Richie Rivera played alternate weekends with Merritt. "His music was dark and serious, mine was light and happy, and the two of us just gelled together very well," adds Merritt, who acquired the nickname "Donna Merritt" after he started to use his promoter position at Casablanca to introduce every Donna Summer single to the scene. "Having a choice kept the members happy."

When Flamingo closed for the summer of 1980, most of its dancers headed to the Pines, an upmarket hamlet on Fire Island, where a new venue called the Pavilion had opened on the site of the old Sandpiper, which had run down its ten-year lease. "There was some nostalgia for the single-story beach feel of the Sandpiper," recalls Marsha Stern, who designed and installed a fresh lighting system with Mark Ackerman. "The Pavilion was a two-story structure with white walls and when it was open as a disco the only visible windows were these little portals behind the bar. It was very sleek and sterile, more New York City than beach." Rivera along with 12 West DJ Alan Dodd DJ-ed at the opening night, after which the venue employed a revolving roster, including Merritt. "It felt like it was history in the making," recalls Sharon White, the principal DJ at the pioneering all-women's discotheque Sahara until the venue's four lesbian owners were forced to close at the end of 1979. "All of the up-and-coming DJs would be playing because this was their breakout spot. If you had a good season on Fire Island you would have a job in the fall in New York."

Used to gathering in a more democratic setting, the 12 West faithful made their way to the inexpensive resort of Cherry Grove, where Roy Thode DJ-ed at the Ice Palace while his dog, Mocha, slept by his feet. "Cherry Grove was more daytrippers whereas the Pines attracted people who had houses," notes White, who had become tight friends with Thode at a Long Island discotheque called the Corral, where Thode made his DJ-ing debut. "There was a bit of a snob factor with the Pines boys, who were much more into their look and the body-building thing. It was a different lifestyle." Even so, Pines partygoers journeyed to the Ice Palace every Saturday night to dance to Thode. "The Pines was a ghost town on Saturdays because everyone went to Cherry Grove to dance," confirms Robbie Leslie, a weekday DJ at the Sandpiper. "I never worked on Saturday nights because the Pines was so dead." The two tribes also converged at Turntables Towers — the house Thode shared with Merritt — after the Island's venues closed for the night. "Roy and I would play music until nine or ten in the morning," reminisces Merritt. "It'd be packed."

That summer attention also turned to the planned autumnal opening of an innovative new venue on the Lower East Side. "Word started to spread that there was going to be a new place that was going to blow everything else out of the water," remembers Leslie, who had started to DJ at 12 West the previous autumn. "There was a great sense of anticipation but nobody had any hard

Robbie Leslie at the Sandpiper on Fire Island, 1977. Photographer unknown; courtesy of Robbie Leslie.

facts." Flamingo owner Michael Fesco called Merritt to advise that he didn't know what would happen to his venue when the new spot opened. "Whatever chances you can get, I'd take them," he advised. Left devastated, Merritt had just interrupted his holiday to guest at Dreamland in San Francisco, and when he returned to New York at the end of the season the owner of the West Coast venue offered him a residency, which he accepted. The culture that had died a public death was about to go through yet another rebirth.

The owner of the soon-to-open location, Bruce Mailman had already de-signed, built, and staged experimental plays at the Astor Place Theater (on Astor Place) and the Truck and Warehouse Theater (on East 4th Street). Com-pact in build and with thinning hair, he had also reopened the Everard Baths (located on St. Mark's Place) as the St. Mark's Baths, turning it into an elec-trifying hangout for bleary-eyed dancers who wanted to gossip, have sex, and continue the party after Flamingo and 12 West wound down on a Sunday morning. Deeply drawn to the "physical, hard-driving, sexual kind of evening" on offer at Flamingo as well as the "imagination and theatricality" of Studio 54, as he told *New York Native* in a later interview, Mailman decided he would combine the two in his next venture. Wrestling with the challenge of how to win over Fesco's crowd as he went to sleep one night, he dreamed of opening a venue with a planetarium. "It wasn't limited to a stage, and it was completely round, and it had a sky; so you had the virtues of dancing outside, and just the whole level of theatricality, I thought, was phenomenal," he added to the newspaper. "Immediately, when I woke up in the morning, I started calling planetarium companies, seeing if it could be done, if it could be built, or if it was affordable. Then I needed a place that was big enough to accommodate the dome."[3]

An East Village resident since the early 1960s, Mailman settled on a boarded-up building on 105 Second Avenue and 6th Street, just a couple of streets down from the St. Mark's Baths, which inspired him to name his new spot the Saint. Once the home of the Loews Commodore Theater and then the legendary rock venue the Fillmore East, the building had drifted into a state of disrepair since the early 1970s and ended up being "used as a toilet," a local noted of the city's decision to seal the spot in 1977.[4] Working with a budget that eventually skyrocketed to $3–6 million, head of design Charles Terrel and head of construction Steve Casko ripped the seats out of the original theater, leveled the floor, and removed the front half of the balcony, installing an oak-covered floor mounted on a floating, circular steel platform.[5] Below, they built a steel and concrete lounge, converting the stage into a refreshment bar and the dressing rooms into banks of private lockers. Above, they created a steel-ceilinged dome that held the planetarium, with the rest of the balcony turned into a dimly lit third level. "If the Saint . . . were a conventional disco, it would not be an overstatement to call it 'the Saint Peter's of discos,'" reported *Lighting Design*. "In fact, what has been created in the city's third largest theater on the lower East Side is appropriately a new dimension in theater — an incredible synthesis of light, sound, and performer (the dance) that has no counterpart on this earth."[6]

Spitz Space Systems fitted the dome after a rival company rejected the job on the grounds it would be put to improper use. Director of lighting Mark Ackerman oversaw the fitting of 1,500 fixtures plus two mushroom-shaped star projectors mounted on hydraulic towers that could be raised to expand the dance floor by 25 percent. "I was knocked out by what I saw," Ackerman recalled of the moment he first viewed the site. "I knew immediately and without a doubt that this project was something very unique and very challenging."[7] Peter Spar of Audio Tech Systems installed the sound system, having completed commissions at the Sandpiper, 12 West, and San Francisco's Trocadero Transfer. Instructed to hide the speakers from view, he placed the equipment inside the dome, under the rise, and other irregular positions. "The object was to make the sound system disappear both physically and sonically so that the dancer would be left with only the music and time and space," *Sound & Video Contractor* reported later. "At the geometric center of the dome where the starfield projector sits, the SPL [sound pressure level] at full power measures more than 145dB. Exactly how much more cannot be determined because the SPL meter scale would not read accurately beyond that point."[8]

Featuring a cyborglike depiction of St. Sebastian with lasers shooting out of his fingertips and eyes, so blending the iconography of suffering, righteousness, and pleasure with male beauty, the artwork for the opening party signaled how the venue's name did more than establish a connection to the St. Mark's Baths. Just as Sebastian was martyred for his Christian beliefs, so the gay male dancer who refused to forsake his homosexuality could experience a form of dance-floor redemption, where the ritual of sacrificing one's body to the rhythm carried the prospect of transcendence. The Coliseum-like proportions of the interior made the narrative seem plausible. With its circular floor, perimeter seating, surrounding balcony area, and celestial ceiling, the venue evoked a scene of epic struggle while Sebastian's seminaked body would have reminded the Fire Island crowd of its penchant for dancing shirtless. "Since the beginning of recorded history the male members of the species have joined together in ritual dance," ran the publicity. "Adorned, semi-naked with rhythm instruments, they used this tribal rite to celebrate their gods and themselves. The Saint has been created to perform the mystery — to continue the rite."

Mailman also circulated a punctilious charter establishing the Saint as a private party governed according to numerous by-laws. In addition to prohibiting members from attending with female guests, the charter set the membership fee at $125, with members required to pay $10 to get in to each party and their guests $18 each, while Sunday Tea, scheduled to run from 6:00 PM to 3:00 AM, would cost $6 and $9, respectively. With a buffet, sodas, and breakfast thrown in, the fee was comparable to the one set at the Paradise Garage, where Michael Brody charged members $100 for a weekend membership card and $75 for a Friday-only pass, with members charged $10 per party and their guests $15 each.[9] Yet Mailman ensured that his membership would be predominantly if not overwhelmingly white and middle-class by focusing his recruitment drive around an inner circle of dancers who holidayed at the Pines. In sharp contrast to Michael Brody's attempt to woo that crowd, word-of-mouth recommendations spread so quickly the owner closed his two-thousand-strong membership list before opening night. If most members brought a guest, Mailman calculated, the turnout would shoot above the venue's legal capacity of 2,800.[10]

The Saint, date unknown. Photographer unknown; courtesy of the Saint at Large.

Held on 20 September, the first night drew in celebrity partygoers Calvin Klein, Paul Jabara, and Egon Von Furstenberg while eyewitnesses recalled Second Avenue coming to a stretch-limo standstill as the queue looped up to the Kiev Restaurant on Second Avenue and Seventh Street, past St. George's Ukrainian Catholic Church on Seventh Street, back down Third Avenue, and eastward into Sixth Street.[11] The challenging situation intensified when a fire lieutenant attempted to shut the venue down on the grounds that the foam-cube seats in the downstairs area were a fire hazard; Casko reckoned he was a homophobe and Mailman felt that he was acting for a competitor.[12] A deputy resolved the stand-off by proposing to move the seats to an alleyway. Meanwhile, Alan Dodd — on a roll following a popular run at the Pavilion — opened his set with the sound of a heartbeat. "The place is striking," noted Andrew Holleran, author of the gay disco novel *Dancer from the Dance*, in a review of the night. "It has that dramatic, black, vaulted, vertical grandeur one sees in those drawings by Piranesi of 18th-century Roman prisons, but very finished, and nothing could be more 21st-century than the Saint."[13]

The party peaked when Dodd introduced the first strains of Donna Summer's "Could It Be Magic," cueing Ackerman to cut from bright light to an artificial dawn. "All of a sudden, we were out in the stars," recalls bookstore worker and until that night 12 West regular Michael Fierman. "For miles around, there were nothing but stars. Everyone gasped. For the twenty seconds of the piano chords, before the drum kicked in, everyone was frozen and in awe."[14] Ackerman adjusted the star machine in sync with the introduction of the drum. "As the song took off, the galaxies began to rotate," Holleran recounted. "There was nothing to do but scream, throw up your hands, and keep screaming. The floor looked like a bacterial culture, the spores the space travelers discover in *Alien*."[15] A little later Ackerman turned off the star machine as the venue's gigantic mirror ball descended from the dome amid ruby red lighting. "The whole place was a departure," adds Fierman. "You really weren't there with your group of friends. We were all connected."[16] When asked "Will you go back?" another dancer replied, "I'll go back every Saturday night until I die."[17]

SELECTED DISCOGRAPHY

ALAN DODD, OPENING NIGHT AT THE SAINT (20 SEPTEMBER 1980)

Ashford & Simpson, "Found a Cure"
Average White Band, "Let's Go Round Again"

Watson Beasley, "Breakaway"

Julie Budd, "All Night Man"

Buffalo Smoke, "Stubborn Kinda Fella"

Cerrone, "Love Is the Answer"

Change, "A Lover's Holiday"

Linda Clifford, "If My Friends Could See Me Now"

Cut Glass, "Without Your Love"

Pierre Dalmon, "Take the Rainbow"

Sarah Dash, "Sinner Man"

Foxy, "Party Boys"

Dan Hartman, "Instant Replay (Replayed)"

Loleatta Holloway, "Love Sensation"

Geraldine Hunt, "No Way"

The Jackson 5, "Forever Came Today"

The Jacksons, "Can You Feel It?"

France Joli, "The Heart to Break the Heart"

Suzi Lane, "Harmony"

Macho, "Roll"

Mark Theodore Orchestra, "Cosmic Wind"

Midnight Powers, "Dance, It's My Life"

Mighty Clouds of Joy, "Mighty High"

Jackie Moore, "Helpless"

Giorgio Moroder, "In My Wildest Dreams"

Giorgio Moroder, "What a Night"

Passengers, "Get Ready"

Passengers, "I'll Be Standing beside You"

Queen Samantha, "Take a Chance"

Quick, "Young Men Drive Fast"

Jimmy Ruffin, "Hold on to My Love"

Salsoul Orchestra, "Magic Bird of Fire"

Jean Shy, "Night Dancer"

Joe Simon, "I Need You, You Need Me"

Candi Staton, "Run to Me"

Martin Stevens, "Love Is in the Air"

Barbra Streisand, "The Main Event (A Glove Story)"

Donna Summer, "Could It Be Magic"

The Supremes, "Let Yourself Go"

Richard Tee, "First Love"

Harry Thumann, "Underwater"

Two Tons o' Fun, "Earth Can Be Just Like Heaven"
John Williams, "The Conversation"
Viola Wills, "If You Could Read My Mind"
Viola Wills, "Up on the Roof"

In the end the Saint wasn't just larger, more futuristic, and more comfortable than Flamingo and 12 West. It was also newer, and that counted for a great deal in the restless terrain of gay male nightlife. "There was no way we could think about staying put," remembers Flamingo diehard Jorge La Torre. "I didn't have a conversation with Michael [Fesco] about this and it was a bit touchy for a while. I had been extremely loyal to Flamingo, but the minute I laid my eyes on the physical aspect of the Saint I was completely enamored with the place. I realized immediately it would accommodate the needs of the gay community." Flamingo appeared to be both spatially and experientially small in comparison. "It was home for us for so many years and you just don't uproot yourself from a place that's been good to you for so many years to go somewhere else," adds La Torre. "But we felt the Saint was created for us to fulfill a specific need in a way that no other club had been before. The pull was so strong and the possibilities were so great we had to move on, in spite of loyalties. There was a mass exodus, basically."

Cherry Grovers and 12 West regulars mightn't have been drawn into the Saint's logic of perfection. "The well-heeled rubbed shoulders with waiters, clerks, and hairdressers," Leslie says of 12 West. "This democratic mix really made the club what it was: not the décor or the location." Yet the Second Avenue venue lassoed a significant proportion of that crowd as well. "It could easily have been a white elephant," Leslie adds of the Saint. "Sometimes the most elegant, sophisticated, and beautiful clubs fail because they're too prissy or highbrow and there's something that doesn't resonate with the gay community. The Saint was so tremendous and high-tech and amazing, but just seeing it before it opened didn't mean you could judge how it would work out because it was really unprecedented in the club world. It was either going to be a huge smash or a huge flop." In the end the opening was so successful 12 West axed Leslie, the less experienced of its two DJs. "Because it was so exciting to be able to go to the Saint on the weekend, I didn't have a feeling of loss," he recalls.

With the venue hitting its stride instantaneously, an average Saturday drew in two thousand to three thousand dancers while some three thousand to five thousand showed up for special theme parties, including the opening party in September, Halloween in October, "Night People" in November, New Year's Eve, the "White Party" in February, the "Black Party" in March, the "Land of Make Believe" party in April and the closing party in June.[18] "The club attracted the clichéd A-list professionals but it also attracted gay men who were in the know — a kind of gay intelligentsia," remarks Leslie. "They could be artists or even waiters and bartenders, and they had an intelligent savviness about them. They knew where to go — the places that were the most fun — and they became part of the core group of the Saint." Mailman later ruminated on the emergence of a pack mentality. "People wanted to be part of this group that all worked out together," he commented. "They all looked great and they all had a kind of bond — they all went dancing every Saturday night."[19]

The membership still took a while to gel, however, in part because the Saint drew such a high proportion of its dancers from the rivalrous Flamingo and 12 West, with the former subset famed for turning the act of looking down on their counterparts into an art form, and 12 West dancers unimpressed by the lightly concealed arrogance of Fesco's regulars. "The crowds did not mix," recalls Fierman. "It's not that they hated each other. But it was like two different country clubs being thrown into one room. . . . Everyone had their section of the dance floor they danced in."[20] Flamingo regular Stuart Lee could barely bring himself to head to Second Avenue. "You didn't dance inside a family but more within a little territory that included people you sort of knew and other families you didn't know, and didn't care to know," he notes. Yet the Saint also brought together an "interesting mix" of dancers, maintains Leslie, while La Torre argues the venue retained the upscale sensibility of Flamingo because "it was the most exclusive club in Manhattan in terms of its design." Sharon White, one of a handful of female cardholders, chipped away at the venue's charter from within. "I got as many memberships as I could possibly get for people who I felt might have otherwise been overlooked because they were a person of color or a woman," she explains.

Neighborhood reaction to the venue was divided. Interviewed for the *SoHo News*, several locals criticized the men-only door policy, with one describing the venue as a "magnificent closet for gays."[21] "The Saint reflects the attitude of a group trapped in the mindless disco of the '70s," added a dancer who returned his membership card during the course of the opening-night party. "The emptiness of human contact in this structure is not comfortable to the eye, the mind or the heart."[22] Father Lawrence of St. George's Ukrainian Catholic Church complained the Saint would "ruin the neighborhood" because its members "don't only do the things they do inside — they bring it right out on the streets."[23] Others, however, embraced the venue's gentrifying potential. "Anytime anybody wants to put in a couple of million dollars, he's welcome," commented Second Avenue Deli owner Abe Lebewohl. "I don't care what he opens up." Another East Village entrepreneur remarked: "They're good customers, good clients, neat people. They seem to have lots of money."[24] The *Daily News* added that, even if the atmosphere inside the spot was feverish, "standards are never less than middle-class." It concluded: "The neighborhood is so relieved."[25]

Mailman showed little interest in nurturing neighborhood relations or cultivating the idea that his venue was embedded in its East Village milieu. As the venue's multistage entrance prompted one dancer to ask, "Are we going dancing or going through customs? I feel like I'm crossing the Swiss border."[26] Yet the Saint was never intended to function as anything other than an entirely distinctive entity that had little to do with the rough and tumble of the neighborhood. "Once you went behind those steel doors you were in nevernever land," explains Leslie. "It could be daylight, there could be riots in the streets, and you'd be listening to Cerrone, ABBA, and Claudja Barry. No effort was spared to keep you in this musical bubble. The Saint was a scene unto itself and the disconnection didn't feel in the least bit strange."

LIGHTING
THE FUSE

Located on the penthouse floor of an office building on 16th Street and Irving Place, Melons attracted a predominantly black and Latin working-class crowd that was never going to sashay into Leviticus, the West 33rd Street venue that targeted the city's "black 'creme de la creme,'" or other spots that aimed for a similar demographic, including Bentley's, the Copa, Down Under, Pegasus, and Silver Shadow.[1] DJ Derrick Davidson helped pull in a regular crowd of fifteen hundred to two thousand. "It was packed," recalls Boyd Jarvis, who decorated, helped with security, and sold black beauties on the side. "It was as big as the Garage and there were more spaces to go because it was the whole floor." But early into 1980 relations between promoter Mike Stone, the onetime cohost of the Soho Place with sound engineer Richard Long, and the Mafia men who controlled the spot turned nasty, prompting the African American promoter to try his hand some forty streets uptown. "Richard said, 'Bring the underground to Studio 54!'" remembers Stone.

The idea wasn't obvious, for although Steve Rubell had once likened the role of Studio 54 doorman Marc Beneke to "tossing a salad," or creating a mix of different social groupings and characters inside the club, the nightly rejection of hundreds of partygoers damaged the venue's democratic credentials, with dancers of color rarely bothering to even join the queue. Charged by Steve Rubell and Ian Schrager to manage the venue according to instructions issued from jail, Michael Overington nevertheless agreed to rent out the venue to Stone for a Friday-night "We Are Family" party in April, aware the promoter's experience in attracting a large crowd to a nonalcohol party made him a handy person to keep the spot ticking over now that it had lost its liquor license. Stone reframed Studio as a downtown party, offering acid-laced juice, a spread of fruit, and a live performance for a $10–12 entry charge, and when his night kicked off he took on Saturdays as well. "I was the first black promoter to come into that kind of setting and I put on a show every week," he claims. "I turned Studio 54 into the Apollo."

Studio 54 began to attract a very different crowd — a development that went unreported by a media that had salivated at the celebrity comings and goings of the Rubell and Schrager era. "The parties had a mix of black and Puerto Rican people, and I'd estimate that about 10–15 percent of the crowd was gay," recalls Kenny Carpenter, who became the resident DJ after Stone concluded that Nicky Siano was using too much heroin and Tee Scott wasn't going to give up his position at Better Days. "The crowd came from all five boroughs and some were even from out of town." Jarvis had reservations about the balcony seating, which made him feel self-conscious when he danced, but recalls that "the energy was excellent and people came out in droves for Mike." Unhappy about the challenge to Melons, the mob sent henchmen to run the crowd out with smoke bombs, yet Stone held firm, convinced he was "the black Steve Rubell," he says. Meanwhile Charles Andre Glenn — known as Afrika Islam to his Zulu Nation friends — became part of the promoter's entourage, having become interested in marketing after he enrolled at the Fashion Institute of Technology that autumn. "I was his PR agent," notes Islam. "In return I got a ten-person guest list, so I would invite people down from school. Meanwhile, I was DJ-ing uptown. But Mike never knew about that because it was in the hip hop scene."

In a further sign that midtown disco culture was lurching toward democracy, Studio 54 rival Xenon gave up chasing celebrities, models, and the moneyed when resident DJ Tony Smith advised owner Howard Stein to abandon the bankrupt ethos of the velvet rope. "When Xenon opened they made the minorities wait outside," remembers Smith. "I said, 'The minorities make the party, Howard!'" Stein also beat a retreat from exclusivity. "Once it got integrated Xenon had its own identity, which meant I could do what I wanted," adds Smith. "I could play these imports that radio wasn't even playing and my crowd was screaming to it." John "Jellybean" Benitez, Smith's alternate, remembers crowds of two thousand showing up on a Monday night, which made him think, "How is disco dead?"

Other midtown spots found it harder to adjust to the promise of the new decade. Co-owned by cousins John Addison and Maurice Brahms, New York, New York was deemed by *New York Magazine* to be suitable only for "those who can't or won't cope with a heavy disco scene."[2] Also owned by Brahms, the Underground attracted celebrities, luminaries, and local fashionistas yet failed to attract the cutting-edge gay crowd targeted by its owner. Owned by

Addison and Brahms, Bond's International Casino seemed to be trapped in time when it unveiled a marble staircase and programmable fountain at its July launch.[3] And although Steven Greenberg opened the Roxy with the cry that Rubell and Schrager's "snob-appeal" version of disco was in decline, he clung to the faux-elitist model.[4] "He wanted the Roxy to be the "Studio 54 of roller skating," comments Danny Krivit, who began to work at the West 18th Street venue in January 1980, just as it opened, having lost his job at Trude Heller's. "The general hardcore rollerskating crowd was quite ethnic but he wanted it to be a white club, so he put a red rope outside and kept a lot of them out."

The transformation of Studio 54, and to a lesser extent Xenon, nevertheless showed how even midtown was loosening up as the denizens of high disco either abandoned the culture or explored other, more integrated ways of partying. The poor, the foreign, the marginalized, and the adventurous had migrated to New York since the mid-nineteenth century in order to seek out opportunity and reinvention, and now that the major money had drained out of disco, the city was ready for another spin. "Do you think there is something unique about New York that people can come here from all over the world and get involved and start doing things here?" the *East Village Eye* asked Rudolf Piper in its Thanksgiving issue. The promoter replied that cities change over time and that the moment had arrived for New York to seize center stage. "It also depends on us New Yorkers," he added. "I consider myself a New Yorker now. It depends on us to make this an inhabitable place."[5] Creativity, hedonism, humor, and partying — not cleaner streets and more luxurious apartments — lay at the heart of his agenda.

Displaying a commitment to community, creativity, and pleasure that knew no obvious precedent in the city, a sprawling coalition of artists, beatniks, bohemians, dancers, feminists, hedonists, libertarians, musicians, queer activists, socialists, and socializers contributed to a migratory pattern that comprised hundreds if not thousands of journeys leading to New York. Brought up in a Marine Corps family in Pittsburgh, Keith Haring knew he had to move to the city from a young age because, as he told John Gruen, that was "the only place where I was going to find the intensity that I needed and wanted. I wanted intensity for my art and I wanted intensity for my life." Traveling from Milwaukee, James Chance wanted to play jazz and where else was there to go? "At one point the *Voice* ran an article about the end of New York," recalls the musician. "I thought, 'I'd better get there before that happens.'" As they and others set up camp, often on the Lower East Side, Michael Brody, Jim Fouratt and Rudolf Piper, Ann Magnuson, David Mancuso, and Steve Mass won the argument that the most entertaining party spaces in the city were those that attracted the dispossessed. "I wanted to be clear that we wanted the relatively unknown artists — the people who would be important in the future, not the establishment," posits Mass.

It was, in short, a time of elastic self-fashioning as well as one in which the self was usually conceived within some form of improvised collectivity; a time when everyone, seemingly, could re-make themselves as an artist, a musician, a film director, a video artist, a performance artist; a time when showing up at a club could lead to a chance encounter that could lead to an improbable idea that could lead to a dynamic venture; a time when staging a party became one of the highest forms of expression, because these inventive, fluid, transient occasions did indeed evoke some kind of pinnacle of existence; and a time when DJ-led dancing inadvertently increased the capacity for people to interact and collaborate. Seduced by the "vigour of the local art-scene" as well as the way New York artists were much more willing than their U.K. counterparts to "incorporate whatever they can into their own work," Brian Eno became so enamored with the party scene he extended his planned three-week stay to seven months.[6] "You could look at all this activity as being an indulgence," argues Magnuson. "Or you could look at it as a group of people who decided they didn't want to live a nine-to-five existence and fit into the particular roles that were expected of us."

Power resided in the ability to re-make one's immediate world via the party network. James Nares joined the Contortions. Anya Phillips appeared in the underground films *The Foreigner* (Poe), *Kidnapped* (Mitchell), and *Rome '78* (Nares). Sylvère Lotringer provided commentary to Kathryn Bigelow's fight documentary *Set-Up*. Even David Wojnarowicz — awkward, lonesome, lacking in confidence — made an audacious move into the art-band scene by teaming up with Danceteria coworkers Max Blagg, Brian Butterick, and Jesse Hultberg to form 3 Teens Kill 4 — No Motive (a name Blagg pilfered from a *New York Post* headline). Illustrating the precarious nature of such ventures, the subsequent closure of the 37th Street venue knocked back the band's planned debut and left Wojnarowicz feeling desperate. Yet the experience of forging friendships with other artists at Fouratt and Piper's spot provided him with focus and confidence, argues biographer Cynthia Carr, and, although he never discovered the same level of satisfaction when he followed the promoters to the Peppermint Lounge, the work still helped him make ends meet.[7] When 3 Teens Kill 4 made their debut in early December at the Danceteria Christmas party held at TR3, Wojnarowicz, untrained, contributed tape recordings as well as improvised percussion, vocals, and lyrics taken from his poems. It had simply become normal to try something one had no experience in and to do so with conviction and integrity while finding a way to make ends meet.

As it became commonplace for party spaces to offer not only DJ-ing or live music but often the two together plus art exhibitions, performance art, video, and film, so it became more likely for practices to bleed into one another. A TV show and a party wrapped into one, *TV Party* typified the way discrete elements combined in ways that were carefree, collective, and nontraditional in terms of political expression. "THE PARTY is the highest expression of social activity — the co-operative production of FUN," Glenn O'Brien argued in March. "THE PARTY is the first step in organizing society for mutual interests. TV PARTY believes that SOCIAL affinity groups will provide the foundation for any effective political action."[8] O'Brien mightn't have been joking when he claimed that the spread of cable television offered citizens an alternative way of governing themselves, and he even spoke of organizing a *TV Party* slate during the next mayoral election — with the policy of turning New York into a free port that would generate enough revenue to offer tax-free services. "I guess it was punk TV," O'Brien wrote later. "We were anti-technique, anti-format, anti-establishment, and anti-anti-establishment. We liked to break all the rules of good broadcasting."[9] As Bernard Gendron notes of the Mudd Club and the wider downtown scene, "borderline aesthetics" were "running rampant."[10]

Already widespread during the first half of the 1970s and reinvigorated when the big money drained out of disco, the democratic modus operandi of its party spaces contributed to the city's integration and sense of well-being by encouraging people from different backgrounds to meet and get along in an informal setting. "You could develop surprisingly deep friendships with people who you only saw in these environments," notes music writer Carol Cooper. "It would never occur to you to invite these people to come and have dinner with you at your home or go bowling with them because that wasn't the nature of the relationship. But this alternative reality had real substance for the people who experienced it." Evoking the organic interaction described by urban writer Jane Jacobs in *The Death and Life of Great American Cities* as well as the interclass contact extolled by Samuel Delany in *Times Square Red, Times Square Blue*, revelers would head out not in pre-established friendship groups that would stick together but as part of a spontaneously formed colony of like-minded people who, with answering machines yet to come into popular use, gathered in order to socialize, experience culture, and exchange information. "Warhol was interested in encountering these people who came from distant suburbs," recalls Mass. "He was so pleased when someone threw up on his shoes. In other words, he was intrigued to meet this person who had no idea who he was."

Even if it was inevitably incomplete and flawed, the shift toward democracy and integration was hardly coincidental inasmuch as Mancuso was a self-identifying child of the Rainbow Coalition; Brody and Stone were profoundly influenced by the Loft; Mass drew on Situationism, punk, the downtown art scene, civil rights, and third-wave feminism; Magnuson was imbued with the ethos of the countercultural movement and iconoclastic theater; Fouratt was a cofounder of the Yippies and the Gay Liberation Front; and Piper cultivated a philosophy of decadent freedom that rejected outmoded institutions and practices. "My theory was to have a place where people just came to party and it transcended all levels of difference," Tee Scott noted of the credo he attempted to instill into Better Days. "No matter what your preference or life-style was, when you came in those doors it was to dance and you forgot about all the barriers."[11]

Admittedly partygoers didn't necessarily think of themselves as partici-pants in a citywide network or coalition. Private parties such as the Loft and the Paradise Garage were so determinedly subterranean that large swaths of the art-punk scene didn't even know they existed. Meanwhile revelers were mistrustful of movements in general, having witnessed how counterculture, disco, and punk had ended in disappointment. Yet the desire to party proved to be infectious during 1980, as demonstrated by the expansion of the art-punk-discotheque scene, the take-off of the Paradise Garage, and the open-ing of the Saint, and although everyone often had favorite hangouts, for the most part the city resembled a huge nocturnal adventure park. "Johnny and I liked to go hopping around as if we were these urban anthropologists," remi-nisces Chi Chi Valenti. "We would go to some mad club that was in Bay Ridge where strippers danced for women, or this wonderful underground drag club that was on Third Avenue right above St. Mark's called Frida's Disco where these black and Latin trannies performed. So there was always this cross-pollination and all these Malkovich doorways. There were all these scenes that were running at the same time." She adds: "It's not like we were in some kind of downtown ghetto. The whole city could be your stomping ground."

The party scene also contributed to New York's identity as a music and en-tertainment capital. Mayor Ed Koch recognized as much when he introduced an official "Disco Week" back in June 1978, and while that kind of public support didn't survive the backlash against disco, at its most commercially successful the party scene could draw on new wave, disco, and rap to produce an international hit such as "Rapture."[12] If records like Blondie's didn't erupt

Chi Chi Valenti, 1979. She made ends meet by putting together window displays as well as working a couple of nights a week at the Mudd Club. Photograph by and courtesy of Richie Williamson ©.

out of the city's substratum on a daily basis, the creative and social exchanges that occurred in between kept a substantial network of venues and record labels in business. That, in turn, provided employment to any number of bar staff, cleaners, DJs, managers, lighting operators, performers, and sound engineers — the kind of work that enabled Klaus Nomi to give up his day job working as a pastry chef in the World Trade Center and Magnuson to give up temping. "Steve, Jim Fouratt, Rudolf, they were like movie producers. I didn't need love from them, like an actor would. I just wanted them to help me put on a show. For me, back then it was, 'My god, we're going to have fun and we're going to get paid!'" notes Magnuson.

Beyond the world of record sales, wage packets, small businesses, and occasional corporate deals, a much more ephemeral set of economic considerations permeated the city's party scene. They began with the way ideas were almost always hatched and developed collectively rather than individually, with clubs providing participants with an opportunity to meet and enter into networks of like-minded people. They continued when parties doubled as crucial spaces within which a new generation of artists, fashion designers, and filmmakers could bypass the established gallery and film hierarchies in order to present their work and get feedback from peers. Much of the activity also fed into a noncommodifiable economy that revolved around ephemeral performance, xerox art, and recycled objects, with thrift-store vinyl and clothing emerging as a related sphere of cut-price exchange. Few would have given much thought to the way a small battalion of writers, lawyers, accountants, and City Hall workers regulated this activity. Long before the notion of the creative class became a catchword within city planning, the party scene also gave regenerative life to down-and-out areas that were deemed by many to be virtually no-go.

The social and economic equilibrium that encouraged this activity to happen remained delicate, however, and Mancuso started to wonder about the future of his own parties as SoHo metamorphosed during the 1970s. "I was there before the gentrification began but the people who would gentrify the area were already there," he says. "It was like a chess game. They knew what they wanted to do and they succeeded in doing it. The SoHo artists were interested in real estate, not art. They would get together and buy a building on the cheap, and some of these people also came from real estate families, so they knew where the neighborhood was going." The battle came to the fore when Mancuso sought permission to reopen on Prince Street. "One woman turned to me and said, 'David, if I try and sell my space and they look out of their window and see niggers and spics . . .' That was what she said. I thought she would say, 'Car traffic.'"

Tied by the stringent deal struck by the banks in return for bailout money when the city went bankrupt, Mayor Koch introduced generous tax abatements worth hundreds of millions of dollars to property developers in an attempt to create future employment and revenue streams that would help the disadvantaged; a deputy recalls how he would joke "the taller the building, the more taxes there are."[13] Despite the graffiti, the abandoned buildings, and the chronic fiscal crisis, New York was "beginning to enjoy a revival . . . known by the curious name of 'gentrification' — a term coined by the displaced English poor and subsequently adopted by urban experts to describe the movement of social classes in and around London," writer Blake Fleetwood noted in the *New York Times* in early 1979.[14] Fleetwood also observed how the city's economy was shifting from the production of goods to the production of services and ideas, and he added that "as the nature of the jobs the city has to offer is changing, so is the population the city attracts."[15]

Mancuso began to stare down the barrel of eviction when his landlord sold 99 Prince Street for a couple of million dollars toward the end of 1979, expressing disappointment that the host didn't take up the option of buying the building himself. The new owner put the property into a holding company and invited Mancuso to stay so he could generate rental income and keep the insurance rate down while waiting for an opportunity to resell. Increasingly disillusioned with SoHo, Mancuso signed an agreement that allowed the landlord to evict him with 30 days' notice and immediately started to scour cheaper parts of the city for a permanent home. "I loved the space in SoHo but not the neighborhood, or at least not the way it developed, because it became too expensive," he reasons. "The local artist residents finally accepted us because they had to, but as far as moving into the area and starting a business, it was getting tougher and tougher and tougher. There was a breaking down of boundaries but boundaries were also being created."

Real estate prices started to rise in 1979, according to SoHo artist, owner-occupier, and chronicler Richard Kostelanetz, and from then onward the area started to attract "people who weren't primarily artists."[16] Some defended their turf by campaigning against Pravda, just as they had battled Mancuso several years earlier, and although Rudolf Piper calculates that the profit accrued from the sale of his SoHo building outstripped anything he could have made if the club had opened, he would have preferred to stay and make less money than become a discontented beneficiary of the real estate boom. In January 1980 Colab's *Real Estate Show* drew attention to the escalating problem of landlord speculation. In February the *Times* reported that the only artists moving into SoHo and TriBeCa were those who could afford a $100,000 mortgage. "The real paintbrush pioneers are braving Williamsburg," it added. "Yes, Williamsburg."[17] After a long slump, the real estate business was in "high gear," reported architecture critic Ada Louise Huxtable in the summer of 1980.[18]

Held in Michigan that summer, the Republican Party National Convention voted for onetime B-movie actor and former governor of California Ronald Reagan to stand as a hawkish candidate in the November presidential election. The politician's comfortable manner, winning smile, and Brylcreemed hair certainly complemented his promise to return the United States to a pre-counterculture, pre-stagflation milieu that would prioritize traditional family values, social order, low taxation, individual enterprise, economic growth, and international dominance — or the conservative scenario lampooned by Piper in his parody of 1950s culture. Aided by the debilitating recession and Iran hostage crisis, the Republican Party had already done much to reverse the vast lead that President Carter's Democrats enjoyed at the turn of the year, and although the Democrats edged to within a couple of points of the Republicans following their own convention in mid-August, Reagan eased to victory in the 4 November poll with 50.7 percent of the national vote and 489 votes in the electoral college to Carter's 41 percent and 49 electoral seats. Jerry Falwell's evangelical Christian lobbying organization the Moral Majority, along with traditional white working-class Democrats who felt ignored by Carter, were key to his success.[19] "Everybody knew that Carter had no chance because his tenure was considered disastrous, except by me," comments Piper. "But then again, I love impotent governments because they are a guarantee of personal freedom."

For many downtowners Reagan's victory unfolded in a faraway land. Valenti recalls that she and her friends didn't feel national politics mattered to their "own tiny world," while Mark Riley maintains that the Better Days/Loft/Paradise Garage crowd "didn't care who was president, only who was playing records." Others, however, feared that Reagan's election would lead to an eventual clampdown. "Considering that America's golden age of the 1950s was something totally anachronistic and ridiculous, I thought that Marx was right when he said that history repeats itself but only as a farce," comments Piper. "I also felt, however, that the return to the past would be accompanied by the more sinister aspects of that era, including McCarthyism, militarism, and predatory capitalism." Leonard Abrams argues that downtowners gave up on mainstream politics because it was so conservative but adds that "underneath all the throwing out of received ideas, many of us were clear we were pro–human rights, anti-exploitation, and socially very liberal." Steve Mass ran mock ads in the *SoHo News* and the *Village Voice* that welcomed Reagan's "glorious victory" and announced that the Mudd Club would assemble artists for a ticker-tape parade down White Street. "Stand in formation behind your new leader," ordered a straight-faced Dr. Mudd. "There will be amnesty for all youth who reject the corrupt devices of the foreign devils. Turn in your punk accessories: studded bracelets, choke collars, spandex, s&M devices and drugs. No questions will be asked . . ."[20]

The assassination of John Lennon by born-again Christian Mark David Chapman on 8 December 1980 reminded the city's partygoers that their lives could never be wholly disentangled from the rest of the country; the ex-Beatle was holding a fresh mix of "Walking On Thin Ice" — a danceable new wave track recorded by his Japanese American wife Yoko Ono that contained lines about the fragility of life — at the time of the shooting. Yet some held onto the belief that New York existed as a quasi-independent city state and that Republican victory wouldn't bear on their daily and nightly existence. "New York City had already been abandoned, especially downtown, so Reagan's election wasn't going to change that," remarks Magnuson. "Reagan wasn't about to challenge the fringe." Others might have gone about their business with even more determination after Reagan amped up hostilities with the Soviet Union and promised to stockpile nuclear weapons. "Some artists became intensely political, others intensely apolitical, and nearly all became, in one way or another, more hedonistic," adds Magnuson. "Expecting the holocaust to arrive on the tip of an ICBM [intercontinental ballistic missile], our collective subconscious knew that our time was limited and so we played that time for all it was worth. Seeing that the end was near we intended to go out with a bang. Nineteen-eighty lit the fuse."

PART II

1981

ACCELERATING TOWARD PLURALISM

EXPLOSION OF CLUBS

On 20 January 1981 Steve Mass staged an inaugural ball to co-incide with Reagan's own inauguration. Troubled by the incoming president's comment in his victory speech that he hoped future generations would look on him as someone who "did protect and pass on lovingly that shining city on the hill," the Mudd Club owner sought to show how Reagan was repeating the promise of John Winthrop, who spoke of delivering the Puritans to a new land, his own version of the shining city on the hill, and attempted to convince the Indians of his good intentions too, only to emerge as a trickster. "Reagan's point wasn't so much to deliver people to the shining city but to make sure the wrong people didn't get close," he argues. "He was clear that those people who weren't chosen were going to be marginalized." Mass also believed that Reagan's apparent inappropriateness for office made him more dangerous than his Republican predecessors. "He was seen as being this wooden man, a Howdy Doody, like a person who had no depth whatsoever," explains Mass. "How could he do anything good or bad? But he started hiring these religious fundamentalists who were warning against sex before marriage, so he was slippery." For all of his folky wisdom and jokey manner, Reagan was also a "hardcore elitist," so Mass resolved to forewarn his crowd that "things might be very good right now, but under Reagan the majority of artists are going to starve to death."

Mass researched Reagan's tenure as governor of California, a period when he sent two thousand National Guard troops to Berkeley to quash a student demonstration, commenting that "if it takes a bloodbath, let's get it over with."[1] The Mudd Club owner proceeded to create placards that displayed phrases from Reagan's speeches, including "morality gap," "filthy speech advocate," and "scruff of the neck," and he also adapted British pop artist Richard Hamilton's collage "Just What Is It That Makes Today's Homes So Different, So Appealing?," recasting the male nude as Reagan, the female nude as the anti–gay rights campaigner Anita Bryant, the tape recorder as a General Electrics product (because Reagan had acted as a spokesperson for the company), the window view as a scene of South Bronx decay, and the old man in the picture frame as Disney (because he and Reagan were "thick as thieves"). Ann Magnuson took charge of the stage show, having published a faux *Vogue* piece in the *SoHo News* about the return of the ballgown. Responsible for staging a linked fashion shoot for the same publication, Animal X prepared outfits for a gown competition. "The youth gala will celebrate the idealism of American youth, downplaying the themes of decadence and rock 'n' roll," trumpeted the flyer. "Dr. Mudd is creating this beautiful many-splendored evening in an effort to steer the Mudd Club on a new course for the '80s towards strength, growth and progress."

On the night of the event, women arrived dressed in mimosa yellow, white, and pink chiffon, avoiding red in deference to the First Lady's renowned preference for that color, as the invite specified, while men wearing dark suits, ties or bow ties, and ruffled shirts were introduced by a chief of protocol and photographed for the venue's "First Family album." Mass also cast Mudd Club regulars as characters that Reagan might surround himself with, including men who wore shades and spoke into walkie-talkies. On the music front, DJs selected patriotic songs, the spoof Jack Adato Orchestra played swing jazz, and Magnuson led the Ladies Auxiliary of the Lower East Side and the newly configured Moral Majority Singers through renditions of "Song of Democracy," "Thumbs Up, America!," and other flag-waving numbers. Capping the variety show, Kenny Scharf serenaded Magnuson, just as Frank Sinatra had serenaded Nancy Reagan at the White House earlier that evening. The ballgown competition finally began at 3:00 AM, with $500 awarded to the winner. "The kids are wearing ballgowns to demonstrate a concept," Mass told the *New York Times*. "The whole idea of Nancy Reagan running the cultural and fashion life of the country now like Catherine the Great is gradually dawning on them."[2] Mass recalls that the night came easily to him. "All I had to do was copy what Reagan was doing," he observes.

For the rest of the year, Mass continued to piece together a music program that amounted to a shadow map of dissident sound. Punk, new wave, punk-funk, and a growing number of hardcore bands made up the club's bread and butter, with A Certain Ratio, Black Flag, Boris Policeband, the Cramps, the Dead Boys, the Dead Kennedys, the Fall, Johnny Thunders and the Heartbreakers, Konk, Malaria!, Pere Ubu, Polyrock, R.E.M., Alan Vega, Was (Not Was), the Waitresses, and the Del-Byzanteens (featuring Jim Jarmusch and occasionally James Nares) among the performers. Mass also booked artists

The "Inaugural Party" at the Mudd Club, held to mark Ronald Reagan's inauguration as president. Lori Montana of the band ART, the Only Band in the World, signs and grimaces on the right. Photograph by and courtesy of Ande Whyland ©.

who messed with the venue's punk discotheque profile, including rockabilly outfit the Blasters, reggae lineup Steel Pulse, composer Rhys Chatham, and Salsa artists Joe Cuba, Tito Puente, and Dave Valentine. Finally he continued to call in legendary performers to White Street, such as R&B artist Screamin' Jay Hawkins, Southern soul mainstay Joe Tex, the "First Lady of Southern Soul" Candi Staton, country architect Ernest Tubb, and Nigerian drummer Babatunde Olatunji. "Sometimes more credit is given to the person who re-creates a song than the original artist," observes Mass. "There's this idea that they are more imaginative, more creative. I wanted to dispel this myth. I wanted to confront the punks with the original artists because they could perform just as abstractly. This was the core of the Mudd Club philosophy."

The interlocking program of fashion, performance, film, and video unfolded in a less compelling manner than it had previously. Yet events featuring avant-garde video artist Naim June Paik, John Waters movie star Edith Massey, and fashion editor Sophie V.D.T.'s curated ballgown selections contributed to 1981 being a "quite rich" year, recalls Mass. Meanwhile the launch of a gallery on the third and fourth floors toward the beginning of the year, which involved him cutting a hole between the two levels in order to create a perimeter balcony and a unified space that could also be used for live performance, confirmed the venue's ongoing inventiveness. Mass hired Keith Haring to work as his first curator, having been introduced to the young artist by Tony Shafrazi, a Mudd Club regular, and he looked on proudly as Haring curated and facilitated exhibitions that included the *Lower Manhattan Drawing Show*, Tseng Kwong Chi's *East Meets West*, and Fred Brathwaite and Futura 2000's *Beyond Words*. "I don't know what I was thinking about the art gallery because it certainly didn't bring in any money," comments the owner. "I said any proceeds should go to the artist. They would have been so small; someone selling something for $200."

Back on the second floor, Anita Sarko locked into the potential of the lounge space by drawing on the easy listening music and exotica of artists such as Juan Garcia Esquivel and Martin Denny. "Because I didn't have a style people said, 'Oh, she doesn't know what the fuck she's doing,'" she recalls. "But August Darnell used to hang out by my booth. He would give me a sly look and then collapse into laughter because he totally understood." Sarko intensified her range in the new setting, playing Shostakovich over tribal drums, or introducing sounds of metal being bashed along with swinging rat pack records and 1950s prom songs. "As far as our regulars were concerned, this was just as much 'dance music' as anything that had a thumping beat," she maintains. Although there was no compulsion to make people dance, however, Mass continued to cast a sufficiently hostile shadow for her to accept Howard Stein's standing offer to work at the Rock Lounge in early 1981, shortly after Haoui Montaug started to work as the doorman at the venue. "She quit," is all Mass remembers. "I was happy and delighted. We didn't have good chemistry."

SELECTED DISCOGRAPHY

ANITA SARKO, MUDD CLUB (1980–1981)

A Certain Ratio, "Shack Up"
Adrian Munsey, His Sheep, Wind, and Orchestra, "The Lost Sheep"
[Anonymous], "RIAA Equalisation — 15,000 to 40 Cps"
Bauhaus, "Bela Lugosi's Dead"
Blondie, "Rapture"
Pat Boone, "April Love"
Earl Bostic, "Harlem Nocturne"
Brains, "Money Changes Everything"

The Bush Tetras, "Too Many Creeps"

Buzzcocks, "Ever Fallen in Love . . . (With Someone You Shouldn't've)"

Cabaret Voltaire, "Nag Nag Nag"

John Cale, "Chicken Shit"

The Clash, "Train in Vain"

The Cramps, "Goo Goo Muck"

Dead Boys, "Sonic Reducer"

Jimmy Dean, "To a Sleeping Beauty"

Defunkt, *Defunkt*

Martin Denny, *Exotica*

Bo Diddley, "Bo Diddley"

DNA, "Blonde Redhead"

Dr. Alimantado, "Best Dressed Chicken in Town"

Echo & the Bunnymen, "Do It Clean"

Duke Ellington, "Autumn Leaves"

ESG, "Moody"

Esquivel and His Orchestra, *Latin-Esque*

Marianne Faithfull, "Why D'Ya Do It?"

Fela Ransome-Kuti and the Africa '70 with Ginger Baker, "Let's Start"

Aretha Franklin, "Rock Steady"

Funkadelic, "(Not Just) Knee Deep"

Funky 4 + 1, "That's the Joint"

General Echo, "Arleen"

Don Ho, "Tiny Bubbles"

Michael Jackson, "Don't Stop 'Til You Get Enough"

Wanda Jackson, "Let's Have a Party"

The Jam, "In the City"

James White & the Blacks, "Contort Yourself"

Joy Division, "She's Lost Control"

Killing Joke, "Change"

Last Poets, "OD"

John Lennon, "Stand by Me"

Link Wray, "Rumble"

Lounge Lizards, "Do the Wrong Thing"

Magazine, "Shot by Both Sides"

Marie et les Garçons, "Re-Bop"

MC5, "Sister Anne"

Ken Nordine, *Colors (A Sensuous Listening Experience)*

Orchestral Manoeuvres in the Dark, "Julia's Song"

PiL, "Swan Lake"

Iggy Pop, "Lust for Life"

Pop Group, "She Is beyond Good and Evil"

Louis Prima, featuring Keely Smith with Sam Butera and the Witnesses,
  "Just a Gigolo"

Prince, "Head"

The Ramones, "I Wanna Be Sedated"

Lou Reed, "Intro/Sweet Jane"

Gil Scott-Heron/Brian Jackson, "The Bottle"

Shostakovich, *Symphony No. 4*

Siouxsie and the Banshees, "Eve White/Eve Black"

The Slits, "In the Beginning There Was Rhythm"

Spandau Ballet, "To Cut a Long Story Short"

Stiff Little Fingers, "Alternative Ulster"

The Stooges, "Loose"

The Stranglers, "Peaches"

Sugarhill Gang, "8th Wonder"

Sugarhill Gang, "Rapper's Delight"

Suicide, "Dream Baby Dream"

Yma Sumac, *Voice of the Xtabay*

The Supremes, "Rock-a-Bye Your Baby with a Dixie Melody"

Thelonious Monk Quartet, "Bye-Ya"

Throbbing Gristle, "Discipline"

Tommy James & the Shondells, "Crimson & Clover"

Tuxedomoon, "No Tears"

Pere Ubu, "Final Solution"

Scott Walker, "The Seventh Seal"

Was (Not Was), "Wheel Me Out"

Wire, "I Am the Fly"

A graduate in political science and the son of a union-activist father, Montaug had already run the door at Hurrah and Danceteria, where he cultivated the notion that downtowners weren't so much marked by poverty, as they liked to think, as "privileged poverty," because they lived "off the rich" and had various taste preferences to match.[3] Montaug's relaying of the news that Rudolf Piper was about to reopen Pravda and wanted to employ her as his DJ sealed Sarko's decision to leave White Street. "Haoui and I thought we'd go to Rock Lounge for a month or two, make some money, and then go to Pravda," she recalls. "But Pravda never opened and we were stuck at this horrible place." Remembering the scenario differently, Piper insists he wouldn't have asked someone to give up a steady job for "pie in the sky," and he adds that by the time he opened Danceteria he had "exhausted every possible means" of mollifying local opposition to Pravda, which led him to tell his business partner in the venture that he was out. Whatever the ins and outs, Sarko found herself stuck playing for Howard Stein, who in her opinion didn't have a "creative bone in his body."

Mass responded by hiring one-time Xenon busboy Ivan Baker to fly the flag of madcap eclecticism. "I worked twenty-eight days straight without a day off," recalls DJ, who got his break when Stephen Saban of the *SoHo News* organized a party at the spot and asked him to play. "All of a sudden I was in the hippest club in the world, playing whatever I wanted, and getting laid left and right. I was nineteen years old and in heaven." Settling into a schedule that saw him play upstairs on Wednesdays and Thursdays, and downstairs on Fridays and Saturdays, Baker juxtaposed James Brown, Funkadelic, and Taana Gardner with the Flying Lizards, Billy Idol, and Bostich in a manner that was entirely of the moment. "Songs were like words and we built sentences and paragraphs over the night," he muses. "We told a story and we threw in a disco song if it was part of the story. Then we'd work in rap versions of the disco records to show where they came from. I'd play 'Fame' by David Bowie and then James Brown 'Hot (I Need to Be Loved),' which had the same rhythm track." Baker adds that he and his good friend Justin Strauss embraced rap as a form of black punk. "There was a lot of back-and-forth. I could barely keep track."

With Dany Johnson employed to play a midweek slot and Pittsburgh-raised doo-wop and soul fan Walter Durkacz also picking up turntable responsibilities, the Mudd Club started to attract a less glamorous but arguably more receptive crowd. "It was always amazing to me that the people who were the most open-minded and the most thirsty for new music were the lower-middle-class bridge-and-tunnel kids," observes Baker, who took to calling himself Ivan Muddski.[4] "You'd have thought they'd be the most close-minded, but they were the most enthusiastic about coming and hearing stuff they couldn't hear anywhere else. The most close-minded were the Studio 54 types who could afford to wear Halston." Certain cliques only wanted to listen to one type of music yet the general demand was for new music to be played in a new way. "You couldn't sustain one beat all night long," adds the DJ. "That's what people were rebelling against — the idea that there should only be one style. It was anti-fascist."

There was no sudden changing of the guard, with the likes of Jean-Michel Basquiat, Keith Haring, Arto Lindsay, and Klaus Nomi still a presence. Others could leave disillusioned, only to return, as happened with Johnson, who headed to the Mudd Club regularly until the night a woman climbed out of a limo holding a small dog, waltzed to the front of the queue, turned to face the milling crowd, and sang "*Disco, disco, disco-disco-disco*," but she later came back to work at the spot. By the time Brian Butterick started to work the door around the summer of 1981, New Jerseyites and tourists who "lacked flair" were still being turned away, he recalls, yet "the Mudd Club had started to change" and "Steve Mass was getting greedy." The owner reasons that the "explosion of competition" led many scenesters to hang out and find work in other spots, which made it harder to sustain his rebel-artist core as well as draw on like-minded people to help him stage happenings, with the "Inaugural Ball" one of the last to be staged. "I thought I was welding together a Dada or Bauhaus community and we'd all stick together," ponders Mass. "But as 1981 wore on I saw that these people were flying off like sparks into whatever entrepreneurial ventures they could find. So this fantasy I had of forming a tribal group started splintering." Still a White Street regular, even though he had gone to work for Jim Fouratt and Rudolf Piper at the Peppermint Lounge in November 1980, Richard Boch nevertheless recalls that the Mudd Club was "still vital" during 1981.

Club 57 also splintered after Magnuson stepped back from managing the venue in September 1980. "I remember Dany [Johnson] trying to talk me out of quitting," she recalls. "'Where will we go?' was the question. But I just could not do it anymore. I was doing something different every single night at Club 57 and I was very worn out. I was also being asked to perform in places like the Kitchen and the Walker Art Center, and wanted to pursue my career in performance art, theater, film, and music." Picking up the role and supported by Dale Ashman, a committed regular who took on bar and drudgery duties, Andy Rees introduced more musical theater and cabaret until his penchant for a drink too many led Kai Eric to take on the job, possibly as part of an unsuccessful ploy to win back the affections of Magnuson. With Stanley Strychacki having stood in the way of Johnson taking over for reasons unknown to those involved, the DJ supported Eric as he introduced more live bands and art shows into the weekly offering. Assuming the directorial role around the autumn of 1981, Ira Abramowitz badmouthed Eric with false

Dany Johnson and Steve Mass at the opening of Club Tabu, 1981. Photograph by and courtesy of Ande Whyland ©.

allegations about misappropriating funds for drug use, performed under the provocative name of Needles Jones, and instilled the venue with a renewed if darker sense of purpose. "By this time I didn't even care anymore," recalls Magnuson. "I was so involved with other things. The fact the club went on for another year or two and still had creative output is pretty amazing."

The turnover at the top didn't result in any obvious slowdown in the level of activity. Part of the expanded theatrical program, Scot Whitman and Marc Shaiman channeled their love of musicals into the Barbie-themed "Living Dolls" and *The Sound of Music* spoof "The Sound of Muzak." Contributing to the dramatic repertoire, Warhol superstar Ondine appeared in *The Life of Burr,* an original play that explored the fetishistic urges of *Ironside* actor Raymond Burr. Other highlights saw Magnuson and Rees step into the personas of evangelists Jim and Tammy Bakker, and John Sex deliver his first burlesque show. "The 57 Performance Expo" featured the contributions of more than forty poets, photographers, and other artists. Special theme parties included a "Rites of Spring Bacchanal," during which the homegrown, thirteen-member female percussion band Pulsallama made its debut. On the art front, Michael Holman organized a two-night graffiti exhibition and Haring staged a "Two Black Light Nights" show. The movie program included a screening of the soft-core thriller *Sugar Cookies*. And the scaled-up live music schedule featured appearances by the likes of Certain General, Rhys Chatham, Liquid Liquid, Snuky Tate, 3 Teens Kill 4, and the in-house simulation act Velvet Mania, which had Magnuson taking on the part of Velvet Underground's Nico.

With the Peppermint Lounge, the Ritz, and TR3 also going strong, the competition within the art-punk party scene rose a notch when Jim Fouratt and Rudolf Piper struck a deal with Maurice Brahms to launch "Modern Classix" at the Underground in May 1981. Aligning themselves with the New Romantic movement that was gathering pace in the United Kingdom, they opened with a fashion show and the U.S. debut of Spandau Ballet. After that they spiced up their weekly slot with occasional "Art Attack" events that showcased the experimental music and performance art of Glenn Branca, Diamanda Galas, and Philip Glass, and at one point they even staged a spoof "Royal Wedding" party starring Magnuson and Scharf to coincide with the marriage of Prince Charles and Lady Diana. "I didn't want to work in high art or avant-art because they were intellectual and elitist," Fouratt notes of his consolidating vision. "I wanted to work in pop culture and bring those elements into it. I wanted to fuse the intellectual and the physical and the emotional together, and I thought that's what pop culture had the potential to do." He and Piper encouraged their crowd to dress up. "If you have a little flair you can make nice clothes and it'll cost you hardly anything at all," Fouratt told the *East Village Eye*. "That's the thing with Spandau. These are basically working class kids. Grovelling in misery is what the Government would like them to do. This is their way of getting back."[5]

That summer, around the time that Fouratt and Piper staged a showcase party for the second New Music Seminar, Steve Rubell asked the promoters if they would take over the running of Studio 54 while he and Ian Schrager completed the sale of the spot. Rubell and Schrager had been released from prison and assigned to a halfway house at the beginning of the year, only for the judge to rule that their venue would be refused a new liquor license if they became re-involved in its operation. That compelled them to sell while seeking out promoters who could re-inject it with a shot of its old glamour in order to smooth the transition to a new owner. "Piper decided it was an offer we could not refuse," Fouratt recalled later. "In fact, other than Pravda, it was the first time I saw Piper really excited. Not only was Studio 54 the most famous nightclub in the world, but because it was an old Broadway theatre, it had extraordinary potential as a live-performance space as well."[6]

Rubell and Schrager were never going to hand the promoter job to Mike Stone. There had already been times when, following his release from prison, Rubell struggled to abide by the court order to keep his hands off the spot.

Ann Magnuson, 1981.
Photograph by and courtesy
of Robert Carrithers.

"I remember Steve coming up to the DJ booth with Calvin Klein and asking me to play Lime," says Kenny Carpenter. "I said, 'No,' and he replied, 'But I am the club!' The next week he hired the band." Stone just got on with his job, scheduling weekly performances by the likes of Change, Taana Gardner, France Joli, Grace Jones, and Chaka Khan. "I got everybody that had a hit record," remembers the promoter, who also hosted regular fashion shows plus a performance by the Alvin Ailey American Dance Theater. "There was a big rivalry with the Paradise Garage over that. We'd both try to get artists to perform exclusively. By 1981 I hated Mike Brody and vice versa." In June *Billboard* pointed out that the venue had been "enjoying a quiet rejuvenation" for several months and that "party rules have been relaxed to encourage attendance by a broader cross-section of the disco dancing public."[7] But Rubell and Schrager didn't see money, status, or a social life in Stone's cross-section and in the summer ended his involvement abruptly. "There was a big robbery and Rubell tried to pin it on me," recalls the promoter. "He gave me a chance to get out and find another place."

At the end of August, Rubell and Schrager sold Studio 54 for $1.15 million to Mark Fleischman, a hotelier with no prior experience in running a discotheque. Meanwhile Fouratt and Piper left the Underground to prepare for the obligatory media circus that was bound to greet the re-launch of the venue on 15 September. "It didn't seem to matter to anyone inside or out that it all seemed a little déja vu," reported *New York Magazine*. "The mobs, the desperation, the potential danger. That was what they had missed."[8] The *Village Voice* even suggested that Stone's eviction had been necessary for the venue to once again be noticed. "For those who loved the place, the last 18 months has been like spending evenings sitting in a bus station," it reported, apparently without blushing.[9] Yet as the *SoHo News* noted, whereas the earlier Studio crowd featured "models and millionaires," now it sported "millionaires and purple hairs," suggesting that a punk-art element turned up, even if it wasn't as prominent as it had been at Danceteria. "Everybody downtown, it seemed, came uptown and actually got it," Fouratt recalled later, "and everyone uptown came to greet them."[10]

Two days after hosting an Andy Warhol party for author and *Interview* contributor Fran Lebowitz, Fouratt and Piper got on with the business of staging regular "Modern Classix" nights on Wednesdays and Sundays, scheduling Bow Wow Wow, Nina Hagen, Heaven 17, and Lene Lovich to perform live and dedicating another night to Soca.[11] They also retained overall creative control of the venue, scheduling disco-oriented nights during the rest of the weekly cycle. "We changed the mix of people in the room," recalls Fouratt. "We also put in some female bartenders and tried to make it more representative of the aesthetic of Danceteria. When I told Steve he said, 'Women bartenders? Do they take off their shirts?'" But then Fleischman ruled that it was necessary to bump up the entrance price and started to complain about the live music. "Bow Wow Wow were too loud, Fleischman pulled the plug on them and that was it," recalls Fouratt. "We left." Piper concurred that the position with the new owner was untenable. "Fleischman bought Studio 54 as a way to become famous and as a way to make money," notes the German. "He didn't have an eye for aesthetics or crowds or how to get different tribes into one space. We were really uncomfortable because we were not understood and we were not getting the support we needed."

Vito Bruno, Chuck Rusinak, and Roman Ricardo made the most of Fleischman's resistance, having opened AM/PM as a de facto after-hours alternative to the withering culture of midtown disco in the spring of 1981. "Studio 54, Xenon, and New York, New York were all about glitz, glamor and limos," points out Bruno, a graduate from the Pratt Institute in Brooklyn. "If you

Jim Fouratt and Rudolf Piper at Studio 54, 1981. "They have become two of the most imaginative and versatile impresarios in New York in the last few years," noted *SoHo News* in September 1981. ("It Was Easier to Get into Heaven," *SoHo News*, 22 September 1981.) Photograph by and courtesy of Allan Tannenbaum/SoHo Blues ©.

were beautiful or looked fabulous you were let in. They had this Hitler-esque mentality. So I said, 'We're not going glam, we're going to do something different.'" Located on Murray Street, a couple of blocks north of the World Trade Center, AM/PM's interior spelled out the message. "Where there were cracks in the walls, we took the cracks and made them bigger," explains Bruno. "Upstairs there was a huge concrete block with bars coming out of it that we couldn't move, so we bent the bars, put flowers on them and lit the thing. We turned this waste material into a sculptural piece." Warhol and his entourage showed up on opening night — Bruno's PR guy knew Richard Bernstein, the artist who created the covers for *Interview* magazine — and promised to return. The *East Village Eye* reported that the "familiar line up of faces" was "almost as painful as looking in the mirror."[12]

The soul-oriented Ricardo shouldered DJ-ing duties until Bruno concluded that the venue needed someone who could deliver a "mixed bag of music," if only because all manner of revelers gravitated to the spot once the city's licensed outlets closed for the night. Invited to step in by Ricardo on a Wednesday, François Kevorkian headed to Bonaparte Records on West 3rd Street in order to transform himself into a "mixed rock format" DJ by the weekend and remembers his debut going down "a storm — like killer." The Prelude mixer combined Stevie Wonder and James Brown with Kraftwerk, Billy Idol, and the Go-Go's, or linked Depeche Mode with the Stray Cats with Eddie Cochran. When the Rolling Stones released "Start Me Up" in August, he teased the crowd with the guitar intro until they went "nuts" and then cut to James Brown, at which point they let out a collective "Oh, shit!" but kept on dancing. He gave the crowd what it most obviously wanted: Blondie, the B-52's, ESG, Liquid Liquid, and Talking Heads. Yet he also tried out records that could be heard at Better Days, the Gallery, the Loft, and the Paradise Garage, just to see how they would work. It turned out that funk-driven African American tracks went down well but "syrupy, soulful diva records" along with the orchestral end of Philadelphia International, and Salsoul didn't appeal at all.

Kevorkian pieced together a mutant sound palette that melded rock, reggae, rockabilly, punk, and new wave with funk, disco, and soul, with Talking Heads' "Once in a Lifetime," from the album *Remain in Light*, a pivotal hybrid selection. If someone complained about the music, he took to saying, "I'll play what you want, just give me time." If another asked him to play a style he hardly knew, he asked for a specific recommendation so that he could buy it for the following week. "I would go to Bonaparte Records and I would go to Ed Bahlman at 99 Records, and I would say, 'School me in industrial German music and the English new wave,'" he reminisces. "I kept acquiring this knowledge little by little." Along the way he came to appreciate that some old DJ tricks could thrill the AM/PM crowd. "I didn't know much about beat-mixing," acknowledges Justin Strauss, who heard and then met Kevorkian at AM/PM. "I was just playing what I thought were good records. Then I heard François play and he opened me up to a world I really didn't know anything about. He showed me how to beat-mix and I started to incorporate that into what I was doing at the Ritz."

A hyena in search of a fight, Jerry Brandt frequently stole the limelight from Strauss and the bands that played on 11th Street. The owner of the Ritz outmuscled smaller venues in booking contests, nonchalantly crammed customers into his venue, and spewed out a shamelessly unreconstructed view of the world that poisoned the underlying atmosphere. "I'm a womanizer, I admit it," he told *After Dark* in September. "I don't think women should go to war, they should stay home and fuck."[13] *New York Magazine* confirmed that the "chic New Wave crowd" judged the Ritz to be uncomfortable and oversized.[14] But a number of the shows were indisputably spectacular, and although it could take a while for the floor to warm up after the act left the stage, underage club kid Tim Broun remembers "dancing a lot at the Ritz." Strauss acknowledges that "some people just came to see the band, so after the band finished I'd have to try to tap into the crowd that wanted to stay."

Held on 11 March, Sylvia Robinson's Sugar Hill review featured a rapping and DJ-ing display that attracted "anyone who'd heard this funny talking stuff at a club or on a passing box and got hooked," reported Richard Grabel in the *New Musical Express*.[15] During Public Image Ltd.'s appearance on 15 May, lead vocalist and ex–Sex Pistol John Lydon refused to come out from behind the venue's unique fifteen-by-thirty-foot video screen, which prompted members of the audience to hurl bottles at the vocalist's video image, storm the stage, and vandalize the equipment. When the aggression died down, Strauss "tried to salvage something out of the situation," starting his set with T. Rex's "Rip Off." Two months later Kraftwerk hoodwinked the audience by having four mannequins open the show in near-darkness. "When they came on, everybody's jaw dropped," recalls Strauss. "It was like, 'Oh shit, you don't even need people to do this!'" Gathering to the left of the stage, the Zulu Nation danced hard. "They had sticks in the air and other accoutrements," remembers Ivan Baker, who viewed the spectacle from Strauss's booth. "They were going crazy."

In the meantime Bond's had switched to a live performance format, and an Internal Revenue Service raid on the apartments of Maurice Brahms, John Addison, and their partners yielded findings of $100,000 in cash (all courtesy

Kraftwerk live at the Ritz, 1981. Photograph by and courtesy of Laura Levine ©.

of a tip-off from Rubell and Schrager, who were looking to cut short their stay in prison).[16] Taking over the midtown spot in the new year, a four-person management group that included ex-cbgb booking agent Charlie Martin replaced its fountain with a stage and began to schedule live shows by groups such as the Bush Tetras and the Lounge Lizards.[17] Then, in April, Martin announced that he wanted to "take the big bands, which we can get here, and glue them to the bands that should make it," and proceeded to put his words into action when he booked the Clash to play eight nights at the spot, with the band invited to select an array of punk, rap, and dub support acts that represented the breadth of their taste (as well as hire Futura 2000 to paint a banner for the stage).[18] The arrangement married an eclectic punk outfit to a city that had become a melting pot of sound. Indeed, such was their focus on New York, the Clash didn't bother to schedule any further appearances in the States. Meanwhile the development thwarted Michael Brody's attempt to book the band to play at the Paradise Garage.

Held on Thursday, 28 May, the first night of the series nevertheless revealed the Bond's management to be as unscrupulous as Brandt as they rammed 3,700 people into a venue with a legal capacity of 1,725. The following day the Clash agreed to play an extra seven nights, the entire series having been oversold, only for the buildings department to run an inspection and pronounce the venue's exits inadequate. Officials deferred the order because fans were already assembling, yet they canceled the Saturday afternoon matinee and all subsequent shows, sparking a "mini-riot" among fans and a media storm that surpassed the "wildest dreams" of any publicist, reported the *SoHo News*.[19] Then, on the Sunday morning, the buildings commissioner reached an agreement that additional security, fire, and crowd regulations would be provided, met with the Clash's representatives at the Gramercy Park Hotel, and appeared alongside the band to announce that the show would go on after all. "Landmines are buried on a road paved with good intentions," observed Michael Hill in the *Village Voice*.[20]

The furor had faded by the time Bond's hosted the tenth-anniversary festival of the Kitchen on 14–15 June and in so doing gave further succor to the kind of exchange that dated back to the mid-1970s, when composers such as Rhys Chatham, Peter Gordon, Arthur Russell, Ned Sublette, and David van Tieghem ventured from the safe haven of the Kitchen into the alternative world of CBGB, the Mudd Club, and, in the case of Russell, the Gallery, the Loft, and the Paradise Garage as well. Chatham went on to write earsplitting pieces for the electric guitar, Russell to record mutant disco with Dinosaur and Loose Joints, and Gordon and van Tieghem to form a downtown dance band, the Love of Life Orchestra. All snapped up invitations from Jim Fouratt, Steve Mass, and other owners because they wanted to perform in a club setting and welcomed the higher fees they could earn. Even the comparatively senior Philip Glass threw himself into the maelstrom while coproducing the minimalist rock band Polyrock. "I used to feel in competition with the clubs," Chatham admitted in February, having recently stopped working as the Kitchen's music director. "I wanted to premiere things, to have the first place where Teenage Jesus and the Jerks or the Contortions happened. But then I realized that it was impossible for the Kitchen because we don't have a club format. It doesn't feel the same."[21]

Capturing the extraordinary range and interactivity of the city's music scene, the program included orchestral works by Glass and Steve Reich; art-pop performances by Laurie Anderson and the Love of Life Orchestra; a show organized by Fab 5 Freddy; screenings of video works by Robert Ashley, Robert Wilson, Nam June Paik, Brian Eno, and Talking Heads; contemporary dance featuring Arnie Zane's company; and blasts of experimental guitar from Branca, Chatham, the Bush Tetras, DNA, the Feelies, Lydia Lunch and 1313, the Raybeats, and Red Decade. Chatham had already argued that he considered the musicians of DNA, Mars, the Contortions, and the Lounge Lizards to be composers.[22] In his preview of the show, John Rockwell added that while the significant band presence might have come as a surprise to those who assumed compositional music and rock to be antithetical, the two had become intertwined in downtown New York. "This grouping attests to the links among the members of the downtown community, which unlike some applications of that word really is a community," he declared.[23]

Four days later Anya Phillips died, her fast-deteriorating condition the reason James Chance and the Contortions didn't appear at the Bond's event. The manager/designer/scenester/muse had told her friends about the first symptoms of what would later be diagnosed as cancer during a Thanksgiving gathering held the previous November that included Patti Astor, Steven Kramer (Astor's artist husband, from whom she had split), Kristian Hoffman (a member of the Mumps, a downtown punk band), and Bradley Field (a member of Teenage Jesus and the Jerks) plus Phillips and Chance. Astor and Kramer cooked, only for everyone to get so stoned the turkey turned to ashes. "We had what I remember as the 'Heroin Thanksgiving Dinner' which marked the end of my association with that drug," recalls Astor. "It was down on the overstuffed velvet Victorian couch in Kristian's loft, with all of us there, that Anya confided to us that she had a strange lump on her neck."[24]

A benefit show for Phillips held at Bond's on 11 May featured a supergroup that included Blondie's Debbie Harry, Chris Stein, and Jimmy Destri; Chic's Nile Rodgers, Bernard Edwards, and Tony Thompson; and violinist Walter Steding. After opening with "Rapture," the lineup closed off with a "Good Times"/"Rapper's Delight" medley that included rapping contributions from Fred Brathwaite and the Funky 4 + 1.[25] "Anya worked the crowd as if she was promoting James Chance and not her life," recalls Steve Mass — not an entirely welcome guest. "I couldn't detect any difference in her basic persona. She still had that enormous, manic drive. It was like, 'I'm not sick and anyone who alleges I won't get better is crazy.'" Acerbic to the last, Phillips passed her time in a hospital designing fashion collections, including one titled "Sadistic Nurses."[26] "Anya was a mascot in that she really dressed for the party," reminisces Diego Cortez. "She always had heels and spiky hair, and she had many sexual liaisons with many rock people. Some people would call her a groupie but she was more of a kind of glamorous genius that these musicians wanted to be with. She was a visual spokesperson. What she looked like and who she was represented the scene." Phillips was also an enigmatic figure whose influence suffused a scene. "Nobody could ever really figure out what Anya did," observes Chi Chi Valenti. "But that was very common then."

Mass, meanwhile, contemplated the rush of competition that had been gathering pace since the spring of 1979, when Fouratt's transformation of the

Anya Phillips in a rubber latex suit attending a Cramps show at CBGB, 1977. She cultivated an influential S&M dominatrix aesthetic and knowing ennui. Photograph by and courtesy of Bobby Grossman ©.

flailing Hurrah amounted to the first clear sign that a broader alignment between punk and discotheque culture was about to unfold. "By 1981 there was this explosion of twenty-odd clubs," notes the owner. "Everyone was starting a club based on the fact that it cost no money. One of my bartenders went down the block and started doing nights in a strip club." AM/PM, Bond's, Club 57, Hurrah, the Peppermint Lounge, the Ritz, the Rock Lounge, Tier 3, and the Underground contributed a sharp-elbowed market that saw the Peppermint Lounge introduce a one-cent "Pep Penny Party" entrance charge for revelers who arrived before 11:00 PM on Sundays through to Thursdays.[27] "I was being outbid by everybody," adds Mass. "Jerry Brandt invited me to his apartment and I said, 'Oh, that's nice.' Then he told me he wanted to put the Mudd Club into the Ritz, which turned me off. It began to dilute the romance of the Mudd Club to some extent. But how could you help it? That's just the nature of culture."

Frank Rose framed the rush of activity as a movement when he published an extended article featuring interviews with Mass, Magnuson, filmmakers Beth and Scott B., photographer Jimmy DeSana, Richard Boch, Lydia Lunch, Chris Stein, and others in the April issue of *Esquire*. The writer argued that the current generation of downtowners contrasted with their punk predecessors inasmuch as they favored art and irony to rage and nihilism, and they preferred to mine the past rather than break with it, which positioned them as "America's first reactionary bohemians."[28] Rose quoted Mass wondering if hockey would become the next hip trend, Magnuson citing that psychedelia and Eastern Europe had become her favorite parodic sources, DeSana revealing that Woolworth's was one of his main sources of inspiration, and Lunch discussing her ambition to become a Hollywood star, form a psychedelic rock band, and settle down in the country with a husband, pets, and toys. Stein thought out loud that everybody had "given up." Rose thought to himself: "Modern youth has no dream. It's empty inside. It's as cold and as hard as the graphics."[29]

Perhaps Rose underestimated the extent to which the city's first generation of punk bands also advocated a self-consciously artistic and often ironic worldview. Perhaps he didn't spend enough time with his interviewees to discover their near-unanimous contempt for Reagan or their opposition to conservatism. Perhaps he didn't appreciate their determination to construct an alternate reality out of the energy of the countercultural movement, the resourcefulness of punk, and the pleasure of the dance floor. He certainly failed to dig beneath the superficial critique of disco as a form of mindless, narcissistic hedonism, and he also showed no awareness of the culture's transformational influence on punk. Yet he did offer a sense of hope at the end of his somewhat despondent survey when he charted the uptown journey of Stein and Debbie Harry plus the release of "Rapture." "Rapping and graffiti are both reminders that New York is predominantly a Third World city," he argued. "They are postcards from America's new underclass."[30] The night he went to hear the Funky 4 + 1 More perform at the Rock Lounge appeared to be a "voodoo response to reality," a form of "magic from the survivors in the zone of wild dogs and charred masonry," a "brave noise from the victims, passed on to other victims."[31]

It didn't matter that those gathered, black and white, wouldn't have thought of themselves as victims. A new alliance was about to take the city by storm.

ARTISTIC MANEUVERS
IN THE DARK

The opening months of 1981 witnessed a hectic, even chaotic intensification of the conversation that had begun to take place between downtown artists, new wave musicians, graffiti writers, and even DJs at the *Times Square Show*.

A skilled provocateur, Diego Cortez got things going when he launched the *New York/New Wave* exhibition at the alternative Long Island City gallery PS1 on 15 February. The show included nearly 1,000 works from nearly 150 artists, among them Kathy Acker, Jean-Michel Basquiat, William Burroughs, David Byrne, Brian Eno, Keith Haring, Arto Lindsay, Lydia Lunch, John Lurie, Ann Magnuson, Maripol, Rene Ricard, Kenny Scharf, Chris Stein, Alan Vega, and Andy Warhol; photographers Nan Goldin and Robert Mapplethorpe; and graffitists Crash, Dondi, Fab 5 Freddy, Futura 2000, Lee Quiñones, Rammel-lzee, and Zephyr. If the *Times Square Show* presented the sprawling energy of the downtown art scene, Cortez's countereffort foregrounded the connected-ness of punk, new wave, graffiti, and contemporary art. "For me the *Times Square Show* was boring," comments the curator. "There was little good art. I saw griping white kids pretending to be political, talking about the discon-nect between the rich and the poor. My PS1 show was culturally political as opposed to politically political. It was about a radical new music scene and the detritus which resulted from it. Many people who created that music scene were renegade art people who escaped the art context, whereas Collab-orative projects [Colab] and the Kitchen music scene remained entrenched in the art scene. It was a turf war between SoHo and the Bowery."

Cortez turned to new wave in order to challenge conventional notions around art. Questioned by an art critic if he thought the contributors were professionals, he asked in reply if the musicians who made "most of the good music for the last four years" were professionals, implying that they weren't, and went on to note that his aim was to bring together a "sociology of elements" that make up a scene.[1] In an ensuing conversation with Edit deAk, he added that he wanted to "attack" the gallery system by "supplanting it with a whole new business," which prompted deAk to add that the art world was afraid of new wave because "it happened between midnight and five o'clock in the morning."[2] Among the reviewers who pronounced themselves disappointed, Kay Larson argued in *New York Magazine* that the show resembled "an advertisement for a Club Med–Mudd Club party" in which Cortez documented not "the scene" so much as punk's "in-groupiness" and "eagerness to skewer the bourgeoisie," yet acknowledged that the "outrageous vitality that somehow didn't find its way into the Whitney Biennial has popped up, for better or worse, in New York/New Wave." The exhibition also maintained the "raw emotive energy" of the *Times Square Show*. "Out of these *'salons de refuses'* comes the art of the next year or the next decade," concluded the critic.[3]

Displayed prominently on the ground floor, fifteen paintings by Basquiat—his first fully realized efforts on canvas—crackled with the explosive spontaneity and impulsive directness of the downtown party scene. "Jean-Michel was this Lower East Side figure who was part of this scene where graffiti, Burroughs, and no wave all mixed together," observes Jeffrey Deitch, who took a number of collectors to see the show. "He was not academically trained, but you would see one of his portraits of Andy Warhol or Arto Lindsay and the likeness would be shockingly accurate yet dissonant. There were a lot of parallels with these punk and no wave musicians who never learned how to play guitar but just started doing it." At the end of the opening party Basquiat headed home and told his accountant father, "I made it."[4] But although his work attracted some offers—$1,000 here, $2,500 there—the Swiss gallery owner and collector Bruno Bischofberger, who had championed the work of Jasper Johns, Roy Lichtenstein, Robert Rauschenberg, and Andy Warhol in Europe, didn't make a purchase.

Keith Haring's *Lower Manhattan Drawing Show* opened in the Mudd Club's gallery a week later, the first exhibition to appear in the new space. "[Steve Mass] said he wanted to buy the talent of Club 57—he wanted to put fresh blood into his own club," the artist noted later. "This was good, because people at Club 57 really needed jobs. . . . It was great because I now had a job I really liked!"[5] Mass said that he gave the young artist the role because of his hands-on gallery experience, and his judgment seemed sound as Haring whisked together the *Lower Manhattan Drawing Show* in time for a 22 February opening. "The new gallery space will exhibit the works of some of the most talented young artists in lower Manhattan, many as yet unrepresented by dealers," announced the press release. "Many of them have shown their works outside of Soho at Fashion Moda, Group Material, A.B.C. No Rio and the Time Square Show. They will now have the advantage of the convenience of Soho as well as a full length THREE WEEK EXHIBITION with gallery hours extending as late as 2:00 AM."[6]

The exhibition displayed contributions from ninety-nine artists, among them Fred Braithwaite, Crash, Dondi, Futura 2000, Lady Pink, and Zephyr alongside Charlie Ahearn, Jean-Michel Basquiat, Kenny Scharf, and David Wojnarowicz — the latter's first public invitation. "Anyone can draw," Haring told Kim Levin of the *Village Voice*. "If I had gotten drawings from people off the streets they probably would have fit in just as well." Levin observed that the exhibition could "almost be called a postscript" to PS1 except that "it was Haring who put together the one-day exhibitions at Club 57 last spring where Diego Cortez found a number of the artists for his PS1 'New Wave' show." (In fact, Cortez met Daze et al. when he attended several uptown meetings of the United Graffiti Artists with Haring.) Levin also argued that if PS1 was "full of the glamour and the grotesquerie of the music scene," the drawings at the Mudd Club "get closer to the sound." Haring's "real heroes," she added, are the "legendary young graffitists," who possess "the raw energy artists are trying to get their teeth into."[7] Back in October, the *New York Times* had somewhat skeptically noted the "inrush of upper-income whites" who were adopting graffiti.[8] Yet Colab artist Jane Dickson, another contributor, adds that the show marked the breakthrough of "white guys who weren't copying graffiti but aligning themselves with the energy of graffiti and minority artists through postering and stenciling. It felt less self-consciously about posing as an art star and more about a shared outlaw sensibility and reckless energy."

Five days later Haring was at it again, this time curating the *First Annual Club 57 Group Erotic and Pornographic Art Exhibition*. Basquiat, Holliday, Magnuson, Scharf, and Wojnarowicz were among the sixty-six contributors, with Wojnarowicz's depiction of a naked man with a dog's head among the most striking. Participants scrambled to take down the image of a giant penis from the entrance when the church's bishop paid a visit to the basement club to tell Stanley Strychacki that people had contacted him to complain that the basement venue was being used to display a pornographic show. Having studied art at a Catholic seminary, the Club 57 caretaker-manager replied that sexual symbolism ran through a great deal of religious art. A group of sanitation workers who regularly dropped by to get a cold drink confirmed that in their eyes it was art, not pornography. "Yes, Michelangelo had the same problem when he painted the Sistine Chapel," concluded the bishop, before he made his exit.[9]

Back at the Mudd Club, Haring invited Fred Brathwaite and Futura 2000 to curate a full-blown *Beyond Words* graffiti show in the gallery, his own subway graffiti drawings having quickly risen to the iconic status of Basquiat and Diaz's SAMO. Proclaiming that the street style amounted to a form of "visual terrorism" that could lead "towards a possible cultural revolution" in the publicity for the exhibition, Brathwaite and Futura 2000 included pieces by Dondi, Haring, Lady Pink, Iggy Pop, Rammellzee, Lee Quiñones, SAMO, Alan Suicide [Vega], and Zephyr plus graffiti photographer Martha Cooper alongside their own.[10] Coordinated by Brathwaite and plugged as a "very special hip hop rap jam," the 9 April opening party showcased Busy Bee, the Cold Crush Brothers, the Jazzy Five, and Afrika Bambaataa. Scores of teenagers armed with cans of Krylon showed up from the Bronx as well as the nearby Jacob Riis Housing Projects to meet their pioneer heroes and tag the venue's walls before heading to the depots. "Nobody had heard or seen anything like it," reminisces Brathwaite. "These clubs were 95 percent white on any given night, so when you had a lot of young African American males and Puerto Ricans in the mix it just changed the dynamics — and that was a good thing."

Brathwaite's decision to hire Bambaataa to play to the newly forming art-punk-graffiti-discotheque crowd was perfectly judged, the DJ having come to see party culture as a means to promote peace. "I always thought music could cross racial barriers," Bambaataa says of his odyssey from gang culture to the formation of the Zulu Nation. "*American Bandstand* was all white and then after a while you'd have black stars singing to an all-white audience. I was thinking, if they hate each other, how come they're vibing to the music?" The opposition to the Vietnam War, the murder of student demonstrators at Kent State University, the protests of the inmates at the Attica Correctional Facility, the countercultural movement's message of peace, and the damage caused by gang violence strengthened the DJ's resolve. "When it was my time I said, 'I want to try to bridge the gap between all the nationalities,'" he adds. "I wanted everyone to dance under one roof — or one nation under a groove, as George Clinton said." Promoting social integration through sonic integration, the DJ soon earned himself the title of "Master of Records." "Bambaataa played everything from Aerosmith to Sly Stone to the Beatles," points out Afrika Islam. "I heard the Clash before I knew who they were, 'Trans Europe Express' before I even knew where Germany was. He would take thirteen cases of records with him, and he would play everything from soca to Fela Kuti and Miriam Makeba to the Rolling Stones to the Plasmatics. There was no limit."

When Brathwaite met onetime Hurrah manager Arthur Weinstein, who opened the Jefferson as an illustriously decorated after-hours spot in an abandoned theater on 14th Street on New Year's Eve 1980, he persuaded him to book Bambaataa, having met the DJ during one of his documentary recon-

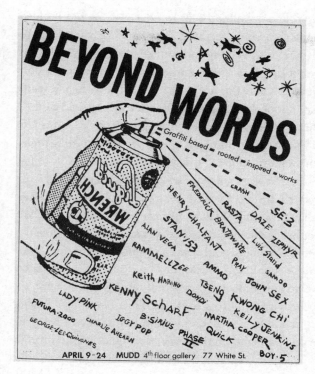

Poster for *Beyond Words*. Designed by and courtesy of Fred "Fab 5 Freddy" Brathwaite.

naissance trips to the Bronx. "Arthur Weinstein used to put together these really stylish after-hours venues that had fifties and sixties motifs," recalls Brathwaite. "I told him, 'Flash is fast but Afrika Bambaataa would be the best hip hop guy to play at the Jefferson because he has the broadest spectrum of music.' He would play the Beatles and the Stones and the Monkees and Fela and James Brown, and he'd incorporate all of these influences into his rap parties in the Bronx." The crowd tuned into the DJ's aesthetic without bowing at his feet or jumping through the roof. "It wasn't like people were running around saying, 'Who's the DJ?'" remembers Brathwaite. "People just wanted to be out amongst each other. It was a fun party and people were having a great time dancing." Two or three months later Bambaataa played the *Beyond Words* opening. "I was surprised at first," he says of his reception, "but then I always knew music transcends barriers."

The show challenged a skeptical art world to acknowledge that graffiti amounted to more than tagging and signatures — that it went "beyond words." "I think they [the writers] are producing some of the best work by young artists today," a supportive Leo Castelli told writer Steven Hager, who had purchased a Futura 2000 photograph at *New York/New Wave* and decided there and then to research the culture further. "They have the talent to make it in the art world; all they need is the opportunity."[11] But while Mass was pleased to integrate graffiti into his spot because it was "part of the whole cultural fabric," he wasn't especially taken with the Wild Style form and made swift moves to have staff remove the guerrilla artwork that kids had daubed on his venue's walls during the opening — according to Haring because he was fearful that graffiti wars were "converging" on the venue, according to the owner because he "didn't want the club to be defined by Jean-Michel Basquiat or Keith or the graffiti artists."[12] Mass judged Haring's graffiti to be "totally different" yet also observed that the artist would "clam up" in his presence. Magnuson confirms that as far as she and the likes of Haring were concerned, "We were young kids who didn't like authority and he was an authority figure."

Haring quit soon after, convinced that Mass was about to fire him anyway and confident that he could start to earn a living from his work, given that he had recently sold some drawings for decent money. Continuing his curatorial work, the Pennsylvanian artist organized *Two Black Light Nights* at Club 57 on 1 and 4 June 1981, and he encouraged Brathwaite to bring in Bambaataa to play the second night. Bambaataa's selection of Richie Rivera's remix of Anita Ward's "Ring My Bell" went down particularly well with the giggly crowd. Then, a month later, Jim Fouratt booked Bambaataa to play at his New Music Seminar showcase after he told a hipster friend that he wanted to bring "more U.S. experimental black acts" to play at the Underground and the friend mentioned the Bronx DJ to him.[13] Mark Kamins advised Fouratt that if he booked Bam he'd get the Zulu Nation tribe as well. "Jim, think black be-in," added the DJ, remembers Fouratt.

Meanwhile Basquiat came away from the PS1 show convinced he needed to quit Gray if he wanted to make it as a famous painter, recalls Michael Holman, and that marked the end of the band as a live entity. The previous summer the Brooklyn artist had taken on the role of playing himself in *New York Beat*, released many years later as *Downtown 81*, a semifictional movie that veered between neorealism and urban fairytale. Parisian designer and Mudd Club regular Maripol, along with her Swiss photographer boyfriend Edo Bertoglio, had come up with the idea to capture the downtown scene. Basquiat became involved after Glenn O'Brien became producer, insisted his friend become the movie's lead, and rewrote the script. "He was a star," O'Brien notes. "So I put him in the starring role of the film *Downtown 81*, playing a kid trying to make it as an artist. For the first time he had enough money to make pictures on canvas and good paper, and a place to sleep where he had the key. I knew

Keith Haring and Dany Johnson, 1981. "We were dressed
for a photo shoot for *SoHo News*," says Dany Johnson. "We
were supposed to look like conservative suburbanites. The
other couples were Ande [Whyland] with Diego Cortez and
Stacey Elkin with Jack Smith." Photograph by and courtesy
of Ande Whyland ©.

he was great — he was electric. A tesla coil with dreadlocks — cool fire emanat-
ing wherever he went."[14]

With Bertoglio directing, the film's loose narrative follows Basquiat's attempt to sell a painting after his landlord evicts him from his apartment. After
he finds a wealthy buyer who will only write him a check, he drops by Gray's
rehearsal studio, only to discover Holman tied up and the band's equipment
stolen. Basquiat stumbles into the likes of Fred Brathwaite, Arto Lindsay,
David McDermott, Steve Mass, Amos Poe, and Lee Quiñones as well as live

performances by James White and the Blacks, Kid Creole and the Coconuts, and rapper Kool Kyle Starchild/DJ partner Sinbad as he searches for the gear as well as a German model he met earlier in the day. Finally he chances on a bag lady (played by Debbie Harry, who had already appeared in Poe's *Foreigner*). When he kisses Harry, she turns into a princess and gives him a million dollars in cash as a reward. "I think he thought about art magically," O'Brien noted in a later conversation with Diego Cortez and Jeffrey Deitch, referencing Basquiat's use of masks, voodoo priests, and other Haitian symbols in his work. "I see the movie as magic. He was a hougan [a male priest in Haitian voodoo]."[15]

As the production progressed, Diego Cortez arranged for Basquiat to stage his first solo show with Bischofberger rival Emilio Mazzoli, in Modena, Italy, in May. The Brooklyn artist returned to give a sit-down dinner at John's, a family-style Italian restaurant on East 12th Street, for Glenn O'Brien, Diego Cortez, Futura, Keith Haring, Arto Lindsay, John Lurie, and Suzanne Mallouk that left his guests "sort of amazed and dazed, realizing Jean was about to do big things," recalls Brathwaite.[16] Basquiat then joined the other members of Gray in the studio in early June to record "Drum Mode," a tense, minimalist, percussive piece for the opening scene of *New York Beat*. The artist attempted to capture the maelstrom of the band on his mix of the track, but the result was an "acoustic mess," says Holman, who claims that he and Nick Taylor "fixed it up." Soon after, however, an Italian corruption scandal led the film's major backer to withdraw from the venture just as it was going through its final edit. "We were just a drop of water," comments Maripol. "I thought it was not meant to be."[17] Basquiat wasn't bothered, having already started to wonder if the film might detract from his artist trajectory.

Running in parallel to the making and unmaking of *New York Beat*, European public-service broadcasters Channel 4 (the United Kingdom) and ZDF (Germany) provided Charlie Ahearn and Fred Brathwaite with $75,000 to make their film—this after the Corporation for Public Broadcasting had turned the duo down, commenting that they "didn't know the garbage on the train was an art movement."[18] The European support affirmed Brathwaite's decision to pursue the film in the first place. "I knew it would be at least accepted in other places around the world because these people had embraced and understood the music we were making and put musicians like Max [Roach] . . . on a par with the greatest European musicians ever," he commented later. "I felt that these people would at least appreciate the things we were doing, because at that time it was not in any way appreciated by mainstream culture here in America."[19]

Fred "Fab 5 Freddy" Brathwaite after the filming of *TV Party*, 1980. Photograph by and courtesy of Bobby Grossman ©.

With Ahearn directing, producing, and writing, the cast featured Lee Quiñones and Lady Pink as the romantically involved leads along with rapper Busy Bee Starski; pioneering breakers the Rock Steady Crew; Bronx MC crew the Cold Crush Brothers; Grandmaster Flash; virtuoso scratcher Grand Mixer D.ST.; graffiti artist Zephyr; plus Patti Astor (who plays a reporter), Fred Brathwaite (an impresario), and Glenn O'Brien (a museum curator). "Most of the characters in the movie are doing what they do in real life," observed Brathwaite. In contrast to *Fort Apache, the Bronx*, a crime drama starring Paul Newman released in February, the absence of pimps, hustlers, and criminals aimed to show that "there's a lot more happening in the Bronx," added the Brooklyn graffiti artist.[20] A skeptical Pink wondered if Ahearn was "just another entrepreneur trying to profit from graffiti," but as filming unfolded during the autumn she concluded that he was a "real sweetheart."[21]

Astor's inclusion epitomized the way borough-downtown meetings were becoming almost commonplace. Raised by physician parents in a family where strong, politicized women who knew how to dress were predominant, she had opted to study at Barnard College rather than another Ivy League institution because of its proximity to the Fillmore East. Immersing herself in radical politics, she became embroiled in confrontations that led her to be arrested and jailed three times, after which she left and then returned to New

York, determined to become a movie star. A face-to-face meeting with Amos Poe led to an appearance in *Unmade Beds*, a 1976 new wave remake of Jean-Luc Godard's *Breathless*, and numerous other films, including *Snakewoman* (L'Hotsky, 1977), *The Foreigner* (Poe, 1978), *Rome '78* (Nares, 1978), *Kidnapped* (Mitchell, 1978), *Long Island Four* (Grafstrom, 1980), and *Underground U.S.A.* (Mitchell, 1980) — the latter a punk version of *Sunset Boulevard* that screened at St. Mark's Cinema for six months. Then she met Brathwaite at a downtown party — the social setting from which so many things seemed to spring — and listened on as the artist told her that she was his favorite movie star and asked for her autograph.

Astor only started to pay proper attention to graffiti after Brathwaite invited her to the opening of *Beyond Words*. Like many of her peers, she had managed to more or less miss the subway art phenomenon because she "walked everywhere," only cramming into a cab with friends every now and again when she needed to go farther afield. The scale of the graffiti phenomenon even remained a mystery after she met and befriended Keith Haring, the artist having approached her while she was walking through Astor Place to ask if he could take her photograph. But at the Mudd Club show she clocked something that hadn't been so apparent to her at the *New York/New Wave* exhibition. "PS1 was a bit more diluted," she explains. "'Beyond Words' was when the hip hop scene came downtown. Afrika Bambaataa was the DJ and that was the first time I saw these little kids armed with these spray cans ready to go out to bomb. It was, 'OK, this is what's happening now.'" Having become friendly with Basquiat before she knew he was an artist, Astor searched out a quiet spot with him on the first of the *Black Light* nights at Club 57. "We were both tripping on mushrooms so we just went into these bushes," she reminisces. "We were like little kids and we had our own playground." When the artist confided that he made $30,000 from his show in Modena, they fantasized about how he was going to become king of Egypt.

A childhood friend of Ahearn's — their families used to go on vacation together by a lake outside Binghamton in upstate New York — Astor badgered the director for the part of the female reporter who wants to explore the South Bronx party scene, only to be told she wasn't mousey enough for the part. The actor calculated that Ahearn was stalling, maybe because he hoped Debbie Harry would fill the role, but when she bumped into him at the second annual Sugar Hill Rap Convention held in Harlem she left an impression. "Patti was wearing a silver jumpsuit and she was probably the only white woman there," he recalls. "She was really throwing out her stardom vibes. People were moving out of her path and staring at her like she was made of gold."[22] Astor and

Ahearn then found themselves taking the same subway home after gunshots broke up the party, and later that night he told her she had the part. "The character she plays in the film is the same character she was playing that night at the rap convention," he notes.[23]

Inspired by the way Haring was already "doing all these one-off shows" and "never cared if anything sold, or if the works were on paper, or if people turned up or if they didn't," Astor made a lighthearted move into the gallery world after Futura told her he wanted to give her a painting. The actor had befriended the graffiti artist along with Dondi and Zephyr when she saw them standing in front of the Peppermint Lounge one night and offered to get them in, but instead of accepting Futura's offer she asked him if he would create a mural in her Third Street apartment — because "in the graffiti world a mural was more prized and special than something that could be bought or sold."[24] They agreed that Futura would spend a morning creating the work, which would then be unveiled during an art opening and barbecue in the afternoon. In the end Kenny Scharf joined in as well, customizing Astor's blender, toaster, and clock, before Basquiat, Brathwaite, Dondi, and Haring along with perhaps five more friends joined them for beer, ribs, and joints. Then, to Astor's shock, Diego Cortez and a besuited Jeffrey Deitch climbed out of a cab, wove their way through the rubbish-strewn sidewalk, and knocked on the door of her apartment. "She got a big kick out of it," recalls Deitch. "She said, 'Now we've made it!' I became a client."

Soon Bill Stelling, a downtown friend who ran a roommate referral service, invited Astor to help him run a makeshift eight-by-twenty-five-foot storefront that was set to open as a gallery on East 11th Street between Second and Third Avenues. Asked if she could recommend an artist for the opening show in August, Astor suggested Steven Kramer and watched on with interest as all twenty of his colored-pencil drawings sold for $50 each. Astor took sole charge of the second show, which opened in September and featured Scharf. Invited by Astor to give the spot a temporary name, Scharf plumbed for the Fun Gallery. "When the roof fell in before Kenny's show, we didn't even have time to clean it up," she remembers. "We just left it there. People were climbing over all this wet cement to get into the door and they were like, 'What a great installation!'"

Scharf only sold one drawing but his Fun Gallery moniker stuck when Astor asked Brathwaite to stage the next show and rename the spot for its duration, only to balk at his suggestion of the Serious Gallery as well as wonder about the cost of creating new stationery for every show. "There was never a discussion like, 'Well, shall we show graffiti art?'" Astor notes of the selection

Futura and Patti Astor at their "art opening and barbecue," 3rd Street, 1981.
Photograph by and courtesy of Anita Rosenberg ©.

process. "We just wanted to show the new art and picked the artists that we really liked. So we had Fred next, since he had been so influential in my life and everything." Held in October and plugged via a $500 ad in *Artforum*, the show amounted to the first solo effort by a graffiti artist in the United States. Meanwhile Astor made the most of working on Ahearn's film. "That's where I picked up all my inside knowledge on graffiti," she recounted later. "All of these writers were sitting around with nothing to do but tell stories."[25]

Other galleries had already challenged the system. Located on Greene Street in SoHo, the 112 Workshop supported the process-oriented work of artists such as Gordon Matta-Clark. Located on Wooster Street, also in SoHo, AIR gallery opened as the first co-op for female artists. Operating out of TriBeCa, Artists Space provided young artists with a nonprofit home. Better known as Colab, Collaborative Projects formed as a not-for-profit artist collective before it staged exhibitions such as the *Manifesto Show*, the *Real Estate Show*, and the *Times Square Show*. Anticipating Astor's work with graffiti artists, the Bronx-based Fashion Moda sought to "challenge the assumption that art is an elitist thing" by "bringing a community of people and artists together," as founder Stefan Eins told the *New York Times*.[26] A precursor to the Fun Gallery in terms of its East Village location and community ethos, Group Material opened as a community-oriented activist gallery in a storefront on East 13th Street. Then came Astor and Stelling, who brought together elements of Fashion Moda (of which they were very aware) and Group Material (of which they were much less aware), mixing both with a splash of Mudd Club and *Wild Style* for good measure.

Fashion Moda had already ramped up its activity as John Ahearn made plaster casts of Bronx locals in the spring of 1979, the Ladies Auxiliary Wrestling team performed there in the spring of 1980, Charlie Ahearn showed the *Deadly Art of Survival* around the same time, its members coproduced the *Times Square Show* in the summer, Jane Dickson created the cardboard installation *City Maze* with neighborhood kids contributing tags in September of 1980, and the nineteen-year-old Johnny "Crash" Matos curated a *Graffiti Art Success for America* show in October, prompting the *East Village Eye* to argue that graffiti had "become a kind of symbol of success" for "non-white and illegal art."[27] Having met Crash through Lee Quiñones, Brathwaite appeared in the show alongside the likes of Ali, Futura 2000, Lady Pink, Quiñones, Zephyr, Crash himself, and John Fekner, whose politicized phrases had become the backdrop to a speech Ronald Reagan gave in the Bronx in 1979. Brathwaite also tapped up Crash for possible locations where he and Charlie Ahearn could film *Wild Style*. Then, in December, Fashion Moda staged a show that included Ali, Crash, Futura 2000, Lady Pink, Quiñones, Rammellzee, and Zephyr alongside the likes of John Ahearn, Eins, and Haring. When *New York/New Wave* followed in February 1981 "critics compared it unfavourably to Fashion Moda," argues art commentator Sally Webster.[28]

At the beginning of 1981, Group Material ran its most successful show, *The People's Choice*, which displayed objects contributed by local residents with accompanying stories. Then, in the late spring, founding member Tim Rollins recorded an impromptu conversation with a local resident of eighteen years, Richard. "Everybody here on the block wonders—why are you here? What are you all doing this for?" Richard asked, remembering how, for the group's first show, everybody on the block came out to stare at all the white people who turned up. He didn't begrudge the punks, students, and artists who took up residence in the area because they were "broke like everyone else," but he questioned their aesthetic preferences. "All I'm saying is that while a lot of the art and stuff I see happening around here is new and interesting and is kind of directed to the people who live here, I've also seen some real lily-white shit spring up—in art exhibitions, in new bars and eating places—like everywhere," he continued. "It's like a lot of bored people from good backgrounds getting into the bad of the neighborhood. And here we are struggling like hell to get rid of the bad, you know? . . . We find no romance in junk and shit."[29]

In September, Group Material announced amid internal rancor that their tenancy on East 13th Street was about to come to an end, leaving Astor and Stelling to work out their own community template in isolation. "It was like a clubhouse from the beginning," remembers the actor-turned-gallerist. "We were only open to the public for three hours on a Sunday afternoon, but then we would just be there. Everybody'd be hanging out." Brathwaite, Dondi, Futura, Haring, Scharf, and the rest were fixtures from the get-go. Crash and Lady Pink started to head to the Fun Gallery once they got to know Astor through *Wild Style*. Rene Ricard dropped by for a coffee every morning. Sculptor Kiely Jenkins became romantically linked with Astor and showed his work in December. Jeffrey Deitch also returned regularly. "I was into the whole sixties thing, you know, *go with the flow*," adds Astor. "There was never any formal anything. The guys were allowed to do what they wanted to do for their show. I think that's why I was successful with them all. They knew I was with them, I was for them; I was on their side."

The rapport was shaped through music as well as art. "Somebody would always have a boom box," recalls Astor. "I never had a real one. I didn't need to, 'cos these guys were bringing in these things that were like the size of a vw! That's how we heard hip hop. Somebody was out on the street with a boom box — 'Yo, check this out!'" Graffiti kids descended on the gallery from the Brathwaite show onward, the school system having given up on them, at least as far as Astor could tell. "They didn't have the art and music classes I remembered from the public schools of my youth," she notes. "From rap, break dancing, and graffiti, they had created a culture of their own. Their piece books were filled with drawings they labored over unceasingly, designs (outlines) for planned subway or wall murals and 'tags' by their idols such as Zephyr, Dondi, Futura, Keith, and Fab 5. If the writers came in, the graffiti kids would swarm them." Astor's receptiveness to good times and glamor also struck a neighborhood chord. "I was always asked to do my 'Astor' tag and kept a special gold marker for the occasions," she recalls.[30]

The good vibes darkened only when Astor learned that Basquiat had taken up residence in Annina Nosei's SoHo gallery and was contributing to her forthcoming *Public Address* show, scheduled for late October. Nosei had passed over Basquiat's wall at *New York/New Wave*, but when she met Diego Cortez in Berlin after the Brooklyn artist's Mazzoli show she announced she wanted to represent the artist. Unsure if it would be the right move for Basquiat, Cortez returned to New York two weeks later to discover he had already started to work for Nosei and at that point Basquiat stopped returning his calls. "He wouldn't speak to me, and it was just, like, over, you know?" remembers Cortez.[31] Astor raged at the "pieceworker" arrangement that saw Nosei house Basquiat in her basement, pay him $1,000 for each painting, and treat him like a "performing seal" when she brought collectors to meet him.[32] Brathwaite also criticized the situation. "I said, 'A black kid painting in the basement. It's not good, man,'" he recalls. "But Jean knew he was playing with this wildman thing. Annina would let these collectors in, and he would turn, with the brush in the hand, all wet, and walk towards them . . . real *quick*."[33]

SoHo wasn't incapable of hosting black culture in a nonexploitative way. Beginning his stint as music director of the Kitchen the previous September, the African American composer, trombonist, and member of the Association for the Advancement of Creative Musicians George Lewis curated a program that helped to "shift the debate around border crossing to a stage where whiteness-based constructions of American experimentalism were being fundamentally problematized."[34] Other black musicians who had established a dissonant-dissident presence in the area through the so-called loft jazz scene retained a foothold as that movement ground to a halt. (Bernie Gendron maintains that "for all practical purposes" the jazz loft scene was "dead" by 1980.)[35] Meanwhile the Loft and the Paradise Garage continued to welcome thousands of black and Latino/a dancers into the area over the course of a weekend. But SoHo's art scene lagged behind its music scene, and for those who wanted to shake up the status quo the East Village was very much the place to be. As far as Astor was concerned, the Fun had only just begun.

DOWNTOWN CONFIGURES HIP HOP

Paralleling the downtown art/borough graffiti encounter, Bronx-based DJs, MCs, and even breakers started to appear on the stages where punk, new wave, and no wave bands were continuing to explore the outer reaches of live performance. Flash and the Sugar Hill roster led the way, which made sense to audiences already familiar with rapping as well as the sight of musicians jamming up a storm. A short while later, Bambaataa took to the stage along with Zulu Nation MCs, the Rock Steady Crew, and a graffiti artist, which was a little more surreal, given that the only instrument in sight was a turntable. Along the way, breakers from the Bronx and Brooklyn started to show off their skills to disbelieving spectators in Manhattan. Then, toward the end of the year, a tiny club spot became the first to dedicate a regular night to the distinctive yet overlapping elements that were now being referred to as hip hop. The partially imagined culture that Fred Brathwaite wanted to give shape to in *Wild Style* was becoming a cohesive entity.

Sylvia Robinson staged the first of the breakthrough events on 11 March at the Ritz. The Funky 4 + 1 More set the Sugar Hill review rolling, the guys wearing white turtleneck suits and Sha-Rock dressed in fuchsia pants, a matching vest, and a ribbed sweater. Sequence, Spoonie Gee, and guest artist Coati Mundi followed in a parade of autobiographical boosterism. Then came Flash, who took to the stage dressed in a black cape, followed by the Furious Five, who wore swanky black and white outfits and executed Temptations-style moves that were so sharp the Sugarhill Gang's finale turned out to be anticlimactic. Working the crowd between the acts and after the show, DJ Justin Strauss interspersed rap records with songs such as "I Hear Music in the Streets." Fearful that "the trendists who sit in the trees of the music industry like vultures will soon be ready to swoop down on rap and pick it to the bone as they did with disco in 1978 and 1979," *Dance Music Report* noted that the moment when Flash dedicated the evening to disco and the DJs was "exhilarating."[1] Even skeptics were seduced. "I still change the station when I hear a rap record on the radio," Vince Aletti wrote in the *Village Voice,* having gone back to writing for music after he parted ways with Warner Bros., "but I haven't had this much fun at a concert since I saw the old Motown Revue at the Brooklyn Fox."[2]

Grandmaster Flash & the Furious Five returned to midtown in less conducive circumstances when the Clash began their eight-night run at Bond's and scheduled the Sugar Hill lineup to appear as their first supporting act. What with the overcrowding, tensions were already rippling through the venue when Flash executed a quick-fire mix and the Furious Five joined him dressed in glitzy outfits. "At first the audience seemed bewildered by this single black man using nothing but two record players amid the cacophony [of the venue's faulty sound system]," reported Michael Hill in the *Village Voice.* "Then, as the Furious Five attempted to rap away the technical difficulties, a vocal minority that grew louder as the show progressed shouted the group down and, after one rapper tried to reason with the audience only to be greeted by a hail of paper cups, drove them offstage just as they began 'The Birthday Party' with 'Hey, y'all, we're havin' a ball, hope you're doin' fine."[3] The following night the Furious Five dressed in street clothes and managed to complete their set as they side-stepped the somewhat less intense volley of paper cups. "But this time they weren't 'havin' a ball' and told the audience so," noted Hill.[4]

The incident reflected badly on the audience. "Aside from the losers who felt they had to throw stuff because they were at 'a punk show' and such behavior was expected, the only reason there was any disappointment by the audience in those shows was because American kids tend to be spoiled," reasons Carol Cooper, who attended the show. "They were of an age and a mindset that led them to believe that the only thing worthy of their attention was the thing they thought was exclusively 'theirs.' These kids were coming to hear 'White Riot,' thinking lyrics like 'I want a riot of my own' advocated separatism when they really alluded to oppressed whites feeling a rebellious kinship with oppressed minorities." Yet the meltdown also unfolded because of the casual approach of the organizers, who made partial amends for neglecting to give Flash and the Furious Five a proper introduction when they welcomed the Treacherous Three as friends of the Clash during a subsequent show. Rapper Kool Moe Dee then consolidated the rapport by delivering a rhyme about the Clash. Looking back on the Bond's flare-up in September, Flash conceded that he and the Furious Five had been too flamboyant, given that the kids in the audience were "prejudiced." If asked to do it again, he would do his homework on what Clash fans wanted to hear and try his best to be flexible, "rather than just go on playing disco, which they can't relate to."[5]

Michael Holman doesn't remember how he came to organize the next major demonstration of Bronx party power in Manhattan: a Zulu Nation show at the Ritz that became the first to present DJ-ing, MC-ing, breaking, and graffiti as one integrated culture (breaking having been absent at the *Beyond Words* opening). But his diary records that on 5 February he filmed a breaker dancing on Plexiglas paneling, on 22 April he met the breaking outfit International Break Masters (IBM), on 22 May he called Bambaataa, on 23 May he went to hear Bambaataa DJ at the T-Connection, on 27 May he met Fred Brathwaite at the Mudd Club, on 28 May he went to see Bambaataa DJ at the Peppermint Lounge, on 8 June he filmed IBM at the Mudd Club, on 15 August he shot a breaking battle between the Rock Steady Crew and the Dynamic Rockers at the Lincoln Center, and on 21 August he phoned the *East Village Eye* to discuss publishing a photojournalism story on the Lincoln Center battle plus an interview with Bambaataa. If Brathwaite's first connection to the scene was graffiti, Holman's was turning out to be the dance.

Breaking had grown out of rocking, or up-rocking, a Latin-based, citywide style that included moves such as the jerk, a four-step sequence that saw dancers drop down and spring back up on the third and fourth count of the bar while battling their opponent through gestural insult and mimed attack. Brooklynites argue that Apache and Rubberband pioneered the style in Bushwick in 1968, but Willie "Marine Boy" Estrada, a Puerto Rican–born dancer who grew up alongside Rubberband in the South Bronx, points out that Rubberband was a "Bronx native before his mother moved to Brooklyn in the early seventies." Deepening the Bronx connection, Kool Herc coined the term "b-boy" to describe two young brothers called Kevin and Keith who — dressed in Pro-Keds, double-knit pants, windbreakers, and hats — evolved the dance style of James Brown at his Sedgwick Avenue parties. "There was no such thing as b-boys when we arrived," one of the brothers recalled later, "but Herc gave us that tag."[6] Integrating moves they'd witnessed in 1970s kung fu movies, b-boys and b-girls went on to embrace the nonviolent competitiveness of the mobile sound systems, with the Zulu Kings of the Zulu Nation the first to travel around the Bronx in search of rivals to battle. "When the music hit, the Holy Ghost got inside of us and breakdancing developed," comments Afrika Islam, the thirteenth member of the Zulu Kings. "We didn't slip on a soap bar. We had musical influences that went back to entertainers like James Brown plus there was this heavy Latin influence in the South Bronx."

Breakers preferred to dance in front of others, tagging in and out of a circle one at a time, often to the anthem "It's Just Begun," which opens with the apposite lines "Watch me now/Feel the groove/Into something/Gonna make you move." In fact breakers had minimal opportunity to "feel the groove," so short was their stay in the center, which helps explain hip hop critic Joe Schloss's observation that breaking's six-step foundational move was often performed out of time with the music.[7] With many of them too young to get into a nightclub, they combined peacock athleticism, flexibility, stamina, and bravado to establish their worth, navigate deprivation, and have some fun. Outsiders, meanwhile, struggled to read the exchange, so when *New York Post* staff photographer and graffiti documentarian Martha Cooper went to shoot a riot that was unfolding in Washington Heights in January 1980, she arrived at the scene to find a bunch of teenage boys sitting in the police station inside the subway with hangdog faces. They told her they had just been dancing. "I thought this was a great story, so I called the *Post* editors and said, 'They weren't having a riot, they were having a dance contest,'" recalls Cooper. "But the *Post* didn't like the idea. No riot, no story."[8]

Determined to capture the action on camera, Cooper contacted University of Pennsylvania folklorist professor and Bowery resident Barbara Kirshenblatt-Gimblett, who advised her to contact PhD student and *SoHo News* contributor Sally Banes. Cooper returned to Washington Heights with Banes to hunt down a breaking crew to photograph, interview, and invite to perform at a forthcoming conference on the Bronx organized by the New York Folklore Society, only to be told by the kids who had participated in the nonriot that they were now into rollerskating and that breaking was over. Others repeated the line until Cooper thought to ask Henry Chalfant if he could help, having befriended the graffiti documentarian during his OK Harris exhibition. Chalfant was preparing for another show, this one planned for SoHo performance space Common Ground, where he planned to include MC-ing alongside his slideshow in order to boost the performative element. Chalfant put the breaker question to graffiti artist Take 1, who proceeded to tell the photographer about the time he did eight head spins on the Staten Island Ferry. "The next day he showed up with Crazy Legs and Frosty Freeze of the Rock Steady Crew," Chalfant recalled in a 1982 interview with the *East Village Eye*.[9] Banes and Cooper now had their documentary evidence while Chalfant had another element for his Common Ground show.

With Cooper contributing photos, Banes published her trailblazing feature on breaking in the *Village Voice* in April 1981. "Breaking is a way of using your body to inscribe your identity on streets and trains, in parks and high school gyms," she wrote. "It is a physical version of two favorite modes of street rhetoric, the taunt and the boast. It is a celebration of the flexibility and budding sexuality of the gangly male adolescent body. . . . But most of all, breaking is a competitive display of physical and imaginative virtuosity, a codified dance-form-cum-warfare that cracks open to flaunt personal inventiveness." Banes identified the basic movements of the breaker: the stylized walk of the entry, the circular movements of the one-hand turn, the urbane pose of the freeze, and the exit. "Part of the macho quality of breaking comes from the physical risk involved," she continued. "It's not only the bruises, scratches, cuts, and scrapes. As the rivalry between the crews heats up, ritual combat sometimes erupts into fighting for real. And part of it is impressing the girls." Banes added that, like graffiti and rapping, which amounted to parallel expressions of ghetto street culture, "breaking is a public arena for the flamboyant triumph of virility, wit, and skill. In short, of style."[10]

The Banes article was the first to connect breaking, graffiti, and rapping, as Jeff Chang points out, yet it contained no mention of hip hop and only a fleeting reference to DJ-ing — probably because breakers spent a good proportion of their time away from the party setting, turning to boom boxes for music.[11] Indeed, Ahearn and Brathwaite didn't come across breaking crews when they started to head to Bronx parties to research *Wild Style*, and even when its practitioners did head to a DJ-led party, they danced alongside free-stylers, hustlers, poppers, and lockers. "Everybody who could breakdance could hustle as well so if a classic disco record came on, you grabbed a girl," recalls Islam. "And sometimes if you put on some breakdance records, people were still hustling anyway because most of those b-boy records were only the breaks of a disco record anyway." DJs also had to play to the wider party. "We were constantly looking for new breaks to play because they energized the dance floor," adds Long Island mobile DJ Hank Shocklee. "But if your set went on for three hours you might have half-an-hour of breaks when you're rocking it and in-between you'd play all this other good stuff that would get people in the mood, like Jocelyn Brown. We weren't just playing breaks for the b-boys."

If anything, breaking hovered on the periphery of hip hop consciousness when Chalfant invited the Rock Steady Crew along with MCs Fred Brathwaite (Fab 5 Freddy Love) and Rammellzee (an MC as well as a graffiti artist) to prepare for the *Aspects of Performance: Graffiti Rock* slideshow scheduled for 3 May plus two further dates.[12] But instead of ushering breaking into its first public combination with graffiti, MC-ing, and DJ-ing — because as Chalfant told the *East Village Eye*, the Banes-Cooper article led him to be "deluged" by the media — the photographer was forced to cancel the event when a gang showed up to settle a beef during the Saturday dress rehearsal.[13] Even so, the Chalfant initiative had enabled Banes and Cooper to locate the breaking scene and they proceeded to call on the Rock Steady Crew to illustrate the talk they gave at the Bronx folk culture conference, held at the Lehman College Center for the Performing Arts in the Bronx in mid-May.[14] "Breaking was on the wane and the *Voice* article revived it," claims Cooper. "Even though many kids both wrote and danced, including breaking with rap music and graffiti was something the media created."

Holman published his own article on breaking in the *East Village Eye* in the summer. Noting that top rockers used theatrical elements to "intimidate or humiliate their dance opponent," and bottom rockers, or breakers, executed spectacular, floor-based "ass spins, head spins, and assorted other contortions," he concluded that crews such as IBM were "so incredibly talented and innovative" he couldn't understand "why they haven't made modern dance an obsolete concept."[15] Holman went on to "film the hell" out of an outdoor battle between the Dynamic Rockers and the Rock Steady Crew, staged on 15 August by Chalfant in the refined setting of the Lincoln Center; the Rock Steady Crew torched the Dynamic Rockers during the up-rocking part of the contest but struggled to keep up when they went to the floor, he recalls. Then Stan Peskett introduced him to Malcolm McLaren at a Canal Zone party, because the ex–Sex Pistols manager wanted to know more about rap culture, and Holman suggested they travel to watch Bambaataa play in the Bronx. "I thought the world of Malcolm and I knew somehow that introducing him to Bambaataa would be important — that it would be a game changer," comments Holman. "We exchanged info and I'm like buzzing." Holman called Bambaataa as soon as he got home. "He didn't know about Malcolm McLaren, but he knew about punk rock and the Sex Pistols. So I said, 'When's your next throwdown, your next park jam?' It was a couple of days away."

On 29 August, Holman went to pick up McLaren and RCA's A&R rep Rory Johnston at the Park and Meridian Hotel on Park Avenue and 56th Street. Holman, dressed for the occasion in khakis, a nylon T-shirt, and a nylon tank top, or the kind of outfit that would help him avoid being "vicked," or "victimized," almost gagged when his guests emerged wearing outfits that made them look like "pirate clowns on acid." After struggling to even find a cab driver who

Rock Steady Crew's Take One breaks at Lincoln Center, 15 August 1981. Photograph by and courtesy of Martha Cooper ©.

was willing to drive to the Bronx, they made their way from the closest drop-off point into the Bronx River Community Center, which was at the center of a cluster of giant project buildings. "There were probably a thousand kids, predominantly boys, with an average age of fourteen or fifteen, I'd say 70 percent black, 25 percent Puerto Rican, and 5 percent white, and they were all going wild dancing to Bambaataa's music," recalls Holman. "As we walked in we would witness a fight break out and then a whole mass of kids would run to see the fight, and then another fight would break out and they'd rush to that one. Bottles were flying out of the windows from the council flats with people shouting, 'Turn the music off!'" McLaren's jaw dropped and his eyes widened as he turned to Holman and said, "Oh my god, Michael, we've got to get out of here!"

Bambaataa surprised Holman and McLaren when he selected Hugh Montenegro's "Jeannie" — the theme song for the TV sitcom *I Dream of Jeanie* —

and they shook their heads some more when the kids started to dance ar-rhythmically instead of funkily to the track, as if they were emulating white kids, because the record didn't obviously fit into an outdoor jam, notes Hol-man. Then the DJ switched to the Monkees' "Mary, Mary," replaying the be-ginning section again and again, and although the dancers wouldn't have known who the Monkees were, they could tell it was a white rock sound and started pogoing. But Holman became nervous that McLaren was still dis-tracted, so he turned to Bambaataa and said, "We're losing this guy, you need to get Jazzy Jay on the turntables." McLaren observed Bambaataa and his as-sistants "acting almost like witchdoctors, struggling with these decks, turning records around, and using the needle like a guitar, scratching certain grooves, and spinning them backwards and forwards," while other guys "were handing each other microphones and suddenly stepping into the throng and starting to tell stories," he recalled later.[16] Then, escorted by three of Bam's guys, they made their exit, having stuck around for maybe half an hour. As their cab drove toward Manhattan, McLaren turned to Holman and said, "Here's what I want you to do. I want you to put on a show to open up for Bow Wow Wow at the Ritz." Once again Bronx party culture was set to breach Manhattan in a Tro-jan Horse called new wave.

Working with a $3,000 budget, Holman opened the 15 September show with a screening of his five-minute breaker film *Catch a Beat*, the first of its kind, and a graffiti artist at work. The intensity stepped up when Bambaataa took to the decks, Ikey Cee and the Soul Sonic Force grabbed some mikes, and the Rock Steady Crew stormed the stage, Holman having tracked them down following the Lincoln Center battle. The performance closed with Jazzy Jay quick-cutting on the turntables. "It was the first hip hop show with all the elements put together," claims Holman, correctly, even if Fred Brathwaite had hatched the idea with Charlie Ahearn. "There had been shows before — rap shows at the T-Connection, rap shows at the Fever — but they didn't have breakdancers and graffiti. I put all those things together." Along the way, adds Holman, he and others made an anthropological error they had no reason to regret. "Hip hop's something us downtown kids thought was going on up-town and we wanted to bring it downtown, but all these elements were all disparate elements," he argues. "Rappers didn't hang out with breakers and breakers didn't hang out with graffiti artists. Downtown kids created a sub-culture by mistake. We were toying with evolution."

Bambaataa's warm-up show didn't earn a mention in the *New York Times* review of the night, but the Zulu Nation leader remembers Annabella from Bow Wow Wow "really feeling" the Zulu Nation's high-intensity performance

ruza blue

Ruza Blue at Danceteria,
1984. Photograph by
and courtesy of Rhonda
Paster ©.

as well as McLaren being "amazed" at the range of music. A onetime regular at Rusty Egan's and Steve Strange's New Romantic, pioneering Blitz Club in London, Ruza Blue also bugged out, having traveled to New York to "check out the punk scene" earlier that spring. "I couldn't believe my eyes it was so extraordinary," she reminisces. "Here was a DJ totally mashing up all these different styles of music, these dancers spinning on their heads, and an MC cheering them all on and entertaining the crowd with interactive gestures and shout-outs. It was so different and so cutting-edge." By this point Blue had picked up work with Malcolm McLaren and Vivienne Westwood, and along with a friend (Nina Huang) she had also taken over the Thursday-night slot at a dub-reggae spot located on Second Avenue and 11th Street called Club Negril from Clash manager Kosmo Vinyl. Now, as the Zulu Nation left the stage, she approached Holman and told him she "wanted to book all his Bronx talent at the club." Hip hop — barely conscious of its new unity — was about to get a weekly showcase.

Blue and Huang relaunched their night on 24 September, two weeks after the Ritz show, turning to Holman to facilitate the creative element. He threw himself into the task, hiring Bambaataa, Fred Brathwaite, Futura, Jazzy Jay, the Rock Steady Crew, and Rammellzee to create a storm of DJ-ing, MC-ing, breaking, and graffiti, and renting TV monitors so he could run *Catch a Beat* on loop. He even arranged for Nick Taylor to make a cameo appearance as DJ High Priest that saw him scratch and cut records in time with a taped loop of funky beats, which he ran into the system via a reel-to-reel. "I called the talent, I made the flyer, I set up the space," notes Holman. Viewing downtown to be an "archaeological site" within a "city of ruins" where Roman gods wandered around, the up-and-coming Italian neorealist artist Francesco Clemente joined a crowd that was very much art-punk in orientation, as did Rene Ricard.[17] "The performers were all hip hop but the people who came were downtown kids," adds Holman. "It was as much a downtown hipster club as a hip hop club."

SELECTED DISCOGRAPHY

AFRIKA BAMBAATAA, NEGRIL (1981)

Abaco Dream, "Life and Death in G & A"

Afrika Bambaataa & the Jazzy 5, "Jazzy Sensation (Bronx Version)"

Babe Ruth, "The Mexican"

The B-52s, "Planet Claire"

Blondie, "Rapture"

Kurtis Blow, "The Breaks"

James Brown, "Funky Drummer"

James Brown, "Funky President (People It's Bad)"

James Brown, "Get Up I Feel Like Being a Sex Machine"

The Busboys, "Did You See Me"

Bobby Byrd, "I Know You Got Soul"

Chic, "Good Times"

Chuck Brown & the Soul Searchers, "Bustin' Loose"

The Clash, "London Calling"

The Clash, "This Is Radio Clash"

Lyn Collins, "Think (about It)"

Manu Dibango, "Soul Makossa"

Dyke and the Blazers, "Let a Woman Be a Woman — Let a Man Be a Man"

Shirley Ellis, "The Clapping Song (Clap Pat Clap Slap)"

ESG, "Moody"

Foreigner, "Urgent"

Aretha Franklin, "Rock Steady"

Free, "All Right Now"

Friend & Lover, "Reach Out of the Darkness"

Funky 4+1 More, "Rappin' and Rocking the House"

Taana Gardner, "Heartbeat (Club Version)"

Glitter Band, "Makes You Blind"

Grandmaster Flash & the Furious Five, "It's Nasty (Genius of Love)"

Eddy Grant, "California Style"

Eddy Grant, "Living on the Frontline"

Daryl Hall & John Oates, "I Can't Go for That (No Can Do)"

Herman Kelly & Life, "Dance to the Drummer's Beat"

Incredible Bongo Band, "Apache"

Bob James, "Take Me to the Mardi Gras"

Rick James, "Super Freak"

Jimmy Castor Bunch, "It's Just Begun"

Joan Jett & the Blackhearts, "I Love Rock 'n Roll"

Grace Jones, "Pull Up to the Bumper"

Kool & the Gang, "Jungle Jazz"

Kraftwerk, "Numbers"

Kraftwerk, "Trans-Europe Express"

Fela Ransome Kuti, "Shakara"

Lakeside, "Fantastic Voyage"

Little Sister, "You're the One"

Michigan & Smiley, "Diseases"

Miracles, "Mickey's Monkey"

The Mohawks, "The Champ"

Gary Numan, "Cars"

The O'Jays, "For the Love of Money"

Prince, "Controversy"

Queen, "We Will Rock You"

Ram Jam, "Black Betty"

Rolling Stones, "Honky Tonk Women"

Rolling Stones, "Start Me Up"

Rufus, featuring Chaka Khan, "Once You Get Started"

Sequence, "Funk You Up"

Slave, "Slide"

Sly & the Family Stone, "Family Affair"

Spoonie Gee and the Treacherous Three, "Love Rap"

Sugarhill Gang, "Rapper's Delight"

Talking Heads, "Once in a Lifetime"

Tom Tom Club, "Genius of Love"

Jazzy Jay at Negril. Photograph by and courtesy of Martha Cooper ©.

Treacherous Three, "Yes We Can Can"
Yellow Magic Orchestra, "Firecracker"
Zapp, "More Bounce to the Ounce"

Holman proceeded to bring in Phase II to design flyers, booked the Cold Crush Brothers to perform, busied himself "calming angry Rastas" who had showed up on the wrong night, and watched on as the Rock Steady Crew became the main attraction. "The crowd were super-supportive, super-curious," notes the facilitator. "They really wanted to see the dancing more than anything. The fact the DJs did special stuff was novel but you could see DJs everywhere. Everyone had seen graffiti on the trains since the mid-seventies plus the rapping was not seen as being something terribly new. But the dancing was seen as radical. That was the draw." But with Bambaataa, Jazzy Jay, and Rock Steady Crew quickly established as fixtures, Blue took on the role of scheduling additional talent after Brathwaite took her up to Disco Fever. "Freddy introduced me to everyone," recalls the promoter, who took down phone numbers as they circulated around Sal Abbatiello's rap hotspot, where a procession of Bronx-based DJs and MCs had made their mark. "He took me to the Fever and that's how Negril got booked from then on." Holman felt jilted but Blue believed she had no reason to pause. "Michael was only involved to the extent of initially providing some talent for the club," she maintains. "He wasn't my partner. He was like an agent. There was no parting of ways because there was never a way in the first place."

Bambaataa, Jazzy Jay, the Rock Steady Crew, and friends didn't miss a beat. "The Zulu Nation was the heart and the nucleus of uptown coming downtown," asserts Afrika Islam. "Then again, Negril was Negril before we got there, and Negril was already a club that played another ethnic sound in lower Manhattan. Hip hop was just the new ethnic sound and it caught on." Switching between names such as "The Corporation," "Sure Shot Party Crew," and "Wheels of Steel," Blue nevertheless thought of her night as a "dance party" rather than a hip hop party. "I was asking the DJs to play all types of music and often would hand them cool vinyl records from Great Britain like Eurythmics, David Bowie, and the Clash," she remarks. "Hip hop happened to be in the mix and I wanted to expose the entire culture within a dance-club environment."

With the likes of Jean-Michel Basquiat, Suzanne Mallouk, and Bruno Bischofberger joining a crowd that was 90 percent white, with the remaining 10 percent made up of Bronx performers and their crews, Negril forged an important connection with a constituency that had never experienced the Loft or the Paradise Garage yet was beginning to crave a more rhythmic form of DJ-ing. "The music immediately blew my mind. So did the way Jazzy Jay and Bambaataa put all of these different types of music together in a cohesive way," reminisces Jonny Sender, raised in Sunnyside, Queens, and Manhattan, who was used to hanging out at spots such as Hurrah, Danceteria, the Mudd Club, and an after-hours hangout called Berlin, and had come to experience a nagging dissatisfaction with the way records were "thrown into the pot" with no sense of an arc. Justin Strauss also thought that Negril was "new" and "fresh." "Bambaataa and I got to be friends," adds the Ritz DJ. "He would hang out at the Ritz with me. He would turn me onto breaks and I'd turn him onto little rock records like Medium Medium, 'Hungry, So Angry.' He was very open to new sounds."

Along with Holman's one-off Ritz show, Negril's Thursday-night Zulu Nation party marked the moment when borough-based DJ-ing, MC-ing, breaking, and graffiti appeared alongside one another in integrated unison for the first time. The hip hop moniker might've dated back to the time when DJ Hollywood coined the line "hip hop de hippy hop the body rock," with Lovebug Starski said to have come up with the coinage around the same time. After that the Sugarhill Gang referenced hip hop as they rolled out the opening couplet of "Rapper's Delight." But none of these usages suggested that DJ-ing, MC-ing, graffiti, and breaking formed an interconnected culture, and Bambaataa recalls that the Bronx party scene "didn't have a name" when it started, with hip hop only gathering conceptual weight as Brathwaite framed *Wild Style* and curated the *Beyond Words* opening and as Chalfant prepared for his *Graffiti Rock* show.[18]

Just as the distinctive parts that came to be known as disco began to take shape and cohere several years before the culture and its music acquired a name during 1974, so hip hop's elements germinated in the Bronx before they were encouraged to share a space and take conceptual form during the early 1980s. Given that Bronx-style DJ-ing, MC-ing, graffiti, and breaking were connected by their emphases on speed, skill, appropriation, improvisation, interruption, dynamism, expression, bravado, and the self, their coming together turned out to be so seamless it appeared peculiar that it hadn't quite happened before. Yet if it seemed counterintuitive that the four elements should coalesce in spaces such as the Mudd Club, the Ritz, and above all Negril rather than the Bronx; it was in downtown New York that a swarm of party-conscious artists, musicians, and filmmakers from all over the city gathered to reinvent culture on a nightly basis, often through the interweaving of different cultural forms. Above all else, downtowners were drawn to the idea of synergy, or the belief that separate elements could resonate with a new and unexpected force when brought together, and so the fashioning of hip hop by the likes of Brathwaite, Holman, and Blue was in many respects rooted in their nightly work. The cultural laboratory was shifting into overdrive.

THE SOUND
OF A TRANSCENDENT
FUTURE

Diminutive and sweet, as his nickname had it, John "Jellybean" Benitez grew up with his mom, who had emigrated from Puerto Rico to the South Bronx during the early 1950s. As a kid he listened to his sister's record collection, checked out Bambaataa and others at local jams, and became an ardent devotee of Walter Gibbons, whose technical skill and emotional range surpassed everyone else he had heard. Obsessed, Benitez joined a subset of Puerto Rican DJs who counted Flamingo stalwart Richie Rivera as its most proficient practitioner. Lacking the connections that helped many Italian DJs get work in Mafia-connected discotheques and many African American DJs become fast friends with record-company promoters, the Latin contingent grouped around Eddie Rivera's record pool, the International Disco Record Center (IDRC), frustrated by the way Salsa strongholds such as Fania cold-shouldered them. When Vince Aletti and Michael Gomes published a state-of-the-union conversation about disco in *Mixmaster* in the summer of 1978, however, they agreed that Benitez was one of the brightest new talents on the scene, and by the end of 1981 he could claim to have become the most prominent Puerto Rican DJ in the city.[1]

Benitez advanced from bright talent to major player after he quit his alternate spot at Xenon in April, disillusioned by the hardening radio preferences of the crowd. When Howard Stein sacked Tony Smith a few weeks later because his resident had refused to play "Happy Birthday" for Bianca Jagger, it began to look like he had timed his exit particularly well, and Stein's ensuing announcement that he wanted to convert Xenon's unused third floor into a "glass-walled disco within a disco" called Xenophobia did nothing to alter that impression.[2] But whereas Smith headed into a cul-de-sac of frustration when he took on work at an Upper East Side pickup joint called Magique — or Tragique, as Tee Scott nicknamed the spot — Benitez swerved to the Funhouse, a struggling spot located on West 26th Street between Tenth and Eleventh Avenues. "I went with the intention of turning it into a late-night party," Benitez notes of his move. "Only the Garage, the Loft, and the Saint went on until 10:00 or 11:00 AM, and I wanted to bring that to the predominantly straight world."

The Puerto Rican DJ's vision appealed to owner Joe Monk, who had planned for the Funhouse to operate as a gay venue when he hired Jim Burgess and Bobby "DJ" Guttadaro to play at his opening-night party back in April 1979, only for a "very singles-oriented" crowd to take to its floor by the time author Vita Miezitis toured the New York club scene to research her 1980 book *Night Dancin'*.[3] By 1981 the singles had given way to a group of sixteen- to nineteen-year-old Italian and Latin dancers who weren't bothered that it didn't sell alcohol, and who positively appreciated its sprawling interior, which featured a clown's-face DJ booth, mirrored walls, and an adjoining video-games room. But when it became clear that Jonathan Fearing was struggling to connect with the teenage borough crowd, Monk turned to Benitez as a fairy-tale alternative, and the Xenon alternate accepted the offer on the basis that the Funhouse would enable him to combine the funk sensibility of his upbringing with the classic disco sound he had cultivated at the midtown spot. His decision coincided with the opening of *Beyond Words* and the publication of the Banes-Cooper feature in the *Village Voice*. The Bronxification of the city — it almost seemed to be synchronized.

Jellybean took to selecting radio-friendly records from 10:00 PM until showtime at 2:00 AM, after which he would peak the floor with records such as Martin Circus ("Disco Circus") and Ian Dury and the Blockheads ("Reasons to Be Cheerful, Pt. 3") through to 6:00 AM, when he would stop the music, kill the lights, and take a breather as the crowd clapped and barked its appreciation. "Then I would start the next part of the evening, which was this sort of throwback in time," he recalls. "That's when I got to play the records that influenced me to become a DJ." Staples included Babe Ruth, "The Mexican"; Booker T., "Melting Pot"; James Brown, "Give It Up or Turnit a Loose"; Manu Dibango, "Soul Makossa"; the Jackson 5, "Hum Along and Dance"; the Jimmy Castor Bunch, "It's Just Begun"; Kraftwerk, "Trans-Europe Express"; M.F.S.B., "Love Is the Message"; and Lonnie Liston Smith, "Expansions." "Jellybean came in with a more purposeful sense of what he wanted to play," notes Brian Chin, who took over the "Disco File" column when Vince Aletti went to work at Warner Bros. "His music was eclectic and exciting."

Within a couple of months the Funhouse started to attract a crowd of 1,800 on Fridays and 2,800 on Saturdays, with some 500 dancers pumping their bodies until 8:00 or 8:30 AM, after which, weather permitting, they would head to the beach to continue the party. The fact that they rolled in from all five boroughs, often as part of tight-knit crews that sported a name, a stylistic identity, and rehearsed dance moves, confirmed that the producers of *Saturday Night Fever* had strayed when they ended their movie by having John Travolta's Tony Manero leave Brooklyn for Manhattan in order to leave the party scene behind and come of age. In fact hardcore suburban dancers were heading to Manhattan for the opposite reason. "The Funhouse changed from being a pick-up bar to a dance club," remarks Jellybean. "I had been playing at the glamour clubs and they were fun, but at the Funhouse I got back into the underground."

Not every DJ had it so good when it came to employer relations, however, and Tee Scott, also raised in the Bronx, as it happens, stepped into a battle too many with his irascible employer toward the end of the year and was told that his nine-year residency at Better Days had just come to an end. "Tee didn't say much," remembers David DePino. "He was very diplomatic. But Larry and I were shocked and felt no matter what had happened, Tee deserved better. He was always a class act." Scott had established an indelible imprint on the New York scene as he mixed every record, interspersing driving selections with slower tracks, and making the most of the floor-level position of the Better Days booth as he eyed his dancers. "Of all the crowds, Better Days was the fiercest," notes François Kevorkian, who filled in for the DJ when invited. "When you played the right Chaka Khan record at the right moment and the queens would lose it, it was so spectacular." He adds: "Tee was a kind, gentle soul and an amazing DJ. He was stylish, powerful, and elegant."

An inexperienced DJ from Binghamton, New York, Bruce Forest stepped into the vacant Better Days booth in late 1981 after he spotted the owner walking across the dance floor, a gun in one hand and a coffee tin filled with money in the other, and asked what was going on with Scott. The owner let out some expletives and offered Forest — an unmistakably white DJ — an audition the next day. "I thought it was hysterical," reminisces Forest. "I told Leslie [Doyle, Forest's DJ girlfriend] about it and she goes, 'Huh, you're going to audition in Tee Scott's club? *Good luck!*' " Debuting before news of Scott's dismissal spread, Forest learned from a regular that his selections had been all wrong — he should have played Jimmy "Bo" Horne's "Spank," not "Is It In?"; it had been a mistake to select Xavier's "Work That Sucker to Death" in a gay club; and so on. But the advice counted for little when the crowd learned that Scott had been fired. "People were giving me the finger, whacking my booth as they went by trying to mess the turntables up, chucking beer bottles at me, telling me to 'Get the fuck out of here, white boy,' all sorts," recalls For-

Dancers taking a break in the back room at Better Days, 1979.
Photograph by Bill Bernstein ©; courtesy of David Hill.

est. "People weren't dancing. They were standing around in a circle looking
at me." Danny Tenaglia, a Better Days and Paradise Garage regular who was
also starting out as a DJ, remembers that Scott's successor "wasn't a credible
DJ when he started out."

When numbers sank, Forest asked African American DJ Timmy Regisford
to play Wednesdays, Fridays, and Sundays, the club's busiest nights, and for
the first week Regisford's nights picked up while Forest's emptied out even
more. But when it turned out that the stand-in couldn't make the second
Friday, Forest stepped in and, making the most of construction work that was
being carried out, hung a drop cloth in front of the booth. As the night ran
its course, Forest heard the crowd chant, "Oh, Tim-my! Oh, Tim-my!" Then,
as the dancers applauded at the end of the night, Forest pulled a cord, sent
the drop cloth to the floor, and lapped up the laughter and applause. "They

thought it was great!" he remembers. "I never had a problem after that." Starting to work Wednesdays through to Sundays, he rebuilt the crowd to capacity. "It was usually so hot the mirrors ran with condensation and the oversaturation of bass was primal," he adds. "I never saw any other place with the same vibe. The Garage was more refined, if you will, whereas Better Days was raw and tough."

Scott experienced the softest of landings when he started to work at Zanzibar, a predominantly black straight venue that hoteliers Bruce and Miles Berger had opened in the Lincoln Motel, Newark, New Jersey, in August 1979. Brought in to provide the venue with a Paradise Garage–style sensibility a couple of months later, onetime Loft regular and party host Al Murphy replaced resident DJ Hippie Torales by hiring Larry Levan, François Kevorkian, and the newly free Scott to play Wednesdays, Fridays, and Saturdays, respectively, with the likes of Grace Jones, Eddie Kendricks, and Two Tons o' Fun booked to perform live. "Hippie is an excellent DJ so I really don't know what Al Murphy was unhappy about," notes Kevorkian. "Perhaps it had more to do with politics. Bringing in Larry Levan had a certain aura around it, as did Tee Scott, and I think Larry was the one who specified that he wanted me to play as well." Mark Riley maintains that it was "interesting" to see Levan play in a different setting. "It worked OK but it didn't work like it worked in the Garage," he observes. "It was different acoustically and there was also a different ambience. It just wasn't Larry's space." Locals nevertheless came to regard Zanzibar as their equivalent of the King Street venue, while Kevorkian judged it to be "definitely phenomenal."

There were fewer power struggles to report on Prince Street and King Street as David Mancuso entered the twelfth year of his unparalleled run and the now-untouchable Larry Levan relaxed into his own position. Yet whereas Mancuso concerned himself with fine-tuning his setup, introducing only the subtlest of adjustments, Michael Brody completed a major renovation that already encompassed an overhaul of the lighting system by opening a 25,000-square-foot roof deck complete with a cedar tree, fountains, and perimeter seating; demolishing the back wall of Levan's half of the DJ booth to create space for an amplifier room as well as a spaceship-style carousel for record storage; and installing a new stage in time for Grace Jones to appear in front of two packed parties.[4] The diva made the most of the platform, dragging an audience member onstage during the rendition of her recent release "Pull Up to the Bumper" during one of the shows. In line with the song's lyrics, she "humped his bumper," reported the *Village Voice*.[5]

Flyer for the "Beauty and the Beast: A Gay Liberation Celebration" party held at the Paradise Garage, 27 June 1981. The event marked the grand opening of the "rooftop jungle." Larry Levan DJ-ed. *Beauty and the Beast* plus *King Kong* were screened in the cinema. Courtesy of Louis "Loose" Kee Jr.

Whereas the Saint's infrastructure maximized the visual, the Garage focused attention on the sonic, and this aspect of the venue's imposing setup came to the fore when *Billboard* ran a couple of articles on sound engineer Richard Long in late 1980 and early 1981.[6] A mechanical engineering graduate who wore glasses that were improbably large, even for a geek, Long started out as an amateur hi-fi enthusiast before he began to adapt designs developed by RCA, Western Electric, MGM, and Lansing, testing the results at the Soho Place, the Loft-style private party he staged in his downtown workshop/home with Mike Stone. As he went about installing some three hundred discotheque systems worldwide, he might have faced his greatest challenge at the Roxy, where the hum was louder than the music and skaters experienced intermittent sound holes as they moved around the rink, notes Danny Krivit; to solve the problem he removed half of the perimeter speakers and took the other half to form an island in the center of the room so they pointed outward, dispersing the sound evenly and using the venue's walls to provide reflection. In terms of notoriety, that effort paled in comparison to the system he installed at Studio, where visiting discotheque entrepreneurs handed him commissions aplenty.[7] Yet the technical pinnacle of Long's work could be found on King Street, which doubled as a laboratory for testing new equipment, and trebled as a showroom for entertaining those who grasped the limits of the Studio setup. *Billboard* noted that Brody had given Long "carte blanche to test all his new equipment," winning several awards for "sound excellence" along the way.[8]

If it hardly mattered that the eulogies glossed over an earlier wrangle that denied Long the first shot at the King Street commission, the details of the struggle were informative. Heavily influenced by the Loft, Brody had initially employed Mancuso's principal sound engineer Alex Rosner to install a system at his first venture on Reade Street, and the owner turned to the engineer again when he set about opening the Garage. On hearing the news, an entirely happy Levan told Rosner he "wanted Klipschorns all over the place," Klipschorns being the iconic "Class A" home-stereo speakers Mancuso used in his own setup (which also included Mark Levinson amplifiers, Koetsu cartridges crafted by a Japanese sword specialist, and other audiophile components).[9] Rosner proceeded to export the fundamentals of the Loft system to the construction room at the Paradise Garage, after which he began to calculate the requirements of the yet-to-open main room. But then Levan experienced a change of heart.

SELECTED DISCOGRAPHY

LARRY LEVAN (1981)

Gayle Adams, "Love Fever"
Barbara Roy and Ecstasy, Passion and Pain, "If You Want Me"
Central Line, "Walking into Sunshine"
Change, "Paradise"
Chemise, "She Can't Love You"
The Clash, "The Magnificent Dance"
"D" Train, "You're the One for Me"
Jeanette "Lady" Day, "Come Let Me Love You"
Donald Byrd and 125th Street, N.Y.C., "Love Has Come Around"
Ian Dury, "Spasticus Autisticus"
Eighties Ladies, "Turned on to You"

Empress, "Dyin' to Be Dancin' "

Brian Eno and David Byrne, "The Jezebel Spirit"

ESG, "Moody"

Frontline Orchestra, "Don't Turn Your Back on Me"

Funk Masters, "Love Money"

Taana Gardner, "Heartbeat"

Eddy Grant, "Time Warp"

Ednah Holt, "Serious, Sirius Space Party (Club Version)"

Inner Life, "Ain't No Mountain High Enough (The Garage Version)"

Inner Life, "Make It Last Forever"

Chas Jankel, "Glad to Know You"

Grace Jones, "Feel Up"

Grace Jones, "Pull Up to the Bumper"

Quincy Jones, featuring Patti Austin, "Betcha' Wouldn't Hurt Me"

Junior, "Mama Used to Say"

Kebec Flektrik, "War Dance"

Chaka Khan, "I Know You, I Live You"

Kraftwerk, "Numbers"

Logg, "I Know You Will"

Gwen McCrae, "Funky Sensation"

Gwen McCrae, "Poyson"

Ullanda McCullough, "Bad Company"

Modern Romance, "Salsa Rhapsody (Dub Discomix)"

Alicia Myers, "I Want to Thank You"

Nick Straker Band, "A Little Bit of Jazz"

Northend, featuring Michelle Wallace, "Tee's Happy"

Billy Ocean, "Night (Feel Like Getting Down)"

Yoko Ono, "Walking on Thin Ice"

Powerline, "Double Journey"

Jimmy Ross, "First True Love Affair"

Rufus and Chaka Khan, "I Know You, I Live You (Special Disco Edit)"

Gino Soccio, "Try It Out"

Sparque, "Let's Go Dancin' "

The Strikers, "Body Music"

Suzy Q, "Get on Up and Do It Again"

Syreeta, "Can't Shake Your Love"

Talking Heads, "Once in a Lifetime"

Third World, "Dancing on the Floor"

Tom Tom Club, "Genius of Love"

Tom Tom Club, "Wordy Rappinghood"
Touchdown, "Easy Your Mind"
Unlimited Touch, "I Hear Music in the Streets"
Unlimited Touch, "Searching to Find the One"
Various, "X Medley"
Was (Not Was), "Tell Me That I'm Dreaming"
Tracy Weber, "Sure Shot"
Weeks and Co., "Rock Your World"
Esther Williams, "I'll Be Your Pleasure"
Yello, "Bostich"

Whereas Mancuso believed that dancers cultivated the greatest level of sustainable energy if he shaped his system around the principle of accurate sound reproduction and ran it at 100 decibels, or a level that wouldn't damage their ears, the Garage DJ found himself agreeing with Long's argument that a sound system should ideally run at 130 decibels or higher, leaving dancers overwhelmed by the force of the music. In fact Long had sold Mancuso his first set of Klipschorns, yet his Soho Place experiments led him to conclude that a sound system should generate the power of a live concert as well as re-create the warmth, detail, and nuance of a home stereo, and his theory made compelling sense at the Paradise Garage. "Everybody felt the Loft had a beautiful sound system," explains Kenny Powers, who started to work for Long in 1980. "It was really sweet and it sounded really nice in David's room. But the Garage was bigger than the Loft and it was also a more intense room." Levan was particularly drawn to Long's specially designed sub-bass horn, the Bertha, which challenged the Klipschorn for bass coverage and efficiency, and so he urged Brody to employ Long to build a system that would combine precision and force. The owner agreed to go with his DJ's irrepressible flow. "Michael didn't know all that much about audio," adds Powers. "That kind of thing was left to Larry. The changes were made because that was what Larry wanted."

With the Studio 54 installation recently completed, Long insisted during discussions with Levan that Klipschorns were "incapable of clean bass reproduction, particularly the deep bass at the high sound pressure levels required" (as he recounted to *Billboard* in December 1980).[10] With the construction phase still unfolding, he replaced four of the corner speakers with modified Waldorf bass speakers and JBLs for the high end. Then, as the construction phase drew to a close, he placed four modified sub-bass Berthas along with four tri-amplified Ultimas in the corners of the main room, positioned the Waldorfs plus smaller sub-bass woofers along the sides, and hung six dispersed tweeter clusters from the ceiling. Inspired by a Levan suggestion, and judged to be the transformative component, the modified sub-bass Berthas consisted of a main W-shaped hyperbolic folded horn, two custom-built drivers, and a flared extension that bolted to the mouth of the horn. "The horn is capable of awesome reproduction at very high sound pressure levels down to 30 hertz," noted Long, who named the piece of equipment the Levan Horn. "One of these speakers was found to overwhelm four of the scaled-up klipsch horns all playing together."[11] Having sided with Mancuso until the challenge of filling the larger room on King Street gave him pause for thought, Levan had come to believe in the power of power.

The Garage DJ might have wondered about his decision when the Garage opened its five-thousand-square-foot main room in January 1978. That night the sound was so awful Brody whisked his parties back to the smaller room and agreed to Long's request to bring Alan Fierstein of Acoustilog, Inc., into the sound team. "I came on board just as they were starting to equip the big room, whose acoustic problems were so severe that they needed help," recalls the consultant. "When I first walked in I couldn't understand what someone was saying if they were more than about fifteen feet away." Deducing that the problem lay with the building's concrete infrastructure, which provided minimal bass absorption, Fierstein designed a series of upside-down fiberglass pyramids and hung them from the ceiling, packing the side walls with the same material. He also oversaw the introduction of extra gear: a new electronic four-way X3000 crossover, a DBX Boom Box, a DBX Dynamic Range Expander, and a Deltalab Acousticomputer. "In Disco installations, and particularly at the Garage, it is important to coordinate the design of the DJ console and control electronics with the desires of the DJ whenever possible," Fierstein and Long noted in a coauthored paper delivered at an Audio Engineering Society convention in the autumn of 1980. "The special console of the Garage . . . satisfies all of the needs of the Garage DJ, putting all control electronics which he uses immediately at his fingertips."[12]

Delivering three-dimensional accuracy with reverberant power in an acoustically balanced space, the revamped Garage setup threatened to leave rivals in its wake. "Nicky Siano had a sound system that was like 10 watts and David had one that was 100 but he would play it at 5," notes Kevorkian, who DJ-ed at the Garage in May 1981 when Levan went away for a weekend, after which he stepped in a couple more times before the year was out. "Larry had a sound system that was 10,000 watts so there was, you know, a bit of a difference. The peak at the Gallery was amazing but the peaks at the Garage were just so *gigantic*. There was just nowhere else you could experience this kind of thing." The system even instigated a new form of listening for some. "Up until the Garage, the Loft was hands down the best sound I had ever heard," notes Danny Krivit. "But once the Garage came along, it became a little hard to hear the refined quality of David's system. It was about progression. The Loft was supersized by the Garage and once the Garage came in it was difficult to go to the Loft afterwards. Most people would just think, my ears are gone."

It made sense to shower Long with praise, with Fierstein also deserving of acknowledgment, and that was how the story played out in front of the Audio Engineering Society and beyond. It was Long, after all, who held a degree in mechanical engineering, who had innovated bass reproduction technology since the early 1970s, and who had become a superlative cabinet maker. Long also designed the Levan Horn and mapped out the fundamentals of the Garage system. "Larry was not a technical person," reasons Fierstein. "It wasn't his technical suggestions that drove Richard and me to build things, but his 'need suggestions' instead." Then again, those suggestions were integral to the system and Long rated the DJ's input highly. "Larry would throw something out to Richard as to what he was trying to achieve, and Richard would jump and say, 'Yeah, we can do this' or 'No, it won't work,'" recalls Powers. "Richard was very open to Larry's feedback. He named the Levan Horn after Larry because Larry inspired him to tune a great box even lower. The design was Richard, the inspiration was Larry." A conspicuous figure at the Garage, Judy Weinstein maintains that Levan was a "scientist" as well as a DJ and remixer. "He built the room and the system with Richard Long," she comments.

Matching Mancuso's relentless development of the Loft system, Levan often delayed starting a party by a couple of hours so he could rewire some speakers or tweak their position, and during the course of a night he would also adjust and readjust the setup to take account of the shifting number of people in the room. Scott, who studied electronics before he took up DJ-ing, remembers Levan "kept Richard Long's head reeling with ideas and innovations," and adds that whenever the engineer "put a thing together the way he liked it" Levan would turn it "around and backwards" in order to make it work in "a different way."[13] The system was a work in constant progress. "Larry just never stopped playing around with it. It was never good enough," confirms Powers. "It was never complete. He was 100 percent involved in the evolution of the system." Contracted to reset the equipment every Monday morning, a sanguine Long came to regard King Street as an organic workshop as well as a significant source of business. "Richard would take clients to the Paradise Garage or Studio to show them the sound system," adds DePino. "If they wanted a glitzy club he went to Studio and if they wanted a more underground club he showed them the Garage."

Rosner questioned the Garage ethos. "Records have more than adequate dynamic range for most environments," he *Billboard*. "It depends on what you believe is the role of the DJ — whether he is there to reproduce the record as it was recorded or to do other things. I think a DJ ought to reproduce a record and not fool around with dynamic range or response."[14] Convinced that Long could have simply introduced more and more Klipschorns until he achieved the desired decibel level, Mancuso took comfort in the publication of *The Life Energy in Music* by behavioral kinesiologist John Diamond in 1981. He agreed with the author's argument that "the function of music since its beginning has been the spiritual uplifting of the listener so that his life energy is enhanced by the experience," argued Diamond.[15] He also sympathized with Diamond's belief that the recording engineer (and, following the logic, the DJ) is part of a "God-given, therapeutic chain passing from the composer through to the populace," who should attempt to transmit music in its purest, most complete form.[16] The party host purchased a hundred copies of the book and handed them to friends, including Levan. "It was very important," he says.

SELECTED DISCOGRAPHY

DAVID MANCUSO, THE LOFT (1980–1981)

Edwin Birdsong, "Rapper Dapper Snapper"

Brian Briggs, "Aeo"

David Byrne, "Big Business"

Central Line, "Walking into Sunshine"

The Clash, "The Magnificent Dance"

Convertion, "Let's Do It"

"D" Train, "You're the One for Me"

Dinosaur L, "#5 (Go Bang!)"

Donald Byrd and 125th Street, N.Y.C., "Love Has Come Around"

Ian Dury, "Spasticus Autisticus"

Brian Eno and David Byrne, "America Is Waiting"

ESG, "Moody"

Frontline Orchestra, "Don't Turn Your Back on Me"

Funk Fusion Band, "Can You Feel It"

Funk Masters, "Love Money"

The Gap Band, "Yearning for Your Love"

Taana Gardner, "Heartbeat (Club Version)"

Eddy Grant, "California Style"

Eddy Grant, "Living on the Frontline"

Eddy Grant, "My Turn to Love You"

Johnny Harris, "Odyssey (Part II)"

Heaven 17, "Play to Win"

Loleatta Holloway, "Love Sensation"

Ednah Holt, "Serious, Sirius Space Party (Club Version)"

Frank Hooker & Positive People, "This Feelin'"

Geraldine Hunt, "Can't Fake the Feeling"

Jah Wobble, Jaki Liebezeit, and Holger Czukay, "How Much Are They?"

Grace Jones, "Pull Up to the Bumper"

Chaka Khan, "Clouds"

Patti LaBelle, "Spirit's in It"

Level 42, "Starchild"

Loose Joints, "Pop Your Funk"

Rita Marley, "One Draw"

Barbara Mason, "Let Me Give You Love"

Pat Metheny & Lyle Mays, "As Falls Wichita, So Falls Wichita Falls"

Pat Metheny & Lyle Mays, "Estupenda Graça"

Pat Metheny & Lyle Mays, "It's for You"

Modern Romance, "Everybody Salsa"

Nick Straker Band, "A Little Bit of Jazz"

Nicodemus, "Bone Connection"

Northend, featuring Michelle Wallace, "Tee's Happy"

Pleasure, "Take a Chance"

Powerline, "Double Journey"

Project, "Love Rescue"

Rolling Stones, "Emotional Rescue"

Steve Miller Band, "Macho City"

The Strikers, "Body Music (Instrumental)"

Tom Tom Club, "Genius of Love"

Tom Tom Club, "Wordy Rappinghood/Elephant"

Touchdown, "Ease Your Mind"

Twennynine with Lenny White, "Fancy Dancer"

Two Tons o' Fun, "Do You Wanna Boogie, Hunh?"

Two Tons o' Fun, "Just Us"
Unlimited Touch, "I Hear Music in the Streets"
Theo Vaness, "I Can't Dance without You"
Fred Wesley, "House Party"
Lenny White, "Fancy Dancer"
Stevie Wonder, "All I Do"

Levan would have appreciated the gift, given that the Loft remained his most important reference point. Having mimicked Mancuso's practice of living in his party space until Brody decreed that the heating bill was unsustainable and bought him an apartment on Gold Street, Levan instructed Long to keep two rows of Klipschorns by the side of the stage, even though he didn't want Klipschorns to dominate the speaker provision, "because Larry insisted that the legacy of David be there in the Garage," recalls Kevorkian. Levan subsequently followed Mancuso's decision to introduce a new cueing system that used tiny little speakers rather than headphones to preview a record, yet his appreciation ultimately stretched beyond the technical. "Larry would pick up on all the things David was playing and sometimes Larry would bring his new acetates to David so David could get filled in on all the freshest things that nobody else had," adds the Prelude mixer. "Larry had a lot of respect for what David was doing."

Levan regularly walked over to the Loft when he finished work on a Sunday morning, often with Kevorkian in tow. "To Larry, David was a quasi-mystical figure with supernatural power because David was so dedicated to providing people with the ultimate experience of the song," continues Kevorkian. "Larry understood how deep David went in order to focus strictly on the essential part of the music, which was to play the song in the closest possible form to the original recording without adulterating it in any shape or form whatsoever. Although you could get a lot more bass and sound pressure when you heard a record at the Garage, at the Loft every single detail and quality would come through." Kevorkian got to appreciate the contrast when he hand-delivered mixes to Levan and Mancuso. "David would pick out a certain hi-fi quality, the sound spectrum of a record, its sound stage, whereas Larry would pick up on the energy or the wild breaks, the madness," observes the Frenchman. "They were both looking at different elements of what I was doing."

The spirit of conviviality continued to flow between Prince Street and King Street, even after Levan broke with Mancuso's exacting recommendations. The Garage DJ would regularly make his way to Prince Street once he had closed for the night, with Mancuso always ready to welcome his onetime protégé into his home. "He didn't have to be Larry Levan at the Loft," Mancuso notes of Levan's relaxed demeanor during these encounters. "He could just be without having to become." Recalling that Levan had been a regular at his Broadway parties long before he broke into DJ-ing, he adds: "One day he told me, 'The Loft is my spiritual home.'" Mancuso might have wondered about some of the decisions taken at the Garage, but as far as Levan was concerned, the King Street venue maintained a tight grip on the Loft's party principles as he adapted the model to a larger home.

Convinced that even seemingly minor, technical modifications fed crucially into a cumulative process that transformed the dance-floor experience, Levan and Mancuso in tandem with Long and Rosner set about calibrating the sound systems at the Garage and the Loft with a remarkable intensity and passion, and as they challenged each other to new heights of technical-holistic innovation they carried New York City toward a thrilling apogee in sound reproduction. Augmented by the notable setups at Better Days, Melons, the Roxy, and the Saint as well as the explosion in boom-box culture, the peak arguably marked the moment when sound systems exerted their greatest influence over New York City. In so doing they encouraged inhabitants from disparate backgrounds to meet and bond with one another in settings where the emphasis on connective sound facilitated the breaking down of boundaries. The city was awash with sound and with that sound came the promise of a transcendent future. Manhattan didn't so much shimmer as reverberate.

THE NEW URBAN
STREET SOUND

As disco hurtled toward its denouement, promoters who worked in the black departments of the major labels started to argue that the genre was harming African American musicians. There was some truth in the allegation inasmuch as Eurodisco (disco minus its R&B swing-groove) had become a significant presence on the charts, while the monumental success of the Bee Gees gave the impression of a whitewash. Yet an impressive list of black artists achieved national hits through disco, with Ashford & Simpson, Brass Construction, B.T. Express, Chic, Lamont Dozier, First Choice, Gloria Gaynor, Harold Melvin and the Bluenotes, Thelma Houston, Michael Jackson, Grace Jones, Eddie Kendricks, Evelyn "Champagne" King, Kool and the Gang, LaBelle, Cheryl Lynn, M.F.S.B., the O'Jays, Teddy Pendergrass, Diana Ross, Sister Sledge, Donna Summer, Sylvester, T-Connection, the Three Degrees, the Trammps, and Barry White among the most prominent. If anything, the real hurt was experienced on an institutional level, where black departments struggled to fight off the colonial tendencies of their upstart disco counterparts regarding the matter of artist ownership. But by early 1980 the battles had dissolved for the simple reason that there were no disco departments left, and during 1981 black music and dance music rediscovered a common lexicon.

As references to R&B began to once again populate record-company press releases and discussions about music, Larry Levan delivered mix after mix that fed into the resurgent groove, including Central Line, "Walking into Sunshine"; Taana Gardner, "Heartbeat"; Ednah Holt, "Serious, Sirius, Space Party"; Inner Life, featuring Jocelyn Brown, "Ain't No Mountain High Enough" and "Make It Last Forever"; Grace Jones, "Feel Up"; Jimmy Ross, "True Love Affair"; Syreeta, "Can't Shake Your Love"; Tracy Weber, "Sure Shot"; and Esther Williams, "I'll Be Your Pleasure." All of them were major club records. All of them grew out of a sensibility that Levan had helped cultivate on King Street. And all of them contributed to the growing impression that disco had never been more than a marketing term for a historically rooted sound. "We never called the music we played at the Garage 'disco,'" points out David De-Pino. "It was R&B. Disco was a commercial sound. It was the music you heard on white radio."

Released on West End in early 1981, "Heartbeat" became a standout re-lease thanks to the way Levan and producer Kenton Nix slowed the pace until the track prowled along at a heavy, funkified ninety-eight beats per minute. Gardner delivered her guttural, sassy vocal over the top, luxuriating in the space created by the deceleration from disco. "'Heartbeat' was so ob-scure when it first came out," remembers DePino. "There was no way to make it fit with another record so Larry would let the last record fade out before he played it. He made it into a moment." On the first hearing, dancers fled to the concession stand, unsure how to move to its down-tempo beat, but a month later everyone was "running to the floor when they heard it," remem-bers Krivit. Featuring viscose synthesizer lines, space-age sound effects, and crunching beats, Ednah Holt's "Serious, Sirius, Space Party" consolidated the shift from authoritarian pulse to a plurality of tempos, as did Gwen McCrae's grinding "Funky Sensation." Nix, increasingly influential, produced both.

Levan's other standout track, his up-tempo remix of "Ain't No Mountain High Enough," blasted away the druggy sleaziness of "Heartbeat." Coproduced by Patrick Adams and Greg Carmichael, who had already worked several major disco mixes, the effort amounted to a risk, Diana Ross having appar-ently recorded a definitive version of the record in 1970. Levan responded by introducing soaring synthesizer lines, booming kettle drums, and belting vocals into two extended mixes, one lasting ten-and-a-half minutes. It was as if steroids and drama had been injected into the Motown original. "I said, 'It'll never work, it's too long!'" remembers Brown. "Larry said, 'Watch!' He took the song where it had to go and put it in another market altogether. It became the theme song at the Garage." When Brown performed the song on King Street, she looked on in awe as the crowd erupted. "Jesus, baby, baby, baby!" she recalls of the experience. "There was no comparison because it was so spectacular."

Already a significant figure thanks to his mixes of First Choice's "Love Thang" and Twennynine with Lenny White's "Fancy Dancer," Tee Scott came as close as anyone to keeping pace with Levan as he contributed three cuts to Inner Life's eponymous debut album plus several other major mixes, includ-ing Junior, "Mama Used to Say"; Material, featuring Nona Hendryx, "Bust-ing Out"; Northend, featuring Michelle Wallace, "Happy Days" backed with "Tee's Happy"; Sparque, "Music Turns Me On"; and Stone, "Time." Released on

A private release party for "Borderlines," mixed by Judy Weinstein and Larry Levan, 1981. In the booth at the Paradise Garage that night were (from left to right) Danny Krivit, David DePino, Judy Weinstein, Jeffrey Osborne, Billy Carol, and John Brown (A&M promotions). Bottom center is Larry Levan. Photographer unknown; courtesy of Danny Krivit.

Emergency, where label head Sergio Cossa also busied himself issuing Italo disco tracks such as Kano's "I'm Ready" and "It's a War" via Italian connections, "Happy Days" was his biggest mix of the year. "I took it apart and put everything on that record," Scott recalled later, aggrieved that he hadn't been granted a coproduction credit for an effort that saw him record new drums, a new bass, new synthesizer lines, and a new guitar. "That record sounded like a piece of garbage when I got it!"[1] The flip side of "Happy Days" featured "Tee's Happy," a uniquely named instrumental B-side groove that turned out to be just as popular as the A-side vocal with DJs and dancers. "Tee was getting into long instrumentals that emphasized the feel of the music," points out Emergency promoter Curtis Urbina. "It was a big record for the label." Highlighting solid rhythm section grooves and breakdowns, Scott's mixes captured the driving, soulful sound of his DJ sets. "Tee made so many big records and a lot of them were unavoidable," says Kevorkian. "It was just like, 'Damn!' "

Scott and Levan came to be known as the Dynamic Duo. "We were constantly being pitted against each other," Scott told the writer and DJ Daniel

Wang. "It was a toss-up supposedly as to who was number one, but we our-selves didn't allow ourselves to be put in that position. The media did so, and Larry had the bigger club, which was a tremendous vehicle, so he got more recognition. But for a while we were the only two in the market doing mixes and it was like, 'Larry Levan's in the studio! Tee Scott's in the studio!' And the companies called us up alternately."[2] It was during 1981, though, that Levan demonstrated that he could set as well as ride a trend, and that gave him a compelling edge over his friend and mentor. "Nobody could compare to Larry because Larry had a visionary sense," argues François Kevorkian. "Whereas Tee Scott was playing all the great music of the day, and was making hot remixes and appearing on the radio, Larry was a trendsetter. Larry would go, 'No, no, no, that's not enough! Let's do this and make it completely different from everything that's ever been done.'" Then again, Urbina took "Happy Days" to Scott because "Larry was becoming unapproachable."

Continuing to mesh innovative production values with a rhythm and blues groove, Kevorkian completed his own flurry of releases, including the standout "Can You Handle It" by Sharon Redd, "Body Music" by the Strikers, "Search-ing to Find the One" by Unlimited Touch, and "You're the One for Me" by "D" Train. For the Strikers, Kevorkian arranged for Prelude to license "Body Music" from Cesaree Records International after first hearing the record in Better Days, and he headed into the studio with Levan to remix. For "D" Train, he worked alongside producer, arranger, and comixer Hubert Eaves III, who was "pretty clear on how he wanted the vocals to sound and how he wanted the keyboards to stick out with some reverb." During the year Kevorkian also persuaded Marvin Schlachter to license "Journey"/"Double Journey" by Pow-erline, an Elite issue from 1981 that Levan and Mancuso supported heavily (and were thanked in the credits). Partly motivated to loan money to Michael Brody to open the Paradise Garage because he believed the venue would pro-vide West End with an ideal marketing platform, Mel Cheren responded to "Body Music" by commissioning Kevorkian and Levan to remix Sparque's "Let's Go Dancin'." "We each brought good ideas to the pot and we went for it," Kevorkian remembers of the studio session with Levan, who had taken to call-ing him "Frenchman." "Larry had this raw, vibrant, boundless energy."

The new wave of releases — by "D" Train, Taana Gardner, Inner Life, Northend, Sharon Redd, Sparque, the Strikers, and Unlimited Touch — carried dance music into terrain that was grittier and tougher than anything occupied by late disco. Perhaps best captured by "D" Train, a Brooklyn-based band whose name referenced the subway line that ran from Brooklyn to Manhattan to the Bronx, there was something inevitable about the shift.

François Kevorkian DJ-ing at a Mike Stone party at Studio 54, ca. 1980. "We didn't play at the Studio 54 of Bianca Jagger and Halston and Warhol," says Kevorkian. "Steve Rubell and Ian Schrager were in jail, and people like Mike Stone were allowed to throw parties to keep the name going." Photograph by David Brockington; courtesy of François Kevorkian.

Grounded in the recessionary moment, which witnessed budgets that might have been used to hire an orchestra or to fund an elongated studio session shrink, the sound was stripped of its flourishes and even its make-believe fantasy. The stripped-down result brandished disco's rhythm and blues heritage. "The music has become slower—funky/sleazy instead of frantic— progressively stripped down . . . , and rawer, especially in the vocals," Vince Aletti noted in the *Village Voice*. "Like rap records, this is the new urban street sound—jagged, nervy, bright though at times purposely dumb—and much of it is made in New York."[3]

Enough records had simultaneously climbed the dance and black music charts by July for Brian Chin and Nelson George (the respective authors of the "Disco File" and "Black Music Report" columns in *Record World*) to co-author a piece on the crossover trend. "The thumping beat of club music in New York, Boston and Los Angeles usually failed to interest stations in black music's backbone, the southeast and deep south," they argued. "The opposite was also true, as the syncopated rhythms of contemporary funk clashed with the sophisticated ambience of many urban discos. But in 1981, those barriers have crumbled."[4] All it took was a loosening of attitudes and interdepartmental rivalries to rekindle an industry-level conversation that had never broken down on the floor. "Maybe there were no disco departments left but that music was still being made," says Prelude's Michael Gomes. "They were now just calling it R&B and R&B had loosened up a great deal as well."

The new point of contention turned out to be rap, for while Chin and George generally reviewed the sound enthusiastically, the major labels were resistant. Ahmet Ertegun of Atlantic Records didn't suggest a deal when he shook hands with Sylvia Robinson at the Ritz, and when Malcolm McLaren attempted to persuade RCA to support the genre the following day his words were stonewalled. "I said, 'What you witnessed last night is going to explode, it's going to be a phenomenon, you must try to sign this act if you really know what's good for you. I highly recommend . . .'" McLaren recalls. "I was really trying to induce, seduce and inspire this A&R department to really take what they had seen the night before seriously." Corporate politics obstructed the way. "They said, 'That's black music, you must go across the corridor and maybe speak to the black department.' So I wandered across the corridor and the black department of course were only interested in George Benson."[5] With the exception of Mercury's release of Kurtis Blow, the culture didn't coincide with major-label strategy. "The black music departments were selling strings and what they considered to be sophisticated black music," comments Mark Riley. "Into that world stepped these totally unsophisticated kids with their totally unsophisticated music, so at first the black music departments were like, 'Get out of here!'"

With the majors faraway, Sugar Hill held on to its vanguard position when it released "The Adventures of Grandmaster Flash on the Wheels of Steel" a month or two after the Ritz show. Recorded by Flash using two turntables, the track showcased a breathtaking sequence of quick-fire cuts that included Bronx party classics (Chic, "Good Times"; the Incredible Bongo Band, "Apache"), intertextual records (Queen, "Another One Bites the Dust"; Blondie, "Rapture"; and the *Flash Gordon* soundtrack), recent Sugar Hill releases ("Monster Jam," "8th Wonder," and "Birthday Party"), and humorous miscellany (a mock children's story lifted from *Singers, Talkers, Players, Swingers & Doers* by the Hellers). "After months of asking, the Good Queen [Robinson] finally let me do my thing," Flash recounts in his autobiography. "After months of standing around the studio, letting live musicians play what I could be mixing on two turntables, and showing the engineers how to mix everybody's voice so the record sounds right, I finally got my own record. Finally got to punch-phase, cut, cue, spin back, rub, and zuka-zuka on wax."[6] Interviewed by Richard Grabel in the *New Musical Express*, Flash noted of the recording process: "Maybe I'd set the cue down too soon and have to stop and go back all over. Or I might cue in too late. Too late, too soon. If you listen to it, even down to the spaces where there's no music, where it pauses and then comes in, the timing is absolutely perfect."[7]

Other DJs had been quick-cutting for years. Early discotheque DJs used the technique as a standard trick, Nicky Siano took it to new levels of intensity at the Gallery, and Walter Gibbons and Kool Herc deployed the technique to extend the break (the former executing his mixes with remarkable precision). But whereas his predecessors related to quick-cutting as one element of their work, Flash deployed the technique with such ferocious intensity it defined his entire practice; rather than hearing records he heard fragments of records. The only exception to this state of affairs — the fleet-handed DJ Mikey D'Merola, who rifled through twenty-five records in just under nineteen minutes on the "Bits & Pieces 1: Disco '79" bootleg twelve-inch — anticipated none of Flash's sense of disjuncture, humor, and manipulative intent as he went about his work. "Programmers: some of your clientele (and especially the staff you work with) will think your turntable is stuttering," a reviewer warned of "Adventures" in *Dance Music Report*, "but most of your dancers will love this."[8] Composed entirely of other people's records, this was the sound of the DJ at work minus the MC/rapper.

If Flash implicitly raised the question of what a rap record should be called if it didn't contain a rap, Tom Tom Club demonstrated how rapping could migrate from the Bronx with minimal bother. Formed by Talking Heads musicians Tina Weymouth and Chris Frantz, the group took its name from the Bahamas dancehall where they made their first recordings. "In the old jazz style, everybody would be playing, then one person would solo and that would create the excitement," Weymouth told the *New York Rocker*. "We take the opposite approach. Rather than someone stepping out and playing a top line, we use the dub style where the featured instrument is simply barred."[9] Signed to Sire and Island, the group released the rap-heavy "Wordy Rapping-hood" in the summer and their eponymous "electro-funk-art-fusion" album (as Chin described it) in the autumn.[10] Dropping the names of Kurtis Blow, Bohannon, and James Brown over an innocent funk riff, "Genius of Love," the second single, also included a quirky rap.

Other records drew Bronx-style rapping into the mutant vortex. "Wikka Wrap" by the Evasions featured a parodic English-accented rapper who referenced the "lingua franca of the funk business." Mean Machine rapped in English and Spanish over "Pull Up to the Bumper" on "Disco Dream." Sweet G and the Treacherous Three respectively reworked "Heartbeat" on "A Heartbeat Rap" and "Feel the Heartbeat." Dr. Jeckyll and Mr. Hyde recycled "Genius of Love" as "Genius Rap," the breakthrough single for Profile Records, formed by Cory Robbins and Steve Plotnicki earlier in the spring. Grandmaster Flash & the Furious Five recorded their own version of the Tom Tom Club hit on "It's Nasty (Genius of Love)." And across the Atlantic, the Clash introduced a rap onto "This Is Radio Clash." "When we came to the U.S., Mick [Jones, the Clash lead guitarist,] stumbled upon a music shop in Brooklyn that carried the music of Grandmaster Flash and the Furious Five, the Sugarhill Gang," Joe Strummer, the band's lead vocalist, commented later. "These groups were radically changing music and they changed everything for us."[11]

Tom Silverman entered the fray when he released his first rap track at the end of the year. Raised in Westchester County, New York, Silverman founded *Disco News* as a subscription newsletter back in September 1978, changing the title of his publication to *Dance Music* when the backlash against disco hit its peak. Around the same time the entrepreneur started to head to the Mudd Club and the Paradise Garage, keen to clock fresh developments that might provide him with a renewed sense of focus. Then he visited a Brooklyn record store the day it shifted something like one hundred copies of "Rapper's Delight" in ten minutes. "*Dance Music* was limping along, and I also had DJs and artists bringing me new music because of the magazine, so I decided to start a label, just in case something good came along," he recalls. "Dance music grew out of this independent network. The marketplace was very disparate."

Silverman met the DJ who would provide him with the information and know-how he needed at the T-Connection. "Bambaataa was playing along with Jazzy Jay and Red Alert, his two assassins," remembers the publisher. "They were quick-cut turntablists. They would work the wheels of steel and Bambaataa would hand them records. They mixed funk with rock; the Monkees, the Eagles, 'Take Me to the Mardi Gras' by Bob James, 'Trans-Europe Express' Kraftwerk, James Brown, Sly and the Family Stone, George Clinton, B.T. Express 'Do You Like It,' Billy Squier 'The Big Beat,' Cerrone 'Rocket in the Pocket' played at 45 instead of 33. Some records were played backwards. It was *refreshing*." Silverman invited the DJ to mix "Havin' Fun," a funk-disco song by Cotton Candy, the first release on his new label, Tommy Boy. Aside from an incongruous rap by the Soul Sonic Force, who received a mix credit along with Bambaataa Aasim, the track offered little in the way of South Bronx aesthetics or dance-floor traction. But Silverman had his man and for his next

Grandmaster Flash and Tina Weymouth, posing for the front cover of the *New York Rocker*, 1981, after the release of "Genius of Love" and before the Grandmaster Flash & the Furious Five release of "It's Nasty (Genius of Love)." Chris Franz recalls of the photo shoot: "We met him [Flash] and he said to us, 'You know this is a very cool beat. You're gonna be hearing a lot of this.' I said, 'Oh really?' He said, 'Oh definitely!'" Photograph by and courtesy of Laura Levine ©.

release he paired him up with the Boston-born producer Arthur Baker, an acquaintance made during a Disco Forum party held in the summer of 1978. The result would provide all three with the breakthrough they craved.

A rock head who got into danceable R&B through black radio in Boston, Baker started out DJ-ing with the help of local turntable heroes, but his dream was to break into production, so he took an engineering course and talked the studio owner into giving him enough time to record "Losing You" by the Hearts of Stone, which ended up coming out on a Canadian label in 1977. Baker went on to release a string of disco records for Casablanca and Posse before the opportunity to coproduce an album with the Latin soul artist Joe Bataan broke down when the commissioning label's parent company went bust just before the record's release. He also worked on North End's "Kind of Life (Kind of Love)" for West End and "Happy Days" for Emergency, only to find himself out of work by the time Tee Scott repaired the latter. Taking up menial work at a record distributor, Baker started to write record reviews for *Dance Music Report* (as Silverman had retitled his publication) in his spare time. Then Silverman offered him a way back into the studio — with Bambaataa.

Baker knew about rap from the time Bataan took him to Mount Morris Park by 125th Street to witness "these guys talking over records — over breaks." The producer thought that the rapping element was fresher than the practice of extended drum breaks because Boston DJs had already fine-tuned the latter using seven-inch singles. "There was no such thing as scratching at that time but John [Luongo] would just go back-and-forth and extend it," reminisces Baker. "[Joey] Carvello could do it a bit, too." Bataan went on to release his half of the album as "Rap-O Clap-O" and *Mestizo* with Salsoul in late 1979. Then, a year and a half later, Silverman told Baker he wanted to "start making rap records" and invited him to produce a track. Baker took up the offer, spurred on by the memory of hearing Larry Levan play "Rapper's Delight," one of the relatively small number of rap tracks Levan liked to play (others included Edwin Birdsong's "Rapper Dapper Snapper," Kurtis Blow's "Christmas Rap," and T-Ski Valley's "!Catch the Beat!"). "Larry played it right when it came out," he remembers. "I heard it and I was, 'What the fuck is this? Is it Chic?' And then the rap came on. I thought it was amazing."

Baker and Bambaataa chose to version Gwen McCrae's "Funky Sensation" rather than "Genius of Love" on the basis that others were reworking the Tom Tom Club song. Baker then contacted the Queens-based musicians who re-recorded "Happy Days" and on Silverman's suggestion laid down two takes of "Jazzy Sensation," the first featuring Bambaataa and the Jazzy 5 (another

Zulu Nation rap outfit), the second the sung vocals of Tina B., Baker's wife. With Kenton Nix credited as the writer, the crosstown collaboration notched up sales of 35,000 to 40,000, easily outstripping "Havin' Fun." Baker had no problem producing two versions of the same song. "The way I look at it, it's sort of like a jazz music," he told the musician and rap historian David Toop. "It's like rearranging. Like when John Coltrane does 'My Favourite Things' it doesn't sound like it's gonna sound if some lounge singer does it. They rearrange it and it comes out differently."[12]

"Jazzy Sensation" fed into the flow of the city. "When disco first came out it didn't matter what label it was on or which language it was in; it was about the groove," argues Baker. "It was the same with hip hop. Bambaataa didn't care who was making the beat, just as long as it had a beat. It was just music that people danced to." Carol Cooper agrees that Bambaataa didn't think of himself as creating a sound that was "completely other" as he presented himself as a cross between the Village People and Parliament/Funkadelic. The South Bronx DJ "got it" when he headed downtown and heard "this grinding, thrashing energy," adds Ivan Baker, who had started to work at Rockpool and thought of the Bronx DJ as a "warm" and "friendly" peer. "Bambaataa, Russell Simmons, the DJs from the Zulu Nation and people from all different backgrounds were coming to hear what we played because they wanted to hear different sounds," he argues. "It either rocked the floor or it didn't. There was a great deal of kinship between the rock underground and the hip hop/rap world." When the Mudd Club DJ submitted a "wise-ass" playlist to Rockpool that only included groups with double names, among them Duran Duran, Liquid Liquid, Medium Medium, and Talk Talk, Bambaataa greeted him with a wry smile and the words "Hey, Ivan Ivan" on their next encounter. The name stuck.

Extracting themselves from the culture of departmental wars and spreadsheet calculations, dance-music producers and remixers were returning to their core mission: to lay down recordings for an extended community of partygoers who wanted to dance. They recognized that disco, funk, new wave, rap, and rock had served their purpose. They also grasped that none of these sounds entirely captured the kaleidoscopic roots of the urban landscape or the range of sound combinations that dancers were willing to embrace. Meanwhile Afrika Bambaataa, Grandmaster Flash, François Kevorkian, Larry Levan, and Tee Scott established the DJ not just simply as a remixer but as an important source of sonic invention as they drew on their DJ booth perspectives to create dance music that was compound in form. A new epoch was under way and its namelessness didn't matter a jot.

IT WASN'T
ROCK AND ROLL
AND IT WASN'T
DISCO

A self-described New Jersey kid and son of a police officer, Sal Principato needed to go through punk before he felt able to weigh up other modes of being. "I couldn't relate to my upbringing," he remembers. "The whole milieu I was brought up in didn't speak to my aspirations artistically, culturally, politically — none of it." When his friend Richard McGuire went to study at Rutgers in New Brunswick, Principato tagged along, pursued some art projects, and then took off to San Francisco. "At one point I tried to fit into the LSD mode, which seemed to be the most revolutionary thing around, but it didn't express the totality of what I was feeling," he adds. "Then Patti Smith came along and she seemed to address the total spectrum of anger, joy, transcendence and revolution. I realized I had to blow up my personality in order to rebuild myself."

In the summer of 1979 Principato traveled to New York to stay with Mc-Guire and another ex-Rutgers student Scott Hartley, who had cofounded a primitive punk band called Liquid Idiot while at the university and were now living in a run-down building on West 80th Street. Principato jammed alongside them and, having agreed they should play at least one concert before Principato headed home, they appeared fifth on what was supposed to be a three-band bill at CBGB. "We had so much fun I never went back to San Francisco," recalls Principato. "We were just hanging out, not really paying rent, taking our electricity from the hallway, doing whatever we had to do to make a little money, and going out mostly to downtown clubs such as Mudd Club, CBGB, Danceteria, and Tier 3." With Harley already on drums, percussionist Dennis Young joined the group in early 1980. Meanwhile Principato sang knotted vocals and, having tried his hand at beginner's bass, started to "hit some sticks" instead. At that point McGuire put down his electric guitar and picked up the bass from Principato. The band also changed its name to Liquid

Liquid Liquid, 1981. (Left to right) Richard McGuire, Scott Hartley, Salvatore Principato, and Dennis Young. Photograph by and courtesy of Laura Levine ©.

Liquid because they had become "too idiosyncratic for punk," which had also started to appear "old hat and corny," notes Principato.

Released on 99 Records in June after McGuire dropped off a five-song demo to Ed Bahlman, Liquid Liquid's eponymous debut EP combined the Bo Diddley beat, the rototoms in Curtis Mayfield's "Super Fly," the percussive crescendos of Fela Kuti, the subtractive spatial dimension of dub reggae, and the deconstructive rock of DNA. "Less is more became this recurring theme in our music and in the way we presented our music," notes Principato. "There was a lot of open space, or unstated space, and some tracks wouldn't have structure until we went into the studio to record them. They were recurring jams. Ed was totally supportive." Liquid Liquid's follow-up EP, *Successive Reflexes*, foregrounded a complex percussive aesthetic that meshed the improvised, the structured, and the composed. Locating the band within a "p‑‑k f‑‑k" movement that was accelerating, even though innovator James Chance had started to receive an "increasingly lukewarm local response," the *Village Voice* described its performance at a 99 Records–sponsored festival at Tompkins Square Park in August as "the hottest thing . . . besides the weather."[1] Two months later the *New York Rocker* credited the group with developing a form of "intense, spontaneous psychedelic trance music."[2] Meanwhile Principato began to think of Liquid Liquid's sound "in the context of dance music" after he started to tune in to WBLS and WKTU.

Also signed to 99 Records, ESG (short for Emerald, Sapphire, and Gold) formed when the mother of Deborah (nine), Valerie (eleven), Renee (thirteen), and Marie Scroggins (sixteen) decided that her daughters were in need of some indoor activity. "We lived in a very rough neighborhood in the Bronx and my mom didn't want us hanging out on the streets," explains Renee. "She wanted us to do something positive so she bought us instruments." With Valerie on drums, Deborah on bass guitar, Renee on vocals, and Marie plus friend Tito Libran on congas, ESG went on to perform raw, percussive covers as well as their own songs at talent shows. "My mother sang in a church choir, my dad played jazz sax, and my older brother was into rock and heavy metal," adds Renee. "I was into gospel and James Brown." Developing instrumental parts that emulated and extended the funk jams demanded by Brown after he took the J.B.'s to the bridge, with lyrics introduced only after the track's dynamics were in place, ESG's players came to think of themselves as a dance band. "When we write a song, we try to have what we call 'the part' right," they told the *New York Rocker*. "And the part is, you know, the part that breaks loose and make you feel the rhythm."[3]

Bahlman first heard ESG while working alongside Jim Fouratt as a panelist at a CBS-sponsored talent competition. "Ed called me up and he said, 'I love the band,'" remembers Renee. "He explained he could help book us shows and work as our unofficial manager. We said, 'Sure!'" When Fouratt arranged for ESG to play at the Pop Front, a short-lived, collectively run Sunday-night showcase for live bands, they "brought the house down with a dance-crazy set of minimalist salsa," reported the *SoHo News*.[4] Fouratt organized additional shows at Danceteria and the Peppermint Lounge while Bahlman facilitated an appearance at Hurrah, where the youth group appeared as an opening act for A Certain Ratio, a funk-oriented new wave lineup from Manchester, England, signed to Factory Records. "This teenage space/salsa/soul outfit from the outer boroughs has brightened many a long night at Hurrah and Danceteria, opening for bigger names," reported the *New York Rocker*. "It's a sound so minimal (one note reverb guitar, bass, drums, congas, group-chant vocals) as to be almost pure rhythm, with hilarious but heartfelt TV-cartoon lyrics on top. Totally fun and totally for real."[5]

ESG made their studio debut after Tony Wilson of Factory offered them a deal while they were preparing to go onstage at Hurrah. Three days later the band headed into the studio to record a seven-inch single with Martin Hannett, the producer of Manchester band Joy Division and its reincarnation New Order, who had traveled to New York with A Certain Ratio so he could record their debut album in the city. Bahlman went on to issue an eponymous twelve-inch EP that included "You're No Good," "UFO," and "Moody" on the A-side and three takes from the band's Hurrah performance on the flip. Soon after, David DePino heard the record while walking past 99 Records as he made his way from the Loft to the Paradise Garage and went inside to pick up a copy. "They hadn't even heard of Larry and the Garage," he remembers. "I was like, '*Really?*'" Levan checked "You're No Good" over and over until he left the booth to think something through on the floor, after which the record ran through to "Moody." "Aaaggghhh!" he shouted out. "This is the better song!" DePino remembers the DJ played the record something like fifteen times that night. "It was completely different from everything else," he reasons. "It sounded like a garage band. It sounded raw. ESG were obscure and Larry loved obscure." The record climbed the SURE charts during the autumn — SURE being the Bronx-based record pool that Bobby Davis set up as an alternative to For the Record — before Levan invited the band to play live at the Garage on New Year's Eve. "Larry loved 'Moody,'" notes Renee. "He started playing that a lot and everybody pretty much followed suit."

Over at ZE, meanwhile, Michael Zilkha declared in a February interview that he was planning to release "lots of disco records in the next six months." His new formula was to lay down a funk track, interweave weird guitar riffs and bebop horns, and watch the city's dance floors go "crazy" to such an extent he wouldn't need to use radio as a promotional outlet.[6] During a prolific year, the label owner came out with releases by Cristina, Kid Creole and the Coconuts, Gichy Dan, Material, and the Waitresses. He also told bass player and cofounder of Material, Bill Laswell, that he wanted "a disco record with heavy metal guitar," and after rejecting his first effort explained further, "I want a proper dance record but I want it to be aggressive." At that point Laswell turned to Black Panther George Jackson's prison letters for inspiration, came up with "Busting Out," and brought in ex-LaBelle vocalist Nona Hendryx to belt out the vocals. Still DJ-ing at Better Days at the time, Tee Scott mixed the result to Zilkha's total satisfaction. "Tee was a really cool guy," remembers the label head. "He was a lot warmer with me than Larry Levan. I went to Better Days more than the Paradise Garage out of choice. I just thought it was a better club for people who were interested in music and not the scene."

Zilkha furthered the cause of sonic deviance when he released Kid Creole's second album *Fresh Fruit in Foreign Places*. "It is too black and/or Latin for white rock stations, but does not fit into the formats of most black pop and

ESG, 1981. Photograph
by and courtesy of
Laura Levine ©.

disco stations, either," mused songwriter and coproducer Andy Hernandez
of the Kid Creole effort. "We're trying to get past the categorization of music,
and it's tough. But little by little we'll gain acceptance. When we play for the
people, there's never any problem."[7] Zilkha then advanced the mutiny when
he spent two consecutive nights recording Was (Not Was)'s eponymous debut
album along with the twelve-inch single "Out Come the Freaks," during which
time he didn't leave the studio once. "It was heaven," recalls the label head, who
took a particular interest in lyrics, the concept of a record, how its elements
would fit together, and its texture. "Don [Fagenson] was open to anything and
I had all these ideas stored up." When the Detroit band made their New York
debut at the Mudd Club, even the sound check was rammed.

With ZE on a roll — "It was my best period creatively," reminisces Zilkha.
"I felt like I was on autopilot" — Rob Partridge, a promoter in Island's London
office, came up with the idea that the label should release a compilation album.
Containing six cuts from Material with Nona Hendryx, Was (Not Was), Cris-

tina, Gichy Dan, Don Armando's 2nd Ave Rhumba Band, and Coati Mundi,
the result captured the strange coherence that underscored the label's aesthetic of mayhem. Titled *Seize the Beat (Dance Ze Dance)* in the United States
and *Mutant Disco: A Subtle Discolation of the Norm* in the United Kingdom,
the result flaunted its miscreant credentials. "I used to say 'a subtle disloca-
tion of the norm,' and they turned it into 'discolation of the norm,'" remembers Zilkha. Interviewed by the *New York Times* in June, August Darnell flew
the flag on intercultural transformation. "To me, the beauty of music is its
possibilities for mutation. And that mutation represents a larger ideal: global
coexistence."[8]

Contributing to the mutant movement, David Byrne and Brian Eno began
the recording of *My Life in the Bush of Ghosts* by laying down a sparse instrumental track that featured two guitars and a synthesizer. Scanning the radio
for "interesting voices," the coproducers then introduced religious extracts
"not so much because of what they were saying but because of the passion
with which they said it," as Eno explained to the *East Village Eye*.[9] Homemade instruments added to the atmosphere of invention. "In one case we
needed a sound that was like a resonant, deep bass drum, so we used a large
wooden cabinet which we found in the studio, miked it in a particular way
and got a lovely resonant boom out of it," added Eno of the February release.
"Frequently we used old pieces of wood or tin or any scrap metal we found
and by recording them in a particular way and treating them in a particular way we could change their sound characteristics enough to use them as
instruments."[10]

Connecting with the live discotheque scene that had superseded CBGB,
Byrne also invited Mark Kamins to remix "Big Business," a track taken from
Songs from the Catherine Wheel, an album he recorded for the choreographer
Twyla Tharp. "When the guitar solo came on I pushed the fader really high,"
recalls the DJ, who made his studio debut back in 1979 when he borrowed
money from his father to coproduce a Dolores Hall album with a schoolfriend Bobby Thiele Jr., the son of Impulse! Records head Bob Thiele. "David
said, 'Do you want the guitar so loud?' And I said, 'Yes!'" Kamins also inspired
the name-dropping featured on "Genius of Love" when he scratched in references to the names of James Brown and Bohannon while DJ-ing at one of
Frantz and Weymouth's parties in their Long Island City loft. "That's where they
got the idea of mentioning those artists," claims the DJ, who went uncredited
on that occasion.

Once close with Byrne, Arthur Russell pursued his own idiosyncratic path
by working on a series of album tracks recorded with a wild assortment of

musicians, among them the Philadelphian rhythm section Ingram Brothers; downtown composers Julius Eastman, Peter Gordon, Jill Kroesen and Peter Zummo; new wave guitarists Denise Mercedes and Ed Tomney; and Loft dancer-percussionist Rome Neal. Running identical copies of the recordings through two twenty-four-track tape machines, Russell created a scrambled jigsaw out of the lurching combinations that came out yet wondered who might release his angular concoction of disco, new wave, free jazz, and orchestral minimalism. West End was a nonstarter, Russell having broken off relations with Mel Cheren once he became convinced the label owed him money for undeclared sales of Larry Levan's remix of "Is It All over My Face?" So too was Sire, its executives having tired of Russell's idiosyncratic methods during the Dinosaur recording of "Kiss Me Again." But then he bumped into Will Socolov, the somewhat directionless son of David Mancuso's lawyer, whom he had met at the Loft, and asked him if he wanted to start a record company. Just back from traveling, the teenager agreed, hopeful it would help him to head to Prince Street as more than a "middle-class white Jewish kid watching all these people dancing."

Naming their label Sleeping Bag as a whimsical anti-disco gesture, Russell and Socolov issued Russell's $24 \rightarrow 24$ *Music* as their first release toward the end of 1981 under the artist name of Dinosaur L. Opening the album, "#5 (Go Bang!)" featured Eastman's virtuosic keyboard playing and orgasmic opera, Kroesen's discordant semisinging, Neal's homoerotic chants and percussion, Zummo's chromatic trombone, Gordon's pop-art tenor sax, creaking guitar lines from Mercedes and Tomney, and the foundational rhythm section of the Ingram brothers. The resulting jam resembled a new style of warped disco that, bored of all the studio formalities, revealed how error, chance, and chaos could align themselves into an insistent, organic funk. David Mancuso selected the indelibly strange yet insistently funky dance jam regularly. Larry Levan took to it as well.

Grace Jones, her body already a study in cubist perspectives, furthered her own move into warped sound when she released *Nightclubbing* in May. The heavy rhythm section, fairground synth lines, and discordant car toots of "Pull Up to the Bumper," the album's standout track, provided the artist with a fitting stage on which she could parade her low, affectless voice. "It doesn't have the kind of monster bass line that powers most funk hits, but lyrics that demand you 'drive it in between' and 'let me blow your horn' nestled into a throbbing groove and whipped along by that dominatrix voice couldn't miss in these freaky times," commented the *Village Voice*. "The sound through-

Arthur Russell at home with boyfriend Tom Lee, 1980. Photographer unknown; courtesy of Tom Lee/the Estate of Arthur Russell.

out the album is consistent, wide open, and uncluttered."[11] Performing at the Savoy, Jones dressed as an ape and later donned a plastic nude torso. "Not since David Bowie's glitter days has androgyny been exploited to more spectacular effect in a pop context," reported Stephen Holden in the *New York Times*.[12] Whereas *Warm Leatherette* received encouraging reviews yet sold modestly, *Nightclubbing* catapulted Jones to international fame. "It just cooked," notes Blackwell.

The death of Bob Marley, which coincided with the release of *Nightclubbing*, extinguished any uplift the Island boss might have derived from Jones's success. "I lost a lot of interest in the music business after that," recalls Chris Blackwell. "It wasn't just music with Bob. It was the world." Island continued to thrive, however, thanks to the emergence of Jamaican dub outfit Black Uhuru and Irish rock band U2, the remaking of Steve Winwood, and the fruitful collaboration with ZE Records, as well as the ongoing success of Jones. The syndrums and bass duo Sly Dunbar and Robbie Shakespeare, innovators of the harder "rockers" drum beat in reggae, who worked on Black Uhuru's *Red* album and Ian Dury's "Spasticus Autisticus" as well as their own space-funk version of "Don't Stop the Music" by Yarbrough & Peoples, also made a significant contribution. Locating the duo within the wider performance of Blackwell's company, *Record World* commented that Island was enjoying its "most successful period in its U.S. history."[13]

With Marley's impact largely felt in the dorms of white middle-class students, Island's showcasing of the interlocking efforts of Black Uhuru, Grace Jones, and Sly Dunbar and Robbie Shakespeare contributed to the breakthrough of a set of Jamaican sounds that had previously enjoyed only an episodic presence on the New York party scene. Back in 1973 Kool Herc had introduced live MC-ing techniques alongside figures such as Eddie Cheba and DJ Hollywood, but although it is often claimed that Herc only started to play up-tempo funk and soul records after his dub and reggae selections flopped at his first party, Herc knew in advance that his peak cuts would include the funk-rock of "Get Ready" by Rare Earth and also the live version of James Brown's "Give It Up or Turnit a Loose," because, as he told Steven Hager, "people would walk for miles just to hear that [James Brown] record."[14] Jamaica also appeared to have minimal bearing on Herc's decision to start mixing between the breaks given that island DJs (in contrast to their New York counterparts) mixed in the studio and not behind the turntables. Having paralleled Herc's venture into breakbeat mixology, Walter Gibbons executed the city's other notable foray into Jamaican aesthetics when he saturated his 1979 remix album *Disco Madness* with dub's spatialized and reverberating priorities.

Dub reggae also wound its way into New York via the United Kingdom, where Jamaican migrants started to settle in significant numbers ahead of their accelerated influx into the United States. Released on Movers Records in 1976, "For the Love of Money" by the Disco Dub Band might have been the first single to weave echo and reverb into a disco pulse; Tom Moulton's review of the record in *Billboard* confirmed that its influence extended to the East Coast.[15] Soon after, bands such as the Clash and PiL expressed their disillusionment with British politics by embracing Caribbean culture as a rebellious gesture, as Dick Hebdige outlines in *Cut 'n' Mix*.[16] Then, in 1981, the Clash released "The Magnificent Dance," an echoey, drum-and-bass version of "The Magnificent Seven" that thundered out of the sound system at the Paradise Garage week in, week out. "That was the showcase record where reggae met dance music," argues François Kevorkian. "When we heard the Clash, it was like, 'What the fuck just dropped in the room?' That was Larry's favorite record of the year."

Kevorkian's personal dub epiphany arrived when he purchased "Re-Mixture," a five-track jazz-funk compilation released by Champagne Records in the United Kingdom a little earlier in the year. Along with "Powerline," the collection included a 7:34 version of "Love Money" by T. W. Funk Masters, a sparse, slurry, dub-dance number produced by the Jamaican-born, London-based radio presenter Tony Williams, who asked lyricist friend Bo Kool to write new lines for "Money in My Pocket" by Dennis Brown.[17] The result was released as "(Money) No Love" by Bo Kool and "Love Money" by the Funk Masters on Tania Music in 1980, but it was the Champagne mix that amazed Kevorkian, who first heard it while shopping at Downstairs Records with Tee Scott. "I was completely transfixed with the big reverb hits and also the way the music just stopped, moved to the effects, and then went back to the music," recalls the mixer. "It was just so dramatic." Already drawn to the heavy processing, flanging effects, reversed sections, and time-warp delays used by Herbie Hancock, Led Zeppelin, Miles Davis, Soft Machine, and Jimi Hendrix, yet unaware of King Tubby and Lee Perry, Kevorkian maintains that the Champagne version of "Love Money" was "part of that same reggae-dub atmosphere that suddenly took over." The record gave him "a lot of ideas," he adds.

Vince Aletti located "Love Money" within a larger flow of U.K. releases that were making a mark in New York. "Even at the peak of the disco boom a stack of esoteric imports was standard equipment for any self-respecting New York disco deejay, but if they were largely exotic specialists then, in the past year import records have become meaty basics again," he argued in the *Village Voice*. "The big difference is, instead of coming from Eurodisco strongholds in Germany, Italy, or France, the best imports right now are from England, where a peculiar confluence of styles — rap; reggae; power pop; fusion jazz; a cool, raceless R&B; plus a subversive touch here and there of new wave anarchy and irony — has produced an especially vivid and appealing brand of post-disco dance music."[18] The Nick Straker Band's "A Little Bit of Jazz" was "the slickest of the lot." As for "Love Money," it had become "the big underground record" of the moment as well as "the import that comes closest to street music's funky eccentricity."[19]

The glistening, bass-rich "Body Talk" by Imagination, released right after Aletti's piece went to print, added weight to the writer's argument that British artists were "not merely reprocessing American soul and sending it back" but were developing "playful, idiosyncratic variations" that amounted to a "new slant."[20] Level 42, a jazz-funk outfit signed to Elite, contributed with the release of the lush, sparkling "Starchild." Meanwhile other cuts by A Certain Ratio, Depeche Mode, Cabaret Voltaire, the Cure, the Durutti Column, Gang of Four, Heaven 17, the Human League, Joy Division/New Order, Killing Joke, Orchestral Manoeuvres in the Dark, Soft Cell, and Pere Ubu — many of them issued on Factory and the London-based independent label Rough Trade — contributed to the infectious dynamism of Britain's music scene. "All of these records that were coming out of England had this dance beat, but the music affected the body in a different way than rock and roll," notes Jim Fouratt, who booked scores of U.K. acts to perform at Hurrah, Danceteria, the Peppermint Lounge, and Studio 54. "The sound that came out of these synthesizers and Linn drum machines, it wasn't rock and roll and it wasn't disco, either."

Released in the spring of 1981, Kraftwerk's "Numbers" and *Computer World* counterbalanced the Anglo influence, with Brian Chin declaring the stilted off-beats, rapidly modulating synthesizer lines, static effects, and vocoder voices of "Numbers" to be "one of the underground successes of the season."[21] "Larry broke 'Numbers,'" claims Boyd Jarvis. "The fags were like, 'What the hell is he [Levan] doing up there? What is he playing?' And they left the dance floor. Two weeks later they were running out to the floor whenever he played that record." Afrika Bambaataa also latched onto the new release, as did Kevorkian. "Everyone was so in awe of this mutant, futuristic music," remembers the Frenchman. "Giorgio Moroder already existed, but his productions were sugary and orchestral and incorporated pop textures, whereas 'Numbers' was radical. It was the first time many of us heard a song that was just one long breakdown. Kraftwerk were like electronic gods."

The European imports fed in to a musical mix that, in contrast to the party soundtrack of the 1970s, was largely based on music recorded in New York. For much of the previous decade DJs turned to Detroit and Philadelphia when searching for party music, with Los Angeles and Europe contributing more as the decade progressed. Beginning in the late 1970s and gaining momentum during the early 1980s, however, New York DJs turned with ever greater frequency to artists, producers, and remixers who lived in the city and, what's more, recorded music that seemed to capture its complex social rhythms. "What we feel around us, that's what we write," ESG told the *New York Rocker* in November. "Like, we hear this in the park, and this in the street and it brings sounds to your head. . . . Someday somebody might say, 'They sound like ESG; they've got that NY sound.'"[22] With Afrika Bambaataa and the Jazzy 5, David Byrne, "D" Train, Dinosaur L, Taana Gardner, Grandmaster Flash & the Furious Five, Inner Life (featuring Jocelyn Brown), Grace Jones, ESG, Liquid Liquid, Material (featuring Nona Hendryx), Talking Heads, and Tom Tom Club among the notable contributors, a new form of advanced social intelligence was coming into formation.

FROZEN IN TIME
OR FREED
INTO INFINITY

Damaged by the opening of the Saint, 12 West closed in early 1981. "The crowd was thinning out and my partners became greedy," recalls owner Alan Harris. "My feeling was, reinvest in the club because there was enough room in town for multiple venues. But my partners wanted the same financial arrangement they had when the club was in its heyday. They were straight and didn't care." After a brief hiatus the venue reopened as the West and then the River Club. DJ John Ceglia notes that the crowd contained more women, was a little older, and preferred a more intimate dance experience than its Saint counterpart. But Robbie Leslie remembers the venue was "never a hit" and wonders if it even made a profit. "The River Club was a haunt of the bridge-and-tunnel folks or those disenfranchised by the Saint," he comments.

Meanwhile Michael Fesco's diehard membership clung to Flamingo as if it were a cherished shirt that had a frayed collar and was in last season's shade. "I thought that we would survive but in the end we only managed to stick it out for six months," recalls the owner. Howard Merritt flew over from San Francisco to play the final party. "I contacted everyone I knew in the business and said, 'If there's a record out that's going to be huge I need it,' and everybody came through for me," he reminisces. "It was probably one of the best nights of music I ever played." Packed to capacity, the room became so hot the DJ stripped down to his jockstrap and used a towel to wipe away the condensation that dripped from the ceiling onto the turntables. Then, at the end of the last song, Merritt sat down and "cried like a baby" because Flamingo had been his home. "Where were you when the club needed your support?" he responded when dancers came up to him to declare their regret that the party had reached its denouement.

Fesco's party received a fitting tribute in the *New York Native* in March 1981. "[Flamingo] showed that there could in fact be a gay society, that one could in fact make this society and make one's way in it," wrote George Stambolian.

"If you didn't know already, this was where you learned how to perfect your dancing style, how to take, contour, and hold your drugs, how to walk, talk, and carry yourself, how to dress better and look better, how to improve your body and occasionally your mind, how to make friends and influence people."[1] If a quasi-totalitarian idea of perfection that revolved around whiteness, good looks, and muscularity also dominated this very unique form of finishing school, insiders experienced the process of selection as an overdue intervention on behalf of an ostracized community. "You sensed that beauty was more than pecs and proportion, it was in all those bodies moving to the same beat," added Stambolian. "You understood that pride was not only in personal accomplishment but in the fact that these men in this space could create such joy. And you recognized that power was not wealth or position, but the incredible energy you could generate with others on that floor and beyond."[2]

Bruce Mailman attempted to re-create the collectivity of the gay male dance floor by employing a roster of DJs who, by dint of their revolving employment, could never be more important than the club itself. The owner also calculated that he and his investors needed to institute a business model that didn't rely on the ongoing presence of a high-profile DJ, as was standard across the city, just in case relations turned sour and threatened the huge cost of their investment. Contributing to a scenario that saw the supply of first-rate DJs outstrip the number of venues where they could play, the decline of Flamingo and 12 West strengthened Mailman's position. Yet the owner also recognized that some kind of continuity was necessary, so he established a pool of principal DJs to play on Saturdays plus a secondary group of up-and-coming DJs to perform on other nights. If it remained the case that the Saint roster couldn't match the profound relationship Levan cultivated with his dancers at the Garage, they still got to play ten-hour sets, often on a regular basis, and that gave them plenty of scope to strike up lines of intense communication. For many, the act of DJ-ing in the Saint's slightly raised, Plexiglas-surrounded booth came to represent the pinnacle of their careers.

Three DJs provided a mix of continuity as well as variety on Saturday nights during the opening 1980–1981 season. Alan Dodd anchored the lineup with an uncomplicated approach that emphasized cut-glass smoothness and effortless flow. "People just wanted to dance," he remarks. "My role was to help them get there and just let the music speak for itself." Roy Thode, a significant presence in Manhattan after Steve Rubell hired him to work Studio 54's gay nights, was a busier DJ who liked to cut between back-beated copies of the same track to create an echo effect. "Roy could take a record and restructure it better than anyone," notes Marsha Stern, a close friend of the DJ and a Saint regular. "We would tease him and say he was getting too knobby, but the re-arranging was part of the art form. He had an innate sense of magic-making and a real rapport with the crowd." A trained opera singer and prolific studio hand who had mixed records such as "A Lover's Holiday" (Change), "Run-away Love" (Linda Clifford), and "Do Ya Think I'm Sexy?" (Rod Stewart), Jim Burgess combined skill, theatricality, and mercurial unpredictability. "He was probably the most talented mixologist," argues Robbie Leslie. "Sometimes he was on and sometimes not. But when he asserted himself, nobody could touch him for technique. He could do things that were so amazing you would almost stop dancing."

Dressed in black tie and tails, Burgess played his last party on 31 January, having announced his retirement in advance. A monstrous crowd clung to his every selection, elated to witness the grandest exit ever made by a DJ. Then, at the climax of his set at 6:00 AM, Burgess selected the extract from the film *Now, Voyager* when Bette Davis says, "If we both try hard to, to protect that little strip of territory that's ours . . . Oh, Jerry, don't let's ask for the moon. We have the stars." As the sound clip tailed off, lightman Richard Tucker turned on the star projector and illuminated the dome with a night sky, bedazzling the congregants gathered on the floor. "It was the most spectacular marriage of sound and light and people, all in harmony," reminisces Leslie. "It was prob-ably the most amazing moment in disco history." Burgess received a bouquet of two dozen white, long-stem roses, accepted his ovation, put on a Barbra Streisand record, and left the booth to enter a prebooked, chauffeur-driven white Bentley, leaving in his wake some several thousand men. "I said, 'Oh my god, he thinks he's at the Met!'" recalls Sharon White. "I was laughing. And then everyone realized there was not going to be any more music." The exit "almost precipitated a riot," adds Robbie Leslie, who left the venue a few minutes later. To add to the drama, Burgess had prepared an assistant to in-form anyone who deigned to fill the void that his record collection was not to be used. It was as if the Wicked Witch of the North had cast her spell and swooshed her cloak, leaving her kingdom in a state of despair and disarray.

Sitting on a banquette near the booth, and the DJ closest to the eye of the storm, White was told to put on a record or a tape by a manager, even though she had yet to make her debut at the venue. She threw on a copy of "I Don't Wanna Lose Your Love" by the Emotions before receiving her comeup-pance from Burgess's assistant. A moment later Mark Ackerman appeared, having made his way down from his third-floor apartment. Enjoying his first night off since opening, Ackerman had hurtled to the floor when he heard

Marsha Stern and Mark Ackerman in Maryland, Baltimore, ca. 1984. Stern got her Saint membership through Sharon White, who was best buddies with Ackerman. Photograph by Robbie Leslie ©; courtesy of Marsha Stern.

the music stop and, with White in tow, hurtled back up to grab some records. With another friend instructed to race to her home to gather more vinyl, White turned to Ackerman and admitted, "Now I know what it feels like to be a dead man walking." When the Emotions song "ended cold," as she knew it would, White selected a record with a message, Sumeria's "Dance and Leave It All behind You." "The crowd just went, 'Wow!'" she remembers. "It was like everybody had whiplash." The DJ played until 1:30 that afternoon. "Every title that I put on was thematic. I played my heart out."

In defiance of Mailman's declaration that no woman should DJ at the Saint, Mark Ackerman had already booked White to play on 29 March, declaring that he would resign if the owner didn't reverse his position. The lightman got his way, only for Mailman to insist that, in contrast to the male DJs who played at his venue, White should be listed as S. White and not by her full name (thus masking her sex). A furious Ackerman saw off that proposition as well, but a tone had been established that led White to gasp when Mailman — who had been traveling at the time of the Burgess farewell party — thanked her on his return. "He said he was very excited about the fact I was scheduled — *hello* — and asked me what fee I wanted for the performance," she recalls. "I said, 'I didn't do it for the money.'" White faced off skeptics following her formal debut. "They were like, 'Miss thing, let me see you do that again!'" she remembers. "I kicked some ass, no doubt about it!" White concluded it was "1,000 percent easier" to play for an all-male crowd than an all-female crowd. "To have people walk away as though you never existed for the night hurts and that's what happened at Sahara," she explains. "For me DJ-ing was a craft and it was something I was trying to hone. I worked really, really hard and the gay male audience rewarded me with their appreciation."

Dodd's decision to retire from DJ-ing at the end of the summer left Thode to play the major parties during the opening months of the second season, including Opening Night, Halloween, and New Year's Eve. George Cadenas, Leslie, and White also picked up Saturday nights during the final weeks of 1981, while Cadenas, Chuck Parsons, and finally Robbie Leslie debuted at the Sunday Tea slot. "I was quite upset about losing my job at 12 West when it happened, but it turned out to be advantageous because it freed me up to work at the Saint," remarks Leslie, who took to the turntables on 25 December 1980. "My reputation at that point was really quite sterling." Even if the memory of Burgess was fading, Leslie amounted to an antidote. "I wasn't a prima donna," he notes of his outlook. "If anything, I saw myself as an entertainer, as if I was doing a Broadway run and the show had to go on. I aspired to be in the lead but I knew that DJs — like actors — could be replaced so I was always pragmatic. I helped pioneer the concept of DJ freelancing."

SELECTED DISCOGRAPHY

ROY THODE, THE SAINT (1980–1981)

ABBA, "Lay All Your Love on Me"
Herb Alpert, "Manhattan Melody"
Ann-Margret, "Everybody Needs Somebody Sometimes"
Area Code (212), "Manhattan Shuffle"
Claudja Barry, "Love for the Sake of Love"
Claudja Barry & Ronnie Jones, "The Two of Us"
Watson Beasley, "Breakaway"

Leonard Bernstein, *West Side Story*

Blondie, "Rapture"

Cerrone, "Trippin' on the Moon"

Teri De Sario, "Ain't Nothing Gonna Keep Me from You"

Taana Gardner, "Heartbeat (Club Version)"

Gibson Brothers, "Que Sera Mi Vida"

Peter Griffin, "Step By Step"

Daryl Hall & John Oates, "I Can't Go for That (No Can Do)"

Harlow, "Take Off"

Thelma Houston, "Too Many Teardrops"

Instant Funk, "Got My Mind Made Up"

The Jacksons, "Can You Feel It?"

The Jacksons, "Walk Right Now"

Chas Jankel, "Glad to Know You"

Carol Jiani, "All the People of the World"

Carol Jiani, "Hit 'n Run Lover"

Evelyn "Champagne" King, "I Don't Know If It's Right"

Kat Mandu, "The Break"

Suzi Lane, "Harmony"

LOI, "Body Contact"

Kelly Marie, "Feels Like I'm in Love"

Gwen McCrae, "Funky Sensation"

Buddy Miles, "Pull Yourself Together"

Ennio Morricone, "Chi Mai"

Olivia Newton-John, "Magic"

Yoko Ono, "Walking on Thin Ice"

Ozo, "Anambra"

Bruni Pagán, "Fantasy"

Passengers, "Hot Leather"

Bonnie Pointer, "Heaven Must Have Sent You"

Bonnie Pointer, "I Can't Help Myself (Sugar Pie, Honey Bunch)"

The Pointer Sisters, *Black and White*

The Pointer Sisters, "Happiness"

The Pointer Sisters, "We Got the Power"

The Police, "Voices inside My Head"

Poussez! "Come On and Do It (Special Disco Mix)"

Quick, "Young Men Drive Fast"

Raes, "Don't Turn Around"

Sharon Redd, "Can You Handle It?"

Barbara Roy and Ecstasy, Passion and Pain, "If You Want Me"
Dee Dee Sharp Gamble, "Breaking and Entering"
Softones, "That Old Black Magic"
Spider, "Better Be Good to Me"
Stevie B, "Midnight Music"
Rod Stewart, "Passion"
Stylistics, "Driving Me Wild"
Suzy Q, "With Your Love"
Talking Heads, "Once in a Lifetime"
Jean Terrell, "Rising Cost of Love"
Two Tons o' Fun, "I Got the Feeling (The Patrick Cowley Megamix)"
Westside Strutters, "The Man I Love/Embraceable You"
Jessica Williams, "Queen of Fools"
Viola Wills, "If You Could Read My Mind"

To a man plus one woman, Saint DJs selected records according to an arc of intensity that was more precisely calibrated in terms of tempo and energy than anything attempted by the wider profession. Tuning the room with a record that incorporated variations in pitch and volume while making a taste statement, they often opened with an orchestral selection as dancers settled down on the banquettes that surrounded the floor and took in the light show. After that they played bright, mid-tempo songs as they built to the peak, which ran from 2:00 to 6:00 AM and featured high-tempo tracks that raced along at 132 BPM (beats per minute) upward. After that they would let the final record of the peak set fade, accept the applause of the crowd, acknowledge the work of the lightperson, and begin an elongated down-tempo "sleaze" or "morning music" set. "In a symphony there would be all of these movements and you could transpose that to a night at the Saint, where it would start off allegro, move to presto, and then peak with a crescendo," comments Leslie. "After the encore you would take it down and then build it up again and then end with something sentimental, romantic, or thought-provoking."

Leslie would go on to characterize the communication that took place between the DJ and the Saint crowd as a "third-person consciousness" in an interview with the *New York Native*.[3] Yet he also acknowledges that the crowd demanded "a very smooth flow" during the middle part of the set, when the playing of certain records was almost mandatory. White confirms that while the DJs weren't clones of one another, they were "expected to play the things that were popular with the crowd at that particular moment," which led her to half-joke that they "played the same records but in a different order." DJS could take a left turn and reclaim the initiative during the morning music set because by then the crowd had been satiated. "We shined as individuals after 6:00 AM," continues White, who would begin her final stretch "in the 80s" and claims she could stay at 105 BPM for hours. "I stretched BPMs like nobody I knew."

The variation, contrast, and drama introduced at 6:00 AM could rival anything experienced on the party scene, as White demonstrated when she told Ackerman to turn off all the lights (including the fire exit lights) as the post-peak applause rang out, and selected an acetate copy of Patti LaBelle singing "Somewhere over the Rainbow." "Mark brought everything down," she recalls. "Everything that was visual just melted away. Then I started 'Over the Rainbow' and he started to slowly heat up the room by light." Dancers held hands, hugged each other, cried. "Mark and I had to take a moment to collect ourselves. Then we took a bow, I threw them a kiss and said, 'We're going to go back up!'" The DJ selected a Cerrone number, turned to Ackerman, and told him that that was the moment she had been waiting for her whole life. "Everyone was feeling the same thing. It was a moment of synchronicity." The morning set could stretch well into the afternoon, with White's personal record ending at 6:00 PM. "I kept saying, 'Please let me stop!'" she recalls of the final stretch. "'I can't do any more coke! I can't do any more downs! I can't drink any more champagne! I can't play any more records!'" White played from a cellular level as Ackerman spurred her on. "Honestly, I was unapproachable," she recalls of the moment she took the tone arm off the final selection. "I was like, 'Don't talk to me!' I locked the door of the booth, lay down, and cried. There was just nothing left to do. Every ounce of energy and emotion had gone into the night."

To varying degrees, the Saint DJs meshed African American artists with synthetic, up-tempo Eurodisco sounds during 1981, just as they had during the final months of 1980. Moving without obvious inhibition at the Black Party, for instance, Thode blended the soulful R&B sounds of "Heartbeat" (Taana Gardner), "Can You Feel It?" (the Jacksons), "Can You Handle It" (Sharon Redd), and "Hot Shot" (Karen Young) with pop, rock, and electronic disco selections such as "Feels Like I'm in Love" (Kelly Marie), "Passion" (Rod Stewart), "Magic" (Olivia Newton-John), and "Cherchez Pas" (Madleen Kane).[4] San Francisco remained a rich source of music for Thode and his colleagues, especially thanks to Patrick Cowley, a onetime music student at the City College of San Francisco, who forged a thick, pulsating synthesizer sound that augmented the pioneering efforts of Giorgio Moroder on Sylves-

Robert Mapplethorpe flyer for the "Saint Black Party," 20–22 March 1981. Designer unknown; courtesy of the Saint at Large.

ter's disco-era hits "You Make Me Feel (Mighty Real)" and "Dance (Disco Heat)," only for Sylvester to back away from disco during the recording of *Sell My Soul* and *Too Hot to Sleep*. ("I like midtempo tunes where I get a chance to work the lyrics," Sylvester told *Billboard* in 1981. "I settle in with this type of song easier than when I'm jumping around doing disco tunes.")[5] Fronted by the gospel-trained Sylvester sidekicks Izora Rhodes and Martha Wash, Two Tons o' Fun compensated with the release of "Just Us," "I Got the Feeling," and "Do You Wanna Boogie, Hunh?" Meanwhile Cowley released a "Megamix" of "I Got the Feeling" along with "Menergy" and "Megatron Man." "From 2:00 to 5:00 in the morning, we would play all of these really fast, popular records," comments Leslie. "They were very masculine and a lot of them came out of San Francisco or were released by San Francisco labels."

The Saint DJs also looked to Europe and Canada, where the mainstream backlash against disco was less marked, selecting songs such as Peter Griffin's "Step by Step," Carol Jiani's "Hit 'n Run Lover," Phyllis Nelson's "Don't Stop the Train," the Passengers' "Hot Leather," and Tantra's "The Hills of Katmandu" along with cuts from ABBA's *The Visitors*. "The twelve-inch import market

Sylvester (left) and Howard Merritt photographed at a record-pool party in San Francisco ca. 1981. Merritt was DJ-ing at Dreamland at the time. Photographer unknown; courtesy of Howard Merritt.

became a major part of our weekly purchases," explains Leslie. "Record companies sprang up in Canada, Italy, England, and to a lesser extent the Benelux countries. Producers were shopping around music productions that were already in the can. They couldn't sell them to American record labels so they shopped them to smaller labels. The level of creativity did go down a step but there were notable exceptions." Mailman's roster maintained standards by returning to late disco classics such as "Without Your Love" (Cut Glass), "Hold on to My Love" (Jimmy Ruffin), "Touch Me in the Morning" (Marlena Shaw), and "Souvenirs" (Voyage). Meanwhile slower, funkier productions were very much edged to the margins. "We would have been lynched in our DJ booth if we played Taana Gardner at 3:00 or 4:00 AM on a Saturday night," insists Leslie. "That would have been heretical. The [white] gay clubs demanded a high-energy format, and they wanted to dance hard and long, especially during the peak hours."

Spending a lot less time at the Saint than they had at the most influential white gay venues of the 1970s, New York record promoters and writers began to critique what they perceived to be the increasingly conservative taste of the affluent gay audience. "Demanding 1977-model disco almost nostalgically, they refuse to accept the new black music as theirs," argued *Dance Music Report*. "And that represents a crucial breakdown in the coalition that launched hits with combined black/gay salespower. The ascendancy of the gay population culturally and politically has stalled."[6] Once proud of the way he had "started breaking records right out of Fire Island," Ray Caviano, now an independent promoter, declared that white gay dancers on both coasts were stuck in a musical time warp that involved them listening to a sound that had been established three years earlier, adding that "Euro up-tempo records have trouble crossing over."[7] Mel Cheren maintains that while "a Garage hit translated into a record store hit almost overnight," this was "not so at the Saint."[8] White acknowledges that "the Garage attracted a record-buying public, the Saint less of a record-buying public."

Inside the venue, however, any sense of stagnation was offset by the ongoing awe generated by the Saint's futuristic infrastructure, the consummate skill of its DJs, and the transcendental energy of the tribal dance. Characterizing the Saint as the "Vatican of clubs," the gay-leaning entertainment magazine *After Dark* maintained that the Second Avenue spot amounted to an "incredible symbiotic environment." It added: "Not everyone is enthralled. Some complain about clone clubs, outmoded music and macho attitudes that need a dose of adulthood. But the chemistry that kicks off some ancient impulse has inflamed the troops every time since The Saint opened last September. The effects at the place are indeed special, and its technology is the freshest state of the art."[9] Record promoters couldn't sell the theatrical interior of Mailman's venue while the shift toward sonic homogeneity distanced its DJs and dancers from the citywide embrace of mutation. But neither factor concerned those who continued to flock to the venue in the thousands.

IT FELT LIKE
THE WHOLE CITY
WAS LISTENING

Dance music slumped to a national sales nadir during 1981. Although Kool and the Gang hit number one on the Hot 100 with "Celebration" early in the year, the rest of the chart featured few black, up-tempo recordings, and while the successes of Blondie's "Rapture" and Queen's "Another One Bites the Dust" indicated that dance music could still cross over, the majors declined to develop these records beyond a pop context. "The disco person at Chrysalis had gone so there was nobody to notice that they could have sold 150,000 pieces of vinyl if they had put out a remix of 'Rapture,'" points out Brian Chin, who started to submit fortnightly rather than weekly "Disco File" columns to *Record World* due to the slowdown in output.[1] Warner Bros. "weren't enthused" when the Kid Creole and Was (Not Was) albums — precisely the kinds of recordings that might have appealed to the departed Ray Caviano — came to them via Sire and Island. Although the majors started to issue twelve-inch singles again in the summer, with Spandau Ballet's "Chant No. 1 (I Don't Need This Pressure On)" among the most notable, the trend was hesitant. The corporates, Chin observed in August, were hoping to "delve into the specialist market without upsetting it as they had in 1979."[2]

The corporate exodus presented the city's independents with an opportunity. Arguing for the need to bypass the majors in *Dance Music Report*, Tom Silverman name-checked Downstairs, Rock & Soul, and Vinyl Mania as examples of stores that were "owned by people who know and love the music they sell," with club exposure and in-store play regarded as key to their survival now that radio had also pulled away.[3] While the corporations remained convinced that disco had died, Silverman added, clubs and record stores were forming the "nucleus" of a new network that would "probably remain a very profitable 'underground' operation."[4] Three months later the publisher teamed up with Mark Josephson and two other colleagues to stage the second New Music Seminar, where panelists discussed the term "new music," racism within the music business, the rise of Anglophilia, and the reluctance of AOR (album-oriented rock) radio stations to play new wave. Disco, rap, and R&B featured more prominently than they had before.[5] "This get-together of dissidents came at a time when the big-time, mainstream music business is in considerable trouble," commented John Rockwell in the *New York Times*. "New club circuits and musical forms are springing up and clinging to life without major record contracts and radio play."[6] By the end of the year the *Daily News* was reporting that "small record labels and self-produced singles make small but real profits" within a down-town music scene that's "limited and self-contained but alive."[7]

Initially located in a tiny space on Carmine Street, Vinyl Mania sold rock, rock, and more rock until owners Charlie and Debbie Grappone realized they were generating more business out of a small box of twelve-inch singles than the rest of the store put together. The explanation for the pattern could be found two blocks away on King Street. "Larry Levan was a very powerful DJ and he dictated what we should sell," adds the entrepreneur, who says he went from being Mr. Rock and Roll to Mr. Disco in next to no time. "He could have played Indian sitar music and the Paradise Garage crowd would have bought it." The Grappones moved into larger premises on Carmine Street during 1981, and they hired roommates/Garage regulars Manny Lehman and Judy Russell to work in the store. "Charlie talked to me and saw that I understood the value of the twelve-inch single," says Lehman, who came recommended by Bobby Shaw, a Warner Bros. dance promoter. "DJs would come in and say, 'What's hot?' I soon got to work the counter because I was dependable and smart." Russell bonded with Levan over a mutual love of Harrison Ford mov-ies. "Larry would leave our names at the door and invited us into the booth," she recalls. "We could go in and look at what he was playing."

Heading to the Garage on Saturdays because to go there on Fridays would have left them too tired to work, Lehman and Russell were among the first to learn the titles of Levan's selections. "They became very close with Larry Levan," recalls Charlie. "They were in that DJ booth and they loved the music. They were my 'in' there. Manny and Judy's knowledge of the Garage made my business." When Levan stopped by the store for the first time and picked out records worth $125, Grappone waived the bill, having recently cleared some five thousand copies of "Heartbeat." All he and his wife had to do was show up on a Saturday morning and unlock the store so the queue of fifty Garage dancers could start to purchase what they had heard during the night.

Vinyl Mania was no subsidiary operation, however, and gained credibility for the way it catered to the city's wider party network. "From the late seventies through to the mid-eighties, clubs were very, very powerful in New York," says Grappone. "Three clubs in particular sold records — the Paradise Garage, the Loft, and the Funhouse." John "Jellybean" Benitez, Mark Kamins, and Robbie Leslie were among those who headed regularly to the store. "Vinyl Mania sold domestic product like Megatone, Moby Dick, Prism, and other independent labels that were difficult to find anywhere else, but their stock in trade was basically imports from Italy, Germany, and London," points out Leslie. "They supplied their customers pretty much equally. Everyone who went there got along. There was no attitude that this was Saint music and this was Garage music." Referred to by Grappone as his "human dictionary of dance music," Lehman remained pivotal. "I knew which crowds liked which songs," states the salesman.

As national disco radio crashed in tandem with the disco juggernaut, New York's party DJs re-asserted themselves as preeminent taste connoisseurs who could break records locally and regionally but not nationally — because the national market had evaporated. They did so with the help of the city's radio DJs, who monitored their selections in order to feed their own listeners with fresh sounds. Frankie Crocker of WBLS led the way, having shifted the black station's mix of activism and avant-garde jazz toward popular jazz, R&B, and disco back in the early 1970s. The first radio DJ to play tracks such as Manu Dibango's "Soul Makossa" and Donna Summer's "Love to Love You Baby," Crocker modified the station's slogan from "The Total Black Experience in Sound" to "The Total Experience in Sound," only for unproven allegations of payola to force him out in 1977. He introduced the "Disco and More" moniker upon his return two years later and rode the backlash. Mark Riley, a co-employee of Crocker's, notes that the catchphrase became ubiquitous and helped the station get back to number one. "Disco sucks was like saying eating sucks," points out Crocker. "It was like, hang on a second, I'm still eating!" Even after disco's crash, the DJ knew that sales could increase by fifty thousand if he supported a record. "Anything that was being played in the clubs might end up on Frankie Crocker's playlist," notes Carol Cooper. "He was a genius and never gets enough credit for it."

Crocker became a regular presence in the booth at the Paradise Garage and even arranged for Levan to play several spots on WBLS's Saturday Night Dance Party until Michael Brody "got pissed off because he thought people wouldn't come out," notes David DePino. A subsequent scuffle broke out when the Garage owner and the self-styled "Chief Rocker" battled to book Gwen McCrae to perform "Funky Sensation" at rival events during 1981, but they got over the row because Crocker appreciated the value of Levan's selections, many

Judy Russell and Manny Lehman. Photograph by and courtesy of Joey Llanos.

of which he worked into his show, while Brody recognized that Levan accrued important cultural capital from the relationship. "Frankie understood
very clearly what club records worked on the radio and what club records
only worked in a club," observes Riley. "Radio is incredibly compressed so
what sounded wonderful at the Garage didn't always translate if someone was
listening to the same record in their car or even at home. You could see that
Frankie would go on certain songs and not go on others." Nor did Crocker see
his visits to the Garage in terms of work. "I went there to enjoy it," he notes.
"Larry and I, we recognized each other."

Crocker enjoyed a less mutually supportive relationship with the National
Black Committee for Economic Justice, which called for African Americans
to boycott WBLS until it became more responsive to black-owned labels in the
spring of 1981. A few months later *Dance Music Report* claimed that the committee was made up of "an extremely small group of black NY-based record
companies" that had become "frustrated by their inability to get their records
(largely of the rap variety) on the air."[8] The group's charge was nevertheless
solid. "Frankie wasn't playing no rap, not in 1980, because it didn't fit in with
the kind of sophisticated sound and image he had spent the last decade building," explains Riley. "What was fascinating is the established clubs shunned

rap, and the black music departments of most of the record companies also shunned rap, and so did black radio. It was like, 'This is going to go away. This is going to go away. I know it's going to go away.' And it never went away."

At the time Crocker must have been more worried about the defection of Shep Pettibone from WBLS to WRKS, otherwise known as Kiss FM, a new black-oriented station that first aired on 1 August 1981. A fan of Roy Thode and Jim Burgess, Pettibone wanted to break into club DJ-ing but landed his steadiest work at WKTU, where he picked up tips from Ted Currier, a skilled tape editor who pioneered Studio 92 (WKTU's response to WBLS's Saturday Night Dance Party). Then, in late 1979, Pettibone met Crocker and accepted his offer to work at WBLS. "Frankie Crocker began to use my mixes in his show," recalls the mixer. "He would say, 'And here's a new supermix by our own Shep Pettibone.' It was at BLS that I made my name. Working for BLS was a dream." When Crocker learned that Kiss-FM program director Barry Mayo wanted to sign Pettibone, he told his "secret weapon" he'd be sorry if he left. "But BLS wasn't paying me," Pettibone notes of his decision to accept the offer. "That summer I ended up producing fifteen hours of dance parties and three mastermixes every week. I played every lunch hour and Saturday nights. There were a lot of tapes."

An aspiring DJ from Brooklyn who worked in the mailroom at the *New York Daily News*, Tony Humphries teamed up with Pettibone at Kiss after he became friendly with a "very close clique" of black and Latin gay men during vinyl-gathering trips to record companies. Pioneering DJ David Rodriguez introduced him to the Loft and the Paradise Garage, where he discovered "the perfect world of partying." David Todd, another trailblazing DJ, encouraged him to stick at it after he burst into his office at RCA and shouted, "Fuck this business! Nobody can get in, man! What, do you have to be gay to get in this business?" Michael Gomes proceeded to introduce Humphries to Pettibone during a chance meeting at the Prelude office, which gave Humphries the opportunity to hand Pettibone a tape. A week later the Kiss DJ asked him to deliver a four-hour show for the next day, a Saturday. Then, in the autumn of 1981, Humphries started to record mix shows for the weekends. "Shep made sure that all of the shows were produced by him so they would be promoted as 'mixed by Tony Humphries, produced by Shep Pettibone,'" he recalls. "It was a great marketing tool. He was huge."

Meanwhile John Rivas, another Brooklyn DJ, provided rap producers with consistent airtime on his show, "Mr. Magic's Disco Showcase," launched in the spring of 1979 on WHBI, a for-hire station that sold airtime to "vanity" buyers. Combining disco and funk with rap, Magic kept going thanks to advertising support from Sal Abbatiello at Disco Fever plus a dedicated audience that navigated the station's French, Greek, Slavic, and West Indian programs.[9] A number of downtowners joined the listenership after WPAIX cut back on its punk and new wave programming. "Mr. Magic wasn't scratching," points out Leonard Abrams. "He was just segueing from one song into another. Thematically it was as good as anything else out there. It was apparent that black radio was more alive than white radio." When Magic started to play "Jazzy Sensation," remembers Silverman, the phones lit up in the Tommy Boy office, and the next week he received orders for five thousand to ten thousand units.

For the time being, however, the Paradise Garage and WBLS continued to provide promoters with their key axis. "Larry had a lot of people who were trying to get him to play their records six months before they were released," reasons François Kevorkian. "There were all these people vying for position and trying to assert power and control. Ray Caviano would come into the booth a lot and when Ray was in other people had to get out of the way because he was the big dog." Crocker's presence in the booth counted for a great deal to Kenneth Reynolds, now director of publicity in the black music department at PolyGram, because the WBLS figurehead had "thousands and thousands of listeners" and "would come to the Garage to check what Larry was doing to keep his program on track." Caviano confirms that during this period "all roads led to the Paradise Garage because Frankie Crocker was listening to what was breaking on the dance floor."

Indifferent to the task of promoting records, Levan nevertheless became a sales machine by dint of his commitment to introducing music with the maximum possible impact. "Larry had this ability to focus with pinpoint accuracy, with a killer instinct, on what was good about the song," argues Kevorkian. "He knew how to work a record so that the crowd would beg for it. Larry would *break* records whereas other DJs would just *play* them." The Garage DJ would also select a record several times during the course of a night so that it became imprinted on the memory of his crowd, "and the next day you'd walk past Vinyl Mania and you'd find yourself asking for it," recalls Danny Krivit. Promoters even began to arrange for acts to perform at the Garage for free because "it was far more important to 'break a record' through the Garage than receive a fee of $1,000–$10,000," adds Reynolds. David DePino maintains that people went to the spot "not to hear the music that was happening but to hear the music that Larry was making happen." All understood that the venue operated as an unrivaled if not unprecedented platform for the presentation of new music. "There was no such reach from anyone else," concludes Kevorkian. "It felt like the whole city was listening."

In charge of a record pool that counted the Saint DJs among its highly re-garded number, Judy Weinstein developed her closest relationship with Levan. "I acted as Larry's manager but I didn't call myself a manager," she says. "I was definitely a go-between when he worked on remixes." Weinstein also staged a party for For the Record at the Garage on Monday 1 June 1981 that doubled as "an opportunity for deejays and industry folk to get re-acquainted," reported *Billboard*.[10] Record pool members, artists, and industry representatives enjoyed a buffet before a crowd of 2,500 filed in to listen to performances by Gloria Gaynor, Chaka Khan, and Billy Ocean, each introduced by Crocker. Benitez, Jonathan Fearing, Krivit, and Kenny Morgan along with Levan worked the turntables. "The community turned out in vast numbers to show that the dance movement is very much alive," proclaimed an increasingly confident *Dance Music Report*.[11]

Levan's proximity to Weinstein and Crocker along with Mel Cheren, his unmatched remixing profile, and his ability to break records set the Paradise Garage apart from the Loft, where Mancuso kept his dealings with the indus-try to a minimum. That had always been his way, even when he cofounded the New York Record Pool, the first organization of its type. Mark Riley re-calls going to a meeting at Warner Bros. in which the Loft host showed up wearing mismatched socks and possibly mismatched shoes. "When we walked into the lobby the receptionist looked at us as though she was about to call security," recalls Riley. "David never identified himself by his full name unless he was asked, so when she said, 'What's your name?' David replied, 'David.' There was a pause. 'David . . . who?' Then he said, 'Mancuso.' And as soon as he said that everything changed instantly. It was an amazing thing to see." When Mancuso wound down the pool in order to focus exclusively on his parties and Weinstein picked up the slack by opening For the Record, the balance of promotional power slipped inexorably toward King Street. "If you brought David a record he'd play it, but David didn't go after records and he didn't work the sound system, so the industry people gravitated to the Garage and the Garage became the hub," points out Michael Gomes. "The Garage was the only game in town."

SHROUDED
ABATEMENTS
AND
MYSTERIOUS
DEATHS

In 1981 William K. Tabb published *The Long Default*, a caustic analysis of the consequences of New York City's descent into bankruptcy in the mid-1970s that outlined how the city's desperate financial situation left it vulnerable to the banking sector, which demanded redundancies, a wage freeze, cuts to welfare and services, a bump in the cost of public transport, and the abolition of free tuition fees in return for bailout money. Deeming New York to be the naughtiest child in the federal union, President Ford's Secretary of the Treasury advised that the terms of any bailout should be "so punitive, the overall experience so painful, that no city, no political subdivision would ever be tempted to go down the same road."[1] A senator observed that while the "imminent fall of Saigon drove the Ford administration to demand another billion dollars of aid," the "imminent fall of New York finds that Administration resistant even to a bond guarantee."[2]

Although Ford softened his approach a couple of months later, handing the city a $2.3 billion loan to tide it over the next three years, Mayor Ed Koch carried forward the budget-tightening program to the point where Republicans began to openly admire the way he valued economic discipline over the needs of his citizens. Reagan didn't need to interfere in the city's affairs after his election victory in November 1980 because it was already turning itself into a model of fiscal discipline. Whereas Ford had criticized New York for lagging behind the rest of the country, Reagan regarded it as exemplary. "The shift to neoconservative reprivatization that is proceeding rapidly under the Reagan administration is merely the New York scenario [of the 1970s] writ large," observed Tabb.[3]

Koch let it be known that he admired Reagan shortly after his election victory. In part the mayor was simply relieved he wouldn't have to continue his strained relationship with Carter. Yet he also thought Reagan could benefit the city and told a student gathering at Princeton University that voters hadn't moved to the right but were instead saying they wanted decision making to shift from the center to the local. "Is that conservative?" he asked. "I happen to think that is liberal."[4] Koch won additional admirers in the White House when budget cuts and tax rises enabled him to balance the city's finances a year ahead of schedule. "This does not mean that the days of wine and roses have returned, or that fiscal discipline can be relaxed," he noted of his more relaxed budget of January 1981. "It does mean, though, that the worst pain is behind us, that cutting can be balanced with new initiatives."[5]

Koch felt less sanguine when Reagan slashed spending by just under $700 billion in his March budget and in so doing withdrew funds that were earmarked for the country's struggling cities. The development amounted to a significant shift in policy, for while Carter, in tandem with Federal Reserve chief Paul Volcker, had initiated belt-tightening monetarist measures during 1979 to combat inflation, the Democrat president had also believed that union and the welfare state should remain strong, whereas Reagan intensified the cutting without holding on to any such principles — and that, argues critic David Harvey, was one of the key elements that marked the Republican's lurch into neoliberalism.[6] In response, Koch proposed a $2 billion capital budget that would mark the beginning of a ten-year reconstruction program and set about stimulating a property-development boom that would attract business and create jobs.[7] The initiative helped him romp home to victory in the November mayoral election, after which he deigned to criticize Reagan's budget as a "sham and a shame" that threatened the well-being of cities. "In withdrawing Federal involvement from the needs of the people and the cities, President Reagan protests that he is returning to the states responsibility that is properly a local concern," argued the mayor. "In truth, he is employing the mask of federalism for a systematic campaign of abandonment."[8]

During 1981 real estate space expanded at eighteen times the rate of Koch's first three years in office.[9] The most conspicuous tycoon to enter the grab, Donald Trump bought the Barbizon-Plaza Hotel at Sixth Avenue and 58th Street plus a fourteen-story apartment house on Central Park South while other developers completed the Park Avenue Plaza, the Vista International Hotel, and the Hotel Parker Meridien. But if the activity gave the impression of a city returning to health, officials started to ask if its economy had been on the verge of a recovery anyhow and also if the heavy tax cuts offered to private investors were necessary. "There is virtually no building going on in the city which is not subsidized," a tax consultant told the *New York Times* in July. "The city is giving away its tax base."[10] Koch tried to stem the flow by denying Trump a $20 million sweetener to build Trump Tower, a $155 million, sixty-story luxury complex on Fifth Avenue, only for the mogul to successfully sue on the grounds that he was the victim of a "purely political act."[11] Property developers appeared to be becoming more powerful than the hands that fed them.

The surging real estate market would go on to suffocate large sections of the city's party scene, but for now the scene continued to flourish. In his reflections on a year almost ended, Brian Chin argued that discotheques still constituted the most socially and musically open settings in the country, and that 1981 had ushered in the rebirth of dance. "There's no reason to be defensive about disco any more," he argued. "It is here in its many forms, here to stay, and forever transforming itself with unexpected discoveries and alliances."[12] In another piece published in December, the *Record World* columnist maintained that the enfants terribles of new wave and rap had been assimilated into the dance mainstream. "The big trend was *quality*," he eulogized. "Fans of dance music haven't feasted on such a consistent flow of truly distinguished music since late 1977."[13]

But the talk of rebirth was countered by reports that a mysterious infection was leading gay men to contract rare illnesses such as Kaposi's sarcoma, a cancer that featured lesions on the skin, and PCP, or pneumocystis pneumonia, a lung infection. Larry Mass — Steve Mass's brother, a gay doctor who had become distant from his family — published the first story about the "exotic new disease" in the *New York Native* in May 1981.[14] The *New York Times* began its coverage two months later. "The cause of the outbreak is unknown, and there is as yet no evidence of contagion," wrote Lawrence K. Altman. "But the doctors who have made the diagnoses, mostly in New York City and the San Francisco Bay area, are alerting other physicians who treat large numbers of homosexual men to the problem in an effort to help identify more cases and to reduce the delay in offering chemotherapy treatment."[15] Later in the year the appearance of PCP in drug users who used needles confirmed that women and straight men weren't immune, although contamination rates remained far higher among gay men.

Not yet named, HIV/AIDS is believed to have passed from a chimpanzee to a human during the late nineteenth or early twentieth century, arriving in the United States in the late 1960s or early 1970s. "There was a big party called Beach and in 1979 it held a fund-raiser to buy a fire truck for the Pines," recalls Howard Merritt. "That was the last big season when everyone was there. I noticed the change in 1980." A friend of a friend of Jorge La Torre became infected that summer. "He was isolated in this hospital room," recalls the dancer. "He was wrapped up in this plastic. Nobody was allowed to go in.

The doctors didn't know what was going on." La Torre adds: "I didn't know what to make of it and neither did anyone else so we didn't do much about it. But it began to take shape very soon after that." Having moved to San Francisco at the end of the summer, Merritt and his boyfriend adopted a kid who was "put in a ward with twelve other guys." By the summer of 1981 two of the men who shared a Pines house with Merritt had also passed away. "It was, 'Hush-hush, what did he die of?'" recounts the DJ. "Nobody knew how you got it or why."

In August Larry Kramer, the author of *Faggots*, a contentious 1978 novel that critiqued the level of promiscuity and drug consumption in the gay bathhouse and dance scene, arranged for eighty men to gather in his Manhattan apartment in order to map out a response. They agreed to set up an organization that would soon be called the Gay Men's Health Crisis and for volunteers to head to Fire Island to raise money over Labor Day weekend. "Kramer and Paul Popham, a poised vice president of Irving Trust and a fixture of the Island's social scene, sat outside the Ice Palace, a Cherry Grove disco, from midnight to dawn," record Dudley Clendinen and Adam Nagourney in *Out for Good*. "That Saturday night they raised a total of $126 — the equivalent of twelve admissions to the disco — at a club which easily held a thousand people. Their entire take for Labor Day weekend, one of the busiest weekends of the season, was $769.55."[16] Although the *New York Times* story indicated that the new disorder carried a greater threat than other sexually transmitted diseases, few wanted to interrupt the festivities with thoughts of mortality.

The spread of the disease wasn't limited to the white gay scene. "The AIDS horror was just starting as the first Danceteria opened," notes Max Blagg. "There were a couple of people struck down while we were open." It was also during 1980 that Rochester-raised Barry Walters lost his virginity to a clubbing friend, having enrolled to study at Fordham University in August 1979. "This is not the best time to be gay," Walters remembers the friend telling him. "There's this thing going around." It was a scary time, sexually. "Herpes and syphilis and gonorrhea were all prevalent in the gay community, even before AIDS," adds Walters. "By 1981 the word was out." The disease spread rapidly and with impunity. "I found out that friends of mine were in the hospital," remembers David Mancuso. "They seemed to be OK, and then they would get violently ill and die. People were going quickly." The level of fear became tangible. "If someone knew someone was sick, my god, people were afraid to be in the same building," adds the party host. "By 1981 people were dropping like flies."

So it came to pass that at the moment of dance culture's rebirth, a viral death sentence started to circulate in its midst.

PART III

1982

DANCE CULTURE SEIZES THE CITY

ALL WE HAD
WAS THE CLUB

On 6 January 1982 the *Village Voice* published a caustic survey of the city's live discotheque scene. Refurbished ballrooms such as the Ritz, the Peppermint Lounge, and Bond's "seemed too large," wrote Michael Hill, while smaller pioneering locations such as CBGB and the Mudd Club had "degenerated into tourist attractions." In other developments, Hurrah and Irving Plaza had closed, Trax was struggling to survive, and rumor had it that Max's Kansas City was about to turn into a Burger King outlet. Responding to charges that the Ritz underpaid local bands, intimidated single women, employed overzealous bouncers, and rammed in customers, Jerry Brandt argued that his spot never became more packed than the subway at rush hour — as if that didn't illustrate Hill's point perfectly — and added that his refusal to introduce a selective door policy countered the "fascism" of other venues. Peppermint Lounge promoter Frank Roccio acknowledged that his willingness to pay higher fees had led to the demise of some smaller venues. Jim Fouratt claimed that the "mega-clubs" had "killed the clubs that developed the acts for the mega-clubs."[1]

The argument between the Peppermint Lounge, the Ritz, and the rest had flared the previous May when Ruth Polsky, Fouratt's successor at Hurrah, told the *New York Times* that the "bigger clubs" had started a price war.[2] Yet the smaller venues were supposed to thrive on the fleet-footedness and creativity that set them apart from the larger spots — something that Roccio happily pointed to when he described himself as a businessman and Steve Mass as an artist in an interview with the *East Village Eye*.[3] Nor were the larger clubs a straightforwardly destructive force. Nobody had complained about the Electric Circus being oversized during the heyday of its countercultural activity, and while the Ritz "wasn't perfect," acknowledges Justin Strauss, it remained the case that "an amazing amount of music was exposed there." Large venues could also compete with one another, as became clear when Roccio relocated to the site of the old Electric Circus in order to challenge the Ritz on down-town turf. Ultimately there was no wipeout, as the *New York Rocker* made clear when it ran a special issue on the "Downtown Sound" in June 1982, list-ing fifteen venues that supported downtown bands.

Of the smaller venues and their owners, Steve Mass continued to run a credible program that kicked off on New Year's Eve with James White and the Blacks, the group's first appearance at the venue. "We wanted to play there," notes James Chance. "It was Steve Mass who kept blowing hot and cold about it. I ended up playing there after Anya died and then he was happy to book me, so that tells you something." Although Mass maintains he was "being outbid by everybody," the program featured blues legend Cocoa Taylor, folk singer Eric Anderson, and Latin jazz maestro Eddie Palmieri along with more punk, new wave, and avant-rock choices, among them the Au Pairs, Bow Wow Wow, Glenn Branca, John Cale, Rhys Chatham, ESG, Flipper, Konk, Klaus Nomi, R.E.M., Sonic Youth, and 3 Teens Kill 4. If the absence of happenings indicated that the venue was no longer surging forward, the scheduling of an *East Village Eye* benefit, a special party for *Details*, a Beat poetry evening, and an event featuring Nam June Paik confirmed that the venue's conceptual mix of 1979–1980 remained in place. The night when Afrika Bambaataa, Dinosaur L, Allen Ginsberg, and the Rock Steady Crew performed at a benefit for the Tibetan guru Rimpochet amounted to yet another extraordinary matching of downtown and uptown undercurrents.

An air of decline nevertheless hung over the Mudd Club. In February the distinctly unhip *New York Post* commented that the venue wasn't "as trendy" as it used to be, and although the *New York Rocker* went on to report that Branca and Chatham were drawing "healthy-to-huge" crowds, the quality of the live music dipped markedly in the autumn, right around the time that Mass agreed to sell his building back to Ross Bleckner.[4] "Graffiti came to the rescue in '81," observes Richard Boch, who continued to head to the Mudd Club regularly after leaving with David Azarch to work at the Peppermint Lounge in the autumn of 1980. "By '82 the fire was out." Mass maintains that he wasn't particularly bothered if the bulk of his original crowd had moved on, having never believed that art should be "some special elite practice," and in normal circumstances would have carried on as before because business remained healthy. But he had become aware that his upper floors didn't meet statutory fire-exit regulations, as was the case with most TriBeCa and SoHo locations that held public events on upper floors. Fearful that he might one day be pulled up, he decided "to buy a new car instead of fixing the brakes." He started to search for a new venue, convinced that it was time to conquer new territory, and in November even stopped charging admission at White Street. "There was no reason for me to promote this old location when I was going to start anew," he reasons. "My strategy was to let everybody wonder, 'Oh, what happened?' and then open up and surprise everybody."

Up on St. Mark's Place, meanwhile, Ira Abramowitz took Club 57 back into the theatrical territory established by Andy Rees. "He added darker, grittier events alongside the camp-oriented musical theater of Marc Shaiman and Scott Wittman," recalls Ann Magnuson. "Marc and Scott were Theater of the Ridiculous, but with show tunes. Ira introduced this element that was grungier, messier." Dany Johnson maintains that the club was still fun but had slid since Magnuson had stepped back from her managerial role. "We started to have more live music, which turned the neighbors against the club," recalls the DJ. "Heroin use by some of the management was also a problem." Magnuson maintains that it was "pretty amazing" the club went on as long as it did, given the circumstances. Stanley Strychacki frets that Abramowitz "brought energies to the club" until his personal life "got in the way."[5]

As one legendary venue faded from view, however, another bounced back from censure when Jim Fouratt and Rudolf Piper reopened Danceteria on the site of Interferon, a struggling venue owned by real estate mogul Alex Di Lorenzo that occupied the first four floors of a thirteen-story ex-industrial building on 21st Street and Seventh Avenue. "Alex owned a hundred buildings and he got it into his head that he wanted to open a nightclub," recalls John Argento, who majored in theater design at NYU before taking on work as Di Lorenzo's bodyguard. "He also brought in this guy Ron Martinez. We were kids and like everybody else we hardly knew what we were doing." Argento dedicated the first floor to live music, the second floor to dancing, and the third floor to a lounge area, only for the venture to run into difficulties after six months. At that point Martinez tried to bring in Roccio, who had yet to move to the old Electric Circus. Argento countered with Piper. "Danceteria [on 37th Street] was very short-lived, but I always liked the name and I always liked Rudolf," reasons Argento. "Alex decided to go with Danceteria instead of the Peppermint Lounge, and Ron Martinez threw up his hands and quit."

Drawn to its multilevel potential and proximity to downtown, Fouratt and Piper preserved the layout of the first two floors, hired video artists Kit Fitzgerald and John Sanborn to design and curate a video lounge for the third, and introduced their style-meets-irony aesthetic into the broader reconceptualization of the club. "The original Danceteria was thrown together in a dark space but the Danceteria at 21st Street was beautiful," Argento notes of the redesign, which also drew on Googie architecture. "Rudolf combined the style, the colors, and the taste of the 1950s with the jaundiced eye of the 1980s. His motto was, 'To the future, through the past.'" Young artist types were hired to staff the spot, including Chi Chi Valenti, who took on bartending duties, having left the Mudd Club after she and Johnny Dynell argued with Steve Mass, and Haoui Montaug, who took control of the door. "He was like a human social network, a repository for culture, and a bunch of great instincts all bundled into one person, and because he was interested in so many aspects of culture he knew all of these people," comments Valenti. "If a brand-new person he had never seen before came along, in an instant he'd know whether they should be a comp, shown where the secret cloakroom was located, and given a drink ticket or not."

Amid an unprecedented level of party activity that wreaked havoc across three floors from the 3 February opening onward, Fouratt booked the likes of DNA, Dog Eat Dog, Durutti Column, Nona Hendryx, Human Switchboard, Medium Medium, Mofungo, Polyrock, the Raybeats, Red Decade, R.E.M., and Alan Vega to play live. He also showcased composers Glenn Branca, Philip Glass, and David van Tieghem alongside D.A.F., the Love of Life Orchestra, and Diamanda Galas at a regular "Art Attack" night; staged a "Pantropical Night" that featured Latin artists such as Alfredo de la Fe and Tipica '73; and invited galleries such as PS1 to curate shows for a recurring "Serious Fun" night. "At places like the Kitchen, this work is perceived in a serious, reverential way," Fouratt told John Rockwell. "At Danceteria, if they like something, they cheer; if they don't, they just move on to another floor."[6]

In other developments, Montaug started to take a regular night off from the door in May to initiate "No Entiendes," a "daffy," "daring," and "definitely different" weekly cabaret that showcased unknown performers who mixed music and theater.[7] "Harry [Haoui] put on the most amazing, bizarre shows," recalls Piper. "He created this balance between the alternative and the intellectual. Every show had the good, the bad, and the ugly." Michigan-raised Madonna, a recent arrival and Danceteria regular, took her turn on the stage. "I thought her music was shit and Harry thought her music was shit, but we decided, 'Let's put it on,' because even if the show was bad, it was great because people would boo," adds the promoter. "The first three shows she did in her life were at this talent search. After her third show at Danceteria she was already beyond our budget." Meanwhile special parties ran with outlandish themes, including one in which Ann Magnuson teamed up with ex-Gray musician and downtown artist Vincent Gallo to stage a "Festivale de San De-Niro" street party that coincided with Little Italy's Feast of San Gennaro, with a Punch and Judy show that reenacted scenes from *The Godfather* part of the

Mark Kamins at Danceteria on 37th Street, 1980. Photograph by
and courtesy of Emily Armstrong ©.

fun and games. A regular performer at the club, Magnuson also cultivated an
"Upwardly Mobile" cabaret performance in the venue's elevator, where she
stood under a spotlight and sang songs. Nobody could complain that the scene
was running low on inventiveness.

On the DJ front Bill Bahlman, Ronda Milliron, and Richard Sweret selected
records before, in between, and after the live shows while Mark Kamins
worked solo on the second-floor dance floor (Sean Cassette having taken up
carpentry). A self-described "black New Yorker" who maintains he drew on
the same pool of music as "David, François, and Larry," Kamins selected records in threes, shifting between genres and other thematic modes as the night
unfolded. "Nobody could ever pin me to a certain sound," he argues, countering those who subsequently labeled him a new wave DJ. "I never wanted to be
trademarked. I was famous for playing everything and being spontaneous."
As on 37th Street, the eclecticism cohered. "Every record had this common
theme, this common vibe, this common heart that enabled me to go from an
Italian record to an English record to a German record into a reggae record
into hip hop," he explains. "Although I can't define it, it existed and it worked."
Kamins even made a point of arriving two hours before opening so he could
play for the busboys and the bartenders, whose praise (or criticism) was the
most important of all. "I wasn't a great mixer but I had an unbelievable choice
of records," he adds. "Whereas a lot of DJs would go for the perfect mix and

give up playing the best record because another one was easier to blend, I always went for the best record, for the best song, for the scream."

SELECTED DISCOGRAPHY

MARK KAMINS (1982)

ABC, "The Look of Love"

ABC, "Poison Arrow"

Afrika Bambaataa & the Soul Sonic Force, "Planet Rock"

Bo Kool/Funk Masters, "Love Money"

Bow Wow Wow, "Baby, Oh No"

Bow Wow Wow, "I Want Candy"

Sharon Brown, "I Specialize in Love"

David Byrne, "Big Business (Dance Mix)"

Cheri, "Murphy's Law"

The Clash, "Rock the Casbah"

Dazz Band, "Let It Whip"

Deutsch Amerikanische Freundschaft, "Der Mussolini"

ESG, "You're No Good"

Falco, "Der Kommissar"

Grandmaster Flash & the Furious Five, "Scorpio"

Gwen Guthrie, "It Should Have Been You"

Heaven 17, "Let Me Go!"

Heaven 17, "(We Don't Need This) Fascist Groove Thing"

Imagination, "Just an Illusion"

Grace Jones, "Nipple to the Bottle"

Grace Jones, "Pull Up to the Bumper"

Junior, "Mama Used to Say"

Kajagoogoo, "Too Shy"

Klein & M.B.O., "Dirty Talk"

Kraftwerk, "The Model"

Lime, "Your Love"

Madonna, "Everybody"

Malcolm McLaren, featuring the World's Famous Supreme Team, "Buffalo Gals"

Modern English, "I Melt with You"

Musical Youth, "Pass the Dutchie"

Northend, featuring Michelle Wallace, "Tee's Happy"

Augustus Pablo, "King Tubby Meets Rockers Uptown"

Man Parrish, "Hip Hop, Be Bop (Don't Stop)"

Peech Boys, "Don't Make Me Wait"

Quando Quango, "Go Exciting"

Raw Silk, "Do It to the Music"

Rockers Revenge, featuring Donnie Calvin, "Walking on Sunshine"

Patrice Rushen, "Forget Me Nots"

Siouxsie and the Banshees, "Spellbound"

Slang Teacher, "Wide Boy Awake"

Spandau Ballet, "Chant No. 1 (I Don't Need This Pressure On) (Extended Mix)"

Trio, "Da Da Da"

Vicky "D," "This Beat Is Mine"

Yazoo, "Don't Go"

Yazoo, "Situation (Dub Mix)"

Fouratt and Piper likened Danceteria to a supermarket that provided its clientele with a range of entertainment options, although unlike a supermarket the promoters expected their crowd to be "open to a range of experiences," as Fouratt puts it. "The entertainment was part of the risk taking," adds the promoter. "It was about, 'What am I going to see? What am I going to discover?' They knew they might hate what they saw, but at the very least it would be engaging." Yet because the venue was open seven nights a week, and because numerous options were available at any one time save for Mondays and Tuesdays, which were quieter, the sheer level of activity also prevented any individual from stamping her or his presence on the venue, and that ostensibly worked against Kamins, who struggled to establish the kind of singular reputation achieved by some of his peers. "Mark was a strong element in Danceteria," remarks Danny Krivit. "But the club was so diversified and spread out it was a little hard for Mark to get that kind of acknowledgment." Argento concedes that although Kamins and the other DJs were included in the venue's publicity and literature the "bigger part of the market" wasn't able to identify them. Paid $300 a night, Kamins dealt with it. "That was like crazy money in those days," he remarks.

Within weeks, however, the apparently seamless reopening of Danceteria careered into a damaging internal conflict. "We became fabulously successful and then the squeeze came on about how much I was paying the bands," recalls Fouratt. "It was Di Lorenzo through Argento who was arguing this. Rudolf kept saying, 'We've got to pay the bands less money,' and I said, 'Why?'" Fouratt maintains that Piper started to "squeeze" him financially. "Then one day

"No Entiendes" flyer, 15 June 1982. Courtesy of John Argento.

I went to the club and I was not allowed in," he recounts. "They had got some kind of legal injunction against me and Rudolf had joined their side." The eviction took place some ten weeks into the venue's run. "One day Rudolf decided he just didn't want to work with the guy anymore," notes Argento. "It came from all of us — from Alex, Rudolf, and myself. We thought we'd be able to deal with Jim but he was just too difficult to work with." Piper confirms Argento's account, adding that Fouratt was "complicated" and "a person who created obstacles out of nothing."

In addition to previous tussles with the owners of Hurrah, the Peppermint Lounge, and Studio 54, Fouratt had also fallen out with Tom Silverman during the New Music Seminar of 1981 when the co-organizer asked him to replace one of the acts he had booked for his artist showcase night at the Underground. Fouratt stood by his lineup of Nona Hendryx, Polyrock, and Pylon plus Bambaataa behind the turntables, only for Mark Josephson to accuse him of profiteering from the seminar the following morning — a charge Fouratt rejected vehemently.[8] Then, toward the end of the year, Fouratt fought with Di Lorenzo during initial negotiations to reopen Danceteria on New Year's Eve 1981. Argento maintains that he and Piper "patched up the deal" yet concluded that they had to get rid of him as soon as possible. They also resolved that they wouldn't let him have his office in the 21st Street building. "How come people think you're a right bastard?" Iman Lababedi asked Fouratt during an interview for the *East Village Eye* in early 1982. "I am difficult to work with, I want everything done my own way," replied the promoter. "But I'm getting better at dealing with people."[9]

A pre-opening flare-up appears to have sealed Fouratt's eventual departure. "It was 4:00 PM and we were installing the heat," remembers Argento. "Jim came in, in front of all these guys who had been working for days, and started screaming at the top of his lungs. Me and Rudolf looked at each other and said, 'This guy's got to go.' " Fouratt's rigorous approach to pleasure, which led him to deliver extended introductions to live acts, contributed to the lingering tension, as did the puritanical leanings that led him to throw out drug dealers at the first Danceteria (only for Piper to shepherd them back in). "Jim was a very sober person," notes Kamins. "He didn't like to see staff drinking, he didn't like to see people partying. Rudolf was the opposite." Fouratt could also be overbearing. "Jim booked the best bands, which I give him so much respect for," adds Kamins. "But what DJ wants to be told what to play from the boss? And that's what he was saying at some points." Kamins adds: "Jim knew what he was doing musically and he wanted everybody to be on his page, but we couldn't all be on his page." And so the tension grew until Argento and Piper took the decision to lock Fouratt out. "Disaster mongers will be wasting their time," announced Argento in a damage-limitation press release sent out on 31 May. "Danceteria will be getting better and better."[10]

Lacking a motive to leave quietly, because his eviction was brutal and underhand, Fouratt took his case to the New York State Supreme Court. "Who owns Danceteria?" *Billboard* asked in August. "The club that now bears the name, or the person who developed the name and concept, and licensed it to the club, but whose services the club no longer wants?"[11] Fouratt argued that Piper and Interferon entered into a conspiracy to force him out, deny him his livelihood, and seize the Danceteria name and concept. Argento, Di Lorenzo, and Piper countered that he had never registered the name, that the original Danceteria was illegal, and that Fouratt overspent his budget regularly. "It was a terrible time," remembers Fouratt, who maintains he took a couple of beatings for his efforts. "It was very hard because Rudolf had violated our contractual relationship. I sued Di Lorenzo for theft of the Danceteria name. I had this plan for Danceteria to be syndicated. It fucked everything up."

Argento and Piper moved to neutralize the loss of Fouratt's curatorial flare by hiring Polsky to take his job in advance of the lockout. Less connected to experimental composers and video filmmakers than her predecessor, Polsky had nevertheless established her own credibility at Hurrah, where she had booked numerous cutting-edge bands, among them New Order, and that combined with the thought that she might be less demanding than her

Jim Fouratt. Photograph
by and courtesy of
Rhonda Paster ©.

onetime mentor made her an obvious substitute. In search of a new job following Hurrah's closure, Polsky slipped into the role at 21st Street seamlessly
as she booked the likes of Cabaret Voltaire, ESG, Richard Hell, Liquid Liquid, Nico, Klaus Nomi, the Raincoats, and James Chance while organizing a
"Bound for Glory!" festival to showcase the "best new local bands."[12] A popular host, she also put up bands that were visiting the city in her downtown
loft. "Ruth had the best connections and the best taste, and she brought in so
many fabulous bands from Manchester and London and Paris," comments
Piper, who paid for the promoter to make biannual trips to Manchester to
spot emerging talent. "She was fabulous. Second Danceteria would not have
had the relevance it did without her."

Piper gave full rein to his whacky, hedonistic sensibility when he opened
Congo Bill on the fourth floor of the venue in the autumn. A private members' club-within-a-club that he named after a colonial hunter character
created by DC Comics during the 1940s, the lounge-styled spot featured retro-
futuristic decor from the 1950s and music selected by Jody Kurilla (a secretary
in the Danceteria office who persuaded Piper to let her DJ).[13] "Rudolf built
it as a 'before after-hours club,'" recalls Argento. "We put together sunken
Greek temples, rooms from 2001: A Space Odyssey, and computers and circuit

Rudolf Piper (far left) singing at a Club 57 benefit held at Danceteria, 25 September 1982. John Sex, at center, eyes him. Photograph by and courtesy of Robert Carrithers ©.

boards. We tried to make it look like a cross between *Blade Runner* and a Soviet-era resort on the Black Sea. This was Rudolf's idea. He kept coming up with these contradictory things that seemed to make sense together." In his review of the year for *Details*, Stephen Saban named Congo Bill the "best new club."[14]

Argento believes that Piper's tongue-in-cheek sensibility underpinned the venue's wild success while Valenti maintains that the promoter was a brilliant thinker and a conceptual innovator. "I would have to call him a visionary — and I don't kick that term around freely," she comments. "Rudolf really understood you need a Noah's Ark approach to building a club." Of the opinion that the "best club owners were warped individuals who worked out their antisocial pathologies by creating events that excited the imagination and offered the illusion of transcendent bliss and erotic fulfilment," Leonard Abrams maintains that Steve Mass edged ahead of Piper, but only "by a nose." Yet the life force of Danceteria didn't so much lie in Piper's social charm and warped creativity, or indeed Fouratt's curatorial brilliance, so much as the different scenes that the two promoters brought together until Fouratt found himself locked out.

"I would call Danceteria a nation," reminisces Kamins. "It was a new country, a new world, a special moment in time when everybody was musically

feeding off each other." Danceteria existed within a continuum of transformative social settings, including Minton's Playhouse, the Factory, the Fillmore
East, Max's Kansas City, and CBGB, claims Kamins, and although the 21st
Street incarnation was more planned and branded than its communelike predecessor on 37th Street, it became a de facto home for many staff members.
"All we had was the club," adds Kamins. "We lived from the club, we lived off
the club. We could eat, we could drink, we could talk, we could party. That's
what we had. You put a match to gasoline and you create a fire. Nobody was
a genius, nobody had a plan for success. It was just pure creative evolution."

INVERTED PYRAMID

Fired by Jim Fouratt during the attempt to open Danceteria in time for New Year's Eve 1981, Interferon employees and boyfriends Bobby Bradley and Alan Mace decided to open a venue of their own that would combine elements of the Mudd Club, a short-lived venue that opened on 25th Street called Club with No Name that featured bizarre installations, and above all the Anvil, a seedy gay club located by the West Side Highway that featured go-go dancers and drag shows. For their location they settled on the Pyramid Cocktail Lounge, an out-of-favor cruise bar situated at 101 Avenue A between 6th and 7th Streets. The idea was to create, Mace explained to the gay porn magazine *In Touch for Men*, "a new image for a gay place."[1]

Held on Thursday, 10 December 1981, the opening-night party blended western movies, the drag-queen allure of John Kelly (a performer at Club 57 and the Mudd Club) and Tanya Ransom (the founder of the Anvil's new wave night), and DJ-ing in the back room (where, according to folklore, Mace opened his set with Dionne Warwick's "Walk on By"). "I met Tanya Ransom at the Anvil," recalls Kelly. "Well, Tanya was lip-synching Nina Hagen. I was at art school, and I would go there and just sketch all night, and I fell totally head over heels for Tanya. Tanya and the other queens at the Anvil used to dance on the bar of the Anvil, so Tanya and I decided to start that at the Pyramid Club."[2] Brian Butterick, who doubled as Hattie Hathaway, recalls the wider gathering was "androgynous, clown-like . . . half drag and half not," and recalls the event being "very exciting" because "there were no other real nightlife venues in the East Village, that far east."[3] Pyramid breathed the same air as other downtown spots yet seemed entirely distinctive at the same time.

Demand surpassed all expectations. "How does an overcrowded, poorly ventilated, terribly narrow, raunchy bar on the edge of Alphaville (Avenue A) and Sixth Street become a Happening Place?" the *SoHo News* asked in February

1982. "I've seen well-dressed couples lined compliantly up on freezing nights, patiently awaiting entrée into the Pyramid Bar as if it were a downtown branch of Studio."[4] By the spring the spot matched Danceteria's seven-nights-a-week parade as Mace and Bradley dedicated Mondays to experimental theater, Tuesdays to alternative bands, Wednesdays to whatever took Bradley's fancy, Thursdays to special theme parties, Fridays and Saturdays to outlandish warm-up acts and popular bands, and Sundays to outré cabaret night "Cafe Iguana." Then again, good intentions could always go astray. "During the week we sometimes wouldn't know what to expect," recalls Joshua Fried, who started to work as a sound engineer after performing there as a self-described one-man, new wave, electronic, dub-reggae dance band.

Although he oversaw the booking of acts and the hiring of staff, Bradley insisted that "the ideas flow freely between the management and workers."[5] Sharing the load, Ransom doubled as Bradley's assistant and hired other go-go dancers while Butterick took charge of the door, began to book bands, and soon became co-creative director. "We appreciated the short attention span of the modern world," remarks Butterick. "The shows were limited to fifteen to twenty minutes each. There would be one at midnight and one at 1:30, and before and after and in the middle there would be dancing." Club 57 came to exert a significant influence as a number of its regulars migrated to the Avenue A spot. "Club 57 was failing at the time we were starting and so many of our performers came from there," Bradley told *In Touch for Men*. "John Sex in particular, John Kelly, Ann Magnuson."[6]

As far as Butterick was concerned, Pyramid also attracted "the more forward-thinking, more thoughtful drag queens that were performing in the West Village." Kelly, the first drag artist to perform at the venue, created a flat-chested character called Dagmar Onassis, the imagined "love child of Maria Callas and Aristotle Onassis," as well as personas such as Narcissus and Saint Sebastien.[7] Ransom, head drag queen, sang stark songs about love and sex over a tape of synthetic disco. Larry Ree, appearing as Madame Ekathrina Sobechanskaya, founded the Original Trocadero Gloxinia Ballet Company, the first all-male ballet company, which performed at the venue during the spring of 1982.[8] Ethyl Eichelberger, a high-octane 6'2" queen, portrayed famous historical women while doubling up as a fashion adviser, role model, and shoulder to cry on. "They call me 'Queen Mother,'" Eichelberger told *Outweek*. "This is the role that I love, because I'm trying to better the world for drag performers."[9] Eager to dance on the venue's long, sturdy bar, which could support the 6'4" Butterick plus ten or so others, drag queens didn't so much define the spot as mark it as a space that welcomed diversity. "But I'd say twenty-four

Ethyl Eichelberger at Pyramid, ca. 1984. Photograph by and courtesy
of Ande Whyland ©.

out of twenty-five people were not in drag unless they worked there," notes
Butterick.

Other types of performing artists took their turn on the venue's backroom
stage, among them Ann Craig (who appeared in a trash can at the first New
Year's Eve party and then as the pivotal host of Sunday's "Cafe Iguana" night),
and film director John Jesurun (who inaugurated the Monday-night serial
play *Chang in a Void Moon*, which featured Kelly and a de-dragged Eichelberger
alongside New York City firefighter Steve Buscemi). "We've gone baroque,"
proclaimed Bradley. "Instead of paring down, we put as much as possible into
the performances."[10] Regular theme parties added to the sense of excess as partygoers dressed up in outer-space costumes for the "Attack of the Vicious Spider
Queen from Crab Nebula Versus the Women of the Moose" night, and South
American nuns seized control of the DJ booth and demanded that only Joan
Baez records be played at the "El Cuspidor" night. The "Naked Savage" party
might have been the only one to go against the venue's counter-minimalist
tendencies as organizers introduced a sliding admission price, with those
wearing the least asked to pay the least.[11] Taken as a whole, the venue oozed
glamour, grunge, and 1960s idealism, recalls Butterick.

Pyramid contributed to the East Village reaction against West Village gay
culture. Performance artist David McDermott had set out the terms of the

John Sex at Pyramid,
ca. 1984. Photograph
by and courtesy of
Ande Whyland ©.

argument in an incendiary article published in the *East Village Eye* two sum-
mers earlier. "No one cares anymore if you are Gay or not, we care about who
you are," he pronounced. "You Gay Culture Fags have made a culture that can
only be your culture, because we do not want your sex-quiche, sex-mustache,
sex-quaaludes, whips, penis-sex literary pretentious love, Gay, natural stories."[12]
He continued: "Well, Mr. and Mr. Gay Culture Fags, you better redecorate
and redo your hair, and make some clothes, because you're out man, real out,
and we from the Lower East Side think you look dreadful. So stay away with
your DISCO and Gay bars and Mustaches instead of hair on your heads."[13]
Complementing Keith Haring's Fags against Facial Hair stencils, the drag
queens, bands, and performance artists who appeared at Pyramid fired the
counteraction. "The West Village was very petrified," observes Butterick. "It

had been running strong from 1971 and in my mind people from small towns were making the style. They were florists and window dressers and shop clerks. We were hoping for something different."

Bradley and Mace took a while to settle on a DJ-ing lineup. At first Mace took on the Sunday slot plus a Friday or a Saturday, stepping in whenever a midweek night went unfilled. "Alan was big on heart and sentiment," remembers Fried. "His selections were always tasteful. He never did any fancy cutting between records." Drawn to Bradley's comment that he wanted to create a Club 57–style environment, Dany Johnson also started to play at the spot but balked at the management's "open heroin use" and Bradley's "sexist comments," and when Bradley refused Grandmaster Flash entry one night because of the derogatory use of the word "fag" in the DJ's latest release, "The Message," she played the record repeatedly until Bradley sacked her "for being a female and refusing to play new wave music." The owner also hired and fired Johnny Dynell, whom he judged to be too close to West Village disco; Butterick conveyed the news to the DJ, being, he says, the only management figure sober enough to make a phone call at 2:00 PM. "I looked like I stepped right out of *Saturday Night Fever*," acknowledges the ex–Mudd Club DJ. "I thought it was brilliant art but it didn't go over well with the new wave Pyramid crowd."

Bradley found his solution in the figure of Ivan Baker, who pronounced himself willing to switch to Avenue A because the Mudd Club was becoming "a little bit too close-minded" and "more of a pure white scene," whereas the Avenue A spot resembled "an uninhibited oasis of creativity" that attracted a "very good mix of gays, straights, bikers, homeboys, college kids, professionals, celebrities, musicians, fashion designers, artists, drag queens, and bridge and tunnel." Insisting that Bradley redesign and reposition the venue's booth, until then an uncomfortable crawlspace located above a toilet, the DJ took to opening his sets at 110 beats per minute, whereupon he would build the crowd to a "sexual, spastic climax," calm the energy, and then repeat the cycle several times before slowing things down at around 2:30 or 3:00 AM. "That way all the people who were high or trying to make the final moves on their romantic targets would feel like I was in tune with their head," says Baker. Acknowledged to be something of a "superstar" by Iris Rose, who staged two shows in the venue, Baker assumed the role of tutor as well as entertainer. "Most club DJs were focused on the flow; they concentrated on smooth mixes and would play particular genres for hours," he explains. "My focus on the other hand was to show where a new song got its influence from. I took great

Ivan Baker, a.k.a. Ivan
Ivan, Danceteria, 1984.
Photograph by and
courtesy of Rhonda
Paster ©.

pride in taking people on an educational journey, going from Led Zeppelin to Boy George to 10CC to Sly and Robbie [Sly Dunbar and Robbie Shakespeare] to New Order."

Selecting a notable proportion of new wave tracks, many of them electronic, many of them disco and funk influenced, Baker recalls that Avenue A dancers would storm the DJ booth to check a strain of music they had never heard before. Yet the crowd was never going to approach the floor with the semireligious distance-runner psychology of dancers who headed to the Funhouse, the Loft, the Paradise Garage, and the Saint, for as Fried points out, revelers thought little of taking a break to buy a drink, get some fresh air, dabble in a bit of flirting, or top up on drugs whenever the moment grabbed them. "We used to call Garage music 'twirly music' as opposed to what we were playing," points out Butterick. "What we were playing had a harder edge." Baker read a deeper meaning into the expressivity and desire of his dancers. "Reaganomics was like, 'Give all the money to the rich people and it will trickle down,' but that never happened. Maybe some of the artists got money from the Wall Street guys who were doing blow and champagne, renting limousines, and going to really fancy restaurants, because those people had money to spend on art, but overall it was a pretty hairy time." Baker adds:

"There was anger and rebellion in the social mix. It was a heady combination, sexual and vibrant in its own way. Pyramid was counterculture."

Over on 11th Street, meanwhile, Patti Astor and Bill Stelling amped up the Fun Gallery, where they mixed shows by downtown artists Arch Connelly and Jane Dickson with the graffiti brigade, beginning with a show by the Brooklyn-born Dondi in February. "Word got out on the graffiti grapevine and kids began showing up with piece books and dreams to meet their heroes," recalls Astor. "The unique Fun audience of beat-boys, downtown artists, hipsters and uptown collectors with their limos and mink coats began to fill the gallery and spill out onto the sidewalk outside."[14] A couple of months later a Futura 2000 show left Astor flabbergasted when she fetched the princely sum of $600 for one of his pieces. By day a pet-store worker, by night the most revered graffiti artist of his generation, Lee Quiñones rounded off the season when he staged a show in June. "Quinone's [sic] talent is indisputable but after years of working on billboard size murals it's understandably difficult to conceive a $3' \times 4'$ painting on canvas," Steven Hager noted in the *East Village Eye*, raising an oft-muttered concern that graffiti lost its edge when it moved from the street to a gallery. "One sometimes wishes the writers would stop even trying, and instead offer sheet metal paintings the size of subway cars for sale."[15]

If the gallery setting might have robbed the style of its contextual immediacy and potential scale, Astor and Stelling preferred to focus on the way the Fun Gallery provided its outsider artists with professional opportunities, critical recognition, and a means of exposure while imbuing the spot with a funky community spirit. "I was at a lot of those openings," recalls Afrika Islam. "To appreciate that type of art you had to have a hip hop DJ play and maybe a couple of dancers as well. It helped buyers from Milan or the affluent areas of New York understand what the streets were like." The liberal end of the collector class lapped it all up. "There was always music, always a boom box," comments adviser Jeffrey Deitch. "This was one of the first places you could hear hip hop in the context of the downtown art world. Patti Astor was just this great character. The whole thing was totally real." As the division that separated the art world and the party scene dissolved, Quiñones used the money he earned from his sell-out show to leave his pet-shop days behind him. "Those who have embraced [the art world], well, I can well understand why," reasoned Henry Chalfant. "It appeals to the same impulses that made them writers in the first place and for the first time they have the opportunity to make money doing what they like."[16]

With the filming of *Wild Style* progressing in tandem — Ahearn shot the spectacular last scene of the film in an East Village amphitheater in

May — Astor and Stelling rode a wave that was partly of their own making when they relocated to larger premises on East 10th Street by First Avenue in August. Barely pausing, they staged a Kenny Scharf *Black Light* installation in September, a second Fred Brathwaite show in October, and a *Graffiti, Thanks a Lot!* open exhibition that featured some five hundred contributions later that same month. A self-portrait by Lady Pink titled "The Death of Graffiti" that critiqued the city's latest effort to eradicate graffiti from the subway by painting cars with a resistant silicon coating appeared in the *Thanks a Lot!* display. (When Diego Cortez met Koch at a city event he told him, "I think I have a better approach to the 'problem' of graffiti than you do. I give the artists museum shows while you throw them in jail." Koch smiled smugly, excused himself, and walked away with his two bodyguards.) "I invited Crash and Daze and Lady Pink and Iz the Wiz and A1 and Rammellzee," recalls Astor. "Then I said, 'Alright, guys, just bring it in, everybody can show at the Fun Gallery,' and I opened it up to all comers. All these little kids just started bringing stuff in and we put it all up." The gallerist adored listening to the questions and plans of the newcomers, and even sold some of their pieces. Then, in November, came Basquiat.

The artist's reputation had risen following his contribution to Annina Nosei's *Public Address* show and the publication of a Rene Ricard article in *Artforum* in December 1981. "What he incorporates into his pictures, whether found or made, is specific and selective," argued the critic, marveling at the artist's ability to apparently express the entire history of graffiti in one or two words. "He has a perfect idea of what he's getting across, using everything that collates to his vision."[17] Held in March 1982, Basquiat's solo exhibition at Nosei's gallery nevertheless left him feeling like an exotic producer of piecework. "Basquiat is likened to the wild boy raised by wolves, corralled into Annina's basement and given nice clean canvases to work on instead of anonymous walls. A child of the streets gawked at by the intelligentsia," observed Jeffrey Deitch in *Flash Art*. "But Basquiat is hardly a primitive. He's more like a rock star, seemingly savage, but completely in control; astonishingly proficient but scornful of the tough discipline that normally begets such virtuosity. Basquiat reminds me of Lou Reed singing brilliantly about heroin to nice college boys."[18]

Having started to work on a second exhibition with Emilio Mazzoli, only to rebel against the "factory" conditions (as he described them) that required him to create eight paintings in the week before opening, Basquiat returned to New York and slashed the unfinished canvases he had left in Nosei's basement.[19] He then got back in touch with Cortez, who recommended he contact Bruno Bischofberger, who agreed to represent Basquiat without hesitation and arranged for him to travel to Zürich that September. "Bruno flew him over, picked him up at the airport, drove him directly to the gallery, and said, 'There's a couch if you want to lie down but here's some canvases, I have people coming over to watch you paint,'" recounts Astor. "Seriously. Jean-Michel told me this after he got back and he had tears in his eyes. They treated him horrible." Nevertheless Bischofberger represented Andy Warhol, whom Basquiat was keen to befriend, and that came to pass when the Swiss dealer introduced the two of them over lunch at Warhol's Factory studio on Union Square in early October, right after Basquiat returned from Switzerland. Basquiat biographer Leonhard Emmerling records that a mistrustful Warhol discreetly asked Bischofberger if he really thought Basquiat was a great artist. When the dealer replied that he would become a great artist, Warhol had a photographer take some Polaroids so he could create a portrait of the newcomer. At that point Basquiat left the table, headed back to his studio, and two hours later sent a still-wet portrait of Warhol and himself to the senior artist. "I'm really jealous," Warhol is said to have commented. "He's faster than me."[20]

After that Basquiat locked himself away to prepare for the Fun Gallery show, which Ricard had set in motion, with Cortez encouraging the artist, unsure of his next steps, to see the commitment through, including when Bischofberger leaned on the Brooklynite to back out. "I had some money; I made the best paintings ever," Basquiat recalled later. "I was completely reclusive, worked a lot, took a lot of drugs. I was awful to people."[21] During preparations for the show Astor and Stelling watched on, amused, when an uninvited collector had her limousine driver carry a jar of gourmet sweets up to his apartment; Basquiat accepted the gift, walked to the window, and poured the contents over her head. After driving the works over to the gallery in the Funmobile, their convertible, they spent three days with Basquiat as he "walked around with a can of paint fixing stuff, deciding what was going to go where." Astor also took out a full-page, Basquiat-designed ad in *Artforum* to plug the 4 November opening party. Even then the artist refused to provide her and Stelling with a list of prices until the very last moment, ostensibly because he was suffering, says the gallerist, from cocaine-induced paranoia.

During the opening Leo Castelli rubbed shoulders with art collectors Don and Mera Rubell (Don being the brother of Studio 54's Steve), while local kids put on an impromptu display of breaking. Cortez felt the works amounted to Basquiat's strongest to date and concluded that the "funkiness" of Astor and Stelling's setting inspired his resurgence.[22] Apparently lost to the spectacle, Basquiat spent most of the night in the corner of the gallery arguing with a new girlfriend, Madonna, who had become something of a local celebrity since appearing at Haoui Montaug's "No Entiendes."[23] Astor ended up selling only a handful of paintings, including one to a friend of Deitch's, who reluctantly paid $10,000 for the piece. "I said, 'Trust me, go for it,'" recalls the Citibank employee. To Astor's dismay, the Rubells passed up her best efforts to persuade them to buy a twelve-foot effort that she and Stelling had carried over by hand because it was too big to fit into the Funmobile. "They thought they could go to his studio afterwards and get it from him there even cheaper," she maintains. "But he didn't do that. Those paintings all got put away in storage because he knew exactly what was going on. Putting his vision up there is what mattered to him. The sales, everything else, was secondary."

Interviewed by a documentary team during the show, Astor cheerily declared that some of the artist's paintings had already been "sold to banks to put in their corporate headquarters," adding that she had never wanted the Fun Gallery to "be considered an alternative space." The interest shown by the financial sector validated her determination to treat graffiti writers as though they were artists with individual styles and deserving of solo shows rather than representatives of a subcultural species who could be dropped when the zeitgeist moved on. "There's good artists and there's bad artists," she argued. "The good ones will last and prevail."[24] Yet the gallerist remained conscious that her turnover had to increase if she hoped to cover expenses as well as pay her artists. For his part, Basquiat was "very hurt" that so few of his paintings were picked up, even if he "knew he was an outlaw" and understood that this counted against him. "A black artist had never been admitted to the premiere ranks of fine art and I had difficulty convincing patrons of his genius," she recalls.[25]

Meanwhile Keith Haring contributed to Nosei's *Public Address* and read Ricard describe his Radiant Child tag as "something so good it seems as if it's always been there" before he found himself placed under arrest for his subway art in January.[26] The Kutztown artist went on to produce a thirty-second animated drawing for a Times Square electronic display, give away twenty thousand posters during an antinuclear rally, and develop a prolific collaboration with graffiti writer Angel Ortiz, author of the LA II tag, with whom he had become fast friends the previous summer. He also concluded that his plan to work as his own dealer had become untenable thanks to the frequency with which collectors were interrupting him as he worked in his Broome Street basement, and so he gave in to the persistent advances of Tony Shafrazi, who now operated on Mercer Street. In between contributing to Shafrazi's *Young Americans* show in the spring and holding his first solo effort for the gallerist in the autumn, Haring participated in the prestigious *Documenta 7* exhibi-

Patti Astor and Fred Brathwaite outside Negril, autumn 1981. Photograph by and courtesy of Anita Rosenberg ©.

tion held in Kassel, West Germany, as did Basquiat and Lee Quiñones. Along the way he dropped by Astor's yet-to-open space on 10th Street to donate a painting that would help her with the move. "I held firm on the price that Keith and I had agreed upon, and we sold it for the asking price of $1,800," she recalls.[27]

An early admirer, Deitch penned one of several contextual essays that appeared in the book that accompanied the Shafrazi show at Haring's request. "He could do something I'd rarely seen," recalls Deitch. "He could start in the upper left corner of a giant canvas on a wall and move across with a perfect rhythm, creating an image that fused a musical rhythm with a dance rhythm with an abstract form and a figurative representation. It was a remarkable thing." Deitch also noted how Haring liked to work to the accompaniment of a boom box, to the point where it seemed as though he worked like he was a dancer, with his work a visualization of the music. Titling his piece "Why the Dogs Are Barking," the critic pointed out that getting a gallery show had never been a problem for the young artist because he would just organize his own in whatever space he could find. "Meshing Madison Avenue and Walt Disney with systemic and contextual art, and laying it all onto a graffiti beat, Haring is creating more than good paintings and drawings," he concluded. "He's not just making art; he's communicating in a totally contemporary way."[28]

Building anticipation for the Shafrazi show, Steven Hager tracked Haring's journey from the subway system to the downtown art elite, noting how he established himself as "New York's favorite uncommissioned public artist" along the way. "It's too early to tell how significant an artist Keith will be, but he is already an emblematic figure who is situated at a nexus point where several styles are converging," Robert Pincus-Witten, the editor of the show's book, told Hager. "One of the great fallacies is that he is an unsophisticated artist. In fact, Keith knows a great deal about art."[29] Shafrazi made no attempt to suppress his enthusiasm. "The excitement over Keith's work is unparalleled," he commented. "I know of certain cases where recent reputations and prices have been exaggerated. I don't mean to boast, but there's never been a need for that in Keith's case."[30] Shafrazi added that Haring remained completely indifferent to money. "He has created a gigantic audience out there, one that he feels very committed to," observed the gallerist. "He's living proof of the phrase by Malraux, 'museum without walls.' The entire city has become his canvas."[31]

Cultivated in the city's clubs, streets, and subways, Haring's conception of art as being public, performative, and socially embedded as well as fun, sexual, and irreverent shone through at the Shafrazi opening. "All these worlds were coming together in this big mishmash of people that never really existed in a gallery before me," the artist recalled of the party that unfolded. "It was the first time that there was this incredible event and atmosphere in a gallery with the CBS cameras whirling and artists from Francesco Clemente to Bob Rauschenberg to Roy Lichtenstein."[32] A slightly overawed grouping amidst the thousand-plus crowd, Haring's parents and sisters traveled from Kutztown, Pennsylvania, to see the show's painted draped tarpaulins, wall-to-ceiling drawings, baked enamel objects, decorated pillars, black-light basement installation, and a giant sculpted figure — much of which also bore the credited handiwork of LA II. "We thought it was just great," recalls Haring's mother, Joan Haring. "That's when people started going up to him and saying, 'Wow! You're Keith Haring! Will you sign this?' "[33]

The alternative end of the gallery scene paralleled the independent-label sector in the way it provided artists with the means to express themselves while making some money — occasionally decent money. Their contribution was crucial, for just as the major labels showed only minimal interest in the dance scene during the early 1980s, so the hard-edged end of the art market kept its distance from the city's up-and-coming artists. "A lot of the clients of Citibank inherited art or had art and needed advice on regarding its worth, on what they should keep, and so on," notes Deitch. "It was more of a service. But when it came to getting people into Haring and Basquiat, it was more a matter of sharing this enthusiasm. In the end it was all a very good investment, but getting someone who would normally buy a Mark Rothko for $250,000 — which is what they went for in those days — to buy a Basquiat for $10,000; that wasn't an investment. I wanted to share something I enjoyed." Deitch argues the money fueled the creativity. "It allowed Jean-Michel to get a studio and an assistant."

Even if it remained relatively confined, the success enjoyed by Basquiat and Haring sometimes rankled with those who struggled in comparison, including David Wojnarowicz. Convinced that Haring stole the image of a naked man with a dog's head he contributed to the *Erotic Show* in 1981, Wojnarowicz started to stencil copies of the radiant baby tag as a wind-up on the basis that he could no longer use his own image.[34] He went on to make his own solo debut at the Milliken gallery in December 1982, bringing a darker, more conflictual set of concerns that revolved around war, discord, and dereliction to the fore, only to have someone spoil his moment by asking him, "Why can't you be like Keith Haring — full of fun?"[35] Scharf also struggled with Haring's rise, to the point where the two of them moved out of their shared Times Square apartment.[36] For his part, Haring became disillusioned with those who claimed he had "sold out" and "gone commercial," which he felt was "bullshit."[37] When someone scrawled "$9,999" over one of his murals after he told the *Village Voice* that he hadn't sold anything for $10,000, he thought, "OK, fuck you, this is the end of the East Village," and resolved to never create a mural there again.[38]

Such altercations, however, were part of the rough-and-tumble of daily life in the art world rather than something that threatened to undermine the effervescent downtown art scene. Indeed as Ricard pointed out in his *Artforum* piece, exhibitions such as the *Times Square Show*, *Beyond Words*, and *New York/New Wave* had encouraged viewers to look at art within a group context, "so much so that an exhibit of an individual's work seems almost antisocial."[39] Thanks to her film-star magnetism, no-nonsense personality, democratic outlook, bombshell style, and dedication to pleasure, Astor had the charisma and wherewithal to even carry the community dynamism of the downtown party scene into the staid setting of the art gallery. Even if they mostly put on individual shows, Astor and Stelling ran the Fun Gallery as a social space to the point where they regarded the task of opening the spot to potential buyers on Sundays as something of an inconvenience — perhaps a necessary evil — that disrupted their club-house modus operandi. With working-class black and Latino artists plus largely moneyless downtowners making up the venue's core crowd, Astor adds that while she and Stelling would have been happy for the gallery and their artists to make money, they "didn't really care" and that, she notes, "drove people freaking crazy, because they had no control over us."

If Astor and Stelling couldn't compete financially with their SoHo counterparts, including Shafrazi, the agreement that Haring would stage a show on 10th Street in the new year suggested they were all set to maintain their finger-on-the-pulse reputation. Meanwhile news that *Artforum* was about to publish another Rene Ricard article, this one arguing that the Fun Gallery and its associated artists had displaced the city's alternative-band scene at the cutting edge of artistic and musical convergence, carried the promise of good times to come. "Rene had written two previous articles for *Artforum*. He made [neo-expressionist artist] Julian Schnabel and then there was the piece about Jean-Michel and Keith. It was like, 'Wow, if Rene does an article about us, we'd hit the big time!' "

ROXY MUSIC

Buzzing like a bee loaded with pollen, Michael Holman spread the word about this thing called hip hop when he published an interview with Afrika Bambaataa in the *East Village Eye* in January 1982. The first of its kind, the piece charted how Bambaataa formed the Zulu Nation out of the combustible energy of gang culture, took his name from his godfather at communion, drew inspiration from the movie *Zulu,* and battled with Kool Herc. Almost in passing, Holman also threw in a definition of hip hop, which he described as the "all inclusive tag for the rapping, breaking, graffiti-writing, crew fashion wearing street sub-culture."[1] Holman, it seems, was the first person to conceptualize the name in print. "It really wasn't used a lot because the term had been a verbal shout out in records like 'Rapper's Delight,'" notes Holman. "Taking something like that and elevating it to the status of encapsulating a culture was a leap. Not everyone was ready to make that move right away." Bambaataa's comment that Kool Herc "knows how to throw down b-beats and that's how he got the reputation of being the godfather of hip hop rock" confirmed that reference points had yet to settle.[2]

Ruza Blue, meanwhile, continued to forge a distinctly Bronx-inspired path at Negril by booking MC outfits the Cold Crush Brothers, the Funky 4 + 1, the Jazzy Five, and the Treacherous Three plus Fab 5 Freddy B, and by inviting Holman to present a breaking battle between the Rock Steady Crew and a newcomer outfit called the Floormasters. Yet the British promoter remained committed to the idea and practice of the mashup and that led her to throw in elements that weren't understood to be part of hip hop's nascent framework, including Kosmo Vinyl, who DJ-ed alongside Bambaataa one night, and also a group of double-dutch rope jumpers. "I saw these incredible girls called the Double Dutch girls jump rope on a McDonald's TV commercial and thought, 'Hmmm, that would work great in the club,' so I got in touch with them and they were a hit in the club," recalls Blue. "Negril was so much more than a hip hop club." Spontaneity lay at the heart of the night. "Each week it was different because we didn't really take it that seriously," Blue told Martha Cooper in a later interview. "It was more about the party and having loads of fun."[3]

The culture's journey from the boroughs to downtown wasn't an entirely seamless affair. Just as some had questioned the ethics of graffiti's transition from the street to the gallery, so Michael Hill wondered out loud in the pages of the *New York Rocker* if Bambaataa's political sensibility would morph into pure entertainment outside its original context. "As appreciative, enthusiastic and envious as the audience might have been, it was hard not to feel a little like part of an awkwardly hip anthropology class," he noted of a Rock Steady Crew performance, before concluding that, in the final instance, the Zulu Nation crew "gave up the funk" and "the beat conquered all."[4] Less concerned about the rights and wrongs of the cross-cultural exchange, at least in her coverage of Negril in the pages of *Dance Music Report*, Monica Lynch described the Double Dutch Girls as "the female counterpart to breaker boys" and saluted the way they had "elevated the simple act of jumping rope to an art form."[5] Of the night that featured Kool Herc on the decks, Rammellzee on the mike, and Futura on the spray can, she wrote, "Blue Ruza's Sure Shot Party Crew continues to pack them in at N.Y.'s Negril."[6] It came as a blow, therefore, when the fire department shut down the spot in late February for occupancy violations.

Hopeful that she would soon be able to return to Negril, Blue took her night to Danceteria. "Jim Fouratt was cool," recalls Bambaataa. "They loved what we was doing. They used to come down and get funky on the dance floor." Yet the 21st Street ambience didn't seem quite right to Blue, and she started to hunt for a new location when it became clear that Negril wasn't about to reopen any time soon. A short while later Fred Brathwaite took her to the Roxy, solely with the intention of partying, only for the promoter to start to dream out loud. The fast-talking Brooklynite hadn't even considered the gargantuan 18th Street venue to be a possible home and told Blue she was crazy to even think about it, only to back down when she explained how she planned to use the space. Blue then approached Steve Haenel, the venue's new owner since the autumn of 1981, who had introduced a more relaxed approach to the door, yet he still resisted her overtures, explaining that he didn't want her crowd "spilling booze over his nice, clean rollerskating rink" or "scratching his floor with their dirty shoes," she recalls.[7] Eventually charm won out. "We just kept moving along," reminisces Bambaataa. "We was going wherever Blue was going. We was with her 100 percent. She was the one that really spearheaded pushing us on from club to club."

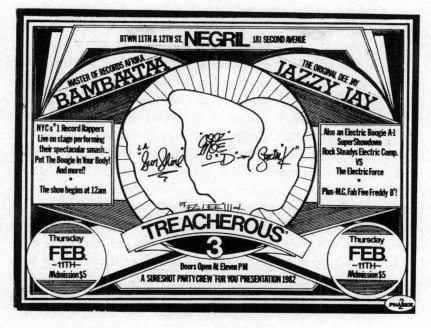

Negril flyer, 11 February 1982. Courtesy of Johnny Dynell.

Blue launched her "Wheels of Steel" party on 18 June 1982, spreading the word with a flyer that trumpeted "The Roxy Rocks. No Skating Just Dance Your Pants Off. Every Friday Nite. B. There." Hosted by Brathwaite, the night featured Bambaataa, Jazzy Jay, Grand Mixer D.ST, and Grand Wizard Theodore on the turntables; a live performance by the Soul Sonic Force; rope skipping by the Double Dutch Girls; breaking by Crazy Legs and the Rock Steady Crew; and Futura's "Super Spray Graffix Experience."[8] A huge drape helped Blue ride the challenge of moving from the diminutive Negril to the sprawling venue. "The place was enormous," remembers the promoter. "There was no way we would fill it up in the beginning, so I had Dondi, Phase 2, and Futura make a graffiti curtain, and we put it up to act like a wall. Only one quarter of the room was open." Worried that "no one would show up to a roller rink," she felt relieved when some three hundred partygoers filed through the door. "As far as I was concerned, it was a success," she recalls.

The night still took a few weeks to find its rhythm. "I liked the idea — it was different," recalls Danny Krivit. "But there were a lot of people who were like, 'What's this? What's scratching? What's hip hop?' Nobody knew what to make of it." Blue inched the curtain back week by week until it reached the back wall after a couple of months, the night having gained visceral momentum the night she screened the Sex Pistols mockumentary *The Great Rock 'n' Roll Swindle* on 30 July. "It took time to build it up," confirms Bambaataa. "The word was getting out that it was a funky club to be at." Although "a little something was lost" when the venue left the tiny Negril for the less intimate Roxy, "the intensity went from like one hundred to one thousand," maintains Jonny Sender. As for the crowd, it amounted to "a big mash-up of b-boys, downtown trendies, punks, famous people, musicians, painters, gays, trannies — everything you can think of," remembers Blue. The Roxy embodied the moment when "uptown and downtown came together," adds Sal Principato, while progressive rock and new wave fan John Hall experienced an epiphany when one of the DJs played "Jailhouse Rock" by Elvis Presley. "It made me walk off the floor but all these b-boys got into the song," he recalls. "I realized at that moment how open-minded the fans and participants of hip hop culture were to all kinds of influences, and how narrow-minded I was being."

The convergence was rooted in sound. "Bambaataa was giving them their music but he was giving them their music *twisted*," points out Afrika Islam. "You can hear 'Honky Tonk Women' from a thousand DJs but if you hear 'Honky Tonk Women' scratched, and you might be on a little bit of a hallucinogenic, you go, 'What was that? This is incredible!' Then it's, 'Wow, Rare Earth!' Then it's, 'Wow, what's this Brazilian shit?' You got to look at the DJ and you go, 'Who is this black dude?'" With Zulu Nation DJ Red Alert joining Bambaataa, Jazzy Jay, and Grand Mixer D.ST a short while into Blue's run, scratching — or the technique of manipulating a piece of vinyl in rapid, rhythmic movements to create a scratchy, percussive sound — became central to the roster's practice, albeit under the watchful and sometimes wary eye of the Zulu Nation leader. "When scratching and cutting first came out every DJ was doing it and going wild," he told Holman. "But what most were doing was too hard to follow and didn't keep a beat."[9] Bambaataa believed Jazzy Jay was "one of only two or three DJs (including Grandmaster Flash)" who could scratch smoothly enough to maintain the beat, but his concerns resurfaced at the Roxy.[10] "Sometimes I had to tell some of them to stop scratching so much," he recalls. "You have some DJs who come and they get into themselves and forget about the dance floor." Regarding his own playing, Bambaataa argues he "didn't have to scratch" because "you was going to get down anyway." The "technical part," Islam noted in a later interview with the *East Village Eye*, simply wasn't Bambaataa's "thing." "He had The Force — a great sense of the crowd. He knew what peaks a night."[11]

AFRIKA BAMBAATAA, AFRIKA ISLAM, GRAND MIXER D.ST, GRAND WIZARD THEODORE, JAZZY JAY, AND RED ALERT, THE ROXY (1982)

Afrika Bambaataa & the Soul Sonic Force, "Planet Rock"

Toni Basil, "Mickey"

The B-52's, "Mesopotamia"

James Brown, "Get on the Good Foot (Parts 1 and 2)"

James Brown, "Get Up, Get into It, Get Involved"

Tyrone Brunson, "The Smurf"

Cameo, "Flirt"

Chic, "Le Freak"

The Clash, "The Magnificent Dance"

The Clash, "The Magnificent Seven"

The Clash, "Rock the Casbah"

George Clinton, "Atomic Dog"

George Clinton, "Loopzilla"

Cotton Candy, featuring Donna Trollinger, "Havin' Fun"

Culture Club, "Time (Clock of the Heart)"

"D" Train, "You're the One for Me"

Defunkt, "Razor's Edge"

Dennis Coffey and the Detroit Guitar Band, "Scorpio"

Eurythmics, "Sweet Dreams (Are Made of This)"

Fab 5 Freddy, "Change the Beat (French and English Rap)"

Falco, "Der Kommissar"

Futura 2000, "The Escapades of Futura 2000"

Peter Gabriel, "Shock the Monkey"

Grand Master Flash, "Flash to the Beat"

Grandmaster Flash & the Furious Five, "The Message"

Eddy Grant, "Time Warp"

The Headhunters, "God Made Me Funky"

The Honey Drippers, "Impeach the President"

Imagination, "Just an Illusion"

Incredible Bongo Band, "In-a-Gadda-da-Vida/Apache"

The Jackson 5, "ABC"

The Jackson 5, "Dancing Machine"

The Jackson 5, "Hum Along and Dance"

Bob James, "Nautilus"

Grace Jones, "Nipple to the Bottle"

Jonzun Crew, "Pack Jam (Look Out for the OVC)"

D.C. LaRue, "Indiscreet"

Led Zeppelin, "Immigrant Song"

Loose Joints, "Go Bang! #5"

Loose Joints, "Is It All Over My Face? (Female Vocal)"

Madonna, "Everybody"

Malcolm McLaren, featuring the World's Famous Supreme Team, "Buffalo Gals"

Melle Mel and Duke Bootee, "Message II (Survival)"

Musical Youth, "Pass the Dutchie"

Nairobi and the Awesome Foursome, "Funky Soul Makossa (Free Beats)"

New Edition, "Candy Girl"

Orange Krush, "Action"

Man Parrish, "Hip Hop, Be Bop (Don't Stop)"

The Peech Boys, "Don't Make Me Wait"

Phase 2, "The Roxy"

Planet Patrol, "Play at Your Own Risk"

Quadrant Six, "Body Mechanic"

Rockers Revenge, featuring Donnie Calvin, "Walking on Sunshine '82"

Patrice Rushen, "Forget Me Nots"

Samba Soul, "Mambo No. 5"

Shades of Love, "Keep in Touch (Body to Body)"

Shalamar, "A Night to Remember"

Sister Nancy, "Bam Bam"

Jimmy Spicer, "The Bubble Bunch"

Rufus Thomas, "The Funky Chicken"

West Street Mob, "Let's Dance (Make Your Body Move)"

Yazoo, "Situation (Dub Mix)"

Instructed by Haenel, Krivit monitored the use of the sound system from the vantage point of a second booth that could control the volume of the first. "As long as D.ST was playing, my job was simple, but the other guys were all over the place," he recounts. "One record would be super low, one would be too loud." Soon into Blue's run, the owner also ordered his longest-standing DJ to tell the Zulu Nation roster to limit the level of scratching because "nobody's dancing," which left him with mixed feelings, for while a minute of the technique could seem "like an eternity" he nevertheless had no desire to fade any of them out. Krivit made it clear he was following orders on the couple of

Afrika Bambaataa (left) and Afrika Islam DJ-ing at the Roxy, 1983. Photograph by and courtesy of Bob Gruen ©.

occasions when he intervened. "Haenel was not very popular with the DJs," remarks Blue. "He was clueless — what can I say? I had my creative agenda and stuck to it. We basically ignored him and that caused a lot of friction." Islam recalls Krivit converting to the Wheels of Steel cause. "He ended up being the white boy who sat there going, 'Man, these guys are cutting this record, maybe I should get this record.' You could see Danny was getting filled with more and more funk."

Bambaataa and his co-DJs cultivated a distinctive sound that wasn't tied to genre. "We was hip hop DJs but we played everything," he comments. "You wasn't just hearing hip hop. You was hearing African music, calypso, reggae, rock, jazz, electro, funk. We even played some funky-style country and western. That's what made it so exciting." An eclectic funk sensibility ran through the night. "The Roxy was a little bit of everything," adds Islam. "It was dance music. We'd play [the Jackson 5's] 'I Want You Back' and we'd also play [AC/DC's]

'Highway to Hell.' We played Loose Joints and we played Donna Summer and we played Hall & Oates. But we didn't have to rock the whole record of Hall & Oates, so you didn't necessarily know it was Hall & Oates. We just had to rock the beginning." The dance styles on show were also wide-ranging, in part because breaking remained a challenging form. "There were rockers and b-boys there, but it was like a show," recalls Willie "Marine Boy" Estrada. "It wouldn't be everyone doing it. It was a hard dance to do. Most people didn't have enough upper body strength." Louis "Loose" Kee Jr. maintains that break-ers "didn't know how to dance with their feet, how to do up work," adding that the dancers who went to the Loft "did both." But Islam contends that breaking amounted to an "extreme statement of freedom" — and that was enough for the style to command the Roxy floor.

Contributing to the downtown framing of the culture, Blue had published an article in *Details* on the eve of her party's relaunch in June in which she argued that hip hop culture had "no hard-and-fast rules." The more it "is ex-posed in its entirety, the more it becomes analogous to the '70s and anarchy — could this be REAL punk?" she added.[12] Looking back, the promoter argues that the Roxy was less of a hip hop night than a "massive dance party where all cultures and races mixed together, and all types of music were played. If a song had a wicked beat or sounded good, we played it." Islam also felt the night was defined by its connectedness to the wider scene. "The Roxy was dance-oriented, which meant it paralleled the Garage," he argues. "It was really about the music. You had your posers that came in — 'I'm higher than every-body else' — but they had to melt into the crowd because people just wanted to have a good time."

The closest anyone got to being an outsider, Krivit located the party within the broader shakeup of the post-disco dance scene. "The whole moment was not predictable and this was a version of that," he reasons. "It was electric. It definitely had a new pulse to it. And this was a new downtown crowd." The social-sonic potential: it seemed limitless.

THE GARAGE EVERYBODY
WAS LISTENING TO EVERYTHING

A trained organist who grew up in Catskill, New York, Michael de Benedictus moved to West 30th Street, found work playing in a local church, and formed an R&B outfit called Snatch, after which a church friend from Catskill who had started to work at the Paradise Garage invited him to the spot in the autumn of 1978. "I immediately fell in love with the place," recalls de Benedictus. "I loved the music. I loved the look of the patrons. I wanted to be there. It was just magnetism."

After meeting the keyboard player, Larry Levan instructed the door staff to admit him whenever he showed up, and they deepened their bond when they met up in Los Angeles during the *Billboard* disco convention of February 1980. Attending as the guest of the Village People's Felipe Rose, de Benedictus proposed they borrow Rose's car and explore the city. A short while later they found themselves driving to Beverly Hills and on to the top of Laurel Canyon, where the road falls away. "Larry was having a ball because here we were, we were going to die if we took one false step," reminisces de Benedictus. "We discovered that we both liked roller coasters and we were daredevils because we kept going. We almost killed ourselves a couple of times." The following weekend Levan couldn't stop talking about the adventure. "That event made me feel close enough to go and watch him play records and talk to him during the course of the night," continues the keyboard player. "The experience established this trust between us."

Levan and de Benedictus started to hang out until, asked to work the lights at the Garage one night, de Benedictus noticed that a police-siren effect connected to the light board was out-of-tune with the music and offered to bring his own synthesizer into the booth because it contained a tuneable siren. With Levan willing to explore, de Benedictus started to reproduce the bass lines of the DJ's selections as well as introduce fresh melodic lines on top. "It was wonderfully natural because it wasn't rehearsed," remembers the musician, who would play for six to eight hours on Fridays and Saturdays. "It was improvisational. It was like disco jazz." Listening to the player through a headphone, Levan would turn up the channel when he felt the keyboard enhanced the musical experience — which was often. "The sound system at the Garage was always rated as one of the best in the world, so to be able to play an instrument through that was amazing," reminisces de Benedictus. "You could feel every nuance."

The duo took their collaboration into the studio, with de Benedictus recording overdubs for "Heartbeat," "Make It Last Forever," and "Serious, Sirius, Space Party." "We spent $80,000 on that," de Benedictus notes of the final track. "Larry just kept adding parts and doing remixes. Mel [Cheren] never made his money back. He was very pissed off." Having turned down the opportunity to cover Snatch's debut single, a cover of "Another Brick in the Wall," Levan joined Snatch around the time they took on the new name of the Peech Boys — a name that was supposed to "capture that realness of being young," Levan explained later.[1] For the new lineup's first recording, "Don't Make Me Wait," Levan contributed to the structuring of the tracks, the equalization of the mix, and the use of additional effects, including a digital delay box that he instructed de Benedictus to trigger repeatedly. "I remember sitting at the board and I turned a knob and sent a handclap into this digital delay," remembers de Benedictus. "Larry jumped. He said, 'Wow, stop, that's it!' It had all the motion and drama that was perfect for Larry. He said, 'Record that!'" De Benedictus printed the result because one slight turn of a knob could have changed everything. "The next day we tried to get it back and sure as shit we weren't able to, so I was thinking, 'Thank god we printed that,'" he remembers. "That was the turning point."

A year in the making, the final mix opened with cluster storms of echo-heavy electronic handclaps and a thick bass line that splurged out massive blocks of reverberant sound — followed by silence. "The bass sounded heavy because of the kind of synth I used," explains de Benedictus. "It was an Arp Odyssey. Everybody else was using Minimoogs." Additional keyboard lines and drum patterns introduced dance elements into a mix that also drew on Jamaican dub effects, spatiality, and out-of-the-box electronics, while Bernard Fowler delivered lyrics on the theme of sexual attraction in a sensual baritone moan that gave the lines an unlikely urgency. "Don't make me wait another night," sang the vocalist. "Tonight I'm gonna love you/Don't make me wait all night/Don't make me wait all night, no no." Robert Kasper contributed raw, Peter Frampton–style guitar. "He was into power chords and screaming solos," explains de Benedictus. "That didn't exist in dance before. But when we put him in the studio, that's what came out."

Released on West End in March after Cheren heard Levan play an early demo version and signed the track, the twelve-inch featured an extended version on the A-side and a dub on the flip. Negotiated by de Benedictus, it also bore a Garage Records logo along with credits for de Benedictus (producer), Levan (producer), Fowler (writer), and the Peech Boys (writer). De Benedictus had to argue for Levan's inclusion. "A lot of the guys in the band were like, 'He's just a DJ,'" recalls the keyboard player. "But Larry always came up with lots of ideas. I said, 'Look, if it wasn't for him, we wouldn't be doing this record, so shut up!'" De Benedictus and Levan also included an a cappella on the seven-inch after they saw the dance floor respond enthusiastically when Levan ran the stand-alone vocal over instrumental sections of other tracks. "People were looking at Larry like, 'You're crazy, man! What the fuck is wrong with you?'" François Kevorkian remembers of the move. "But then everybody went, '*Of course we should put a cappellas on records!*'" Kevorkian adds: "The way Larry preset the claps was so radical. After 'Don't Make Me Wait,' everybody *had* to have claps in their records."

Reviewers swooned over the release. *Dance Music Report* described it as a "highly progressive funk fantasy" that could "initiate a new category of dance music, a name for which has yet to be developed," with "echo effects galore" sending listeners "on a trip from which there is no return!"[2] The *Village Voice* described it as "an undisputed monster," adding that the Peech Boys weren't so much "predicting the future as hastening it."[3] Brian Chin noted in *Record World* how the twelve-inch "makes a succession of changes from dub, to soul, to rock" before remarking that "Levan's mix pretty much sums up all the changes and advances that have happened in disco-mixing over the past two years. Can you pass up such a document?"[4] Garage heads heard the record performed live when the Peech Boys appeared alongside ESG and Two Tons o' Fun for Levan's birthday party in July. Cheren, however, maintains that sales fell short of expectations because Levan mixed and tested the record for so long everyone was "over it" by the time of its release."[5] De Benedictus acknowledges that Levan would never say, "This is the mix," yet also maintains that "if it wasn't for Larry playing it every weekend it would have died altogether."

Levan also began to work with Island Records, reworking Gwen Guthrie's "Seventh Heaven," "It Should Have Been You," and "Getting Hot" for the subsidiary label 4th & Broadway as well as a promo-only, uncredited remix of

Michael de Benedictus on stage at the Paradise Garage, ca. 1981. Photographer unknown; courtesy of Michael de Benedictus.

Grace Jones's "Feel Up." The DJ played the records ruthlessly at the Garage along with additional mixes of "Can't Play Around" by Lace, "Don't Turn Your Back on Me" by the Frontline Orchestra, "Tearin' It Up" by Chaka Khan, and "Changes" by Imagination (which went uncredited until the mix appeared on the group's 1983 album *Night Dubbing*). As momentous as these releases were, Levan's remix output nevertheless slowed during 1982, while his efforts for "Every Way but Loose" by Plunky & the Oneness of Juju and "Let Me Feel Your Heartbeat" by Glass were relatively disappointing. "When most of his attention was on the Peech Boys the remixes fell to the side," observes Judy Weinstein.

Although Levan enjoyed a remarkably low profile in the city and no national profile to speak of, influential figures from the art-punk end of the party network nevertheless began to head to the Garage to hear him play during 1981 and 1982. "My biggest influence was Larry," comments Mark Kamins, who gifted the DJ promotional copies of Junior's "Mama Used to Say" and Central Line's "Walking into Sunshine" following a trip to London. "He was always spontaneous and never had a plan. He was a genius the way he would use sound effects, the way he'd mix a record, the way he'd tell the lighting man what to do, the way he'd have complete control over a situation, the way he'd take two five-minute records and play them for thirty minutes, the way he fucked with the EQ, the way he stopped the music, the way he made people scream." Kamins welcomed Levan when he visited Danceteria as the two of them developed a kinship based on taste and trust. "I'd give him some records, he'd give me some records," says the Danceteria DJ. "We had our own little thing going on that nobody knew about." Kamins adds: "Every trick I learned I learned from Larry Levan."

Other art-punk stalwarts found themselves drawn into the parallel universe of the Garage. "The music and everything else there was just mind-expanding," recalls Justin Strauss, who was introduced to the spot by Kevorkian. "Hearing that music and how Larry played totally changed my outlook on *everything*." Taken to the spot by Strauss, Ivan Baker remembers the Ritz and Garage DJs becoming "very friendly," with Levan hooking up with Strauss whenever he wanted to see a live concert at the Ritz. "People were holding fans, tripping their brains out, doing this interpretive dance, and the sound system was just totally dead perfect," Baker reminisces of the King Street setting. "Nothing hurt your ears. It was just beautiful." Even *SoHo News* nightlife reporter Stephen Saban found himself swept off his feet when he visited the venue for the first time. "You can't fall over because there are 4,000 bodies packed onto the dance floor, dancing as one person," he reported, "and if you fell it would be onto someone who would prop you up from sheer closeness and keep you dancing whether you were conscious or not."[6] Kevorkian argues that the "Garage/Loft/Better Days/Zanzibar world" was separate from the "art gallery, decadent, after-hours, trashed, punky, new wave scene." Yet he also remembers how "all the DJs from those rock clubs started going to the Garage every week" because "they all had to hear what Larry was playing."

Hip hop protagonists also flocked to King Street. Coke La Rock, Kool Herc's onetime DJ and MC partner, "started hanging down in the Village and going to the Paradise Garage because they had the best sound system in New York," he recalls.[7] Name-checking "Don't Make Me Wait" in her 1982 hip hop article, Ruza Blue also headed to the Garage as part of a ritual that saw her and her Negril/Roxy friends head to several parties during the course of a night before winding up in a diner for breakfast.[8] "I went everywhere!" declares the promoter. "I loved the Loft, the Garage, the Funhouse and Danceteria. All

Afrika Islam's Paradise Garage membership card. Courtesy of Afrika Islam.

we wanted to do was dance!" Less of a party animal, Bambaataa nevertheless developed a respect for the King Street setup. "They had their scene and we had our scene, but we played a lot of their records, like the Peech Boys," he comments. "I would visit the Paradise Garage if there was something interesting to go see. Larry Levan was funky with what he was playing for his style of audience. He certainly knew how to drill it down on the turntables."

Bambaataa joined Afrika Islam, who started to go to the Garage "religiously" after he picked up work at Downstairs Records, where Yvonne Turner, head of the imports section, would pick out records for Levan and instruct her assistant to hand-deliver them to King Street. "Yvonne was gay and she was the one who got us into the Garage," notes Islam. "She opened the doors to that culture, and I understood the dance music scene because the hip hop scene was the dance scene too — it was just in the Bronx." Islam argues that the Garage "wasn't disco at all," but was instead "based on music and dance and freedom," doubling as a "place to dance in a community." Whatever its status, he was "open to all of it" because of the philosophical and sonic education he had received from Bambaataa, although even then the scale of the King Street operation was something to behold. "At the Garage you could hear Roy Ayers, the Soul Sonic Force, and Manu Dibango," he reminisces. "And to see such acts as the Peech Boys and Chaka Khan and Grace Jones and France Joli — all of these eclectic underground acts — it was impressionable for a kid from the South Bronx."

Liquefying into a setting that "pulled people from all the boroughs," Islam took to combining soul and funk styles from the 1950s and 1960s with some of the freer moves that were popular on the floor, and although Levan's selections weren't funky enough to make him "go down," the Bambaataa acolyte was more than happy to skip, which "had the same intensity as breaking" yet was executed while standing upright. "I got a chance to express my uptown funk in this downtown setting," he recounts. "If I saw someone do a ballet move, I would say, 'OK, let me see if I can fuck with that.' I saw people do Brazilian capoeira, and I saw body types and tones and shit that could have belonged to professional dancers for all I knew. The Garage was a good melting pot." Part of the team that built the Zulu Nation sound system, Islam made the Garage his primary reference point, acknowledging that "a lot of the stuff we copied came from Richard Long." The King Street system also rendered Bambaataa spellbound. "That was powerful," he remembers. "Richard Long was wild with his speakers."

The interscene exchanges ramped up some more when Brooklyn friends introduced Fred Brathwaite to the venue. "If you weren't homophobic you could experience very hot women and hear the most amazing dance music that has ever been made on the most incredible sound system ever," he comments. "When a tune reached the point when it was the hottest song in New York, that's when the artist would perform at the Garage and that's when I'd be there. I couldn't wait to go." Brathwaite took Keith Haring to the King Street venue when the two of them got stoned one night and went out for a walk. "It's a disco that absolutely blew my mind," Haring recalled to John Gruen. "I mean, I have never been the same since I walked into Paradise Garage!"[9] Drawn to the ethnic mix, the Pennsylvanian artist also valued the way the Garage validated a culture he had come to repudiate. "It's nothing like other gay discos, because the kids here are gay but they're really tough street kids — and they're incredibly, incredibly beautiful!" he added to Gruen. "It's the closest thing to being at a Grateful Dead concert, except that it wasn't this hippie thing, but taking place in a totally urban, contemporary setting. The whole experience was very communal, very spiritual."[10] The fact that Haring painted like a virtuoso dancer drew him deeper into the setting. "The 'elevated spiritual experience' that Haring found at the club was something that he tried to infuse into his paintings and his exhibitions," points out Jeffrey Deitch. "Haring's fluid compositions, with their figures dancing inside abstract curves, paralleled the rhythm and freeform composition of the dance floor. The paintings also embody the sensuality of the communal dance experience. Like the Paradise Garage, they are permeated with sexual energy."[11]

The traffic didn't flow in one direction only, so when Tony Humphries visited the Prelude office and complained to label employee Larry Patterson about how hard it was to emulate the likes of Levan, Patterson told him, "Forget about the Paradise Garage, I want you to come and check out a club in Jersey." A onetime Loft regular, Patterson worked as the key stand-in figure for Levan during the opening years of the Garage, in part because he didn't have a residency of his own, and when Levan tired of traveling to Newark every Wednesday night Patterson took over his Zanzibar slot. None of this persuaded Humphries to feign enthusiasm at Patterson's suggestion — he was, after all, a child of the city — but a subsequent visit reminded him of Melons. "I said, 'What the *hell* is this?'" recalls the Brooklynite. "'This is in *Jersey*?' I was like, 'Holy shit, look at this place!' The sound system was the shit and the people were partying." Humphries was "blown away again" when he returned on Saturday to hear Tee Scott. "I had never been to a club where half the club was in regular baggies and sneakers and tank tops and all that, and the other half was all of these suited people, and they're all getting along partying until ten o' clock in the morning!" recalls Humphries. "I was like, 'Fuck the Garage, I'm going to start coming to New Jersey!'"

Saint DJs were much more straightforwardly hostile, although when Roy Thode headed to the Garage he made a point of complimenting Levan on his work. Concerned that her co-DJs were "too pristine in their presentation," Sharon White organized a group outing to the Garage, telling them that there was something that was the "antithesis" of their world that they had to experience, even if it was just once. "Larry could do anything," she maintains. "He was so unorthodox in his presentation. Sometimes he was a mess but it didn't matter. He waved a magic wand across that crowd and he could do no wrong. He was quite something to behold." In the end, White's colleagues "freaked out" because they were "out of their element," but on another occasion she returned with Robbie Leslie after he insisted he couldn't imagine how a record such as "Weekend" by Phreek could be programmed successfully. "I said, 'Dammit, you come with me!'" she recounts. "When Larry kicked in, I told him, 'Hold on, honey, because the hair on the back of your neck is going to go straight up.' He was like, 'Oh my God!'" Yet Leslie also concluded that Levan's "unpredictability" combined with his penchant for taking "hard-left and hard-right swerves" would have been deemed "heretical" at the Saint.

Of the infinitesimal number of white gay men who divided their time equally between the Saint and the Garage, John Giove could become frustrated with the way the Second Avenue DJs only occasionally "toyed with soul or funk," whereas Levan's selections and technique of building to a peak remained utterly compelling. "The dance energy at the Garage was also something to wonder at," he adds. "Some of the dancers were so smooth and fluid they seemed to be part of the music." Yet the multisensorial experience of the Second Avenue environment and in particular the ability of the DJs to work a "production number" in tandem with the planetarium remained peerless. "When a song was given a treatment like that, under that dome, with that star machine and the rain lights and the mothership all going at the same time, the experience was cathartic. The DJ could evoke just about any emotion," continues Giove. That along with the tribal magnetism of the Saint crowd and the freer availability of sex meant that few Second Avenue regulars journeyed to King Street. "Going to the Garage was like socialites in New York in the 1920s going up to Harlem," comments Saint member Stuart Lee. "I was adventurous. But with a few exceptions, I couldn't get people to go there. They would say, 'It's all black,' and 'We're going to go *there*? I don't think so!'"

Then there were those who didn't feel particularly attracted to or repelled by the Paradise Garage, among them Michael Zilkha, who maintains that although the venue cultivated a sense of abandon, its social mores were "fairly circumscribed." It was "harder to fuck" with the Garage's culture than the Mudd Club's, he argues, conscious that irony didn't circulate freely within the venue's walls. Yet the lack of knowing distance didn't signify any deficit in attitude, with Levan's style sufficiently declarative and streetwise to draw drag queens from the House of Xtravaganza into the Garage during 1981 and 1982—seemingly the first time a drag house subdivided attention that was usually devoted to competing against other houses within the autonomous drag ball scene. Overall, the chorus of awe drowned out expressions of even partial doubt as a coalition of revelers elevated the Garage to a semi-mystical plateau within the city's party network. With the Loft and the Roxy also major contributors, an unprecedented degree of synchronicity had come to define the downtown scene. A different level of partying had begun.

23

THE PLANET ROCK
GROOVE

Tom Silverman hired an office hand to help him build Tommy
Boy and manage *Dance Music Report* toward the end of 1981. "I interviewed
with Tom two or three times," says Monica Lynch, who got the job. "I didn't
have any formal background in music but Tom provided me with an opportunity. He was going out to Long Island City and Queens to pick up the new
Tommy Boy release, which was 'Jazzy Sensation,' and he asked me if I wanted
to come." Lynch was confronted with the heavy-duty currency of the dance
economy: a mini-mountain of fifty-count boxes packed with twelve-inch
vinyl. "These guys brought them out to the curb and I started slinging them
into the back of Tom's hatchback car," she recounts. "At that point I think
Tom thought it could work out. I was bright enough and would work like
a mule. The money was so low I had to continue waiting tables at night for
quite some time."

The boxes piled higher after Silverman teamed up with Bambaataa to map
out an eight-track demo that included sections of Babe Ruth's "The Mexican,"
B.T. Express's "Do You Like It," Captain Sky's "Super Sporm," Rick James's
"Give It to Me Baby," and Kraftwerk's "Numbers" and "Trans-Europe Express." "Me and Tom did the demo together in a studio, upstate New York,"
recounts the DJ. "We was going through records to get the concept; we was
trying different grooves." Kraftwerk were the major influence. "I wanted to
create the first black electronic group," adds Bambaataa. "I always was into
'Trans-Europe Express' and after Kraftwerk put 'Numbers' out I said, 'I wonder if I can combine them to make something real funky with a hard bass and
beat.'" Downtown sensibilities also shaped the sound of the track. "I got the
idea from playing in a lot of punk rock clubs," he revealed in another interview published in the *East Village Eye*, this one conducted by Steven Hager,
who got hold of the Bronx DJ's phone number from Fred Brathwaite at the
Beyond Words opening. "The punkers were getting off on our kind of music

so I decided to make a record that would appeal to the white crowd and still keep the sound that would appeal to the hip hoppers. So I combined the two elements."[1]

Asked to work on the project, Arthur Baker was immediately drawn to the Kraftwerk elements, having considered making a record using "Numbers" and "Trans-Europe Express" himself, he claims. "From the start I was thinking, 'I want to make it so they can play it at Danceteria and they can play it at the Garage and it will also be a rap record,'" comments the producer. "I wanted it to be able to cross all those boundaries." The producer streamlined the demo by removing the B.T. Express and Rick James elements, after which he tracked down the equipment he needed to re-create the beats of "Numbers" by searching the ad section in the *Village Voice*. The "man with drum machine" turned out to be the owner of a Roland TR-808, the successor to the TR-33, TR-55, and TR-77 (which contained presets), and the CR-78 (which was programmable). "Basically, we played him 'Numbers' and we said, 'Get that beat for us,'" adds the producer. "Then Bam played 'Super Sporm' and he said, 'I want that for the break.'"

A guitarist and synthesizer player who loathed disco, John Robie added synthesizer parts. "I came from an era when artists couldn't get a record deal unless they or one of their band members had some incredible talent or quality, and disco basically put an end to that," he notes of his anti-disco position. "You had people playing to metronomes, everyone sounding the same, and lyrics that were nonsensical and generally infantile." Robie particularly resented the way the 1970s dance sound required great musicians to play below their skill level in order to create a hypnotic trance. "From the point of view of someone who had started out as a die-hard rock musician, it was a death knell," he continues. "The producer's job was to make sure everybody played like a robot. It was as if we went from Bob Dylan to 'Let's rollerskate!'" It got to the point where Robie and his friends would walk away if they went into a restaurant and heard disco playing. "It was everywhere; it was like a virus," he concludes. "And it all sounded *exactly the same*."

Robie got to meet Bambaataa after he laid down four Moroder/Kraftwerk-style synthesizer pieces in real time, released one of them with Capitol in Belgium, and, following a tip-off, took the others to "this guy who lives in Co-op City in the Bronx." Bambaataa's mother was watching *Wheel of Fortune* when Robie made his visit. "I played the tracks to Bam and he said I should choose 'Vena Cava,'" recalls the instrumentalist, "so I borrowed $1,200 from a friend and went to a small recording studio to make the record." When the subscriber service Disconet featured the track as its record of the month, Bambaataa

Afrika Bambaataa at Bronx River Project, 1982. Photograph by and courtesy of Sylvia Plachy ©.

called Silverman to say, "I got this keyboard player who is as funky as Kraftwerk — check him out!" The publisher contacted Robie within the hour and arranged for him to meet Baker in Tommy Boy's tiny Upper East Side office. "Nobody could have seen all these disparate elements coming together," posits Robie. "The unlikely mix of talents was as much a phenomenon as the record itself. People from totally different backgrounds with completely dissimilar tastes and styles somehow came together to do this. At the time I remember it feeling pretty bizarre."

Baker, Bambaataa, and Robie headed into the studio soon after the release of "Don't Make Me Wait." "I was definitely influenced by that, so 'Planet Rock' had a drop-down to the bass and then the claps," notes Baker. "I was a dance producer so I was like, 'I want it to be dance.' It had to have drama." Encouraged by Baker to break with the habit of playing the synthesizer like a conventional instrument, Robie used a Multimoog to re-create the melodic lines from "Trans-Europe Express" and "The Mexican" plus orchestra hits, and he employed a Fairlight to generate a quivering orchestral string-line for the break (on the condition he receive a cowriter's credit). Engineer Jay Burnett "contributed greatly to the record" through his inventive use of signal processing, which resulted in the 808 sounding "quite different than it would have in its unprocessed, 'natural' state," maintains the instrumentalist. Later that night Baker played the result to his wife and declared, "We've made musical history." "This was before the rap was on," adds the producer. "The track was so fucking different."

For the vocals, Bambaataa spoke through an electronic mic because vocoder technology failed to provide the precise robotic effect the production team wanted. Globe, Mr. Biggs, and Pow Wow of the Soul Sonic Force fashioned a new, conversational mode of rapping because the track's 130-beat-per-minute tempo ran significantly faster than most funk and rap recordings, making the ubiquitous hippety-hop rhyming style difficult to deliver. Baker claims he came up with the idea to introduce the crowd cheering and chanting that accompanies Bambaataa's opening lines as well as the ensuing "Rock, rock to the planet rock, don't stop," which he grabbed from the "Rock, rock, to the disco rock/Give it all you got" intro of "Body Music" by the Strikers, although Bambaataa went on to tell Hager that those lines came about because the studio gathering started talking about every planet having its own way of rocking. Burnett suggested the rappers shout out the places where the planetary party was about to unfold, just like James Brown would call out to audience members from different cities while onstage. In the final contribution, David Azarch and the band members of Animal Luxury recorded the "Rock it don't stop it" line when Bambaataa hauled them in from the studio's waiting room. "Bam comes out, we recognize each other, exchange high-fives and handshakes, and he says, 'I need more voices — you just have to shout 'Planet Rock,'" recounts the Peppermint Lounge DJ. "We all just casually got up, went in, and did it in two or three takes. That was the beginning and end of my career as a backup vocalist."

The result heralded the breakthrough of a new form of synthetic funk. "I took the techno-pop sound of the Yellow Magic Orchestra and Kraftwerk and Gary Numan, and I flipped it to the funk sound of James Brown, Sly and the Family Stone, and George Parliament-Funkadelic Clinton," explains Bambaataa. "Arthur Baker and John Robie put in sounds and noises. They really took it there. It was the birth of the electro-funk sound." Concerned with complexity and virtuosity, Robie was left unmoved. "Coming from a rock background and being a 'legit songwriter,' I thought 'Planet Rock' was silly," he reasons. "I was playing one-note lines and creating sound effects on a monophonic synthesizer, there was a repetitive drum machine sequence, and people were spouting stuff about saving the universe. Honestly, to me it

East Village Eye front cover featuring "Planet Rock," June 1982. "The gulf between the white and black worlds was still so wide that we could get away with using a cover that had nothing directly to do with Afrika Bambaataa, but was simply a cool-looking image of a young black man that our art director, Glenn Miller, had in his portfolio," says Leonard Abrams. "In our defense, our time and resources were so limited then that we couldn't send someone to the South Bronx to take his picture. But I wish we had've." Courtesy of Leonard Abrams.

was an embarrassment." But Baker had no reservations when he took acetates to the IDRC record pool as well as a Brooklyn record store called the Music Factory. "At the pool it was one of those 'What the fuck is this?' records," he remembers. "Then a guy at the record store offered me a hundred dollars for the acetate."

Released under the artist name of Afrika Bambaataa & the Soul Sonic Force in the spring, the record tore through the city as its first print run of fifty thousand sold out in a week.[2] "'Planet Rock' was the one record that blew everything open," recalls François Kevorkian. "It was just this wild animal, a cyborg let loose. It was just the most astounding, bass-drum-heavy, in-your-face, mother-fucking deadly record we'd ever heard. It was a phenomenon — a tidal wave." In June Steven Hager referred to the twelve-inch as the "monster dance hit of the spring" before Malcolm McLaren lauded it during his keynote address at the third New Music Seminar in July.[3] "'Planet Rock' is the most rootsy folk music around, the only music that's coming out of New York City which [is] directly related to that guy in the streets with his ghetto blaster," declared the impresario. "The record is like an adventure story; it's like that guy walking down the street. And, if Elvis Presley was that in the '50s, then Afrika Bambaataa is that for the '80s."[4] Steve Knutson, a musician, actor, and friend of Lynch's, remembers hearing "Planet Rock" whenever he walked down the street. "It was the day of boom boxes and you'd hear it on WBLS," he reminisces. "It was like there was a big sound system right over the city." When the track played repeatedly on his car radio, Robie "definitely got it at that point," while Bambaataa remembers being amazed when he "started seeing all different types getting into the 'Planet Rock' groove."[5] Sales eventually totaled 650,000 to 700,000 copies — or a solid 13,000 to 14,000 boxes for Silverman and Lynch.

Released in July, "The Message" by Grandmaster Flash & the Furious Five slowed the pulse but maintained the intensity as it built on groundwork established by Brother D, whose 1980 single "How We Gonna Make the Black Nation Rise?" critiqued the outwardly apolitical concerns of party culture with lines such as "Space out, y'all, to the disco rhythm/You're moving to the rhythm but you're wasting time," as well as Kurtis Blow's "Tough," which critiqued the effect of unemployment on male self-esteem. "I noticed the kids around my block in the Bronx doing it [rapping], but there was no message — the stuff they were saying didn't make much sense," Brother D commented in May 1982. "It occurred to me that I could take rap and put a message in it, and it would carry."[6] The record's antimaterialistic lyrics lacked popular appeal, however, while Kurtis Blow's album cover of *Tough*, which had the rapper posing in a decaying urban scene while dressed in a pristine white outfit, illustrated the difficulty of combining social commentary and upward mobility. Then came "The Message," which achieved a better balance between the medium and the message, even if the story of its making turned out to be an unedifying affair.

The track came about after Sugar Hill musicians Ed "Duke Bootee" Fletcher, Keith LeBlanc, Skip McDonald, and Doug Wimbish started to jam in the label's basement studio in Englewood, New Jersey, one day. "I had gone out to get a drink of water, and I started beating on this water bottle," Fletcher recounted later. "Everyone was so in tune that you couldn't fart down there without everyone playing along. We got a groove going and it was really like a jungle track — real intense."[7] Fletcher came up with some lyrics while he was hanging out in his mother's basement with arranger and producer Clifton "Jiggs" Chase. Taking a drag on a joint, Fletcher mused, "Man, it's like a jungle sometimes," which became the lyric "It's like a jungle sometimes/It makes me wonder how I keep from going under." A short while later the sound of glass being broken on the street outside inspired the line "Broken glass everywhere/People pissing on the stairs, you know they just don't care," followed by "I can't take the smell, I can't take the noise/Got no money to move out, I guess I got no choice."[8] Referencing Zapp's "More Bounce to the Ounce" along with the bubbling funk of Tom Tom Club, Fletcher and McDonald then recorded fresh DMX drum-machine beats, a new bass line, and an oscillating synth hook, ran the percussion parts on a backward tape, and, evoking Stevie Wonder's "Living for the City," rounded off the track with the sound of sirens, arguments, and a street arrest.

As far as Sylvia Robinson was concerned, all the track needed was for Grandmaster Flash & the Furious Five to lay down the vocals, only for Flash to protest the song was "way too dark, way too edgy, and way too much of a downer."[9] Melle Mel didn't share Flash's concerns, however, and offered Fletcher additional lyrics he had written for Grandmaster Flash & the Furious Five's "Super Rappin' No. 2" that told the story of a kid who grew up in poverty and died young in prison. Flash's dismay increased when Robinson outlined her intention to have Mel deliver the lyrics solo. "This is what I was afraid of," recalls the DJ in his autobiography. "This is how things fall apart. This isn't about Grandmaster Flash and the Furious Five. This isn't everybody shining at the same time. This isn't about teamwork. This isn't about taking five MCs and making 'em sound like one, which has been our thing from the very beginning. This is about Mel. This is about Sylvia. This is about money."[10] The DJ tried to turn the situation around by having the Furious Five deliver the song, only for Robinson to reject everything save for Flash's name, turning to Mel to deliver the lyrics as a solo rap. "All the rappers, including us, were scared to do something serious," Mel told Steven Hager. "Sylvia Robinson is the only one who believed in 'The Message.' She told us it would be a big song for us."[11]

Unaware of the behind-the-scenes conflict, reviewers welcomed "The Message" as a breakthrough release. Brian Chin described the twelve-inch as rap's "finest, most sophisticated manifestation, an impassioned, emotionally exhausting piece of street art that trivializes by inference almost everything else on the market right now."[12] Hager declared Mel to be the "poet laureate of rap."[13] Robert Palmer of the *New York Times* declared that "The Message" had "radically expanded the horizons" of rap.[14] Kurt Loder of *Rolling Stone* lauded the record as "the most detailed and devastating report from underclass America since Bob Dylan decried the lonesome death of Hattie Carroll—or, perhaps more to the point, since Marvin Gaye took a long look around and wondered what was going on."[15] Loder went on to wonder how anyone "could fail to get the message," but that begged the question: what message?[16] Did the song critique the impact of the Republican right, or the hopelessness of a life of crime, or the failure of politicians to tackle racial inequality, or did it offer a parable of hope? "They pushed a girl in front of a train/Took her to the doctor, sewed her arm on again," ran some lines that pointed to the latter. "Stabbed a man right through the heart/Gave him a transplant and a brand new start." As cultural critic Marshall Berman would note in the *Village Voice* in 1984: "No one has yet written its history or explained how so much creative vitality could emerge, and could keep emerging, from the South Bronx's ashes and dust."[17]

The fortunes of Grandmaster Flash & the Furious Five faltered in the aftermath of the release. Released at the beginning of August, the group's ensuing album, *The Message*, featured "Scorpio," a manic electronic "filler," which began to cause ripples while the group was on tour, but little else of note in terms of fresh material.[18] The subsequent release of the "Message II (Survival)" saw Mel deliver disappointingly paranoid and clichéd musings on the themes of betrayal and survival on top of "Scorpio." Issued by the bootleg label Bozo Meko, Flash's "Flash It to the Beat" featured the DJ punching out beats via a synthesizer for the Furious Five at a Bronx River Center party organized by Bambaataa. But even if "The Message" had catapulted Flash's name into the public consciousness like no other rap track, his relationship to the release remained traumatic, and he also lacked a regular DJ-ing spot in Manhattan.

Steven Hager chose to focus on Bambaataa rather than Flash when he published the first major article to be written on hip hop in the *Village Voice* in September. Titling the piece "Afrika Bambaataa's Hip Hop," Hager set the scene by describing the way Bambaataa defused a violent incident that took place outside a Zulu Nation party held at the Bronx River Community Center by speaking over the microphone and teasing the crowd with James Brown. "It's about survival, economics, and keeping our people moving on," the DJ commented in an interview that covered his background, gang culture, and the rise of the Zulu Nation, whose numbers now ran into the thousands.[19] Hager devoted a solitary paragraph to Flash before claiming that hip hop's b-boys, rappers, DJs, and graffiti writers had developed "their unique artistic vision" in "complete isolation from the rest of the world" between 1974 and 1979 — as if the culture had been born whole and cohesive.[20] "In the future, I just hope all my groups keep piping," added Bambaataa. "See, George Clinton took the music of James Brown and Sly and the Family Stone and made a whole funk empire out of it. That's what I'm trying to do with rap."[21]

Extending Michael Holman's analysis in the *East Village Eye*, Hager speculated if, in five years, hip hop would be considered "the most significant artistic achievement of the decade." He cited Diego Cortez's recent claim in

Flash Art that rap and breaking amounted to "a highly sophisticated art form" and the "soul of the underground scene," which was "just starting to have an effect on the official culture in New York and elsewhere."[22] Hager also argued that if "subcultures are the experimental laboratory where society tests new cultural concepts, then hip hop represents the most imaginative leap forward since the '60s." He even claimed that, echoing the countercultural movement of the 1960s, hip hop had "the capacity to infiltrate and subvert the mass media culture, energizing it with a fresh supply of symbols, myths, and values." It just remained to be seen if figures like Bambaataa could "rise to the occasion, hold onto their principles, and spread the hip hop sensibility across the globe."[23]

Hager felt he had gone "out on a limb" and with good reason. "Even in the East Village, there was intense resistance to recognizing the value of rap music in some quarters," he remembers. "Rap was viewed as a ghetto fad that had no significance for the rest of the world."[24] Others might have wondered how hip hop would fare in relation to disco, which had enjoyed real rather than speculative international influence, even if Hager eschewed any reference to its recent history, and why hip hop should be earmarked for such success when the dance scene that had come to orbit around the Paradise Garage enjoyed greater numbers and turned out more records. But although both scenes were predominantly working-class, the Garage was structured as an inward-looking private party that catered to significant numbers of gay men, many of whom wanted to remain discreet about their sexuality, whereas hip hop operated as a relentlessly outward-facing culture that attracted younger men (and to a lesser extent younger women) who had something to prove. Meanwhile the subplot of Mel's ascendency over Flash illustrated how the rapper's direct communication could trump the circuitous modus operandi of any DJ. Even if the argument between Flash and Robinson indicated that hip hop would inevitably lead a more compromised existence than Hager supposed, the culture was all set to command the public gaze.

Meanwhile Arthur Baker built on the success of "Planet Rock" by releasing a series of twelve-inch singles that held cross-scene appeal. He recorded a Peech Boys–inspired, handclap-heavy cover version of Eddy Grant's "Walking on Sunshine" that featured the vocals of Music Factory record-store employees Donnie Calvin and Dwight Hawkes — or Rockers Revenge. He teamed up with Russell Presto and Tony Carbone, his Boston-based collaborators on the North End lineup, to coproduce Michelle Wallace's "It's Right" and "Jazzy Rhythm" — both mixed by Tee Scott for Emergency. He teamed up with John Robie to coproduce Planet Patrol's "Play at Your Own Risk," which laid vocals sung by a Boston quintet over the 808 beats of "Planet Rock," integrated an additional synth line that Baker had asked Robie to record for the Bambaataa release in case lawyers called them up on their simulation of Kraftwerk, and introduced a playful woofing effect that they knew would appeal to the Funhouse dancers who barked whenever they dug a selection. He and Robie collaborated again on "Funky Soul Makossa" by Nairobi and the Awesome Foursome, a cover of Manu Dibango's "Soul Makossa," which was recorded in real time, even though it sounds sequenced, notes Robie.

With innovative sound techniques part of their arsenal, Baker and Robie led the citywide charge into electronics. "I had struggled for so long so I was just glad to be in a recording studio," recounts Robie. "Getting into a recording studio was a rite of passage; someone was paying $150 an hour so you could go into this rarified environment. I just wanted to play." The instrumentalist and producer added to his catalog by recording Quadrant Six "Body Mechanic," which featured a metallic-sounding voice generated with an MXR Digital Delay, and C-Bank featuring Jenny Burton's "One More Shot," which featured his first foray into sequencing as well as the scratchy percussive sound of breaking glass. "It was like, 'Let's do another record, let's do another record,'" he adds. "We did so many things back-to-back. I didn't care about anyone's perception. Everyone talks about the cultural significance of hip hop now, but giving a label to the music I was making wasn't that important at the time. It's just what we were doing. Now it seems like high art, but there was no design to it. Nobody had a grand plan."

Malcolm McLaren made his own unruly contribution to the mini-boom in synthesizer and drum-machine music with "Buffalo Gals," which he titled after an 1844 song performed by the blackface minstrel John Hodges, who asked if Buffalo gals (women from Buffalo, upstate New York) would "come out tonight" and "dance by the light of the moon." Teaming up with U.K. producer Trevor Horn and the World Famous Supreme Team, broadcasters of a show on WHBI-FM, the ex–Sex Pistols manager combined sounds gathered from South Africa, the Caribbean, and the Appalachia region of the United States with stutter edits, scratching, and vocals, which he delivered in the style of a square-dance caller beamed onto a Bronx playground. The result was so foreign the U.K.-based commissioning label Charisma Records initially rejected McLaren's effort, only to relent. That gave the impresario the green light to make a video that featured poppers, breakers, graffiti artists, and the World Famous Supreme Team interspersed with square dancing that featured men dressed in contemporary streetwear partnering with traditionally clad women. Fire hydrants, skyscrapers, and other urban elements punctuated the song with an explanatory rationale; the chaos made sense in New York City.

Arthur Baker and Rockers Revenge at the Music Factory in Brooklyn. Having asked the Music Factory assistants to recommend a singer, the producer offered them the job when they sang the lyrics back to him. Photograph by Ebet Roberts ©; courtesy of Arthur Baker.

McLaren shed light on his methodology in an interview with *Details* when he noted that Bambaataa's "whole thing" was about "stealing other people's music" as well as "using other people's records like instruments." Referencing, reproducing, xeroxing, and now bare-faced pillaging were the key imperatives to spring out of disco, funk, and even punk repetition. "He had this huge filing cabinet full of stuff like Brenda Lee, the Beach Boys, *everything,*" recounted McLaren. "And when I heard the name of his outfit was Zulu Nation, well, I thought, 'This guy's on my *wavelength*. An African pirate.'"[25] Unconcerned that McLaren had taken it upon himself to substitute the figure of the rapper with a square-dance caller, Bambaataa maintains that the Englishman "took the funk and the new wave and the punk and mixed it up together." Reviewing the record for *Billboard* in December, Chin drew parallels between "Buffalo Gals" and disco, which "was always the source of the most outrageous fusions." In addition to being "strange and fabulous," McLaren's effort amounted to "a wholesale 'x'-ing out of musical boundaries," Chin added.[26]

Contributing to the musical mayhem when he released "Hip Hop, Be Bop (Don't Stop)" around the same time as "Buffalo Gals," the Brooklyn-born Manny Parrish had run away from home at fourteen, whereupon he went to live in the YMCA, "which was worse" (meaning better) "than the bathhouses." He grew into a 6′3″ man-boy; took to dressing in green velvet bell bottoms, blue suede platform shoes, a flower shirt, and a gold chain; and formed an art-fag/new wave/synth pop outfit called Shox Lumania that played at Hurrah, Max's, the Mudd Club, and the New Wave Vaudeville show, which is where he met soprano Klaus Nomi. "We just sat there mesmerized and every night Klaus would bring the house down," reminisces Parrish. "Backstage I said, 'You're amazing,' and he said, 'I think you're amazing too and I'd really like to work with you.'" Parrish recorded "Nomi Chant" for Nomi's eponymous debut album in 1981 and that same year laid down a high-energy, vocoder-happy track titled "Heatstroke" for a porn movie. The release prompted Disconet office assistant Raul Rodriguez to propose they team up to write something funky. Parrish agreed. "I wasn't just a disco bunny," he points out. "I was also into urban dance music."

A George Clinton fan who claims that Kraftwerk's "Numbers" gave him "permission" to combine wholly electronic music with a funk rhythm, Parrish went about his work with limited means and know-how. "I just set the drum machine going and layered in the tracks one at a time by hand," he recounts. "If I had had a choice, I'd have loved to have been a black kid with a funk band, but socially and musically I wasn't there, so the tools I had dictated what I could produce." With Rodriguez assisting, Parrish recorded twenty-four separate tracks of electronic percussion, munchkin voices, a bass line derived from Cymande's "Bra," dog barks, and some keyboard parts. "We included elements of records we heard at the Funhouse," notes Parrish. "I also reflected sounds I heard at Fever in the Bronx because I went there once or twice." With Robie adding tom-tom drums (a preset on the Prophet 5) and a keyboard line, Parrish integrated the twenty-four tracks via random fader movements as if he was on a Warhol-Eno art trip. He and Rodriguez then edited twelve reels of tape down to a hypnotic, jerky, five-minute drum track that featured echo-laden synth lines and sound effects along with Parrish's spoken delivery of the lyric and eventual title of the track—"Hip Hop, Be Bop (Don't Stop)." Like "Planet Rock," the record carried rap further away from its rhythm section roots. Unlike "Planet Rock" it cast the figure of the MC rapper to the outer margins of the recording process.

Parrish crammed a twenty-strong entourage into a van to perform the record in front of club crowds in the Bronx, the Hamptons, and New Jersey, none of them prepared for the moment when he would appear onstage wearing a hooded cape with a dry ice machine attached to his back. Accompanied by Club 57 performer Joey Arias, who twirled around in a little ballerina outfit while young kids moved across the dance floor carrying lanterns, Parrish ended one show convinced he was about to get shot. The drama escalated at Studio 54 when he hung from a trapeze hours after burying his mother. "They turned to me and said, 'How would you like to make an entrance?' And I said, 'Oh, fly me in,' and they did," he remembers. "I was up there for fifteen minutes, my knuckles were white, and I kept coming within inches of these giant neon signs. I was screaming, 'Help! Get me down!'"

Although Parrish judged his record to be a "piece of shit" that lacked "song structure," *Dance Music Report* hailed him a "techno funkster" while Chin argued Kraftwerk's next release would be "hard pressed" to match the track's "high humor and serious groove."[27] By the time Parrish appeared at the Roxy the song was "all over the radio," so that concert turned out to be much more straightforward than some of the earlier ones. But just as the artist wondered if he was about to settle into an urban-electronic niche, Kiss FM removed "Hip Hop, Be Bop (Don't Stop)" when he released his debut album. "There was a backlash in the rap community because I was white and gay," he comments. "I was making music that they played, and then they found that I was white and gay and they pulled it. It didn't hurt sales but it was shocking."

"Hip Hop, Be Bop (Don't Stop)" confirmed that a novel strain of electronic dance music — one that featured funk-oriented beats along with rapped and nonrapped vocals — had surged to the fore. "It wasn't about the lead singer and what they wore and how they sang," observes Parrish. "It was about the sonic composition of the track. It was about the rhythm and the beats and the noise." With "Body Mechanic," "Buffalo Gals," "Funky Soul Makossa," "The Message," "One More Shot," "Planet Rock," and "Play at Your Own Risk" also contributing, the development bolstered the perception that rap's clap-your-hands-in-the-air days were numbered. Even when the figure of the rapper survived, as was the case with the Brooklyn-based group Whodini, synthetic gadgetry still came to the fore, in his case courtesy of U.K. synthesizer whiz Thomas Dolby, with the black disco underpinnings of early rap manifestly in retreat. "There was a change in technology," adds Parrish. "In the beginning, synthesizers were these odd things with oscillators and filters, and like a mad scientist you turned dials. Then computer chips started coming in and Roland released the 808, which was a milestone. All of a sudden I had a drum machine that didn't have a bossa nova beat; it was programmable and I could

John Robie in the
studio, ca. 1984.
Photographer
unknown; courtesy of
John Robie and Tina B.

create my own beats. It was a technological thing and the technology was no longer exclusive."

As expectations disintegrated across the city, it almost seemed appropriate that an eclectic French-owned label should bring the rapidly shifting terrain of rap to an end-of-year conclusion when it cohosted a Zulu Nation tour of France and the United Kingdom. Founded in Paris by leftists Gilbert Castro and Jean Georgakarakos (or Karakos), Celluloid Records had started out licensing records from labels such as Rough Trade and ZE for the French market, after which it began releasing original African, jazz, and no wave tracks. The shift encouraged Karakos to travel to New York to try to market his label's productions and on the last night of his trip he met Bill Laswell. Complaining that nobody had the "guts to go against the system," Laswell told the label head to migrate to the city.[28] Karakos traveled home, mulled over his options, decided to return, and, with his bags barely unpacked, stumbled into a startled Laswell, who proceeded to hand him some Material recordings to kickstart his U.S. operation. Karakos then swerved into rap when French journalist Bernard Zekri turned him onto Negril. Zekri's Second Avenue apartment had become a popular post-party hangout for the Zulu Nation crew, and with Karakos hungry for fresh material, he proposed a hip hop tour of Paris and London. "I thought it was a great idea," recalls Ruza Blue of the moment

Karakos and Zekri approached her as a potential collaborator shortly after she reopened the Roxy, although Zekri remembers her being "cautious" and "unforthcoming" until he took her on a tour of Parisian sponsors, radio stations, and clubs.[29]

Celluloid went on to release four rap records, three of them featuring a graffiti artist as the principal rapper. Recorded in December 1981, "The Escapades of Futura 2000" showcased Futura 2000 stumbling his way through a rapped history of graffiti, with music provided by the Clash and backing vocals delivered by Fred Brathwaite, Dondi, and the Clash lead singer Joe Strummer.[30] For the second release, Brathwaite delivered "Change the Beat" in English and French, with Zekri's French-speaking American girlfriend, Ann Boyle, couching the foreign-language lines out of the Brooklyn artist, prompting him to comment, "Ahhh, this stuff is really fresh!" (When it became obvious that her take was in many respects superior to Brathwaite's, Karakos, and Zekri decided to run it on the B-side and gave Boyle the name Beside.) Next up, "Grandmixer Cuts It Up" brought together scratching pioneer Grand Mixer D.ST and the Infinity Rappers. ("It has the same rhythm as [Miles Davis drummer] Tony Williams," Bill Laswell told Zekri.)[31] Released in July, not even two weeks into Blue's run on 18th Street, "The Roxy" featured Phase 2 on the microphone, with the artist coproducing alongside Laswell.[32] At the end of it all, a French outfit with no background in rap and no prior connection to the Bronx had become a key player within hip hop.

Afrika Bambaataa, Jazzy Jay, Rammellzee, the Rock Steady Crew, and the Double Dutch Girls joined Celluloid artists Grand Mixer D.ST, Fab 5 Freddy, Futura 2000, and Phase 2 for the "New York City Rap Tour." "I decided I was going to start doing things for the planet," Bambaataa recounts of the November trip. "I decided I was going to really start mashing things up and getting more people into this new sound. We wanted it to become intergalactic!" Blue and Zekri had their work cut out keeping the party together. "It was the first hip hop tour to go anywhere and the first tour to go to Europe with all four elements on board," she recalls. "There were twenty-five artists — MCs, DJs, dancers, and graffiti writers — and none of them had been out of the country before. *Can you imagine?*" The party stopped at the Bataclan in Paris and then the Venue in London before heading to Lyon, Metz, Belfort, and Strasbourg, with the performers subdividing to cover the territory. "England embraced the scene immediately," adds Blue, who modeled the shows on the 18th Street experience. "France did not. They were bemused and puzzled." Of the Paris crowd, David Hershkovits of the *New York Daily News* reported, "It's not exactly Friday night at the Roxy."[33]

Afrika Islam held down the decks at the Roxy while Bambaataa and the
other Zulu Nation DJs were away. "It was, 'Who can we get to fill the void?'"
he remembers. "They said, 'You need to get Bam's eight-year-old son.'" Islam
maintains that he had been "groomed" for the role as he watched the Zulu
Nation head go about his work, party in, party out, handing him records
when the moment seemed right, and adds that his background as a breaker
sharpened his DJ-ing sensibility. He also turned out to be razor-accurate with
his mixing. "I knew what Larry [Levan] was playing so I was able to play all
the teaching that my Dad [Bambaataa] gave me, all the records that Flash
gave me and all the records that Larry played," adds Islam. "They could all go
into the same set that we were playing at the Roxy. That's why it was such a
melting pot." Once he was done for the night, the up-and-coming DJ headed
to the Garage, where he would jam with two thousand other dancers when
Levan selected "Planet Rock." "The scenes hadn't been segmented," he remarks. "Everybody was listening to everything." Blue returned to discover that
Islam had made a name for himself. "He did become the star DJ for a while,"
she remarks. "His mixing was incredible."

TECHNO FUNKSTERS

Contributing to the electronic bedlam, François Kevorkian began to incorporate dub elements into his recordings during his mix of the album version of "D" Train's "You're the One for Me (Reprise)." "I was fucking with the reverb, and had drums cutting out and coming back at weird moments," he recalls. "I transformed the song radically — and I still didn't know who King Tubby was." The Frenchman went on to introduce a dub-heavy break in his A-side remix of "D" Train's "Keep On," opening the B-side with an echoed a cappella before keyboards, maracas, bongos, and bass built to a climax. Then, early in the autumn, he wove hard electronic handclaps, dubbed vocals, and dubbed keyboard into his mix of Sharon Redd's "Beat the Street." "They tried to accommodate me," he notes of the engineers who worked with him. "But there was a stage where they didn't understand what I was trying to do, so after a while they said, 'Why don't you do it yourself?'"

Kevorkian completed approximately thirty mixes for Prelude during 1982, with "D" Train's "'D' Train (Theme)," Sharon Redd's "In the Name of Love," Secret Weapon's "Must Be the Music," and Michael Wilson's "Groove It to Your Body" among the most notable. Yet he produced his most compelling work on other labels, beginning with Dinosaur L's "#5 (Go Bang!)," a commission from Sleeping Bag he accepted early into the year. "There were so many parts laid on top of each other that when they were played together they made no sense," he recalls. "Most other records were arranged and had direction, but this one was so utterly chaotic." Self-critical of his first effort, Kevorkian returned to the studio for a second stab, determined to streamline the chaos. "The mix was about peeling away layers of the onion until I found the core," he explains. "The more I stripped the record down, the more powerful it became." Aiming to give the mix shape, Kevorkian also introduced a discarded vocal by James Brown backing singer Lola Blank, brought Julius Eastman's submerged operatic cameo to the fore, and turned a Peter Zummo

trombone coda into the record's opening stanza. "I felt I managed to instill
some sort of structure and continuity and build," he adds. "The final mix had
this progression that drove people insane."

Although he never stopped selecting Russell's original effort, which was
"full of nuances," Mancuso took to playing the remix of the retitled "Go Bang!
#5" when his parties reached a peak. Will Socolov remembers the Prince
Street crowd went "crazy" the first time the Loft host played Kevorkian's
aerodynamic remix. Larry Levan, meanwhile, worked Eastman's operatic-
orgasmic interlude until dancers started "bouncing off the walls." A short
while later Socolov bumped into Levan on Carmine Street and basked in the
glory as the DJ turned to his entourage of friends and introduced him as the
"daddy of 'Go Bang.'" Socolov happened to be taking a shower when he first
heard Frankie Crocker play the twelve-inch on the radio. "I freaked out," he remembers. "I called Arthur. I was screaming." *Dance Music Report* contributed
to the fervor, applauding the record's "exciting blend of organ, bongo and
horns, deep bass, death-defying drums and heavy high hat," while Kevorkian's echo-laden reworking of "Clean on Your Bean," the B-side, also received
play and praise.[1] "Rap was just starting to happen," remembers Peter Gordon,
who coproduced "Clean." "We did this right after Blondie released 'Rapture'
and I remember telling Arthur that rap was dead because Blondie had done
it," remembers Gordon. "He never let me forget that."

Kevorkian extended his extracurricular activity with his remix of "Situation" by Yazoo (renamed Yaz for the U.S. market), heading over to John Robie's house in order to record overdubs. "John was already an accomplished
musician and technical wizard," recalls the Frenchman. "He already had a se-
quencer. In 1982 that was a big deal." The studio hands recorded fresh tom-
toms plus an ascending harmonizer effect that had already been deployed more
moderately by Kraftwerk on "Home Computer" and "Numbers" as well as by
Tom Tom Club on "Genius of Love." "I stuck to the core of the song on the
A-side and I went ape-shit-wild on the B-side dub," remembers the remixer. "I
became really enamored with that harmonizer effect, which had nothing to do
with the original. I used it on the Alison Moyet laugh and on the keyboard line.
For a while it became my kind of electronic trademark." Moyet and Yazoo collaborator Vince Clarke contained their enthusiasm when they were introduced
to Kevorkian at Danceteria. "They came from a synth pop/new wave perspective and they were not sure what inspired me," he recounts. "Their record
was the biggest record in the city and I got a really cold handshake."

Kevorkian turned to the harmonizer effect again on his funk-dub mix of
Michael Wilson's "Groove It to Your Body," even though he could only

deploy it in an elongated form at the beginning and end of the track, where the nonsequenced percussion didn't collide with its regulated pattern. Yet the Frenchman remained more intrigued by spatial dimensions of dub, which he further explored on Jimmy Cliff's "Treat the Youths Right," Forrrce's "Keep on Dancin' (Phase II)," Set the Tone's "Dance Sucker," and Wham's "Enjoy What You Do (Wham Rap)." Arthur Baker's request that he co-arrange, mix, and produce "Play at Your Own Risk" merged into the to-and-fro of his insane schedule. "There were a lot of things going on in the same studios with the same group of people," he notes of his work with Baker and Robie. "The community was very tight."

SELECTED DISCOGRAPHY

FRANÇOIS KEVORKIAN, AM/PM (1981–1982)

The B-52's, "Party Out of Bounds"
Afrika Bambaataa & the Soul Sonic Force, "Planet Rock"
Bauhaus, "Bela Lugosi's Dead"
Black Uhuru, "Sinsemilla"
Blondie, "Rapture"
Boris Gardiner Happening, "Melting Pot"
Bow Wow Wow, "I Want Candy"
Glenn Branca, "The Ascension"
James Brown, "Give It Up or Turnit a Loose (Live Version)"
The Bush Tetras, "Too Many Creeps"
A Certain Ratio, "Shack Up"
The Clash, "The Magnificent Dance"
The Cure, "A Forest"
Depeche Mode, "New Life"
Deutsch Amerikanischen Freundschaft, "Ich Will"
Thomas Dolby, "She Blinded Me with Science (Extended Version)"
Brian Eno and David Byrne, "The Jezebel Spirit"
ESG, "Moody"
Flying Lizards, "Money"
Funk Masters, "Love Money"
Gang of Four, "I Love a Man in a Uniform"
Paul Gardiner, "Stormtrooper in Drag"
Taana Gardner, "Heartbeat"
The Go-Go's, "We Got the Beat"

Grandmaster Flash & the Furious Five, "The Message"

Heaven 17, "(We Don't Need This) Fascist Groove Thing"

Human League, "Don't You Want Me Baby"

Sheila Hylton, "The Bed's Too Big without You"

Ian Dury and the Blockheads. "Reasons to Be Cheerful, Pt. 3"

Impossible Dreamers, "Spin"

Grace Jones, "Pull Up to the Bumper"

Grace Jones, "She's Lost Control"

Joy Division, "Love Will Tear Us Apart"

Kraftwerk, *Computer World*

Fela Anikulapo Kuti, "Sorrow, Tears, and Blood"

Gaspar Lawal, "Kita Kita"

Liaisons Dangereuses, "Los Niños del Parque"

Liquid Liquid, "Bell Head"

Logic System, "Domino Dance"

Lene Lovich, "New Toy"

Rita Marley, "One Draw"

Michigan and Smilie, "Diseases"

Modern Romance, "Salsa Rappsody [*sic*] (Dub Discomix)"

New Order, "Procession"

Nicodemus, "Boneman Connection"

The Normal, "Warm Leatherette"

Orchestral Manoeuvres in the Dark, "Souvenir"

The Police, "Voices inside My Head"

Public Image Ltd., "Public Image"

Romeo Void, "Never Say Never"

Pete Shelley, "Witness the Change"

Simple Minds, "Theme for Great Cities"

Siouxsie and the Banshees, "Spellbound"

Soft Cell, "Memorabilia"

Soft Cell, "Tainted Dub"

The Stray Cats, "Rock This Town"

T-Ski Valley/Grand Groove Bunch, "!Catch the Beat!"

Talking Heads, "Once in a Lifetime"

Tom Tom Club, "Genius of Love"

Tom Tom Club, "Wordy Rappinghood"

Tuxedomoon, "No Tears"

Various, "X Medley"

Wide Boy Awake, "Slang Teacher"

Jah Wobble, "Not Another"

Yazoo, "Situation (Dub Version)"

Z'EV, "Salts of Heavy Metals"

Kevorkian stopped playing at Zanzibar at the turn of the year before he gave up his AM/PM residency in the early summer. "I was living more in the studio than my own house and I found it difficult to stay at the level people expected of me as a DJ," he explains. "So I figured it was better to stop." Around the same time Vince Aletti went to see "D" Train open for Smokey Robinson at Radio City and caught himself longing for Kevorkian's studio version of the tracks. "When they swung into their best song, the anthemic 'Keep On,' all I could think was, will they do the 12-inch version?" he wrote in the *Village Voice*. "I suddenly realized how much more satisfied I'd be if only they could. . . . I missed the Francois K mix."[2] Meanwhile Larry Levan took to turning down the volume at key moments during Kevorkian's dub reworking of "Keep On" in order to give voice to the crowd, which sang every line. "There were very few people who could come to the Garage in the middle of the night and have Larry put on one of their new records without hesitation," remarks David DePino. "François was one of them." Over at Better Days, meanwhile, Bruce Forest appreciated the way Kevorkian remixed artists who were "different" while showing "great concern for audio quality."

The paradigm shift toward electronic dub gathered pace when Tom Silverman commissioned Shep Pettibone to mix and arrange "Jazzy Sensation." Pettibone's contribution to that release was relatively conventional, as it happens, while his subsequent mixes of disco-oriented records such as Aurra's "Checking You Out," Inner Life's "Moment of My Life," and Skyy's "Let Love Shine" suggested he would ultimately save his most dramatic gestures for the airwaves. But the Kiss DJ caught the electronic-dub bug during his remix of Aurra's "Such a Feeling," which he instilled with bright, vibrant echo and reverb as well as an a cappella opening, and from there he delivered a 6:59 mix of Sinnamon's "Thanks to You" that he revved with electronic beats, handclaps, a harmonized synth line, a looped guitar riff, a fattened bass, and searing vocals. "It was very dubby, very out there," remarks Pettibone, who also saturated the track with regulation reverb and echo. "Larry Levan played it two or three times a night. That was my big breakthrough." Kevorkian was blown away by the result. "He caught that whole Peech Boys aesthetic and took it to the next level," argues the Frenchman.

Bobby Shaw (left) and Shep Pettibone, ca. late 1980s. Photograph by and courtesy of Leslie Doyle ©.

A mild-mannered and somewhat timid figure, Pettibone lacked Kevorkian's outré-immigrant presence, intellectual edge, and reputational authority. Yet the Kiss mixer had risen to the front line of remix culture all the same, and he consolidated his standing when Marvin Schlachter invited him to deliver a double album's worth of reedited Prelude tracks, a number of which included Kevorkian's name on the original credits — meaning that the French mixer was about to be remixed. As with his radio mixes, Pettibone combined the raw material of vinyl with whatever tape-recorder echo effects he could find, apparently sanguine that he was about to mess with a series of records that some believed had already received their definitive version. "Pettibone drenches tracks in echo and delay to achieve a kind of dub disco, at the same time acknowledging the B-Boy DJs with his use of repeats and occasional turntable manipulation," the *New York Rocker* noted of *98.7 Kiss FM Presents Shep Pettibone's Mastermixes*. "Climactic moments . . . are accentuated to startling effect."[3] Asked about his segue into dub-inflected dance music, Pettibone commented, "The Peech Boys started that — like what are the handclaps doing?"[4]

Mark Kamins joined the dub parade after he started to date Madonna and expressed an interest in a demo she had recorded of "Everybody." Chris

Blackwell promptly rejected the tape on the basis that he wasn't prepared to sign his "A&R guy's girlfriend," but Seymour Stein turned out to be much more enthusiastic, not because he particularly liked Madonna, maintains Kamins, but because he "believed in Mark Kamins." ("I could break a record in those days," hazards the DJ.) When Baker listened to the demo through Madonna's "fucked-up" headphones, he remarked that it sounded a lot like Patrice Rushen's "Forget Me Nots." Two days later Kamins phoned the producer and asked: "What do I do? Where do I start?" Baker suggested he hire a programmer and passed on the phone numbers of John Robie and Fred Zarr (who had created the instrumentation for "Walking on Sunshine"). "I said, 'It really depends on what vibe you're going for, 'cause John's really good with an electronic vibe and Fred's much better with an organic sound,'" recalls Baker. "John was away at the time so he called Fred." Zarr recorded the record's insistent keyboard hook as well as a hissing snare that he ran backward through an Oberheim 8. "I didn't tell Fred what to play," acknowledges Kamins. "He came up with all that stuff. It became a hit because of what he played."

Wrapped in a sleeve that depicted a dog gripping a red Frisbee between its teeth, a Puerto Rican kid, lopsided tenement blocks, a young rollerskater, and a yellow water hydrant, Madonna's debut twelve-inch came out in late October. "There was a reason why Warner Bros. didn't put Madonna's face on the cover," observes Kamins. "They didn't want people to know if she was black or white. It was just a dance record." Levan loved the track, adds the Danceteria DJ, and so did Frankie Crocker, while *Dance Music Report* remarked on how the 9:23 B-side dub "never lets up as vocals echo over captivating instrumentation."[5] Madonna proceeded to break up with Kamins and enter into a brief relationship with Jean-Michel Basquiat as "Everybody" broke into the *Billboard* dance chart.[6] Then, in mid-November, she appeared live at the Paradise Garage and continued with the show as if nothing was wrong when one of Brody's technical assistants played the back-coding of her tape by mistake. "I just felt she was already a kind of a sensation," remembers Kevorkian. "You have to have nerves of steel to do that on your first live performance." Madonna wasn't spectacular in the manner of Loleatta Holloway or Chaka Khan, adds the remixer, "but she had a good routine, she was organized and together, and she had good dance moves. You could see that no bullshit was going to get in her way."

As the soundscape also hummed with the infectious military snares of Yello's "Bostich," the flickering beats of Klein & M.B.O.'s "Dirty Talk," and the hypnotic instrumentation of Eddy Grant's "Time Warp," Brian Chin traced the "strong resurgence of synthesizer music" back to new wave's embrace of

Mark Kamins in the studio with engineer Butch Jones and also
Kim Davis and Stacey Elkin, members of Pulsallama. Photographs
by and courtesy of Butch Jones ©.

Madonna shot her video for "Everybody" in the Paradise Garage. Larry Levan would go on to list the dub version of "Everybody" as one of his top ten songs from the 1980s. ("Discs of the Decade," *DJ Times*, December 1989.) Photograph by and courtesy of Laura Levine ©.

the technology during 1980–1981 and questioned if there was "really much new technique involved."[7] Carol Cooper, however, remembers the moment being akin to a rupture, with the speed at which different pieces of equipment came into and fell out of fashion "something to behold," while Kevorkian recalls how the onrush of "these new tools" transformed the studio experience, in part because the steady tempo of the drum machine allowed for a different kind of play and creativity. Kamins believed that the arrival of the first drum machines "fundamentally changed the direction of music" by giving producers "the opportunity to be creative with machines and not with your best friend the drummer," especially as getting a drummer to show up in the first place could be challenging. Then again, the presence of figures like Robie confirmed that there could be no absolute break with the immediate past, so fresh modes of electronic production were regularly combined with more conventional instrumental, vocal, songwriting, and studio skills. No single approach dictated and the music was more dynamic as a result.

Nor did anybody hurry to give the wave of new sounds a name, perhaps because the backlash against an overhyped disco remained a recent memory.

Brian Chin introduced an "electro" prefix in several reviews, describing Feel's "Let's Rock (Over and Over Again)" as "sparse electro-funk" and "Funky Soul Makossa" as a "crazy electro-rap number," having already defined "Wordy Rappinghood" as a form of "electro-funk-art-fusion," but the critic didn't claim to have identified and named a new sound, and he didn't repeat the move in any concerted way.[8] Perhaps with disco, dub, and rock among the other sonic elements in play, the idea of attempting to bring order to the mayhem seemed churlish. "I remember Will Socolov gave me a test pressing of 'Go Bang!' and that was the most mind-blowing thing I'd ever heard," recalls Monica Lynch, who listened to every record submitted to *Dance Music Report*. "But did that mean we weren't going to review the new Melba Moore twelve-inch? No, it didn't. These things were coexisting." Meanwhile the mixers and producers stayed focused on the process and the result. "None of us thought, 'Oh, now we're going to take these reggae elements and reinvent dance music,'" remarks Kevorkian. "We were just excited to be able to create these crazy effects."

25

TASTE SEGUES

Steven Harvey executed a dramatic listening somersault during the opening years of the 1980s. He had grown up listening to Captain Beefheart and experimental music before he moved to New York and took his turn hanging out at the Mudd Club and playing in a no wave lineup, Youth in Asia. But then a friend started to play him scratchy R&B records and at that moment he realized that "in punk and new wave there was nobody like Marvin Gaye or Aretha [Franklin]" and also that no band was "defining" his "rhythmic character." "There just came a point where I said, 'I'm reacting against the noisy brittleness of band music,'" he recalls. "It was like a taste segue in my life."

Harvey started to write about music in the autumn of 1981 after he spoke with Grandmaster Flash & the Furious Five on air and set up an interview there and then. Taking the subway up to Cyprus Avenue, where Flash was living with his sister, he talked with the Bronx DJ for hours, only for Robert Christgau to recommend he take his proposal to the *New York Rocker* — it still being a year before the *Village Voice* would print Steven Hager's feature on Afrika Bambaataa and hip hop. Harvey went on to publish a piece about Sly and Robie in the November issue of the *New York Rocker* (he noted that the duo's "hybrid of disco, reggae and funk seems adaptable to any musical context") and saw his Flash interview published the following January ("It's almost impossible to believe that anyone's hands can move so fast," he maintained).[1] Going on to review Flash's "Flash It to the Beat" in his next contribution, he claimed the record "makes rapping and break-mixing sound like some kind of new jazz — just voices and percussion, the beat box pushed way up front in the recording, the voices riffing and diving in horn-like arcs," and asked if it amounted to "punk rap or Afro-American vocal folk jazz?" He concluded: "This shouldn't be a bootleg, it should be on the Smithsonian label."[2]

Harvey soon grasped he could write about any music he liked at the *New York Rocker* because everyone else wanted to write about rock bands. Articles about African music, gospel, and above all dance started to flow from his typewriter, including an overview published in the "Vinyl Exams" review section of the July-August issue. "Contemporary disco productions utilize elements of countless styles to create an increasingly sophisticated musical form, including classic R&B, funk, reggae and dub, electro-pop, hard rock, Latin and African," he noted. "DJs are snatching up everything from the latest London synth duo to samples of tropical musics from around the globe." Harvey went on to describe "Planet Rock" as "totally electronic" and "atonal," "Don't Make Me Wait" as a "magnum opus" that reinvented disco in a "timely blend of dub, rock and electronics," and "Go Bang!" as a source of "abstract, jazz-inflected rhythm-rock with very 'outside' vocals" that sounded "almost Nigerian."[3] Harvey simply lost interest in the rock outfits that could be read about elsewhere in the paper. "There was such a renaissance going on in dance," he argues, pointing to "D" Train's "You're the One for Me" and Afrika Bambaataa & the Jazzy 5's "Jazzy Sensation" as other "definitive" releases from the period. "This was it — this was Valhalla — the room of the Gods. There weren't better records being made anywhere in the world. I thought band music was really fallow in comparison."

The performers who stormed CBGB during the mid-1970s had certainly run out of collective energy given that the year witnessed Blondie break up, Richard Hell and the Voidoids release the low-impact *Destiny Street* on Red Star Records, Patti Smith step back from music after giving birth, and Talking Heads falter with the release of the live album *The Name of This Band Is Talking Heads*. Meanwhile a number of the no wave and punk-funk lineups that had charged the city's live music scene with angular and groove-oriented possibilities struggled to match the searing impact of their breakthrough efforts. Writing in the *New York Times*, Robert Palmer gave *Sax Maniac* by James White and the Blacks a positive review yet also noted that "the basic ingredients in his music haven't changed."[4] Also released during 1982, ESG's EP ESG *Says Dance to the Beat of Moody* contained credible new tracks plus a remake of "Moody" yet didn't come close to matching the impact of the group's debut. The EP also turned out to be the only record released on 99 Records during the year.

Although he lost James Chance to Animal Records, Chris Stein's new label, Michael Zilkha enjoyed a significantly more productive year than Ed Bahlman as he released music by John Cale, Cristina, Suicide, and the Waitresses plus fresh mixes of Was (Not Was)'s "Tell Me That I'm Dreaming" (which sampled Reagan's State of the Union speech from February 1981) and "Out Come the Freaks." The label head then scored his first pop hit when Kid Creole's third album — released as *Tropical Gangsters* in Europe and *Wise Guy* in the United States — reached number three on the U.K. charts. "Darnell has become a favorite interview for the European press," Carol Cooper noted in the *Village Voice.* "Great Britain has been particularly solicitous, zeroing in on his elegance, glib erudition and gigolo mien to iconize their first black American pinup boy."[5] Zilkha reveled in the tension that ran through "Annie, I'm Not Your Daddy," which combined soca-drenched instrumentation with the story of a father telling his daughter he wasn't her biological parent — and that if he had been she "wouldn't be so ugly." "I had quite a debt with Chris [Blackwell] by the time Kid Creole's third album came out because nothing had sold a lot," admits Zilkha. "But then it got paid back very quickly with Kid Creole."

Blackwell accepted his remittance as he continued to build a diverse roster that saw him mix the recognizable (the dub reggae of Black Uhuru, Gregory Isaacs, and Pablo Moses along with the conventional rock of U2 and Steve Winwood) with the mongrel (the dub-vocoder electronics of Set the Tone and Grace Jones's third Compass Point album, *Living My Life*). Of the disappointments, Tom Tom Club's "Under the Boardwalk" was notably lackluster, yet such setbacks were easily offset by his introduction to the Paradise Garage. Bewitched by Larry Levan, he immediately became a regular at the King Street spot. "The Garage was like a temple for me," he reminisces. "I used to go there so often. I went with my girlfriend, who Grace introduced me to, and we'd think we'd been there for half an hour and in fact four hours would have passed."

Island employee and King Street diehard Judy Cacase had already arranged for Levan to remix Gwen Guthrie's "It Should Have Been You" and "Getting Hot" by the time Blackwell arrived in the Garage booth toward the end of the year in time to hear the DJ play "Life Is Something Special," the second Peech Boys single, which came about after Levan suggested to Michael de Benedictus that they make a cover of "Jungle Fever" by Chakachas. Blackwell asked the keyboard player if he knew the name of the recording artist and, when he got his reply, its label. "We're on West End but we're not on West End," replied de Benedictus, who had grown tired of working with Mel Cheren. "The record is available." Blackwell and de Benedictus went to talk in the white room that held the lighting gels and fixtures, because the sound levels were lower there, and struck a deal. Cheren sued, having paid for de Benedictus and Levan to test and tweak the record for six months, at the end of which he believed "there was nothing to release," and then settled when Blackwell offered $50,000 for the single plus the rights to "Don't Make Me Wait."[6] "Chris just had more clout with lawyers and more money than Mel," comments de Benedictus. "Mel buckled."

The money arrived at a critical moment for West End, where Cheren was enduring a difficult run that dated back to the moment when Taana Gardner stopped recording for the label, bemused she had "never received a royalty check."[7] Cheren's difficulties mounted when Shep Pettibone turned down the opportunity to deliver a Prelude-style mastermix of West End releases. Passed on to Tony Humphries, who had completed two run-of-the-mill mixes to date, the resulting "Master Mix Medley" didn't come close to matching the impact of the Prelude effort. Admittedly a degree of respite came in the form of Raw Silk's "Do It to the Music," a bona fide club hit, but the group's follow-up failed to maintain the momentum. Meanwhile a deal with Jacques Morali produced nothing of note. "Unfortunately, we needed a continuous string of hits to stay viable," Cheren remarks in his autobiography, "and 'Do It to the Music' proved to be the exception."[8]

Cheren might have split with de Benedictus and Levan of his own accord if the future of West End hadn't become intertwined with the Peech Boys. The label head maintains that de Benedictus was manipulative and Levan unreliable, plus the two of them were too slow when they worked together at the studio. Yet de Benedictus and Levan were happier with the split, having concluded that Cheren lacked transparency when it came to paying royalties and ambition when it came to developing the band. "We were playing all over the place to support 'Don't Make Me Wait' and it was like pulling teeth to get Mel to do anything," maintains de Benedictus. "Mel gave us the best deal he gave anybody in West End but he had no interest in making an album." Levan might have felt awkward about the break with Cheren, a close if sometimes overbearing supporter. Then again, he considered Cacase a good friend, was familiar with the setup at Island, and appreciated that the label would provide the Peech Boys with an ideal platform. Above all, he looked forward to running the subsidiary label Blackwell said he would fund on his and de Benedictus's behalf: Garage Records. "Working with Chris Blackwell and being on the same label as Stevie Winwood and U2 was the culmination of a dream," notes de Benedictus. "C'mon, who did Mel have?"

Finally released on Island at the end of 1982 under the name of New York Citi Peech Boys — because lawyers representing the Beach Boys had threatened to sue if the band didn't change their name — "Life Is Something Special" featured a smooth, transcendent groove and neospiritual lyrics. *Dance Music Report* described the record as "a near perfect amalgam of R&B, gospel and dance music" and noted how its "drive and intensity just [kept] building and building to frenzied levels."[9] Yet the Peech Boys didn't merely shape a mutant sound — they did so in collaboration with a DJ who could bring a

Jonny Sender (left) and Dana Vlcek of Konk, live at the Peppermint Lounge, 1982. Vlcek formed the band in 1980. Photograph by and courtesy of Jenny Gillespie ©.

fresh sensibility to the group's aesthetic while connecting it to a grassroots audience that he held in the cup of his hand. "Everything Grace released was a hit at the Garage because she was the female Larry," observes David DePino. "She was crazy, she was wild, she was daring, and Larry was like that as a DJ." Blackwell even purchased top-of-the-line equipment so he could record the DJ's sets and relive them outside the party. "You couldn't buy what you were hearing," he explains. "Larry had three turntables going and was weaving in and out music that you couldn't buy. He was incredible." Carol Cooper remembers Blackwell "reaching out to Larry quite a bit at the time."

Formed by the trained jazz saxophonist Dana Vlcek and the definitively untrained ex-Gray trumpeter Shannon Dawson, Konk injected boisterousness into the downtown band scene with the release of "Master Cylinder's Jam" — backed with a short version of "Konk Party" — at the end of 1982. With Geordie Gillespie (drums), Richard Edson (trumpet), Scott Gillis (guitar), Angel Quinones (congas), Daniel Sadownick (percussion), and Jonny Sender (bass) completing the makeshift lineup, the release harnessed the insistent danceability of ESG and the improvisatory mindset of Liquid Liquid within a percussive-cacophonous dance band lineup that drew heavily on jazz, funk, Afro-beat, and Salsa. "We were listening to a lot of Brass Construction, Mandrill, and Fela [Kuti], and we talked about aspiring to their sound, or parts of their sound, but we could never manage it," explains Sender. "We almost sounded like we were out on some dusty road in Benin because we could never quite get our tuning together. It wasn't a conscious choice. It was just the funny mishmash of people playing to the best of their ability — and everybody had different abilities."

With Friday nights at the Roxy lodged into his party schedule and memories of his Negril epiphany still fresh, Sender joined Konk after playing bass alongside some of its members during an open jam session at A7, an East Village bar located on Avenue A and 7th Street. Attracted to the way the band seemed determined to swap the austere element of the downtown band scene for something more syncopated and propulsive, he drifted further from the art-punk network the night he headed home down Prince Street following a night spent partying at the Mudd Club and Berlin, only to notice that the entrance to number 99 — where music piped out gently every Saturday night — was for once unstaffed. Stepping inside, he found himself blown away by the Loft setting. "The sound was incredible, the music sounded great, and downstairs there were all these people breakdancing, except it was like jazz-style breakdancing," he recalls. "Even though David Mancuso didn't mix, the energy would keep building. Again, I had this feeling of, 'What am I doing around the corner at Berlin?'"

Whether opening for Kurtis Blow at the 930 Club or for Eddie Palmieri at the Mudd Club, Konk's musicians burst into life when they could throw themselves into a rough-at-the-edges, good-time, global-funk jam. "Just the fact it was a very big sound with those three horns and the percussion and the congas meant that when we played it became a dance party," adds Sender. "People didn't watch us; they danced. It made for a wild, sweaty musical experience." In comparison, heading into the studio to record "Master Cylinder's Jam" and "Konk Party" left them feeling self-conscious that the recording process threatened to turn innocuous mistakes into permanent stains as well as irritated by the way the introduction of a drum machine to provide the track with its metronome kick drum inhibited their carefree style. But those complications didn't stop David Mancuso, Larry Levan, and then Frankie Crocker from jumping on the record, while Brian Chin reviewed it as "outstanding, polished rock-crossover material."[10] Soon after critics started to cite Konk as one of the progenitors of "naive beat," recalls Sender, and that just about summed them up.

In this way and others, the funk was now driving the punk.

STORMY WEATHER

Synthetic music's spacey, alien quality went down well at the Saint thanks to the way it complemented the cosmic planetarium and the dance-floor journey into a parallel dimension. Yet peak time records still needed to foreground a four-on-the-floor rhythm, a melodic instrumental line or vocal, and a 130-beat-per-minute tempo, so Saint DJs ended up selecting from a subsection of electronic releases that only occasionally crossed over to the Loft and the Paradise Garage, with Patrick Cowley's landmark 16:15 mix of "I Feel Love" (a Mancuso selection) and Cowley's joint effort with Sylvester "Do You Wanna Funk" (briefly popular at the Garage) the most prominent exceptions. As for the syncopated electronic tracks that featured so heavily at the Funhouse and the Roxy, there was almost no crossover at all. "Gay music became high-energy music," points out Man Parrish, who started to go to the Saint (as a guest) around 1982. "The rest of music was going in an urban direction, but the queens didn't want urban music. They wanted fantasy music for their drugs." Already something of an island, the Saint became even more detached from the rest of the New York party scene as the new strain of records took hold.

Robbie Leslie, Roy Thode, and Sharon White chalked up the most appearances during the opening months of 1982, followed by Howard Merritt (who returned to live in New York during 1982), Chuck Parsons, and Wayne Scott, with the special parties divided between White (the "White Party" in February), Merritt (the "Land of Make Believe Party" in April), Parsons (the "Armed Forces Day Party" in May), and Thode (the "Black Party" in March and the end-of-season party in June). Linda Clifford, Melba Moore, Esther Satterfield, and the Patrick Cowley Singers turned in live performances. Laura Branigan's "Gloria," Sharon Redd's "In the Name of Love," Viola Wills's "Stormy Weather," and the Weather Girls' "It's Raining Men"—the last collaboration between Izora Rhodes and Martha Wash—tore up the floor. Special movie nights included screenings of *The Muppet Movie*, *Pink Flamingos*, and *Wizard of Oz*. Meanwhile up-and-coming DJs were given the opportunity to test their ability at the "Hot New Talent Night," inaugurated in May. "Many of these people are into some very progressive music and want to show you their stuff," commented *Star Dust*, the Saint's new journal, in the spring. "Let us know how you like them."[1]

But if it appeared that an equilibrium had been reached, Thode felt troubled, even though his peers, along with Mailman, viewed him as the venue's preeminent DJ, and he expressed an improbable degree of insecurity when he published a letter in the same issue of the in-house publication. "Hi, I'd like to thank you for all the memorable nights and mornings we've shared together," he began. "Actually, that's what it is all about, sharing. A man in the booth playing records to catch your mood, ride it, and take you even higher."[2] The DJ added that the task of selecting records that worked in terms of sound, mood, and message was "hard," with the integration of new music especially challenging.[3] "All nights are not great ones; if they were, we would not have a lever to know what a great one was," he concluded, mixing regret with deference. "Regardless, first record to last, for twelve hours or more, we the Booth Staff strive to entertain you and bring you happiness. Your happiness is ours. Love, Roy Thode."[4]

Thode died of a drug overdose in his apartment in May, shortly before he was due to open the summer season at the Ice Palace. A week earlier he had celebrated his thirty-third birthday, traveling to and from Fire Island with Marsha Stern, and when they disembarked he asked her to pick up Mocha, who had been staying with another friend. Two days later, Stern received a phone call from the police, who wanted to access the DJ's apartment, which had been locked from the inside. On entering they discovered his body. "Roy did die of his own hand," confirms Stern. "Whether it was an accident or suicide, I don't know if anyone can answer that question." Thode hadn't spoken about wanting to commit suicide in the run-up to his death yet experienced ongoing difficulties that were related to his job. "Being the DJ made him the butt of everyone's comments," explains Stern. "He might have played brilliantly, but if the guy writing the editorial page in a magazine happened to have a lousy time, maybe because he had some bad drugs or a fight with his boyfriend, he could be quick to hand out a lashing. There were also some nasty-ass queens who would write letters. Roy even received hate mail. These people are nuts, but if you're a little too sensitive you can let that get to you."

Thode happened to be vulnerable to mood swings. Merritt remembers him being "very sensitive, very dark, very secretive, very much a loner" and also

Roy Thode, 1979. On the back of a copy he gave to Marsha Stern, he wrote, "If I were to marry a woman she would be like you." Photograph by Len Tavares; courtesy of Marsha Stern.

someone who was "way too critical of himself." He could, of course, experience the joys of the profession. "He had such a rapport with the crowd," reminisces Stern, who worked lights with him at the first "Land of Make Believe Party" in March 1981. "People would come up to the booth and say, 'It's just a wonderful party, we wish you could dance with us,' and Roy would always reply, 'I'm dancing with everybody in the room.'" Yet his fragility was long term and it kept on rearing itself at the Saint, where the highs and lows were accentuated. "Roy was exceedingly depressed and he tried to kill himself on numerous occasions," maintains White, who had become close with the DJ at the Corral, the Long Island spot where he made his breakthrough at age sixteen. "He said to me, 'There's nothing worse than playing from your heart and soul for six thousand people and then going home alone.'" White adds: "It got to the point when the accolades and booze went into the same bag and he took his life. That's the final thing he had."

Bruce Mailman staged a memorial party for Thode on 2 June. "We miss him," ran the publicity for the event, which was written in silver ink. "He believed in 'The Party,' therefore, we who loved him should dance and continue to party." Four DJ/light-operator combinations — Sharon White/Mark Ackerman, Howard Merritt/Jim Hicks, Robbie Leslie/Karen Ludemann, and Wayne Scott/Jorge Vilerdell — performed in front of the largest turnout in the venue's short history. "It was a lovely tribute," recalls Stern. "It was a way for Roy's colleagues, some of whom he grew up with, to express their gratitude and enjoy a wonderful night of dance. Every DJ played with their heart to honor someone they respected and loved. The crowd was devastated." Stern adds that "only kind words were spoken and that was the way it should have been." When Viola Wills sang "Stormy Weather" at the Saint's closing pre-summer party, held on 26 June, the song carried added poignancy.

With Thode no longer around to cast his spell, the Ice Palace lost its Saturday-night crowd. "Roy's exit twisted Fire Island into a new animal," Glenn Person, a contributing editor at *Christopher Street* and the *New York Native*, wrote in the second issue of *Star Dust*. "It's almost certain that if there'd still been a Roy, there still would have been a gay Ice Palace on Saturday night, the tradition for Pines men. But with all that rain in June — half the nights the water taxis weren't even running — why go through the trouble of traipsing to the Grove?" When Person eventually made the trip to Thode's old spot, he encountered a setting transformed. "We only stayed a few minutes, not wanting to be surrounded by dolled-up female Ocean Beach imports — or whatever godawful place they came from — when our drugs took effect," he commented. Back in the Pines, meanwhile, the Pavilion became too packed while its DJs seemed unable to feel out "what the crowd wanted to hear." Person called on the Saint roster to take on the "steep challenge" of shaping a sound when the new season began.[5]

Invited to play that first party, which also featured a live performance by Jimmy Ruffin, Leslie believes it had become "quite evident" during the memorial event that he was the "most popular of the new crop of DJs by far," as well as conventional wisdom that he would be the "natural choice to ascend to Roy's lofty position." His claim was buttressed when he was selected to author the second "DJ Speaks" article in the September issue of *Star Dust*. "Roy was probably the most popular DJ at the Saint until he passed away and my performances made it clear that I was the one to continue that tradition," adds the ex–12 West employee. "When he died, it quickly became clear that I was to fill Roy's shoes." White, however, maintains that she had been the "number two draw" when Thode was alive and that upon his death Mailman told her, "We're handing you the baton. You're the head draw and you have to recognize the responsibilities that come with this." Of the opinion that the memorial party had been an occasion where "DJs who were friends or who were influenced by Roy gave a piece of themselves in performance" rather than "a popularity contest," Stern wonders if the owner might have encouraged both

Leslie and White to "think they were 'the chosen one' because he really had no idea who would end up as the 'star of the next season.'"

During the first two months of the 1982–1983 season, Leslie played twice (the opening-night party and one Saturday), White thrice (one Saturday and two Sundays) and Merritt twice (two Saturdays), with Scott, Parsons, and new talent breakthroughs Michael Fierman and Lance Wise sharing the remainder. Yet if the even distribution indicated that Mailman wasn't initially sure which DJ would assume Thode's mantle, he became less hesitant toward the year's end when he handed Leslie a contract and invited him to play the set-piece Halloween and New Year's Eve parties plus three more Saturdays and two more Sundays in close succession. White appears to have picked up just one Sunday slot during the same period, ostensibly because her independent streak became more apparent to her employers and the dancing crowd. "If there was a song that I heard at the Garage that I liked and wanted to introduce it at the Saint, there was no way I was going to not play it," she declares. "There were people who would say, 'I don't think that would fit the Saint format' and I'd say, 'I don't care.' I broke the rules a lot."

A mixed-race lesbian who formed a minority group of one at the venue, White wasn't ideally positioned to take risks. "The Saint was 95 percent white gay men," she notes. "Everything else fell into the remaining 5 percent, whether it be women, blacks, or Latinos. Most of my friends were white but I'm sure people who were used to a more balanced situation might have said, 'Where are the people of color?'" White encountered occasional racism in the setting. "Some people said, 'Take that bone out of your nose and go back to the Garage!' I would say to them, 'It's OK if you don't like me. Read the schedule and don't come back when my name is listed.'" Her sex might have been more incendiary than her race. "I felt very comfortable on the dance floor with these people and to go into the booth was a natural progression," she remarks. "But I knew I had to be good because shit would be thrown at me if I wasn't. If you were a woman you had to work twice as hard."

Airing their views in the letters pages of *Star Dust*, Saint members discussed the issue of the near-total exclusion of women in the autumn of 1982. One argued against the policy of segregation and a second called for limits on their admission to be removed, only for a third to ask: "Whatever happened to the idea of THE SAINT being a place where males could feel at home with each other and form a bond while dancing?"[6] The results of the survey settled the matter: only 2 percent of members believed women should be admitted on Saturdays, while another 48 percent favored their admission at some other point during the week. Henceforth, announced the management, members

Sharon White, ca. 1979–1980 (playing behind a Plexiglas shield). White started to date Stern after they met at Sahara. Photographer unknown; courtesy of Marsha Stern.

would be permitted to show up with female guests on Wednesdays and could also clear female guests in advance on Sundays, with Saturdays to remain male-only (save for the tiny number of women who held memberships).[7] "Bruce had this opinion that gay men danced well together — that they had this body chemistry where they moved on the dance floor as a tribe, as one entity — and he always felt very strongly about not having women there because women's body movements were contradictory to this flow," comments Leslie. "He was quite emphatic about it, which was why he didn't even want gay women there, and there were just a few exceptions."

The number of female dancers might have remained stubbornly low even if Mailman had relaxed his policy. Frustrated when they were refused entry to what had once been a mixed venue, and uninspired by the lesbian bars on offer, Leslie Cohen, Michelle Florea, Linda Goldfarb, and Barbara Russo opened Sahara as the first lesbian discotheque in the spring of 1976. The venue offered a mix of DJ-ing, live performance, political rallies, and art shows until a "two-timing, backstabbing, greedy attorney and a crooked city marshal" (as Florea puts it) padlocked the venue on Christmas Eve 1979. Cohen and Florea went on to launch a new Thursday-night party at a spot called Manhattan in June 1980, with Goldfarb and Russo opening a venue of their own, Moonshadow, during 1982. But when the liquor-licensing authorities delayed Goldfarb and Russo's application, they opened as a juice bar to keep things moving, only for it to become so male-identified the lesbian crowd stayed away (even when Cohen and Florea stepped in to coordinate Saturday nights). "The girls took issue with the open design of the space," notes Russo. "There were no dark corners or nooks and crannies for them to disappear into."

The lesbian scene expanded when advertising employee Joni Rim and her marketing director girlfriend Marcia Picoult moved from putting on occasional parties to signing a one-year lease on a venue called Shescape, located at 58th Street between Park and Madison, also during 1982. "We set up video screens on the dance floor, arranged fresh flowers every week, and employed the most beautiful bartenders," says Rim. "Girls would come from everywhere and we were packed every night. White, black, Latin — we all started to mix." Open from Wednesdays through to Saturdays, Shescape attracted a younger "lipstick lesbian" clientele whose dress consciousness set them apart from the butcher Sahara/Manhattan crowd. But although she was "great friends" with Mailman, Rim notes that "no one was interested" in staging mixed events. "The girls said the guys took up the dance floor and the guys just never cared for the girls," she explains. "Bruce didn't care for women much and adding girls was just not his thing. I think the girls were never that interested in the Saint either because it had no liquor." Having DJ-ed at Sahara and Manhattan, where the lesbian crowd preferred to listen to pop and resisted the twelve-inch format, White confirms that the dance scene was "very much gay territory" and "very much drug-fueled."

Back at the Saint, the near-total absence of black and Latino dancers rivaled the dearth of women thanks in part to social and economic circumstances that were already in place by the time Mailman started to market his venue to the sweepingly white crowd that holidayed on Fire Island. When the owner increased the cost of new (rather than renewed) memberships from $125 to $200 for the 1981–1982 season, or double the charge at the Garage, he made it even less likely that black and Latino dancers would be able to afford to join, thanks to their lower mean earning power. "Should Bruce have initiated an affirmative action policy like 'White Males $10, African Americans Free' and put on chartered buses from 125th Street, Bed-Stuy [Bedford-Stuyvesant, Brooklyn], and the Bronx to the Lower East Side?" asks Terry Sherman, who started to DJ at the venue during the 1983–1984 season and who also thought

nothing of bringing black boyfriends to the spot. "Maybe. But Bruce didn't
care who came and there was no racial profiling specific to the Saint." Then
again, musical taste and social preference also contributed to the division,
while the division itself was also less pronounced than it had been at the
Tenth Floor and Flamingo. "It was a bigger club so there was more room, so,
of course, you saw more blacks," remarks Jorge La Torre. "I think black men
also felt more welcome and you began to see white men with black lovers. But
if you saw a handful of black people that was a lot." Leslie notes that while he
can make the judgment that he "preferred the inclusive approach of 12 West"
with the benefit of hindsight, at the time he was "pretty dazzled" by the Saint.

Rivals operated in the cracks left uncovered by the Second Avenue phenomenon. Michael Fesco launched a Sunday-night party at Studio 54 in the
autumn of 1981 and built a reasonably successful alternative to Mailman's quieter weekend slot, with Leslie his primary DJ. Jimmy Murray integrated an
in-house jazz band, a sunken dance floor, and two mascot macaws when he
opened the Red Parrot on West 57th Street for the white gay crowd, but he had
to make do when a straight clientele showed up instead. Steve Cohn started
to admit women at the River Club as his own numbers dropped away. Only
Goldfarb and Russo's Moonshadow properly flourished as an after-hours spot
for men who wanted to head out on Fridays or continue to party once Mailman's spot wound down on Sundays. "It would open at eight in the morning
and people would come straight from the Saint," recalls Merritt, who DJ-ed
alongside Shaun Buchanan, Kevin Burke, Michael Jorba, and Sharon White.
"I would play two to six on a Sunday afternoon before the Saint started again."
Then again, Merritt would only take work at Moonshadow once he knew he
wasn't needed by Mailman. "After Flamingo closed things really changed,"
notes the DJ. "None of the big clubs had an in-house disc jockey. You had your
calendar and you'd get called by the clubs and gradually you would fill in the
nights. Everyone would wait for the Saint to call before accepting other book-
ings because if you said no to the Saint it wasn't good for you."

The city's white gay party scene was, it appeared, heading in the direction
of one-party rule, and with Thode's death not quite a distant memory, stress
fractures that related to the Saint's quasi-monopolistic control and obsession
with perfection were beginning to show.

During 1982 dancers started to refer to the contagion that was
killing disproportionate numbers of gay men as "Saint's disease," maintains

Randy Shilts in *And the Band Played On*. But Jorge La Torre has no recollection of the usage at all while Michael Fesco maintains that the name might have circulated only "for a moment" alongside a slightly more popular variation — "the Saint Mark's Baths disease."[8] Meanwhile medical researchers and commentators still didn't know if the mystery condition — which they variously referred to as "related immune deficiency," "gay compromise syndrome," and "gay cancer" — was sexually transmitted or related to the use of a toxic substance. During the summer "friends toned down drug intake and meat rack activity, hoping to rescue their immunological systems," Glenn Person observed in *Star Dust*.[9] Yet whereas the absence of fifty residents on Fire Island was noticeable and could lead to a change of behavior, the same number of deaths wouldn't dent the concentration of bodies on the floor of the Saint, where queuing dancers were ready to pounce whenever a membership became available.

When the Gay Men's Health Crisis (GMHC) held a fundraising benefit at Paradise Garage on Thursday 8 April, the Saint crowd headed to the King Street venue en masse for the first and last time.[10] "It was a completely different audience," recalls François Kevorkian, who DJ-ed. "It was the only time I played Cerrone 'Trippin' on the Moon.'" During the event Paul Popham (now GMHC president) declared that the gay community had to show that it had guts and heart as well as looks, brains, talent, and money, yet Kevorkian felt an underlying sadness.[11] "You had all these people going to the mike saying, 'This is an emergency, people are dying left and right, please have sex responsibly,'" he recalls. "But while they were saying this you could see people doing what they always did. People didn't pay a lot of attention." Evelyn "Champagne" King advised the gathering to avoid the bathhouses and back rooms and to stick to "one lover per person," only for the crowd to chant back, "No way!"[12] "That kind of moralizing was out of the question back then," comments Mel Cheren, who ended the night feeling satisfied that "the gay community's fight against [the yet-to-be-named condition of] AIDS" had begun.[13] But Edmund White (who briefly worked as the first president of GMHC) maintains that a strategic mistake had been made. "Instead of instantly enlisting the help of the federal government, we organised a disco fund raiser," he remarks. "We thought small. We thought ghetto. We didn't understand that we were watching the beginnings of an epidemic."[14]

In fact Larry Kramer fully grasped that the disease required a governmental response, but his efforts to jolt Ed Koch into action were frustrated by Herb Rickman, the mayor's gay community liaison, who refused to return his calls and avoided contact with the gay community in general, even though he was a gay man himself. Lee Hudson, Rickman's deputy, later commented in an interview with Koch biographer Jonathan Soffer that Rickman saw his job as "controlling the message that went to the mayor" and became more of an obstacle than a conduit.[15] Arguing that the real energy to tackle the disease needed to come from the community rather than the city's health department, health commissioner Dr. David Sencer told Koch that no increase in spending was necessary, even though cases of Kaposi's sarcoma were spiraling upward. This, observes Soffer, was precisely what Koch wanted to hear, given that he was attempting to balance his 1982 budget.[16] As New York City representatives and officials stalled, Californian Democrat Henry Waxman held congressional hearings on the federal government's inaction and concluded that "if the same disease had appeared among Americans of Norwegian descent, or among tennis players, rather than among gay males, the responses of both the government and the medical community would have been different."[17]

First suggested as a name for the disease in July, AIDS (an acronym for Acquired Immune Deficiency Syndrome) came into general usage in August. Although prevalent among gay men, the disease could be contracted by anyone who engaged in sexual intercourse or the sharing of needles, as well as those who received infected blood through a transfusion, with straight drug users and hemophiliacs among those infected, noted the Centers for Disease Control and Prevention.[18] The National Gay Task Force added that sexually active gay men were most at risk, while no lesbians were known to have contracted the syndrome. Meanwhile the *New York Times* pointed to puzzling scenarios where "one person in a longtime sexual relationship will get the syndrome, while the partner will not."[19] As confusion reigned, patients with skin lesions that in many cases turned out to be bug bites, bruises, or freckles descended on medical staff.

Promoted through a $500,000 ad campaign that featured homoerotic images of the Brazilian Olympic pole vaulter Tom Hintnaus, the summer launch of Calvin Klein's new line in men's underwear suggested that death was an outcome reserved for those who were less dashing, less wealthy, less talented, and less articulate than the libidinous network that gathered at Mailman's venue (where Klein was a regular). If the Adonis-like athlete and the starchy white underwear suggested a certain sterility, the campaign also sexualized the male body like no campaign before it, heading all the way to Times Square, and did so by referencing a look that had taken hold on the floors of Flamingo followed by the Saint. Did Klein grasp the way the male gay body was becoming a site where health and freedom were entering a morbid battle? Cheren's claim that Klein had attempted to gain access to the Garage GMHC benefit without paying suggested he didn't.

AIDS struck at the heart of the dance community when Patrick Cowley died in November. The musician had been sick for a couple of years when Sylvester challenged him to get better and dragged him from his bed to record "Do You Wanna Funk," which the duo released in July.[20] The track featured Cowley's synth recorded high in the mix, the final gesture of one of the instrument's pioneers. "So if I tell you that you're really something baby," sings Sylvester, "will you stay or will you go away (don't go away)?" Several West Coast clubs had held events to support research into Kaposi's sarcoma when Cowley passed four months later.[21] Yet the appearance of an advert for "It's Raining Men" by the Weather Girls alongside an obit for the musician in *Dance Music Report* would have jolted activist readers into remembering the struggle they faced. Bolstering the Klein campaign when it was released in September, "It's Raining Men" stoked the celebration of gay male promiscuity at the moment of its greatest peril.

CUSP OF
AN IMPORTANT
FUSION

When the Yippie activist turned entrepreneur Jerry Rubin launched a new Business Networking Salon on weekend nights at Studio 54 in March 1982, it was settled.[1] The long-running Better Days aside, Bond's stood as the only midtown discotheque that aspired to cultivate a sound and attract a crowd that would contribute to the ongoing vitality of the New York party scene. Mike Stone drove the effort once again, having started to work at the venue in time to book Central Line, "D" Train, and Modern Romance to play on New Year's Eve 1981. When the Peech Boys hit the stage the following summer, making a cacophony of electronic noise that transitioned into a re-creation of the break from Cymande's "Bra," after which Afrika Bambaataa & the Soul Sonic Force took their turn, Steven Harvey concluded that a different order of performance had just occurred. "I was blown away," he reported in the *New York Rocker*. "Any group that can shift instantaneously from pure noise to an exact reading of a timeless rhythmic extract embodies the best-of-both-worlds funk experimentalism I'd always hoped to hear."[2]

Stone maintains that the momentum he created at Bond's was sufficiently powerful to unsettle the owner of the Paradise Garage. "We were attracting different crowds but Mike Brody still felt threatened," claims the promoter. "We fought over who'd be the first with the big shows — Grace, Gwen McCrae, Alicia Myers." David DePino confirms that "Bond's was the competition, if only because of its size," while Michael Gomes recalls it being "packed with street kids." However, DJ Kenny Carpenter struggled to control the room, which was "too big" and "hadn't been acoustically treated," and concedes that the venue was also "a lot more commercial than Studio 54 [during the Mike Stone era] and the Garage." Boyd Jarvis preferred to start out at Bond's rather than end up there. "Bond's was actually very, very nice, but it was just too big and the sound reverberated in there," he recalls. "The teeny boppers liked it. There'd be 2,000 to 3,000 of them there. But it couldn't touch the Garage."

Boyd Jarvis (bottom right), Kirk Leacock (bottom left), and
friends (top left to right) Yolanda Clark (with collar), Andrea Hall,
Mario Grant, and Chenoa (wearing a hat), ca. 1981. "We were at
an evening pool party given by Conran's first department store,"
says Leacock. "Everyone else was dressed for a high-society, stately
home, pool party. Then I showed up with this 'crew' dressed in
our East Village/retro/punk/Patricia Field style. We were the life
of the party. Then we left and went to the Garage." Photographer
unknown; courtesy of Kirk Leacock.

With Bond's hardly alone in that regard, the New York City party scene
ended 1982 in rude health, despite the broader decline of midtown along
with the diminishing influence of Club 57 and the Mudd Club. Danceteria
and Pyramid compensated for the drift on St. Mark's Place and White Street,
while Better Days and the Loft continued their marathon runs. As for the

Paradise Garage, Michael Brody and Larry Levan appeared to be capable of surpassing themselves at will. The simultaneous rise of the Roxy and the Funhouse diversified the scene as they brought breakbeat aesthetics and borough dancers to the heart of Manhattan. Meanwhile the Saint eclipsed earlier white gay private parties in terms of scale, drama, and intensity, even if aspects of its operation raised questions. These venues didn't simply transcend the breathtaking levels set by the New York dance movement of the 1970s, epitomized by a private party network that could be traced back to David Mancuso's Valentine's Day party. With the partial exception of the Saint, they went about their work in conversation with one another, aware of their commonality as well as their distinctiveness.

The music played in these venues matched their momentum step for step. Indeed at one point it even appeared as though the history of dance was being recast as "Don't Make Me Wait" begat "Planet Rock" begat "Go Bang!" begat "Thanks to You" in just a couple of months, with "The Message," "Situation," "Buffalo Gals," and "Hip Hop, Be Bop (Don't Stop)" following in close succession. These and other hybrid records shredded the categories that had defined the 1970s — disco, dub reggae, rock, punk, and new wave — and in so doing revealed how, for all their radicalness, they had fallen short of capturing the complexity of New York. Enabling people from the widest range of backgrounds to inhabit the city, the cheap cost of living produced crowds that wanted to embrace new forms of music — music that spoke to their social experience. As pluralistic sounds catalyzed new modes of being, pluralistic modes of being catalyzed new hybrid sounds. "People were people and no matter what the crowd, we reached them," Renee Scroggins notes of the way the music encouraged new forms of connectivity. "It didn't matter if they were black, white, straight, or gay. It's the music that reached them. There were different atmospheres in each club, but it didn't matter to me. Dancing is dancing."

The relative absence of the corporates provided labels such as Island, Prelude, Sleeping Bag, Tommy Boy, and ZE with the kind of market freedom that had last existed during the first half of the 1970s, when the majors were even more clueless about the percolating energy that was coursing through the city's nascent DJ-led dance scene. Tom Silverman captured the rising confidence of the independent sector when he argued in March 1982 that it had "the power to make disco the backbone of the record industry."[3] Soon after the majors embarked on another round of redundancies and cuts, yet their troubles were sufficiently localized for Nelson George to argue in the autumn that bubbling beneath the talk of gloom and doom, black-oriented independents were "proliferating," with Tommy Boy "the hottest" of the lot.[4] A virtuous circle in which independent labels, DJs, party spaces, and dancers supported one another's creative, social, and financial needs had come to define the city's party network.

Grassroots demand was such that Charlie Grappone started to hang rare disco classics on wires. "This is a very selective market with a very smart clientele," he explained. "Rock'n'roll fans think they know trivia, but these dance music fans are incredible."[5] Prelude, meanwhile, enjoyed one of its most successful years to date. "We signed real artists, and focused on songs and visuals," maintains Marvin Schlachter. "We didn't abandon the club scene. The country embraced the club scene. 'D' Train were accepted in the clubs and in the mainstream." Having spent the year plugging as many "black" records as George had pushed "dance" records, Brian Chin argued that 1982 witnessed music reach "the cusp of an important fusion between black and white" — and "without the distrust and acrimony" that had spoiled the exchange that took place in 1979.[6] George commented that the two biggest records of the year, "Planet Rock" and "The Message," were "products of New York's insatiable dance clubs."[7]

The majors showed little interest in rap, argues historian Dan Charnas, although in truth their indifference extended to the gamut of sounds that vibrated through the New York party scene.[8] First, they remained skeptical that the city's slippery dance sound could establish a national foothold. Second, they remained wary of the ongoing popularity of the twelve-inch single, for while a successful release could achieve sales of five hundred thousand plus, most sold between five thousand and fifty thousand copies, which fell some way short of their bottom-line calculations. Just as importantly, twelve-inch consumers showed minimal interest in buying accompanying album releases, in part because the "giant single" format enabled them to buy an expansive version of a group's best work while avoiding fodder. "With more black youths joining the unemployment rolls, albums became a luxury, while 12-inchers, easily transferrable to cassette tapes, and usable on disco turntables, dominated street music," George pointed out in December.[9] One way or another, the twelve-inch format seemed to be designed to frustrate the industry's most powerful players.

Gail Bruesewitz came face-to-face with these and other challenges when she became marketing and promotions manager of twelve-inch singles at Columbia in August 1982, having started out in artist development three years earlier. "Small independent labels were making money by pressing up ten thousand copies of a twelve-inch record and selling them out of a back of a van," she notes. "It was illegal for the majors to do this. We had contracts with distributors and retailers." Moreover, whereas the independents could nurture local stores and DJs, Bruesewitz had to address a national market in which store owners were often oblivious to local party trends. "I had a weekly printout of what records were selling in what regions," she recalls. "I could see if the number one record in Dallas clubs wasn't for sale in the shops, but when I phoned I was often told, 'Little lady, I don't need to be told how to sell records.'"

Bruesewitz came to better appreciate the chasm that existed between the corporates and the New York party scene when François Kevorkian (her boyfriend) took her to the Loft for the first time, also during 1982. "I wore a bright red dress and François made me change," remembers the promoter. "He said I would stick out like a white girl." The Frenchman also warned Bruesewitz to prepare herself for a culture shock but in the event she segued into the crowd seamlessly, having already run summer camps for working-class black and Latino kids in the Catskills. On the floor, Bruesewitz executed arabesques and piqué turns before she made the first of many visits to Mancuso's home the following week, bearing the gift of Marvin Gaye's soon-to-be-released "Sexual Healing." "I introduced myself as a promoter from Columbia and gave him the record," she recounts. "The first thing he said was, 'Is it virgin vinyl?'"

For a short while Bruesewitz wondered if she could merge her day job with her new passion for the city's subterranean dance scene but soon concluded that the thread linking the two worlds was precariously thin. "I grew to realize that an underground hit in New York might not translate nationally," she explains. "There was a division between what David was playing and the rest of America. I ended up feeling very schizophrenic." Before long, Bruesewitz began to refer to herself as the "compost pile." "Warners had a dance music department whereas Columbia was a conservative label making money on Bruce Springsteen, Billy Joel, Barbra Streisand, Neil Diamond, Gladys Knight and the Pips, Miles Davis, Willie Nelson, Crystal Gayle, James Taylor, and Elvis Costello," she explains. "As far as the label was concerned, dance music was just a tool."

Meanwhile Frankie Crocker responded to the straitened finances of his African American constituency and its sliding share of the consumer market by pioneering the introduction of the urban contemporary format, which combined black music, pop, and rock.[10] Critics rounded on him for seeking to cultivate a crossover audience at the expense of the uncompromising end of black music production.[11] Yet the radio boss was already an old hand when it came to fending off criticism while tweaking his station's offering, and having

The Loft on Prince Street, 1982. "The entrance lobby was decorated with pictures, found treasures, and balloons, and dancers could dip into a jar of candy as they made their way into Mancuso's home," says Louis "Loose" Kee Jr., a regular. "Inside, David Mancuso decorated his ceiling with balloons in order to re-create the atmosphere of a kid's birthday party, and he also kitted out his apartment with found furniture; cast-off Con Edison wire spools were used as tables, and old movie theater seats were attached to the wall to provide seating. All this stuff was taken from the streets. It was very raw and improvised. All of the things you saw there would have been thrown away as trash, and people took them and made them part of the décor." Photographer unknown; courtesy of Louis "Loose" Kee Jr.

pioneered the "Saturday Night Dance Party" show during the 1970s, he got in touch with Timmy Regisford and Boyd Jarvis, who had started to program a dance show for the station toward the end of 1981. (Regisford had invited Jarvis to play synthesizer on the trial tape, having heard him play live alongside DJ Derek Davidson at Melons.) "Guys, whatever you're doing, I love it!" declared the station boss, who proceeded to hand the duo nighttime slots on Fridays, Saturdays, and Sundays. "That was a rare opportunity — a kid bringing a synth into a major radio station," reminisces Jarvis. "After WBLS, all the DJs wanted me to play on their sets. I used to overdub Tony [Humphries]'s sets for Kiss and then Timmy's sets for BLS. It was bad."

Crocker also commissioned his first rap show in the summer of 1982, having initially shied away from the move because rap's rough-and-ready mode of delivery and production values conflicted with the sophisticated style he had nurtured so assiduously. In the end, however, WHBI became "so popular" it "forced mainstream black stations to play rap," observes Carol Cooper, and when Crocker invited Mr. Magic to host "Rap Attack," WBLS became the first commercial station to air a rap show — albeit one that was "ghettoized" to a midnight slot on a Saturday, comments Mark Riley. When Crocker subsequently attempted to de-rap "Rap Attack," perhaps because Magic's deep voice and classy if somewhat arrogant manner seemed a little too close to his own, Magic returned to WHBI in protest, only for Crocker to relax his demands in order to lure him back. As the tussle unfolded, Whodini namechecked Magic in "Magic's Wand" (with Tee Scott delivering the mix). Meanwhile the Supreme Team — DJs Devon and Justice from Queens — started to host shows on Tuesdays from 1:00 to 2:00 AM, Thursdays from 4:00 to 5:00 AM, and Sundays from 4:00 to 5:00 AM on WHBI. "The entire production exudes a positive air," reported Steven Harvey in the *New York Rocker*. "Both hosts are Muslims and stress a message of peace, unity and political consciousness to the kids who check them out."[12] Malcolm McLaren's "Buffalo Gals" — featuring the Supreme Team—came out a couple of months later.

These developments coincided with and in some respects contributed to the breakup of band culture. "When Futura 2000 (appearing in *Wild Style*) or Dondi White (appearing in *Wild Style*) walk into a club it sparks the same sparks usually reserved for rock or movie stars," Rene Ricard argued in *Artforum* in November. "Economics have influenced this power shift; new bands don't make the kind of money that very young painters do. The winning musicians are DJs, and they play wheels of steel, not guitars."[13] Ricard added that the apotheosis of what Edit deAk termed "Clubism" — a coinage that captured the way that club culture was doubling as an artistic movement, even an ideological practice that cultivated the multiple viewpoints fostered by cubism — could be found at the Fun Gallery. After all, the East Village setting was run by an actor and showed paintings by street artists, some of whom also made records and some of whom took on film roles, all of which established it as a "hub of local intelligence operations."[14] Danceteria continued to fill its stage with experimental lineups seven nights a week, yet the trend was toward bands adopting electronics and foregrounding the sensibilities of DJs such as Afrika Bambaataa and Larry Levan. Connecting with the art-punk crowd that had previously headed to spots such as Club 57 and the Mudd Club, Negril and the Roxy championed another set of influences that didn't so much displace band music as lure it into a cornucopia of sounds. "Some rap was hard to dance to," notes David DePino of the way Levan's own sensibility shifted during 1982. "But all those electro records came in big because they sounded great on the sound system."

If 1981 marked the beginning of a new era in which discrete forces came into creative, explosive contact with one another, 1982 carried those combinations to a new level of intensity. "There was this convergence," argues Jeffrey Deitch. "There were the graffiti artists and the art-school artists, the no wave musicians and the disco aesthetic. Several strains that formed the highest energy and the highest innovation in American progressive culture came together. It was graffiti, hip hop, dance, gay culture, the campy Pyramid culture, the conceptual art coming out of the teachings of Joseph Gasoof at SVA [the School of Visual Arts], Andy Warhol's entry into this dialogue, the European intervention with people like Francesco Clemente, and also someone like Diego [Cortez], who was the mixer." The art investment adviser and critic adds: "Music, art school, graffiti, and street culture all came together into something very interesting. Nineteen eighty-two marked the full emergence of the downtown scene."

Divided into three broad and inevitably overlapping groupings, mixers were taking over significant sections of the city. First there were the artistic, cultural, and social mixers (ranging from Patti Astor to Ruza Blue, Fred Brathwaite to Michael Brody, Keith Haring to Rudolf Piper). Then there were the musical mixers and their label heads (including August Darnell, Grace Jones, the Peech Boys, Arthur Russell, and Michael Zilkha). Finally came the DJs, engineers, studio hands, and one musical host, who explored mixing as a form of sonic integration that could inspire parallel social developments (among them Arthur Baker, Afrika Bambaataa, John "Jellybean" Benitez, Bob Blank, Grandmaster Flash, Mark Kamins, François Kevorkian, Larry Levan, David Mancuso, John Robie, Tee Scott, and — until his passing — Roy Thode). Chris Blackwell, the Clash, Kraftwerk, Malcolm McLaren, and Bernard Zekri appeared as honorary visitors. The melting-pot city was entering its liquid phase.

As the city's mixers went about their business, they aimed to pay the rent and maybe even earn a bit extra so they could buy equipment, book studio time, or sign a new act. Their primary drive, though, was to experience what happened when sounds and people from different backgrounds came together, and they did this with the view that they would take their explorations further if the early signs were promising. "What we feel around us, that's what we write," the ESG lineup told Marjorie Karp of *New York Rocker*, capturing the spirit that powered the era. "Like, we hear this in the park, and this in the street and it brings sounds to your head." When Karp asked if the band aimed for a funk audience, an art-rock audience or what, its members replied, "We aim for every-e-body. We don't play for types of people; we play for people." They added: "Someday somebody might say, 'They sound like ESG; they've got that NY sound.'"[15]

The drive to integration and synthesis drew on and inspired recordings that were largely recorded in the city — more so than had been the case on the dance floors of the early 1970s, arguably the first and last time a similarly wide range of sounds had come together spontaneously in a public setting outside of radio. Rather than coalesce into the homegrown genres of disco, punk, and rap, as it had between 1974 and 1979, the New York sound also assumed a kaleidoscopic brilliance that crossed between genres as it surged through dance floors, boom boxes, and car stereos. It had, quite simply, come to embody and express the diversity and complexity of the city's population.

PART IV

1983

THE GENESIS
OF DIVISION

CRISTAL FOR EVERYONE

The punk-art scene shed its lizard skin twice during 1983 as pioneering parties ground to a halt, exuberant challengers gathered momentum, and a sleek newcomer offered revelers such a remarkable visual feast they would wonder if they were at a party at all.

Of the fading originators, Club 57 wound down in early 1983. "The place closed due to noise complaints and then opened briefly and then closed again," remembers Dany Johnson. "There was about $2,000 in fines owed to the city. Someone stole the money that was supposed to be used for the fines. I used to believe that a few junkies ruined everything but now I think that the club had just run its course." Although many onetime regulars had already gravitated to alternative hangouts, some still experienced the venue's ending as a personal closure. "We all worked and performed at other clubs, including Danceteria, and for a while we took over the Mudd Club as we were hired by Steve Mass," recalls Kenny Scharf. "The transition when Club 57 died was sad for me. A lot of regulars went to the Pyramid, including John Sex, and Keith went to the Garage. I never really got into it again." The *East Village Eye* made light of the development. "Ira Abramovitz is now reduced to hawking hot dogs at the Pyramid on Sunday nights. The shame! The ignominy!" it reported. "However, as the space is now going to be used to treat the mentally disturbed a part of the old Club 57 atmosphere is certain to continue."[1]

Steve Mass closed the Mudd Club soon after, having maintained a rudimentary program during April. "I couldn't pay the prices Danceteria paid for a big-name band like the Gang of Four," he reflects. "The bands started to ask for thousands instead of hundreds." The proprietor took out a series of adverts in the *Eye* that listed many of the more prominent artists who had appeared on White Street, perhaps to attempt to lure in nostalgic readers for a final drink, perhaps to remind revelers of his venue's pioneering run. Then, without any announcement, he completed the sale of the building to Ross

Bleckner, leaving an indifferent Stephen Saban to reference its closing in the October issue of *Details*.[2] "My plan was that the club would just disappear and people would say, 'What happened?'" recounts Mass. "Then there'd be a spectacular new opening, at 254 East 2nd Street or somewhere else. A club owner is like Superman. He just goes back to being Clark Kent, a year or two goes by, and then he reopens the hottest scene in the world."

Mass staged a few events in an old catering hall on 254 East 2nd Street, which he dubbed the Earth's Edge, but he quickly grasped that the building was riddled with insurmountable structural problems that ruled it out as a permanent option. Still feeling upbeat about the prospect of finding another spot, he walked away, although time would establish the Earth's Edge events to be his last in the city. Reflecting on his run, Mass expressed fatalistic dismay at the way the media prompted "the average working class guy or girl" to "come down in droves, large and uncontrollable droves," until "eventually the delicacy of the theatrical environment" was "violated."[3] Yet he had succeeded in keeping the venue at the cutting edge of an edge-driven industry for more than two years and relevant if somewhat diminishing for another two and a half years after that. Given that the Mudd Club opened seven nights a week for close to the entire period, clocking up more than 1,500 nights along the way, it was hardly surprising that a certain exhaustion set in. The only problem was that once Mass switched back into civilian attire he forgot where he left his Superman costume.

Of the exuberant challengers, Danceteria continued to stage four events a night, five nights a week, as John Argento supported and sometimes moderated Rudolf Piper's conveyor belt of ideas as they argued over budgets, only reducing the offering along with the price on Mondays and Tuesdays. "Rudolf would have given money to anyone who walked in the door," reasons the manager. "There were a lot of penniless kids from the Lower East Side who had a good idea but didn't know how to publicize it or organize it as an event, and we'd back it." Although he was "more of a businessman," Chi Chi Valenti maintains that Argento "knew enough to weave all of the creative decisions through Rudolf" and "didn't impose himself very much." Turnover increased through a form of creative multiplicity. "If you do a fashion show with fifteen new designers who are going to just completely turn it out, and they all have their models and their models' friends and whatever music they're picking for the show, then that's a party in itself, plus there'll be one or two brilliant people who stand out and go on to make a mark," adds Valenti. "That's a concept that Rudolf reenacted throughout Danceteria's run that I thought was very smart."

With "No Entiendes" still in full flow, the crazed schedule featured special "Gay Parade," "Spring Cleaning," and "Tropical" parties plus one held "In Remembrance of the *SoHo News*"; video lounge encounters that included a "*TV Party* Highlights" compilation, a Bob Marley tribute, a RockAmerica Video Convention, and premieres of films such as Nick Zedd's *Geek Maggot Bingo* and Ed Wood's *Glen or Glenda*; fundraising benefits for the Interactive Art Library System of the Organization for International Artists, the Museum of Holography, Semiotext(e), and a demo against U.S. intervention in Central America and the Caribbean; a "Hip Hop Art Explosion" event with Daze, A1, Lady Pink, and Crash plus music by Grandmaster Caz of the Cold Crush Brothers; an "East Village Look" fashion and hair exposition featuring local clothing stores, hair salons, and makeup artists; a "Polygon" multimedia night that combined bands, avant-garde performance, and art; a "Science Fair" hosted by Tanya Ransom; performances by Jayne (formerly Wayne) County, Tina L'Hotsky, John Sex, and the nonviolent, noncooperative Downtown Sissies in Revolt Ensemble; and a Depravnik Island participatory theater experience conceived by Ann Magnuson and staged by her with Lithuanian-American performer Kęstutis Nakas that refigured Congo Bill as a Soviet-style resort set in the Arctic Circle where, as the flyer put it, "the sun never rises and the fun never sets, where commissars and party members indulge in revisionist entertainment."

The music schedule unfolded at an equally frenetic pace as the supremely able Ruth Polsky scheduled performances by an ocean-wide range of artists, including Laurie Anderson, Aztec Camera, the Beastie Boys, the Bush Tetras, Certain General, Einstürzende Neubauten, ESG, Diamanda Galas, Human Switchboard, Johnny Dynell and New York 88, Arto Lindsay, Lene Lovich, the Lounge Lizards, Quando Quango, Red Alert and the Dynamic Force, R.E.M., Run-D.M.C., Sisters of Mercy, Tin Tin, Yello, John Zorn, and scores of others. With Argento and Piper sponsoring Polsky to visit the United Kingdom twice a year to spot up-and-coming talent, the curator made a point of visiting the Haçienda, a Danceteria-style venue that the band members of New Order along with Rob Gretton and Tony Wilson had opened in Manchester in May 1982. Polsky also scheduled a "Brazilian New Music!" series as well as "Bound for Glory" and "Manhattan Local" festivals that showcased New York bands, with Mon Ton Son, Histerica Passio, and Cool It Reba worth their appearance fee for their names alone. "One of the regular 'super groups' consisted of Marc Almond, Lydia Lunch, Nick Cave, and Blixa Bargeld [founder of Einstürzende Neubauten and a guitarist/backing vocalist in Nick Cave and the Bad Seeds]," reminisces Anita Sarko. "You couldn't beat that combo!"

SUN. MAY 22. 9 PM
The People's Switchboard

BENEFIT BASH $4.00

CONGO BILL CLUB
4TH FLOOR OF DANCETERIA
30 WEST 21 STREET
TEL: 620-0515

DRAWING FOR THE PEOPLE'S SWITCHBOARD K Haring
APRIL-26-83

Flyer for Congo Bill, 22 May 1983. Courtesy of John Argento.

Argento signed off on payments of up to $5,000, which is what it cost to have the British breakthrough vocalist Sade make her New York debut at Danceteria in May. Piper judged such expenses to be "absurd," in part because there was no way the venue could hope to make the money back at the door, yet he acknowledges that the loss-leading strategy helped put the Mudd Club out of business. Then there was the possibility that an unaffordable artist who was destined to perform at the Peppermint Lounge or the Ritz might still drop by to hang out on 21st Street, as happened with Boy George, an ex–Blitz Club regular and lead vocalist of the British synth pop outfit Culture Club, whose single "Do You Really Want to Hurt Me" went to number one the previous autumn. Piper judged the experience of having Boy George socialize with the Danceteria crowd to be "actually better than having the show" and attributes his and other such visits to Polsky. "She had such great relations in the music industry," he notes. "She not only booked acts but she had musicians coming into Danceteria the whole time because it was an ambience for them and she created that ambience."

The year also saw Anita Sarko start to DJ before and after the scheduled live performances on the first floor, having caught Rudolf's eye for a second time at a messed-up party she had started to co-organize on Second Avenue. "Ruth Polsky was a genius and I was proud that she only wanted me to DJ when her discoveries played Danceteria," comments the DJ. "She was

Ann Magnuson ready to perform as Anoushka the Soviet chanteuse, 1983. During 1982–1983 Magnuson appeared in the films *The Vortex* as well as *The Hunger* while pursuing a performance career that included work with Pulsallama, an all-female pots-and-pans percussion group that grew out of the Ladies Auxiliary of the Lower East Side, Magnuson's downtown take on the Junior League. Photograph by and courtesy of Robert Carrithers ©.

beloved by so many up-and-coming bands, who usually slept on her floor when they performed in NYC. Our musical beings were always completely in sync." Soon invited to DJ on the fourth floor as well, Sarko appreciated the way the minuscule dance floor made the purpose of the space clear as well as the way Rudolf's topsy-turvy design elicited imaginative selections. During a "Cold War" party, she switched from "illegal music," such as ABBA and the Carpenters, to "sanctioned music," which included recordings of socialist men's choirs and ensembles, whenever Rudolf (dressed as head commandant) entered the room to arrest someone. She also DJ-ed at hardcore sex parties held in the fourth-floor space (including regular Bad Boy events that featured Times Square go-go boys), "Straight to Hell" nights that included S/M demonstrations, bondage exhibitions, and on one occasion a graphic show by performance artist Karen Finley. "I would play extremely suggestive SM/DS music such as Throbbing Gristle during these events," recalls Sarko. "Danceteria

leonard abrams

haoui montauq

maripol

ruth polsky

Danceteria faces (top left, moving clockwise) Leonard Abrams, Haoui Montaug, Chi Chi Valenti, Rudolf Piper, John Argento, Johnny Dynell, Ruth Polsky, and Maripol, photographed in the club in 1984. "I was a waitress in the restaurant at Danceteria and I was always a cocktail waitress at Haoui [Montaug]'s 'No Entiendes,'" says photographer and occasional party host Rhonda Paster. "I actually quit a job in the garment center as a sales rep to work at Danceteria when I decided I wanted to merge my work life with my social life." Photographs by and courtesy of Rhonda Paster ©.

chi chi valenti

rudolf

johnny dynell

john argento

was Mudd Club, next generation. It takes time for a decade to define itself and leave the previous one behind. Danceteria was where the eighties embraced its own identity, very much existing in the moment rather than the past, which had played such a massive role at kitsch-loving Mudd and Club 57."

Meanwhile Piper hired Johnny Dynell to play Fridays on the second floor at the very moment when, as the DJ puts it, "the disco people were going new wave and the new wave people were going disco." If that enabled him to draw on a reservoir of records that both he and the crowd found acceptable, the ex–Mudd Club DJ didn't go so far as to play the Smiths, because he would have preferred to slit his wrists than do that. He was also initially reluctant to play New Order, even after the band made fun of him for playing disco. "I said, 'Well, if you give me a drum beat in one of your records, maybe I'll play it,'" he recalls. "A few months later they gave me a test pressing of 'Blue Monday,'" a March release that drew inspiration from Klein & M.B.O's "Dirty Talk," Kraftwerk's "Radioactivity," Donna Summer's "Our Love," and Sylvester's "You Make Me Feel (Mighty Real)." Dynell adds of Kamins: "He was the main DJ without a doubt. He was really influential on that whole scene. Mark could take a lot of the music that was coming over from England and mix it flawlessly with disco records. He did that better than anybody."

The second floor was the last to benefit as Piper and Argento oversaw a floor-by-floor renovation. On Friday 13 May they opened the basement to the first of a series of goth-driven "BatCave" parties, inviting all of the London organizers to transplant their original aesthetic to 21st Street. The following month they inaugurated a new roof terrace space on the thirteenth floor of the building, irreverently titled "Wuthering Heights." In September they unveiled the newly decorated first floor as well as the revamped third floor, which they decorated in the style of an Italian American living room, with an island bar providing "access to Chi Chi Valenti on all sides," reported Stephen Saban.[4] Ten days later Piper relaunched Congo Bill as a Soviet bureau adorned with hammer-and-sickle-style cocktail glasses and posters of Lenin — a flagrant and, as far as Magnuson was concerned, annoying borrow from the Depravnik Island event. Finally additional bass bins and lighting were introduced to the second-floor dance floor at the end of the month. Yet even if the venue was more obviously geared up to someone like Valenti, who might venture onto the dance floor for half an hour, but who primarily loved to "be social and be amongst people and watch things and talk about things," Danny Krivit still found himself enjoying the entertainment every time he hit the spot. "It wasn't a rock club," he notes. "It was a club for alternative culture. It was the quintessential place for this."

Steve Mass could have claimed that mantle for the Mudd Club not so long ago, but Danceteria had since pioneered a more democratic and outward-facing avenue, with Piper far less ambivalent than Mass when it came to dealing with the media and seeking out new crowds. Dressed in a yellow blazer adorned with black criss-crosses, the Danceteria promoter even made an improbable appearance on the kids' talk show *Livewire* in October, and he invited the public access cable show *New York Dance Stand* to present an edition of its show from inside 21st Street around the same time. "The responsibility is on the people," Piper put it to the host of *Livewire*, contextualizing his own contribution to the party. "They are the ones that are going to make a great night by the way they dress, by the way they dance, by the way they are around, the new fashions they come up with. So I alone really can't do very much."[5] More of a social touchstone than a barwoman or hostess, Valenti argues that whereas the Mudd Club was an art project that became a business, Danceteria was a creative business that operated as a cultural breeding ground. "Danceteria was much more accessible and advertised and known about than the Mudd Club," she reasons. "It was meant to be that. It was meant to be bigger. It was just the zeitgeist."

Pyramid, meanwhile, continued to drum up a seven-nights-a-week schedule that, given its size, was every bit as frenzied as the one unfolding on 21st Street. In one of the venue's most notable performances during the year, Kęstutis Nakas recruited Steve Buscemi, John Kelly, Ann Magnuson, and John Sex to appear in his production of Shakespeare's *Titus Andronicus*, "the Elizabethan equivalent of a splatter movie," and for the production spectators received a slice of luncheon meat as they came through the entrance.[6] In other developments the prolific Magnuson completed what the *East Village Eye* described as a "solo tour de force," and photographer Nan Goldin showed an early version of her evolving series "The Ballad of Sexual Dependency," a forty-five-minute slide show plus a soundtrack that documented the intimate relationships of the artist and her Lower East Side art friends.[7] Meanwhile Brian Butterick booked the Beastie Boys, Bronski Beat, the Butthole Surfers, Foetus, Joshua, Kristi Rose and the Midnight Walkers, Nico, Martin Rev., the Red Hot Chili Peppers, and They Might Be Giants to play live, with 3 Teens Kill 4 also making an appearance. "Bronski Beat's show was like a visit from a prophet," recalls Joshua Fried (the Joshua of Joshua). "Nico and her equally beautiful son mesmerized us. They seemed drugged the whole time."

The territorial reaction appeared unnecessary when the October opening of 8BC as a nearby performance space prompted Bobby Bradley to tell performers he would only book them if they appeared exclusively at Pyramid.[8] After all, the venue was already benefiting from the opening of some eleven neighborhood galleries in the slipstream of the Fun Gallery.[9] The development prompted the *New York Times* to report that the East Village gallery scene was threatening "to erupt into Manhattan's third art district, after Uptown and SoHo," with the David Wojnarowicz show at the Civilian Warfare gallery commended for being "right at home in the gritty ambiance" of the neighborhood thanks to its violent, erotic, and political images painted over supermarket food posters, garbage-can lids, and found pieces of metal.[10] Then, just as the SoHo galleries closed for the summer, the East Village upstarts staged a succession of high-spirited openings, their crowds primed to head to Pyramid once the first leg of the party closed. As the queues outside the Avenue A spot lengthened, door staff took to charging $10 to those they didn't want to admit and $3 or less for those they did. "I might have felt like Steve Rubell if I'd thought about him," says Butterick, who picked out people on especially busy nights. "But that was more Mudd Club, which was intended as an antithesis of Studio. We were just trying to keep our living room the way we wanted it."

SELECTED DISCOGRAPHY

IVAN BAKER, PYRAMID (1982–1983)

Afrika Bambaataa & the Soul Sonic Force, "Planet Rock"
Art of Noise, "Beat Box"
Bauhaus, "Kick in the Eye"
The Beastie Boys, "Cooky Puss"
The Clash, "Rock the Casbah"
George Clinton, "Atomic Dog (Atomic Mix–Long Version)"
The Cure, "Primary"
Depeche Mode, "Everything Counts (in Large Amounts)"
Fad Gadget, "Collapsing New People"
Gang of Four, "I Love a Man in a Uniform"
The Gap Band, "Burn Rubber on Me (Why You Wanna Hurt Me)"
Nina Hagen, "New York New York"
Hashim, "Al Naafiysh (The Soul)"
Jimi Hendrix, "Fire"
Impossible Dreamers, "Spin"
J.B.'s, "Doing It to Death"
Jimmy Castor Bunch, "It's Just Begun"
Grace Jones, "My Jamaican Guy"
Kraftwerk, "Numbers"
George Kranz, "Din Daa Daa (Trommeltanz)"
Lady B, "To the Beat Y'All"
Laid Back, "White Horse"
Lawrence Welk and His Orchestra, "Calcutta"
Ledernacken and Band, "Amok!"

Led Zeppelin, "Ocean"

Liquid Liquid, "Cavern"

Cheryl Lynn, "Got to Be Real"

Malcolm McLaren, featuring the World's Famous Supreme Team, "Buffalo Gals"

New Order, "Blue Monday"

New Order, "Temptation"

Pigbag, "Papa's Got a Brand New Pigbag"

Public Image Ltd., "Flowers of Romance"

Shriekback, "My Spine Is the Bassline"

Siouxsie and the Banshees, "Israel"

Siouxsie and the Banshees, "Spellbound"

Jimmy Spicer, "Money (Dollar Bill Y'all)"

The Staple Singers, "Respect Yourself"

Steppenwolf, "Magic Carpet Ride"

Donna Summer, "Love to Love You Baby"

Sylvester, "You Make Me Feel (Mighty Real)"

Talking Heads, "Burning Down the House"

Treacherous Three, "The Body Rock"

Trouble Funk, "Pump Me Up"

T-Ski Valley/Grand Groove Bunch. "!Catch the Beat!"

Barry White, "It's Ecstasy When You Lay Down Next to Me"

Yazoo, "Situation"

Thrilled by the publication of Rene Ricard's article in *Artforum* back in late 1982, Patti Astor and Bill Stelling opened the new year with a Futura 2000 show, selling every piece but one before opening night. "I loved Rene and I loved the article," comments Astor. "It definitely captured what we were doing. It was so influential. That article made us." It hardly mattered that Astor had become good friends with Ricard during the filming of *Underground USA* or that the artist-actor-critic headed to the Fun Gallery on a daily basis. As Steven Hager argued in the *East Village Eye*, even if Ricard was an "old chum" it was "already glaringly obvious that Astor had taken a hole-in-the-wall in the East Village and turned it into the hottest gallery in America."[11] Reiterating his *Village Voice* forecast, the writer added that the story of the 1980s would come to revolve around the coupling of the South Bronx and the East Village, and that within that story Astor would "loom very large indeed."[12] For her part the onetime Mudd Club regular was still determined to stave off "the tremendous boredom" she used to feel when she went to other openings. "I think people have a good time when they come to the Fun," she remarked. "Our artists have immediacy and popular involvement."[13]

Running from 3 to 27 February, the next show featured Keith Haring, who had initially expressed concern that if he presented at the Fun Gallery he would take up space that could otherwise go to a less well-known artist. But Astor felt she and Haring shared the objective of making art public and that it was incumbent upon them to collaborate. She and Stelling also needed Haring's support as they attempted to meet their increased rental charge of $1,400 per month along with the general cost of running a larger space. "Keith was always right there," she comments. "When we got together to smoke pot before going to Negril, Keith was totally part of the crew, and when we moved over to the new gallery he gave me this beautiful painting to sell. Then he did a show at the Fun Gallery — *he had to*."

With LA II contributing signatures, lines, and figures to the works, Haring painted the entire gallery in his trademark style, placing a newfound emphasis on images of breakers, electric boogie dancers, and DJs, many of them featuring electric-current arms or spinning on their heads. "The work directly referenced hip-hop culture," Haring told John Gruen. "I then put the work back into hip-hop culture via the subway and the exhibition at the Fun Gallery so they became one and the same."[14] The artist went on to create works on leather hides sourced by Halston handbag designer Bobby Breslau along with a couple of Smurfs made out of plaster casts that he had found on the street. "The whole idea of the Fun Gallery was you could do whatever you wanted to do, go wild, go nuts, so Keith got this idea that he wanted to paint on these hides," comments Astor. "Tony [Shafrazi] would never have let him do this." Haring's simple invite for the show featured three twisting bodies that formed the letters "F," "U" and "N."

A thousand people teemed into the venue and its backyard, spilling out onto the pavement and the street, for the 3 February opening. "It was a very funky East Village scene again, packed with a mix of graffiti artists and other people — much more funky than the Tony Shafrazi opening had been," Haring recalled to Gruen. "Andy [Warhol] decided that he wanted to trade work with me and so we started becoming friends."[15] At one point Stelling turned to Astor and said that he thought the gallery was about to levitate into the sky or crash into the basement it was shaking so much.[16] "The opening attracted a remarkable mix of Puerto Rican kids from the neighborhood and the elite of the art world," adds Jeffrey Deitch. "It was a platform for the mix of music, art, and social strata that Keith's art embodied." Haring's boyfriend, Juan Dubose, eased the interaction with his turntable selections. Yet the show ended up being less successful com-

(Left to right) Keith Haring, unknown, Grace Jones, and Fred Brathwaite at the Fun Gallery, ca. 1983. "Break dancing was a real inspiration, seeing the kids spinning and twisting around on their heads," says Keith Haring. "So my drawings began having figures spinning on their heads and twisting around. My exhibition at the Fun Gallery was really a reference to this whole Hip-Hop culture." (Quotation from Gruen, *Keith Haring*, 90.) Photograph by and courtesy of Ande Whyland ©.

mercially, with the gallery only selling "one freakin' Smurf," recalls Astor, who deduced that the work was too adventurous for the collectors who showed up in their limos the following morning. Undeterred, Haring showed up every day to sign the posters he had printed and give them away for free. On Valentine's Day he also gifted Astor a red velvet heart filled with Godiva chocolates.

Subsequent shows turned out to be lucrative enough for Astor and Stelling to claim midyear that they had sold some thirty paintings by Futura, twenty-three by Dondi, fifteen by Zephyr, and seven by sixteen-year-old Dominican newcomer ERO, with the going rate of $1,000 to $4,000 per piece and the proceeds split evenly with the artists. "People might say graffiti looks really out of place in a gallery," Zephyr told *People Magazine*. "But I think it's good if graffiti is out of place. Sneaking into these places is just what graffiti is supposed to do."[17] Futura ramped up the critique, arguing that "a lot of art-buying is bull" and lambasting visitors who exoticized graffiti artists for being black. "But I play the game because I want their money," he added. "Meanwhile, I'm still painting and getting better."[18] However, even as the likes of NYU film student Spike Lee, the Beastie Boys, Rammellzee recording collaborator K-Rob, and a multitude of local kids started to hang out at the gallery, there was no straightforward way for Astor and Stelling to bubble-wrap their community project, and sometime during the second half of the year, Astor and Stelling lost Futura to Tony Shafrazi. Looking to ward off some of the more opportunistic competitors, Astor printed up T-shirts with the slogan "Fun Gallery: The Original and Still the Best" and handed them out to her artists."[19] Shafrazi, she maintains, proceeded to "ruin" Futura's career by pushing him to "create way too many canvases in a very short time" for his first show.[20]

Haring's simultaneous rise to stardom took him to London, Lucerne, Madrid, and São Paulo as well as galleries in Michigan, Pennsylvania, and Massachusetts, with the London trip notable for a collaborative project he carried out with the U.S. choreographer and dancer Bill T. Jones. The connection with Jones dated back to perhaps 1980 and the moment when he and his partner Arnie Zane performed at Kutztown University, where they were introduced to Haring's art, after which a friend commented on the similarity between their dance aesthetic and Haring's work during a rehearsal later that week. Jones tracked down Haring and when the two of them "hit it off," the dancer asked the artist to create a poster for a forthcoming performance. A couple of years later Jones had Haring paint a backdrop while he performed "Four Dances" at the Kitchen. Then, in 1983, having become good friends, Haring asked Jones if he would strip naked so he could decorate his entire body with white acrylic patterns. "I said, 'Why the hell not?'" recalls Jones. "We were going to be in London at the same time and I thought it would be fun to see the Keith Haring machine on the road."

Taking more than four hours to complete, during which time Jones changed his position intermittently while Tseng Kwong Chi photographed the session, the work extended Haring's exploration of art, the body, black culture, and dance in a manner that spoke directly to his weekly visits to the Paradise Garage. "What I didn't know beforehand is that twenty white British photographers would be there cracking jokes," recalls Jones. "The thing that saved me is I loved what Keith was doing. In fact it turned into a performance with this impromptu light show of the flashing photography, so that was very exciting and testimony to how much I trusted Keith." A child of the countercultural era, Jones was keenly aware of the racial assumptions

Futura (left), Gerb (DJ-ing), Patti Astor, Anita Sarko, and others in the Fun Gallery's backyard, 1983. Photograph by and courtesy of Robin Holland © robinholland.com.

that threatened to overwhelm the session, yet he never held Haring's white middle-class upbringing against him. "As a black man whose body was his primary instrument there was always this uncomfortable feeling that one was on display, somehow or other complicit in an odd kind of meat show wherein people were given permission to look and fantasize, but never had to express their desires publicly," he explains. "But Keith was extremely generous, and a melange of innocence, vulnerability, and idealism. He loved street culture, black and Hispanic men, and women too, I believe. I trusted Keith and actually found him brave, if someone so innocent can be called brave. He was the child of America's heartland and headed out to the big city equipped only with his talent, his desires."

Jean-Michel Basquiat, meanwhile, belatedly released "Beat Bop," a ten-minute experimental rap track he'd laid down some time during Ruza Blue's run at

Negril or immediately after it closed. The record featured homemade percussion instruments played by Al Diaz, a two-chord guitar riff, angular violin shards, bass, and conga, with Basquiat drenching the results in so many effects Diaz's woodblock ended up sounding "absolutely synthetic," the percussionist commented later.[21] Yet the more profound transformation came about when K-Rob (a fresh-faced fifteen-year-old MC whom Basquiat had spotted at Negril) and Rammellzee rejected the lyrics for being both banal and outlandish, and embarked instead on a beguiling, improvised account of drugs, prostitution, poverty, quitting school, and partying that rivaled the reportage of "The Message" while introducing a novel existentialist strain. Just as its title promised, the finished track combined the abstract principles of Basquiat's father's favorite strain of jazz with the beat-driven territory of rap, ushering Gray's space-conscious, experimental, often surreal aesthetic into a new downtown-meets-the-Bronx amalgam. In another first, Basquiat designed crown-and-bones artwork for the cover, which also included the words "test pressing." He then issued five hundred copies of the record — "Beat Bop" by Rammellzee vs. K-Rob — on his own imprint, Tartown Inc.

In March Basquiat won museum recognition when he contributed to the Whitney Biennial, the most important exhibition for contemporary art in the United States. Haring was also selected to contribute, as were emerging artists Jenny Holzer, Barbara Kruger, and Cindy Sherman. The limits of Basquiat's as well as Haring's inclusion were illustrated when the *New York Times* ran an extensive piece on the show that managed to reference neither of them — the stars of the downtown movement had yet to fully convince in New York, never mind beyond.[22] Yet Basquiat made an important connection at the post-opening dinner when he met gallerist Mary Boone, who took on the role of representing him in the United States — a role Bruno Bischofberger never wanted for himself. With his Haitian-born accountant father in tow during an ensuing visit to the show, Basquiat chanced into Jeffrey Deitch, who asked him if he needed help with his tax returns, which were due. "That was kind of a role I had with these artists," remarks the art adviser and critic. "I wasn't that much older than them but I was working at Citibank and had a little more maturity. So the father was astonished. He couldn't believe that his son, whom he saw as a pothead and a loser, had a friend who would offer to do his taxes."

"Beat Bop" enjoyed a second life after John Hall picked up a used copy of the record in Saint Mark's Sounds and took it to Cory Robbins at Profile Records. "I thought it was cool as shit," Robbins recounted later. "It was druggy, it was so out there. All of a sudden there's lots of echo, and then the echo's gone. Nobody made records like that. No record producer would make a record like that. It didn't follow any rules."[23] Hall advised Robbins to get in touch with the Mary Boone Gallery, which had agreed to distribute the artist's leftover boxes of vinyl, and when an assistant provided the label owner with Basquiat's new address on Crosby Street he sent him a mailgram. A couple of weeks later Basquiat agreed to release "Beat Bop" on Profile and, in what Robbins took to be a trusting gesture, delivered the masters to the label office. When Basquiat offered to create new artwork for the re-release, Robbins declined on the false premise that he would make more money if he stuck with the standard Profile jacket.[24]

With "Beat Bop" something of a tangential project, however, Basquiat flickered in and out of the party scene for the first eight months of 1983. After all, the Mudd Club had lost its insider cachet while venues such as Danceteria and the Roxy failed to reproduce its original appeal. Instead he took to partying at home, happy to finally have a place of his own, and increasingly relaxed about turning to recreational drugs for his entertainment. "There was the beginning period, which was 1981–1982, where he was everywhere and connected with everyone — with all the coolest people, with all the most gorgeous women — and he was the center of it all," recalls Deitch, who would visit him on Crosby Street. "Then from 1983 onwards he started to become very successful, the drugs were getting heavy, and he was getting a little more paranoid and suspicious of people. Instead of the circle being the other cool artists and musicians, he had a group of hangers-on who were on his payroll and were trying to sponge off of him."

Four Angelenos lured Basquiat back onto the floor when they opened Area in September 1983. Eric Goode and Shawn Hausman had already started to put on student house parties back in LA, and when they found themselves living in New York with Eric's younger brother Chris and his onetime school friend Darius Azari they joined forces to open an unlicensed party known as Club with No Name on West 25th Street in April 1981. More than familiar with the art-punk end of the downtown scene, Goode and Hausman persuaded the landlord of the fourth floor of a walk-up to give them permission to open an "environmental gallery," which "sounded more respectable than a nightclub," recalls Hausman.[25] For the launch they placed two white rats in a display case inserted into the bar, installed a large Plexiglas area that housed two white rabbits in a fake fur nest, hung forty fresh bones from a ceiling, placed a larger bone surrounded by blood on a pedestal, suspended cages from a wall, lined up porcelain urinals along another, hung a motorbike above a second bar, and projected a mixture of surfing, boxing, nature, Japanese animation, surrealist, and hardcore Super-8 porn films.[26] Those in attendance clocked that a new form of freakishly morbid inventiveness had just gate-crashed the city's nightscape.

The upstart partners closed the spot a short eight weeks later, mainly because they never set out to run a regular party. But they soon discovered they had built a "cult following," remembers Hausman, with "everyone" keen to know when they were going to reopen.[27] Backed by a family friend of a friend, who provided them with the bulk of the $350,000 opening costs, the Californians searched for a permanent location and settled on the former Pony Express Stables, a 12,500-square-foot T-shaped building located at 157 Hudson Street in TriBeCa. Subdividing the space into a 100-foot entrance hallway that featured four giant display cabinets that resembled those used in the American Museum of Natural History, a dance floor driven by a Richard Long sound system, a unisex bathroom/hangout, and a large bar that featured an aquarium, they named their new spot Area, because they wanted to run the venue as a flexible space that could be reconceptualized on a regular basis. They then issued five thousand copies of their first night invite: a ring box that contained a blue pill and a note to drop the pill into a glass of hot water. Recipients knew that the venue was about to take the city's art-oriented party scene to a new level of sophistication when the outer casing dissolved to re-lease details of the event.

Held on Thursday, 15 September, the opening party might have been the most highly anticipated since Danceteria relaunched on 21st Street. "Hundreds of pill-bearers arrived seemingly en masse, each and every one assuming immediate *entrée*," Saban reported in *Details*. "Strange, alien door people lurked. They knew no one, no one knew them. So, like most openings, fragile egos were hurt and the crowd turned ugly."[28] Unable to breach the wall of madness, Johnny Dynell, Chi Chi Valenti, and hordes of others held an impromptu party in the street. Those who found a way inside marveled at the inventiveness of the spectacle, which explored the theme of "Things That Go On in the Night" through dioramas dedicated to a swamp scene, an exhibit of freeze-dried bats, a flashing filament, and a sleeping boy listening to a Walkman, plus other thematized elements such as a live owl, a butterfly collection, fluttering moths, and a masked pseudo-welder who put a blade to a whetstone, sending sparks into the surrounding space. As the night unfolded, the uni-sex toilets hosted a party within the party. "Taped eclectic lounge music was provided by Anita Sarko, a tableaux in herself," added Saban. "What did it all mean?"[29]

Eric Goode (left) and Shaun Hausman (right) with Kimberly Davis of ART, the
Only Band in the World, at a Club 57 afterparty following an ART performance at
Carnegie Hall, ca. 1983. Photograph by and courtesy of Robert Carrithers ©.

Area's purpose became a little clearer a month later when its owners closed
the spot for four days before staging a second Thursday-night launch, this
time to reveal a venue redesigned around the theme of cars, with installations
ranging from a decorated AMC Gremlin to a giant toy racing track. Even if the
theme lacked the unsettling quality of the opening, the mere fact of the breakneck self-reinvention set the venue apart as something additionally new, and
its distinctive modus operandi was confirmed when two more relaunches —
one with the uninspired theme of obelisks and another on the zanier topic of
the future — took place before the year's end. "Many clubs occasionally have
theme nights, but their function is usually limited to being a backdrop for
disco or a diversion between band performances," the organizers declared in
their mission statement, and it was all coming true. "We intend to radically
expand on the concept of themes, creating elaborate environments, utilising
film, video, photography, theatre, sculpture, dance, etc., inviting the participants of the senses. . . . The entire club will be in constant flux."[30]

Many of those from the art-punk end of the downtown party scene swerved
happily toward Area. Dynell took on the role of DJ-ing Wednesdays and Fridays, handing in his notice at Danceteria because he didn't feel he could hold
down both jobs, plus the opportunity to play at Area amounted to a "big step

up" for him careerwise, given that Mark Kamins was the main DJ figure on 21st Street. Valenti started to head to the spot three or four nights a week and not just because her boyfriend was playing there. "I really liked what they were doing artistically and creatively," she explains. "There were all of these performers who were hired to do tableaux, and it was very in keeping with a way of working that was close to certain bigger events I'd been involved with. There were some absolutely phenomenal nights at Area." Also heading regularly to Hudson Street, Patti Astor remembers some "really cool events" during the first year. Ann Magnuson recalls that "everyone in the scene seemed to go there," especially during weekday nights, which turned Area into a "part of the downtown family."

SELECTED DISCOGRAPHY

JOHNNY DYNELL, AREA (1983)

Afrika Bambaataa & the Soul Sonic Force, "Planet Rock"
Blancmange, "Blind Vision"
David Bowie, "Let's Dance"
The Clash, "The Magnificent Dance"
Depeche Mode, "Just Can't Get Enough"
"D" Train, "You're the One for Me"
ESG, "Moody"
52nd Street, "Cool as Ice"
First Choice, "Let No Man Put Asunder"
Taana Gardner, "Heartbeat"
Grandmaster Flash & Melle Mel, "White Lines (Don't Do It)"
Grandmaster Flash & the Furious Five, "The Message"
Eddy Grant, "Electric Avenue (Special Extended Dub Mix)"
Eddy Grant, "Walking on Sunshine"
Gwen Guthrie, *Padlock*
Herbie Hancock, "Rockit"
Hashim, "Al Naafiysh (The Soul)"
Loleatta Holloway, "Love Sensation"
Indeep, "Last Night a D.J. Saved My Life"
Johnny Dynell and New York 88, "Jam Hot"
Grace Jones, "My Jamaican Guy"
Chaka Khan, "Clouds"
Konk, "Konk Party"

Barbara Mason, "Another Man"

Gwen McCrae, "Funky Sensation"

Malcolm McLaren, featuring the World's Famous Supreme Team, "Buffalo Gals"

Modern Romance, "Everybody Salsa"

New Order, "Blue Monday"

New York Citi Peech Boys, "Life Is Something Special"

Yoko Ono, "Walking on Thin Ice"

Peech Boys, "Don't Make Me Wait"

Rockers Revenge, "Rockin' on Sunshine"

Rufus & Chaka Khan, "Ain't Nobody"

Shannon, "Let the Music Play"

S.O.S. Band, "Just Be Good to Me"

Talking Heads, "Burning Down the House"

Talking Heads, "Once in a Lifetime"

Tom Tom Club, "Genius of Love"

UB40, "Red Red Wine"

Womack & Womack, "Baby I'm Scared of You"

Yazoo, "Situation"

Even Basquiat hauled himself out of semi-exile to become a fixture at Area, manifestly drawn to the way it self-consciously styled itself as an exclusive hangout for artists while pursuing the idea that a nightclub could double as a twisted art installation — rather like the Mudd Club. The regularity with which Warhol also headed to Hudson Street was an added bonus, and within weeks of opening Bischofberger facilitated an agreement between the ex-Factory figurehead, Basquiat, and Francesco Clemente to participate in a collaborative project. Relaxing into the spot, Basquiat also DJ-ed in the venue's lounge area when it took his fancy. "He would play the most obscure records, anything from the latest underground reggae dubs and early hip hop to rare jazz recordings," recalls Dynell. "One night we had a very heated discussion. I told him that I just didn't think that two hours of John Coltrane was really 'party music.' He got very defensive, saying that it depended on what kind of party it was, and added, 'Anyone who can't dance to John Coltrane can't dance.'"

In many respects Area amounted to an intensification of the creative and playful sensibility that had attracted Basquiat and others to the Mudd Club and Club 57 in the first place. If Goode and Hausman had made Studio 54 their favorite destination when they arrived in the city in the autumn of

Jean-Michel Basquiat DJ-ing in the lounge at Area, 1986. Photograph by and courtesy of Johnny Dynell ©

1979, they soon gravitated downtown. Magnuson remembers the two of them participating in Club 57's "envirothèque" setting, with the low-budget "Putt Putt Reggae" mock shantytown installation a highlight for them. They also became regulars at the Mudd Club, where Mass hired them to redesign his basement in the style of a Venetian palace, and Goode contributed to the *Lower Manhattan Drawing Show*. "They had these extraordinary skills as set designers," recalls the owner. "They could do almost anything." Mass was struck by the similarities Area shared with the Mudd Club when he visited the new spot. "They were able to incorporate art installation into the flow of nightlife just as I had done with my third-floor gallery, so I was very impressed," he remarks. "The size of it just dwarfed the Mudd Club. I said, 'My God, they really are doing it!'" Dynell confirms that "the whole Area thing really did come out of the Mudd Club."

Area amounted to the latest phase in the downtown art scene's development, even its success. Several years earlier, participants had congregated in the cheapest neighborhoods, relishing the opportunity to demonstrate what they could produce on a shoestring budget, especially given that rents were so low. Come the autumn of 1983, however, a good number of downtowners had started to receive significant recognition and in some cases remuneration for their work, and that came to find its echo in Area, where organizers spent $30,000 — or twice as much as it cost Mass to open the Mudd Club — on its renovation every six weeks.[31] Yet because the Hudson Street spot was so manifestly connected to what had come before, because so many of its participants descended from earlier downtown parties, and because the downtown scene had already spawned its own form of exclusivity, many judged it to be the next evolutionary stage in a restlessly inventive culture rather than a foreign element that broke with the past. "We saw that Area was what was happening creatively in New York," notes Dynell. "It was just my favorite club."

The dazzle shrouded the extent to which the integrationist premise of the downtown scene weakened in the Hudson Street venue. After all, the Mudd Club started out as a social space that brought together artists and like-minded types from different backgrounds, Club 57 followed a similar if more youthful and lighthearted path, and Danceteria, Pyramid, and the Fun Gallery also championed inclusive paradigms. But Area's organizers shaped a crowd that revolved around three groups: first, the now recognizably successful pioneers of the downtown scene; second, a rapidly multiplying and increasingly networked class of artist agents, gallerists, designers, models, stylists, and advertising creatives and executives; and, third, a formative contingent of "uptowners and Europeans" (as the owners would describe them).[32] "Area became a big hangout," confirms Justin Strauss, who became the Thursday and Saturday night DJ at the venue. "People really wanted to get into the place. There was this door guy, who was picking the right mix of downtown and uptown. For a while it was the best of Studio 54 meets the Mudd Club." Some also detected a "major shift" from what had come before. "There was less of a community feel," observes Magnuson. "It was much more uptown and had a lot in common with Studio 54, except the artistic sensibility was much more clever and excellently executed."

Whereas Club 57's relentlessly witty theme parties had been the equivalent of a "third grade school play where you're holding a cardboard tree in front of you," observes Astor, drawing one of several possible comparisons, Area "was Club 57 with money." The qualitative shift could be traced to the very conceptualization of the new venue, when Hausman and Goode approached Mass along with other potential investors. "They had an extraordinary presentation you might see in a cosmetics company," recalls the White Street owner. "You opened a book and figures popped out. You put particles in a tea cup and letters spelling 'Area' came up. Although it was well done it was like a Disney promotion." That presentation segued into the highly professional yet somewhat sterile Hudson Street aesthetic. "When I saw Area's big-budget installations I have to admit to being a bit envious, and Eric and Shawn continuously blew our minds with their beautifully crafted creations," acknowledges Magnuson. "But it did feel like it was the beginning of the scene shifting away from a more DIY approach into something more slick." The change was pronounced. "Before Area, discos were black spaces that would go off into infinity, but Area was this conceptual, postmodern white room, and instead of flashing lights there were projections," points out Dynell. "In a way it was more like a museum than a nightclub."

The dynamic, participatory, and unpredictable modus operandi of the downtown party scene shifted in tandem. Amidst the multitasking mayhem, Mass and Magnuson took on the role of enablers at the Mudd Club and Club 57, empowering participants to give free range to their self-expression through performance and event organization. Danceteria and Pyramid also operated as breeding grounds of grassroots expressivity, immersive experience, and performative interaction, while the Fun Gallery operated as an outlet for community creativity. At Area, though, revelers took on the sensibility of the gallery visitor awed by the artistic brilliance on display, and while a good time could be had by all on the dance floor as well as in the unisex bathroom, the perfectionism of the space simply didn't promote the kinds of rough-and-tumble experience that could still be enjoyed on 21st Street and Avenue A. "Area felt like a mall-ification of the downtown scene," concedes Dynell. "People thought it was so fantastic but the space didn't feel underground. It was a very polished, finished club. They had these glass windows and behind them people would act out these tableaus. The audience was out here and the performance was in there. There was a delineation between the participants and the performers, and that bothered me on some level."

It seems entirely possible that Area was the first downtown venue where someone like Bischofberger felt entirely at ease, in part because it integrated gallery culture into the very heart of its aesthetic in a way that surpassed Mass's efforts at the Mudd Club, in part because its sleek VIP area became a space where it seemed entirely natural to strike art deals. In a serendipitous turn, the Hudson Street venture also embarked on its journey into the heart of sophisticated clubbing at the very moment when the art market began to climb precipitously. "By 1983 the scene was rolling in dough and nightlife reflected that trend," remembers Astor. "The opening of Area upped the ante."[33] While Astor and Stelling tried to figure out how to hold on to their social values and aesthetic sensibility, Area launched its flawless and somewhat soulless aesthetic at the very moment when new money started to smooth out the city's rough underbelly. "Area was unique and classy and had some unbelievable parties," remarks Rudolf Piper. "Whether or not I wanted to go there depended on my mood. It was a bit too posey, too contrived, too artificial, but we all had those languid moments, and for that, Area was perfect and übercool."

The influx of "dough" coincided with changes that were rippling across the city as Reagan's neoconservative agenda of tax and welfare cuts, financial deregulation, and monetary contraction laid the basis for a very specific form of recovery that began during the final quarter of 1982 before establishing 4 percent growth during 1983. Contributing to the trend, the New York economy created seven thousand new jobs, having shed seventy thousand the previous year, with the financial and services sector producing most of the work as manufacturing continued to dive. Structural in nature, the shift also resulted in a growing disparity in earnings, unfolding in New York City with "greater intensity" than elsewhere, notes sociologist Saskia Sassen.[34] Meanwhile the real estate market soared by 15 percent during 1983, having already expanded by 5 percent the previous year, as office building rents rose at an unprecedented rate.[35] Mayor Koch didn't completely fall for the charms of the property developers yet found himself reprimanded by a state court in December 1982 for denying Donald Trump a tax abatement for the development of Trump Tower, which the entrepreneur completed during 1983.[36] Capping the year, the Dow Jones Industrial Average closed at 1,258, up from the previous year-end figure of 1,046, which marked the beginning of a period of exponential growth captured by the figure of the voracious, arrogant, and narcissistic Wall Street broker.[37] An era shaped by deepening inequality, accelerating commodity consumption, and an obsession with surface image was making its presence felt.

If Area appeared to be more obviously entangled in the encroaching culture of materialism and consumption than, say, Danceteria and Pyramid, its owners remained remarkably uninterested in the idea of making money out of the venue. If anything, they headed in the opposite direction as they sunk their door takings back into the most elaborate installations anyone could remember. As Glenn O'Brien notes, Area was both "riotously successful yet insanely oblivious to profit," and some of the venue's most recognizable figures were equally unbothered about money, even if they suddenly had more of it than seemed possible.[38] Happy to demonstrate his newfound wealth while showing his disdain for the etiquette of the rich, Basquiat had already started to paint in designer suits by the time Area opened, splattering them with glee. In another gesture that might have appalled his accountant father, the artist also took to buying bottles of Cristal for everyone who happened to be in the Hudson Street venue during his visits, enabling "colorful but penniless club kids" to "clink glasses of champagne with the richest art dealers," recalls Dynell.

If it was easy to view Area as the pinnacle of the downtown scene, or the moment when club-inspired art had reached its zenith and the champagne flowed in recognition of its success, the venue's arrival also signified an ending of sorts. What, after all, was there to drink after Cristal except more Cristal? "We didn't sense that the scene was changing, but we were young," ponders Dynell. "This was our first scene and we had nothing to compare it to."

DROPPING
THE PRETENSE
AND THE
FLASHY SUITS

Thanks to the promotional efforts of Fred Brathwaite, Michael Holman, and Ruza Blue in particular, the idea that hip hop existed as a cohesive culture that melded the four elements of DJ-ing, MC-ing, breaking, and graffiti had become a reality by the time *Wild Style* premiered in the United States at the New Directors/New Films festival held at the Museum of Modern Art on 18 March 1983. Rudolf Piper staged the after party at Danceteria. "It's a teenage romance that rocks the rap revolution!" he enthused in the venue's newsletter.[1] It was also, as Charlie Ahearn noted later, "an idealization, or a projection of what hip-hop could be rather than what it was." He and Fred Brathwaite, adds the director, "weren't looking backwards, we were looking forwards."[2]

The movie didn't attempt to smooth over the culture's disjointed edges in order to create a seamless subcultural narrative. In the first party sequence, breaking appears as just one of a plethora of compellingly kinetic styles, with graffiti nowhere to be seen. With Lee Quiñones cast as Raymond Zoro assuming the lead and Lady Pink playing his girlfriend, the graffiti writers lead a largely autonomous existence from the party scene as they stalk subway depots by night. There's only one scene when the four elements come together, that being the final party staged in the amphitheater, which was "25 times bigger" than any outdoor jam Ahearn had ever seen.[3] So light is the meshing of the four elements, no actor even gets to utter the words "hip hop." Yet the film's nonhyperbolic approach to its subject matter along with its naturalistic use of Patti Astor playing a white woman who falls in love with the culture plus Busy Bee, Fred Brathwaite, Crash, the Cold Crush Crew, Daze, the Fantastic Five, Grandmaster Flash, Lady Pink, Quiñones, the Rock Steady Crew, and Zephyr dancing, DJ-ing, promoting, rapping, and writing just as they did offscreen turned out to be precisely its strength. Finally, even if Ahearn and Brathwaite had gently cultivated the idea that hip hop amounted to a cohesive culture, by the time of the film's release it had become real enough as Negril and then the Roxy soldered the four elements together.

As the film and accompanying Brathwaite-directed soundtrack started to circulate, Steven Hager applauded Astor's "comical portrayal of herself" as well as Fred Brathwaite's creation of a "new urban hipster," only for the *New York Times* to argue that it "never discovers a cinematic rhythm that accurately reflects and then celebrates the rare energy and wit of the artists within the film."[4] It was regretful but not calamitous that the *Times* failed to get Ahearn's apt combination of neorealist and Warholian techniques — because moving between the street and the depot could be slow, plus the art-downtown connection was palpable. Armed with MOMA's 35-mm print of the movie, Ahearn and Brathwaite traveled separately to screenings in Cannes and Seville before they joined a party of thirty to embark on a twelve-city promotional tour in Japan organized by Ruza Blue. Traveling first class, Busy Bee got the party going by cracking open a couple of bottles of Dom Perignon, Ahearn having handed out per diems ahead of duty free. After that, remembers Astor, the boom boxes went on "full force" as the Boeing 747's multibathrooms were put to use, with "the green bud" smoked in one, "killer cheeba" imbibed in another, and "the zooty" (cocaine) snorted in two more.[5] "It was like Beatlemania," Brathwaite recounted to the *Times*, now more sympathetic. "The Japanese didn't understand a word we said, but they clapped right along."[6] *Wild Style* then played at the Embassy on 46th Street in November. "We never expected any of this stuff," added Brathwaite. "We were just making this picture and expecting to show it on 42nd Street."[7]

Meanwhile Michael Holman set out to extend hip hop's screen presence when he recorded a pilot for a dedicated TV show, *Graffiti Rock*, having busied himself managing the Floormasters for much of 1982. Still smarting from his fallout with Blue, he had also attempted to reopen Negril but gave up the ghost when the scheduling of Afrika Islam, Kool Herc, and Nick Taylor failed to attract a significant crowd. "It was on a Thursday night and it was tough to compete with the Roxy, which was on a Friday," he concedes. "I think I did maybe four or five and then it petered out." Around the same time Holman started to host and produce a weekly cable TV show, *On Beat TV*, that he would begin in the studio before heading out on location, filming in the subway, the School of Visual Arts, squat theaters, hip hop parties, and the like. Then, in April 1983, he resolved that the time was right to emulate how *Shindig!* and *Hullabaloo* had captured the rock and roll movement. Afrika Bambaataa, the Cold Crush Brothers, Jazzy Jay, and Red Alert headed to the Bronx River Community Center to film the pilot, with Jean-Michel Basquiat

Wild Style tour of Japan, 1983. (Left to right) Babylove, Afrika Islam,
Busy Bee Starski, and K. K. Rockwell. Photographer unknown; courtesy
of Afrika Islam.

and Steven Hager showing up to observe developments. "It was a big party
performance," reminisces Holman. "We shot it and we cut it into a teaser."

But if Holman's venture along with *Wild Style* indicated that visual coverage
of hip hop was all set to remain lo-fi, a cameo appearance by Richard "Crazy
Legs" Colón in *Flashdance* suggested that breaking, at least, could crossover
to a wider audience. "When there's a movie you can't send an actor to *breakdance*," Afrika Islam notes of Legs's spiraling reputation. "You got to get the
Rock Steady Crew." Along with *Fame*, a 1980 film set in the New York High
School of Performing Arts, *Flashdance* contributed to the post–*Saturday
Night Fever* rehabilitation of the idea that dancing and the big screen could
combine successfully as it tracks its young female lead through the Pittsburgh
strip club, loft home, and dance studio where she executes her moves — far
away from the discotheque floor. Castigated in reviews when it was released
in April, the movie nevertheless went on to generate $100 million at the box
office, making it the third-highest grossing movie of the year. Even if the breaking sequence was brief, it "made it into a mass cultural phenomenon, not just
something kids did on the streets of the South Bronx," Jim Fouratt observed
in the *Daily News*.[8]

Three further developments boosted hip hop's visibility, beginning with the
autumn announcement by Orion Pictures that it was working on *Beat Street*,

the first major motion picture to depict the culture. "The story is about the friendship between three guys — two black and one Hispanic — who go to high school in the South Bronx," commented Hager, recruited to write the script. "I didn't want it to be about white people going up to Harlem and discovering something."[9] A short while later PBS premiered *Style Wars*, a documentary directed by Tony Silver and coproduced by Henry Chalfant that dated back to the canceled *Graffiti Rock* performance, when an acquaintance told Silver there was a film waiting to be made about the events they had just witnessed. Including footage of the Lincoln Center battle between the Rock Steady Crew and the Dynamic Rockers and further material shot during August 1982, the incisive film meshed together interviews with Mayor Koch, the police, and several artists. Then, in December, ex–Mudd Club regular Stephen Sprouse staged his first major fashion show, having used a $1.4 million parental contribution to open his own business. The collection revolved around graffiti-covered motorcycle jackets that the novice designer had first imagined after taking a walk through the East Village in the spring. Bloomingdale's started to carry Sprouse's line soon after.[10]

Offscreen and away from the catwalk, Bambaataa bypassed the increasingly troubled Flash as the Bronx's most influential DJ, at least in the eyes of Islam, who had acquired the nickname "Son of Bambaataa," thanks to his proximity to the Zulu Nation leader. "I'd like to point out that there's been an overemphasis on Grandmaster Flash and I think that's really been an injustice to Afrika Bambaataa," Islam argued in the *East Village Eye* in June. "I really perceive that he is the Ambassador of Rap. While they both came from the street, Bambaataa was always the major force on the street."[11] Over on West 18th Street, meanwhile, Danny Krivit found himself increasingly influenced by those he was supposed to police. "I could see from my perspective at the Roxy that hip hop was the next thing," he says. "I was really into it and I felt, 'OK, the hip downtown people are embracing it and these are people with insight.'" The DJ started to incorporate "good hip hop" into sets along with scratching techniques. "One of the graffiti artists gave me the nickname Danny Rock," he recounts. "The name stuck." But when Krivit spliced together "Feelin' James," a cut-up bootleg of James Brown's "Funky Drummer," modeling it on D.ST's live mix of the track, he handed a copy to Larry Levan more out of politeness than hope. "The quality was too rough for Larry and also the breakbeat element was too choppy," he figures. "The rap records Larry played were groove-oriented."

Steve Haenel wanted more from the Friday-night slot at the Roxy, however, and approached Vito Bruno to boost the turnout. "Steve wanted us to bring the trendy, hip, downtown crowd to the Roxy and to build up the profile of

Dancers at the Roxy, 1983. Photograph by and courtesy of Bob Gruen ©.

the night," recalls Bruno, who was still working at AM/PM when Haenel made his approach. "Some downtown people were already going there and that might have sparked the idea of, 'Hey, let's get the guys who have got them to work with us.'" Bruno stepped up his involvement — distributing flyers and posters in the Bronx, initiating a word-of-mouth campaign among trendies, and arranging for AM/PM regulars to be driven to Ruza Blue's night — when his after-hours spot closed in February. "Then the whole thing blew through the roof," he claims. Blue, however, maintains the scene was growing of its own accord, with appearances by the likes of Liquid Liquid and the release of *Wild Style* feeding the momentum. "The media realized they were dealing with something that wasn't as taboo as a gay scene," points out Islam. "It was an American scene — *young black Americans breakdancing*! That's newsworthy. Where do they all party? At a place called the Roxy!"

Haenel sacked Blue in late July or early August, just over a year into her run at his venue.[12] "The owner brought in Vito and that's when it all started to go downhill," she recounts. "Haenel got a bit greedy and wanted it all to himself. I was ousted without any notice." Krivit recalls that Blue presented Haenel with a don't-mess-with-me ultimatum that the owner chose to ignore. "She was getting a little less business-oriented, at least from Haenel's perspective," maintains the DJ. "He felt he could do it without her." Bambaataa held on to his position as well as his vision when he resisted Haenel's subsequent proposal to bump up admission to $10. "'Na, man. Na. You can't do that,'" Bambaataa told Haenel during a meeting held in a pizzeria up by the Tommy Boy office, recalls Bruno. "'These kids can't afford $10.' He held his ground and price was raised only $1 or $2, and Bam was right because it would have affected the whole racial balance of the club." The DJ nevertheless regretted Blue's departure. "I was cool with the Roxy people but Lady Blue was the one we paid our respects to," he comments. "She was the one that helped make it happen."

The Roxy's integrationist ethos weakened when Bruno and Haenel started to give more emphasis to guest MC performers in order to drum up numbers. But the strategic shift altered the dynamic of the night, for whereas Bambaataa encouraged a plethora of sounds, people, and activities to come together, the MCs occupied a streamlined world in which they primarily drew attention to themselves. "The management at the Roxy were clueless and didn't get what I was trying to do there," argues Blue. "I was more into the DJ-ing and the dancing than the MC-ing. The scene became one-dimensional instead of three-dimensional, and it also became a bit violent and troublesome. There were mostly men in there. It wasn't very exciting." A sign of the segmenting times, the Roxy "lost its edge" along with its "mash-up of people and culture," claims Blue, who turned her focus to the *Wild Style* tour of Japan and an ensuing trip to the United Kingdom, where the Rock Steady Crew performed in a variety show in front of the Queen. On their return the breakers released "(Hey You) The Rocksteady Crew" on Atlantic, which Brian Chin judged to be "one of the most commercial rap-fusion records yet produced."[13] Some viewed developments with a degree of suspicion. "When we got back and told our best friend in the Bronx what had happened, they didn't go, 'Yo, you got to go to England!'" recalls Afrika Islam. "It was more like, 'Yeah, fuck that! Fuck the queen! She ain't paying my rent!'"

The Funhouse, meanwhile, went through a subtler transition when John "Jellybean" Benitez's studio commitments began to multiply, the DJ having established a foothold during 1982 with edits, coproductions, and mixes of Deodato, the Jonzun Crew, Orange Krush, Jimmy Spicer, Rockers Revenge, and Warp 9 plus the seven-inch of "Planet Rock." Benitez got to move into "a whole different league" in early 1983 when Polygram commissioned him to remix Giorgio Moroder's production of Irene Cara "Flashdance . . . What a Feeling," the theme song for *Flashdance*, and his studio career continued its upward arc when Madonna asked him to remix "Physical Attraction," having ended her collaboration with Mark Kamins (who acknowledges he lacked experience "when it came to producing vocals"). "She came to the DJ booth and was like, 'Oh, I'm working on my album,'" recalls Benitez. "We traded numbers and went out on a date the week after that." The Funhouse DJ had completed three more mixes for Madonna by the time she found herself short of a song, at which point he played her the demo of "Holiday," a number he was working on with an outfit called Pure Energy. Turning to Arthur Baker after Madonna said she "loved it," Baker advised, "Let Madonna do it!" The producer recalls Benitez being "a bit lost" in the studio but maintains that it didn't really matter because Fred Zarr was there. "By this time Fred was Madonna's guy and he played everything," he explains.

That summer Jellybean rented a house in the Hamptons with Baker and Robie, hanging out there in between nights at the Funhouse. With her dancers in tow, Madonna joined them after she performed nearby on the Fourth of July as well as when she wasn't busy promoting her debut album, *Madonna*, which came out in August. "She never had any money," reminisces Baker. "We'd always have to buy her dinner. She loved penny candy." Back at the Funhouse, Jellybean played "Holiday" after every live show, because that was when the highest number of industry people would be in the room, and he also handed copies of the record to every DJ he knew, including Larry Levan, who programmed it heavily. "Sire was gearing up to release 'Lucky Star,'" recalls the Funhouse DJ. "But the day the album came out, all of the radio stations started playing 'Holiday' and Warner had to switch gears. There was this huge buzz around the record." Released in September, "Holiday" went on to become Madonna's first pop hit, eventually reaching number sixteen on the Hot 100. Downtown had just produced its biggest homegrown hit since Blondie came out with "Rapture."

SELECTED DISCOGRAPHY

JOHN "JELLYBEAN" BENITEZ, THE FUNHOUSE (1982–1983)

Afrika Bambaataa & the Soulsonic Force, "Looking for the Perfect Beat"
Afrika Bambaataa & the Soul Sonic Force, "Planet Rock"
Afrika Bambaataa & the Soulsonic Force, "Renegades of Funk"

Area Code 615, "Stone Fox Chase"

Babe Ruth, "The Mexican"

Pat Benatar, "Love Is a Battlefield"

Blackbyrds, "Gut Level"

Booker T. & the M.G.'s, "Melting Pot"

James Brown, "Give It Up or Turnit a Loose"

Jenny Burton, "Remember What You Like"

Irene Cara, "Flashdance . . . What a Feeling"

C-Bank, "One More Shot"

Cybotron, "Clear"

Cymande, "Bra"

Deodato, "Keep It in the Family"

Manu Dibango, "Soul Makossa"

ESG, "Moody"

Freeez, "I.O.U."

Grandmaster Flash & the Furious Five, "The Message"

Grandmaster Flash & the Furious Five, "Scorpio"

Grandmaster Flash & Melle Mel, "White Lines (Don't Do It)"

Johnny Hammond, "Los Conquistadores Chocolates"

Hashim, "Al Naafiysh (The Soul)"

Heaven 17, "Let Me Go!"

Jimmy "Bo" Horne, "Spank"

Imagination, "Just an Illusion"

The Jackson 5, "Hum Along and Dance"

Jimmy Castor Bunch, "It's Just Begun"

David Joseph, "You Can't Hide (Your Love from Me)"

Jonzun Crew, "Pac Jam"

Jonzun Crew, "Space Is the Place"

Kraftwerk, "Numbers"

Kraftwerk, "Tour de France"

Kraftwerk, "Trans Europe Express"

George Kranz, "Din Daa Daa (Trommeltanz)"

Level 42, "Starchild"

Liquid Liquid, "Cavern"

Madonna, "Burning Up"

Madonna, "Everybody (Dub Version)"

Madonna, "Holiday"

Madonna, "Lucky Star"

Madonna, "Physical Attraction"

Martin Circus, "Disco Circus"

Vaughan Mason, "Jammin Big Guitar"

MFSB, "Love Is the Message"

Nairobi and the Awesome Foursome, "Funky Soul Makossa"

New Order, "Blue Monday"

New Order, "Confusion"

Orange Krush, "Action"

Man Parrish, "Hip Hop, Be Bop (Don't Stop)"

The Peech Boys, "Don't Make Me Wait"

Planet Patrol, "Play at Your Own Risk"

Quadrant Six, "Body Mechanic"

John Robie, "Vena Cava"

Rockers Revenge, featuring Donnie Calvin, "Walking on Sunshine '82"

Gil Scott-Heron, "The Bottle"

Shannon, "Let the Music Play"

Sinnamon, "Thanks to You"

Lonnie Liston Smith, "Expansions"

Jimmy Spicer, "Bubble Bunch"

Strikers, "Body Music (Vocal)"

Sweet G., "Games People Play"

Talking Heads, "Slippery People"

Visual, "The Music Got Me"

Warp 9, "Nunk"

Wide Boy Awake, "Slang Teacher"

Yazoo, "Situation"

Steven Hager published a diary-style feature on the Funhouse in the *Village Voice* in May, opening his account with a 5:00 PM preparty exchange between dancers meeting in a Queens pizzeria and closing it when the last record ended at 8:30 AM the following morning.[14] Days later *New Musical Express* journalist Richard Grabel claimed that the venue had reinvigorated the culture of Saturday-night partying. "Perhaps it's the harder economic times, or perhaps it's the fact that they take their dancing more seriously," he observed, "but the Funhouse kids have dropped the pretence and the flashy suits of the last disco generation."[15] Low belts, jeans or shorts or billowy genie pants, bare midriffs, and T-shirts or halter tops signified the arrival of a more functional outlook as some 3,000 to 3,500 revelers executed exuberant, vigorous, athletic moves. "Dancing or drugs — but more often a combination of the two — takes the place of sex, and you don't notice any cruising going on," Grabel continued. "Dancing is the name of the game, and it is pursued with single-minded determination, trained for like a sport, approached with devotion."[16] Although dancers subdivided according to ethnic, borough, neighborhood, school, and sometimes workplace affiliations, the Funhouse was the "most integrated" within the hardcore dance scene, he added. "For all the rivalry, and despite the potential tension in any racially mixed crowd . . . there is never any fighting. All that's left at the door."[17]

Garage and Loft regulars struggled to warm to the energy and taste of the younger crowd. "Dancing there was about showing off, dissing people, a form of kid-play," recalls Louis "Loose" Kee Jr. "There probably wasn't much violence but the atmosphere was highly aggressive." Stepping in when Benitez sneaked out of the booth to spend time with Madonna or found himself occupied in the studio, Tony Smith fitted an earring to make himself look younger. "The Funhouse crowd's taste was eclectic in only one sense; they could be programmed into enjoying old 'street' classics mixed with rap and the Arthur Baker sound," he argues. "But by no means did it have the advanced musical sensibility of the Garage. It wasn't even close." Yet the venue established itself as a linchpin alternative to the Roxy, with Renee Scroggins maintaining that she has "better memories of the Funhouse," even if the West 18th Street venue was "pretty cool and pretty interesting," while Monica Lynch was of the opinion that "the Roxy was a little bit more of a boys' scene than the Funhouse." Bambaataa notes that the Funhouse seemed to have a problem when it came to admitting African Americans and on one occasion he even refused to go on stage "until they let all the different people in," but he recognizes that the atmosphere was "off the hook." The Zulu Nation DJ adds that he "loved what Jellybean was jamming" and thought of him as "a cool brother."

Up in Bambaataa's home borough, Disco Fever continued to double up as a legitimate disco and a clandestine after-hours spot that attracted "pimps and hustlers as well as college kids and aspiring rap stars," notes Carol Cooper, who started to head there in 1983.[18] In May *People* described Sal Abbatiello's hangout as the "rap capital of the Solar System" and the "tom-tom heart of the South Bronx, one of the few places its disenfranchised citizens can go to forget the harsh reality of their lives." A twenty-five-year-old McDonald's employee recounted how he went home to sleep after work at 3:30 PM so he could dance at the Fever until dawn, while a twenty-seven-year-old mother of four and part-time department store cashier described her thrice-weekly visits as her "summertime." When asked how he got away with being a white

Sal Abbatiello (right) and Kurtis Blow celebrate a gold record for "The Breaks" at Disco Fever, 1981. Photographer unknown; courtesy of Sal Abbatiello.

guy running a business for black and Latina/o dancers, Sal Abbatiello commented that all he did was show them "a little kindness." "The Fever's where I go to get ideas for my albums," Kurtis Blow revealed. "You get to see what the street likes."[19]

Abbatiello launched his own label — named Disco Fever — after heavy lobbying from Blow and Simmons. With distribution agreed with West End, the owner brought in Blow to produce Sweet G.'s "Games People Play" for his first release and watch contentedly as the record broke at the Funhouse and the Roxy. Efforts by Love Bug Starski and Gigolette followed as Abbatiello opened a family-oriented roller disco named Skate Fever, led a campaign to restore a rundown playground situated across the road from the rink, staged a telethon to raise money for the United Negro College Fund, introduced bus rides to help local residents visit family members in prison, and staged free parties for kids. "Because he did so much business in the South Bronx, Sal routinely initiated charitable projects in that community intended to improve the general quality of the residents' lives," observes Cooper. "If charity work also helped improve Disco Fever's reputation and the image of rap in general, so much the better."[20] At the end of 1983 the Bronx borough president named Abbatiello Bronx Citizen of the Year.

Back downtown, Brathwaite rapped alongside his godfather-drummer Max Roach in an event held at the Kitchen in November that also featured DJ-ing and the New York City Breakers. "Normally, break dancers work against unchanging rhythm tracks," reported the *Times*, "but Mr. Roach — who has collaborated with a number of dance groups — gave their acrobatics an extra dramatic boost."[21] Overall, however, hip hop was heading in a more market-driven and less experimental direction than had appeared likely just twelve months earlier as Bruno started to plug MCs over DJs at the Roxy, Benitez's studio career drew him away from the Funhouse, Crazy Legs popularized breaking, Orion Pictures began work on what it hoped would be the next *Saturday Night Fever*, and *Wild Style* toured Japan. If the hardcore faithful felt they were proselytizing as well as getting due financial reward for their efforts — which they were — the developments contributed to the sense that 1983 was a transformative year during which the coincidence of hip hop's con-solidation with the national return to economic growth carried the culture far beyond the floors of the Bronx and Manhattan.

"The Roxy came to an end when Blue started traveling with the Rock Steady and all of us," comments Bambaataa. "We had to go to a lot of coun-tries many times to make hip hop happen. I had to play a lot of smaller places until the people got it. Then I started getting big in Paris." The DJ adjusted his focus to the task of making the planet rock. "The more I was doing, the more it was being accepted," he adds. "The news and the media started getting on it and the movies started coming out, so that started changing things. But it was a lot of work going to all those countries."

STRAIGHTEN IT OUT
WITH LARRY LEVAN

After-hours spots proliferated during the early 1980s as they attracted three groups of people: club employees who wanted to go out after wrapping up work in the middle of the night, revelers who didn't want the festivities to end at the times required by New York's cabaret licensing laws, and those who were never ready to go out before 4:00 AM in the first place. Arthur Weinstein's Continental and the Jefferson were two of the most renowned. Located on the corner of Houston and Broadway, where it took over the Reggae Lounge's space midway through the night, Berlin was another popular destination. "I would go to the Mudd Club, I'd stop off at Dave's luncheonette, where they sold hot dogs with sauerkraut and egg creams, and then I'd walk up from Canal Street to Houston and Berlin," recalls Jonny Sender. "There wouldn't be a soul on the street." Haoui Montaug would greet him at the door. Richard Vasquez played records inside. "If you got there early enough you'd catch the last bit of reggae and the Jamaicans hanging around," adds Sender. "Then it'd switch to Tuxedomoon."

The after-hours spots were always vulnerable to raids, however, and investigators gained the upper hand in their long-running battle with their organizers when the FBI told Weinstein he'd have to wear a wire or face six years in prison after he made inadvertent payoffs to a plain-clothes officer at the Continental, which opened following the closure of the Jefferson in the spring of 1981. Weinstein took the wire and wore it until the *New York Times* ran a story on the stitch-up on 22 February 1983.[1] Le Pop, another after-hours venue, was shut down the next day and AM/PM followed two days later. "We made a decision to voluntarily close and had a funeral party," recounts Vito Bruno, who concluded that the venue's position had become untenable after he was quoted talking about cash payments in the *Times* piece (inaccurately, he says).[2] "We had the club filled with floral arrangements and we got busted just as we were about to open. Thank you, Arthur."

The police completed domino raids on Berlin, Elan, and Pink Cadillac by the time Weinstein attempted to clear his name by granting an interview to Stephen Saban at the Munson Diner on West 48th Street on Sunday 27 February. "The first thing I want to say is that I never wore a wire," he announced. "That's number one. What I did do was provide some information that was absolutely necessary about . . ."[3] Saban proceeded to quote a twisted account of partners, deals, truths, and falsehoods that shed minimal light on the events that culminated in the swooping shutdown. "New York, the city that never sleeps, can at last rest," Saban noted of the closures, while the *East Village Eye* reported that the "jaded little microcosm that we call clubland" had been "rocked."[4]

In a sharp response, Dave Peaslee argued in *Dance Music Report* that the *Times* piece constituted "a prelude — by means of public misinformation — to a planned assault on New York's nite-clubs." The choreographed closure of the city's after-hours spots was motivated by a desire to move unwelcome populations out of gentrifying locations, with the official target of criminal activity a chimera. "The operating of these clubs becomes then for some a 'quality of life' issue," continued Peaslee, "their erasure part of the official campaign, and while it can be argued that more patrons possessing cocaine could be found at Elaines or 21, more prostitutes at the Plaza, more tax-evasion on Wall St., and more corruption in City Hall, it is the discos, because of their position as cultural pariahs (and their perceived effect on property values) that come under attack."[5] Later that month the *Times* ran another story on intensifying authority efforts to ensure compliance. "In 1980 and 1981, we didn't seem to be getting anywhere," a fire prevention officer commented. "But now there is a recognition on the part of the cabarets [venues holding a cabaret license] that we're going to get them."[6] Urban geographer Laam Hae points out that as the city pulled out of recession, the Department of Consumer Affairs was "given the funds and authority to step up nightlife regulation" and that the liabilities incurred by business owners when they violated regulations "also grew."[7]

As the property boom gathered momentum, residents exerted not-in-my-backyard pressure on the city to clamp down on those who had helped pave the way for gentrification in the first place. "I don't know of any elected official . . . who does not constantly get calls from people who live near cabarets, discos and even certain restaurants complaining about the loud music that blares forth," the head of the Consumer Protection Committee proclaimed at the end of April, making the case for the urgent introduction of new soundproofing regulations, this after Consumer Affairs had gained new powers to close down clubs that were in violation the previous year.[8] Meanwhile resident-venue disagreements erupted in real estate hot spots such as TriBeCa, where crime rose 2.3 percent in 1982 while falling 5.1 percent city-wide, with some blaming local discotheques for the disparity.[9] "We want to present our suggestion to eliminate the problem once and for all: transform Manhattan into an agrarian community, therefore erasing with one shot all our social plagues," Rudolf Piper opined in a Danceteria newsletter. "No more drugs, no more gambling, no more street crime, no more prostitution, no more nitelife . . . and no more jobs, but in face of these major crimes, who cares about jobs?!"[10]

The New York party scene suffered a further setback when Bond's — the last remaining mega-club to pursue a multicultural agenda in midtown — embarked on its own cleanup exercise after Maurice Brahms came out of jail in January 1983 and, overruling John Addison, kicked out Mike Stone. "Maurice Brahms wanted a white promoter because he preferred the white crowd. It appeared to be racist to me," remarks Stone, who went to work at a small spot called Illusion and who mightn't have been too disappointed when Bond's closed some three months later following further Internal Revenue Service action.[11] Up on West 54th Street, meanwhile, Jerry Rubin argued on the first anniversary of his Business Networking Salon night that his venture was "healthy and hardy and growing" because participants were tapping into the 1980s mantras of networking and success.[12] As syndicated columnist Bob Greene pointed out in the *Chicago Tribune*, Rubin had gone from being a Yippie to a Yuppie — or from being a member of the Youth International Party he had championed during his countercultural days to becoming a young, upwardly mobile professional.[13] Coined a couple of years earlier, the term would soon come to define a group of workers who were individualistic, entrepreneurial, materialistic, and ambitious, and who clothed their opinions with a dash of preppy style. Rubin's approach to party crowds was enough to make Steve Rubell's limited conception of "tossing a salad" look positively revolutionary.

Even Michael Brody faced an ongoing struggle to remain open as the local neighborhood association applied pressure on the King Street building's owner to close the Paradise Garage. The tension went back at least to 1981, when Brody began to receive legal letters after the roof deck opened. "Michael decided to go to one of their meetings to talk to them in person," recalls David DePino, who drove Levan to the forum, recognized the head of the association to be a friend of his father's, and introduced the head to Brody. Everything was settled after the two of them spoke in a corner, with the Garage owner willing to remove the speakers from his roof, hire a team to sweep the streets at the end of every party, and extend the venue's opening hours so that an exodus of dancers wouldn't crash into Sunday-morning worshippers each week at 9:00 AM. But the opening of a new luxury apartment block on the site of an old parking lot on the corner of King Street and Hudson Street during 1983 resulted in additional pressure being placed on the building's owner to force Brody out. "The developer and the local neighborhood association wanted the club gone, so they persuaded the landlord not to renew the lease," remembers David DePino. "Neighborhood associations are powerful. It's not something a landlord wants to have problems with." Although Brody had a lease that ran until September 1987, the Garage's destiny had been sealed.

Aware that the heating up of the real estate market made his eviction inevitable, David Mancuso began his own search for a new location in a less moneyed part of town. "I loved the space in SoHo but not the neighborhood, or at least not the way it developed, because it became too expensive," he notes of his decision to leave. "The local artist residents finally accepted us because they had to, but the SoHo artists were interested in real estate, not art. They would get together and buy a building on the cheap, and some of these people also came from real estate families, so they knew where the neighborhood was going and they developed a plan." The Loft host scoured the Lower East Side for an alternative. "Values went down and it was ripe for development," he recalls. "But the immigrant community saved the East Village from getting totally flipped over like SoHo and NoHo. A lot of people's parents and grandparents grew up there. There were churches and community centers."

Around the middle of 1982 the friend who had introduced Mancuso to 99 Prince Street told him about a small theater that had become vacant on East 3rd Street between Avenues B and C — the part of the city that locals referred to as Alphaville because of the lettered names of its avenues. Mancuso placed a $25,000 down payment on the building and began work soon after, encouraged by the announcement that the area had been earmarked to benefit from a slice of the $250 million Federal Community Development block grant money promised to New York City. Even so, the move represented something of a risk, given that the alphabetized avenues amounted to one of the most destitute areas in the city, with over a third of the local population on public assistance, school enrollment down by close to 40 percent during the previous ten years, the number of residents living in the area down 20 percent for the same period, and property values that were decreasing rapidly, thanks in part to the fact that its housing stock included 360 abandoned buildings and 310 vacant lots. The *East Village Eye* argued that the planned regeneration of the area could be threatened by Reagan's budget cuts. "It may be a long time before construction crews are actually seen on the Lower East Side," it warned. "The overall picture on the Lower East Side, particularly in the south east section, is very grim."[14]

With the Fun Gallery located on First Avenue and Pyramid on Avenue A, the *New York Times* responded to the opening of the Kenkeleba Gallery on the eastern side of Avenue B and 2nd Street with the comment that it was "ensconced in what amounts to a combat zone."[15] Patti Astor notes: "You didn't go over to the Alphabets. If you were on heroin you did, but I wasn't. You just didn't go over there." Yet Mancuso dedicated much of 1983 to his move, employing his old friend Michael Cappello — a pioneering Italian American DJ who had moved into the building trade — to lay a new floor and carry out other construction work. "People who lived in the area said that it was really bad and in some ways they were right," remembers the party host. "But the state had agreed to put money into the area and the city was backing the plan. I was totally optimistic." Aware that a proportion of his crowd would be reluctant to join him, he also held onto the belief that he could secure the longevity of his parties if he purchased his own property. "I looked on it as though these were my kids," he explains. "Maybe they wouldn't understand now but in the long term they would see the benefits."

SELECTED DISCOGRAPHY

DAVID MANCUSO, THE LOFT (1982–1983)

Affinity, "Don't Go Away"

Mike Anthony, "Why Can't We Live Together"

David Astri, "Dancing Digits (Album Version)"

Atmosfear, "What Do We Do (Club Mix)"

Black Uhuru, "Big Spliff"

Black Uhuru, "Youth"

Celestial Choir, "Stand on the Word"

Jimmy Cliff, "Roots Radical (Dub Version)"

Patrick Cowley, featuring Sylvester, "Do You Wanna Funk"

Dinosaur L, "Clean on Your Bean"

Dinosaur L, "Go Bang! #5"

"D" Train, " 'D' Train Dub"

"D" Train, "Keep On"

"D" Train, "Music"

Earl Young's Trammps, "What Happened to the Music"

Exodus, "Together Forever (Dub)"

First Choice, "Let No Man Put Asunder"

Frank Hooker & Positive People, "This Feelin'"

Girls Can't Help It, "Baby Doll"

Eddy Grant, "Electric Avenue (Special Extended Dub Mix)"

Eddy Grant, "Living on the Frontline"

Gunchback Boogie Band, "Funn (Special 12″ Instrumental)"

Gwen Guthrie, *Padlock*

Hashim, "Al Naafiysh (The Soul)"

Heaven 17, "Play to Win"

Geraldine Hunt, "Can't Fake the Feeling"

Imagination, "Burnin' Up"

Michael Jackson, "Billie Jean"

Michael Jackson, "Thriller"

Jago, "I'm Going to Go (Dub)"

Jah Wobble, Jaki Liebezeit, and Holger Czukay. "How Much Are They?"

David Joseph, "You Can't Hide (Your Love from Me)"

King Sunny Adé and His African Beats, "365 Is My Number/The Message"

Klein & M.B.O., "Dirty Talk"

Konk, "Konk Party"

George Kranz, "Din Daa Daa (Trommeltanz)"

Patti LaBelle, "The Spirit's in It"

Lace, "Can't Play Around"

Laid Back, "White Horse"

Level 42, "Starchild"

Liquid Liquid, "Cavern"

Loose Joints, "Tell You Today"

Montana Sextet, "Heavy Vibes"

Odyssey, "Inside Out"

Jeffrey Osborne, "Plane Love"

The Peech Boys, "Don't Make Me Wait"

Prince, "Irresistible Bitch"

Quando Quango, "Love Tempo"

Alexander Robotnick, "Problèmes D'Amour"

Rockers Revenge, featuring Donnie Calvin, "Walking on Sunshine '82"

Rude Movements, "Sun Palace"

Rufus & Chaka Khan, "Ain't Nobody"

Shannon, "Let the Music Play"

Steve Miller Band, "Macho City"

Strangers, "Step Out of My Dream"
Sun Palace, "Rude Movements"
Time Zone, "Wildstyle (Special New Mix)"
Torch Song, "Prepare to Energize"
Various, "X Medley"
Visual, "The Music Got Me"
Fred Wesley, "House Party"
Womack & Womack, "Baby I'm Scared of You"
Michael Wycoff, "Diamond Real"
Yazoo, "Situation"

Back on Prince Street, Mancuso enjoyed a moment of significant recognition when Gail Bruesewitz arranged for the Loft to stage a special prerelease party for Pink Floyd's new album *The Final Cut*, during which invitees could listen to the record play off a first-generation tape. "Lyric Hi-Fi donated a Studer, which is the best tape recorder, and it was modified with Mark Levinson electronics," recalls Mancuso. "It was an optimum situation." By the autumn he had also completed the next stage of his pursuit for perfect sound reproduction by removing the mixer from his system, having concluded that this was the way to go after the world-renowned Levinson said he wouldn't be prepared to build a mixer for him.[16] "The electronics that made the mix possible took away from the sound quality," the host deduced. "Without the mixer there was a three-decibel increase in the sound, which was a lot. It was like I was 97 percent of the way up the mountain and that last 3 percent made a big difference. When you're into high end you don't want to hear 97 percent of a Koetsu; you want 100 percent." The fact that the removal of the mixer meant he couldn't minimally blend records together or even use headphones to line up his next selection was of little concern. "The pause was OK," he explains. "When the life energy is working well, the fact of blending or not blending isn't significant."

In the end, most of those who followed the closure of the after-hours scene would have located it within the city's undulating campaign to control its revelers. As for gentrification, that remained a novel phenomenon that was largely restricted to SoHo, NoHo, TriBeCa, and the western end of the East Village, with Alphaville one of several neighborhoods where the arrival of a new class of city dwellers barely registered as a problem at all. As far as their core dancers were concerned, the Garage and the Loft continued to compel with an unlikely force as they attracted the widest range of dancers. "The parties would go on until six or seven [in the afternoon] but I couldn't stay until then," Afrika Islam recalls of his visits to the Loft, which he started to frequent at seven or eight in the morning when "all the vampires, zombies, and other thrill-seekers" headed over from the Garage. "That's when my parents would put out a bulletin, '*Where's my son?*' I couldn't tell them I was all the way downtown at some party that was primarily full of gay men. '*What's wrong with you?*' "

Yet it remained the case that cracks had started to appear in the Garage and Loft operations that, when connected, would threaten their viability as well as the broader downtown party scene. A transformation was afoot that would tinge the adventures of the year with ambivalence.

Bruce Forest prepared for the arrival of 1983 by revamping the Better Days sound system after the owner asked him if he wanted to pick up any equipment from Alex in Wonderland, a West Village venue fitted out with a Richard Long sound system that had recently closed. "Yeah, baby!" came the DJ's reply. With Shep Pettibone assisting, Forest proceeded to pick up four Bertha subwoofers (without the Levan Horns due to space constraints), four JBL midrange cabinets, four RLA boxes of six twelve-inch Cerwin Vega drivers, a rack of Crown amps, and twenty-four JBL bullet tweeters. A smaller number of the JBL tweeters could already be found in the previous system, designed by Alex Rosner. Little else survived. "Shep and I spent at least four nights redoing the entire system," recalls the DJ. "We powered it up and ran it for the first time on New Year's Eve. All that power in a seventy-five-foot circular room with a twenty-foot ceiling — it was fucking mind-blowing — *the sound system of death*." Forest maintains that only the Garage matched the result, and even then the difference wasn't that great. "The new system broke light bulbs in the apartment building next door, which called every night to tell us to turn it down," he recounts. "The place really took off after I became truly established there, which coincided with the new system going in."

Forest waded into the world of electronic trickery after he and Pettibone installed a second mixer (made by Yamaha) for outboard gear. To begin with, the DJ tried out a simple, two-second sampler known as Instant Reply, which he triggered via a pad. A week or so later he started to use an Emulator (a keyboard sampler released back in 1982) along with an early prototype of a small synth that had been presented to him by Casio (the future CZ101). "As my collection of gear grew, I just piled it on crates, in record bins, and on chairs, rewiring as the night went on," recalls Forest. "But in late 1983 I deci-

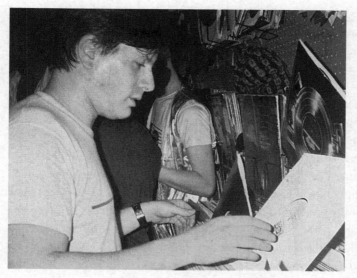

Bruce Forest, circa 1986. "It wasn't glitz," he says of Better Days.
"There were no sightseers." Photography by and courtesy of Leslie
Doyle ©.

ded I couldn't function properly with this mass of samplers, keyboards, and
jerry-rigged wiring, so I started to put all the effects gear in a rack that lived in
the DJ booth permanently." Although still rudimentary, the new equipment
enabled Forest to pioneer a form of DJ-ing that placed more emphasis on
technical cunning than anything Larry Levan along with Michael de Benedictus had attempted at the Paradise Garage. "The Emulator was slow and a
pain in the ass, but I could play prerecorded samples over music, which was
neat," recalls the DJ. "I played solo lines and chords over records, and I got a
lot of questions, like 'How you doing that?'" The 49th Street regulars danced
with a new sense of pleasure and awe.

The integration of electronic toys happened to suit Forest's evolving DJ aesthetic, for while he was never reluctant to turn to the classic disco song so
beloved by the Better Days crowd, he also began to cultivate a sound that was
much more consistently electronic and stable in its flow than anything that
could be heard at the Loft or the Paradise Garage, and much more evenly
regulated than the breakbeat aesthetic that was influential at the Funhouse and ruled at the Roxy. Drilled by Tee Scott, who kept a solid, R&B
groove while mixing every record in a way that was an anathema to Mancuso
and Levan, Better Days dancers wanted to sweat out an aerobic groove and

Forest supplied them with records that, thanks to their programmable nature, seemed as though they could go on forever. Only the DJs at the Saint conjured a smoother, more frictionless mix — yet in contrast to Forest theirs was also a sound that placed little emphasis on funk and bass. "Tee was the house DJ for a long time so when Bruce came in he fitted into what Tee was doing," recalls Better Days diehard and Rock & Soul assistant Keith Dumpson. "But Bruce also brought in his own thing, including a lot — *a lot* — of electronic music and sampling. It was robotic!"

DJ-ing at Better Days on Thursdays, Pettibone cultivated a similar post-disco R&B dance sound yet if anything was an even busier mixer than Forest. "He constantly mixes over-the records, dropping in extra hand claps . . . and effects and hardly ever seems to let a record play through," Steven Harvey observed following a visit to the club. "He is constantly teasing the discs with his finger and tapping the rims of the turntable to bring records into sync." It was enough to make Harvey wonder if, even in the context of the Bronx DJs he had witnessed, Pettibone could be "the new form's Charlie Parker, working with three Technics 1200 turntables and a Bozak mixer."[17] Yet whereas Pettibone preplanned his intricate mixes, drawing almost exclusively on familiar club hits as his source material, he wasn't so good when it came to "working off the emotion of five hundred people right in front of you," maintains Forest, who never preplanned a set, never repeated a mix from one set to another, and followed the mantra "Fuck with their heads! Make them think!" The resident DJ concludes: "Shep was flawless; I was aggressive and would try anything once."

The Paradise Garage, meanwhile, slipped into a turbo-groove. "Saturdays took off in 1980 but they only started to boom in 1983," explains David DePino. "At that point, Saturdays became even busier than Fridays, so then there was a campaign to get Fridays just as packed. It wasn't until 1983, 1984, that both nights were packed out." The special shows continued to attract dancers to the point where they began to turn up, whether or not there was live entertainment, and at that point Michael Brody stopped charging extra for those occasions. "The acts cost $1,500–2,000 each, so they actually made the club money and they also made the club more of a thing you did every week," adds DePino. "Once you come out three weeks in a row it becomes a habit. So Michael was making big bucks, *beaucoup bucks.*"

Scene-shaking shows came through one after the other. First Choice performed their monster anthems before turning it out on the floor with the rest of the crowd. Patti LaBelle appeared with her full band during the peak of a Friday night, blew the place apart, headed to Philadelphia after the sun finally rose to do a walkathon and sing at the World Series, and then returned to per-

Larry Levan DJ-ing at the Paradise Garage during a Columbia Records promotional tour for Herbie Hancock's *Future Shock*, 16 September 1983. David Mancuso stands to Levan's left. Hancock stands to Mancuso's left. Lightman Robert DeSilva stands to Hancock's left. Photographer unknown; courtesy of Gail Bruesewitz.

form at the Garage later that night "and was *even better*," recalls Jim Feldman. Konk relished the moment when Larry Levan mixed the recorded version of "Konk Party" over their live take. New Order and supporting act Quando Quango injected the venue with Manchester sounds as they appeared at King Street for the only New York date of their 1983 U.S. tour. And then there was the party that featured Liquid Liquid, when "the energy was of a different level," recalls Sal Principato. Generating their own mini-shows, celebrities from Mick Jagger to Diana Ross dropped by to witness the setup. "At 4:30 in the morning you'd see the limousines line up from one end of King Street to the other," reminisces Michael de Benedictus. "The kids who were really the heart and soul of the Garage — the street kids — were all gaga-goo-goo over who was in the booth. But Larry wasn't bothered by any of that."

Quando Quango in New York, 1983. (Left to right) Simon Topping (percussion), Mike Pickering (sax and vocals), Gonnie Rietveld (keyboards, programming, vocals). "The Paradise Garage had this fantastic sound system that moved the hair on your arm while it was perfectly possible to have a conversation without shouting," remembers Rietveld of the group's performance on King Street. "The crowd was electric!" Photograph by Kevin Cummins ©; courtesy of Gonnie Rietveld.

Loose became a Friday-night member after a Long Island friend started to head to the venue regularly during 1983. Initially dividing his time between the Loft and the Garage, and occasionally hitting both during the course of a weekend, he came to appreciate that the Loft system "was about subtlety," with Mancuso encouraging his crowd to "listen to every note — to listen to the highs, the lows, the instruments, the vocals," whereas the Garage sound "engulfed" dancers, there being "nothing except the beat." The difference encouraged Loft dancers to bring their own interpretation to each selection, while the Garage compelled its crowd to submit to the disciplinary injunction of the beat and move as part of a tribalistic organism. "At the Loft everyone would clap to different beats, even though they were all listening to the same music," he explains. "At the Garage everyone clapped at the same time to the same beat." In the end the full theatrical power of the King Street party won out, prompting Loose to coin the term "eargasm" to describe the peak moment when dancers would raise their hands in the air and jump and scream as Levan put on a song like "Ain't No Mountain High Enough" or "Clouds" or "Go Bang! #5" as he triggered a confetti cannon and worked the lights. "The intensity of the party rose to a point where you could fly," he reminisces. "Your job didn't matter, your boyfriends didn't matter, your girlfriends didn't matter. Nothing mattered but that one moment on the dance floor. Chaos was there, unity was there, the thrill of a lifetime was there. Everything hit at the same time."

First taken to King Street by Vince Aletti, whom he met when they both started to work at the newly opened Tower Records store on Lower Broadway in 1983, Barry Walters concluded that the venue surpassed the setups he'd experienced at Hurrah, the Mudd Club, and Danceteria. "The night was immersive, immediately," he remembers. "I just loved every record I heard there and at the end of his set Larry played the dub version of 'Love on Your Side' by the Thompson Twins. There's a line that says 'I've played you all my favorite records' and that was an amazing thing to hear at the end of a night." Exiting the venue to discover the day already begun, a novel experience, he went to Vinyl Mania to track down some of the music he had just heard. "Oh, I know where you went last night!" Manny Lehman told him on hearing his list. From that night on, Walters began to head more to the Garage and less to rock-dance clubs. "The energy was so intense and so contagious," he reasons. "It was so happy and blissful, and it was really for people who got off on the music. You felt in every fiber of your being that that was why you were there and I loved that."

Chi Chi Valenti also came to appreciate the power of the King Street party during 1983 when she worked behind a portable bar alongside other

Danceteria staff at the Paradise Garage Rock 'n' Roll Club night, all of them relaxed on mushrooms. "I remember watching one of the people who cleaned in there, and they took the garbage bag on this crazy, crazy night and they reverently wiped the inside of the pan so it was all shipshape in this way I'd never seen," she recalls. "It was totally not meant to be seen. It just made such a deep impression on me because you can't make people behave that way." Valenti wasn't about to give up her more sociable lair at Danceteria for the Garage, but that didn't prevent her from appreciating the fine-tuned intensity of Brody's party. "It was just so epic," she adds. "I love scenes that have their own history and their own star systems and their own references, so without being in the mood to go and do it a lot, whenever I went there I was just so impressed."

Behind such harmonious scenes, however, Levan began to test Brody's patience to the limit as his unbounded lifestyle and additional undertakings threatened to compromise his basic DJ-ing responsibilities. Often the life and soul of the party, Levan could make $4,000 a week and spend every penny of it, recalls Mel Cheren, who observes that "when Larry had money, everybody had money." At the end of a night's work, for instance, he would often head to Balducci's to buy a bag of pork chops and cook for a group of ten to fifteen friends, spending freely until he would "call Michael and ask for more money," adds Diane Strafaci, a close friend of the owner. Appreciative of his DJ's pivotal contribution to the Garage, Brody would meet such requests and would also protect him from any letters of complaint because the good so easily outweighed the not so good. "Larry was Jimi Hendrix with turntables and a mixer," reasons Mark Riley. "Hendrix didn't play at his best on many occasions but when he did play at his best there was nobody better. Larry was the same way. Some nights he would suck — I mean, he would be *terrible* — but other nights he would be fabulous. And when Larry was on top of his game there was nobody like him." Yet Levan's extracurricular commitments seemed to reach new levels of intensity during 1983, with the Peech Boys and Garage Records impinging heavily on his schedule, and by the autumn his perceived lack of attention to his turntable duties provoked Brody to seek out a temporary replacement.

SELECTED DISCOGRAPHY

LARRY LEVAN (1982–1983)

Affinity, "Don't Go Away"
Afrika Bambaataa & the Soul Sonic Force, "Planet Rock (Instrumental)"
Aurra, "Checking You Out"

Pat Benatar, "Love Is a Battlefield"

Black Uhuru, "Big Spliff"

Black Uhuru "Darkness"

Black Uhuru, "Youth"

David Bowie, "Let's Dance"

Sharon Brown, "I Specialize in Love"

Captain Rapp, "Bad Times (I Can't Stand It)"

C-Bank, "One More Shot"

Class Action, featuring Chris Wiltshire, "Weekend"

Patrick Cowley, featuring Sylvester, "Do You Wanna Funk"

Dinosaur L, "Go Bang! #5"

Ronnie Dyson, "All Over Your Face"

Eurythmics, "Sweet Dreams (Are Made of This)"

52nd Street, "Cool as Ice"

First Choice, "Let No Man Put Asunder"

Freeez, "I.O.U."

Girls Can't Help It, "Baby Doll"

Gladys Knight and the Pips, "Save the Overtime (for Me)"

Grandmaster Flash & the Furious Five, "The Message"

Grandmaster Flash & Melle Mel, "White Lines"

Eddy Grant, "Time Warp"

Gwen Guthrie, "Getting Hot"

Gwen Guthrie, "Hopscotch"

Gwen Guthrie, "It Should Have Been You"

Gwen Guthrie, "Padlock"

Gwen Guthrie, "Peanut Butter"

Gwen Guthrie, "Seventh Heaven"

Herbie Hancock, "Rockit"

Hashim, "Al Naafiysh (The Soul)"

Nona Hendryx, "Transformation"

Imagination, "Changes"

Imagination, "Just an Illusion"

Inner Life, "Moment of My Life"

Michael Jackson, "Billie Jean"

Michael Jackson, "Thriller"

Jamaica Girls, "Need Somebody New"

Grace Jones, "My Jamaican Guy"

Grace Jones, "Nipple to the Bottle"

David Joseph, "You Can't Hide (Your Love from Me)"

Chaka Khan, "Tearin' It Up"

Klein & M.B.O., "Dirty Talk"

Konk, "Konk Party"

Koto, "Japanese War Game"

Kraftwerk, "Tour de France"

George Kranz, "Din Daa Daa (Trommeltanz)"

Lace, "Can't Play Around"

Liquid Liquid, "Cavern"

Shirley Lites, "Heat You Up (Melt You Down)"

Madonna, "Everybody"

Madonna, "Holiday"

Mahogany, featuring Bernice Watkins, "Ride on the Rhythm"

Nancy Martin, "Can't Believe"

Montana Sextet, "Heavy Vibes"

New York Citi Peech Boys, "Life Is Something Special"

Stevie Nicks, "Stand Back"

NV, "It's Alright"

N.Y.C. Peech Boys, "Dance Sister (Biofeedback)"

N.Y.C. Peech Boys, "On a Journey"

Jeffrey Osborne, "Plane Love"

Man Parrish, "Hip Hop, Be Bop (Don't Stop)"

The Peech Boys, "Don't Make Me Wait"

Planet Patrol, "Play at Your Own Risk"

Q, "The Voice of Q"

Raw Silk, "Do It to the Music"

Alexander Robotnick, "Problèmes D'Amour"

Rockers Revenge, featuring Donnie Calvin, "Walking on Sunshine '82"

Rufus & Chaka Khan, "Ain't Nobody"

Shades of Love, "Keep in Touch (Body to Body)"

Shannon, "Let the Music Play"

Sinnamon, "Thanks to You"

Steve Miller Band, "Macho City"

System, "You Are in My System"

Talking Heads, "Burning Down the House"

Thompson Twins, "In the Name of Love"

Time Zone, "Wildstyle"

Visual, "The Music Got Me"

Michelle Wallace, "It's Right"

Michelle Wallace, "Jazzy Rhythm"

Womack & Womack, "Baby I'm Scared of You"
Yazoo, "Situation"
Yes, "Owner of a Lonely Heart"

Brody had called in replacements before, sometimes to cover the first couple of hours as he sent out a search party to track down Levan, sometimes to fill in for an entire night or even a weekend on the rare occasions when his DJ was out of town, with François Kevorkian, Gregory Myers, and Robert Moretti the main people the owner would turn to during 1982 and 1983 once Larry Patterson had taken on regular duties at Zanzibar. Yet there were also times when Levan's lack of punctuality, haughty attitude, and increasingly volatile manner could drive Brody to distraction, and on those occasions the owner contemplated just how difficult it would be to find a credible replacement because all of the viable candidates were tight with the resident. "Larry was always rebellious and had a way of his own, and when Michael Brody wanted to teach Larry a lesson, there were only so many people who could play at the Garage and get over," Tee Scott commented later. "If he threw just anybody in the Garage, he'd lose money. So he would ask me if I'd do something, or whatever, and I told him: the only way I'm going to play the Garage is with Larry's blessings. You can't get me to do anything behind his back. If you have a problem with Larry Levan, you have to straighten it out with Larry Levan."[18]

The tension went on and off the boil until a heated fight prompted Brody to invite Bruce Forest to play at the venue. "Larry immediately nixed it," recalls the Better Days DJ. "He was a bit paranoid and I had already taken one of his best friends' jobs, so I fully understood why he was hesitant. David Morales played instead." The Brooklyn-based Morales had started out as a graffiti artist. "I used to sneak out with stolen spray cans and Pilot markers — the ones with the really fat tip — to graffiti the trains with my tag IR159 Dave 1," Morales recounted in an interview with Walters. "My friends and I were crazy. We all slept in the day and hung out at night at my friends' houses, drinkin' beer, smokin' pot."[19] He went on to become a regular at the Prince Street Loft, where he developed an athletic dance style that integrated handstands, twists, and the splits, gravitating to the downstairs area, "where the connoisseur dancers hung out because it was brighter." Morales made his DJ-ing debut at the Ozone Layer, a Brooklyn venue where a friend was dating the owner, in 1981. "The whole idea was based on the Loft, only smaller," he recounts of the monthly affair. "There was fruit and balloons, and I spent money on the system. Disco had gone. I was playing Black Uhuru, Lamont Dozier, 'D' Train."

The invite to play at the Garage for the weekend of 16–17 October, even though Levan was in town and available, arrived after David DePino and Judy Weinstein recommended the twenty-two-year-old to the owner. "Mike Brody phoned me and said, 'Our DJ has been playing like shit lately,'" remembers Morales. "'I've heard a lot of good things about you and I'd like you to come and play at my club.'" Although his growing reputation had enabled him to give up his day job working at a midtown coffeeshop, Morales still wondered if he was the target of a hoax, so he contacted Weinstein, who confirmed that he wasn't. A Loft head at heart, he reflected on the disappointment he had felt during the handful of occasions he had partied on King Street. "I had heard so much about Larry Levan the genius and I was like, 'OK, it must be a bad night,' which is understandable, because we all have bad nights. But the second time I went I was like, 'Oh, another bad night!' And the third time I was like, 'Oh, another bad night!'" In short, he felt he could do better.

Morales ended up enduring a torrid time during his preparatory trip to King Street; Levan showed up late and gave him attitude in front of a group of friends before returning on the Friday to adjust the sound system and behave in a generally obnoxious manner, he claims. "The owner came to me and said, 'Why are the two speakers in the back not on?'" recounts Morales. "I was like, 'I don't know, I didn't touch anything.' They had to call some guy who was working at the Loft to come over and figure out what was going on." Levan's disruptive behavior was based on mistrust. "Larry felt that if David had the chance he would take his job in a heartbeat," comments Danny Krivit, who also filled in for the Garage DJ every now and again, usually when Levan wanted to dance for a few records. Having been made head of security, Joey Llanos tried to help the Ozone Layer resident adjust to the situation. "I picked out some of Larry's records for him that I knew he didn't have and I told him 'If you need anything, just call me. I just hope you enjoy it,'" he recalls. "He had a ball." By the end of the night the security team had to peel Morales off the turntables. "Mike Brody told me I reminded him of Larry when he was young," reminisces the upstart.

The Garage owner must have surely viewed the Morales invite as a cautionary warning that could pave the way for Levan's return the following weekend. Close to completing his seventh year at the venue, the resident had become inseparable from the King Street project, for while the thousands of dancers who filed into the venue every weekend were drawn to its sound system, its sprung floor, its house-party atmosphere, its extended opening hours, and its shows, Levan remained the primary draw, his DJ-ing sensibility and remix catalog effectively untouchable. Conversely, no other venue could conceivably lure Levan away from the Garage because no other entrepreneur had attempted to start a party that combined the scope of the King Street setup with the community ethos of the Loft. "Michael and Larry had a symbiotic relationship," observes DePino. "One couldn't do without the other. Michael needed Larry and Larry needed Michael. At one point Michael realized he'd created this Frankenstein monster and I think if he'd gone back he wouldn't have put all his eggs in one basket. But then Larry made the club for him."

Yet as 1983 hurtled toward its close, the optimism and creativity that had streamed through the decade's opening gave way to a period that was becoming overloaded and strained. It's unlikely that August Darnell had the Garage in mind when he wrote and recorded the Kid Creole song "There's Something Wrong in Paradise" during the year, but Brody and Levan along with DePino, Llanos, Morales, and a small group of others had witnessed a rise in discord, and it would have been strange if Levan hadn't wondered about the secondary connotation of the song when he carried out a remix of the record for Michael Zilkha—a lame affair that could have been his worst to date. If Brody's difficulties with the neighborhood association would ultimately condemn the Garage to closure, something also appeared to be shifting for Levan.

STRIPPED-DOWN
AND
SCRAMBLED SOUNDS

"In the scene now, live rock has receded," a downbeat Jon Pareles remarked in the *New York Times* back in late 1982, and for the next twelve months the supply of band music that appealed to the city's party-based DJs dried up like an overexuberant dancer, starting out strongly before flagging abruptly, dehydrated and shorn of energy.[1] In this respect as well, an epoch appeared to be drawing to a close.

The year had started promisingly when, back from touring in Europe, Liquid Liquid released the minimalistic, percussion-heavy "Cavern" and "Optimo," which crackled through the city in a manner reminiscent of "Don't Make Me Wait" and "Planet Rock." Also charging the new year, Nona Hendryx's "Keep It Confidential" and "Transformation" recounted stories of sexual transgression, with the latter played regularly at the Paradise Garage for a while. Konk contributed when Celluloid gave a domestic release to a long-jam version of "Konk Party" in April, the record having initially come out in Belgium and the United Kingdom. A month or so later, Talking Heads bounced back from an extended hiatus with *Speaking in Tongues*, which included "Burning Down the House," soon to be their first top ten hit, and "Slippery People," soon to receive an extended remix by John "Jellybean" Benitez. When David Byrne and company embarked on an extended tour that would be documented in Jonathan Demme's film *Stop Making Sense* as well as the album of the same name, DJs who liked to draw on danceable tracks recorded by local bands could comfort themselves with the thought that a small number of incandescent tracks had illuminated the period.

The summer, however, turned out to be awkwardly quiet on the live band front, and although ESG livened up the autumn with their debut album, *Come Away with ESG*, which the *New York Times* reviewed as being "as rigorously minimal as anything in SoHo and as tough as anything uptown," the release didn't stop *Dance Music Report* from bemoaning the "formularization" of

dance-oriented rock in the autumn.[2] One of the more compelling groups to
come through during 1982 and 1983, the Swans occupied the abrasive rather
than the funk end of the fading experimental rock scene. Meanwhile artists
who had recently picked up guitars and drumsticks as willingly as brushes
and canvases began to turn to rap and electronics instead. Robert Palmer
would go on to argue that "guitar-rock waged a determined counteroffen-
sive against the inroads of the synthesiser" during 1983, citing Los Angeles
rock quartet X; British guitar bands U2, Big Country, and Aztec Camera; and
R.E.M. as examples.[3] But the downtown production line slowed.

Michael Zilkha's experience encapsulated the shifting fortunes of a band
scene that began to find it harder to reproduce itself internally as well as connect with the city's DJs. The ZE boss maintains he got to make "exactly the record" he wanted when he laid down *Born to Laugh at Tornadoes* with Was (Not
Was), yet despite a strong review in *Rolling Stone*, which lauded it as the best
conceptual album of the year, the effort didn't gain traction in the city or cross
over to the consumers of mainstream rock.[4] In line with the label's irreverent
aesthetic, Caroline Loeb's "Narcissique" amounted to a bouncy punk-freak
reimagining of disco but also struggled to attract DJ attention. Meanwhile
albums by Alan Vega (*Saturn Strip*) and James Chance (*James White's Flaming Demonics*) did less well than previous efforts.

Part of Zilkha's problem could be traced back to his success with *Wise Guy/
Tropical Gangsters*, which prompted August Darnell to leave the label and release his next Kid Creole album, *Doppelganger*, with Island and Sire. "My record label was based on the faulty premise that no artist would resent me taking 50 percent, which is what it took to develop new bands," he explains. "But
once I had a hit they started viewing it as a tax rather than me as an asset. Once
Kid Creole were huge, I was bought out of my contract. It was suggested that
this was what August wanted." The departure of his most influential creative
ally amounted to too much of a blow for Zilkha to feel any strong sense of
vindication when Darnell's ensuing album sold poorly. "At that point I really
lost interest in the whole thing," he remarks of the breakup, which came to
mark the symbolic end of ZE's great, mutant reign.

As the cutting edge of sound shifted from irreverent bands
to conceptual producer-musician-DJ outfits, Arthur Baker, John Robie, and
Afrika Bambaataa consolidated their pivotal position when they teamed up
with the Soulsonic Force (as the group started to spell its name) to record
"Looking for the Perfect Beat." Robie created the track's looped melodic line

Afrika Bambaataa and Michael Holman. Photographer unknown; courtesy of Michael Holman.

with a poly-sequencer and played chords in real time on a Prophet 5. "There was a sense of discovery in 'Perfect Beat,' which is why it was so fresh," comments the keyboard player, who also coproduced the record with Baker. "It was much more ornate, much more musically intricate, than 'Planet Rock.'" Bambaataa & the Soulsonic Force injected their global philosophy in the opening lines of the rap, which ran: "Universal people/Looking for the perfect beat/Mortal motivations/Looking for the perfect beat/Mighty Zulu Nation/They have found the perfect beat/Afrika Bambaataa/I present the perfect beat." The *New York Times* described the result as "a remarkable seven-minute symphony, with electronic textures and colors, melodic themes and rhythmic signatures shifting kaleidoscopically while the momentum never lets up."[5]

For their next release, "Renegades of Funk," Baker and Robie laid down a stuttering electronic-beat track, intertwining synth lines, Afro-Latin percussive elements, and assorted samples, channeling many of the sounds through an Emulator. Afrika Bambaataa & the Soulsonic Force stepped in to contribute words of wisdom once the track was ready. "This was how it worked with Bam," comments Robie. "Everyone would do their thing and Bam would lay down chants after all the other work was completed." Released on Tommy Boy, the record received another strong review in the *Times*, where Robert Palmer noted that its sound was "much harder and more spartan" than earlier Bambaataa singles, which had "already been reduced to a formula by legions of imitators."[6] In *Billboard* Brian Chin applauded the way the record "crosses innovative rhythms" with "pancultural allusions" to Manu Dibango and others.[7] *Dance Music Report* commented that "Baker and Robie certainly are the reigning kings of this particular style of beat music."[8] When asked by the *New York Times* about his and Baker's approach to production, Robie described the process as "William Burroughs-like."[9] Robie adds that he and Baker could spend up to sixty hours working on a single mix.

Moving fast and without obvious inhibition, Robie applied his intricate, uncoiling sensibility to collaborations with Jenny Burton, Cabaret Voltaire, C-Bank, and MC Connection as well as Planet Patrol, whose eponymous debut album he coproduced with Baker. For his part, Baker released a dozen or so productions of his own, including "The Harder They Come" by Rockers Revenge, "I.O.U." by Freeez, and "Candy Girl" by New Edition, channeling profits back into Streetwise, a label he founded in 1982. "Arthur brought New Edition down to the Roxy for an audition," recalls Ruza Blue. "They were babies and they blew me away." With "Candy Girl" and "I.O.U." reaching number one and two on the U.K. pop charts, respectively, Nelson George argued it had become "hard to avoid praising" the Boston-raised producer, who not so long ago had cut an unfortunate figure as he tried to get publicity for productions that merely showed promise.[10] "Streetwise Records is the hottest indie label in black music and, considering the lack of significant indie action on the pop country charts, it may be the most successful indie in the industry right now," argued the *Billboard* reporter.[11]

Baker returned to the studio with New Order after the New York rep of Factory approached him around the time he was working with Freeez (Jim Fouratt and Ruth Polsky having already forged a vital connection with the Manchester-based label). Influenced by visits made to Danceteria, Hurrah, and the Paradise Garage during their autumn 1980 tour of the States, New Order had already integrated terse electronics into the melancholic guitar matrix of Joy Division, most notably on "Blue Monday." When the band returned to the Garage in 1983, guitarist and vocalist Bernard Summer adapted a line from "Blue Monday," singing "How does it feel/To stand in front of bastards like you" when the crowd displayed limited enthusiasm.[12] Interpersonal relations with Baker turned out to be a little awkward as well, at least to begin with, but then they got down to mixing the jittery electronic beats, strained

Arthur Baker (second left) and Freeez in Unique Studio, New York
City, ca. 1982. Photographer unknown; courtesy of Arthur Baker.

vocals, and a synthetic bass riff of "Confusion." The promotional video for
the song joined the dots as it switches between atmospheric shots of a steamy
New York City, Baker at work in the studio, a night at the Funhouse, and a live
New Order show, at the end of which the producer and musicians decamp to
the Funhouse to listen to Jellybean play Baker's fresh-off-the-lathe recording
of "Confusion." Baker maintains that he laid down "Confusion," "I.O.U.," and
"Looking for the Perfect Beat" with the Funhouse in mind.

Meanwhile Celluloid continued to build on its improbably hip inventory
when Jean Karakos persuaded Afrika Bambaataa and Bill Laswell to luxuriate
in the vast pool of their combined musical knowledge before heading into a
recording studio. The collaboration resulted in Shango's "Shango Message"
and "Zulu Groove," with Bambaataa also teaming up with Bernard Zekri to
coproduce Time Zone's "Wildstyle." Refusing to tame the latter's jittery beats,
terrorizing bass, and schizoid samples during his remix of the record, François
Kevorkian brought in Boyd Jarvis to record overdubs and Paul "Groucho" to
engineer. "It had an all-star cast of rappers on it," recalls the Frenchman. "It
was very exciting for me." Bambaataa and Islam drilled every version of the

track at the Roxy, while Mancuso selected it regularly at the Loft. It was, notes Afrika Islam, a "hybrid" record, a "real downtown New York City song."

Other tracks also suggested that, as in 1982, the rapped parts of electronic breakbeat music existed as one optional element among many. Thought up by coproducer Laswell, who had been hanging out at the Roxy and wanted to make a record that featured a DJ, Herbie Hancock's "Rockit" showcased a ferocious scratching performance by Grand Mixer D.ST in place of a regular voice, never mind rap, with Hancock providing catchy keyboard accompaniment. Written as a tribute to the rope skippers of the city, Malcolm McLaren delivered the spoken commentary on "Double Dutch" but was overpowered by the vibrancy of the record's improperly credited South African–style chanting and instrumentation. Most memorably, Shannon's "Let the Music Play" featured Brenda "Shannon" Greene deliver the guttural story of a dance-floor relationship over an instrumental track that took as its inspirational reference point the part in "Looking for the Perfect Beat" where an extended, echo-heavy electronic break cuts to intertwining synthesizer lines. "I remember playing it off reel-to-reel and thinking that it was going to be a smash," Benitez remembers of the cut, which Sergio Cossa released on Emergency. "I played it five times that night. It had a Latin thing to it. It was so perfect for the Funhouse."

Prominent at the Funhouse as well as the Loft and the Paradise Garage, and growing proportionately in the city ever since the passage of the 1965 Hart Cellar Act, which loosened up restrictions on non-European immigrants, the Latin crowd was ready to embrace a sound it could call its own. Salsoul had cultivated a Latinized disco aesthetic during its 1970s heyday, only for R&B to return to the fore in the post-backlash era. Latin lineups started to perform in downtown venues during 1982, and a consortium of concert promoters also initiated a series of "Salsa Meets Disco" concerts at Bond's. However, a chasm between Salsa players, their labels, and younger Latin listeners remained in place, with Eddie Rivera highly critical of the Latin labels' refusal to service DJs.[13] One of the artists to appear at Bond's, Ray Barretto encapsulated the generational divide when he recognized that "the growing Hispanic population is getting into disco" yet maintained the problem could only be solved when younger listeners "rediscover his or her roots."[14] Inescapable in the East Village and Bronx neighborhoods they walked, Latin elements nevertheless suffused the recordings of ESG, Konk, and Liquid Liquid, and while "Let the Music Play" wasn't fronted by a Latina vocalist, its Latin element prophesied a major sonic shift when it broke across the city during August 1983. Manny Lehman and Judy Russell even placed a notice in the window of Vinyl Mania instructing customers not to ask for the yet-to-be-released track, such was the pent-up demand.

Meanwhile Russell Simmons propped up out-and-out rap music through his tireless promotion of Kurtis Blow, Whodini, and Jimmy Spicer plus new signing Run-D.M.C., which featured three middle-class rap enthusiasts from Hollis, Queens — rappers Joseph Simmons (known as Run, the younger brother of Russell Simmons) and Darry McDaniels (one of Joseph's childhood friends, whose initials made up the second half of the group's name) plus DJ Jason William Mizell (who went under the name of Jam Master Jay). Such was the promoter's focus, Afrika Islam maintains he headed to the Roxy "to push Run-D.M.C.," not "to be part of the culture," and he moved through the Funhouse in a similar fashion. On one occasion he even tried to convince Levan of the music's value. "Larry said, 'It'll never catch on,'" remembers David DePino. "Hip hop was very new and it just wasn't Larry. I remember Russell Simmons saying rap music was going to be the future, it was going to be the biggest thing, and Larry said, 'Not here.'" Rap's emphasis on flat riffs and individualized bravado rather than crescendoing journeys and shared emotion meant that it was never going to conquer the most powerful venue in the city, yet François Kevorkian recalls that Simmons "had this energy and he would not give up. He kept pounding the pavement until he got the thing he wanted." Ultimately the promoter's main port of call remained Sal Abbatiello's South Bronx haunt. "If a rap record doesn't go around in the Fever, it's fake," he told *People*.[15]

Simmons reshaped rap music's future through Run-D.M.C. when he instructed producer Larry Smith to avoid embellishing the group's beat-box instrumentation and semishouted raps during the recording session of "It's Like That" and "Sucker M.C.'s" for Cory Robbins and Steve Plotnicki's Profile Records, in part because he wanted to cultivate a rap sound that reproduced the cut-up beats that could be heard at borough party jams, in part because he had come to dislike Baker and Robie's hyperactive sound. "Russell used to hear some of my records and he goes, 'Man, they're too nervous for me,'" confirms Baker. "'I can't get with that nervous shit.'" Featuring crunching beats, minimalistic synth stabs, and bursts of scratching, the resulting twelve-inch forged a slow groove, sparse arrangement, and aggressive rapping style that swerved away from the jittery funk of the Baker-Robie-Bambaataa axis and broke altogether with the disco-funk rhythm sections that had defined the earliest incarnation of the genre. Lyrical references to unemployment, death, hardship, competition, money, and disillusionment indicated that, at least as far as the surly Queens rappers were concerned, the party was over, at least when it came to lyrical content. Nor was there anything there "for the breakers," as Gary Jardim observed in the *Village Voice* in June.[16]

Although Simmons believed that "It's Like That" and "Sucker M.C.'s" augured an overdue break with Sugar Hill's old-school rhythm section aesthetic, that shouldn't obscure the way he had cultivated a rap career within the terms established by that camp, or the way he was still plugging records that recycled rap's founding thematic, including Kurtis Blow's "Got to Dance." Tracks such as "Planet Rock," "The Message," and a host of others had already made it clear that synthetic bass lines and drum-machine beats were displacing the rhythm sections that had created music in real-time jam sessions. Moreover, while Sugar Hill's output slowed during 1983, that had more to do with Sylvia Robinson's deteriorating relationship with Flash than her view of hard-edged electronics. Run-D.M.C.'s appearance at an outdoor "Dance Music New York" concert held at Pier 84 in August further complicated the soundscape. With thousands of music fans attending the show, which also featured Afrika Bambaataa & the Soulsonic Force, Kurtis Blow, the Crash Crew, the Fearless Four, Grandmaster Flash, and Starski, Simmons calculated that he could reach more people if he focused his marketing efforts away from the party spaces of New York. He also duly noted that the rappers rather than the DJs stole the show.

Released as the follow-up to "The Message" in mid-October, Grandmaster Flash & Melle Mel's "White Lines (Don't Do It)" opens with tingling chimes, utterances of "Fun, baby," a bass hook plundered from Liquid Liquid's "Cavern," and electronic beats, after which Mel raps out verses on the theme of cocaine culture — with the "don't do it" warning introduced belatedly for commercial motives. The record picked up heavy play at Area, the Funhouse, and the Roxy while Larry Levan tested out its rap and instrumental sides at the Garage, only for Flash to rage against Robinson's decision to reuse his name on a track that didn't feature his input. Robinson replied that the DJ would forfeit his moniker if he left Sugar Hill and proceeded to repeat her ruse on "New York, New York," a taut electronic track that Nelson George pronounced to be "even meaner and more hardcore" than "The Message."[17] When Flash sued, Robinson whipped out a reissue of "White Lines" under the artist title of Grandmaster Melle Mel, all before the year's end. "Sylvia's been feeding 'em some kind of Reaganomics trickle-down garbage about how if the label doesn't do good, they don't do good, and how if we don't stay hot, the train doesn't leave the station," Flash wrote of his failure to persuade the rest of the Furious Five to resist Mel and Robinson. "But what they don't understand is that she's eating cake and we're crumb-snatching. Fuck Reaganomics."[18]

A second conflict opened when Ed Bahlman asked Robinson to pay for her use of the Liquid Liquid bass line in "White Lines." By then a stranger had approached Sal Principato in Tompkins Square Park and asked him if he had heard the new Grandmaster Flash record — the one that sounded like Liquid Liquid. The vocalist "wasn't that impressed" when he listened to "White Lines," yet he had applauded when rap outfits versioned other records and felt enthused the night NYU undergraduate and punk affiliate Rick Rubin staged an "Uptown Meets Downtown" night featuring Liquid Liquid alongside the Treacherous Three in the spring of 1982. "I couldn't get that mad, given what a big influence Grandmaster Flash was on me," he comments. "I was partly flattered, partly flabbergasted, partly confused." In the meantime, Bahlman clocked the record's international chart success and took Sugar Hill to court, ignoring intimidation tactics that allegedly stretched to the label sending someone equipped with a machete into the label's MacDougal Street store. "They were doing all these scare tactics so Ed would drop the case," Liquid Liquid bass player Richard McGuire commented years later. "We [eventually] won the case and then Sugar Hill filed bankruptcy."[19]

Although it wouldn't reach a resolution for a couple of years, the dispute joined a list of proprietary tensions that had sprung into play when Kraftwerk's publishing company squeezed Tom Silverman for 27.5 cents per single (or six times the standard cost of covering an entire song) following the release of "Planet Rock."[20] That prompted the label head to hire an in-house lawyer to advise on intellectual property matters and proceed with caution when he launched a Tommy Boy competition that invited contestants to custom mix GLOBE & Whiz Kid's "Play That Beat Mr. D.J.," an electronic rap track released earlier in the year. "Tapes should not exceed 6 minutes in length," specified the entry blurb, published in the 29 October edition of *Dance Music Report*. "Entries will be judged on originality and technical proficiency."[21] Arthur Baker, Afrika Bambaataa, Jellybean Benitez, Brian Chin, GLOBE, Barry Mayo, Shep Pettibone, Raul Rodriguez, and Tom Silverman lined up on the dream-team panel charged with the task of awarding the winner $100, the Tommy Boy catalog, a Tommy Boy shirt, radio play on participating stations, and a Disconet release. Clearly the perils of copyright law had become too obvious for a regular release to be considered. "I was aware that the world of hip hop was intrinsically tied to sampling and expertise in this area was essential," recalls Silverman. "Tommy Boy was the first cautious navigator in the new world of derivative works. Most labels in this period were less concerned with the law than we were."

One half of the duo who took the prize, advertising creative and fanatical record collector Steve "Steinski" Stein had started to buy rap after he "straightened up like a bird dog" while listening to a radio show hosted by Debbie Harry and Chris Stein that featured records they'd heard at a South Bronx party the night before. On his next visit to Downstairs Records he tracked down a copy of Family's "Family Rap" and handed it to the woman who worked behind the store's elevated cash register. "There was this long silence and she came over the edge and said, 'This is a rap record,'" recalls Stein. "'If you don't like it you can't bring it back.'" The next day he returned to buy the store's five remaining rap records and then headed to Negril after he spotted an ad for the venue in the *Village Voice*. When Blue migrated to the Roxy, Stein eyed up the records Bambaataa placed in front of his crates. "There were things by Mardi Gras Indians like the Wild Magnolias and I knew damn well that nobody else knew what these records were," he remembers. "I was like, '*He knows about the Wild Magnolias*. Oh, shit!'"

Stein met studio engineer Doug "Double Dee" DiFranco during a work project in early 1983. They started to share sushi, listen to records, and head to the Roxy before one of DiFranco's major-label clients showed him the Tommy Boy ad. Armed with six boxes of records selected by Stein, the tape library of the studio where DiFranco worked, and equipment that included a state-of-the-art Studer eight-track tape deck, a turntable, two stereo tape machines, and a splicing tape, they started to work on their entry on a Saturday morning. Fresh memories of the Roxy along with older memories of Bill Buchanan and Dickie Goodman records that interspersed mock reportage of an alien landing in New York with clips of popular songs provided them with cut-up inspiration as they integrated quotations from Culture Club, Grandmaster Flash, Herbie Hancock, Indeep, Little Richard, Malcolm McLaren, the N.Y.C. Peech Boys, Elvis Presley, the Supremes, Rufus Thomas, and Yaz with speech extracts from Humphrey Bogart, the National Aeronautics and Space Administration, Dr. Saint, Betty White's dance instructor, and ex–New York mayor Fiorello LaGuardia, who asked the final question, "And say, children, what does it all mean?" According to Stein, he and DiFranco "just had this little party in the studio for two days."

When the judges heard the entry, the last of ten to be shortlisted, they broke into spontaneous applause. Like "The Adventures of Grandmaster Flash on the Wheels of Steel," only more so, DiFranco and Stein's mashup foregrounded a form of semiotic intelligence that far exceeded the solid groove ambitions of most dance tracks. Recorded in the spirit of the Roxy dance floor, it also embodied a form of heightened integration. Yet although the duo were fleet-ingly welcomed as stars at the 18th Street venue, their effort ultimately received its heaviest play on radio. If a tipping point existed where danceability and complexity became difficult to sustain, the victorious mix of "Play That Beat" camped right at its edge.

The hemorrhage rush of the new contributed to Ken Cayre's decision to wind down Salsoul's activity during 1983. "I got married in September 1981 and wasn't free to spend time on music like I used to," explains the label boss. "There were no more hits from the Philadelphia crowd and rap was also starting to come in, so it wasn't as much fun as it used to be. I didn't have the same desire to go forward." That didn't mean Cayre felt quite the same way about going backward, however, and having broken new ground as the first label head to release a commercial twelve-inch single as well as to employ a DJ to carry out the remix, he turned to Shep Pettibone to breathe new life into his label's catalog by carrying out an unprecedented series of remixes. The beat was set to go on and back and on.

Pettibone began with the Salsoul Orchestra's "Chicago Bus Stop" after Les-lie Doyle pointed out that parts resembled "Love Is the Message"; his effort was released as "Ooh, I Love It (Love Break)." He then went on to inject a crisp, electronic sheen into First Choice's "Doctor Love," Candido's "Jingo," and Loleatta Holloway's "Love Sensation" plus several other sets of dust-gathering tapes. Yet it was his mix of an obscure album cut, First Choice's "Let No Man Put Asunder," that made the greatest impression. "I did overdubs on it, and the drums and the bass were really in your face," notes Pettibone, who concluded his mix with a mesmeric, five-minute bass-voice-percussion break. "Nothing had anything to do with the original mix." Bruce Forest judged Pettibone to be the only figure who could rival Kevorkian "in terms of raw production" and maintains that the remix of "Let No Man" was his "big-gest record ever" at Better Days. Others were less enamored, including Tom Moulton, Salsoul's onetime leading remixer alongside Gibbons, who thought the newcomer's remake of "Doctor Love" to be particularly "horrible," and Levan, who played "Let No Man" while steering clear of Pettibone's other Sal-soul reissues. Nevertheless Pettibone's "Let No Man" mix alongside "Thanks to You" remained definitive, and Danny Krivit remembers that it soon got to the point where if a record didn't have Pettibone's stripped-down sound it would get lost. "He was the first one who was really mixing with that mental-ity," argues the Roxy DJ.

Marvin Schlachter, meanwhile, entered the new year in good spirits. Releases by "D" Train, Shep Pettibone, and Sharon Redd had prompted Carol Cooper to argue in the *Village Voice* in December that, with apologies to Motown and Tommy Boy, "Prelude just has that extra touch of class."[22] Interviewed by *Billboard* a couple of weeks later, Schlachter's label partner, Stan Hoffman, painted a picture of a label at ease with itself as he asked why it was necessary to "assign different names to what is essentially the same kind of music."[23] Prelude's seamless run seemed set to continue when Visual's "The Music Got Me" caught fire at Better Days, the Loft, and the Paradise Garage. As the twelve-inch scaled the dance chart, the *Voice* posited that Prelude had cultivated a coherent "sound" even though it had never employed a house band in the manner of Motown, Philadelphia International, Stax, Sugar Hill, or T.K. "It's perched about halfway between the old disco sound and the grittiest modern funk; it's equally at home on the street, on the dance floor, or in the penthouse," observed the author of the piece. "It is to Sugarhill's rock-hard attack what Philly International was to T.K. in the mid-'70s: a little sleeker and more ornate, it still gets the job done."[24]

The genesis of "The Music Got Me" stretched back to late 1981, when Boyd Jarvis and Timmy Regisford recorded two bedroom demos — "One Love" and "Stomp" — for their new dance show on WBLS. Lacking a drum machine, Jarvis laid down bass and melodic lines over the naked drum patterns of "Mix Your Own 'Stars,'" a DJ-only release issued by the fleetingly popular Dutch novelty act Stars on 45. A strong audience response encouraged them to take the tapes to Tee Scott, who tested "One Love" during one of his twilight appearances at Better Days. "As soon as he put it on, the crowd whooshed to the dance floor," recalls Jarvis. "We were like, 'Wow, we've got a track that people like!'" Offered the cassettes, Schlachter latched onto "Stomp." Then he handed the duo $5,000 to produce a more polished version.

Granted the freedom to play, Jarvis turned to "long jam" influences that ran from James Brown's "Sex Machine" to Herbie Hancock's "Chameleon" to South Shore Commission's "Free Man." "Just because I was playing a synth didn't mean I was thinking electronic because I always wanted to try and play a bass line like a real bass player," he notes. "I wasn't thinking Kraftwerk or Thomas Dolby or Wendy Carlos. If anything I was thinking electronic like George Duke." Above all, Jarvis thought of the Paradise Garage, because although Larry Levan could be "a crabby bastard," musically speaking "he was a bad motherfucker," while the dancing experience was so intense he would take three pairs of pants with him in the knowledge that — what with doing the splits and the rest of it — he'd probably destroy two during the course of a night. "I thought of being in the middle of that floor and being moved," he remembers of the recording process. "I thought of the people and the mood and the smells and the bodies and the sweat and coming home with cramp." Jarvis also made the record long because during the course of a night he would always think, "Play the long version — *take me out!*" "That stuff was gymnastic for us," he adds. "My shit is influenced by all kinds of things. But the Garage fulfilled my inspiration because that's where I lived, so I wanted to make a record that would be played at the Garage."

Mixed and edited by Tony Humphries — who had spent enough time loitering around Larry Patterson to land the Wednesday-night slot at Zanzibar in late 1982 — the result opens with interplaying four-on-the-floor bass kicks, racing symbols, a thick bass line, breeze effects, and echo-laden synthesizer arpeggios, its approach to composition matching the dramatic spatialization of "Don't Make Me Wait." But whereas the Peech Boys song hits full stride after a minute and a half, the Jarvis-Regisford cut shifts back to pure bass around the same point, remaining on the substratum of the musical spectrum thereafter. The first of vocalist Jason Smith's hoo-hoo-hoos arrives around 2:30, with Jarvis hitting the full jam mode around 3:30. Garage-inspired lines such as "Move . . . /Move . . . /Move . . . /Free your bo-dy" and "The music's got me movin'" follow as the track rides a primitive-electronic plain, mobilizing its rudimentary parts into a bewitching range of combinations. Released as "The Music Got Me" under the artist name of Visual in February, three months ahead of Pettibone's brighter, more playful remix of "Let No Man," the result amounted to a haunting, bass-heavy seven-and-a-half-minute workout that engaged the spiritual and the visceral, the spartan and the sophisticated. "It got major, major radio airplay in New York," remembers Jarvis. "It became this cult record."

Instead of heralding an exultant future, however, "The Music Got Me" turned out to be the last of Prelude's major contributions to the city's dance floors, in part because two of its most successful artists opted to change direction. "France Joli decided that dance music wasn't good enough for her," recalls Schlachter. "She wanted to sing rock and roll because she thought that it would give her more visibility and take her up the ladder. We battled over that and we let her go. She went to Epic and was never heard from again." "D" Train followed a similar route after the release of the moderately successful "Music" in the spring. "We had an argument," continues the Prelude boss. "There was a clause in our contract that stipulated that I had to approve of six songs on any given album and they kept submitting material to me that I didn't like. I said, 'Fine, those are your six, now find my six.' They wouldn't write the kind of music that I felt that they should be doing. Eventually they left to go to Columbia and that was the end of 'D' Train."

Schlachter also started to find it harder to balance his books in a market in which syncopated electronics and rapping were gathering momentum at the same time that white gay consumers retreated from black-identified sounds. "The club scene started to segment," he reasons. "You couldn't get the concentration you needed to land a big hit." Michael Gomes rated releases such "All I Need Is You" by Starshine, "Falling" by the Biz, "Memories" by Diva, and "Ride Like the Wind" by Taka Boom, but none achieved straightforward traction with the city's DJs. Meanwhile the label started to push a slower, sweeter R&B aesthetic while the purchase of Savoy signaled its intention to mine the gospel market. Featuring only two Prelude cuts from 1983, the September release of *Kiss 98.7 FM Mastermixes Vol. II*, a double album mixed half-and-half by Shep Pettibone and Tony Humphries, didn't paper over the cracks. "The music was changing," argues Gomes, who accepted a severance offer in the summer, just before the label relocated to New Jersey. " 'The Music Got Me' was a *huge* club record, but overall 'disco' wasn't selling, not for Prelude or the other labels."

By then Kevorkian had also parted ways with Schlachter. "I started doing all these things for other labels and Prelude was not having it," comments the mixer. "Marvin said, 'We don't want you to do all these things for other people' and I was like, 'I can't pass up the kind of money they're offering me.' " When Kevorkian announced that he wanted to break into production, Schlachter offered him that opportunity so long as he worked exclusively for Prelude. "I was like, 'No fucking way am I doing that!' " recalls the mixer. "I had all these big hits in 1982 — Dinosaur L 'Go Bang,' Yazoo, this, that. I was getting hired to do mixes for other labels and I was getting paid five or six times in one day what I would be making in a whole week at Prelude. What do you do?" Kevorkian quit at the end of 1982 and traveled to London in January 1983 when Chris Blackwell offered him the opportunity to produce an album. "I've got to be honest with you, some of the music Prelude was signing was great but some of it wasn't so exciting," adds the Frenchman.

Given free rein by Blackwell to work with whomever he wanted, Kevorkian teamed up with Jah Wobble, Can's Holger Czukay and Jaki Liebezeit, and the U2 guitarist the Edge plus studio engineer Paul "Groucho" Smykle — because the mixer of Black Uhuru's *Dub Factor* "had it worked out seventeen layers deeper than any of us who were doing dub." When Madonna asked Kevorkian to mix her new single at the beginning of 1983, he told her he couldn't spare the time because he was "so taken with this other project," which became the

François Kevorkian at Sigma Sound Studios, 1983. Photograph by Gail Bruesewitz ©; courtesy of François Kevorkian.

Snake Charmer EP, a five-track release that hovered between dubbed-out rock and spaceship dance. He maintained his purist intentions on mixes of "What Is Life?" by Black Uhuru, "Let's Start the Dance III" by Bohannon, and "The Wildstyle" by Time Zone plus Kraftwerk's *Tour de France* EP, the latter having come about after the group bought twenty to thirty records during a trip to the city. Kevorkian's name "always seemed to be on the best of them," percussionist Karl Bartos recalled later.[25]

Kevorkian also took on more obviously commercial collaborations with the Eurythmics, Midnight Oil, Robert Palmer, the Smiths, and U2 in order to support himself as a fresh-faced freelancer, and he made a point of keeping as many elements of the original as he could on these mixes. That didn't stop the Smiths from letting him know that they "truly hated" his light-touch remix of "This Charming Man." "I was not born to work with rock artists," he remarks. "I was into Hendrix and Led Zeppelin to a point, and that was it. There were lots of forgettable records in that time period." Spending more and more time in Europe, Kevorkian started to detach himself from the New York party scene, and while he still got to see a decent amount of Levan thanks to their mutual involvement with Island, their friendship became less intense. "Larry played *Tour de France* but not like he played 'Numbers,'" acknowledges the mixer.

In the end Kevorkian left a somewhat spectral imprint on the New York party scene after his contribution to "The Wildstyle" — his only notable dance-floor hit of 1983 — went uncredited.

With opportunities at Prelude and Salsoul curtailed, and West End out of favor as well as in retreat — the year was a "disaster" for the label, notes Mel Cheren — Levan carried out the bulk of his studio work for Island and various subsidiaries.[26] Primarily focused on the Peech Boys' album, the Garage DJ took time out to inject freakish dub effects, drops, and spatiality into Sly Dunbar's and Robbie Shakespeare's productions of "Hopscotch," "Padlock," and "Peanut Butter" by Gwen Guthrie, all remixed at Compass Point in Nassau. With Steven Stanley engineering, the results were released alongside additional mixes of Guthrie's "Seventh Heaven" and "Getting Hot" on an EP titled *Padlock*, the first release on Garage Records. Cementing his relationship with Blackwell, Levan also transformed David Joseph's "You Can't Hide (Your Love from Me)" for Mango, an Island subsidiary. "All the formulaic details are gone," an admiring Brian Chin declared of the remix.[27]

Released in October, the Peech Boys album *Life Is Something Special* ran at a short thirty-five minutes and contained relatively little new material. The jolty and disjoined "Dance Sister (Biofeedback)," which had come out in July, featured alongside the seven-inch versions of "Don't Make Me Wait" and "Life Is Something Special." Beyond that, the album included three more tracks of little more than passing appeal: the regimented rock of "Love Kills Pain on Contact," the middle-of-the-road ballad "Warm Summer Night," and the straight-up piano solo "Steinway & Synergy." Only the more groove-oriented if somewhat subdued "On a Journey" was likely to appeal to the group's hardcore followers. Yet Brian Chin hailed the album as "amazingly well-rounded" in *Billboard*, Jim Feldman described it as "an especially home-user-friendly club record" in the *Voice*, and Robert Palmer welcomed the way it sidestepped "the bloodless, all-electronic cliches of so much current funk" in the *Times*.[28] Michael De Benedictus certainly seemed upbeat, having made contact with the Allen Organ Company to request they build him an instrument that would look like a church organ but would combine several synthesizers. "I would be able to use my organ technique and perform funk music live," he told Palmer. "That would be like home for me."[29]

Behind the glow, however, the Peech Boys began to founder when drummer Steven Brown contracted food poisoning during the promotional tour of England. "The most successful part of the trip was the press we generated," de Benedictus recounted on his return. "Otherwise, it was a little disconcerting. The audiences reacted strangely to our guitar solos and big drum sound. They were expecting the techno-funk-drum-machine sound on the record. I was disappointed that they weren't more open."[30] On the band's return, Bernard Fowler made it clear he wanted out, in large part because he had met Herbie Hancock during the tour and the two of them had discussed a possible collaboration. To make matters worse, Blackwell concluded that the album was "disappointing for everybody." DePino believes the release still did well enough in terms of press and sales for Island to consider the option of a second deal, but Fowler's departure ruled that out. "I didn't feel it was a real group, somehow," adds Blackwell. "I sometimes thought there were too many of them doing too many drugs."

At least Garage Records remained intact, because that was the part of the Island deal that most excited Levan, points out DePino. Yet the DJ also experienced an overly complicated relationship with Sleeping Bag, the only other label he worked with regularly during 1983, even if the collaboration started out sunnily enough when Bob Blank proposed the label should re-record Phreek's "Weekend," a Garage classic that had only ever been released as a promo. Studio partners John Morales (renowned for his bootleg releases on Sunshine Sound) and Sergio Munzibai (the managing director at WBLS) mixed one side of the track, leaving Levan to add his signature to the other. Released under the name Class Action, the result generated sales of fifty thousand, but King Street regulars judged it to be inferior to the original. Levan went on to deliver two mixes of "Need Somebody New" by the Jamaica Girls, one poppy and upbeat, the other sparse and dub-inflected, yet Will Socolov maintains that the Garage DJ arrived six hours late for the session and then added $9,000 worth of edits after the record was signed off on. Worse followed when Levan showed up two and a half days late for the three-day remix of Dinosaur L's "Cornbelt," only to submit an effort Socolov deemed unworthy of release. The owner also rejected Levan's mix of "Tell You (Today)" by Loose Joints, although that effort found a home on 4th & Broadway.

Blank and Socolov believe that drugs impeded Levan's ability to complete his remix obligations. "Larry had a tremendously severe drug problem to the extent he was incapacitated a lot," maintains the engineer. "He would be flat on his back, so I would work in the style of Larry and then wake him up around five and say, 'What do you think?' Like with 'Weekend'—he wasn't there for any of that." If Garage dancers might have concluded that that explained why the record disappointed, the Sleeping Bag co-owner concluded it was close to impossible to work with the most successful remixer in the city. "Larry was like a preacher in a black church," he argues. "He knew how to whip up the parishioners until they were going crazy. But in the studio he was hit and miss. He did a lot of incredible records but he also did some pretty shitty ones. He was starting to get high and I had mixed feelings about working with him." Socolov adds: "Although I wanted Larry to play my records I didn't know if I wanted him to mix them because he was always late for sessions and he would fall asleep."

It's possible that Levan was simply exhausted. After all, no other high-profile DJ or remixer faced an equivalent schedule, and if he ended up turning out something like half the number of dance-floor smashes during 1983 as he had during the previous two years, his coproduction of *Life Is Something Special* and cofounding of Garage Records were major factors. Whatever the particulars of his Sleeping Bag efforts, de Benedictus and DePino insist that Levan's drug consumption didn't impede his work until later. "Larry always did drugs," points out DePino. "He'd smoke in the studio and he also liked to mix records while he was on acid. But drugs only really became a problem for him during 1985." De Benedictus confirms that he and Levan started to use heroin in September 1984, after which their relationship deteriorated steadily until they stopped working together around the middle of 1985. Yet 1983 amounted to a "good year" for Levan, stresses DePino, and even if his workload was "taking a toll," the DJ remained in demand and in control of his own destiny. "Larry was busy but he was young and could handle it!" he adds. "He didn't say that things had gone somewhere he didn't want them to go." Levan's end-of-year remix of Jeffrey Osborne's "Plane Love" reminded the small number of insiders who had started to cast doubt that his transformational powers remained intact.

Featuring intricate electronic beats, dexterous scratching, a synthesizer melody, and a squelchy version of the "Planet Rock" bass, all created on a Casio keyboard, Hashim's "Al Naafiysh (The Soul)" came out around the same time as the Osborne twelve and traveled across the city in a manner that reaffirmed the open, hybrid identity of the dance network. Yet while "Cavern," "Holiday," "Let the Music Play," "One More Shot," "Rockit," "White Lines," and "Wildstyle" also amounted to locally produced records that crossed scenes as if part of a connecting force, the cumulative impact of these records didn't quite reach the heights of the nomadic party hits of the previous year, among them "Don't Make Me Wait," "Everybody," "Go Bang! #5," "Hip Hop, Be Bop (Don't Stop)," "The Message," "Planet Rock," "Situation," and "Walking on Sunshine '82." Moreover, the most influential records to be played at the Funhouse and the Roxy ("Looking for the Perfect Beat" and "It's Like That") as well as Better Days, the Loft, and the Paradise Garage ("Let No Man Put Asunder" and "The Music Got Me") didn't travel with the conviction of the previous year's interparty hits. Although still operating at a high level, the movement toward integration had slipped past its peak.

Four significant subtrends had come into focus. First, the scene that fed the city's DJs with danceable music recorded by bands entered a period of relative decline, with Konk the only lineup to exit the year in better shape than it had begun it. Second, the cluster of independent labels that held street-level sway during the heyday of disco and its R&B-driven aftermath — Prelude, Salsoul, and West End — more or less stopped releasing original music that was targeted at the New York dance network. Third, the rhythm sections that had driven the R&B end of disco and post-disco dance music became an endangered phenomenon. Fourth, the rush to electronics championed by Celluloid, Profile, Sugar Hill, Streetwise, and Tommy Boy spearheaded a shift from a four-on-the-floor to a breakbeat rhythmic matrix that offset these developments yet left someone like Bruce Forest feeling shortchanged. "Shep's mix of 'Let No Man Put Asunder' was my number one record at Better Days for six months," comments the DJ, who partly compensated by completing his debut mix, an electronics-meets-disco cut by UDM titled "To Please You" that combined elements of "D" Train, Inner Life, and Sylvester. "There wasn't that much else to play."

Admittedly the ability of a record to cross over from one scene to another wasn't going to give dancers or DJs much pause for thought. Yet the underlying movement was toward an incremental segmentation that would intensify as a decade defined by economic and social division wore on. In this respect as well, the era of mutant unpredictability and aesthetic openness appeared to be giving way to something more defined and hardheaded.

WE BECAME
PART OF
THIS ENERGY

In contrast to the city's more gregarious club owners, Bruce Mailman nurtured his anonymity to the point where he was able to stand at the entrance of the Saint and overhear strangers claim to be on his guest list. Head of maintenance Steve Casko even maintains that as many as half of Mailman's employees didn't know "who the hell he was," and if that set him apart from someone like Michael Brody, who treated staff members like they were part of an extended family, the Second Avenue entrepreneur was happy to prioritize competence and professionalism above friendship and intimacy, convinced that if the Saint was to survive at the apex of the white gay dance scene it had to provide consistent excellence.[1] Every detail was subject to scrutiny, from the cleanliness of the bathrooms to the efficiency of the cloakroom service, with the owner also ready to respond to any written criticisms of his DJs. "Bruce or one of the managers would say, 'You need to come into the office when you have a chance. We have some mail we need to discuss with you,'" recalls Sharon White. "They would want you to explain what the letter writer was talking about and how true their statement was. Because it was a private club, they felt the members had a right to do that and they wanted to give you a chance to defend yourself."

The development would have been an anathema to the majority of the venue's dancers, who went out to enjoy themselves and didn't dwell on what were perceived to be the machinations of Mailman's inner circle. Yet Roy Thode's *Star Dust* letter of the previous spring revealed how even the most respected DJ could adopt a humble tone in relation to the perceived power of the floor, while Jorge La Torre recalls how Second Avenue insiders started to become more casually judgmental shortly into the venue's run. "Did they have a peak experience?" asks the charismatic dancer. "If they did, they went home happy. If they didn't, then they blamed the DJ. I am not certain people actually meant it; they were not critical enough or observant enough of why sometimes it happened and why sometimes it didn't. But I heard it from everybody. It was just the thing to say."

As it happens the A-list crowd had already started to pressurize DJs at Flamingo. "When you had a good night, you really knew it, and if you had a bad night, by Sunday morning my phone would be ringing from the critics," recalls Howard Merritt. "Most of the time I'd say I knew when I had a bad night but there'd be those who would let you know." However, whereas a less-than-stellar performance at Flamingo might have generated a few comments from "the family," an equivalent showing at the Saint would result in "key people — friends of the owners — the first fifty members" lodging a complaint. "If the drug didn't hit them right, or they didn't get laid, or their friend stood them up, it was the disc jockey's fault," continues Merritt. "I thought that was sort of sad because I'm a firm believer that if I go out on a Saturday night I'm in charge of my own good time." Although the DJ appreciated the standing ovations he received, the lows came to outweigh the highs. "I was so on edge," he explains. "The dance floor was a circle. The DJ booth was 12 o'clock, and I knew the people at 3, 6, and 9 o'clock, and if I didn't see those groups of people, I knew that I would get a bad review."

Sticking with the competitive logic that had enabled him to lure the A-list crowd from Flamingo, Mailman tended to side with the perceived will of the dance floor whenever tensions escalated. George Cadenas became one of the first to experience the axe when he played "White Rabbit" by the Great Society with Grace Slick at the peak of a night to calamitous effect. "He planned so much around the song and he worked with the lightman on it," remembers Merritt. "But the place fell apart and that was the end of him." Called in to account for some of her own performances, White pointed out that the letter-writing dancers formed the tiniest of minorities. "I did explain to Bruce, 'This customer complaint is one person out of *how many?*'" she recalls. "'And how much is it to do with me, or did I just happen to be the person who was playing when they felt shit?'" White wrote to her detractors to suggest they drop their "shit at the door" and would normally receive a letter of apology. As long as the Saint came out "smelling like a rose," Mailman would back the DJ, she adds.

White's perfume ran dry sometime between the winter of 1982 and the early spring of 1983. "Bruce just didn't feel that I was doing my best," she remembers. "I don't know whether it was because I was playing what I wanted to play, or whether he thought I was lazy. He just fired me." Already annoyed that Mailman would ask her to account for her work even though he never stayed for the duration of a night, she accepted the decision without argu-

Flyer for a "Land of Make Believe Party" at the Saint, 2 April 1983.
Courtesy of the Saint at Large.

ment. "The responsibility got to be too large for the reward, so I was more than willing to say, 'Whatever.'" White went on to take solace from the moment Wayne Scott ended a set by playing Gene Pitney's "Town without Pity." "He was saying, this is like a little town with a mayor and a sheriff, and there are criminals and the good guys," she explains. "It's a town without pity because if you don't fit the mold, you're just gone." Every rule "went out of the window" for Larry Levan at the Paradise Garage, she adds, but if a Saint DJ "pulled a stunt like not coming in at the beginning of the night or being on the floor when the record ran out" they "wouldn't have a job." And now she didn't have a job.

When Mailman introduced a requirement that his DJs prepare a playlist in advance of a Saturday night shortly after her departure, White looked on aghast, convinced that the "people upstairs" were exerting too much control on those who were "supposed to be creative." Merritt, meanwhile, began to plan his exit. "I always had that one record I held back, just in case I needed it," he remembers. "But when the playlist thing happened, I said to myself, 'It was great playing for you, people, but I'm out of here!' This is when I knew this place was not for me. All of a sudden it was about product and it wasn't fun anymore." An exit strategy presented itself when the owners of the Copa, a huge venue located in the gay holiday destination of Key West in Florida, traveled to the Pines that summer and invited Merritt to work as their new resident. Having concluded that the Saint lacked the "family feel" of Flamingo and that its managers "really weren't that nice," Merritt accepted, only for Mailman to approach him at the Pavilion at the end of the season and ask him if he was glad it was over. "No, I'm not happy, and as for the Saint, you can shove it up your ass!" replied the DJ. "You have destroyed so many nice people."

Booked to play a set number of nights at the venue per month in return for a "handsome salary" plus a commitment that he wouldn't DJ elsewhere without Mailman's permission, Robbie Leslie became the most accessible face of the Saint. The May issue of *Star Dust* included an interview with the DJ, whose neatly parted hair and handsome features radiated from the front cover.[2] Working alongside Mark Ackerman, he then played the final party of the 1982–1983 season. "Leslie is arguably New York's premier club disc jockey," proclaimed Jan Carl Park in the *New York Native*. "He is, at any rate, the most popular of the Saint's several disc jockeys — from my post as the disco's part-time cashier I see the crowds, I hear the roar from the dance floor, and when I get off at 6 AM the floor looks like it does on other nights at 3 or 4 AM."[3] Initially concerned the playlist policy would impinge on his creativity and add to his workload, Leslie soon came to believe it encouraged him to be more versatile. "When you're performing on the fly you tend to be a little bit safer and grab the records that are surefire, but when you program in advance you're more likely to insert newer records and try different styles and different artists," he reasons. "Bruce believed that the concept of preprogramming encouraged us to expand our musical palette and play more progressive sets." Leslie adds that neither he nor anybody else ever "played a playlist from beginning to end."

SELECTED DISCOGRAPHY

ROBBIE LESLIE, THE SAINT (1983)

ABBA, *The Visitors*
Azul y Negro, "The Night (La Noche)"
Baiser, "Summer Breeze"
Big Ben Tribe, "Heroes"
Blancmange, "That's Love, That It Is"
Laura Branigan, "Solitaire"
Julius Brown, "Party"
Miquel Brown, "So Many Men, So Little Time"
Irene Cara, "Hot Lunch Jam"
Cerrone, "Trippin' on the Moon"
China Crisis, "Wishful Thinking"
China Crisis, "Working with Fire and Steel"
Sarah Dash, "Lucky Tonight"
F. R. David, "Pick Up the Phone"
Hazell Dean, "Searchin' (Special Remix)"
Eurythmics, "Sweet Dreams (Are Made of This)"
Frankie Goes to Hollywood, "Relax"
Gloria Gaynor, "I Am What I Am"
Gazebo, "I Like Chopin"
Gazebo, "Love in Your Eyes"
Jock Hattle, "Crazy Family"
India, "Stay with Me"
Lama, "Love on the Rocks"
Amanda Lear, "Love Your Body"
Limahl, "Only for Love"
Lime, "Angel Eyes"

Lime, "Come and Get Your Love"

Lotus Eaters, "You Don't Need Someone New"

Nancy Martinez, "So Excited"

Nancy Martinez, "Take It Slowly"

Menage, "Memory"

Men without Hats, "I Got the Message"

Oh Romeo, "These Memories"

The Pointer Sisters, "Automatic"

The Pointer Sisters, "Jump (For My Love)"

Stefano Pulga, "Love Taker"

Marsha Raven, "Catch Me (I'm Falling in Love)"

Chris Rea, "I Can Hear Your Heartbeat"

Sharon Redd, "In the Name of Love"

Jimmy Ruffin, "Hold on to My Love"

Marlena Shaw, "Touch Me in the Morning"

Sleeping Lions, "Sound of My Heart"

Spandau Ballet, "True"

Donna Summer, "She Works Hard for the Money"

Sylvester, "Band of Gold"

Sylvester, "Don't Stop"

Taco, "Puttin' on the Ritz"

Technique, "Can We Try Again"

Thompson Twins, "Hold Me Now"

Womack & Womack, "Baby I'm Scared of You"

The most obvious beneficiary of the semi-vacuum created by White's sacking and Merritt's resignation, Baltimore DJ Chuck Parsons played the "Black Party: Rites IV," Memorial Day weekend, Halloween, New Year's Eve, and numerous Saturday-night parties during 1983. In other developments, Shaun Buchanan and Warren Gluck also came to the fore, Michael Fierman clocked up several Sunday Tea appearances, Wayne Scott started to largely play down sets and tea parties, and Terry Sherman made his debut. "Shaun sprang upon the scene as an almost instant success and crowd favorite," recalls Marsha Stern. "It seemed that the membership loved Shaun as much as it could ever love a DJ." Even though he was "never a favorite with the crowd," however, Parsons played most of the special parties because Mailman was "very progressive about dance music" and "loved" his selections as well as the fact that "he was a brilliant technician and almost never had a bad mix," argues Sher-

Shaun Buchanan, ca. 1984. Photograph by and courtesy
of Leslie Doyle ©.

man. For his part, Sherman notes that he received work because he "was not
afraid to play 'unusual things,' even though some of the crowd might not like
them," including funkier numbers such as Gwen Guthrie's "Padlock," Chaka
Khan's "Clouds," Teena Marie's "Square Biz," and Grandmaster Flash & Melle
Mel's "White Lines."

As the roster chopped and changed, the African American component that
had been so integral to the white gay dance scene during the 1970s became
harder to hear. As Stern observes, Jim Burgess, Alan Dodd, Howard Merritt, and Robbie Leslie were all known for being more "white-sounding" than
Richie Rivera and Roy Thode, yet all of them "played a lot more R&B than
some of the newer DJs." Buchanan and Parsons pioneered the playing of hard,
ultra-fast dance tracks that were rock rather than disco-tinged, including Devo's "That's Good," Billy Idol's "White Wedding," Olivia Newton-John's "Twist
of Fate," Rational Youth's "City of Night," and Van Halen's "Jump." A heavily
electronic, rhythmically monosyllabic, harmonically adventurous, high-
tempo aesthetic also took hold through popular selections such as Azul y Negro's "The Night (La Noche)," Blancmange's "That's Love, That It Is," Miquel

Brown's "So Many Men, So Little Time," China Crisis's "Wishful Thinking" and "Working with Fire and Steel," Lime's "Come and Get Your Love," Lotus Eaters' "You Don't Need Someone New," Menage's "Memory," Chris Rea's "I Can Hear Your Heartbeat," Technique's "Can We Try Again," and the Thompson Twins' "Hold Me Now." Music that seemed to have little in common with the tradition of African American music was taking hold in a venue where the membership was overwhelmingly white.

The rupture hardened during 1983 as the Saint DJs felt increasingly compelled to draw on sounds that could be mixed into an arc of seamless intensification. "We resisted the format change in the New York market," reasons Leslie. "The boys liked their R&B but preferred it to be more soulful and Philly-influenced. With the exception of just a few isolated tracks, the new sound just wasn't 'pretty' enough for them. It was too 'raw' and stripped down." The taste shift resulted in Saint DJs receiving fewer and fewer offers to play in other venues. "Gay music is a very specialized sound, and once you become fluent with it you lose contact with all the other things that are going on musically," a regretful Leslie told the *New York Native*. "You tend to get a little too narrow. That is the benefit of playing at a black club or a straight club: broadening yourself."[4]

But breadth wasn't of particular concern to the Saint crowd, and it was through distillation rather than expansion that the venue's dancers reached a new level of immersive experience as the year ran its course. It got to the point where the DJs "would drag the same beat for what seemed like a very long time, just to maintain that feeling, that peak experience, for as long as possible," recalls La Torre. Michael Fierman confirms that when he took his turn he would maintain a steady energy, punctuating his selections with additional "anthems" that generated "evanescent convergences," with "unification of the room" his "main goal."[5] Individual moves gave way to a more constricted style of dancing as dancers sought transcendence through regimented collectivity. "The Saint seemed almost synchronized," observes La Torre. "If someone was doing a certain move, the others would start to follow. The goal was the moment of unity, the moment when time and space disappeared. When we got there this pure energy, this friendly force, made itself available. It was extremely welcoming and extremely powerful. Within it everything seemed possible. It was what we aimed for every time we went to the Saint." A qualitative change in the history of the dance floor had come to pass. "People really lost themselves more at the Saint than they did at 12 West and Flamingo," confirms Leslie. "It was more divorced from reality."

Robie Leslie at the Underground, 1981. By 1983 DJs such as Leslie were receiving fewer offers to play outside of the white gay scene. Photographer unknown; courtesy of Robbie Leslie.

Evolving cultural codes helped establish the Second Avenue venue as a space where dancers executed circumscribed, micro-organic movements. The Anglo-Saxon, Protestant upbringing of the majority of the dancers prepared them for a ritual that emphasized obedience, control, and self-discipline — or what critic Walter Hughes calls the "empire of the beat."[6] A reaction against the feminization of early gay male identity, the growing sway of macho culture further encouraged participants to rein in the way they used their bodies. Those who dedicated hours to gym work in order to build deific upper-body muscles lost flexibility and mobility, which in turn encouraged more modest movements. If clone culture had become "*the* look for the postcloset urban denizen of the gay ghetto" by the end of the 1970s, as participant-observer Martin P. Levine notes in *Gay Macho*, the Saint became the epicenter for its relentless reproduction during the early 1980s.[7] "To express themselves in dance would have been considered flamboyant," points out La Torre. "It would have attracted attention and they just wanted to blend in. The crowd at the Saint were really self-conscious of themselves and their bodies. They were conformist at heart."

The physical design of the Saint fostered the shift into mutual anonymity. With no right angles available on the circular floor or the surrounding walls, revelers entered into a destabilizing environment, especially on opening night, when the floor was painted black to enhance the experience of bottomless isolation, only for dancers to complain that they felt giddy because they couldn't see anything below their feet. "People couldn't tell if they were up, down, or sideways," recalls Leslie. "The management had to immediately sand the floor down and varnish it." The alteration modified rather than eradicated the sense of disorientation. "I couldn't find where the walls were and I was very disoriented," Man Parrish remembers. "There was the light tree in the center, there were banquets around the outside, and I was like, 'Where's the sound coming from?' The whole thing fucked your mind until you got your bearings." The shifting patterns generated by the planetarium bolstered the impression of journeying into a utopian plane of outer-body being. "The lighting works heavily on the subconscious and has a rather subliminal effect on people while they are dancing," Mark Ackerman explained to *Star Dust*. "Some people on the dance floor claim they don't really notice the lighting. But they do. Sometimes they even claim they see things that aren't even happening or may not even be there."[8]

Prevalent within the wider private party scene, where alcohol consumption was minimal and parties stretched way beyond regular opening hours, drugs were consumed with particular relish at the Saint, with combinations of amyl nitrite, cocaine, ethyl chloride, and MDA popular. "Drugs were a major part of the dance experience back in the 1980s," notes Leslie. "There was a segment of the crowd who would dance 'unenhanced' but they were certainly a minority." Starting the night at home alone, La Torre would smoke half a joint made up with phencyclidine, or PCP, commonly referred to as angel dust, a drug that can result in a lack of balance, slurring, and a loss of ego, before heading to the Saint, where he'd take some more PCP on his arrival. "I'd have peak experiences at home but they were of a different nature to the ones at the Saint," he reminisces. "My mind traveled in a different way when I did it by myself at home." The dancer took dust because it best enabled him to enter a sensorial vortex. "Most people would probably see it as an addiction but I didn't see it that way," he adds. "I worked all week and only did it to go out dancing. It was a tool, a means to get me to that place where we entered this void and became part of this energy."

Heading to the Paradise Garage on a Saturday night once every two months or so with a group of close Puerto Rican friends, La Torre surveilled the contrasting dynamic of the two floors. "There was a real physicality to the dance, where you moved all of your limbs," he recalls of Brody's spot. "Everyone was in self-expression mode." Although he maintained the same drug intake, La Torre remained "totally aware" of everyone who danced around him at the Garage, whereas at the Saint "everything disappeared." The fact that Larry Levan selected a higher proportion of vocal records than his Saint counterparts contributed to the contrast, as did the King Street crowd's more obsessive focus on their DJ. "We didn't want to miss any of his work, any of his moves, any of his talent," continues La Torre. "He could be very subtle at times and very in-your-face at other times. His personal mood on a particular night could determine what the night was going to be like. At the Saint it was completely different." Of the white Garage regulars who tried out the Saint, Jim Feldman acknowledges that Mailman's venue was "very high-tech and exciting" yet maintains that the dancing "revolved around white boys showing off pecs." Introduced to the venue a short while after the Garage, Barry Walters remembers the mixes being much smoother than he was used to and the variations between the records being "almost infinitesimal."

There was, however, no demand for the Saint to journey down the mutant path taken by so many other New York venues. Its purpose was to provide a route to collective bliss for a homogeneous group of dancers, and it pursued its utopian if circumscribed mission through its tailored combination of music, architecture, and lighting. "I remember entering the dance floor for the first time and noting that there was this pectoral fascism going on," recollects actor and Broadway assistant Brent Nicholson Earle, who first headed to the venue in the spring of 1981. "But the overriding thing was this feeling of being welcomed and absorbed into the tribe." Previously a 12 West regular, Earle's jaw stayed agape for something like three hours that night. "It was, 'Oh my god, all my dreams have come true,'" he adds. "I'd only fantasized about this sense of freedom and theatricality, and it had become real and it was ours. It was absolutely transcendent. That night I said to myself, 'I have to be part of this.' I became obsessed."

Earle joined some three thousand others in the attempt to become one. As La Torre observes, "At times it felt like we were levitating."

SEX AND DYING

Intercourse and oral sex rarely took place in New York clubs during the 1970s, and if dance floors brimmed with the frisson of sexual energy, few left the floor early in pursuit of the act itself. Admittedly the gap that separated desire and sex diminished when Michael Fesco introduced leather and fetish acts into his annual black parties at Flamingo. But whereas these thematic elaborations were suggestive — at one Black Party Fesco employed a carpenter to build a series of jail cells and then had performers act out a sin — Bruce Mailman arranged for what he termed "sex-associated" acts to take place during his own version of the event, with the snake that entered a man's anus perhaps the most extreme.[1] "Believe it or not, most members do not like to be grossed out," complained one member in *Star Dust* in September 1982.[2] However, another declared that the party was "one of the hottest" he had attended anywhere.[3] A third objected only to the person he heard complain. "Who do these guys think they're fooling?" he asked. "I thought the Black Party was supposed to be about sex and reflective of our current sexual lifestyles."[4]

Saint dancers also broke with the end-of-night-only protocol when they began to head to the balcony area that overlooked the dance floor early into the venue's run. "It was expensive to go to the Saint, but if someone wanted to suck my dick they would take me along, which was socially acceptable in those days," recalls Man Parrish. "You could go up to the balcony and fuck and have sex. I remember tongue-kissing somebody who had MDA on their tongue. I walked home tripping my brains out." Thousands of others enjoyed the opportunity. "I was no different from the other guys," notes Brent Nicholson Earle, who was in a committed, open relationship at the time. "I went up to the balcony — up to heaven — and did things I probably shouldn't have been doing." Others approached the balcony in a more circumspect manner or not at all. "It bothered me that the balcony took something away from the dance floor," remarks Jorge La Torre. "I personally left it for the end of the night. I would never consider sex until I was satisfied on the dance floor. But I thought it was a valid form of self-expression and I wanted it to be available."

The balcony action became politically explosive shortly after medics announced that AIDS was in all likelihood caused by a virus that spread through bodily secretions such as blood and semen and that while the diseases associated with AIDS had the potential to be treated, the underlying collapse of the immune system seemed to be irreversible. "Medical detectives are calling it the century's most virulent epidemic," reported the *New York Times* in February. "It is as relentless as leukemia, as contagious as hepatitis, and its cause has eluded researchers for more than two years." The *Times* added that despite the efforts of hundreds of investigators and a fresh funding grant of $2 million, scientists appeared to be forever trailing the disease. "That makes us very, very concerned," a doctor at the Centers for Disease Control commented. "The disease could be anywhere now."[5]

Horrified by the intensification of the crisis and the lack of a proportionate response, Larry Kramer published an incendiary article titled "1,112 and Counting" in the *New York Native* in March. "If this article doesn't scare the shit out of you, we're in real trouble," he wrote. "If this article doesn't rouse you to anger, fury, rage, and action, gay men may have no future on this earth. Our continued existence depends on just how angry you can get." Kramer listed a series of alarming figures. There were 1,112 cases of AIDS. Between 13 January and 9 February there were 164 new cases and 73 new deaths. The number of people who had died from the disease totaled 418. And almost 50 percent of AIDS cases were from the New York metropolitan area. Kramer tore into local and national politicians, health care organizations, and media outlets before he turned his wrath on the hedonistic gay men he had already lambasted in *Faggots*. "I am sick of guys who moan that giving up careless sex until this blows over is worse than death," he declared. "How can they value life so little and cocks and asses so much? Come with me, guys, while I visit a few of our friends in Intensive Care at NYU. Notice the looks in their eyes, guys. They'd give up sex forever if you could promise them life."[6]

Although history would demonstrate Kramer to be correct in many ways, the perceived moralism of his tone weakened the impact of his message. The Gay Men's Health Crisis (GMHC) even decided he shouldn't be included as one of two representatives it was about to send to attend a meeting between the New York AIDS Network and Ed Koch — a development that prompted Kramer to resign from the organization. At the subsequent 20 April meeting Koch agreed to declare a "state of concern" during the week of a GMHC candlelight march and fundraising performance of the Ringling Bros. and Barnum & Bailey Circus at Madison Square Garden. But although Koch agreed to other requests, he refused any that would have required him to spend money, and that left Paul Popham concerned that he "did not seem vaguely concerned about the epidemic," notes Randy Shilts in *And the Band Played On*. The resignation of Kramer left the GMHC to pursue a "timid policy of constructive engagement with a mayor who seemed petrified of being highly identified with any gay issue, perhaps because of his status as a perennial bachelor," adds Shilts.[7]

Held on Saturday 30 April, right after the circus benefit at Madison Square Garden, the Saint held a fundraising event that featured Robbie Leslie, Mark Ackerman, and a live show by Nona Hendryx. Mailman relaxed his normal guest policy for the event in order to raise as much money as possible and also agreed to forward proceeds from a cash bar for the following night's "Tea Party."[8] "The Saint did step up with the 'Circus Party' and it left a big impression in New York," argues Tim Smith, a Saint member and GMHC volunteer. "There was some criticism at the time that the club could have done more, but it was not singled out and it was as involved as any other entertainment organization. There wasn't much of a tradition in those days of clubs hosting fundraisers. Philanthropy in the gay community for the gay community was a novel thing as well."

AIDS also made its indiscriminate advance through the part of the East Village scene that lived locally rather than in the West Village (as was the case with most Saint members). "I've had too many beloved friends die lately from diseases contracted when the immune system breaks down," wrote Cookie Mueller in her "Ask Dr. Mueller" health advice column in the April edition of the *East Village Eye*. "I'm tired of going to wakes. I miss these people." Everybody believed the CIA and the American Medical Association were "creating strange diseases to eliminate certain segments of society" — queers, voodooists, drug users, and hemophiliacs — claimed Mueller, who advised readers diagnosed with AIDS to seek the advice of a nutritionist, a homeopath, or a kinesthesiologist rather than a doctor. The approach had worked for three of her friends, who were now "virtually cured," she claimed, before adding: "So there is some hope."[9] If the advice turned out to be naive, the mainstream medical profession had nothing better to offer at the time.

The same issue of the *East Village Eye* carried information about a Danceteria benefit to be held "for ailing Klaus Nomi" on 21 April, with David McDermott and John Sex among the performers.[10] "We had to put masks and rubber gloves on when we went to see him," remembers Man Parrish of the visits he made to his friend. "We were very freaked out. We thought there was an airborne virus." A regular visitor to a public health clinic, Parrish suspected that a vaccine against gonorrhea might have been the cause of Nomi's illness. "I had to have this vaccine and they told me that if I refused the social worker would come and get me," he remembers. "I walked up Ninth Avenue and had this really bad feeling about it and never showed up. I lived in a loft with no bell, so calculated I would be able to avoid anyone who came calling." Parrish was relieved to have evaded the treatment. "Everyone had gonorrhea — it was a fuck fest — and there was a huge, huge push for this vaccine in the gay community. Whether the vaccine weakened your immune system or helped you get the virus quicker, I don't know, but everyone I knew who had this vaccine died. Klaus was one of the guys who got that vaccine." One of the first public figures to succumb to the virus, Nomi passed away on 6 August 1983.

Patti Astor and Bill Stelling came knowingly face-to-face with the killer virus for the first time when a young Lebanese critic, Nicolas Mouffaregge, became sick. One of those who would drop by the Fun Gallery for coffee every morning, Mouffaregge also created hand-embroidered versions of master-works of such exquisite quality the gallerists offered him a show in the spring, only for the artist to fall ill during planning. Astor and Stelling took Mouffaregge regular batches of chicken soup bought from the Second Avenue Deli, but before long he couldn't get out of bed. He ended up going to a hospital in Queens and was placed in a room festooned with bright "Infected" signs. "It was obvious no nurse had been near him for some time," Astor recalls of her and Stelling's first visit. "Bill delicately suggested I withdraw while he assisted Nicolas to re-lieve himself and clean his poor sick body." Mouffaregge's opening took place as planned. His memorial followed right after. "No one, no matter how celebrated, could stop the unforeseen cataclysm that was to come," notes Astor.[11]

That spring, experts informed the Senate Investigations Committee that AIDS appeared to have reached epidemic proportions. It now amounted, they added, to "one of the most threatening public health problems in modern times," with the number of cases doubling every six months.[12] A congressio-nal committee went on to reject activist claims that the government's response to the crisis was slow, but Ronald Reagan had already described gay sexuality as an abomination during the 1980 election campaign and did nothing to qualify that position. The Republican administration had also championed a traditional agenda around sexuality that saw it propose cuts to child and family support, attempt to limit a woman's right to choose to have an abor-tion, and block the passage of the Equal Rights Amendment (which proposed to guarantee equal rights for women in the U.S. Constitution). Perhaps mindful

Klaus Nomi performing at Xenon, 1980. Photograph by and courtesy of Allan Tannenbaum/SoHo Blues ©.

of the 58 percent of U.S. citizens who rejected homosexuality as an acceptable lifestyle in a *Newsweek* poll, the president declined to make a public statement on the disease and in so doing created an enormous credibility gap that reeked of homophobic opportunism.[13] Moral majoritarians polarized the issue further by using the disease to intensify their attack on gay culture. "The sexual revolution has begun to devour its children," conservative columnist Pat Buchanan wrote in the *New York Post* in May. "The poor homosexuals. They have declared war upon nature, and now nature is exacting an awful retribution."[14]

The Saint became a battleground where those concerned with the escalating crisis clashed with those determined to protect the rights of gay men to sexual freedom. When a member wrote a letter to the management asserting that another member who was sick with AIDS was "using the facilities," Mailman confronted the concern head-on in the May edition of *Star Dust*. "We designed the balcony as a viewing platform," he replied. "We cannot brighten the lights because it would destroy the dome lighting, and we will not be put in the position of policemen. If the balcony disturbs you, DO NOT GO THERE, but do not name those who do. This is FASCISM, and we will close The Saint before we tolerate it."[15] The owner argued that pointing fingers and judging other people's behavior "is almost worse than the disease itself," and he added that "it is only by maintaining a community that we can all live."[16]

June brought a mixture of good news as well as overly optimistic news. The good arrived when the New York State Senate passed a bill to provide $5.25 million to expand laboratory facilities, intensify research, boost hospital care, increase educational programs, and monitor blood supplies. "We must not permit AIDS sufferers and their families to be subjected to irrational and unscientific behavior born out of fear rather than fact," commented Governor Mario Cuomo.[17] The overly optimistic followed when the New York City Health Commissioner claimed that the number of cases of AIDS had started to increase at a slower rate in the city, to the point where it "appears pretty much to have leveled off and reached a plateau." Even the head of the AIDS task force at the National Centers for Disease Control in Atlanta predicted that "the number of cases will continue to increase gradually, but more slowly and accompanied by a leveling off."[18] Nobody forecast that the number of people dying from AIDS would rise from 1,508 a year in 1983 to a peak of 49,897 during 1995.[19]

The disease made its first conspicuous incursion into the Paradise Garage when a manager, Emilio, his surname unknown to friends at the venue, passed away. "It was a secret for a while," remembers Judy Russell. "Nobody wanted to face the truth or to scare anyone. It was a weird time. We ended up losing at least five staff members to the disease." Yet the Saint lost far more dancers and it was during 1983 that the trend became more noticeable. "People weren't freaking out about AIDS when Roy Thode passed away, but during the 1982–1983 and 1983–1984 seasons people started to get sick at an alarming rate," observes Marsha Stern. "Nobody understood the cause of the disease. Everyone stopped doing poppers because they thought that that must have been the cause. Who knew?" Terry Sherman confirms that AIDS didn't appear to have a significant impact on the venue until 1983, when the dance floor wasn't quite as packed as before. "Lots of people died, a lot were sick, and a lot of the friends of the members who had died or were sick stopped coming because it was too painful to go to a place with so many memories of the fun times they had enjoyed with their friends and lovers," he comments.

The spread of the disease was enough to prompt a partial shift in behavior. "I would still wander up to the balcony area during the night, but I wouldn't go all the way to the point of having sex without a condom," explains Earle. "I wouldn't go past oral sex." Yet Barry Walters found it "a little scary" when he discovered that guys were still enjoying casual sex on the balcony, and he positively "hated" Miquel Brown's "So Many Men, So Little Time," a June release cowritten and produced by the U.K. DJ and Saint frequenter Ian Levine that became the venue's biggest hit of the year. Any doubt about the song's meaning was dispelled by the accompanying video, which featured the vocalist moving through a steamy gym populated by muscular, seminaked, gyrating men sporting the clone look so popular at the Second Avenue party. "It felt like an unintentional commentary on gay men's predicament at the time," comments Walters. "This was before we knew what safe sex was; we just knew that many of the people who were the most promiscuous were among the first to die, and the willful denial in that record terrified me."

Many, of course, were concerned, among them author Edmund White, who packed his suitcases and migrated to Paris because he wanted to go on having "industrial quantities of sex" and believed it would only be possible on the Continent.[20] Earlier he and coauthor Charles Silverstein had considered revising their book *The Joy of Gay Sex* to include information about AIDS but hesitated because "no one knew how to frame that cautionary advice."[21] By 1983 the atmosphere had shifted in the New York gay community. "A feeling of dread was now in every embrace," he recalls. "Whereas in the late 1970s everyone wanted to be bisexual, the height of trendiness, now people were starting to deny they'd ever had experiences with members of the same sex. People who'd been fashionably skinny the year before now were beefing up to prove they weren't besieged by a wasting disease."[22]

Because AIDS accentuated the way many gay men experienced time as fragmented, ephemeral, and urgent, as Judith Halberstam notes, many remained committed to the dance floor as a space of expression and community.[23] With participants often compelled to conceal their sexuality in everyday life, venues such as Better Days, the Paradise Garage, and the Saint celebrated gay identity as something positive, even during negative times. "AIDS didn't make me consider not going out," argues La Torre. "That would have only been an option if I had gotten sick or had known someone who was afflicted with it." Robbie Leslie even wondered if the health crisis would boost dance-floor numbers. "The aspect of going out to find someone to trick with is becoming secondary, I think, to perhaps going out to have a good time," he told the *New York Native*. "Perhaps there will be a resurgence in nightclubbing."[24]

As if confronting Kramer's belief that dancing and promiscuous sex distracted gay men from activist pursuits, Earle became politicized after his lover (sculptor Ignacio Zuazo) introduced him to Mel Cheren. "Mel started pressing me about the AIDS crisis," recounts Earle. "He was trying to get me to become a true member of the community, and that meant not just enjoying the benefits of the community but also giving something back. Since I was not a person of means, that giving back had to take some other form." Earle went to Gay Pride for the first time in 1983 and participated in a fundraising run organized by the GMHC in the autumn. After that he went into training for a solo, awareness-raising run that would cover the perimeter of the United States. "Being at the Saint, being part of a tribe, being part of this glorious community, went hand-in-hand with my becoming an AIDS activist," he reasons. "I would never have dreamt I could become a hero if I hadn't had that image of transcendent glory, that iconized version of myself, bestowed to me under the dome of the Saint."

The singularity and separateness of the Saint also left its members partially stranded when the AIDS crisis spiraled, their focus having been inward rather than outward. Yet responsibility for the drift also lay elsewhere, for while the white gay men who gravitated to Second Avenue were often slow to engage with the concerns of the black community, so African American activists were shy when it came to addressing homophobia. As a siege mentality began to take hold, the pre-AIDS sound of disco came to signify a nostalgic moment when unprotected sex didn't carry the threat of death, even if its recycling added force to the argument that the Saint was trapped in sonic time. For these and other reasons, music industry reps became even more disengaged from the venue. "Because all the early victims of AIDS were gay white males, it was no longer considered 'cool' by straight people in the domestic record industry to dance in gay white clubs," argues Sherman. "It was definitely homophobia, although perfectly understandable since nobody knew what AIDS was, where it came from, or how you could 'catch' it, and there was a bit of reverse racism thrown in for good measure. Hanging with white gay males was definitely not sexy by 1983."

Dancers still flocked to the Saint in huge numbers. Few believed the highs they experienced were compromised. But the atmosphere began to acquire a darker edge during 1983 and AIDS played a major part in that development. The same was true of the wider downtown scene. Death had become an urgent concern on the New York dance floor.

WE GOT THE HITS,
WE GOT THE FUTURE

Previously defined by the Jackson 5 and the Motown conveyor belt, Michael Jackson began to assert himself as an African American icon of unparalleled popularity with *Off the Wall*. Released just weeks after Steve Dahl staged his melodramatic disco sucks rally in Chicago, the album provided the artist with four top ten singles and a slew of awards at the February 1980 Grammys. The coincidence of the economic downtown with the anti-disco upturn probably meant that was all Jackson could have realistically hoped for; indeed, the prize for best album went to the consummately safe *52nd Street* by Billy Joel. But a disappointed Jackson told his new entertainment lawyer that it was "totally unfair" he didn't win the album of the year category and vowed "it can never happen again."[1] Almost three years in the making, *Thriller* amounted to his reply.

Expectations were low when Jackson issued "The Girl Is Mine," an insipid duet with Paul McCartney, as the first single, almost a month ahead of the LP, which came out at the end of 1982. But "Billie Jean," the second single, a study in orchestrated tension, shot to number one on the pop charts, its accompanying video also the first by a black artist to gatecrash its way onto MTV, the video channel that had launched back in August 1981. "Beat It," the third single, maintained the pressure thanks to the introduction of Eddie Van Halen's raucous guitar into a dance structure — a move that made Michael Zilkha smile when he thought of its proximity to Material's "Busting Out." The fourth single, "Wanna Be Startin' Somethin'," referenced Manu Dibango's "Soul Makossa" as it moved toward its percussive-chant finale. "Human Nature" and "P.Y.T. (Pretty Young Thing)," the fifth and sixth singles, confirmed that Jackson's fans had become uniquely willing to collect even some of the weaker tracks on an album they had already purchased. The *Thriller* cycle climaxed with the December release of the title track's fourteen-minute video, directed by John Landis, and the *Making Michael Jackson's "Thriller,"* a sixty-minute documentary that tracked its genesis. The choreographed moves of the lithe-footed Jackson alongside a cast of gyrating ghouls and zombies captured the popular imagination in a way that hadn't happened since John Travolta took to the floor in *Saturday Night Fever*. By the year's end, sales of the LP alone topped fifteen million.[2]

After the epoch-defining successes of Elvis and the Beatles, it was the turn of an African American to seize the musical moment and in so doing revive the national profile of black music. Although no major-label executive would have admitted as much, the retrenchment of the early 1980s amounted to a turn against black pop as well as disco. By late February 1983 the situation was sufficiently dire for Robert Palmer to argue that black and white pop had become segregated in a way that was "reminiscent of the mid-1950's, when the pop mainstream was almost all-white except for a few exceptional cross-over artists."[3] With black artists laying claim to only two top ten singles and one top ten album in the week before the article went to print, the decline coincided with Ronald Reagan's attack on affirmative action and social welfare programs, his firing of members of the U.S. Commission on Civil Rights who criticized his agenda, his opposition to the introduction of sanctions against apartheid South Africa, and his invasion of Grenada. As Thomas Edsall and Mary Edsall note, the president also attacked policies targeted toward blacks and other minorities without referring to race and in so doing shaped "a conservative politics that had the effect of polarizing the electorate along racial lines."[4] It was in this context that John Rockwell described *Thriller* as a sign that "the destructive barriers that spring up regularly between white and black music — and between whites and blacks — in this culture may be breached once again."[5]

But Jackson didn't just challenge the present; he also articulated it. Instead of spreading the message of collective pleasure and dance-floor democracy, as he had on *Off the Wall*, he wrote lyrics that spoke of betrayal, split identities, sick babies, breakdowns, and gang battles as well as lying, stealing, and crying. His sound also changed with the times as the percussive layerings and symphonic rushes of his debut gave way to stuttering electronic beats, spatialized synth stabs, and prowling bass lines. Even the spatial imaginary of *Thriller* suggested a departure, with the communal bliss of the discotheque displaced by the darkened street, the abandoned yard, and the decaying cemetery. Of the release's numerous subplots, the uncredited and unpaid-for usage of the Dibango chant suggested a certain level of unscrupulousness. Meanwhile Epic's unprecedented release of six (running in 1984 to seven) singles from the album encapsulated the wider shift to market intensification. *Thriller* still spoke of multicultural promise, sonic integration, and a national renaissance for dance. Yet whereas *Off the Wall* was grounded in the late 1970s, when integration and unity were part of a common language, Jackson's new album was at least partially rooted in the harsher, more materialistic 1980s.

As the *Thriller* phenomenon surged, the majors turned to dance culture with renewed enthusiasm. The turnaround announced itself in March when David Bowie released *Let's Dance*, an album coproduced by Chic's Nile Rodgers, and gained momentum when Irene Cara and Giorgio Moroder's "Flashdance . . . What a Feeling" came out in April. Billy Joel's issuing of a twelve-inch remix of "Tell Her about It" in July signified that another milestone had been passed — because Joel, unlike Bowie, Cara, Rodgers, and Moroder, enjoyed no obvious connection to dance. Pat Benatar and Cyndi Lauper rattled out dance-oriented Hot 100 hits ("Love Is a Battlefield" and "Girls Just Want to Have Fun") before Paul McCartney and Michael Jackson released an extended mix of "Say Say Say" in October. A month later Warner Bros. came out with "Ain't Nobody" by Rufus and Chaka Khan, perhaps the outstanding major-label twelve-inch single of the year. Rounding off the volte-face, RCA invited Bob Clearmountain — whose earlier mixes of the Rolling Stones' "Miss You" and Roxy Music's "Dance Away" harked back to the last time the majors flexed their muscles in dance — to reshape and extend "Adult Education" by Daryl Hall and John Oates.

A go-to remixer who could infuse twelve-inch releases with a dance personality while leaving the seven-inch and album versions free to circulate in a nonremixed state, John "Jellybean" Benitez became the most influential intermediary between major labels and the dance floor. With the Cara commission completed, the Funhouse DJ picked up further remix work with Joel ("Tell Her about It") and Talking Heads ("Slippery People"), after which friends asked him who he would most like to work with next. "Michael Jackson and the Beatles," he joked, only for Paul McCartney to phone the next day to ask him if he'd be willing to remix "Say Say Say." "Yeah, right," replied Benitez, wise to what he wrongly assumed to be a trick, something he only clocked when the president of Columbia Records called to explain his error — and to request he avoid making the same mistake when Barbra Streisand got in touch. Coinciding with the Funhouse DJ's mix of "Automatic" by the Pointer Sisters in December, Brian Chin remarked that Jellybean was "cornering the top 40 market."[6]

The year also came to be marked by the accelerating influx of British new wave lineups that foregrounded synthetic sounds and danceable beats, among them Aztec Camera, Big Country, Bow Wow Wow, Cabaret Voltaire,

Culture Club, Depeche Mode, Thomas Dolby, Duran Duran, the Eurythmics, Freeez, Heaven 17, the Human League, Madness, New Order, the Police, Soft Cell, Spandau Ballet, the Thompson Twins, and Yazoo/Yaz—not to mention Bowie and the Clash. Staged in midtown Manhattan in July, the fourth New Music Seminar capitalized on the trend as it attracted some three thousand participants through its door—enough to encourage *Billboard* to finally acknowledge it had grown into the most successful event of its kind. As talk of a second British invasion circulated, Danceteria hosted the showcase party while Haoui Montaug and Rudolf Piper appeared on the Club Management and Promotion panel; Mark Kamins spoke on the DJs and Remixers panel; and Ruth Polsky contributed to the Talent and Booking Panel. "Ladies and gentlemen, the new music has happened," Police manager Miles Copeland declared in his keynote. "The record companies are signing it; the radio stations are playing it; the people are buying it. We got the hits. We got the future. Whip out the champagne and drink up."[7]

With so many "new music" releases attracting heavy play at the openly Anglophile Danceteria, Kamins's studio diary came to reflect the shifting transatlantic current after Malcolm McLaren approached him at the West 21st Street venue, told him he was "fucking great," and asked him to remix "Baby, Oh No" by Bow Wow Wow. Having accompanied Madonna on her first tour of the United Kingdom, the DJ also got to meet Quando Quango member Mike Pickering, who invited him to mix "Love Tempo." Domestic commissions still came through in the form of "Oui-Oui" by Pulsallama, "Don't Go Away" by the Brooklyn-based Affinity, and Johnny Dynell and New York 88's rap-gospel-electronic-funk "Jam Hot," but the U.K. artists started to command the bulk of his attention. "I would make the beat a little funkier and I would make the sound a little bit brighter for American radio," says Kamins. "If there was a hit record in England, I was hired to do the American mix when it was released in the States."

The heating market spilled into radio and in particular Kiss FM when Shep Pettibone called program director Barry Mayo and asked, "How come I don't get paid more money? I should be making $25,000. I'm the biggest thing on this station. You know, I *am* Kiss. Shep Pettibone *is* Kiss" (or at least that's what Mayo told Tony Humphries). The director fired his star mixer on the spot and, in a bittersweet development, asked Humphries to step in. "Shep was my *best friend*; he got canned and I get offered his job," recounts Humphries, who bought a $1,200 Technics 1500 reel-to-reel tape machine with his severance money from the *Daily News*—the same one Pettibone used. "And you're talking about radio, man. You're talking about serious shit

Johnny Dynell performing "Jam Hot" at Danceteria, 1983.
Photograph by Chris Savas ©; courtesy of Johnny Dynell.

here." Pettibone left a series of expletives on his successor's answering machine and then devoted himself to remixing old Salsoul records and DJ-ing at
Better Days, only for Mayo to rehire him some six months later to maintain
his challenge to WBLS. "Tony was more underground than me," observes Pettibone. "He'd play records that I wouldn't play because I didn't think they
worked on the radio. I could be underground, but I'd give it a commercial fla-
vor." Meanwhile Mayo boosted his rap profile by recruiting Jazzy Jay to host
a "Dance Mix Party" show and by turning to Red Alert after Jay grew tired
of working for no money. "Unlike Jay," notes Dan Charnas, "Red understood
the true compensation of an unpaid radio show: exposure."[8] Russell Simmons
kept his eye on the dial, convinced, as he told Carol Cooper, that "white audiences and radio stayed loyal longer than black radio."

Television continued to keep its distance from the locally produced music that surged through New York's party spots, with MTV's attitude to black music resolutely backward, even after it agreed to play Jackson's "Billie Jean." In the aftermath of that forced decision, one station executive even argued that "the mostly white rock audience was more excited about rock than the largely black audience was about contemporary rhythm and blues," adding that black video play remained so low because black and white popular music had always been segregated—a reminder that Reagan's support for the South African regime enjoyed echoes at home.[9] Yet the icy disconnect that marked the post-backlash period did begin to thaw as MTV executives moved to court rather than deflect Jackson and Epic, and by the end of the year the station— still unprofitable—could claim to have boosted the sales of visually charismatic artists such as David Bowie, Culture Club, Def Leppard, and Duran Duran, plus Jackson, as it reached into more than sixteen million homes.[10] "Performers who made videos attractive enough (and slick enough) to go into heavy rotation on MTV sold spectacular quantities of records," observed Palmer.[11]

By the year's end, critics could point to evidence that the music industry was experiencing a rebound after four consecutive years of depressed sales, even if the 5 percent yearly increase only returned the total to its 1981 level. Adding to Jackson's till-pinging run, David Bowie, Def Leppard, Men at Work, the Police, and *Flashdance* each hit the four-million-plus mark, which amounted to a significant improvement on 1982, when the best-selling John Cougar and Asia each struggled to reach three million. CBS, the parent company of Epic, Jackson's label, announced a $75 million profit for the first three months of the year, up 600 percent on the previous year, with the figures aided by the group's dismissal of three hundred employees and the closure of half of its distribution and pressing-plant facilities. Industry executives attributed the improvement to the economic recovery, the popularity of the Sony Walkman, and the decline of video-game technology.[12] *Time* argued that *Thriller* had restored confidence to an industry that found itself "stuck on the border between the ruins of punk and the chic regions of synthesizer pop."[13]

Back on the New York music scene, the reaction to *Thriller* was largely although not overwhelmingly positive. Brian Chin described "Wanna Be Startin' Somethin'" as "the best shot of high energy around," Arthur Baker picked "Billie Jean" as a likely DJ selection in *Dance Music Report*, and Larry Levan "played 'Thriller' to the point where people were sick of it," recalls Michael de Benedictus.[14] The Garage DJ also took a copy of the album to David Mancuso and told him, "It's a pop song, but it's good," remembers David DePino.

"'Billie Jean' was too commercial for the Garage," he adds. "'Thriller' was bigger. But Michael was Michael, you couldn't go wrong." Over at Danceteria, Anita Sarko played "Wanna Be Startin' Somethin'," even if she thought the album was "a bit bland," while David Azarch played selections at the Peppermint Lounge because, aside from judging it to be "a great musical work from certain points of view," people were requesting it. Up at Disco Fever, Starski cut back and forth between the first eight bars of "Billie Jean" until he had "the whole house rocking to the rhythm," reported *People*.[15]

Meanwhile Benitez's rise to studio stardom was greeted somewhat skeptically. Observing that the Funhouse DJ gave Madonna "credibility" and that she "made him famous," Baker felt that his friend was a "major" DJ-ing talent but didn't take enough risks with his remixes and "ended up going incredibly pop." Often sharing the same studio, John Robie came to regard him as a good editor yet recalls times when he and Baker would be working while Jellybean would be "on the phone doing PR." "I always thought that caring about making great music was all you needed," adds Robie. "Jellybean, on the other hand, worked both ends of the spectrum simultaneously." Garage heads also wondered about the underlying impact of Benitez's work. "Larry did a lot of mixes that made a nobody become somebody, but Madonna was Madonna, Irene Cara sang on a movie soundtrack, and Michael Jackson was Michael Jackson," points out DePino. "They didn't need Jellybean." Then again, Benitez never planned for many of his mixes to find a dance-floor audience. "A lot of the records I mixed I didn't play at the Funhouse," he explains. "The Funhouse was very underground and different. I got away with some of my mixes in the early part of the night. Otherwise I played the dub mix or my own special version that I created for myself."

With Jellybean a notable factor, Chin pronounced himself to be "amazed" at the "resurrection" of dance in April. "The very notion that *anyone* should put out a single titled 'Let's Dance' and expect it to be a big crossover hit was more than many of us (deep down inside) thought was likely or possible," he wrote of the Bowie-Rodgers collaboration.[16] Admitting that the "dance underground" couldn't match the sales of a hit such as "Let's Dance," he added: "It's merely responsible for the idea, that's all."[17] Yet the majors were responsible only to their shareholders, and having backed away from disco-dance at speed they reentered not to engage with the culture but to cherry-pick artists who displayed national potential or to commission remixes for those who were never going to record a bona fide dance hit. "The major labels never really supported the genre," comments Judy Weinstein, still the primary intermediary between DJs and the rest of the industry. "It was an annoying format and didn't sell as much as rock, pop, and R&B. Very few artists came out of the scene because it was hard to build an artist profile out of a drum machine. The major labels were embarrassed to be associated with the music, even though they were adding dance mixes to every release."

Whereas independents were largely accountable to their artists, the majors maintained their distance, especially from those who occupied the middle and lower rungs of the food chain. "Columbia was releasing six or seven club records a week, and I would hear these old businessmen talk about the record with Paul McCartney and Michael Jackson being a priority, and they would have three priorities and those priorities had to get charted," remarks Michael Gomes, who went to work for Gail Bruesewitz after leaving Prelude. "There were lots of other good records but they weren't happening because the person who was doing the calls was pushing the priority records. I would see these young producers come in and they would say, 'What's happening with my record?' And I would know that they would sit on the shelf and that was it." Gomes adds: "If it wasn't a top artist, Columbia wasn't promoting it and they could write it off as a loss at the end of the year, big deal."

Some also started to wonder if MTV would inadvertently dull the city's party scene. When the Saint management instructed its roster to start watching the cable station in order to keep up, Howard Merritt calculated that he had one more reason to quit because New York DJs were in the business of establishing trends, not following them. Meanwhile Jim Fouratt believed the music station helped establish a culture in which participants started to want to experience something "they'd already seen on TV" rather than head out in the spirit of adventure and discovery. The buzz of the surprising seemed to fade a little more when Robert Shalom opened Private Eyes as the city's first video nightclub on 21st Street — a novel initiative that soon fell flat. "The whole VJ [DJ-ing with videos] thing was about playing to a dead audience," comments Danny Krivit, who tried the new approach but soon got fed up with it. "They didn't dance, they didn't yell, they didn't drink. They just sat there until you stopped playing this stuff."

Having committed himself to the production of confrontational music, even activist music, Michael Zilkha wondered if an era was drawing to a close, not just for ZE Records but for the city as a whole. "It became a lot more commercial in 1983 and expectations changed," he recalls. "Elektra invested $70,000 in my Alan Vega record, so they needed that record to sell a certain number of copies. I never had that pressure before because the previous Alan Vega record cost $6,000 to make — so a whole different set of realities came into play." Zilkha maintains that he'd never worried about the microdebts he

Gail Bruesewitz dancing at the Paradise Garage, 1983. Photographer unknown; courtesy of Gail Bruesewitz.

accrued with Chris Blackwell because the *Face* and *Interview* reviewed his records in glowing terms while insisting the label was on the cusp of breaking through. "Chris didn't worry about it either," he adds. "But the negative balance on Alan Vega — I didn't know how that was going to be paid back."

Zilkha also started to wonder if he still had his finger on the pulse of the city after he failed to recognize the potential of the Beastie Boys, a hardcore punk outfit whose members graduated from sweeping the floors at Danceteria, to playing live at the venue and the Kitchen, to laying down the improvised "Cooky Puss" (which included funk beats, scratching, and a prank phone call to Brooklyn ice cream parlor Carvel, inventor of the ice cream character Cookie Puss) and "Beastie Revolution" (a spoof Rastafari number). Certain she was the first to turn the band's members onto rap when they used to put in requests at the Rock Lounge, Anita Sarko felt vindicated. "They'd come and say hello and ask me to play Stiff Little Fingers," she remembers. "I said, 'I'll play that for you if you'll dance to this new music that's out called rap and also this great African music by Fela Kuti." Zilkha, though, felt only distance. "They were friends with my sister and they'd always be in my office," he recounts. "I realized they were really cool but I wasn't getting it. I figured if I couldn't see the Beastie Boys then my time had passed."

Zilkha pondered the shifting climate some more when Dave Robinson, who became CEO of Island after Blackwell stepped back, listened to his latest

NED SUBLETTE BAND & THE BEASTIE BOYS

THE KITCHEN · MONDAY · DEC 12
59 WOOSTER STREET · 8:30PM · $5/3.50 MEMBERS/TDF + 50¢

Poster publicizing a Kitchen double bill featuring Ned Sublette and the Beastie Boys, 12 December 1983.

offering, the Breakfast Club, and instructed him to deliver a "multicultural dance troop" in the spirit of Kid Creole instead. "I didn't know how to do that," reasons the ZE boss. "I didn't put together Kid Creole as a multicultural dance band. I loved August's songwriting and we were going to do something cool together." Breakthrough bands such as the Thompson Twins also left Zilkha cold. "When I recorded a record it was all instinct and suddenly it was all calculated," he explains. "There were these records that seemed offbeat but they weren't offbeat at all. It was about having hits and because you could have hits with strange records, manufactured originality became something commercial." New York changed as well. "Our friends who were bankers and things like that were securitizing mortgages and making these ridiculous amounts of money by doing things that I didn't understand at all," he concludes. "I was always interested in the thing you were making and all of a sudden there was no longer a product, so New York became alienating as well. Music and the economy started to become synchronized with one another and money started to change everything."

Finally, although more dance records were coming out than at any time since 1979, a higher percentage were deemed unplayable by New York's party DJs than had been the case at any time since the peak of disco. It wasn't just the fault of the majors, although their instincts were more profit-oriented than the independents that had fed the city's dance floors during the opening years of the 1980s. But at a time when the art market was beginning to overheat, when the effects of gentrification were beginning to make themselves felt, when AIDS reached epidemic proportions, and when the independent dance sector was fragmenting, participants could have been forgiven for wondering if the New York party scene had slipped past its creative-integrationist peak.

BEHIND
THE GROOVE

Steven Harvey had a story he wanted to publish. "People didn't accept disco and thought it murdered R&B, but the renaissance was happening and there was all this energy," he recounts. "I decided that club music was the continuation of R&B." The writer decided to compose an oral history of dance told through the figure of the DJ after artist-turned-songwriter Lotti Golden introduced him to Better Days, the Funhouse, the Loft, and the Paradise Garage, because DJs "were channels, really, and they were also incredibly hip and influential." His eventual piece would become the first one dedicated to New York DJ culture.

Harvey conducted interviews with the six "defining" DJs of the moment: John "Jellybean" Benitez, Walter Gibbons, François Kevorkian, Larry Levan, David Mancuso (still more of a musical host than a DJ), and Shep Pettibone. "David defined the modern house party and was a musical influence on everybody," he explains of his choices. "Larry defined the extraordinary post-Mancuso house-party sensibility for the early 1980s. François defined the sonic architecture of the moment and was an after-hours DJ. Shep Pettibone also defined a kind of studio and mixing virtuosity. Jellybean defined the white Latino drum-machine club sound of that moment. And Walter was the historical inventor of the remix and to a certain extent club DJ-ing. Each of them were definitive characters within the genre." Harvey omitted Kenny Carpenter, Billy Carroll, Bruce Forest, Tee Scott, and Nicky Siano due to "lack of space," while Bambaataa and Flash were judged to be tangential to the disco-dance continuum.[1] As for the DJs who played at the Saint, Harvey simply notes that he wasn't interested in "white dance music."

Golden's tour was transformative. At the Funhouse, Harvey registered Jellybean's hard-hitting, beat-box aesthetic and noted the DJ's intense connection with his *West Side Story* crowd. At Better Days he sweated it out to Shep Pettibone's selections and highly technical mixing style, amazed at the DJ's dexterity. At the Loft he marveled at the "children's wonderland" setup, high-end stereo sound system, and best-of-the-1960s ambience. And at the Paradise Garage the clear door policy, courteous staff, awesome sound system, serious music, and interconnected dance floor seemed antithetical to the "glazed poses" he had experienced as a Mudd Club regular. The writer found himself returning to the Loft more or less every Saturday night and remembers it being "the first place where I felt my heart open up completely." Studying the interplay between Mancuso and his crowd for hours at a time, he observed how the dancers were "virtuosic in an offhand, almost casual manner. The energy was quite extraordinary." Magnetized by the way Levan "would speak in sentences as he developed his repertoire" and intrigued by the connection with the Loft, he also returned regularly to King Street. "It was complete emulation," he comments. "But as is the way with many good pupils, Larry also went past David in many ways as well." The first time Harvey saw the Peech Boys play live, he thought to himself: "This black/white, gay/straight instrumental dance music with the DJ doing the sound is the future."

Publishing his thoughts in an eight-page feature titled "Behind the Groove" in the September edition of *Collusion*, Harvey launched into his argument from the get-go. "The brief 10 years of disco history have provided popular music with one of its most creative periods — one too often passed over by critics," he declared. "Even the faddish embrace of all things danceable has failed to encourage critics to muster the same seriousness for the synth-anthems of Brooklyn duo D Train as they do for Soft Cell or Yazoo." Few credited disco as being the legitimate heir to the rhythm and blues tradition, while the likes of Grandmaster Flash alleged that disco was responsible for "killing off" funk, "despite its means of production being the same" and "despite its embrace of great black voices like Loleatta Holloway, Aretha Franklin, Bettye Lavette, Gwen McCrae and many others."[2] Harvey also argued that DJs rather than musicians or producers were the most influential figures within disco thanks to the way they communicated the music with such "extraordinary power." Who else could remember the thousands of one-off releases, he asked, and who else could claim to be as modernist as the DJs who transformed their found materials into a collage? "Disco has always revolved around the cult of the DJ and the club," he concluded, "and, as such, record spinners have shaped the music in a way that is unique."[3]

Harvey opened his DJ-by-DJ survey with Walter Gibbons, the "least known" of the mixers featured, yet the one responsible for the "revolution" of the first commercially available twelve-inch single, "Ten Percent" by Double Exposure, which he extended "from a three minute album track into 11 minutes of break

Steven Harvey, ca. 1982. Photographer unknown; courtesy of Steven Harvey.

after break," turning it into a record "designed specifically for the underground club scene in New York." Gibbons also anticipated break-style mixing with his percussion blends of tracks such as "Two Pigs and a Hog" from the *Cooley High* soundtrack, only to drift from the scene after he became a born-again Christian. "You really have to think that every time you change the record, the title or something about the record is going into people's heads," the DJ told Harvey, pointing to one of the reasons his opportunities had dried up. "For me, I have to let God play the records. I'm just an instrument."

Next up, Harvey turned to Kevorkian, recounting his entry into the scene as a live drummer employed to work alongside Gibbons, his studio mixes of Musique and others, his DJ-ing work at AM/PM, and his occasional contributions at the Loft and the Paradise Garage. "Francois' mixes have all possessed a sterling sound quality, the result of carefully cleaning up each individual track before reshaping them, and a radical sensibility in terms of the shaping of music as architecture," noted the writer. "His first D Train mixes suggested what a marvellous marriage there could be between Jamaican dub mixers like Augustus Pablo and the street/studio musicians of the New York dance scene." Kevorkian, though, had become pragmatically negative about dance aesthetics, which had drifted toward uniformity and one-dimensionality. "The way we perceive the music, digest it, assimilate it, like it and then reject it because we are sick of it has become alarming," the Frenchman explained. "There's too much fast food music and we become addicted to it instead of looking forward to something a little more challenging."[4]

As if to offset Kevorkian's skepticism, Harvey turned next to Levan, yet even here a certain wistfulness permeated the interview. When Harvey asked Levan about his turntable style, the DJ cited Nicky Siano, David Mancuso, Steve D'Acquisto, Michael Cappello, and David Rodriguez as forming "the school of DJs" that had influenced him. "When I listen to DJs today they don't mean anything to me," he added. "Technically some of them are excellent — emotionally they can't do anything for me. I used to watch people cry in the Loft for a slow song because it was so pretty."[5] Harvey went on to describe Levan's break into DJ-ing, his connection to Richard Long, his fascination with the Loft sound system, and his plans to add two turntables fitted with superior Grace cartridges to the Garage system. Then, asked by Harvey to paint an image of the Peech Boys, Levan described the group as resembling a group of "energetic men" who had "captured that realness of being young, because that's something you lose very fast in New York City."[6] Even with the world at his feet, Levan felt a pang for the recent past.

Harvey's overview of Mancuso was an altogether tighter affair, in part because his short interview with the host was conducted during a Prince Street barbecue. "It's very simplified," Mancuso explained when asked to define his house parties. "We don't sell food. We don't sell cards (memberships). Therefore, we are able to keep it in the spirit of an invitation. It was my own way of socially rebelling." Harvey pressed Mancuso on the question of sound. "Music came before the word and I've found over the years that music has become an expression of individuals, of groups, of tribes, etc.," came the reply. "Each one has its own sonic personality to it." The host went on to explain his sonic objective: to transcribe as closely as possible the intention of the musician as expressed in the groove of a record. "The person who made the cartridge did it by hand," he remarked, holding up a Koetsu. "He used to make swords. If the ambience is in the groove it'll come out. When you can listen to a recording and tell what make the instruments are, you're getting close."[7]

Turning to John "Jellybean" Benitez, Harvey maintained the DJ had transformed the Funhouse into the "seedbed for electro-bop" as well as a hotbed for producers who wanted to test their latest beat-box pressings. Benitez maintained that Gibbons had been his primary inspiration, with "hip hop culture from the street" also influential. "Everything he was doing back then, people are doing now," he observed of Gibbons. "He was phasing records — playing two records at the same time to give a flange effect — and doubling up records so that there would be a little repeat. He would do tremendous quick cuts on record sort of like b-boys do. He would slam it in so quick that you couldn't hear the turntable slowing down or catching up. He would do little edits on tape and people would freak out."[8] Benitez noted how DJs brought the immediacy of their experience to the craft of remixing records yet also sounded a cautionary note about the present. "A lot of people seem to be copying the Baker/Robie sound which is going to get boring," he remarked. "I got to the point where I was playing and it seemed like I was in a video arcade."[9]

Finally, Harvey turned to Pettibone, who received confirmation of his pay raise from Barry Mayo just as the piece was about to go to print. Pettibone explained that his radio tapes were all prerecorded because spinning live on air didn't work, there being "zero audience response," and added that he put his tapes together with vinyl plus tape-recorder echo effects, avoiding tape-to-tape maneuvers because they would result in a loss of sound quality. Then, when Harvey asked him about the excitement shown by the Better Days crowd when he selected a classic, the DJ responded with a comment that was beginning to sound like a mantra. "The music right now is not good," he remarked. "I'm sick of hearing drums and synthesisers. I'd like to hear music again."[10] Harvey commented that, like a number of his other interviewees, "you don't seem very positive about current trends in disco."[11]

Harvey shared some of the concerns expressed by his interviewees. The previous year marked the period when New York City disco "expanded its perimeters to include dub, electronics, jazz, latin, afro, new wave — a cauldron capable of melting down any ingredient." Leading the way, the Peech Boys, Sinnamon, and D Train allied black R&B with high-tech electronics while Arthur Baker and John Robie pushed the beat-box sound to the fore. "To turn on one of the city's three dance radio stations and hear a DJ mixing three records together at once seemed like an impossible dream of the avant garde infiltrating the market place," he declared. Yet the specter of disco's collapse now loomed over dance music's resurgence. "Will the major labels, now practically insatiable in their quest for new dance music, retract as they did before?" Harvey asked. "Will the formularisation of production styles and techniques eliminate inspiration? Will the gentrification of disco by dance rockers and Flashdancers effect the same loss of visceral soul as it did before?"[12] If these seemed like hard-edged questions to raise in a largely celebratory feature, Harvey judged them to be necessary because commercial imperatives had once again come to the fore.

A second tribute to New York party culture followed in late October when U.K. music show the *Tube* broadcast a film of Leslie Ash and Jools Holland touring the city's clubs.[13] In a sign of the times, the presenters started out in front of CBGB but instead of going inside made their way to Danceteria, where Ruth Polsky, cool and engaging in red lipstick and red earrings, explained how the venue operated as a "place where anything goes." Asked by Ash if New Yorkers had a particular musical preference, Mark Kamins replied that tastes had opened out. "There's no specific genre of music," he commented. "It's whatever's got that magic feeling to it." Next up, Rudolf Piper, dressed sharp in a black turtleneck and checkered jacket, chipped in with his latest personal predilection: transvestite singers playing accordion. Asked about the venue's Klaus Nomi exhibition, Piper said he wanted the Danceteria crowd to see Nomi for "what he was" — an artist raised like himself in Germany who was "quintessentially from New York."

Ash and Holland appeared to be playing ignorant when they asked their guide about street gangs as they made their way over to the Roxy. He explained that instead of entering into violent conflict, gangs had "evolved certain cultural forms" that included dancing, rapping, and heading to the Roxy. Once inside, Holland asked Arthur Baker about his habit of having DJs test his demos on dance crowds. "I probably did like 15 or 20 different mixes," Baker noted of "Confusion." "I kept going into the clubs and testing them out and they really didn't live up to what I wanted, so I'd go back into the studio and used that as the barometer of whether the record was where it should be as far as the people were concerned." The key, he continued, was to get the kick and snare drums right, because "if you don't have the power then you can lose the dance floor." Holland asked the producer if he thought dance music would evolve to the point where records were purely rhythmic. Baker replied that rap records had more or less reached that point already. "If you have the right beat, the record can get over just on the beat and the chant," he observed. Then he added: "I am actually trying to get away from that."

Ash and Holland completed their night out at the Garage, joking about the headaches Roxy breakers must experience as they walked up the venue's ramp entrance. "They're supposed to have the best sound system and at ten-to-four in the morning I think one really has to have the best sound system to really appreciate exactly these rhythms," mused a wry Holland, "because at ten-to-four in the morning one has to be uplifted, so we're going to go in here and be uplifted." After surveying the dance floor, he segued into an interview with the (subdividing) Peech Boys. "Basically we come here and enjoy ourselves here in a party atmosphere and then the music comes from that as well," Michael de Benedictus explained. "It all has an inspiration from that point." Fresh back from their tour of the United Kingdom, another member interjected: "Bognor Regis, you know who you are, hi, we love you!"

Intercut with dance-floor scenes and video clips of locally produced dance hits, the film captured the sense of wonder that must have been felt by any stranger who encountered the party scene's in-house art shows, scratching DJs, breakers, and homegrown bands for the first time. There were even times when it conveyed the community-spirited soulfulness that ran the city's dance floor, including the moment Ash interviewed a gray-hatted, gray-scarfed Nona Hendryx at the Roxy. (Everyone seemed to be stylishly coordinated that night.) "Well, it's a place that you can come to after a week of being, I guess, a busboy, a waitress, a hairdresser, a dancer, a mother, a husband — you know, any of those things — and give it off, get rid of it, and dance," eulogized the vocalist. Of the omissions, perhaps Klaus Nomi's cause of death was judged too downbeat and Ruza Blue's ousting from the Roxy too complicated to explain, with Larry Levan's and Bambaataa's absences from the Garage and Roxy sections probably related to them being too busy or too wary. Then again, perhaps these and other omissions simply spoke of a culture too vast to relay in a short film.

Come the year's end, then, the overriding impression was of a scene either peaking or just passed its peak. In late December Brian Chin touched on the doubts raised in Harvey's "Behind the Groove" when he asked if success was about to "spoil" disco. After all, dance music's recent history had been marked by the "rise-and-fall cycle" of several styles, including those cultivated in Philadelphia, New York, Miami, and Europe during the 1970s. "Make no mistake about it," the *Billboard* columnist argued. "Even the most ardent partisans of club culture admit that there is occasional exhaustion among record producers, DJs, even the audience." Chin observed that no "distinct new musical trend" had emerged during the year and referenced a recently published Rockpool newsletter that warned its readership to wake up "lest the term 'new music' make itself a code name for formularized music with a more saleable image." Despite success stories such as Madonna, New Order, and Shannon, dance music had apparently arrived at another critical juncture. "There is much history behind it and a vigorous future waiting to be created," concluded the writer.[14]

Harvey concluded his own year of writing by arguing that a geographical swing in energy from New York to Europe appeared to be under way. The first of four illustrative examples, "White Horse" by the Dutch duo Laid Back, foregrounded a "resolutely minimal arrangement," "punchbeat mechanics," and "gruff vocals." The second, "Din Daa Daa (Trommeltanz)," presented George Kranz scatting in German "over furious drums and organ blasts in chaotic ascension." The third, U.K. producer Trevor Horn's production of Art of Noise's *Into Battle* EP, included "Beatbox," a "symphonic B-boy mix." Finally, François Kevorkian's production of Jah Wobble's *Snake Charmer* EP included "Hold on to Your Dreams," which featured Arthur Russell lyrics and plotted "a kind of jazz-dance fusion of genuine lyricism and graceful transition." Harvey noted that although many European producers sought to replicate the sound and spirit of New York dance, "their inability to tap into an ingrown formal vocabulary is often taken for originality here." He concluded that the "hybrid originality" of all four tracks "is exactly what New York City dance music fans are waiting for."[15]

If some kind of local drift was under way, it wasn't straightforwardly the fault of the corporations. All they did, after all, is release a series of twelve-inches that weren't terribly memorable while luring a small number of DJs and recording artists away from their single-minded focus on dance floors. Along the way, they also started to make amends for their reactionary post-disco-sucks retrenchment around white male rock acts by giving more support to black and female artists who had at least one foot planted in R&B and funk—most notably Michael Jackson, Madonna, and Prince (whose album *1999*, released shortly before *Thriller*, established his reputation as a funk-rock force). Even if there was some kind of decline, it started out from a very high level indeed—even Valhalla high. If the view from the summit now seemed a little less spectacular than it had at the end of 1982, it was still a view that couldn't obviously be bettered anywhere else in the world. Any scene worthy of its cutting-edge status could negotiate such developments.

But the New York party network had to deal with a whole lot more because in addition to the familiar challenge of a corporate sector becoming belatedly interested in its activity it also had to contend with a radically shifting economic and social milieu. In a somewhat gruesome list of developments, the art market was beginning to overheat, real estate values were skyrocketing, the ripple effects of gentrification were making themselves felt, AIDS was tearing through the nightscape, and a mixture of city and national policy decisions were ushering in an age of lurching growth, ruthless materialism, and heightened inequality. Given all of this, it was hardly surprising that tastes began to segment as market choice and social divisions widened or that creativity became increasingly rooted in commercialism as the cost of living in the city spiraled. Within this context the marauding behavior of the majors was merely symptomatic of the changing environment and not the reason

for its ascent. "A lot of it had to do with the Reagan ethos," reasons Zilkha.
"Everything became fucked because it all started to revolve around money.
The more you retained your leftist ideals the more alienated you became."

Born out of hardship, resistance, and the desire for communal pleasure,
the New York party scene wasn't about to give up the ghost. It had already
negotiated the reaction against the counterculture; ignored laws that prohib-
ited gay men from dancing with one another; provided women, people of
color, drag queens, artists, bohemians, and pleasure-seeking others with a
self-sufficient system of expression, entertainment, employment, and communal support; survived the challenge of two recessions; and negotiated the
sometimes antagonistic advances of punk, the hyper-commercialization of
disco, and a second backlash against the culture's easiest targets. The combination of Reaganite dog-eat-dog economics, the largely unreported spread
of the consumption of crack cocaine, and the ongoing advances of AIDS was
ushering in an era of conflict and strife that would test the city's embrace of
hybrid mutation and social integration to the limit. But for now, as the year
reached its climax, the city's party tribes subdivided in preparation for New
Year's Eve (which happened to fall on a Saturday night) in the only way they
knew how.

They headed to Danceteria, where Piper promised his crowd that "George
Orwell was wrong" and that 1984 would turn out to be a "fabulous year."[16]
They traveled to the Paradise Garage, where Michael Brody thanked his staff
by giving each one of them an all-expenses-paid trip to Rio for carnival.
They journeyed to the Loft, where Mancuso staged what would turn out to
be his last New Year's Eve party on Prince Street without fear of the future.
They gravitated to the Saint, where Bruce Mailman summoned France Joli
out of her major-label cul-de-sac to perform alongside Chuck Parsons. They
trekked to the Roxy, where Frankie Crocker hosted a night that featured Afrika Bambaataa and Jazzy Jay, live performances by Fonda Rae and Rockers
Revenge, and the graffiti of Dondi White, Zephyr, and Futura.[17] And they
congregated at Area, Better Days, CBGB, Disco Fever, the Funhouse, the Peppermint Lounge, Pyramid, the Ritz, Shescape, the honorary Zanzibar, and
scores of other locales, because the city's party network remained extraordinarily diverse, and its patrons wanted to *give it off, get rid of it, and dance.*

Even when confronted by the specter of decay and even death, New York's
partygoers lived for the night — for the meeting of friends, for the embrace of
strangers, for the performance, for the immersion, for the surge, for the scream.

EPILOGUE
LIFE, DEATH, AND THE HEREAFTER

Get up and get down to the funky sound
Everybody out there, come on and get down
Uptown, rock the house, and
Downtown, rock the house, and
Eastside, rock the house, yeah
Westside, rock the house, and
Manhattan, rock the house,
Wherever you are keeping grooving out
—*Sha Rock of the Funky 4 + 1 at the Kitchen,*
22 November 1980

New York serves as a reminder of how fragile hedonistic
lifestyles can be, how ephemeral all true cosmopolitan
entertainment is. And to think that all of us who were
immersed in the vertigo of those times believed that it
would never end . . . that it would get better and more crazy
instead! The only consolation is that, like in the past, this
sad state of affairs will change too, sooner or later, for better
or worse. The outcome depends on all of us.
—*Rudolf Piper, interview*

It's hard to disagree with Will Hermes when he argues in *Love Goes to Buildings on Fire* that New York City reached a peak of sonic creativity during 1973–1977 that fell away during the 1980s and 1990s.[1] How could anything compare to the era that produced disco, punk, the loft jazz scene, the breakout of experimental minimalism and post minimalism, Salsa, and the first articulations of what would later be known as hip hop? But although they mightn't have displayed the same level of streamlined coherence, the sounds and scenes that defined the opening years of the 1980s reached a comparable level of dynamism, their rootedness in intermixing and synthesis transforming what was supposed to have been a cooling-down period into the convulsive climax of 1970s inventiveness. At times it seemed as though a circus of sounds had stopped off in town and everyone was invited to play.

The 1980–1983 period certainly didn't lack in ferociously inventive homegrown music thanks to Afrika Bambaataa, Blondie, the Bush Tetras, "D" Train, Doug "Double Dee" DiFranco and Steve "Steinski" Stein, Brian Eno and David Byrne, ESG, Grandmaster Flash & the Furious Five, Gwen Guthrie, Hashim, Inner Life, Grace Jones, Kid Creole, Konk, Liquid Liquid, Material/Nona Hendryx, Malcolm McLaren, Man Parrish, the Peech Boys, Run-D.M.C., Arthur Russell's Dinosaur L and Loose Joints, Shannon, Talking Heads, Tom Tom Club, the Treacherous Three, Visual, and scores of others. The period also witnessed a studio vanguard that included Arthur Baker, Bob Blank, August Darnell, François Kevorkian, Larry Levan, Shep Pettibone, John Robie, and Tee Scott stretch out the sonic spectrum as they combined traditional rhythm sections with new electronic gadgetry. Meanwhile Bambaataa and Flash released records as artists, rap consolidated its opening salvos and began to mess with electronics, disco refocused its energies around R&B and more electronics, dub spread through the city like a contagion, punk-funk rose out of the nihilistic discontent of no wave, the downtown band scene reached a raucous climax, and a good number of records successfully attempted to do everything at once — among them Dinosaur L's "Go Bang! #5."

The same period saw party spaces reach a level of intensity that knew no historical precedent. The Loft sustained its unrivaled run as David Mancuso perfected his sound system and dancers packed the Prince Street floor. The Paradise Garage overcame a sometimes difficult opening period as it multiplied the scale and power of Mancuso's inspirational private party while holding onto its community feel. Negril followed by the Roxy carried Bronx-style DJing into Manhattan on a weekly basis and, with *Wild Style*, shaped hip hop into an integrated culture. After an indifferent run, the Funhouse employed John "Jellybean" Benitez, who transformed it into a pulsating venue for a young Italian and Latin crowd. Even if they were situated on the periphery, Disco Fever and Zanzibar cultivated vital local scenes in the Bronx and Newark that were on a par with their Manhattan counterparts. Growing out of punk's encounter with art, the Mudd Club, Club 57, Danceteria, Pyramid, and Area forged a novel form of art-punk partying. Meanwhile the Saint carried the white gay scene to unprecedented levels of synesthetic dance-floor immersion. If the 1970s reinvented the parameters of party culture, then, the early 1980s scaled new levels of immersive socio-sonic possibility.

The period also came to be defined by its shift into sonic convergence and mongrel transformation, for if the 1970s had already produced the fusion sounds of disco and Salsa, the very late 1970s and early 1980s witnessed musicians champion a form of postgeneric freedom that all but forgot to codify its sounds. It helped that the city's music corporations backed away from a setting they judged to be devoid of national potential because that gave independent labels free rein to target the DJs and diehard crowds that had grown weary of join-the-dots disco and reductionist punk. It also helped that dub followed by cheaper electronic gear washed into New York at the very moment when musicians, producers, and remixers were on the lookout for new ways to feed the frenzy. Meanwhile the noncoincidental emergence of rap — itself a form of mutant disco-funk — provided music makers with an unorthodox vocal style that could work on just about any instrumental track. Already rooted in the practice of creating fresh combinations out of found material, Bronx DJs were predisposed to embrace the paradigm shift and discovered a particular affinity with downtowners already immersed in cutup, collage, intertextuality, juxtaposition, DIY, and recycling. A spectacular period of mutant exploration ensued.

Thoughts of convergence also seemed to be hardwired into the psyche of promoters as Hurrah, Club 57, Danceteria, the Mudd Club, and Pyramid pursued the novel idea that participants should enjoy both DJ-ing and live music along with, variously, themed happenings, video and film screenings, performance art, and art exhibitions. It became almost mandatory for participants to open themselves up to new experiences, sensations, and forms of expression, with Jim Fouratt a particularly avid proponent of experiential/critical consciousness. Even Michael Brody put on movies and live performance, although the path to convergence at the Paradise Garage revolved around the cross-generic vinyl journey orchestrated by Levan, with Mancuso pursuing a similar goal at the remarkably purist Loft. Meanwhile Charlie Ahearn, Afrika Bambaataa, Fred Brathwaite, Michael Holman, and Ruza Blue brought the somewhat disparate elements of DJ-ing, MC-ing, breaking, and graffiti into enough contact for Negril, the Roxy, and *Wild Style* to establish hip hop as the quintessential convergent form. The fact that the Jamaican-raised, definitively angular, disco-rock-dub artist Grace Jones would have been welcomed as the ultimate diva in any of these settings as well as Bruce Mailman's Saint shows how aesthetic preferences were coinciding.

The shift reflected and reinforced parallel social developments as powerful women became pivotal figures, drag queens collectively entered the party scene for the first time, anticlone queers forged an alternative form of partying, straight Latin kids found their first Puerto Rican DJ megahero, and African Americans began to access areas of the city's party scene that were previously closed off. By facilitating what city philosopher Iris Marion Young evokes as a "being together of strangers," the party network engineered a form of accelerated integration that facilitated encounters between revelers from diverse backgrounds, their interactions anticipated and supported by the compound sounds that surged throughout the city, among them "Don't Make Me Wait," "Planet Rock," and "Go Bang!" which were themselves re-corded by DJs, musicians, and producers from diverse backgrounds.[2] The party scene also supported a form of democratic socializing in which par-ticipants could gain what urban activist Jane Jacobs describes as "a feeling for the public identity of people, a web of public respect and trust, and a resource in time of personal or neighborhood need."[3] Andy Warhol might not have struck up a friendship with the suburban kid who puked on him in the Mudd Club, but the fact that he was thrilled by the encounter hints at the spirit of the times. So is the way thousands of Bronx, Brooklyn, Harlem, and Queens residents came to view downtown Manhattan as a second home.

As an unprecedented number of artists and musicians converged on down-town, a period of boundless action — or, in philosopher Hannah Arendt's terms, freedom and plurality — unfolded, much of it through or within the city's party spaces.[4] Leisure and work also converged as New Yorkers com-bined the pleasure of going out with the possibility of entering into any num-ber of collaborative possibilities, some of which helped pay the rent. With digital communication barely on the horizon, answering machines a rarity, and even landlines a premium expense, participants went out as a matter of social and, increasingly, professional necessity. After all, it was in the city's clubs that one could find out what was going down — where the next party was happening, what band was looking for a new drummer, who needed help with a performance, when the next low-budget film or fashion show required volunteers, which venue was offering door/coat check/bar/DJ-ing work, and so on and so forth, deep into the night. In this manner the city's party scene became a hive of informal networking that engendered a cornu-copia of creative ventures. "The number of pairing-offs that came out of the Mudd Club was astronomical," comments Mudd Club owner Steve Mass. "As Robert Louis Stevenson said, it's not how much money you make but how many seeds you sow, and the seeds that were sown at the Mudd Club were facilitated by dance-floor experiences and drinking."

It's hardly surprising that the activity didn't acquire a name to match disco, punk, or new wave. For a while music industry figures discussed the pros and cons of sticking with disco or twisting with dance, but that discussion faded when the majors backed out of the party scene. Rap referred to a fairly cohesive set of features, but these were dramatically unsettled by the rush of breakbeat electronic sounds released in the slipstream of Kraftwerk's "Numbers," and there followed only half-hearted attempts to name that phenomenon until the British music entrepreneur Morgan Khan chose the term "electro" when he released the first *Street Sounds Electro* compilation album in the summer of 1983. Hip hop only began to assume its full form in the autumn of 1981 and even then the going was initially tentative. Also late to the party, "mutant disco" started to circulate around the same time, the coinage having been thought up (again) in London rather than New York. Even if the popularity of Simon Reynolds's *Rip It Up and Start Again* has popularized the term to the point where its original absence seems anomalous, even the postpunk moniker was also barely in usage. "We're living in an age where people have this need to define genre," comments Robie. "But when people look back at the early 1980s there's a whole lot of music that can't be easily analyzed and understood because it didn't fit into any generic category."

Brian Eno encountered this fomenting, polyglot synergy when he traveled to New York in the spring of 1979. "People are just much more willing to talk to one another, because everyone is desperate for an idea," he explained in a reflective interview. "People really regard it as important that they should find out what everyone else is doing, and surely part of the reason is that they want to incorporate whatever they can into their own work."[5] The producer noted that even the most ambitious ideas seemed possible to him in New York, only to seem unrealizable back in London, where the music, art, dance, and theater scenes were more segmented. That was because his creativity was rooted in the scene he inhabited more than his own ideas, with the New York setting particularly enabling. "Scenius stands for the intelligence and the intuition of a whole cultural scene," Eno commented later, proposing a theory of creativity that focuses on scenes that encourage risk taking, sharing, and collaboration — an analysis that might have been inspired by his stay in Lower Manhattan. "It is the communal form of the concept of the genius."[6]

Artist and critic David Brody has gone on to claim that no common factor connected downtown's most influential artists and that without the "fiction of revolutionary alignment" their work amounted to "just a loose, vibrant locus of activity."[7] Yet the scene's poverty/street aesthetic; its guerrilla/punk strategies; its focus on the collective, the performative, and the ephemeral; and its thematic concerns with sex, violence, power, race, urban decay, and real estate recurred again and again, all of them seemingly rooted in the city's writhing, coiling personality. "The vernacular of Downtown was a disjunctive language of profound ambivalence, broken narratives, subversive signs, ironic inversions, proliferate amusements, criminal interventions, material surrogates, improvised impersonations, and immersive experientiality," comments art critic Carlo McCormick. "It was the argot of the streets, suffused with the strategies of late-modernist art, inflected by the vestigial ethnicities of two centuries of immigration, cross-referenced across the regionalisms of geographic and generational subculture, and built from the detritus of history on the skids as a kind of cut-up of endless quotation marks."[8]

Admittedly such a complex combination could never produce a streamlined body of work. Yet the scene's indeterminacy — or its "refusal to settle into a stable collective identity," as critic Jeremy Gilbert has noted of postpunk — contributed to its democratic modus operandi as participants opened themselves to thoughts and experiences, forged connections and relationships, and expanded their potential.[9] The carnivalesque result turned out to be effective (in Gilbert's terms) because, first, its activities were shareable and extendable, and not merely attractive to discrete and homogeneous groups, and, second, the activity didn't merely reinscribe existing social hierarchies but consistently sought to displace them.[10] As Eno intuited, participants experienced a heightened sense of creativity and freedom not because they discovered an ability to express themselves as individuals, but because they were able to enter into a boundless set of social relations, which heightened their ability to feed back into downtown's infinitely complex "affective alliance," each in their own unique way.[11] "Everybody was very much on the same page," argues Ann Magnuson. "That's why we were all down there. The place was such a cauldron of frenetic activity and a lot of people were having similar ideas at the same time."

The socially grounded, process-focused, collectively authored work and play of the downtown era realized John Cage's 1967 observation that "instead of being an object made by one person," art "is a process set in motion by a group of people," or "people doing things, giving everyone (including those involved) the opportunity to have experiences they would not otherwise have had."[12] Magnuson along with the likes of Patti Astor, Ruza Blue, Fred Brathwaite, Michael Brody, Diego Cortez, Jim Fouratt, Michael Holman, Tina L'Hotsky, Steve Mass, and Rudolf Piper became influential because of their ability to make connections, run with ideas, and inspire participation. DJs Ivan Baker, Afrika Bambaataa, John "Jellybean" Benitez, Johnny Dynell, Grandmaster Flash, Bruce Forest, Grandmaster Flash, Dany Johnson, Mark

Kamins, Larry Levan, Anita Sarko, and Tee Scott plus musical host David Mancuso rose to prominence because they operated as highly sensitized readers (of their crowds) and processors of information (or vinyl). Of the most influential lineups from the period, Gray, Konk, and Liquid Liquid cultivated a deconstructed anti-artistry, August Darnell pursued a form of multicultural pastiche, ESG went about their work with the innocence of a high school band, and Arthur Russell assembled eclectic lineups and novel artist names at every possible turn. Meanwhile Arthur Baker, François Kevorkian, Larry Levan, Shep Pettibone, and John Robie carried out their subterfuge studio work behind the cover of sometimes unknowing recording artists. Everyone seemed to be charged by the city's cross-currents, able to gain power and force of expression according to the depth of their immersion.

Even those who were most committed to producing singular, authored works were immersed in the scene's collective personality. In particular, the artist cohort that included Jean-Michel Basquiat, Keith Haring, Kenny Scharf, and David Wojnarowicz plus Fred Brathwaite, Futura, and Lee Quiñones created art on the streets, evoked the city's energies in these and other more conventionally executed works, drew inspiration from one another, and channeled their early careers through spots such as Club 57, the Mudd Club, Danceteria, the Fun Gallery, and Area. Appreciative of the way Club 57 provided a built-in audience while operating as a space that meshed together a wide range of practices, Haring became a particularly responsive vessel for the era's major cultural movements. "In a single painting, Haring could invoke break-dancing and a hip-hop beat from the Bronx, the fluidity and sexuality of the Paradise Garage dance floor, and a Lower East Side street sensibility, all within a rigorous semiotic structure," points out Jeffrey Deitch. "Perhaps more than any other artist, Haring's work embodies the mixture of underground subcultures in '80s New York. His work helped to create the cross-fertilization that ignited one of the most dynamic periods in American vanguard culture."[13]

None of this is intended to suggest that the city's party scene came to resemble a frictionless, utopian movement for change. Everyday resentments rumbled as artists wondered if others were stealing their ideas or receiving undeserved acclaim or earning more money than sense dictated. Although the low cost of living provided a sense of freedom, and although actual muggings were rare, the discomfort of surviving in a rundown apartment or getting by with next to no money or walking about with a lingering sense of fear could be grueling. For all of the openness, a number of divisions persisted, with the art-punk scene and the crowd that gathered at the Saint stubbornly white. Some club owners displayed autocratic tendencies during their efforts to nurture a pluralistic milieu. Yet downtown participants overwhelmingly opted to live with these and other limitations rather than seek out a more comfortable alternative because their ability to remake their immediate world according to participatory and pleasurable objectives more than compensated.

The activity multiplied because New York held itself together while negotiating the challenges of a complicated and at times perilous historical conjuncture. First, the countercultural movement spurred the city's multicultural and polysexual population to seek out new forms of community, expression, and transformation while inspiring a generation of Americans to migrate to its downtown setting. Second, the early 1970s witnessed growth seep out of the national economy, the industrial sector spiral into decline, the white middle class flee to the suburbs, and the international oil crisis trigger a recession. Third, the city careered into bankruptcy during the middle of the 1970s as President Ford forced it to go cap in hand to the banks, thereby buck-passing City Hall to a sector that demanded severe cuts in expenditure in return for bailout money. Fourth, Ford reneged on the rhetoric soon after, handing the city a $2.3 billion loan to tide it over the next three years and avoid Armageddon. Fifth, the recession of the early 1980s encouraged the major music labels to back away, no longer sure that they could sell downtown taste to a shrinking and increasingly suspicious national audience. Intertwined with these developments, the rental and real estate market dipped, paving the way for the city's party scene to surge toward a sonically immersive, multichannel, Technicolor peak.

Part of the epochal shakeup, the city became a home to those who wanted to break with the comfortable norms of the postwar era, with the Beatniks followed by downtown's cultural workers united in their rejection of Fordist conformism.[14] "We were living this alternative life compared to the mundanes who were going out to their daily jobs just as we were coming home," observes Chi Chi Valenti. "We were constantly in this creative hubbub, always mounting some big production that we'd thought up. So we lived this alternative life that was not just nocturnal but communal, a small circle of people who were very important to each other." Living out their collective dream, participants pursued a new form of freedom (because rents were low and regulation light) and a new form of collective creativity (because never before had so many like-minded people converged to live in a concentrated part of a city). Even the triple threat of real estate inflation, AIDS, and a tightening regulatory framework did little to dent the mood come the end of 1983. But it was in that year that the conditions of the party machine's imminent demise made themselves apparent. "We thought New York was and always would be like this," recalls Johnny Dynell. "We were wrong."

Many of the synergistic elements that defined the New York party scene during the opening of the decade weakened during 1984–1988. The city remained productive as it witnessed the rise of hard-edged rap, free-style, the drag-street party Wigstock, and a local house-music scene (after that sound took root in Chicago). Yet on balance the scene diminished during the period that more or less coincided with Ronald Reagan's second term of office as the AIDS epidemic, the crack epidemic, real estate inflation, and the introduction of national legislation that raised the legal drinking age from eighteen to twenty-one contributed to the closure of its most influential venues. During the same period, newer spots were founded on more explicitly mercenary prerogatives, local musicians made music that appealed to increasingly segregated audiences, and demographic shifts weakened the communities that helped define the scene. Participants were left shell-shocked by the transformation of their culture.

The private network shrank at a particularly alarming pace, beginning in late April 1984, when Mancuso's landlord instructed him to move out of 99 Prince Street, possibly on the very same day that Ed Koch published an article in the *New York Times* acknowledging that Alphabet City — where Mancuso was preparing to reopen — continued to suffer from a "stubbornly persistent plague of street dealers in narcotics whose flagrantly open drug dealing has destroyed the community life of the neighborhood."[15] Mancuso lost two-thirds of his crowd within a month of reopening. "The state had agreed to put money into the area, the city had agreed as well, but it all came to a grinding halt," he recalls. "You didn't go over there unless you lived over there or were buying drugs."[16] Outwardly thriving, the Paradise Garage experienced its own corrosive challenges when Levan began to use heroin in September, while Michael Brody's relationship with the local neighborhood association unraveled with enough speed for the owner to announce in September 1985 that the venue would close at the end of its ten-year lease in September 1987. Confirmation that he was HIV-positive persuaded Brody to not bother scouting for alternative venues and he ended up dying two months after the Garage closed. Levan never recovered emotionally from these developments. Following a tough run, Mancuso went on an extended sabbatical in 1988.

Over at the Saint the escalating AIDS epidemic tore into Bruce Mailman's membership with such ferocity the owner lowered his prices and opened certain nights to straight promoters. "One of my best friends was Bruce Mailman's assistant, and she said that toward the end the number of letters for membership renewals that were coming back marked 'addressee unknown' or 'addressee deceased' was just unbelievable," remembers Robbie Leslie. "It wasn't that the living were canceling their memberships. It was just that they were dying off and there was nobody to fill the gap. It became an unfeasible operation." Mailman only closed the venue in April 1988 when a real estate developer offered him an eight-figure sum that at least doubled his initial outlay and promised to mollify investors, who had long blamed the cost of running the club for their lack of return. "Bruce was very ambivalent about selling the club because he loved it so much and the last season [1987–1988] was actually crowded again on Saturday nights," recalls Terry Sherman. "He did say to me, 'Maybe I shouldn't sell it this year.' " Other venues opened in the Saint's wake, but none rivaled its scale and ambition.

The rap and hip hop scene went through its own traumas, beginning the night a staff member at Disco Fever was shot because he tried to stop a kid from snorting coke at the bar, which prompted Sal Abbatiello to install an airport-grade metal detector at his entrance. Tensions rose as crack consumption reached epidemic proportions in the city during 1984 — a development that led to a doubling of homicides for black men aged fourteen to seventeen. "During the worst of the crack years, he [Abbatiello] would have staff supervise patrons walking back to the subway to make sure they got there without being mugged," remarks Carol Cooper.[17] But that wasn't enough to save the club, which closed in 1985, and in that same year the Roxy reopened with a new name, 1018, after violent clashes led to problems with residents and the police. "The ethnic balance started to change in the room and we started having trouble and then it was gone," remembers Vito Bruno. "There would be fights and chain snatching, and then angel dust started coming into fashion. Basically it wasn't *if* there was going to be violence but *when* there was going to be violence." Bambaataa notes: "The Roxy had problems and they changed their format and some other things happened and that was it."

The art-punk scene experienced its own set of tensions when the crowd that gravitated to Rubell and Schrager's Studio 54 started to head to Area, prompting Eric Goode and Shawn Hausman to instruct door staff to make sure that the venue wasn't overrun by "uptowners and Europeans."[18] In the end the main threat came from elsewhere, as Magnuson experienced the night she took the part of pretending to sleep while blindfolded on a bed in an installation. "These awful Wall Street frat boys or drunk Jersey types — I had a blindfold on so I couldn't see — were pounding on the Plexiglas screaming, 'WAKE UP, BITCH!'" she recalls. "I tried to ignore it but got really scared when they wouldn't stop. I said, 'To hell with this!' and got up and left." Within a couple of years of opening, a new type of preppy clubber had colonized Area. "The influx of money on Wall Street led to this tremendous number of coked-up brokers going to clubs, and that changed the dynamic," explains Valenti. "They were these hideous geeks with a tie. At Danceteria there were one or two of them. But by the end of Area there were so many of them they weren't just an irritant, they were a threat."

The growing popularity of Jerry Rubin's Networking Salon nights at Studio 54 augured the rise of a brazen form of network-driven partying, with the yippie-turned-yuppie promoter staging separate nights for lawyers, doctors, brokers, and advertisers.[19] If such an achingly narrow form of partying made Rubell and Schrager's run on West 54th Street look positively democratic, the ex–Studio 54 owners reentered the scene in heavy-handed style when they opened the gargantuan Palladium on East 14th Street in May 1985, decorating its interior with a frescoed ceiling by Francesco Clemente, lounge decorations by Kenny Scharf, and a wall mural by Keith Haring. "They tried to copy the creative element of Area but it just didn't work," comments Valenti. "With the Mudd Club, art merged organically into the club whereas at Palladium it was just tacked on. I remember turning around on the stairs at the opening and saying, 'I have to get out of this temple of shit.' 'Temple of Shit' became our codename for it." Employed as program director, Piper staged six or seven events a night in order to fill the venue with three thousand to four thousand and avoid it looking empty. "It was a nightmare," he recalls.

With competition from Palladium a significant factor, the art-punk scene imploded as the Fun Gallery closed in 1985, Danceteria followed in 1986, and Area concluded the sequence in 1987. "The kind of events often found in clubs in the past, with installations and performances conceived and pro-duced independently of mainstream institutions, mixing different crowds and fields and resulting in exciting syntheses, are rare now," Leonard Abrams reminisced in January 1987 in the last issue of the *East Village Eye*, which coincided with the closure of Area. "This is a shame: firstly, because the sale of liquor at such events has probably afforded more money for art and music than any other source apart from institutions; and secondly, because a club setting allows for immediacy, informality and a diverse audience."[20] Captur-ing the broader shift in an April feature titled "The Death of Downtown,"

Michael Musto lamented the fragmentation of a scene. "Downtown '87 is by Ralph Lauren out of the Reagan White House," he wrote. "The trend is toward exclusive palaces of the faux elite, tailor-made for the black-Azzedine-clad new conservatives whose goal in life is to get their loose jaws to lock."[21] A scene once marked by its vibrant, organic, spontaneous character had been supersized and hollowed out.

Real estate inflation played a major part in developments. As early as 1 January 1980 Colab staged the *Real Estate Show* in a boarded-up city building on Delancey Street in order to draw attention to the way "mercantile and institutional structures" used artists for the purpose of gentrification.[22] A little more than a year later, a local Lower East Side resident invited Tim Rollins of Group Material to look across the street at buildings that were about to undergo renovation. "Those fucking buildings have been standing empty over there for two years now," commented the resident. "In five years I bet you won't even see our asses on this block. Only this time, I don't know where people will go. There's always the Bronx." In May 1984 *New York Magazine* noted how apartments that had been let for $115 per month under rent control were now going for $700 per month.[23] "If an East Village resident didn't have a place nailed down they would be forced to either leave or spend a lot more time working for somebody else instead of doing their own stuff," confirms Abrams. "So the new blood, the young enthusiastic artists, were confronted with a whole different set-up."

Such developments were related to a city-led strategy that saw Mayor Koch grant $1 billion in tax abatements (dubbed "corporate welfare" by critics) that "reduced real estate taxes for a period of years in return for a particular kind of development," notes Jonathan Soffer.[24] The strategy recast the social life of the city, including those who frequented Times Square, where the "economic attack on the neighborhood by the developers" irrevocably changed the nature of the gay male sexual encounters that took place there between 1984 and 1987, recalls novelist and critic Samuel Delany.[25] Meanwhile the property market inflated by a frenetic 19 percent, 20 percent, 25 percent, and 17 percent in 1984–1987 before dropping back to 4 percent in 1988.[26] "We were heading into the reheating of the real estate market," recalls Steve Mass of his failure to land a venue after leaving White Street. "You couldn't find anything." Although the development appeared benign for those locked into a good lease, he adds, "These rich owners were now saying we want the whole neighborhood to be improved because our property will be devalued if there's a needle on the sidewalk." As it happens, nightlife businesses that held a lease faced rental increases of 35 percent between 1983 and 1985, while those without a lease faced a 66 percent rise, notes law professor and civic activist Paul Chevigny.[27] Danceteria eventually closed down due to incontrovertible real estate imperatives. "We rented the whole building for $1.20 per square foot and he [Di Lorenzo] was getting offers of $25 per square foot," recalls John Argento. "His siblings pressed him to rent the building for more money."

The income of some downtowners rose in line with the real estate bonanza, the corporate reentry, and the rise of Wall Street, among them Jean-Michel Basquiat, Keith Haring, and Madonna. The response of their peers ranged from the generous to the hostile, with Lounge Lizard John Lurie inclined to critique when he alleged that Basquiat's becoming wealthy marked the end of the downtown scene.[28] The popularity of Piper and Warhol, along with the members of Blondie and Talking Heads, suggests that the real issue wasn't one's success or wealth, but rather the way some were seen to celebrate money, such as Basquiat when he posed in a paint-splattered Armani suit with $100 bills overflowing from its pockets, just as his paintings started to sell for $20,000 each during 1984, or when Madonna released "Material Girl" as a provocative zeitgeist celebration of consumerism and avarice. Cortez points out that by 1983 the poverty aesthetic had become "boring" and "that "change was necessary," and perhaps he's right. Yet the flagrant embrace of consumption could seem traitorous to those who built a scene out of DIY resourcefulness, only for the rising cost of living to price many of them out of downtown. "When I got to New York [in 1978] my feeling was the most uncool thing you could be was rich," recalls Magnuson. "Then what started happening was the most uncool thing you could be was poor because being a struggling artist became unsustainable, and it sort of switched like that very dramatically. It shifted for me when Reagan got into office for the second four years [in November 1984]."

With Reagan's support for deregulation, competition, and individualism making it difficult for the downtown scene to enter into a cycle of renewal, onetime commodities broker Jeff Koons became the next figure to break through after his 1988 show *Banality* presented large porcelain sculptures of figures such as Michael Jackson and his chimpanzee Bubbles that referenced the pop art/kitsch prerogatives of the Mudd Club, Club 57, and Danceteria — yet did so without their irony, humor, and political intent. Having taken out ads to publicize his show in four different trade magazines, Koons went on to champion a shiny, surface-focused aesthetic that was intentionally empty of meaning. Art critic Jed Perl noted that Koons's production of "oversized versions of cheap stuff in extremely expensive materials" amounts to the "apotheosis of Walmart."[29] Art historian and curator Robert Pincus-Witten observes: "Jeff recognizes that works of art in a capitalist culture inevitably are reduced to the condition of commodity. What Jeff did was say, 'Let's short-circuit the process. Let's begin with the commodity.'"[30]

Whereas the backlash against disco didn't dampen the downtown scene, its synergistic capacity diminished significantly between 1984 and 1988. Increasingly, cultural exchanges took place in well-heeled galleries and fashionable restaurants rather than inclusive party spaces. Entrepreneurs and investors displaced curator-promoters and party hosts as the demand for creative surprise and dance-floor immersion drained away. The city came to focus less on the creation of culture and more on its licensing, marketing, showcasing, and consumption as it hurtled into an era of gentrification, global finance, and tourism. Meanwhile Reagan's framing of the poor as being welfare scroungers and the newly wealthy as pioneering heroes brought to the surface the "alienations" and "anomie" that social geographer David Harvey maintains are integral to the operation of neoliberalism.[31] "There was a Darwinian aspect to the notion of cutting welfare that asked the question: Why should we who make money think in any way, shape, or form about helping other people, about helping the less fortunate?" says Mark Riley. "It was like, 'You're doing OK, later for everybody else.' Places like the Garage and the Loft maintained their sense of collectivity, but what was around them changed. To some extent the people who went to these parties felt they were almost under siege." Reagan's refusal to speak publicly about AIDS until May 1987 contributed to their sense of embattlement.

The city's music makers struggled to maintain the extraordinary standards set during the 1970s and early 1980s. If Brian Chin stuck to his argument that 1983 hadn't been a "particularly distinguished" year for dance music when he reviewed the year a second time in the autumn of 1984, he did so from within a setting that saw Michael Zilkha wind down ZE Records, 99 Records grind to a halt, Liquid Liquid break up, Arthur Baker swerve into rock, François Kevorkian maintain his distance from the dance floor, Shep Pettibone go on sabbatical, the Peech Boys break up, and Larry Levan become less productive.[32] Countering the slide, John "Jellybean" Benitez ramped up his studio work — at one point during February he had thirteen records in the Top 100 — and Madonna broke through as an international artist with the release of *Like a Virgin*. "Of all the people, Madonna had the genius to dig out the best part of the downtown scene and put it all together into a production that appealed to the general population," argues Kevorkian. Yet major-label efforts generally struggled to gain traction in the city's party scene, while Benitez's success led him to quit the Funhouse booth in the summer of 1984. "The majors clearly

wanted to capitalize on the success of the street sound," comments instrumentalist and producer John Robie, who devoted most of his year to major-
label commissions. "But they came to the show too late and were never able
to successfully promote these records nor translate the scene into something
commercially viable."

There was, of course, no total wipeout. Releases by Boyd Jarvis and Timmy
Regisford along with newcomers Colonel Abrams and Paul Simpson appealed
to the crowds that gathered at Better Days, the Loft, and the Paradise Garage.
Meanwhile hip hop DJs looked to Sleeping Bag, Tommy Boy, and new entrant
DefJam for fresh sounds. Yet Strafe's "Set It Off," an eerie, electro-funk track
mixed by Walter Gibbons in 1984, became one of only a tiny number of records
to cross between the city's diverse party scenes with the convergent force that
characterized so many releases from the opening years of the decade, and the
number shrank some more during 1985 as the subdivision of the city's party
scene around rap and house hardened. Whatever the explanation — and it's
hard to avoid concluding that the sonic separation was rooted in wider social
and economic developments — the open exchange of the early 1980s diminished as records started to assume clearer generic identities.

The subdivision of the city's party scene became more explicit when Chicago house broke in New York during 1985. Bruce Forest followed by Larry
Levan locked into the new sound, alive to its call to communal togetherness
and physical release. "A lot of house lyrics were like commands, such as 'Jack
Your Body,' but a lot of them were about the importance of friendship," points
out Riley. "I think there was a collective sense of loss for what was disap-
pearing from the 1970s and house music helped counter that." But hip hop
protagonists didn't go for the sound at all, with Public Enemy rapper Chuck
D convinced that whereas rap "could offer a very thorough shot at criticiz-
ing something and not be mistaken for what it was talking about, house was
too sparse on the ideology of it all." Public Enemy producer Hank Shocklee
matched hard-hitting syncopated beats to Chuck D's high-octane vocals.
"You looked at the black community and it was a shambles," he recounts.
"Crack was at an all-time high plus there were no jobs. It was *insane*. I didn't
want to pacify the situation; I wanted to wake people up. And I realized that if
it was a dance record it would be a distracted statement because when you're
dancing you're thinking about girls and sex." Nelson George cemented the
break when he argued in his 1988 book *The Death of Rhythm and Blues* that
disco diluted and then led to the downfall of R&B, only for rap to emerge as
black music's fighting reply. In so doing he established the enduring myth that

rap and hip hop emerged apart from and as a cohesive reaction against disco. Meanwhile rap's journey into harder, more aggressive territory didn't appeal to crowds that included a significant percentage of gay men, including the ones that gathered at Better Days, the Loft, and the Paradise Garage.

Whereas taste tribes formed in unpredictable patterns during the opening years of the 1980s, from 1983 and 1984 onward they subdivided around house, rap, and (in the case of the Saint crowd) Hi-NRG, drawn to the way these sounds offered some kind of solution to the crises they were experiencing around homophobia, racism, and inequality. "In the early '80s, everything was progressive," Afrika Bambaataa commented later. "People listened to funk, soul, reggae, calypso, hip hop all in the same place." But by the late 1980s, continued the Zulu Nation DJ, club culture resembled a form of musical apartheid. "If you wanted house music, you went to this club, reggae another club, and hip hop yet another club."[33] The flight into generic obedience threatened to wipe out the memory of a time when music couldn't be straightforwardly subdivided. "I remember there was a real mix of music," notes Barry Walters. "I think that is really what defined the first half of the 1980s in a way that is hard to understand from the perspective of what came after, where DJs would play one sound throughout the entire night and beatmix everything and become famous for one particular sound."

Three ensuing periods saw the Manhattan party scene undergo a revival before it was sucked into a semicomatose state. First, the economic slowdown of the late 1980s, the recession of 1990–1991, and the concomitant becalming of the real estate market created a window of possibility that saw influential new venues such as the Sound Factory and Shelter open, even as AIDS, heroin, and crack continued to devastate the city's party scene, with Haring (1988), Basquiat (1990), Wojnarowicz (1992), and Levan (1992) all dying young. Second, Mayor Rudolph Giuliani initiated a sweeping "zero tolerance"/"quality of life" crackdown on nightlife institutions between 1994 and 2001 that "dwarfed" measures introduced by Koch and before him David Dinkins, notes urban geographer Laam Hae, and while crime and the number of AIDS deaths fell during his tenure, both trends began in the pre-Giuliani era.[34] Finally, multibillionaire Mayor Michael Bloomberg toned down the regulatory attack on nightlife yet did little to encourage its revitalization as the wealth divide widened during his 2002–2013 tenure, with the offshoot Brooklyn scene quickly was sucked into the logic of gentrification. And so the streets of downtown and other parts of Manhattan have become largely moribund zones, the city's remarkable outpouring of music and dancing during the 1970s and early

1980s a fading memory that hangs over buildings long since converted to retail outlets and luxury apartments.

Were the participants in the Manhattan party scene of the early 1980s and the preceding years somehow responsible for its demise? In *Loft Living*, her classic study of the artistic colonization of SoHo, Sharon Zukin details the way the artistic daughters and sons of real estate investors hoovered up as many loft spaces as possible while pressuring the city to rezone them as residential, so they could be legally inhabited and gain in value, and she also notes how property developers encouraged artists and musicians to decamp in run-down, low-rent neighborhoods as part of a "'historic compromise' between culture and capital."[35] Developing the critique, David Harvey argues that cultural producers became entangled in the neoconservative agenda during the 1970s and 1980s. "The narcissistic exploration of self, sexuality, and identity became the leitmotif of bourgeois urban culture," he maintains. "Artistic freedom and artistic licence, promoted by the city's powerful cultural institutions, led, in effect, to the neoliberalization of culture [and] . . . erased the collective memory of democratic New York."[36] Even if the downtown scene isn't named as such, Harvey and Zukin heavily imply that its protagonists at best inadvertently and at worst knowingly championed the shift from industrial to postindustrial capitalism. It was on their watch that the collective gave way to the individual, nowhere articulated more clearly than in the demise of union power and the rise of freelance creativity. Upon this disaggregation the wealthiest members of society oversaw the rollout of policies that promoted deregulation, competition, individualism, and rising inequality.

Although the complexity of this argument cannot be fully addressed here, it can be acknowledged that many downtowners became alarmed at the manner in which the wider SoHo artist community became embroiled in the process of gentrification. David Mancuso warded off artist opposition when opening on Prince Street, only for Rudolf Piper to face unyielding pressure to abandon Pravda, after which the Colab artist collective brought attention to the struggle in the *Real Estate Show*. Then again, the financial yields made by a minority of artists who managed to buy property in SoHo couldn't disguise the experience of the majority of downtowners, who were displaced from both SoHo and the less salubrious neighborhoods that surrounded it as rents went through the roof (including recently leaking roofs that landlords were now much quicker to mend). At the same time, there can be no straightforward celebration of the Fordist era, which promoted conservative conformism as well as forms of collectivity. The radical protest movements of the late 1960s challenged that conformism head-on and the artistic community that took root in downtown New York became one expression of that energy — an energy that encompassed an explosive range of ideas and groupings that had struggled to find voice and expression in established political settings. The broader will to freedom contributed to the emergence of an alternative form of progressive politics that sought to eke out space between the traditional lines of political struggle. A new form of engagement beckoned.

That much was clear to the French literary critic, cultural theorist, and CBGB-turned-Mudd Club regular Sylvère Lotringer, who had made it his mission to introduce French and Italian political theory into the United States via the establishment of the journal *Semiotext(e)* and the staging of a "Schizo-Culture" conference at Columbia University. Lotringer drew particular inspiration from the writings of Gilles Deleuze, Michel Foucault, and Félix Guattari, who critiqued the traditional left for being too authoritarian, too centralized, and too narrow in its definition of the working class, and as he started to frequent downtown venues during the second half of the 1970s he came to believe their decentralized, fluid, pluralistic modus operandi unknowingly articulated the cultural, philosophical, and political principles laid out by Deleuze, Foucault, and Guattari. Sharing a Fashion District loft with Diego Cortez, Lotringer meshed together post-1968 philosophy with contributions authored by downtown artists, filmmakers, and musicians in a special issue of *Semiotext(e)* titled "Schizo-Culture."[37] "Artists then resisted commercialism in every possible way," remembers Lotringer. "Only when they were touring in Europe did they get some attention. They were living in precarious conditions, but they didn't mind it then. They were making up a tight and self-supportive community and we didn't much care for outside recognition." He adds of the Mudd Club: "It was so loud that no one could ever talk with each other. Just dancing among this crowd was meaningful enough. We all knew each other and there was a sense of togetherness."[38]

With the energy, openness, and inventiveness of their activity taking the place of a political manifesto, the downtown coalition of hosts, promoters, curators, and partygoers overturned aesthetic conventions; parodied conservative values; ironized kitsch; recycled and improvised; carried the rainbow energies of the countercultural movement into third-wave feminism, queer politics, and new forms of black expressivity; bypassed established models of success; and renounced corporate prerogatives as they shaped a form of entrepreneurialism that showed no more than a passing interest in money. Lotringer must have wondered if his "Schizo-Culture" belief in the need for the creation of a "nomadic entity" that displayed a "libidinal fluidity" and an "irreducible multiplicity," through which "desire could be directly coupled to the socius" as it rid itself "step-by-step" of repressive prohibitions, had started to take shape.[39] Grounded in a heady mix of creativity, pleasure, participation, work, collaboration, critique, humor, friendship, community, and openness, New York's proliferating happenings, concerts, art shows, screenings, and dance nights certainly existed as a radical alternative to the conservative environments in which so many participants had grown up. At times it seemed as if the countercultural movement of the 1960s was on replay, only this time with the utopian hopes of global transformation reined in.

The idea that a broader political plane existed — one that could change the way life was being experienced in downtown — only occasionally came into focus. Colab staged shows that explored politics and power, Glenn O'Brien toyed with the idea of turning New York into a never-ending episode of *TV Party*, and the city's art-punk clubs hosted political benefits when they didn't need to skimp for their own survival. But participants were more or less unified in the belief that the established political parties along with trade unions and the church had no understanding of their desire to break with the hierarchical, ordered, and often regressive status quo. Of the opinion that New Yorkers were already experiencing "everything that the French had already thought," Lotringer set about coediting a special issue of *Semiotext(e)* on the Italian Autonomist movement, which saw students, workers, and intellectuals forge a new anti-authoritarian framework for work and politics, until the state crushed their activity.[40] Raising money for the issue, Lotringer teamed up with Cortez to auction off donated downtown artworks, only for gallerist Annina Nosei to withdraw her offer to host the event when she became concerned she would be arrested next time she set foot in Italy. Cortez sold the works separately, organized a *Semiotext(e)* benefit at the Mudd Club with Frank Zappa as DJ, and designed the ensuing issue. "The audience was a mixture between the political world — which actually didn't react too much to it — then the artworld and the punk world," recalls Lotringer. "It didn't matter what audience was reading it and I didn't worry what they were getting from it, as long as they had one way of connecting to it."[41]

Although it didn't produce an overarching political philosophy, the downtown scene intersected with Autonomism in numerous ways. Founding theorist Antonio Negri would later recall in an interview with Lotringer how Italian workers demanded "new forms of work, of culture, of life" as they self-organized to the point where entire neighborhoods became de facto no-go areas for the police, not because of the level of violence but because workers "were able to organize the social fabric."[42] The movement and its theorists introduced a new Marxist vocabulary that called for workers to redefine work rather than fight to improve existing conditions as well as to separate themselves from capitalism rather than overthrow the capitalist class. "People always talk about the necessity of power, but power is necessary only for the boss," Negri added to Lotringer, reflecting on the movement's break with the traditional left. "It is not necessary for life."[43] Much of this would have chimed with downtowners who picked up the Autonomia issue of *Semiotext(e)*. "The prevailing feeling was that it was more important to discover the capabilities of human existence than to actually control society," observes Leonard Abrams, "so the reigning mood was to lose control rather than gain control."

Negri and coauthor Michael Hardt would go on to argue that post-Fordism came about not because capital needed to forge new ways of making money following the decline of Western industrialism but because the workers, students, women, young people, people of color, and other participants in the social movements of the late 1960s grew tired of the regulations and repressions of the old order and sought out something different. Although disputed by those who attribute a greater role to capital, the account captures the reason so many artists and musicians headed downtown.[44] Correspondingly, there can be no argument that capital engineered the cultural movements that grew out of the Loft, the Kitchen, and CBGB when music corporations remained so oblivious to their early incarnations and took so long to profit from their creative power. But capital intensified its power and profitability under Augusto Pinochet, under the cloak of the New York banking crisis, and under Reagan, as Harvey recounts, while the cultural history offered in these pages indicates that the shift into an epoch rooted in individualism, competition, and rising concentrations of wealth started to take effect in New York during 1983.[45] Unleashed by ongoing waves of deregulation and market liberalization, the drive to profitability has subsequently reshaped post-Fordism as an era driven by individual rather than collective freedom. Downtown's shifting ratio of shops to party spaces during the last forty-five years tells this story with admirable precision.

If the political weakness of the downtown scene was ultimately exposed by its breakup and eviction, it remains the case that no political party, trade union, or activist group managed to halt the forward march of neoliberalism, even though they were more obviously qualified to understand and act upon developments. Perhaps both groups would have discovered more resilience if they had tapped into one another's capacities, but few foresaw the scale or consequences of the neoliberal turn, and few felt compelled to explore their shared strategic concerns. When Lotringer and Cortez saw their rent go up from $300 to $2,500 a month, they moved out, and equivalent detonations resulted in the displacement of artists and musicians all over the city. At least some remnants of the party network survived as places of refuge and community. "Pyramid was completely mixed and really amazing and really liberating and very anti-what was going on with Reagan," argues Ivan Baker of one. "You had this antithesis of what was going on nationally and what was going on in New York. There was this polarization between class and sex and art and music. It almost felt in those Reagan days that creativity was under attack and here you had this little gem of freedom, of creativity, and of expression. It was like an oasis."

More than thirty years after the downtown era began to implode, interest in the era is growing exponentially, from the establishment of the "Downtown Collection" at New York University to the steady stream of reissues and compilation albums that pepper record release schedules, from James Murphy's formation of LCD Soundsystem as a ca. 1982 electro-punk-disco-dub outfit to the release of the footage shot for *New York Beat* as *Downtown '81*, from the steady stream of downtown art and no wave publications to the staging of *East Village USA* at the New Museum. Meanwhile the legacy of the early 1980s and the years that preceded their spectacular unfolding is in good health, with DJ-ing ubiquitous; punk continuing to circulate as the most recognizable sound of rebellion; the principles of disco absorbed within international dance culture; rapping, breaking, and graffiti known the world over; synthesizers and drum machines along with techniques such as mash-ups and sampling omnipresent; the principle that musicians should be free to move between genres commonplace; and the likes of Bambaataa, Basquiat, Blondie, Flash, Haring, Mancuso, Levan, and Talking Heads identified as legendary innovators, with Madonna one of the most successful pop stars of all time. Clearly culture has continued to evolve in ways that don't reference these developments and figures. Clearly culture can draw its inspiration from other epochs, not to mention other cities. Yet the frequency with which contemporary practices can be traced back to the early 1980s and that period's umbilical connection to the socio-sonic movements of the previous decade remains remarkable, and the phenomenon prompts interest in the past.

The flurry can be partly explained by the way pop culture has become "obsessed with the cultural artifacts of *its own immediate past*," as music critic Simon Reynolds argues in *Retromania*, and the accumulating parade of YouTube clips, reunion tours, reissues, and retro-driven sounds certainly suggests that the mining of the early 1980s is part of a wider phenomenon.[46]

Within the pantheon of eras that can be revisited, the early 1980s stands out for being the first to thoroughly forge its music through the recombination of already existing sounds — namely disco, punk, funk, and dub reggae. It was also the last to produce music that was largely grounded in analogue combinations, with the release of the Yamaha DX7 synthesizer in 1983 a key marker of the digital tsunami that would soon unfold. If those troubled by the rise of digitization can find refuge in the era, others who are at one with the phenomenon can look back to it as a window when connectedness and creativity — two of the defining characteristics of digitization — came into sync, with the added romance that they did so in the flesh rather than via a phone, tablet, or computer.

Viewed from the vantage point of any number of global cities where the cost of living has driven organic culture to the periphery and beyond, however, the downtown era resonates with particular force because of the way an economically battered yet spiritually resilient city fostered a socio-sonic eruption of parties, recordings, artworks, happenings, and performances. If New York encountered a treacherous combination of spiraling debt, declining services, exploitative landlords, and stubbornly high crime rates, it also enjoyed a reputation for being the preeminent destination for anyone who wanted to make a stand, a place where dreams could be fulfilled as what sometimes seemed like the whole world squeezed into its perimeter, and during the early 1980s inhabitants new and old headed out to the city's party spaces with renewed democratic intent. The contrast between the version of the city that used to attract moneyless people who wanted to build a life and the one where the best those without capital can hope for is to commute to its center to carry out jobs that will never enable them to establish a home in its increasingly exclusive landscape is dramatic and continually charges the fascination with this bygone era. Memories of this earlier period support the idea that the present remains contingent. As a result they inspire hope.

The music that followed captured the multiple energies of a city in which different communities came into kaleidoscopic contact with one another, bursting with soul-sonic force (as one Zulu Nation lineup encapsulated it). There were times when New York sounded like it was one giant speaker system as car radios, boom boxes, and sound systems ushered in a period of "sonic dominance," as critic Julian Henriques describes any situation where the aural holds sway over the visual.[47] Even the most compelling art of the era — of Basquiat, Futura, Haring, Quiñones, Scharf, Wojnarowicz, and others — grew out of and in many respects embodied the steamy, vibrant, tactile personality of the city's party scene. When these artistic works and musical recordings are encountered today, a city that pulsated with a gritty, resilient, electrifying energy bursts through, announcing "this is what it felt like to be alive back then."

To argue that things aren't as good as they used to be is not only boring but also insensitive to the way each generation throws up new energies as humans do what they're preprogrammed to do: seek out each other and find ways to communicate. Brooklyn has provided the most obvious home to such activity in recent years, having started to attract artists fleeing inflationary Manhattan since the early 1980s, with Williamsburg, DUMBO, Greenpoint, and Bushwick the key hot spots. Yet if asked to compare the two, Jeffrey Deitch maintains that the Brooklyn scene has never matched downtown's concentrated energy and inventiveness, and with a one-bedroom apartment in Williamsburg going for $2,000 a month, the type of artist who can hope to make a stand there has become circumscribed. That could simply mean that each successive scene will take root that little bit further away from the center, with artists and musicians forging concentric circles of cultural action, spreading culture, wealth, and gourmet cafés as they plough their path. The underlying trend, however, is one of displacement, or what Harvey terms "accumulation by dispossession," whereby high-value land is captured from low-income inhabitants, many of them tenants forced to move out because of spiraling rents, and the culture that survives any such gentrifying revival is usually restricted, especially if it has anything to do with sound.[48]

The process can only logically conclude with musicians and artists heading to the outskirts of New York until they abandon the city altogether. Indeed many started to relocate to Jersey City during the late 1990s, with cultural producers also contributing to the doubling of the number of Americans living in Berlin between 2005 and 2014.[49] "I came to Berlin and the canvas is insane," Brooklyn party promoter Dan DeNorch told the *New York Times* in 2014. "There's so much that's possible here, because of the spaces, because of the music culture that's grown up around here. I mean, in New York it's so hard to find a small club or a medium-sized club with a subwoofer, because of noise complaints."[50] As easy as it is to be seduced by downtown's legendary reputation, the migration away suggests that its importance lay in its discarded unimportance, its down-and-out affordability and off-the-radar ventures establishing it as a space where New Yorkers from all five boroughs could contribute to its steamy range of activity. Participation and possibility were all. "Nothing is impossible," reasons Chi Chi Valenti, "but it's less possible now to open a club like the Mudd Club or Danceteria or Area in Manhattan than any of the thirty-plus years I've been there."

The point isn't to make a judgment about contemporary art and music, but instead to draw attention to the way shifting conditions have led the home- grown art and music scene to lose its hold over the workings of the city. Critic Elizabeth Currid argues that New York risks undermining the art and cultural quotient of its economic turnover, with the sector the fourth largest employer in the city, because the prohibitive cost of living combined with the punitive approach toward nightlife has undermined the "the very means by which the cultural economy operates."[51] Yet if that doomsday scenario remains real, it's conceivable the city could sustain and even boost its art and cultural sector through the basic licensing, marketing, and showcasing of nonlocal art, both old and new, integrating its historic fomentation of disco, punk, and hip hop into a brand identity. It follows that the value of an indigenous art, music, and party culture should be assessed in terms of not only naked economic statis- tics but also the immense social contribution it makes to the life of the city. If culture continues to circulate through New York, the aggregation is manifestly diminished, and that constitutes a loss for any city that aspires to nurture a sense of participation, democracy, and well-being as well as economic activity.

It can be sobering to conduct a tour of the locations that used to host the city's thriving party network. The building at 77 White Street (once the Mudd Club) is now a block of luxury apartments, 99 Prince Street (once the Loft) houses a J. Crew store and a high-end restaurant, 84 King Street (once the Paradise Garage) operates as a Verizon office, the Crosby Street apartment where Basquiat lived can be rented out for $650/night, and 30 West 21st (once Danceteria) has been turned into a luxury residential unit known as Alma ("soul" in Spanish) with units marketed at $5,995,000 to $10,000,000 in the spring of 2008. "The building sure has come a long way from club kids and Madonna performances," ran the sales blurb, "though maybe Madge will buy in the building just for nostalgia's sake."[52] Having returned to Brazil, Piper wonders about the well-being of the city he once called his home. "It seems that, in the future, the New York of the early eighties will be remembered as one of those mythical places, like Paris in the twenties or Shanghai and Ber- lin in the thirties — places where freedom was so absolute it could not last," comments Piper. "A once grand, magical, venomous center of the world has been transformed into a ridiculous, self-pitying village of Wall Streeters, all looking for the next trendy restaurant serving the finest zucchini, all text- messaging feverishly night and day."

At least a chorus of dissenting voices can now be heard. They range from the Brooklyn DJ team Mister Saturday Night, who wonder what it might have been like to participate in the "rich culture of dancing" that "existed before the Giuliani regime," to David Byrne, who warned in 2013 that "bit by bit, the resources that keep the city vibrant are being eliminated," to critic Jason Farago, who noted in the *New Republic* that "it's a testament to how constrained and inert the city has become that the 1970s, the most unloved decade of the recent past, now seems to so many young New Yorkers like a golden age."[53] Then, in early 2015, Mayor Bill de Blasio announced a plan to create eighty thousand new affordable homes in the city by 2024, including two thousand live/work homes and affordable workspaces for low-income artists and musicians. Perhaps the memory of living through the peak of the downtown scene and tracking the rise of Grandmaster Flash while majoring in Metropolitan Studies at NYU (where De Blasio enrolled in 1979) contributed to the move. "We know that New York is the city it is today in part because of the contributions from generations of artistic visionaries who at one point struggled to make ends meet," explained the mayor, before adding that New York's reputation as a "city that unleashed human potential" was now at risk because "the city has for decades let developers write their own rules when it came to building housing."[54]

Even if there can be no straightforward return, a discussion is under way as to what the period signifies. Conservatives juxtapose images of homeless people, hypodermic syringes, and subway graffiti in order to damn the era as terminally poverty-stricken, violent, and anarchic. At the same time nostalgists fetishize its "outward signs of hardship and violence," as Charlie McCann observes in *Prospect*.[55] Both groups have made a habit of representing tough times as being cataclysmic, so the *New York Daily News* 29 October 1975 headline "Ford to New York: Drop Dead" is routinely cited in relation to the city's near bankruptcy, yet rare reference is made to the president's ensuing loan. The dangerousness of the era is also routinely hyped, so while just over 2,220 murders were recorded in 1980, making it the most murderous year since records began, it is rarely added that the rate went on to peak at just over 2,600 in 1990, perhaps because that statistic doesn't fit the grand narrative of New York's market-driven revival during the 1980s.[56] If squalor was widespread, those who camped in run-down apartments weren't homeless, and while heroin is regularly glamorized, usage was restricted and contributed little in the way of creativity, with totemic figures such as Basquiat and Levan producing their best work before they became regular users. In short, the era wasn't quite as down-and-out as many make it seem. "Don't romanticize having no money!" warns Ann Magnuson. "But would I rather be a twenty-two-year-old now or back then? Back then, absolutely."

The recollections of those who contributed to the party scene of the early 1980s go well beyond the clichés of addiction, dereliction, fear, and suffering. Instead they describe the potential of a city locking into a pulsating rhythm of such insistent energy it burst into a musical and artistic renaissance of historic proportions. The early 1980s were a time of full-throttle expressivity and immersive community, a time that witnessed the city's party network become a source of pleasure, hope, expression, community, and interaction; a time when the vibrations of art-punk, hip hop, and transcendental dance riffed off one another as they forged a democratic, pluralistic movement that seemed to know no limit; a time that only subdivided and diminished when confronted by the omni-assault of neoliberalism, AIDS, and crack. Clearly the task of redemocratizing New York and indeed other global cities remains daunting, yet the gathering desire to listen to music, dance, and engage creatively with a level of public freedom that was once taken for granted is visceral. Feeding the appetite for change, the downtown era and its scarcely believable level of activity attest that, given the right conditions, a different kind of city can exist.

NOTES

PREFACE

1. José Muñoz, "Ephemera as Evidence: Introductory Notes to Queer Acts," *Women and Performance: A Journal of Feminist Theory* 8, no. 2 (1996): 5–18, quote on 16; also quoted in Halberstam, *In a Queer Time and Place*, 161.

2. Halberstam, *In a Queer Time and Place*, 169.

3. Lefebvre, *Writings on Cities*, 173.

4. Zukin, *Naked City*, 23.

INTRODUCTION

1. Both polling figures are included in "Distrust, Discontent, Anger and Partisan Rancor," Pew Research Center for the People and the Press, 18 April 2010, available at http://www.people-press.org/2010/04/18/section-1-trust-in-government-1958-2010/, retrieved 5 September 2014.

2. Lester Thurow, "The Editorial Notebook: Enough of Economic Fits and Starts; Slow, Steady Growth Will Work Better than Induced Spasms," *New York Times*, 31 December 1979.

3. "The Seventies and How We Got Away with It," *New York Magazine*, 31 December 1979, 34.

4. Ibid.

5. Jack Egan, "Future Hock: The Economy," *New York Magazine*, 31 December 1979, 38.

6. "Seventies and How We Got Away with It," 35.

7. "Editorial: Dumping Koch," *Village Voice*, 26 August 1981, 3.

8. Joe Conason and Jack Newfield, "The Men Who Are Burning New York," *Village Voice*, 2 June 1980, 15–19. Quoted arson figures are also drawn from this article.

9. Lunch, untitled essay, in Taylor, *Downtown Book*, 95.

10. Baker, *New York Noise*, 157.

11. Taylor, *Downtown Book*, 31.

12. Gallup poll data for January 1980, available at http://www.gallup.com/poll/110548/gallup-presidential-election-trialheat-trends-19362004.aspx#2, retrieved 8 September 2014.

1 **STYLISTIC COHERENCE DIDN'T MATTER AT ALL**

1. Leonard Abrams, "Steve Mass," *East Village Eye*, November 1983, 10.

2. Debord, *Society of the Spectacle*.

3. Cortez, *Private Elvis*.

4. Masters, *No Wave*, 14.

5. Richard Williams, "Energy Fails the Magician," *Melody Maker*, 12 January 1980, available at http://eno-web.co.uk/interviews/melma80b.html, retrieved 15 September 2014.

6. Brien Coleman, "Tina L'Hotsky . . . High Priestess," *East Village Eye*, summer 1979, 31.

7. "Etc.," *East Village Eye*, 15 June 1979, 14.

8. Flyer, "War Games: Combat Love Party," 20 June 1979. Scan held by the author.

9. Gendron, *Between Montmartre and the Mudd Club*.

10. "Why Are Lines Shorter for Gas Than the Mudd Club in New York? Because Every Night Is Odd There," *People Magazine*, 16 July 1979, available at http://www.people.com/people/archive/article/0,,20074119,00.html, retrieved 13 September 2014.

11. John Holmstrom, *Punk*, January 1976, reprinted in Holmstrom, *Punk*.

12. Miezitis, *Night Dancin'*, 209.

13. Richard Fatina, "Johnny Dynell: Too Hot to Handle," *East Village Eye*, July 1983, 17.

14. Pablo "Cuchi-Frito" Cordova, "How I Beat Cancer by Listening to Disco Music," *SoHo News*. No date or page on photocopy.

15. Fantina, "Johnny Dynell," 17.

16. Chance quoted in Moore and Coley, *No Wave*, 13.

2 **THE BASEMENT DEN AT CLUB 57**

1. Strychacki, *Life as Art*, 24–25.

2. Ibid., 46.

3. Ann Magnuson, "I Dreamed I Was an Androgynous Rock Star in My Maidenform Bra," *ZG*, winter 1982; reprinted in Moore and Miller, *The Book: ABC No Rio Dinero*, excerpt available at http://98bowery.com/return-to-the-bowery/abcnorio-the-neighborhood.php, retrieved 21 May 2014.

4. Information drawn from the August calendar for Club 57 (original held by Ann Magnuson; scan held by author); Ann Magnuson, "Ann Magnuson on Club 57" in "The East Village 1979–1989," *Artforum*, October 1999, 121.

5. Strychacki, *Life as Art*, 57, 59.

6. Judy Jones and William Wilson, "The Late Shows: New York from Eleven to Three," *New York Magazine*, 10 March 1980, 73.

7. Gruen, *Keith Haring*, 46, 47.

8. Hager, *Art after Midnight*, 72.

9. Advertisement, *East Village Eye*, summer 1980, 41; "Benefit," *New Yorker*, 8 September 1980, 28.

10. "Mudd Club Playboy Party," 23 October 1980. Original flyer held by Steve Mass; scan held by author.

11. Elkin information from Candy Clandestine, "Pooper Scoopers," *East Village Eye*, Christmas 1980, 11.

12. Jones and Wilson, "Late Shows," 72.

13. Mudd Club advertisement, *East Village Eye*, summer 1980, 7.

14. Flyer, "War Games: Combat Love Party," 20 June 1979. Scan held by author.

15. Leonard Abrams, "Steve Mass," *East Village Eye*, November 1983, 11.

16. Brien Coleman, "Tina L'Hotsky . . . High Priestess," *East Village Eye*, summer 1979, 31.

3 DANCETERIA

1. Michael Shore, "Jim Fouratt: One Step Beyond," *SoHo News*, 16 April 1980.

2. Alan Platt, "In Defense of Pravda," *SoHo Weekly News*, 27 December 1979, 8.

3. Mary Breasted, "The Truth about Pravda," *SoHo Weekly News*, 20 December 1979, 7; Eric Nadler, "Debating Pravda," *SoHo Weekly News*, 24 January 1980, 4; Judy Jones and William Wilson, "The Late Shows: New York from Eleven to Three," *New York Magazine*, 10 March 1980, 70.

4. Video information drawn from Richard Fantina, "NuVue << >> Video," *East Village Eye*, summer 1980, 32.

5. Malu Halasa, "New and Used Clubs," *East Village Eye*, summer 1980, 26. Spelling correction made.

6. Iman Lababedi, "Average Normal: Jim Fouratt," *East Village Eye*, January 1982, 21.

7. Date reference is from Roman Kozak, "Peppermint Rocks Off Times Square," *Billboard*, 3 October 1981, 34.

4 SUBTERRANEAN DANCE

1. Cheren, *My Life and the Paradise Garage*, 219.

2. Author holds a dated recording of the night; from the private collection of Conor Lynch.

3. Cheren, *My Life and the Paradise Garage*, 219.

4. Mark Riley, interview with Tee Scott, broadcast on WWRL-FM in 1994. The precise date of the interview is not traceable. A recording of the interview is held in the private collection of Simon Halpin.

5. Undated letter from Michael Brody, addressed to the Paradise Garage membership list. The letter referred to the introduction of a new Thursday men-only night beginning on 5 June, which makes it likely it was written in the spring. Transcription of the letter held by author.

6. Riley, interview with Scott.

7. Alex Pe Win, "Victor Rosado (Paradise Garage, NYC). Interviewed by Alex, 16/02/05," *Voices*. Original publication date unknown, retrieved 19 December 2008.

8. Riley, interview with Scott.

9. Ibid.

1. Howard Smith and Cath Cox, "Scenes," *Village Voice*, 12 February 1979, 30.

2. Philip Faflick, "The SAMO Graffiti . . . Boosh-Wah or CIA?" *Village Voice*, 11 December 1978, 41.

3. Quoted in Nicola Vassel, interview with Fred Brathwaite, "Rapping with Fab 5 Freddy," in Deitch et al., *Jean-Michel Basquiat 1981*, 118.

4. Ibid.

5. Glenn O'Brien, "The TV Party Story," available at http://www.tvparty.org, retrieved 6 January 2010.

6. Tamra Davis, dir., *Jean-Michael Basquiat: The Radiant Child*, Arthouse Films, 2010.

7. Deitch, "A Dialogue between Diego Cortez and Glenn O'Brien," in Deitch et al., *Jean-Michel Basquiat 1981*, 19.

8. Ibid., 14.

9. Glenn O'Brien, "Graffiti '80: The State of the Outlaw Art," *High Times*, June 1980, 52.

10. Susana Sedgwick, "Times Square Show," *East Village Eye*, summer 1980, 21.

11. Jeffrey Deitch, "Report from Times Square," *Art in America*, September 1980, 61.

12. Quote from Bill Brewster, interview with Charlie Ahearn, "Charlie Ahearn," 22 March 2001, available at http://www.djhistory.com/interviews/charlie-ahearn, retrieved 13 September 2014.

13. Chang, *Can't Stop Won't Stop*, 149.

14. Chris Chase, "At the Movies," *New York Times*, 25 November 1983.

15. Brewster, interview with Ahearn.

16. Troy L. Smith, interview with Coke La Rock, available at http://www.thafoundation.com/coke.htm, retrieved 27 October 2010.

17. Alex Gayle, "The Oral History of 'Wild Style,'" 11 October 2013, available at http://www.complex.com/pop-culture/2013/10/oral-history-wild-style/page/2, retrieved 15 December 2013.

18. Cooper, *Hip Hop Files*, 178.

19. Chang, *Can't Stop Won't Stop*, 132.

20. "Dubbed in Glamour" press release, November 1980. An original copy is held in the archives of the Kitchen Center; electronic copy held by author.

21. Video recording of Funky 4+1 performance at the Kitchen, available at http://www.egotripland.com/funky-four-plus-one-the-kitchen-1980-video/, retrieved 5 January 2015.

22. Gruen, *Keith Haring*, 65.

23. Ibid., 66.

24. Ibid.

25. Ibid., 45, 62.

26. Ibid., 60.

27. Ibid., 58, 60.

28. Ibid., 60.

29. Ibid., 57.

30. Flyer dated 29 October 1980. Scan of flyer held by author.

31. Ronald Smothers, "Koch Calls for Dogs in Fight on Graffiti," *New York Times*, 27 August 1980.

32. "Henry Chalfont: Photographer to the Car," *East Village Eye*, August 1982, 24.

33. "Crying Wolf," *New York Times*, 29 August 1980; Caryl S. Stern and Robert W. Stock, "Graffiti: The Plague Years," *New York Times*, 19 October 1980.

34. Stern and Stock, "Graffiti."

35. Gruen, *Keith Haring*, 68.

36. Ibid., 70.

37. Ibid.

38. Ibid., 68.

39. Grandmaster Flash and Ritz, *Adventures of Grandmaster Flash*, 149.

6 **THE SOUND BECAME MORE REAL**

1. Quoted in Moore and Coley, *No Wave*, 98.

2. Quoted in Reynolds, *Rip It Up and Start Again*, 68.

3. James White, "White & Co. Move Uptown," *East Village Eye*, May 1979, 8.

4. Barry Lederer, "Disco Mix," *Billboard*, 16 February 1980, 50.

5. "Christina, Christina Monet," *Dance Music*, 1 February 1980, 5.

6. Peter Holsapple, "Back in the Public Eye," *New York Rocker*, February 1980, 34. Minor spelling correction made.

7. TAS [Thomas A. Silverman], "Kid Creole & the Coconuts, Kid Creole & the Coconuts," *Dance Music*, 1 March 1980, 5.

8. "Industry Update," *Dance Music*, 29 March 1980, 1.

9. Stephen Barth, "Chasing the Bush Tetras," *East Village Eye*, March 1980, 11.

10. Marguerite Van Cook, "Snuky Tate and Octaroon," *East Village Eye*, summer 1980, 31.

11. Greg McLean, "Byrne Gets the Third Degree," *New York Rocker*, November 1980, 13.

12. "Remain in Light," *Dance Music*, 8 November 1980, 6.

13. Robert Ford Jr., "Jive Talking N.Y. DJs Rapping Away in Black Discos," *Billboard*, 5 May 1979, 3.

14. "Rap Records: Are They Fad or Permanent?" *Billboard*, 16 February 1980, 57.

15. Lawrence, "Mixed with Love"; Lawrence, "Disco Madness," 15.

16. Cheren, *My Life and the Paradise Garage*, 266.

17. Lawrence, *Hold on to Your Dreams*, 171.

18. Ibid., 153.

19. "Reviews," *Dance Music Report*, 29 March 1980, 5.

20. Cheren, *My Life and the Paradise Garage*, 264.

21. Ibid., 267.

7 MAJOR-LABEL CALCULATIONS

1. Information drawn from "Disco — The Real Story — Part V: Dance Music — Does It Sell?" *Dance Music*, 26 April 1980, 7–8.

2. Brian Chin, "Dance Trax," *Billboard*, 22 December 1984, 44.

3. Barry Lederer, "Disco Mix," *Billboard*, 19 January 1980, 46. Minor grammatical correction made.

4. Tom Topor, "Disco Boss," *New York Post*, 5 January 1980. No page number on photocopy.

5. Ibid.

6. "Industry Update," *Dance Music*, 1 March 1980, 1, 3.

7. "Forum Attendees Unite, Vow to Aid Disco," 23 February 19890, *Billboard*, 3.

8. "'It's Simple Dance Music,' Enthusiasts Agree," *Billboard*, 22 March 1980, 50.

9. "Neil Bogart's Keynote Highlights," *Billboard*, 5 April 1980, 14.

10. Steve Singer, "Sales Action: The Spinner's Circle," *Dance Music*, 1 March 1980, 10.

11. "Presidents' Panel Topics Strikes a Sensitive Nerve," *Billboard*, 16 August 1980, 46; "Disk Breakers," *Billboard*, 16 August 1980, 52.

12. Radcliffe Joe, "No Nonsense Forum Attacks '80s Problems," *Billboard*, 16 August 1980, 45.

13. Howard Smith, "The Record Biz: Where Is It Going?" *Village Voice*, 4 February 1980, 26–27. Minor spelling correction made.

14. "Industry Update," *Dance Music*, 26 April 1980, 1, 3.

15. "Who's Who in A&R at RFC/Warner Brothers: Interview Notes with Ray Caviano," *New on the Charts*, September 1980, 17.

16. Ibid.

8 THE SAINT PETER OF DISCOS

1. White, *States of Desire*, 259.

2. Ibid., 272.

3. Darrell Yates Rist, "A Scaffold to the Sky and No Regrets," *New York Native*, 2 May 1988, 17.

4. Pamela C. Smith, "Fillmore East Changing Its Tune," *East Village Eye*, June 1980, 5.

5. A range of figures are quoted in Claudia Cohen and Cyndi Stivers, "I, Claudia," *New York Daily News*, 15 September 1980; Nathan Fain and Jil Lyne, "The New Boogie Merchants," *After Dark*, September 1980, 47–51; and Jan Hodenfield, "A Gay Disco on a Grand Scale," *Daily News*, 17 November 1980.

6. George Finley, "A Star Is Born in the Man-Made Environment," *Lighting Design*, January/February 1981, 30. Minor grammatical correction made.

7. Ed Constantly, "Profile: Mark Ackerman," *Star Dust*, September 1982, 14.

8. "The Saint," *Sound & Video Contractor*, 15 April 1984, 36, 40.

9. According to InflationData.com, inflation from October 1980 to October 2010 totals 157.91 percent, so the $125 membership would have cost $322.38 in 2010, the $10 entry for members $25.79, and the $18 charge for nonmembers $46.42.

10. The capacity figures are drawn from Hodenfield, "Gay Disco."

11. "Second Avenue," *SoHo News*, 22 October 1980, 10; Yates Rist, "Scaffold to the Sky," 17–18.

12. Jeff Dupre, interview with Steve Casko for a documentary about the Saint, undated; Yates Rist, "Scaffold to the Sky," 17–18.

13. Andrew Holleran, "Marching into the Saint," *SoHo News*, 24 September 1980, 4.

14. Jeff Dupre, interview with Michael Fierman for a documentary about the Saint, undated.

15. Holleran, "Marching," 4.

16. Dupre, interview with Fierman.

17. Holleran, "Marching," 4.

18. In a 1988 interview Bruce Mailman asserted that the Saint attracted three thousand dancers every week during its peak years (Yates Rist, "Scaffold to the Sky," 18). The figures quoted here are based on estimates provided by Mailman's assistant in an email exchange dated 12 August 2011 with Robbie Leslie.

19. Yates Rist, "Scaffold to the Sky," 17.

20. Dupre, interview with Fierman.

21. "Second Avenue," 10.

22. Ibid.

23. Pamela C. Smith, "Fillmore East Changing Its Tune," *East Village Eye*, June 1980, 5.

24. "Second Avenue," 10.

25. Hodenfield, "Gay Disco."

26. Andrew Holleran, "Adiós, Sebastian," *New York Native*, 2 May 1988, 20.

9 LIGHTING THE FUSE

1. Herschel Johnson, "The Discotheque Scene," *Ebony*, February 1977, 56.

2. Judy Jones and William Wilson, "The Late Shows: New York from Eleven to Three," *New York Magazine*, 10 March 1980, 67.

3. Don Weinbrenner, "Disco to Fill 3 Floors with Palatial Splendor," *New York Daily News*, 27 April 1980.

4. Radcliffe Joe, "N.Y. Roxy Owner Sees Sunshine," *Billboard*, 15 November 1980, 72.

5. Richard Fantina, "Rrrudolf," *East Village Eye*, Thanksgiving 1980, 9.

6. Richard Williams, "Energy Fails the Magician," *Melody Maker*, 12 January 1980, available at http://eno-web.co.uk/interviews/melma80b.html, retrieved 15 September 2014.

7. Carr, *Fire in the Belly*, 170, 200.

8. Richard Fantina, "TV Party Interview with Glenn O'Brien," *East Village Eye*, March 1980, 9.

9. Glenn O'Brien, "The TV Party Story," available at http://www.tvparty.org/, retrieved 6 January 2010.

10. Gendron, *Between Montmartre and the Mudd Club*, 301.

11. Mark Riley, interview with Tee Scott, broadcast on WWRL-FM in 1994.

12. *Mixmaster*, 1 July 1978.

13. Quoted in Soffer, *Ed Koch*, 259.

14. Blake Fleetwood, "The New Elite and Urban Renaissance," *New York Times*, 14 January 1979.

15. Ibid.

16. Kostelanetz, *SoHo*, 223.

17. Randall Rothenberg, "Hey, This Way (➡) To Brooklyn!" *New York Times*, 4 February 1980.

18. Quoted in Soffer, *Ed Koch*, 259.

19. Chafe, *Unfinished Journey*, 437.

20. Quoted in Frank Rose, "Welcome to the Modern World," *Esquire*, April 1981, 32.

10 EXPLOSION OF CLUBS

1. Jeffery Kahn, "Ronald Reagan Launched Political Career Using the Berkeley Campus as a Target," *UC Berkeley News*, 8 June 2004, available at http://www.berkeley.edu/news/media/releases/2004/06/08_reagan.shtml, retrieved 19 November 2014; quoted in Cannon, *Governor Reagan*, 295.

2. Georgia Dullea, "Mudd Club Regulars Celebrate Inaugural," *New York Times*, 22 January 1981.

3. Stephen Saban, "Haoui Does It," *SoHo News*, 24 June 1981, 22.

4. Van Gosse, "Dancing in My Booth," *Village Voice*, 23 September 1981, 93.

5. Iman Lababedi, "Average Normal: Jim Fouratt," *East Village Eye*, January 1982, 21. Lababedi notes she first interviewed Fouratt back in June. The quote is from that interview.

6. Fouratt references Bambaataa's appearance at the New Music Seminar showcase in Jim Fouratt, "How I Made a Scene: Notes from a Club Impresario," *Village Voice*, 23 October 1984, 49.

7. Radcliffe Joe, "Studio 54 Is Regaining Popularity," *Billboard*, 6 June 1981, 71.

8. Marie Brenner, "Can Studio 54 Be Born Again?" *New York Magazine*, 28 September 1981, 38.

9. Clovis Ruffin, "Can Souffle Be Reheated? The Reopening of Studio 54," *Village Voice*, 23 September 1981, 23.

10. Jim Fouratt, "How I Made a Scene: II. My Life in Clubland," *Village Voice*, 23 October 1984, 50.

11. John Duka, "Notes on Fashion," *New York Times*, 25 August 1981.

12. "E," *East Village Eye*, summer 1981, 18.

13. Jil Lynne and Nathan Fain, "New Boogie Merchants," *After Dark*, September 1980, 50.

14. Henry Post, "New Wave after Dark: The Big Clubs," *New York Magazine*, 3 November 1980, 55.

15. Richard Grabel, "Rap, Rap, Rap," *New Music Express*, 30 May 1981, 32.

16. Arnold H. Lubasch, "Cash Skimming at Discothèques Alleged by I.R.S.," *New York Times*, 16 August 1980.

17. Richard M. Nusser, "4 Disco Men Admit Income Tax Evasion," *Billboard*, 11 October 1980, 6; Radcliffe Joe, "N.Y. Bond's Casino Up for Sale," *Billboard*, 15 November 1980, 72.

18. Roman Kozak, "Bond's Becomes 'Everything' Club," *Billboard*, 4 April 1981, 63.

19. Mick Farren, "The Longest Week," *SoHo News*, 10 June 1981, 70.

20. Michael Hill, "The Clash at the Clampdown," *Village Voice*, 10 June 1981, 74.

21. Jan Westervelt, "Rhys Chatham Interview," *East Village Eye*, February 1980, 19. Minor spelling correction made.

22. Information from "Aluminum Nights: The Kitchen's Birthday Party and Benefit," 14–15 June 1981. PDF of brochure held by author.

23. John Rockwell, "Avant-Gardists in Midtown for Benefit," *New York Times*, 13 June 1981.

24. Astor, *Fun Gallery*, 92–93.

25. Bond's benefit information is available at http://www.youtube.com/watch?v=Sg69WMIVIj4, posted 9 February 2011, retrieved 5 November 2014.

26. Posted by Daddy on 16 February 2004 at http://motherboards.infopop.cc/eve/forums/a/tpc/f/23310500341/m/3616064165/p/1, retrieved 18 February 2010.

27. Peppermint Lounge flyer, July 1981. Scan held by author; original held by David King.

28. Frank Rose, "Welcome to the Modern World," *Esquire*, April 1981, 32.

29. Ibid., 39.

30. Ibid.

31. Ibid.

11 ARTISTIC MANEUVERS IN THE DARK

1. Diego Cortez with Marc Miller," ART/*new york* no. 5, 1981, www.artnewyork.org, available at http://artforum.com/video/id=30181&mode=large&page_id=8, retrieved 4 September 2014.

2. Diego Cortez and Edit deAk talk, "The Night Time Is the Right Time," date unknown, published in Moore and Miller, *The Book*; also available at http://98bowery.com/return-to-the-bowery/abcnorio-the-neighborhood.php, retrieved 26 May 2014.

3. Kay Larson, "History's Fickle Finger," *New York Magazine*, 16 March 1981, 60.

4. Deitch et al., *Jean-Michel Basquiat 1981*, 90.

5. Gruen, *Keith Haring*, 62.

6. Press release, *Lower Manhattan Drawing Show*, 10 February 1981. Original held by Steve Mass; scan held by author.

7. Kim Levin, "Anarchy in the M.C.," *Village Voice*, 4 March 1981, 70.

8. Caryl S. Stern and Robert W. Stock, "Graffiti: The Plague Years," *New York Times*, 19 October 1980.

9. Strychacki, *Life as Art*, 85–86.

10. *Beyond Words* press release. From the personal collection of Johnny Dynell; scan held by author.

11. Steven Hager, "Is the Art World Ready for Graffiti?" *New York Daily News*, 9 April 1981.

12. Gruen, *Keith Haring*, 74.

13. Fouratt references Bambaataa's appearance at the New Music Seminar showcase in Jim Fouratt, "How I Made a Scene: Notes from a Club Impresario," *Village Voice*, 23 October 1984, 46.

14. Glenn O'Brien, "Basquiat: The Show Must Go On." Written for an exhibition of works by Basquiat at Sotheby's, available at http://glennobrien.com/?p=1086, retrieved 13 August 2014.

15. Deitch et al., *Jean-Michel Basquiat 1981*, 19.

16. Quoted in ibid., 120.

17. Anthony Haden-Guest, "The Roving Eye," *Artnet*, 22 September 1999, available at http://www.artnet.com/Magazine/features/haden-guest/haden-guest9-22-99.asp, retrieved 17 May 2014.

18. Chris Chase, "At the Movies," *New York Times*, 25 November 1983.

19. Willard Jenkins, "Fab 5 Freddy: The Max Roach Influence," *JazzTimes*, 26 May 2011, available at http://jazztimes.com/articles/27743-fab-5-freddy-the-max-roach-influence, retrieved 5 May 2011.

20. Chase, "At the Movies."

21. Alex Gale, "The Oral History of 'Wild Style,'" *Complex Pop Culture*, 11 October 2013, available at http://www.complex.com/pop-culture/2013/10/oral-history-wild-style/page/3, retrieved 2 December 2013.

22. Steven Hager, "Patti Astor," *East Village Eye*, February 1983, 8.

23. Ibid.

24. Astor, *Fun Gallery*, 113.

25. Hager, "Patti Astor," 8.

26. Grace Glueck, "The New Collectives — Reaching for a Wider Audience," *New York Times*, 1 February 1981.

27. Pat Wadsley with Leonard Abrams, "(More Than) Fashion Moda," *East Village Eye*, Thanksgiving 1980, 38.

28. Sally Webster, "Fashion Moda: A Bronx Experience," 1996, available at http://www.lehman.cuny.edu/vpadvance/artgallery/gallery/talkback/fmwebster.html, retrieved 8 April 2014.

29. "Tim Rollins Interviews Richard of East 13th Street," published in Moore and Miller, *The Book*; also available at http://98bowery.com/return-to-the-bowery/abcnorio-the-neighborhood.php, retrieved 26 May 2014.

30. Astor, *Fun Gallery*, 173.

31. Deitch et al., *Jean-Michel Basquiat 1981*, 16.

32. Astor, *Fun Gallery*, 115.

33. Haden-Guest, *True Colors*, 129. Minor grammatical correction made.

34. Lewis, *Power Stronger Than Itself*, 384.

35. Gendron, "Downtown Music Scene," 50.

12 DOWNTOWN CONFIGURES HIP HOP

1. "MCs Invade the Ritz," *Dance Music Report*, 28 March 1981, 11.

2. Vince Aletti, "Golden Voices and Hearts of Steel," *Village Voice*, 18 March 1981, 57.

3. Michael Hill, "The Clash at the Clampdown," *Village Voice*, 10 June 1981, 74.

4. Ibid.

5. Richard Grabel, "Flash Is Fast: Flash Is Cool," *New Musical Express*, 26 September 1981, 15, 49.

6. Hager, *Hip Hop*, 32.

7. Schloss, *Foundation*, 88.

8. Cooper, *Hip Hop Files*, 70.

9. "Henry Chalfant: Photographer to the Car," *East Village Eye*, August 1982, 24. Minor spelling correction made.

10. Sally Banes, "To the Beat, Y'All: Breaking Is Hard to Do," *Village Voice*, 22 April 1981, 31.

11. Chang, *Can't Stop Won't Stop*, 157.

12. Fab 5 Freddy Love's name was cited in publicity for the Common Ground performance at the end of Banes, "To the Beat," 33.

13. "Henry Chalfant," 24.

14. Barbara Crossette, "A Three-Day Celebration of Bronx Folk Culture," *New York Times*, 15 May 1981.

15. Michael Holman, "Breakdown, Top Rock," *East Village Eye*, summer 1981, 43.

16. McLaren quotes taken from the track "It Was a New York Phenomenon," released on Malcolm McLaren, featuring the World's Famous Supreme Team vs. Rakim, KRS-One, Soulson, Hannibal Lechter, Da Boogie Man, and T'Kalla, *Buffalo Girls: Back to the Old School* (Virgin, 1998).

17. Lisa Dennison, *Clemente*, exhibition catalog, Guggenheim Museum, New York, 1999, available at http://www.ubs.com/microsites/art_collection/home/the-collection/a-z/informations/clemente-francesco/perseverance.html, retrieved 2 June 2014.

18. Fricke and Ahearn, *Yes Yes Y'all*, 45.

13 THE SOUND OF A TRANSCENDENT FUTURE

1. "A Dialogue between Two Editors: Vince Aletti and Michael Gomes," *Mixmaster*, summer 1978.

2. Albin Krebs and Robert McG. Thomas Jr., "Notes on People; Expanding Disco Sees Better Nights Ahead," *New York Times*, 11 June 1981.

3. Miezitis, *Night Dancin'*, 115.

4. The installation of the new lighting system is noted in "New Lighting for Paradise Garage," *Billboard*, 24 May 1980, 41.

5. Vernon Gibbs, "Grace Jones Has Great Cheekbones," *Village Voice*, 5 August 1981, 55.

6. "Sound Secrets of Paradise Garage Unveiled," *Billboard*, 27 December 1980, 25, 27; Radcliffe Joe, "Home Sound Go," *Billboard*, 14 March 1981, 52.

7. Joe, "Home Sound Go," 51.

8. Ibid., 52.

9. Steven Harvey, "Behind the Groove," *Collusion*, September 1983, 30.

10. "Sound Secrets of Paradise Garage Unveiled," *Billboard*, 27 December 1980, 25, 27.

11. Alan Fierstein and Richard Long, "State-of-the-Art Discotheque Sound Systems — System Design and Acoustical Measurement," presented to the sixty-seventh convention of the Audio Engineering Society, 31 October to 1 November 1980, available at http://www.acoustilog.com/disco1.html, retrieved 13 January 2010.

12. Ibid.

13. Mark Riley, interview with Tee Scott, broadcast on WWRL-FM in 1994.

14. George Kopp, "Sound Systems," *Billboard*, 16 August 1980, 53.

15. Diamond, *Life Energy in Music*, 7, 30.

16. Ibid., 37.

14 THE NEW URBAN STREET SOUND

1. Daniel Wang, interview with Tee Scott, 14 July 1994. Download of interview posted at www.geocities.com/jahsonic/TeeScott.htm, held by author.

2. Ibid.

3. Vince Aletti, "Disco Takes to the Streets," *Village Voice*, 4 March 1981, 53.

4. Nelson George and Brian Chin, "Dance Clubs, Black Radio Interacting More Closely," *Record World*, 4 July 1981. Page number is missing from the photocopy.

5. Taken from Malcolm McLaren's spoken-word history on "Bow Wow Wow Show (Live)," from *Buffalo Girls: Back to the Old School*.

6. Grandmaster Flash and Ritz, *Adventures of Grandmaster Flash*, 150.

7. Richard Grabel, "Flash Is Fast: Flash Is Cool," *New Musical Express*, 26 September 1981, 15.

8. TL, "Grandmaster Flash: 'The Adventures of Grandmaster Flash on the Wheels of Steel,'" *Dance Music Report*, 23 May 1981, 4.

9. Kristine McKenna, "Tom Tom Club," *New York Rocker*, January 1982, 16.

10. Brian Chin, "Disco File," *Record World*, 3 October 1981, 18.

11. Strummer was talking to Antonino D'Ambrosio in 2002, quoted in D'Ambrosio, "'Let Fury Have the Hour': The Passionate Politics of Joe Strummer," *Monthly Review*, June 2003, available at http://www.monthlyreview.org/0603ambrosio.htm, retrieved 4 March 2010. Minor spelling corrections made.

12. Toop, *Rap Attack 3*, 110.

1. Perry Meisel, "A P -- k F -- k Glossary," *Village Voice*, 19 August 1981, 58.

2. David Keeps, "Beat. Sound. Motion," *New York Rocker*, October 1981, 40.

3. Marjorie Karp, "ESG: One Household under a Groove," *New York Rocker*, November 1981, 22.

4. Michael Shore, "Jim Fouratt: One Step Beyond," *SoHo News*, 16 April 1980.

5. Ira Kaplan, Greg McLean, and Andy Schwartz, "30 New York Bands," *New York Rocker*, December 1980, 26–27.

6. Richard M. Nusser, "Indies Find Sweet Success on Disco's Top 100 Chart," *Billboard*, 14 February 1981, 44.

7. Robert Palmer, "The Pop Life: Kid Creole: He Mixes a Heady Brew of Styles," *New York Times*, 10 June 1981.

8. Ibid.

9. Axel Gros, "Eno/Interview," *East Village Eye*, summer 1981, 11.

10. Ibid.

11. Vernon Gibbs, "Grace Jones Has Great Cheekbones," *Village Voice*, 5 August 1981, 55.

12. Stephen Holden, "Pop-Disco: Grace Jones," *New York Times*, 8 August 1981.

13. Phil Dimauro, "Island Records: Musical Diversity Yields Commercial Success," *Record World*, 4 July 1981, 8.

14. Hager, *Hip Hop*, 32.

15. Tom Moulton, "Disco Mix," *Billboard*, 8 May 1976.

16. Hebdige, *Cut 'n' Mix*.

17. Greg Wilson, "For the Love of Money: The Untold Story of an Underground Classic," 2004, available at http://www.electrofunkroots.co.uk/interviews/tony_williams.html, retrieved 10 February 2010.

18. Vince Aletti, "England's New Slant on Soul," *Village Voice*, 5 August 1981, 55.

19. Ibid.

20. Ibid.

21. Brian Chin, "Disco File," *Record World*, 5 September 1981, 46.

22. Karp, "ESG," 22. Minor grammatical corrections made.

16 **FROZEN IN TIME OR FREED INTO INFINITY**

1. George Stambolian, "Requiem for a Great Pink Bird," *New York Native*, 9 March 1981, 14.

2. Ibid.

3. Jan Carl Park, "The A-Gay's Disc Jockey: Robbie Leslie and the Politics of the Turntable," *New York Native*, 20 June 1983, 37. The "smooth flow" quote is from an interview with author.

4. Roy Thode set at the Black Party, the Saint, held in early 1981. MP3 recording provided by Marsha Stern.

5. Jean Williams, "Why Sylvester Has Altered His Sound," *Billboard*, 20 June 1981, 62.

6. "The New Segregation," *Dance Music Report*, 23 May 1981, 2.

7. Jesse Kornbluth, "Merchandising Disco for the Masses," *New York Times*, 18 February 1979; "Fragmentation," *Dance Music Report*, 24 October 1981. No page on author's photocopy.

8. Cheren, *My Life and the Paradise Garage*, 319.

9. William Alvis, "The Saint: The Vatican of Clubs," *After Dark*, May 1981, 66, 68–69.

17 IT FELT LIKE THE WHOLE CITY WAS LISTENING

1. The information on Chin's column appears in "Industry Update," *Dance Music Report*, 11 April 1981, 1.

2. Brian Chin, "Disco File," *Record World*, 22 August 1981, 40.

3. Tom Silverman, "Dance Music Retailing: The New Specialty," *Dance Music Report*, 11 April 1981, 14. Spelling correction made.

4. Ibid. Spelling correction made.

5. "Industry Update," *Dance Music Report*, 20 June 1981, 1.

6. John Rockwell, "New-wave Rock Seeks 'Chart Penetration,'" *New York Times*, 16 July 1981.

7. Martha Hume, "Old, Borrowed, but Nothing New," *New York Daily News*, 27 December 1981.

8. "WBLS Unfair to White Record Companies!" *Dance Music Report*, 18 July 1981, 16.

9. Information on the content of the other shows is drawn from Steven Harvey, "Supreme Team: Rockin' the Air," *New York Rocker*, October 1982, 6.

10. "Disco Mix," *Billboard*, 4 July 1981, 69.

11. "Industry Update," *Dance Music Report*, 20 June 1981, 13.

18 SHROUDED ABATEMENTS AND MYSTERIOUS DEATHS

1. Harvey, *Brief History of Neoliberalism*, 46.

2. Tabb, *Long Default*, 2.

3. Ibid., 15.

4. *New York Times*, 6 November 1980. Quoted in Soffer, *Ed Koch*, 223.

5. Clyde Haberman, "Koch Calls for Expanding Services in $14.8 Billion Fiscal '82 Budget," *New York Times*, 17 January 1981.

6. Harvey, *Brief History of Neoliberalism*, 24–25.

7. Edward A. Gargan, "Rebuilding Plan for City Property Offered by Koch," *New York Times*, 13 May 1981.

8. Clyde Haberman, "Reagan's Policies 'Sham and Shame,' Koch Says in Talk," *New York Times*, 2 December 1981.

9. Soffer, *Ed Koch*, 259.

10. Edward A. Gargan, "Try to Work In: Is the City Building Its Tax Base or Eroding It?" *New York Times*, 26 July 1981.

11. Ibid.

12. Brian Chin, "Disco File," *Record World*, 14 November 1981, 16.

13. Ibid., 26 December 1981, 62.

14. Larry Mass, "Disease Rumors Largely Unfounded," *New York Native*, 18 May 1981, 7. According to Dudley Clendinen and Adam Nagourney, Mass believed the title of the article misrepresented its contents (*Out for Good*, 451).

15. Lawrence K. Altman, "Rare Cancer Seen in 41 Homosexuals," *New York Times*, 3 July 1981, available at http://www.nytimes.com/1981/07/03/us/rare-cancer-seen-in-41-homosexuals.html, retrieved 17 April 2010.

16. Clendinen and Nagourney, *Out for Good*, 463.

19 ALL WE HAD WAS THE CLUB

1. Michael Hill, "Clubs Will Tear Us Apart," *Village Voice*, 6 January 1982, 33–39.

2. Robert Palmer, "Pop Jazz: The Bloom Has Faded at Small Rock Clubs," *New York Times*, 29 May 1981.

3. Richard Fatina, "Interview with Frank Roccio," *East Village Eye*, April 1982, 24.

4. Merle Ginsberg, "Venues," *New York Rocker*, June 1982, 38.

5. Strychacki, *Life as Art*, 65.

6. John Rockwell, "Notes: Rock Comes to the Aid of Art," *New York Times*, 13 June 1982.

7. "No Entiendes" flyer, 22 September 1982. Original held by John Argento; scan held by author.

8. Jim Fouratt, "How I Made a Scene: II. My Life in Clubland," *Village Voice*, 23 October 1984, 50.

9. Iman Lababedi, "Average Normal: Jim Fouratt," *East Village Eye*, January 1982, 21. Minor spelling correction made.

10. Danceteria press release, 31 May 1982. Original held by John Argento; scan held by author. Date provided by John Argento.

11. Roman Kozak, "Danceteria Rights Contested," *Billboard*, 21 August 1982, 50. Minor spelling correction made.

12. "Bound for Glory!" flyer. Original held by John Argento; scan held by author.

13. Jon Pareles notes the 1950s decor in "Dance and Music Clubs Thriving in Era of Change," *New York Times*, 12 November 1982.

14. Stephen Saban, "Oh, Mama, Can This Really Be the End?" *Details*, December 1982, 4–5.

20 INVERTED PYRAMID

1. Kęstutis Nakas, "Behind the Scenes at Manhattan's Wildest Performance Club," *In Touch for Men*, 1983, available at http://www.johnkellyperformance.org/Site/clubPress.html, retrieved 16 July 2010. No information is provided on the publication month of the magazine.

2. Tricia Romano, "Nightclubbing: New York City's Pyramid Club," *Red Bull Music Academy*, 4 March 2014, available at http://www.redbullmusicacademy.com/magazine/nightclubbing-pyramid, retrieved 23 September 2014.

3. First quote from Rose, "Judy and Mickey's Bohemia." No pages included in the digital version.

4. Merle Ginsberg, "We Tell You Where to Go," *SoHo News*, 16 February 1982, 16.

5. Nakas, "Behind the Scenes."

6. Ibid.

7. Quoted in C. Carr, "Silence=Life: John Kelly Represents in Mime," *Village Voice*, 10 September 2002, available at http://www.villagevoice.com/news/silence-life-6412564, retrieved 19 July 2010.

8. Information taken from http://orangeexplainsitall.blogspot.com/search/label/Larry %20Ree, posted 29 April 2008, retrieved 20 July 2010.

9. Joe E. Jeffreys, "Queen of a Thousand Faces: The Illustrious Life of Ethyl Eichel-berger," *Outweek* 66, 3 October 1990, 41. Quoted in Rose, "Judy and Mickey's Bohemia."

10. Nakas, "Behind the Scenes."

11. The details of the theme party nights are drawn from Rose, "Judy and Mickey's Bohemia."

12. David McDermott, "Gay Shame," *East Village Eye*, summer 1980, 5.

13. Ibid.

14. Astor, *Fun Gallery*, 114.

15. Steven Hager, "Lee Quinones at the Fun Gallery," *East Village Eye*, July 1982, 34.

16. "Henry Chalfont: Photographer to the Car," *East Village Eye*, August 1982, 24.

17. Rene Ricard, "The Radiant Child," *Artforum*, December 1981, available at http://artforum.com/inprint/issue=198110&id=35643, retrieved 3 July 2014.

18. Jeffrey Deitch, "Jean-Michel Basquiat: Annina Nosei," *Flash Art*, May 1982, 50.

19. Cathleen McGuigan, "New Art, New Money," *New York Times*, 10 February 1985.

20. Emmerling, *Jean-Michel Basquiat*, 57.

21. McGuigan, "New Art, New Money."

22. Cortez interviewed by Deitch et al., *Jean-Michel Basquiat 1981*, 16.

23. Astor, *Fun Gallery*, 150.

24. *ART/New York No. 19 — Young Expressionists*, directed by Marc. H. Miller and Paul Tschinkel (Inner-Tube Video, 1982), available at from http://www.youtube.com/watch?v =kSEAyxs6MEQ, retrieved 4 March 2013.

25. Astor, *Fun Gallery*, 151.

26. Ricard, "Radiant Child."

27. Astor, *Fun Gallery*, 148.

28. Jeffrey Deitch, "Why the Dogs Are Barking," in *Keith Haring: New York City*, fall 1982, 17–20 (New York: Tony Shafrazi Gallery, 1982). Reprinted in Sussman, *Keith Haring*, 88.

29. Steven Hager, "Art on the Block," *East Village Eye*, October 1982, 8.

30. Ibid.

31. Ibid., 9.

32. Original transcript of John Gruen's interview with Keith Haring, published in Deitch et al., *Keith Haring*, 212.

33. Gruen, *Keith Haring*, 88.

34. Carr, *Fire in the Belly*, 244.

35. Ibid., 231.

36. Gruen, *Keith Haring*, 75–76.

37. Deitch et al., *Keith Haring*, 172.

38. Ibid.

39. Ricard, "Radiant Child."

21 ROXY MUSIC

1. Michael Holman, "An Interview with DJ Africa [*sic*] Bambaata [*sic*] of the Zulu Nation," *East Village Eye*, January 1982, 22.

2. Ibid.

3. Cooper, *Hip Hop Files*, 130.

4. Michael Hill, "DJ Afrika Bambaataa and Zulu Nation/Rock Steady Crew: Club Negril NYC," *New York Rocker*, March 1982, 45.

5. Monica Lynch, "Red Hot," *Dance Music Report*, 6 February 1982, 11.

6. Ibid., 6 March 1982, 11.

7. "Roxy Roller Disco Is Sold; Refurbished," *Billboard*, 19 September 1981, 65, 67.

8. The flyer is reproduced in Brewster and Broughton, *Last Night a DJ Saved My Life*, 231.

9. Holman, "Interview," 29.

10. Ibid.

11. Tony Heiberg, "Afrika Speaks," *East Village Eye*, June 1983, 12.

12. Ruza Blue, "Beating the Rap," *Details*, June 1982. No pages provided in the issue.

22 THE GARAGE

1. Steven Harvey, "Behind the Groove," *Collusion*, September 1983, 30.

2. Terry L. Lind, "Peech Boys: 'Don't Make Me Wait,'" *Dance Music Report*, 20 March 1982, 3.

3. Marjorie Karp Spencer, "Peech Buzz," *Village Voice*, 27 April 1982, 68.

4. Brian Chin, "Disco File," *Record World*, 13 March 1982, 33.

5. Brewster and Broughton, liner notes to *Larry Levan's Paradise Garage*.

6. Stephen Saban, "It Was Very Nice. . . . It Was (Not Was) Paradise," *SoHo News*, 9 February 1982, 26.

7. Troy L. Smith, interview with Coke La Rock, available at http://www.thafoundation.com/coke.htm, retrieved 27 October 2010.

8. Ruza Blue, "Beating the Rap," *Details*, June 1982. No pages provided in the issue.

9. Gruen, *Keith Haring*, 88–89.

10. Ibid., 89.

11. Deitch et al., *Keith Haring*, 18.

1. Steven Hager, "It's the Sure Shot," *East Village Eye*, June 1982, 11.

2. Brian Chin, "Where the Beat Meets the Street," *Billboard*, 19 June 1982, DD-8.

3. Hager, "It's the Sure Shot," 11.

4. Steven Hager, "Afrika Bambaataa's Hip Hop," *Village Voice*, 21 September 1982, 73.

5. Bambaataa quoted in ibid.

6. Richard Grabel, "Brother to Brother," *New York Rocker*, May 1982, 54.

7. JayQuan, interview with Ed Fletcher, February 2007, available at http://www.thafoundation.com/dukebootee.htm, retrieved 11 June 2010.

8. Fletcher's account of the writing process is provided in JayQuan, interview with Fletcher.

9. Grandmaster Flash and Ritz, *Adventures of Grandmaster Flash*, 157.

10. Ibid., 158.

11. Steven Hager, "Melle Mel: Behind the Message," *East Village Eye*, September 1982, 10.

12. Brian Chin, "Dance Trax," *Billboard*, 24 July 1982, 44.

13. Hager, "Melle Mel," 10.

14. Robert Palmer, "Pop Jazz," *New York Times*, 3 September 1982, C4.

15. Kurt Loder, " 'The Message': Grandmaster Flash and the Furious Five," *Rolling Stone*, 16 September 1982, 52.

16. Ibid.

17. Marshall Berman, "Roots, Ruins, Renewals," *Village Voice*, 4 September 1984, 25.

18. Tompkins, *How to Wreck a Nice Beach*, 220.

19. Hager, "Afrika Bambaataa's Hip Hop," 72.

20. Ibid.

21. Ibid., 73.

22. Ibid.

23. Ibid.

24. Steven Hager, "The Pied Piper of Hip Hop," February 6, 2012, available at http://stevenhager420.wordpress.com/tag/jean-michel-basquiat/, retrieved 1 May 2013.

25. Alan Patt, "Monsieur Butterfly," *Details*, November 1984, 87.

26. Brian Chin, "Dance Trax," *Billboard*, 11 December 1982, 46.

27. Michael Robinson, "Man Parrish: Hip Hop Be Bop," *Dance Music Report*, 27 November 1982, 4; Brian Chin, "Dance Trax," *Billboard*, 8 January 1983, 60.

28. "Part One of Celluloid Records Documentary Series with Bill Laswell, DXT and Jean Karakos," Strut Records, 11 March 2013, available at http://www.strut-records.com/part-one-of-celluloid-records-documentary-series-with-bill-laswell-dxt-jean-karakos/, retrieved 11 July 2013.

29. Bernard Zekri, "Is Europe Ready for Hip Hop?" 26. In Andrea Caputo (curator), *All City Writers: The Graffiti Diaspora* (Bagnolet, France: Kitchen93 / Critique Livres, 2009), 26–27.

30. Date provided by Becker, "The Adventures of Futura 2000," *East Village Eye*, January 1982, 23.

31. Zekri, "Is Europe Ready for Hip Hop?," 27.

32. Date provided by Celluloid, available at http://www.celluloidrecords.net/releases /CEL102.php, retrieved 11 June 2014.

33. David Hershkovits, "London Rocks, Paris Burns, and the B-Boys Break a Leg," *New York Daily News*, 3 April 1983; reprinted in Cepeda, *And It Don't Stop*, 30.

24 TECHNO FUNKSTERS

1. "Dinosaur L: 'Go Bang #5,'" *Dance Music Report*, 1 May 1982, 3.

2. Vince Aletti, "'D' Train Live," *Village Voice*, 29 June 1982, 86.

3. Ibid.

4. Steven Harvey, "LP Reviews: Various Artists: Mastermixes (Prelude)," *New York Rocker*, September 1982, 38.

5. Steven Harvey, "Behind the Groove," *Collusion*, September 1983, 33.

6. "Madonna: 'Everybody,'" *Dance Music Report*, 30 October 1982, 8.

7. Astor, *Fun Gallery*, 150.

8. Brian Chin, "Dance Trax," *Billboard*, 12 June 1982, 62.

9. Brian Chin, "Dance Trax," *Billboard*, 3 July 1982, 40; Brian Chin, "Dance Trax," *Billboard*, 27 November 1982, 36; Brian Chin, "Disco File," *Record World*, 3 October 1981, 18.

25 TASTE SEGUES

1. Steve Harvey, "Taxi Drivers: Sly and Robbie Cross All Over," *New York Rocker*, November 1981, 45; Steven Harvey, "Spin Art," *New York Rocker*, January 1982, 27.

2. Steven Harvey, "Singles: Rappin' about Rappin'," *New York Rocker*, June 1982, 22.

3. Steven Harvey, "Vinyl Exams: Dance Stance: On the Floor with Steven Harvey," *New York Rocker*, July–August 1982, 22.

4. Robert Palmer, "They Stake Out the Frontiers of Pop," *New York Times*, 31 October 1982, Section 2, 21.

5. Carol Cooper, "August Darnell and the Creole Perplex," *Village Voice*, 27 July 1982, 61.

6. Cheren, *My Life and the Paradise Garage*, 293.

7. Undated interview with Dayna Newman, available at http://www.discomusic.com /people-more/9568_0_11_0_C/, retrieved 16 April 2009.

8. Cheren, *My Life and the Paradise Garage*, 318.

9. "New York Citi Peech Boys: 'Life Is Something Special,'" *Dance Music Report*, 25 December 1982, 10.

10. Brian Chin, "Dance Trax," *Billboard*, 20 November 1982, 54.

1. "Hot New Talent: Saint Opens Wednesday Nights for Seven Weeks Only," *Star Dust*, spring 1982, 9.

2. Roy Thode, "A Letter from a DJ," *Star Dust*, spring 1982, 2.

3. Ibid.

4. Ibid.

5. Glenn Person, "Dancing on without Roy Thode," *Star Dust*, September 1982, 12.

6. "Letters to the Editor or . . . ," *Star Dust*, September 1982, 11.

7. "Star Dust Speaks: An Editorial," *Star Dust*, September 1982, 3.

8. Shilts, *And the Band Played On*, 149; Jeff Dupre, interview with Michael Fesco for an unfinished documentary about the Saint, undated.

9. Person, "Dancing on without Roy Thode."

10. Mel Cheren records the date as 10 April in *My Life and the Paradise Garage*, 314, but the Thursday-night date indicates it was 8 April, as recorded in Andriote, *Victory Deferred*, 53.

11. Reported in Michael Ver Meulen, "The Gay Plague," *New York*, 31 May 1982, 54, quoted in Andriote, *Victory Deferred*, 53.

12. Ibid., 54.

13. Cheren, *My Life and the Paradise Garage*, 315, 316.

14. White, *City Boy*, 287.

15. Soffer, *Ed Koch*, 307.

16. Ibid., 308.

17. *New York Native*, 26 April 1982, quoted in Soffer, *Ed Koch*, 308.

18. Robin Herman, "A Disease's Spread Provokes Anxiety," *New York Times*, 8 August 1982.

19. Ibid.

20. Diebold, *Tribal Rites*, 9–10.

21. Brian Chin, "Dance Trax," *Billboard*, 27 November 1982, 36.

27 CUSP OF AN IMPORTANT FUSION

1. "Rubin's Charity a Runaway," *New York Magazine*, 26 April 1982, 13.

2. Steven Harvey, "Afrika Bambaataa & the Soul Sonic Force, Peech Boys, Bond's, NYC," *New York Rocker*, September 1982, 46.

3. Tom Silverman, "Dance Biz: The Disco Army," *Dance Music Report*, 6 March 1982, 12; Tom Silverman, "The Vinyl Glut Is Coming!" *Dance Music Report*, 3 April 1982, 22.

4. "Industry Update," *Dance Music Report*, 4 September 1982, 1; "Industry Update," *Dance Music Report*, 18 September 1982, 1; Nelson George, "Independent Labels Are Proliferating," *Billboard*, 6 November 1982, 48.

5. Nelson George, "Limited Editions, Remixes Are Key for Vinyl Mania," *Billboard*, 10 July 1982, 17.

6. Brian Chin, "Dance Trax," *Billboard*, 25 December 1982, 60, 61.

7. Nelson George, "Black '82,'" *Billboard*, 25 December 1982, TIA-8.

8. Charnas, *Big Payback*, 147–148.

9. George, "Black '82,'" TIA-8.

10. David Mills, "Disco Didn't Suck," *Washington Times*, 28 August 1989.

11. Jean Williams, "Black Radio Debates Urban Contemporary," *Billboard*, 9 January 1982, 1, 15.

12. Steven Harvey, "Supreme Team: Rockin' the Air," *New York Rocker*, October 1982, 6.

13. Rene Ricard, "The Pledge of Allegiance," *Artforum*, November 1982, available at http://artforum.com/inprint/ord=2&id=3677, retrieved 4 July 2014.

14. Ibid.

15. Marjorie Karp, "ESG: One Household under a Groove," *New York Rocker*, November 1981, 22. Minor grammatical corrections made.

28 CRISTAL FOR EVERYONE

1. "Etc. Etc.," *East Village Eye*, July 1983, 16.

2. Stephen Saban references the closing of the Mudd Club in "Season to Taste," *Details*, October 1983, 11.

3. Leonard Abrams, "Steve Mass," *East Village Eye*, November 1983, 11.

4. Saban, "Season to Taste," 12.

5. Rudolf Piper, interviewed on *Livewire*, 30 October 1983, available at http://www.youtube.com/watch?v=haHXisfvoeI, retrieved 20 February 2014 (minor correction made); *New York Dance Stand* episode, 1983 (precise date unknown), available at http://www.youtube.com/watch?v=jGHWNvNiAqc&feature=share, retrieved 22 February 2014.

6. Kęstutis Nakas, "Behind the Scenes at Manhattan's Wildest Performance Club," *Touch for Men*, 1983, available at http://web.mac.com/johnkellyperformance/Site/clubPress.html, retrieved 16 July 2010. No additional information is provided on the date of publication.

7. Tony Heiberg, "Ann Magnuson," *East Village Eye*, August 1983, 8.

8. Rose, "Judy and Mickey's Bohemia." No pages included in the digital version.

9. Art gallery figure from Hoban, *Basquiat*, 152.

10. Grace Glueck, "Gallery View; A Gallery Scene That Pioneers in New Territories," *New York Times*, 26 June 1983.

11. Steven Hager, "Patti Astor," *East Village Eye*, February 1983, 8. Minor spelling correction made.

12. Ibid. Minor spelling correction made.

13. Ibid., 9.

14. Deitch et al., *Keith Haring*, 236.

15. Ibid., 232.

16. Astor, *Fun Gallery*, 179.

17. "When Graffiti Paintings Sell for Thousands, the Art World Sees the Writing on the Wall," *People Magazine*, 22 August 1983, available at http://www.people.com/people/article/0,,20085742,00.html, retrieved 12 August 2014.

18. Ibid.

19. Astor, *Fun Gallery*, 177.

20. Ibid., 175.

21. Andrew Nosnitsky, "Basquiat's 'Beat Bop': An Oral History of One of the Most Valuable Hip-Hop Records of All Time," *Spin*, 14 November 2013, available at http://www .spin.com/articles/beat-bop-basquiat-k-rob-rammellzee-freak-freak/, retrieved 12 August 2014.

22. John Russell, "Why the Latest Whitney Biennial Is More Satisfying," *New York Times*, 25 March 1983.

23. Nosnitsky, "Basquiat's 'Beat Bop.'"

24. Ibid.

25. Goode and Goode, *Area*, 25.

26. Information on décor drawn from Stephen Saban, "The Night of the Iguana," *SoHo News*, 27 May 1981. Reprinted in Goode and Goode, *Area*, 26–27.

27. Goode and Goode, *Area*, 25.

28. Saban, "Season to Taste," 12. Minor spelling changes made.

29. Ibid.

30. Goode and Goode, *Area*, 32.

31. The estimated costs of the changes are drawn from Jesse Kornbluth, "Inside Area: The Wizardry of New York's Hottest Club," *New York Magazine*, 11 March 1985, 33.

32. Ibid., 40.

33. Astor, *Fun Gallery*, 177.

34. Sassen, "New York City," 91–92.

35. Figures drawn from forecastchart.com, available at http://www.forecast-chart.com /estate-real-new-york.html, retrieved 26 February 2010.

36. Sydney H. Schanberg, "Strictly Beau Monde," *New York Times*, 18 December 1982.

37. Damon Stetson, "New York Area Economy on the Mend as '83 Ends," *New York Times*, 1 January 1984.

38. Glenn O'Brien, "Culture Club," *New York Times*, 27 August 2006.

29 DROPPING THE PRETENSE AND THE FLASHY SUITS

1. Danceteria newsletter, untitled, undated (event range 16–19 March 1983). Original held by John Argento; scan held by author.

2. Michael Zelenko, "No Concessions: Legendary *Wild Style* Director Charlie Ahearn on Hip Hop's Unlikely Genesis," *Fader*, 27 September 2013, available at http:// www.thefader.com/2013/09/27/no-concessions-legendary-wild-style-director-charlie -ahearn-on-hip-hops-unlikely-genesis/, retrieved 17 August 2014.

3. Alex Gale, "The Oral History of 'Wild Style,'" *Complex*, 11 October 2013, available at http://www.complex.com/pop-culture/2013/10/oral-history-wild-style/page/2, retrieved 2 December 2013.

4. Steven Hager, "Patti Astor," *East Village Eye*, February 1983, 8, minor spelling correction made; Vincent Canby, "'Wild Style,' Rapping and Painting," *New York Times*, 18 March 1983.

5. Astor, *Fun Gallery*, 172.

6. Chris Chase, "At the Movies," *New York Times*, 25 November 1983.

7. Ibid.

8. Rob Baker, *Daily News*, 18 December 1983. No article title on photocopy.

9. Stephen Holden, "The Pop Life," *New York Times*, 28 September 1983.

10. Patricia Morrisroe, "The Punk Glamour God," *New York Magazine*, 5 April 2004, available at http://nymag.com/nymetro/arts/features/n_10106/index1.html, retrieved 9 July 2014.

11. Tony Heiberg, "Afrika Speaks," *East Village Eye*, June 1983, 12. Spelling correction made.

12. Reported in Kathy Nizzari, "DOR," *Dance Music Report*, 6 August 1983, 16.

13. Brian Chin, "Dance Trax," *Billboard*, 3 December 1983, 49.

14. Steven Hager, "Bugging Out on the Endless Peak," *Village Voice*, 17 May 1983, 1, 44–46.

15. Richard Grabel, "Burn This Disco Out," *New Musical Express*, 21 May 1983, available at http://www.djhistory.com/features/burn-this-disco-out-1983, retrieved 2 October 2010.

16. Ibid.

17. Ibid.

18. Carol Cooper, "Remembering the Fever," liner notes for various, *Hip Hop Fever*, Warlock Records, 2001.

19. Bill Adler, "The South Bronx Was Getting a Bad Rap until a Club Called Disco Fever Came Along," *People Magazine*, 16 May 1983, available at http://www.people.com /people/archive/article/0,,20084997,00.html, retrieved 7 October 2010.

20. Cooper, "Remembering the Fever."

21. Jon Pareles, "Rhythm in the Kitchen: Be-bop Meets Hip Hop," *New York Times*, 15 November 1983.

30 STRAIGHTEN IT OUT WITH LARRY LEVAN

1. Weinstein provided the information within Haden-Guest, *Last Party*, 247–248.

2. Bruno denied the accuracy of the quote in an interview with Spencer Rumsey and Richard Fantina, "Arthurgate," *East Village Eye*, March 1983, 4.

3. Stephen Saban, "The Lost Weekends," *Details*, March 1983, 4.

4. Ibid., 3; Rumsey and Fantina, "Arthurgate," 4.

5. Dave Peaslee, "Persecution and Prejudice: Their Effect on the NY Club Scene," *Dance Music Report*, 19 March 1983. No page on photocopy.

6. David W. Dunlap, "Two-thirds of City's Cabarets Violating the Fire Safety Law," *New York Times*, 28 March 1983.

7. Hae, "Dilemmas of the Nightlife Fix," 6.

8. Shawn Kennedy, "Consumer Saturday: New Move to Reduce City Noise," *New York Times*, 30 April 1983; Chevigny, *Gigs*, 81.

9. Dylan Landis, "If You're Thinking of Living in Tribeca," *New York Times*, 15 May 1983.

10. Danceteria press release, 15 March 1983. Original held by John Argento; scan held by author. Ellipsis in original.

11. Information on the date of the closure of Bond's is contained in Maurice Brahms's petition to the State of New York Tax Tribunal, filed on 9 May 1996, available at http://www.nysdta.org/Decisions/801441.dec.pdf, retrieved 27 August 2011.

12. William McKibben, "The Talk of the Town: Network," *New Yorker*, 28 March 1983, 29.

13. Bob Greene, "From Yippies to Yuppies," *Chicago Tribune*, 23 March 1983. Cited in Leslie Budd and Sam Whimster, eds., *Global Finance and Urban Living: A Study of Metropolitan Change* (New York: Routledge, 1992), 316.

14. Suzanne Present, "Lower East Side Housing Master Plan?" *East Village Eye*, summer 1981, 5, 40.

15. Grace Glueck, "Gallery View; A Gallery Scene That Pioneers in New Territories," *New York Times*, 26 June 1983.

16. Reported in Steven Harvey, "The Perfect Beat," *Face*, October 1983, 57; Steven Harvey, "Behind the Groove," *Collusion*, September 1983, 31.

17. Harvey, "Behind the Groove," 33.

18. Daniel Wang, interview with Tee Scott, 14 July 1994. Download of interview posted at www.geocities.com/jahsonic/TeeScott.htm, held by author.

19. Barry Walters, "Last Night a DJ Saved My Life: David Morales Remakes Dance Music," *Village Voice*, 7 June 1988, 22.

31 STRIPPED-DOWN AND SCRAMBLED SOUNDS

1. Jon Pareles, "Dance and Music Clubs Thriving in Era of Change," *New York Times*, 12 November 1982.

2. Jon Pareles, "The Pop Life," *New York Times*, 19 October 1983; Kathy Nizzari, "DOR," *Dance Music Report*, 15 October 1983, 13.

3. Robert Palmer, "Energy and Creativity Added Up to Exciting Pop," *New York Times*, 25 December 1983.

4. "Born to Laugh at Tornadoes," *Rolling Stone*, 13 October 1983, 77.

5. Robert Palmer, "The Pop Life," *New York Times*, 2 February 1983.

6. Ibid., 25 January 1984.

7. Brian Chin, "Dance Trax," *Billboard*, 4 February 1984, 37.

8. Terry L. Lind, "Afrika Bambaataa & Soulsonic Force: 'Renegades of Funk,'" *Dance Music Report*, 18 February 1984, 19.

9. Stephen Holder, "The Pop Life," *New York Times*, 28 September 1983, C22.

10. Nelson George, "The Rhythm and the Blues: Streetwise Baker Branching Out," *Billboard*, 10 September 1983, 50.

11. Ibid.

12. Mick Middles, "State of Independence: Confusion Reigns as New Order Corrupt the USA," *Sounds*, 23 July 1983, 29.

13. Enrique Fernandez, "Mercado's Record Pool Is New Force in Latin Mart," *Billboard*, 21 August 1982, 54, 58; "Latin Concerts Set for Bond's," *Billboard*, 20 March 1982, 58.

14. Mary Bruschini, "Ray Barretto: Going for Broke," *East Village Eye*, June 1982, 15.

15. Bill Adler, "The South Bronx Was Getting a Bad Rap until a Club Called Disco Fever Came Along," *People Magazine*, 16 May 1983, available at http://www.people.com /people/archive/article/0,,20084997,00.html, retrieved 7 October 2010.

16. Gary Jardim, "John Who?" *Village Voice*, 21 June 1983, 93.

17. Nelson George, "The Rhythm and the Blues: Motown Rapped; Rap Happening," *Billboard*, 4 June 1983, 38.

18. Grandmaster Flash and Ritz, *Adventures of Grandmaster Flash*, 175.

19. McLeod and DiCola, *Creative License*, 113.

20. Ibid., 115.

21. Advertisement, *Dance Music Report*, 29 October 1983, 21.

22. Carol Cooper, "Ear to the Street," *Village Voice*, 7 December 1982, 73.

23. Irv Lichtman, "Prelude Execs Tell Why They Keep on Dancing," *Billboard*, 18 December 1982, 54.

24. John Morthland, "Prelude Is as Prelude Does," *Village Voice*, 5 April 1983, 59.

25. Bussy, *Kraftwerk*, 124.

26. Cheren, *My Life and the Paradise Garage*, 332.

27. Brian Chin, "Dance Trax," *Billboard*, 26 March 1983.

28. Brian Chin, "Dance Trax," *Billboard*, 1 October 1983, 49; Jim Feldman, "A Disco Is Not a Home," *Village Voice*, 10 January 1984, 69; Robert Palmer, "The Pop Life," *New York Times*, 5 October 1983, C24.

29. Robert Palmer, "The Pop Life," *New York Times*, 5 October 1983, C24.

30. Leo Sacks, "Peech Boys 'Journey' to Charts," *Billboard*, 12 November 1983, 59.

32 WE BECAME PART OF THIS ENERGY

1. Jeff Dupre, interview with Steve Casko for a documentary about the Saint, undated.

2. Jan Carl Park, "Interview: Robbie Leslie," *Star Dust*, May 1983, 4–5.

3. Jan Carl Park, "The A-Gay's Disc Jockey: Robbie Leslie and the Politics of the Turntable," *New York Native*, 20 June 1983, 36.

4. Ibid., 37.

5. Jeff Dupre, interview with Michael Fierman for a documentary about the Saint, undated. The original transcript is held by Stephen Pevner. A copy of the transcript is held by author.

6. Hughes, "In the Empire of the Beat," 148.

7. Levine, *Gay Macho*, 58.

8. Ed Constanty, "Profile: Mark Ackerman," *Star Dust*, September 1982, 14.

33 SEX AND DYING

1. Darrell Yates Rist, "A Scaffold to the Sky and No Regrets," *New York Native*, 2 May 1988, 17.

2. S.P., NYC, "Letters to the Editor or . . . ," *Star Dust*, September 1982, 11.

3. G.H., NYC, "Letters to the Editor or . . . ," *Star Dust*, September 1982, 11.

4. J.E., NYC, "Letters to the Editor or . . . ," *Star Dust*, September 1982, 11. Minor spelling correction made.

5. Robin Marantz Henig, "AIDS a New Disease's Deadly Odyssey," *New York Times*, 6 February 1983.

6. Larry Kramer, "1,112 and Counting," *New York Native*, 14 March 1983, available at http://la.indymedia.org/news/2003/05/58757.php, retrieved 20 October 2010.

7. Shilts, *And the Band Played On*, 277.

8. Elliott Siegel, "*Star Dust* Speaks: An Editorial," *Star Dust*, March 1983, 5.

9. Cookie Mueller, "Ask Dr. Mueller," *East Village Eye*, April 1983, 24.

10. "Benefit," *East Village Eye*, April 1983, 42.

11. Astor, *Fun Gallery*, 180.

12. Ronald Sullivan, "Experts Testify AIDS Epidemic Strikes the City," *New York Times*, 17 May 1983.

13. Anna Mayo, "Grandstanding on AIDS," *Village Voice*, 1 November 1983, 1, 9–13, 36. The *Newsweek* poll is noted by John-Manuel Andriote in *Victory Deferred*, 70.

14. Quoted in Clendinen and Nagourney, *Out for Good*, 484.

15. Ibid.

16. Ibid.

17. Susan Chira, "Cuomo Says State Will Step Up AIDS Research and Assist Victims," *New York Times*, 23 June 1983.

18. Ronald Sullivan, "Case of AIDS in City Increase at Slower Rate Than Was Predicted," *New York Times*, 28 June 1983.

19. "AIDS Work: Chronology of HIV/AIDS," available at http://www.aidswork.org/tag /death-cases/, retrieved 26 August 2014.

20. White, *City Boy*, 288.

21. Ibid.

22. Ibid., 287.

23. Judith Halberstam discusses the temporal condition of queers in *In a Queer Time and Place*, 2.

24. Jan Carl Park, "The A-Gay's Disc Jockey: Robbie Leslie and the Politics of the Turntable," *New York Native*, 20 June 1983, 37. Minor spelling correction made.

34 WE GOT THE HITS, WE GOT THE FUTURE

1. Taraborrelli, *Michael Jackson*, 191.

2. Robert Palmer, "Energy and Creativity Added Up to Exciting Pop," *New York Times*, 25 December 1983.

3. Robert Palmer, "Brazil's Beat Alters Black Pop," *New York Times*, 27 February 1983.

4. Edsall and Edsall, *Chain Reaction*, 87.

5. John Rockwell, "Michael Jackson's Thriller: Superb Job," *New York Times*, 19 December 1982.

6. Brian Chin, "Dance Trax," *Billboard*, 3 December 1983, 49.

7. Roman Kozak, "New Music's Growth Reflected at Seminar," *Billboard*, 16 July 1983, 3.

8. Charnas, *Big Payback*, 98.

9. Ed Levine, "TV Rocks with Music," *New York Times*, 8 May 1983.

10. Stephen Holden, "Pop Music Surges along New and Unexpected Paths," *New York Times*, 20 November 1983.

11. Palmer, "Energy and Creativity."

12. Jon Pareles, "Pop Record Business Shows Signs of Recovery," *New York Times*, 28 November 1983.

13. "Why He's a Thriller," *Time*, 19 March 1984.

14. Brian Chin, "Dance Trax," *Billboard*, 18 December 1982, 27; Anonymous, "Michael Jackson: 'Thriller,'" *Dance Music Report*, 25 December 1982, 10. (Baker confirmed in an interview with me that he wrote the *Dance Music Report* review.)

15. Bill Adler, "The South Bronx Was Getting a Bad Rap until a Club Called Disco Fever Came Along," *People Magazine*, 16 May 1983, available at http://www.people.com/people/archive/article/0,,20084997,00.html, retrieved 7 October 2010.

16. Brian Chin, "Dance Trax," *Billboard*, 30 April 1983, 41.

17. Ibid.

35 BEHIND THE GROOVE

1. Steven Harvey, "Behind the Groove," *Collusion*, September 1983, 33.

2. Ibid., 26. Minor grammatical and spelling corrections made.

3. Ibid., 28.

4. Ibid., 29.

5. Ibid., 30. Minor grammatical correction made.

6. Ibid. Minor grammatical correction made.

7. Ibid., 31.

8. Ibid., 32.

9. Ibid.

10. Ibid., 33.

11. Ibid.

12. Ibid., 27.

13. *The Tube*, broadcast 27 October 1983, available at http://www.popyourfunk.com/2009/07/the-tube-a-night-in-nyc/, retrieved 2 September 2014. All subsequent quotes from the program are from this source.

14. Brian Chin, "Dance Trax," *Billboard*, 24 December 1983, 73.

15. Steven Harvey, "Imported Bliss," *Village Voice*, 27 December 1983, 92, 94, 98.

16. Danceteria newsletter, December 1983. Original held by John Argento; scan held by author.

17. Roxy information from Jon Pareles, "Night on the Town with Pop or Rock," *New York Times*, 30 December 1983.

Video recording of Funky 4+1 performance at the Kitchen, from the first epigraph, available at http://www.egotripland.com/funky-four-plus-one-the-kitchen-1980-video/, retrieved 5 January 2015.

1. Hermes, *Love Goes to Buildings*, 286.

2. Young, *Justice and the Politics of Difference*, 237.

3. Jacobs, *Death and Life*, 73.

4. Arendt, *Human Condition*.

5. Richard Williams, "Energy Fails the Magician," *Melody Maker*, 12 January 1980, available at http://eno-web.co.uk/interviews/melma80b.html, retrieved 15 September 2014.

6. Quoted at http://www.kk.org/thetechnium/archives/2008/06/scenius_or_comm.php, retrieved 22 May 2012.

7. David Brody, "Brooklyn DIY: A Story of Williamsburg Art Scene 1987–2007 Directed by Martin Ramocki," *Artcritical*, 1 March 2009, available at http://www.artcritical.com/2009/03/01/brooklyn-diy-a-story-of-williamsburg-art-scene-1987-2007-directed-by-martin-ramocki/, retrieved 23 September 2014.

8. McCormick, "A Crack in Time," in Taylor, *Downtown Book*, 69.

9. Gilbert, *Common Ground*, 199.

10. Ibid., 196–197.

11. Lawrence Grossberg refers to "affective alliance" in *Dancing in Spite of Myself*, 31.

12. Quoted in Nyman, *Experimental Music*, 130.

13. Deitch et al., *Keith Haring*, 19.

14. Jeremy Gilbert makes the point about the Beatniks' relationship to Fordist conformism in *Anticapitalism and Culture*, 170.

15. Ed Koch, "Needed: Federal Anti-Drug Aid," *New York Times*, 27 April 1984.

16. Roland G. Fryer Jr., Paul S. Heaton, Steven D. Levitt, and Kevin M. Murphy, "Measuring the Impact of Crack Cocaine," National Bureau of Economic Research Working Paper Series, 11318, p. 6, available at http://www.nber.org/papers/w11318, retrieved 26 June 2012.

17. Carol Cooper, "Remembering the Fever," liner notes for Various, *Hip Hop Fever*, Warlock Records, 2001.

18. Jesse Kornbluth, "Inside Area: The Wizardry of New York's Hottest Club," *New York Magazine*, 11 March 1985, 40.

19. *Growing Up in America*, 1988, available at https://www.youtube.com/watch?v=2ONemV4ztAk#t=592, retrieved 20 April 2015.

20. "Editor's Note: About the Issue," *East Village Eye*, January 1987, 3. Minor grammatical correction made.

21. Michael Musto, "The Death of Downtown," *Village Voice*, 28 April 1987, 20.

22. Committee for the Real Estate Show, "The Real Estate Show: Manifesto or Statement of Intent," 1980, available at http://www.abcnorio.org/about/history/res_manifesto.html, retrieved 12 October 2014.

23. Craig Unger, "The Lower East Side — There Goes the Neighborhood," *New York Magazine*, 28 May 1984, 33.

24. Soffer, *Ed Koch*, 259.

25. Delany, *Times Square Red, Times Square Blue*, 123, 159.

26. Figures drawn from forecastchart.com, http://www.forecast-chart.com/estate-real
-new-york.html, retrieved 26 February 2010. Figures have been rounded up or down.

27. Chevigny, *Gigs*. Quoted in Hae, "Dilemmas of the Nightlife Fix," 6.

28. Danhier, *Blank City*.

29. Jed Perl, "The Cult of Jeff Koons," *New York Review of Books*, 25 September 2014, available at http://www.nybooks.com/articles/archives/2014/sep/25/cult-jeff-koons/, retrieved 26 January 2015.

30. Kelly Devine Thomas, "The Selling of Jeff Koons," *ARTnews*, 1 May 2005, available at http://www.artnews.com/2005/05/01/the-selling-of-jeff-koons/, retrieved 26 January 2015.

31. Harvey, *Brief History of Neoliberalism*, 205.

32. Brian Chin, "Dance Trax," *Billboard*, 22 September 1984, 54.

33. Frank Owen, "Back in the Days," *Vibe*, December 1994, 68.

34. Hae, *Gentrification of Nightlife*, 138, 125.

35. Zukin, *Loft Living*, 5, 193.

36. Harvey, *Brief History of Neoliberalism*, 47.

37. Lotringer, "Schizo-Culture."

38. Juliette Premmereur, "From New York No Wave to Italian Autonomia: An Interview with Sylvère Lotringer," *Interventions*, 13 March 2014, available at http://interventionsjournal
.net/2014/03/13/from-new-york-no-wave-to-italian-autonomia-an-interview-with-sylvere
-lotringer/, retrieved 18 September 2014.

39. Lotringer, "Introduction to Schizo-Culture," 43, 45, 47.

40. Leo Edelstein, interview with Sylvère Lotringer, "Pataphysics Interview," *Pataphysics*, 1990, retrieved from http://www.egs.edu/faculty/sylvere-lotringer/articles
/pataphysics-interview/, retrieved 1 September 2015; Lotringer and Marazzi, eds., "Autonomia: Post-political Politics," *Semiotext(e)*, 1980.

41. Sylvère Lotringer, "A Revolutionary Process Never Ends: Sylvère Lotringer Talks with Antonio Negri," *Artforum* 46, no. 9 (May 2008).

42. Ibid.

43. Ibid.

44. Hardt and Negri, *Empire*.

45. Harvey, *A Short History of Neoliberalism*.

46. Reynolds, *Retromania*, xiii.

47. Henriques, "Sonic Dominance."

48. Harvey, *Rebel Cities*, 18.

49. Kostelanetz, *SoHo*, 223.

50. Zeke Turner, "Brooklyn on the Spree: Brooklyn Bohemians Invade Berlin's Techno Scene," *New York Times*, 21 February 2014, available at http://www.nytimes.com/2014/02/23
/fashion/Brooklyn-Bohemians-Berlin-Techno-Scene.html?_r=0, retrieved 23 September 2014.

51. Currid, *Warhol Economy*, 11, 49.

52. Joey Arak, "Development du Jour: Alma," *Curbed*, 19 June 2008, available at http://ny.curbed.com/archives/2008/06/19/development_du_jour_alma.php#reader _comments, retrieved 6 October 2014. Minor grammatical correction made.

53. Gabriel Szatan, "House, in Motion: Exploring NYC Dance Culture with Eamon Harkin and Justin Carter," *Boiler Room*, 27 January 2015, available at http://boilerroom.tv /mister-saturday-night-episode-001/, retrieved 4 February 2015; David Byrne, "If the 1% Stifles New York's Creative Talent, I'm Out of Here," *Guardian*, 7 October 2013, available at http://www.theguardian.com/commentisfree/2013/oct/07/new-york-1percent-stifles -creative-talent, retrieved 8 October 2013; Jason Farago, "Our Odd, Revealing Obsession with 'Gritty' Photos of the 1970s NYC Subway," *New Republic*, 12 March 2014, available at http://www.newrepublic.com/article/116991/our-love-gritty-1970s-subway-photos-says -lot-about-new-york, retrieved 7 October 2014.

54. "Text of Mayor de Blasio's State of the City Address," *New York Times*, 3 February 2015, available at http://www.nytimes.com/2015/02/04/nyregion/new-york-mayor-bill -de-blasios-state-of-the-city-address.html?_r=0, retrieved 9 February 2015.

55. Charlie McCann, "Longing for New York's Bad Old Days," *Prospect*, 30 May 2014, available at http://www.prospectmagazine.co.uk/arts-and-books/bring-back-the-bad-old -days-will-hermes-rolling-stone-love-goes-to-buildings-on-fire-review, retrieved 4 February 2015.

56. "New York City Crime Rates 1960–2014," available at http://www.disastercenter .com/crime/nycrime.htm, retrieved 11 January 2015.

SELECTED
DISCOGRAPHY

This discography includes artist, title, label and year of release information for all records cited in the main text of the book but it does not include those that only appear in the DJ discographies. Unless otherwise stated, references are to the twelve-inch singles that would have been purchased and played in New York City during 1980–1983. In the case of records featured on the B-side of a twelve-inch single, information on the A-side is also provided. Album and seven-inch references are introduced for records that didn't receive a twelve-inch release. Further discographical information can be found at www.discogs.com.

ABBA. *The Visitors*. Atlantic, 1981.

AC/DC. "Highway to Hell." Atlantic, 1979.

Adams, Gayle. "Stretch In Out." Prelude, 1980.

Affinity. "Don't Go Away." Mango, 1983.

Afrika Bambaataa & the Jazzy 5. "Jazzy Sensation (Bronx Version)." Tommy Boy, 1981.

———. "Jazzy Sensation (Manhattan Version)." Tommy Boy, 1981.

———. "Jazzy Sensation (Remix)." Tommy Boy, 1982.

Afrika Bambaataa & the Soulsonic Force. "Looking for the Perfect Beat." Tommy Boy, 1983.

———. "Renegades of Funk." Tommy Boy, 1983.

Afrika Bambaataa & the Soul Sonic Force. "Planet Rock (Vocal)"/"Planet Rock (Instrumental)." Tommy Boy, 1982.

Afrika Bambaataa and the Zulu Nation Cosmic Force. "Zulu Nation Throwdown." Paul Winley, 1980.

Art of Noise. "Beat Box." ZTT, 1983.

———. *Into Battle*. ZTT, 1983.

Aurra. "Checking You Out." Salsoul, 1982.

———. "Such a Feeling." Salsoul, 1982.

Azul y Negro. "The Night (La Noche)." Mercury, 1982.

Babe Ruth. "The Mexican." From the album *First Base*. Harvest/EMI, 1972.

Bataan, Joe. "Rap-O Clap-O." Salsoul, 1979.

Bataan, Joe, and His Mestizo Band. *Mestizo*. Salsoul, 1980.

Beastie Boys, The. "Cooky Puss"/"Beastie Revolution." Rat Cage, 1983.

Benatar, Pat. "Love Is a Battlefield." Chrysalis, 1983.

Beside. "Change the Beat (French Rap)." From the twelve-inch by Fab 5 Freddy and Beside, "Change the Beat (French and English Rap)." Celluloid, 1982.

B-52's, The. "Rock Lobster." DB Recs, 1978.

Birdsong, Edwin. "Rapper Dapper Snapper." Salsoul, 1980.

Bits & Pieces. "Don't Stop the Music." Mango, 1981.

Biz, The. "Falling." Prelude, 1983.

Black Uhuru. *The Dub Factor*. Mango, 1983.

———. *Red*. Mango, 1981.

———. "What Is Life?" Island, 1983.

Blancmange. "That's Love, That It Is." London, 1983.

Blondie. *Autoamerican*. Chrysalis, 1980.

———. "Call Me." Chrysalis, 1980.

———. "Rapture." Chrysalis, 1980.

Blow, Kurtis. "The Breaks." Mercury, 1980.

———. "Christmas Rappin'." Mercury, 1979.

———. "Got to Dance." From the album *Kurtis Blow, the Best Rapper on the Scene*. Mercury, 1983.

———. "Tough." Mercury, 1982.

Bo Kool. "(Money) No Love." Tania Music, 1980.

Bohannon. "Let's Start the Dance III." Compleat, Phase II, PolyGram, 1983.

Booker T. & the M.G.'s. "Melting Pot." From the album *Melting Pot*. Stax, 1971.

Boone, Pat. "April Love." Dot, 1957.

Bowie, David. *Let's Dance*. EMI America, 1983.

———. "Let's Dance." EMI America, 1983.

Bow Wow Wow. "Baby, Oh No." RCA Victor, 1982.

Branca, Glenn. "Lesson No. 1 for Electric Guitar"/"Dissonance." 99, 1980.

Branigan, Laura. "Gloria." Atlantic, 1982.

Brother D with Collective Effort. "How We Gonna Make the Black Nation Rise?" Clappers, 1980.

Brown, Dennis. "Money in My Pocket." Lightning, 1979.

Brown, James. "Feelin' James." Uncredited edit by Danny Krivit. T.D., undated.

———. "Funky Drummer." King, 1970.

———. "Give It Up or Turnit a Loose (Live Version)." From the album *Sex Machine*. King, 1970.

———. "Sex Machine." King, 1970.

Brown, Miquel. "So Many Men, So Little Time." TSR, 1983.

Brown, Peter. "Do You Wanna Get Funky with Me." T.K. Disco, 1977.

B.T. Express. "Do You Like It." From the album *Do It ('Til You're Satisfied)*. Scepter, 1974.

Bush Tetras, The. "Too Many Creeps." 99, 1980.

Byrd, Bobby. "Hot Pants — I'm Coming, I'm Coming, I'm Coming." Brownstone, 1972.

Byrne, David. "Big Business (Dance Mix)." Sire, 1981.

———. *Songs from the Catherine Wheel*. Sire, 1981.

Candido. "Jingo." Salsoul, 1979.

———. "Jingo." Salsoul, 1983.

Captain Sky. "Super Sporm." Dynamic Sounds, 1978.

Cara, Irene. "Flashdance . . . What a Feeling." Casablanca, 1983.

C-Bank, featuring Jenny Burton. "One More Shot." Next Plateau, 1982.

Central Line. "Walking into Sunshine." Mercury, 1981.

Cerrone. "Rocket in the Pocket." CBS, 1979.

———. "Trippin' on the Moon." Malligator, 1981.

Chakachas. "Jungle Fever." Polydor, 1972.

Change. *The Glow of Love*. Warner Bros./RFC, 1980.

———. "A Lover's Holiday." Warner Bros./RFC, 1980.

Chic. "Good Times." Atlantic, 1979.

Chicago. "I'm a Man." Columbia, 1970.

China Crisis. "Wishful Thinking." Virgin, 1983.

———. "Working with Fire and Steel." Warner Bros., 1983.

Clash, The. "The Magnificent Dance." From the twelve-inch single "The Call Up." CBS, 1981.

———. "The Magnificent Seven." CBS, 1981.

———. "This Is Radio Clash." CBS, 1981.

———. "White Riot." CBS, 1977.

Class Action, featuring Chris Wiltshire. "Weekend." Sleeping Bag, 1983.

Cliff, Jimmy. "Treat the Youths Right." Columbia, 1982.

Clifford, Linda. "Runaway Love." Curtom, 1978.

Collins, Lynn. "Think (about It)." People, 1972.

Contortions, The. *Buy*. ZE, 1979.

Cotton Candy, featuring Donna Trollinger. "Havin' Fun." Tommy Boy, 1981.

Cowley, Patrick. "Megatron Man." Megatone, 1981.

———. "Menergy." Fusion, 1981.

Cowley, Patrick, featuring Sylvester. "Do You Wanna Funk." Megatone, 1982.

Cristina. *Cristina*. ZE/Island, 1980.

———. "Disco Clone." ZE, 1978.

Culture Club. "Do You Really Want to Hurt Me." Virgin, 1982.

Cut Glass. "Without Your Love." 20th Century Fox, 1980.

Cymande. "Bra." Janus, 1973.

Devo. "That's Good." Warner Bros., 1983.

———. "Whip It." Warner Bros., 1980.

Dibango, Manu. "Soul Makossa." Fiesta, 1972.

Dinosaur. "Kiss Me Again." Sire, 1978.

Dinosaur L. "Go Bang! #5"/"Clean On Your Bean #1." Sleeping Bag, 1982.

———. "#5 (Go Bang!)." From the album *24 → 24 Music*. Sleeping Bag, 1981.

———. *24 → 24 Music*. Sleeping Bag, 1981.

Disco Dub Band. "For the Love of Money." Movers, 1976.

Diva. "Memories (Theme from the Broadway Musical *Cats*)." Prelude, 1983.

Don Armando's Second Avenue Rhumba Band. "Deputy of Love." ZE/Buddah, 1979.

Double Exposure. "Ten Percent." Salsoul, 1976.

Dr. Jeckyll and Mr. Hyde. "Genius Rap." Profile, 1981.

"D" Train. " 'D' Train (Theme)." Prelude, 1982.

———. "Keep On." Prelude, 1982.

———. "You're the One for Me." Prelude, 1981.

———. "You're the One for Me (Reprise)." Prelude, 1982.

Dury, Ian. "Spasticus Autisticus." Polydor, 1981.

Emotions, The. "I Don't Wanna Lose Your Love (Special Disco Version)." Columbia, 1976.

Eno, Brian. *Discreet Music*. Obscure/Island, 1975.

Eno, Brian, and David Byrne. *My Life in the Bush of Ghosts*. Sire, 1981.

Equals, The. "Black Skin Blue Eyed Boys." President, 1970.

ESG. *Come Away with ESG*. 99, 1983.

———. *ESG Says Dance to the Beat of the Moody* (EP). 99, 1982.

———. "You're No Good"/"UFO"/"Moody." Factory, 1981.

———. "You're No Good"/"Moody"/"UFO"/"Earn It"/"ESG"/"Hey!" From the EP *ESG*. 99, 1981.

Evasions, The. "Wikka Wrap." Sam, 1981.

Fab 5 Freddy. "Change the Beat (French and English Rap)." Celluloid, 1982.

Faithfull, Marianne. "Why D'Ya Do It?" From the album *Broken English*. Island, 1979.

Family. "Family Rap." Sound of New York, 1979.

Feel. "Let's Rock (Over and Over Again)." Sutra, 1982.

First Choice. "Doctor Love (Special Mix)"/"Doctor Love Doctor Love (Mega Dub Remix)." Salsoul, 1983.

———. "Double Cross." From the album *Larry Levan's Greatest Mixes Vol. Two*. Salsoul, 1980.

———. "Let No Man Put Asunder." From the album *Delusions*. Salsoul, 1977.

———. "Let No Man Put Asunder." Salsoul, 1983.

———. "Love Thang." Gold Mind, 1979.

Flying Lizards, The. "Money." Virgin, 1979.

Forrrce. "Keep on Dancin' (Phase II)." West End, 1982.

Franklin, Aretha. "Mary Don't You Weep." From the album *Amazing Grace*. Atlantic, 1972.

Freeez. "I.O.U." Beggars Banquet, 1983.

Freeman, Bobby. "Betty Lou Got a New Pair of Shoes." Josie, 1958.

Frontline Orchestra. "Don't Turn Your Back on Me." Quality Records/RFC, 1982.

Funk Masters. "Love Money." From the twelve-inch single by Bo Kool, "(Money) No Love." Tania Music, 1980.

Funky 4 + 1 More. "Rappin and Rocking the House." Enjoy, 1979.

Futura 2000. "The Escapades of Futura 2000." Celluloid, 1982.

Gardner, Taana. "Heartbeat (Club Version)." West End, 1981.

Gaye, Marvin. "Sexual Healing." Columbia, 1982.

——. "What's Going On." Tamla, 1971.

Glass. "Let Me Feel Your Heartbeat." West End, 1982.

GLOBE & Whiz Kid. "Play That Beat Mr. D.J." Tommy Boy, 1983.

Grandmaster Flash. "The Adventures of Grandmaster Flash on the Wheels of Steel." Sugar Hill, 1981.

Grandmaster Flash & the Furious Five. "The Birthday Party." Sugar Hill, 1981.

——. "Freedom." Sugar Hill, 1980.

——. "It's Nasty (Genius of Love)." Sugar Hill, 1981.

——. *The Message.* Sugar Hill, 1982.

——. "The Message." Sugar Hill, 1982.

——. "New York New York." Sugar Hill, 1983.

——. "Scorpio." Sugar Hill, 1982.

——. "Superappin'." Enjoy, 1979.

——. "Super Rappin' No. 2." Enjoy, 1980.

Grandmaster Flash & Melle Mel. "White Lines (Don't Do It)." Sugar Hill, 1983.

Grand Mixer D.ST and the Infinity Rappers. "The Grandmixer Cuts It Up." Celluloid, 1982.

Grant, Eddy. "Time Warp." On the twelve-inch single "Can't Get Enough of You." Ensign, 1981.

——. "Walking on Sunshine." Epic, 1978.

Gray. "Drum Mode." Unreleased, 1981. Later released on the soundtrack album *Downtown 81.* Recall, 2007.

Great Society, The, with Grace Slick. "White Rabbit." Columbia, 1968.

Griffin, Peter. "Step by Step." Electrola, 1981.

Guthrie, Gwen. "Getting Hot." From the EP *Padlock.* Garage, 1983.

——. "Hopscotch." Island, 1983.

——. "It Should Have Been You." Island, 1982.

——. *Padlock.* (EP). Garage, 1983.

——. "Padlock." From the EP *Padlock.* Garage, 1983.

——. "Peanut Butter." Island, 1983.

——. "Seventh Heaven." From the EP *Padlock.* Garage, 1983.

Hall, Daryl, & John Oates. "Adult Education." RCA, 1983.

Hancock, Herbie. "Chameleon." Columbia, 1974.

——. "Rockit." CBS, 1983.

Hartman, Dan. "Vertigo"/"Relight My Fire." Blue Sky, 1979.

Hashim. "Al Naafiysh (The Soul)." Cutting, 1983.

Hearts of Stone, The. "Losing You." Disco 1, 1977.

Hellers, The. *Singers . . . Talkers . . . Players . . . Swingers . . . & Doers.* Command, 1968.

Hendryx, Nona. "Keep It Confidential." RCA Victor, 1983.

———. "Transformation." RCA, 1983.

Holloway, Loleatta. "The Greatest Performance of My Life." From the album *Larry Levan's Greatest Mixes Vol. Two*. Salsoul, 1980.

———. "Love Sensation." Salsoul, 1983.

———. "Love Sensation." Gold Mind, 1980.

Holt, Ednah. "Serious, Sirius Space Party (Club Version)." West End, 1981.

Horne, Jimmy "Bo." "Is It In." TK, 1980.

———. "Spank." Sunshine Sound Disco, 1978.

Ian Dury & the Blockheads. "Reasons to Be Cheerful, Pt. 3." Epic/Stiff, 1979.

Idol, Billy. "White Wedding." Chrysalis, 1982.

Imagination. "Body Talk." MCA, 1981.

———. "Changes (Remix)." From the twelve-inch single "Just an Illusion (Remix)" and the album *Night Dubbing*. Unidisc, 1982/MCA, 1983.

Incredible Bongo Band, The. "Apache." From the album *Bongo Rock*. Pride, 1973.

Inner Life. "Ain't No Mountain High Enough." Salsoul, 1981.

———. "Make It Last Forever." Salsoul, 1981.

———. "Moment of My Life." Salsoul, 1982.

Instant Funk. "I Got My Mind Made Up." Salsoul, 1978.

Isley Brothers. "Get into Something." T-Neck, 1970.

Jackson, Michael. "Beat It." Epic, 1983.

———. "Billie Jean." Epic, 1983.

———. "Human Nature." Epic, 1983.

———. *Off the Wall*. Epic, 1979.

———. "P.Y.T. (Pretty Young Thing)." Epic, 1984.

———. *Thriller*. Epic, 1982.

———. "Wanna Be Startin' Somethin'." Epic, 1983.

Jackson, Michael, and Paul McCartney. "The Girl Is Mine." Epic, 1982.

Jackson 5, The. "Hum Along and Dance." From the album *Get It Together*. Tamla Motown, 1973.

Jacksons, The. "Can You Feel It?" Epic, 1980.

Jamaica Girls. "Need Somebody New." Sleeping Bag, 1983.

James, Bob. "Take Me to the Mardi Gras." From the album *Two*. CTI, 1975.

James, Rick. "Give It to Me Baby." Motown, 1981.

James White & the Blacks. "Contort Yourself." ZE/Buddah, 1979.

———. *Off White*. ZE/Buddah, 1979.

———. *Sax Maniac*. Animal, 1982.

Jimmy Castor Bunch, The. "It's Just Begun." From the album *It's Just Begun*. RCA Victor, 1972.

Joel, Billy. *52nd Street*. Columbia, 1978.

———. "Tell Her about It." Columbia, 1983.

Johnny Dynell and New York 88. "Jam Hot." Acme Music Corporation, 1983.

Jones, Grace. "Feel Up." Island, 1981.

———. *Living My Life*. Island, 1982.

———. *Muse*. Island, 1979.

———. *Nightclubbing*. Island, 1981.

———. "Pull Up to the Bumper." Island, 1981.

———. *Warm Leatherette*. Island, 1980.

———. "Warm Leatherette." Island, 1980.

Joseph, David. "You Can't Hide (Your Love from Me)." Mango, 1983.

Junior. "Mama Used To Say." Mercury, 1981.

Kane, Madleen. "Cherchez Pas." Uniwave, 1980.

Kano. "I'm Ready." Emergency, 1980.

———. "It's a War." Emergency, 1980.

K.C. & the Sunshine Band. "That's the Way (I Like It)." T.K., 1975.

Kendricks, Eddie. "Girl You Need a Change of Mind." Tamla, 1972.

Khan, Chaka. "Clouds." Warner Bros., 1980.

———. "Tearin' It Up." Warner Bros., 1982.

Kid Creole and the Coconuts. "Annie, I'm Not Your Daddy." Island/ZE, 1982.

———. *Doppelganger*. Sire, 1983.

———. *Fresh Fruit in Foreign Places*. Sire/ZE, 1981.

———. *Off the Coast of Me*. Antilles/ZE, 1980.

———. "There's Something Wrong in Paradise." Island/ZE, 1983.

———. *Tropical Gangsters*. ZE/Island, 1982.

———. *Wise Guy*. Sire/ZE, 1982.

Klein & M.B.O. "Dirty Talk." Zanza, 1982.

Knight, Jean. "Mr. Big Stuff." Stax/Polydor, 1977.

Konk. "Konk Party"/"Konk Party (Uptown Breakdown)"/"Konk Party (Master Cylinder Jam)." Celluloid, 1983.

———. "Master . . . Master Cylinder's Jam (New York City Club Mix)"/"Konk Party." Interference, Les Disques du Crépuscule, 1982/Rough Trade, 1982.

Kool and the Gang. "Celebration." De-Lite, 1980.

Kraftwerk. *Computer World*. Warner Bros., 1981.

———. "Home Computer." From the album *Computer World*. Warner Bros., 1981.

———. "Numbers." Warner Bros., 1981.

———. "Radioactivity." Capitol, 1976.

———. *Tour de France* (EP). Warner Bros., 1983.

———. "Trans-Europe Express." From the album *Trans-Europe Express*. Capitol, 1977.

Kranz, George. "Din Daa Daa." Pool, 1983.

Kryptic Crew, featuring Tina B. "Jazzy Sensation (Manhattan Version)." Tommy Boy, 1981.

LaBelle, Patti. "Somewhere over the Rainbow." White label, date unknown.

Lace. "Can't Play Around." Atlantic, 1982.

Laid Back. "White Horse." Sire, 1983.

Lauper, Cyndi. "Girls Just Want to Have Fun." Portrait, 1983.

Levan, Larry. *Larry Levan's Greatest Mixes Volume 2*. Salsoul, 1980.

Level 42. "Starchild." Polydor, 1981.

Lime. "Come and Get Your Love." Unidisc, 1982.

Lipps Inc. "Funkytown." Casablanca, 1979.

Liquid Liquid. *Liquid Liquid* (EP). 99, 1981.

——. "Optimo"/"Cavern." 99, 1983.

——. *Successive Reflexes* (EP). 99, 1981.

Loeb, Caroline. "Narcissique." From the album *Piranana*. ZE, 1983.

Loose Joints. "Is It All Over My Face?" West End, 1980.

——. "Is It All Over My Face? (Female Vocal)." West End, 1980.

——. "Tell You Today." 4th & Broadway, 1983.

Lotus Eaters, The. "You Don't Need Someone New." Sylvan, 1983.

Lunch, Lydia. *Queen of Siam*. ZE, 1980.

Machine. "There But for the Grace of God Go I." RCA Victor/Hologram, 1979.

Madonna. "Everybody"/"Everybody (Dub Version)." Sire, 1982.

——. "Holiday." Sire, 1983.

——. *Like A Virgin*. Sire, 1984.

——. "Lucky Star." Sire, 1983.

——. *Madonna*. Sire, 1983.

——. "Material Girl." Sire, 1984.

——. "Physical Attraction." From the twelve-inch single "Burning Up." Sire, 1983.

Malcolm McLaren and the Ebonettes. "Double Dutch." Island, 1983.

Marie, Kelly. "Feels Like I'm In Love." Calibre + Plus!, 1981.

Marie, Teena. "Square Biz." Motown, 1981.

Martin Circus. "Disco Circus." Prelude, 1979.

Material with Nona Hendryx. "Busting Out." Island/ZE, 1981.

Mayfield, Curtis. "Super Fly." Curtom, 1972.

McCrae, Gwen. "Funky Sensation." Atlantic, 1981.

McLaren, Malcolm, featuring the World's Famous Supreme Team. "Buffalo Gals." Supreme Team Production, 1982.

McLaren, Malcolm, featuring the World's Famous Supreme Team vs. Rakim, KRS-One, Soulson, Hannibal Lechter, Da Boogie Man, and T'Kalla. *Buffalo Girls: Back to the Old School*. Virgin, 1998.

Mean Machine, The. "Disco Dream." Sugar Hill, 1981.

Medium Medium. "Hungry, So Angry." Cachalot, 1981.

Melle Mel & Duke Bootee. "Message II (Survival)." Sugar Hill, 1982.

Menage. "Memory." Profile, 1983.

MFSB. "Love Is the Message." Philadelphia International, 1973.

Michael Jackson and the Jackson 5. "I Want You Back." Motown, 1969.

Monkees. "Mary, Mary." RCA Victor, 1966.

Musique. "In the Bush." Prelude, 1978.

Nairobi and the Awesome Foursome. "Funky Soul Makossa." Streetwise, 1982.

Nelson, Phyllis. "Don't Stop the Train." Tropique, 1981.

New Edition. "Candy Girl." Streetwise, 1982.

New Order. "Blue Monday." Factory, 1983.

———. "Confusion." Streetwise/Of Factory New York, 1983.

New York Citi Peech Boys. "Life Is Something Special." Island, 1982.

Newton-John, Olivia. "Magic." MCA, 1980.

———. "Twist of Fate." MCA, 1983.

Nick Straker Band. "A Little Bit of Jazz." Prelude, 1981.

Nomi, Klaus. *Klaus Nomi.* RCA Victor, 1981.

———. "Nomi Chant." From the album *Klaus Nomi.* RCA Victor, 1981.

Northend, featuring Michelle Wallace. "Happy Days"/"Tee's Happy." Emergency, 1981.

North End. "Kind of Life (Kind of Love)." West End, 1979.

N.Y.C. Peech Boys. "Dance Sister (Biofeedback)." Island, 1983.

———. *Life Is Something Special.* Island, 1983.

———. "On a Journey." Island, 1983.

O'Jays, The. "Back Stabbers." Philadelphia International, 1972.

Ono, Yoko. "Walking on Thin Ice." Geffen, 1981.

Osborne, Jeffrey. "Plane Love." A&M, 1983.

Parrish, Man. "Heatstroke." Disconet, 1981.

———. "Hip Hop, Be Bop (Don't Stop)." Importe/12, 1982.

Passengers. "Hot Leather." Moby Dick, 1981.

Paulette and Tanya Winley with the Harlem Underground Band. "Rhymin' and Rappin'." Paul Winley, 1979.

Peech Boys, The. "Don't Make Me Wait." West End, 1982.

Perren, Freddie. "2 Pigs and a Hog." From *Cooley High (Original Soundtrack).* Motown, 1978.

Phase 2. "The Roxy." Celluloid, 1982.

Phreek. "Weekend." Promotional copy. Atlantic, 1978.

Pink Floyd. *The Final Cut.* Columbia, 1983.

Pitney, Gene. "Town without Pity." Musicor, 1961.

Planet Patrol. *Planet Patrol.* Tommy Boy, 1983.

———. "Play at Your Own Risk." Tommy Boy, 1982.

Plunky & the Oneness of Juju. "Every Way but Loose." Sutra, 1982.

Pointer Sisters, The. "Automatic." Planet, 1983.

Powerline. "Double Journey"/"Journey." Prelude, 1981.

Prince. *1999.* Warner Bros., 1982.

Pulsallama. "Oui-Oui (A Canadian in Paris)." Y, 1983.

Quadrant Six. "Body Mechanic." Atlantic/RFC, 1982.

Quando Quango. "Love Tempo." Factory, 1983.

Queen. "Another One Bites the Dust." Elektra, 1980.

———. *Flash Gordon (Original Soundtrack Music).* EMI, 1980.

Rammellzee vs. K-Rob. "Beat Bop." Tartown, 1983/Profile, 1983.

Rare Earth. "Get Ready." Rare Earth, 1969.

Rational Youth. "City of Night." Yul, 1982.

Raw Silk. "Do It to the Music." West End, 1982.

Rea, Chris. "I Can Hear Your Heartbeat." Magnet, 1983.

Redd, Sharon. "Beat the Street." Prelude, 1982.

———. "Can You Handle It." Epic/Prelude, 1980.

———. "In the Name of Love." Prelude, 1982.

Reed, Lou. *Transformer*. RCA Victor, 1972.

Richard Hell & the Voidoids. *Destiny Street*. Red Star, 1982.

Robie, John. "Vena Cava." Disconet Program Service, 1982.

Rockers Revenge. "The Harder They Come." Streetwise, 1982.

Rockers Revenge, featuring Donnie Calvin. "Walking on Sunshine '82." Streetwise, 1982.

Rocksteady Crew. "(Hey You) the Rocksteady Crew." Atlantic, 1983.

Rolling Stones, The. "Honky Tonk Women." London, 1969.

———. "Hot Stuff." Rolling Stones, 1976.

———. "Miss You." Atlantic, 1979.

Ross, Diana. "Upside Down." Motown, 1980.

Ross, Jimmy. "First True Love Affair." Quality/RFC, 1981.

Roxy Music. "Dance Away." ATCO, 1979.

Ruffin, Jimmy. "Hold on to My Love." RSO, 1980.

Rufus & Chaka. "Ain't Nobody." Warner Bros., 1983.

Run-D.M.C. "It's Like That"/"Sucker M.C.'s." Profile, 1983.

Rushen, Patrice. "Forget Me Nots." Elektra, 1982.

Salsoul Orchestra, The. "Chicago Bus Stop (Ooh I Love It)." Salsoul, 1976.

———. "How High." From the album *Larry Levan's Greatest Mixes Vol. Two*. Salsoul, 1980.

———. "Ooh, I Love It (Love Break)." Salsoul, 1983.

Scott-Heron, Gil, and Brian Jackson, "The Bottle." Strata-East, 1974.

Secret Weapon. "Must Be the Music." Prelude, 1981.

Set the Tone. "Dance Sucker." Island, 1982.

Shango. "Shango Message." Celluloid, 1983.

———. "Zulu Groove." Celluloid, 1983.

Shannon. "Let the Music Play." Emergency, 1983.

Shaw, Marlena. "Touch Me in the Morning." Columbia, 1979.

Sinnamon. "Thanks to You." Becket, 1982.

Skyy. "Let Love Shine." Salsoul, 1982.

Slits, The. "Heard It through the Grapevine." From the seven-inch single "Typical Girls." Island, 1979.

Small, Millie. "My Boy Lollipop." Fontana, 1964.

Smith, Lonnie Liston. "Expansions." Signature, 1975.

Smiths, The. "This Charming Man (U.S. Remixed)." On the twelve-inch single "This Charming Man." Virgin/Rough Trade, 1983.

Snatch. "Another Brick in the Wall." Millenium, 1980.

Snuky Tate. "He's the Groove." Emergency, 1980.

Soccio, Gino. "Dancer." Warner Bros./RFC, 1979.

South Shore Commission. "Free Man." Wand, 1975.

Spandau Ballet. "Chant No. 1 (I Don't Need This Pressure On) (Extended Mix)." Chrysalis, 1981.

Sparkle. "Handsome Man." From the album *Larry Levan's Greatest Mixes Vol. Two*. Salsoul, 1980.

Sparque. "Let's Go Dancin.'" West End, 1981.

———. "Music Turns Me On." West End, 1981.

Spoonie Gee Meets the Sequence. "Monster Jam." Sugar Hill, 1980.

Squier, Billy. "The Big Beat." Capitol, 1980.

Starr, Edwin. "War." Motown, 1972.

Stars on 54. "Mix Your Own 'Stars.'" WEA, 1981.

Starshine. "All I Need Is You." Prelude, 1983.

Stewart, Rod. "Do Ya Think I'm Sexy? (Special Disco Mix)." Warner Bros., 1978.

———. "Passion." Warner Bros., 1980.

Stone. "Time." West End, 1981.

Strafe. "Set It Off." Jus Born, 1984.

Strikers, The. "Body Music." Prelude, 1981.

Sugarhill Gang. "8th Wonder." Sugar Hill, 1980.

———. "Rapper's Delight." Sugar Hill, 1979.

Suicide. "Dream Baby Dream." Island, 1979.

Sumeria. "Dance and Leave It All behind You." Casablanca, 1978.

Summer, Donna. "Could It Be Magic." Oasis, 1976.

———. "I Feel Love/I Feel MegaLove (Patrick Cowley MegaMix)." Disconet Program Service, 1980.

———. "Love to Love You Baby." Oasis, 1975.

———. "Our Love." From the twelve-inch single "Sunset People." Casablanca, 1980.

Sweet G. "Games People Play." Fever, 1983.

———. "A Heartbeat Rap." West End, 1981.

Sylvester. "Dance (Disco Heat)." Fantasy, 1978.

———. *Sell My Soul*. Fantasy Honey, 1980.

———. *Too Hot to Sleep*. Fantasy Honey, 1981.

———. "You Make Me Feel (Mighty Real)." Fantasy, 1978.

Syreeta. "Can't Shake Your Love." Motown, 1981.

T. Rex. "Rip Off." From the album *Electric Warrior*. Fly, 1971.

Taka Boom. "Ride Like the Wind." Prelude, 1983.

Talking Heads. "Burning Down the House." Sire, 1983.

———. *More Songs about Buildings and Food.* Sire, 1978.

———. "Once in a Lifetime." From the album *Remain in Light.* Sire, 1980.

———. *Remain in Light.* Sire, 1980.

———. "Slippery People." Sire, 1983.

———. *Speaking in Tongues.* Sire, 1983.

———. *The Name of This Band Is Talking Heads.* Sire, 1982.

Tantra. "Hills of Katmandu." Importe/12, 1981.

Technique. "Can We Try Again." From the twelve-inch single "(Looking for Someone to Love) Tonight." Arial, 1983.

Thompson Twins. "Hold Me Now." Arista, 1983.

———. "Love on Your Side." Arista, 1983.

Time Zone. "Wildstyle." Celluloid, 1983.

———. "Wildstyle (Special New Mix)." Celluloid/Island, 1983.

Tom Tom Club. "Genius of Love." Sire, 1981.

———. "Under the Boardwalk." Sire, 1982.

———. "Wordy Rappinghood." Sire, 1981.

Treacherous Three, The. "Feel the Heartbeat." Enjoy, 1981.

T-Ski Valley. "!Catch the Beat!" Grand Groove, 1981.

T. W. Funk Masters. "Love Money." From the album Various, *Re-Mixture.* Champagne, 1981.

Twennynine with Lenny White. "Fancy Dancer." Elektra, 1980.

Two Tons o' Fun. "Do You Wanna Boogie, Hunh?" From the twelve-inch single "Taking Away Your Spaces." Fantasy Honey, 1980.

———. "I Got the Feeling (The Patrick Cowley Megamix)." Fantasy, 1981.

———. "Just Us"/"I Got the Feeling." Fantasy Honey, 1980.

UDM. "To Please You." Kadabra, 1983.

Unlimited Touch. "I Hear Music in the Streets." Prelude, 1980.

———. "Searching to Find the One." Prelude, 1981.

Vaness, Theo. "I Can't Dance without You." Prelude, 1980.

Van Halen. "Jump." Warner Bros., 1983.

Various. "Bits & Pieces 1: Disco '79." Bootleg, 1979.

———. *Disco Madness.* Salsoul, 1979.

———. "Flash It to the Beat." Bozo Meko, 1982.

———. *Kiss 98.7 FM Mastermixes Vol. II.* Prelude, 1983.

———. "Master Mix Medley by Tony Humphries." West End, 1982.

———. *Mutant Disco: A Subtle Discolation of the Norm.* Island/ZE, 1981.

———. *98.7 Kiss FM Presents Shep Pettibone's Mastermixes.* Prelude, 1982.

———. *No New York.* Antilles, 1978.

———. *Re-Mixture.* Champagne, 1981.

———. *Seize the Beat (Dance Ze Dance).* Island/ZE, 1981.

———. *Street Sounds Electro 1.* Street Sounds, 1983.

———. *Wild Style.* Animal, 1983.

———. "X Medley." Bootleg, 1980.

Vega, Alan. *Saturn Strip*. Elektra/ZE, 1983.

Visual. "The Music Got Me." Prelude, 1983.

Voyage. "Souvenirs." T.K. Disco, 1978.

Wallace, Michelle. "It's Right." Emergency, 1982.

———. "Jazzy Rhythm." Emergency, 1982.

War. "City, Country, City." From the album *The World Is a Ghetto*. United Artists, 1972.

Ward, Anita. "Ring My Bell." T.K. Disco, 1979.

Warwick, Dionne. "Walk on By." Scepter, 1964.

Was (Not Was). *Born to Laugh at Tornadoes*. Geffen/ZE, 1983.

———. "Out Come the Freaks." Island/ZE, 1981.

———. "Out Come the Freaks (Dub Version)." Island/ZE, 1982.

———. "Tell Me That I'm Dreaming." Island/ZE, 1981.

———. *Was (Not Was)*. Island/ZE, 1981.

———. "Wheel Me Out." Antilles, 1980.

Weather Girls, The. "It's Raining Men." Columbia, 1982.

Weber, Tracy. "Sure Shot." Quality/RFC, 1981.

Wham. "Enjoy What You Do (Wham Rap)." Inner Vision/Columbia, 1982.

White, James. *James White's Flaming Demonics*. ZE, 1983.

Whodini. "Magic's Wand." Jive, 1982.

Williams, Esther. "I'll Be Your Pleasure." RCA, 1981.

Wills, Viola. "Stormy Weather." Sunergy, 1982.

Wilson, Michael. "Groove It to Your Body." Prelude, 1982.

Wobble, Jah, The Edge, and Holger Czukay. "Hold on to Your Dreams." From the EP *Snake Charmer*. Island, 1983.

———. *Snake Charmer*. Island, 1983.

Wonder, Stevie. "Living for the City." Tamla, 1973.

Xavier. "Work That Sucker to Death." Liberty, 1981.

Yarbrough & Peoples. "Don't Stop the Music." Mercury, 1980.

Yaz/Yazoo. "Situation"/"Situation (Dub Mix)." Sire, 1982.

Yello. "Bostich." Stiff America, 1981.

Young, Karen. "Hot Shot." West End, 1978.

Younger Generation, The. "We Rap More Mellow." Brass, 1979.

Zapp. "More Bounce to the Ounce." Warner Bros., 1980.

Zappa, Frank. "Dancin' Fool." From the album *Sheik Yerbouti*. Zappa, 1979.

SELECTED
FILMOGRAPHY

Alphaville. Directed by Jean-Luc Godard. Athos Films, 1965.

Beat Street. Directed by Stan Lathan. Los Angeles: Orion Pictures, 1984.

Blank City. Directed by Celine Danhier. New York: Insurgent Media/Pure Fragment Films, 2011.

Breathless. Directed by Jean-Luc Godard. Films around the World, 1961.

Catch a Beat. Directed by Michael Holman. Unreleased, 1981.

Deadly Art of Survival, The. Directed by Charlie Ahearn. Unreleased, 1979.

Downtown 81 (originally *New York Beat*, unreleased). Directed by Edo Bertoglio. New York: Zeitgeist Films, 2000.

Fame. Directed by Alan Parker. Beverly Hills: United Artists, 1980.

Flashdance. Directed by Adrian Lyne. Los Angeles: Paramount Pictures, 1983.

Foreigner, The. Directed by Amos Poe. Unreleased, 1978.

Fort Apache, The Bronx. Directed by Daniel Petrie. Los Angeles: 20th Century Fox, 1981.

Geek Maggot Bingo. Directed by Nick Zedd. Unreleased, 1983/Eclectic DVD, 2002.

Great Rock 'n' Roll Swindle, The. Directed by Julien Temple. PolyGram Video, 1980.

Jean-Michel Basquiat: The Radiant Child. Directed by Tamra Davis. Los Angeles: Curiously Bright Entertainment, 2010.

Kidnapped. Directed by Eric Mitchell. Unreleased, 1978.

Long Island Four, The. Directed by Anders Grafstrom. Unreleased, 1980.

Making of "Thriller," The. Directed by Jerry Kramer. Optimum Productions/Vestron Video, 1983.

Night Porter, The. Directed by Liliana Cavani. New York: Criterion Collection, 1974.

Pink Flamingos. Directed by John Waters. Dreamland/Saliva Films, 1972.

Rome '78. Directed by James Nares. Unreleased, 1978.

Saturday Night Fever. Directed by John Badham. Los Angeles: Paramount Pictures, 1977.

Set-up, The. Directed by Kathryn Bigelow. Unreleased, 1978.

Snakewoman. Directed by Tina L'Hotsky. Unreleased, 1977.

Stop Making Sense. Directed by Jonathan Demme. New York: Cinecom Palm Pictures, 1984.

Style Wars. Directed by Henry Chalfant and Tony Silver. Public Art Films, 1983.

They Eat Scum. Directed by Nick Zedd. Unreleased, 1979.

Underground U.S.A. Directed by Eric Mitchell. Los Angeles: New Line Cinema, 1980.

Unmade Beds. Directed by Amos Poe. Unreleased, 1976.

West Side Story. Directed by Robert Wise and Jerome Robbins. Mirisch Corporation/ Seven Arts Productions, 1961.

Wild Style. Directed by Charlie Ahearn. London: Metrodome Distribution, 2007.

SELECTED
BIBLIOGRAPHY

Andriote, John-Manuel. *Victory Deferred: How AIDS Changed Gay Life in America*. Chicago: University of Chicago Press, 1999.

Arendt, Hannah. *The Human Condition*. Chicago: University of Chicago Press, 1998.

Astor, Patti. *Fun Gallery . . . The True Story*. thefungallery.com, 2012.

Baker, Stuart, ed. *New York Noise: Art and Music from the New York Underground, 1978–88*. London: Soul Jazz Records, 2007.

Brewster, Bill, and Frank Broughton. *Last Night a DJ Saved My Life: The History of the Disc Jockey*. London: Headline, 2000.

Bussy, Pascal. *Kraftwerk: Man, Machine and Music*. London: SAF Publishing, 1997.

Cannon, Lou. *Governor Reagan: His Rise to Power*. New York: PublicAffairs, 2003.

Carr, Cynthia. *Fire in the Belly: The Life and Times of David Wojnarowicz*. London: Bloomsbury, 2012.

Cepeda, Raquel. *And It Don't Stop: The Best American Hip Hop Journalism of the Last 25 Years*. London: Faber and Faber, 2004.

Chafe, William H. *The Unfinished Journey: America since World War II*. New York: Oxford University Press, 1999.

Chang, Jeff. *Can't Stop Won't Stop: A History of the Hip Hop Generation*. London: Picador, 2005.

Charnas, Dan. *The Big Payback: The History of the Business of Hip-Hop*. New York: New American Library, 2011.

Cheren, Mel. *My Life and the Paradise Garage: Keep on Dancin'*. New York: 24 Hours for Life, 2000.

Chevigny, Paul. *Gigs: Jazz and the Cabaret Laws in New York City*. New York: Routledge, 1991.

Clendinen, Dudley, and Adam Nagourney. *Out for Good: The Struggle to Build a Gay Rights Movement in America*. New York: Simon and Schuster, 1999.

Cooper, Martha. *Hip Hop Files: Photographs 1979–1984*. Cologne: From Here to Fame, 2004.

Cortez, Diego, ed. *Private Elvis*. Stuttgart: FEY, 1978.

Currid, Elizabeth. *The Warhol Economy: How Fashion, Art and Music Drive New York City*. Princeton, NJ: Princeton University Press, 2007.

Debord, Guy. *Society of the Spectacle*. London: Rebel, 1987.

Deitch, Jeffrey. "A Dialogue between Diego Cortez and Glenn O'Brien." In Deitch et al., *Jean-Michel Basquiat 1981*, 14–20.

Deitch, Jeffrey, Suzanne Geiss, and Julia Gruen. *Keith Haring*. New York: Rizzoli, 2008.

Deitch, Jeffrey, Franklin Sirmans, and Nicola Vassell, eds. *Jean-Michel Basquiat 1981: The Studio of the Street*. Milan: Edizioni Charta, 2007.

Delany, Samuel R. *Times Square Red, Times Square Blue*. New York: New York University Press, 1999.

Diamond, John. *The Life Energy in Music*. Valley Cottage, NY: Archaeus, 1981.

Diebold, David. *Tribal Rites: San Francisco's Dance Music Phenomenon 1977–1988*. Northridge, CA: Time Warp, 1988.

Edsall, Thomas, and Mary Edsall. *Chain Reaction: The Impact of Race, Rights, and Taxes on American Politics*. New York: W. W. Norton, 1992.

Emmerling, Leonhard. *Jean-Michel Basquiat: 1960–88*. Cologne: Benedikt Taschen Verlag, 2011.

Fricke, Jim, and Charlie Ahearn. *Yes Yes Y'all: The Experience Music Project Oral History of Hip-hop's First Decade*. Cambridge, MA: Da Capo, 2002.

Gendron, Bernard. *Between Montmartre and the Mudd Club: Popular Music and the Avant-Garde*. Chicago: University of Chicago Press, 2002.

———. "The Downtown Music Scene." In Taylor, *Downtown Book*, 41–65.

George, Nelson. *The Death of Rhythm and Blues*. New York: Penguin, 2003.

Gilbert, Jeremy. *Anticapitalism and Culture*. London: Bloomsbury, 2008.

———. *Common Ground: Democracy and Collectivism in an Age of Individualism*. London: Pluto, 2014.

Goode, Eric, and Jennifer Goode. *Area: 1983–1987*. New York: Abrams, 2013.

Grandmaster Flash and David Ritz. *The Adventures of Grandmaster Flash: My Life, My Beats*. New York: Crown Archetype, 2008.

Grossberg, Lawrence. *Dancing in Spite of Myself*. Durham: Duke University Press, 1997.

Gruen, John. *Keith Haring: The Authorized Biography*. London: Thames and Hudson, 1991.

Haden-Guest, Anthony. *The Last Party: Studio 54, Disco, and the Culture of the Night*. New York: William Morrow, 1997.

———. *True Colors: The Real Life of the Art World*. New York: Grove, 1998.

Hae, Laam. "Dilemmas of the Nightlife Fix: Post-industrialization and the Gentrification of Nightlife in New York City." *Urban Studies* (April 11, 2011): 1–17.

———. *The Gentrification of Nightlife and the Right to the City: Regulating Spaces of Social Dancing in New York*. New York: Routledge, 2012.

———. "Zoning Out Dance Clubs in Manhattan: Gentrification and the Changing Landscapes of Alternative Cultures." Dissertation submitted for PhD in Geography, Syracuse University, 2007.

Hager, Steven. *Art after Midnight: The East Village Scene*. New York: St. Martin's, 1986.

———. *Hip Hop: The Illustrated History of Break Dancing, Rap Music, and Graffiti*. New York: St. Martin's, 1984.

Halberstam, Judith. *In a Queer Time and Place: Transgender Bodies, Subcultural Lives*. New York: New York University Press, 2005.

———. *The Queer Art of Failure*. Durham: Duke University Press, 2011.

Hardt, Michael, and Antonio Negri. *Empire*. Cambridge, MA: Harvard University Press, 2000.

Harvey, David. *A Brief History of Neoliberalism*. Oxford: Oxford University Press, 2005.

———. *Rebel Cities: From the Right to the City to the Urban Revolution*. London: Verso, 2013.

Hebdige, Dick. *Cut 'n' Mix: Culture, Identity and Caribbean Music*. New York: Routledge, 1987.

Henriques, Julian. "Sonic Dominance." In *The Auditory Culture Reader*, edited by Michael Bull and Les Back, 451–480. Oxford: Berg, 2003.

Hermes, Will. *Love Goes to Buildings on Fire: Five Years in New York That Changed Music Forever*. New York: Faber and Faber, 2011.

Hoban, Phoebe. *Basquiat: A Quick Killing in Art*. New York: Viking, 2004.

Holmstrom, John, ed. *Punk: The Original*. New York: Trans-High, 1996.

Hughes, Walter. "In the Empire of the Beat: Discipline and Disco." In *Microphone Fiends: Youth Music and Culture*, edited by Andrew Ross and Tricia Rose, 147–157. New York: Routledge, 1994.

Jacobs, Jane. *The Death and Life of Great American Cities*. New York: Modern Library, 1993.

Kostelanetz, Richard. *SoHo: The Rise and Fall of an Artists' Colony*. New York: Routledge, 2003.

Lawrence, Tim. "Disco Madness: Walter Gibbons and the Legacy of Turntablism and Remixology." *Journal of Popular Music Studies* 20, no. 3 (2008): 276–329.

———. *Hold on to Your Dreams: Arthur Russell and the Downtown Music Scene*. Durham: Duke University Press, 2009.

———. *Love Saves the Day: A History of American Dance Music Culture, 1970–1979*. Durham: Duke University Press, 2004.

———. *Mixed with Love: The Walter Gibbons Salsoul Anthology*. Suss'd Records, 2004.

Lefebvre, Henri. *Writings on Cities*. Translated and edited by Eleonore Kofman and Elizabeth Lebas. Oxford: Blackwell, 1996.

Levine, Martin P. *Gay Macho: The Life and Death of the Homosexual Clone*. New York: New York University Press, 1998.

Lewis, George. *A Power Stronger Than Itself: The AACM and American Experimental Music*. Chicago: University of Chicago Press, 2008.

L'Hotsky, Tina. *Muchachas Espanola Loca (Crazy Spanish Girls)*. New York: Self-published, 1978.

Lotringer, Sylvère. "Introduction to Schizo-Culture." Reprinted in *Schizo-Culture: The Event, the Book*, edited by Sylvère Lotringer and David Morris, 9–49. Cambridge, MA: MIT Press, 2013.

———. "Schizo-Culture," *Semiotext(e)* 3, no. 2 (1978). Reprinted in *Schizo-Culture: The Event, the Book*, edited by Sylvère Lotringer and David Morris. Cambridge, MA: MIT Press, 2013.

Lunch, Lydia. Untitled essay. In Taylor, *Downtown Book*.

Masters, Marc. *No Wave*. London: Black Dog, 2007.

McLeod, Kembrew, and Peter DiCola. *Creative License: The Law and Culture of Digital Sampling*. Durham: Duke University Press, 2011.

Miezitis, Vita. *Night Dancin'*. New York: Ballantine, 1980.

Moore, Alan, and Marc Miller, eds. *The Book: ABC No Rio Dinero: The Story of a Lower East Side Art Gallery*. New York: ABC No Rio with Collaborative Projects, 1985.

Moore, Thurston, and Byron Coley. *No Wave: Post-Punk, Underground, New York, 1976–1980*. New York: Abrams Image, 2008.

Nyman, Michael. *Experimental Music: Cage and Beyond*. Cambridge: Cambridge University Press, 1999.

Reynolds, Simon. *Retromania: Pop Culture's Addiction to Its Own Past*. London: Faber and Faber, 2011.

———. *Rip It Up and Start Again: Post-Punk 1978–84*. London: Faber and Faber, 2005. Also New York: Penguin, 2006.

Rose, Iris. "Judy and Mickey's Bohemia: East Village Performance from 1981–1986." Unpublished thesis for the Master of Arts degree in the Department of Performance Studies, New York University, September 1992.

Sassen, Saskia. "New York City: Economic Restructuring and Immigration," *Development and Change* 17, no. 1 (January 1986): 85–119.

Schloss, Joseph. *Foundation: B-boys, B-girls, and Hip-Hop Culture in New York*. New York: Oxford University Press, 2009.

Shapiro, Peter. *Turn the Beat Around: The Secret History of Disco*. London: Faber and Faber, 2005.

Shilts, Randy. *And the Band Played On: Politics, People and the AIDS Epidemic*. New York: St. Martin's, 1987.

Soffer, Jonathan. *Ed Koch and the Rebuilding of New York City*. New York: Columbia University Press, 2010.

Strychacki, Stanley. *Life as Art: The Club 57 Story*. Bloomington, IN: iUniverse, 2012,

Sussman, Elizabeth, ed. *Keith Haring*. New York: Whitney Museum of American Art in association with Bulfinch Press and Little, Brown, 1997.

Tabb, William K. *The Long Default: New York City and the Urban Fiscal Crisis*. New York: Monthly Review Press, 1981.

Taraborrelli, Randy J. *Michael Jackson: The Magic and the Madness*. London: Pan, 2004.

Taylor, Marvin J., ed. *The Downtown Book: The New York Art Scene, 1974–1984*. Princeton, NJ: Princeton University Press, 2006.

Tompkins, Dave. *How to Wreck a Nice Beach*. New York: Melville House, 2010.

Toop, David. *Rap Attack 3: African Rap to Global Hip Hop*. London: Serpent's Tail, 2000.

White, Edmund. *City Boy: My Life in New York during the 1960s and 1970s*. London: Bloomsbury, 2011.

———. *States of Desire*. London: Picador, 1986.

Young, Iris Marion. *Justice and the Politics of Difference*. Princeton, NJ: Princeton University Press, 1990.

Zekri, Bernard. "Is Europe Ready for Hip Hop?" In *All City Writers: The Graffiti Diaspora*, edited by Andrea Caputo, 26–27. Bagnolet, France: Kitchen93/Critique Livres, 2009.

Zukin, Sharon. *The Cultures of Cities*. Hoboken, NJ: John Wiley and Sons, 1996.

———. *Loft Living: Culture and Capital in Urban Change*. London: Radius, 1988.

———. *The Naked City: The Death and Life of Authentic Urban Places*. Oxford: Oxford University Press, 2010.

INDEX